Panic Disorder with Agoraphobia

Agoraphobia Without History of Panic Disorder

Specific Phobia

Social Phobia

Obsessive-Compulsive Disorder

Posttraumatic Stress Disorder

Acute Stress Disorder

Generalized Anxiety Disorder

SOMATOFORM DISORDERS

Somatization Disorder

Undifferentiated Somatoform Disorder

Conversion Disorder

Pain Disorder

Hypochondriasis

Body Dysmorphic Disorder

FACTITIOUS DISORDERS

DISSOCIATIVE DISORDERS

Dissociative Amnesia

Dissociative Fugue

Dissociative Identity Disorder

Depersonalization Disorder

SEXUAL AND GENDER IDENTITY DISORDERS

Sexual Dysfunctions

Sexual Desire Disorders

Hypoactive Sexual Desire Disorder

Sexual Aversion Disorder

Sexual Arousal Disorders

Female Sexual Arousal Disorder

Male Erectile Disorder

Orgasmic Disorders

Female Orgasmic Disorder

Male Orgasmic Disorder

Premature Ejaculation

Sexual Pain Disorders

Dyspareunia (Not Due to a General Medical Condition)

Vaginismus (Not Due to a General Medical Condition)

Paraphilias

Exhibitionism

Fetishism

Frotteurism

Pedophilia

Sexual Masochism

Sexual Sadism

Transvestic Fetishism

Voyeurism

Gender Identity Disorders

Gender Identity Disorder in Children

Gender Identity Disorder in Adolescents or Adults

EATING DISORDERS

Anorexia Nervosa

Bulimia Nervosa

SLEEP DISORDERS

Primary Sleep Disorders: Dyssomnias

Primary Insomnia

Primary Hypersomnia

Narcolepsy

Breathing-Related Sleep Disorder

Circadian Rhythm Sleep Disorder

Primary Sleep Disorders: Parasomnias

Nightmare Disorder

Sleep Terror Disorder

Sleepwalking Disorder

IMPULSE-CONTROL DISORDERS NOT ELSEWHERE CLASSIFIED

Intermittent Explosive Disorder

Kleptomania

Pyromania

Pathological Gambling

Trichotillomania

ADJUSTMENT DISORDERS

Adjustment Disorder

With Depressed Mood

With Anxiety

With Mixed Anxiety and Depressed Mood

With Disturbance of Conduct

With Mixed Disturbance of Emotions and Conduct

PERSONALITY DISORDERS
Note: These are coded on Axis II.

Paranoid Personality Disorder

Schizoid Personality Disorder

Schizotypal Personality Disorder

Antisocial Personality Disorder

Borderline Personality Disorder

Histrionic Personality Disorder

Narcissistic Personality Disorder

Avoidant Personality Disorder

Dependent Personality Disorder

Obsessive-Compulsive Personality Disorder

MULTIAXIAL SYSTEM

Axis 1

Clinical Disorders
Other Conditions That May Be a Focus of Clinical Attention

Axis II

Personality Disorders
Mental Retardation

Axis III

General Medical Condition

Axis IV

Psychosocial and Environmental Problems

Axis V

Global Assessment of Functioning

Essentials of
Understanding Abnormal Behavior

David Sue
Western Washington University

Derald Wing Sue
Teachers College, Columbia University

Stanley Sue
University of California — Davis

Houghton Mifflin Company   Boston   New York

To our parents, Tom and Lucy Sue, who never suspected they would produce three psychologists, and to our wives and families who provided the emotional support that enabled us to complete this edition.

Vice President & Publisher: Charles Hartford
Senior Sponsoring Editor: Kerry Baruth
Development Editor: Laura Hildebrand
Senior Project Editor: Aileen Mason
Editorial Production Assistant: Neil T. Reynolds
Senior Composition Buyer: Sarah Ambrose
Art & Design Manager: Gary Crespo
Senior Art & Design Coordinator: Jill Haber
Senior Manufacturing Manager: Florence Cadran
Marketing Manager: Jane Potter
Marketing Assistant: Erin Lane

Cover Image: Eric Dinyer, Graphistock, Inc.

All chapter openers © James Endicott/The Stock Illustration Source. Chapter 1: *Head /Building/Orbiting Spheres*; Chapter 2: *Faces Holding Up Road Network*; Chapter 3: *Doctor Examining Profiles*; Chapter 4: *Portrait Of Phobias*; Chapter 5: *Man Floating On Leaf*; Chapter 6: *Hand Holding Hatched Egg*; Chapter 7: *Figures Emerge From Face*; Chapter 8: *Woman Catching Water Drop From Pipes*; Chapter 9: *Man And Woman Standing On Puzzle*; Chapter 10: *Head of Man With Figure Climbing It*; Chapter 11: *Two Faces As Bridge*; Chapter 12: *Man Peering At Mask*; Chapter 13: *Figure Looking Through Large Face*; Chapter 14: *Man With Nutritious Diet*; Chapter 15: *Man Carrying Mountaintop On Highwire*.

Credits continue on page C-1 at the end of the text.

Printed in the U.S.A.

Library of Congress Catalog Card Number: 2003110147

ISBN (student text): 0-618-57409-3

ISBN (library edition): 0-618-37633-X

5 6 7 8 9-WC-08 07

Brief Contents

Contents

Features

Preface

Abnormal behaviors are both a fascination and a concern of scientists and the general public. Why people exhibit abnormal behaviors, how they express their disturbances, and how such behaviors can be prevented and treated are questions that continue to intrigue human beings. We now know that all human beings are touched in one way or another by a mental disturbance in their lives, either directly through their own struggles to deal with mental disorders or indirectly, through affected friends or relatives. Over the years, major research discoveries in genetics, neurobiology, and psychology have made unprecedented contributions to our understanding of abnormal behaviors. This is clearly evident in the Human Genome Project, where scientists have mapped the location of all genes in the human nucleus. The hope among mental health professionals is that the "map of life" will allow for increased understanding of mental disorders and their subsequent treatments. In addition to this tremendous biological breakthrough, we also know that psychological forms of intervention are effective in treating abnormal behaviors. Finally, research has revealed the great cultural variations in abnormal behaviors and what other cultures consider to be effective treatments.

Essentials of Understanding Abnormal Behavior retains the approach and style of the full-length text, while providing concise, yet thorough, coverage in a convenient 15-chapter format. In *Essentials,* we have maintained the hallmark multicultural coverage of our full-length text, along with our engaging writing style, and commitment to providing students with scholarship of the highest quality. We offer an evenhanded treatment of abnormal psychology as both a scientific and a clinical endeavor, giving students the opportunity to explore topics thoroughly and responsibly. *Essentials* presents complex material in a dynamic, highly readable format that challenges students, encourages them to think critically, and provides them with a solid background in the field of Abnormal Psychology.

Special Features of the *Essentials* Text

Even the most well-aimed textbook will miss its mark if not presented in a way that engages students' interest, follows through with clear explanations, and reinforces concepts to keep students on track. Contributing to the strength of *Essentials* are carefully planned presentation and learning aids that assist students in reflecting on chapter concepts and internalizing the material covered. Each chapter includes the following pedagogical elements:

- *Focus Questions* frame the chapter and stimulate active learning—with questions in mind, students begin thinking about the concepts they are about to explore within the chapter.

- *Checkpoint Reviews* are modular summaries that punctuate the chapter and provide an opportunity for students to recap the central concepts and key terms covered up to that point. These reviews enable students to digest the material more easily and efficiently, helping them to form an integrated understanding of the chapter content.

- *Glossary* with key terms boldfaced in the text, and defined both in the margins and in the glossary at the end of the book. Ready access to term definitions in the text margins facilitates students' comprehension of these terms.

- *Disorder, prevalence, onset, and course charts* provide information not only about the DSM-IV-TR diagnostic category but also about the prevalence rate, onset, and course of various disorders. These charts are expressly designed to help students conceptualize and define disorders.

- *Mental Health and Society boxes* provide factual evidence and thought-provoking questions that focus on key research issues, examine widely held assumptions about abnormal behavior, and challenge the students' own understanding of the text material. They will doubtless stimulate critical thinking, evoke alternative views, provoke discussion, and draw students into issues that help them to better explore the wider meaning of abnormal behavior in our society.

- *Cross-cultural and diversity issues* are infused throughout the text. Because we are convinced that cross-cultural comparisons of abnormal behavior and treatment methods can greatly enhance students' understanding of disorders, we pay special attention to cultural, gender, and diversity phenomena. Research findings include rates of each mental disorder and the prevalence of disorders according to gender, ethnicity, and age.

- *New updated case studies and research findings* make issues of mental health and mental disorders "come to life" for students and instructors. Many of the cases are taken from actual clinical files and have a colored background to draw students' attention to them. The latest scholarly research is incorporated throughout the text to reflect recent breakthroughs in the etiology and treatment of mental disorders.

- *Format and design of the book* include a new single column design and softened palette throughout the text, art, and tables. Along with a fresh presentation, and the pedagogical features previously outlined, *Essentials* contains numerous tables, illustrations, figures, and photographs to enhance students' understanding of concepts or controversies in the field.

Our Approach

We take an eclectic, multicultural approach to the field, drawing on important contributions from various disciplines and theoretical stances. The text covers the major categories of disorders listed in the *Diagnostic and Statistical Manual of Mental Disorders* (DSM-IV-TR), but it is not a mechanistic reiteration of DSM. We believe that different combinations of life experiences and constitutional factors influence behavioral disorders, and we project this view throughout the text.

Essentials continues our tradition of providing the most extensive coverage and integration of multicultural models, explanations, and concepts available. We not only discuss how changing demographics have increased the importance of multicultural psychology, but also introduce multicultural models of psychopathology in the opening chapters. As with other models of psychopathology (e.g., psychoanalytic, cognitive, behavioral, biological), we address multicultural issues throughout the text whenever research findings and theoretical formulations allow. For example, to add richness to the students' understanding of mental disorders, we outline cultural factors as they affect assessment, classification, and treatment. To aid students in integrating new research and work in abnormal behavior, in Chapter 2 we present a tripartite approach to viewing disorders through the lens of individual, group, and universal dimensions.

As psychologists (and professors) we know that learning is enhanced whenever material is presented in a lively and engaging manner. We achieve these qualities in part by providing case vignettes and clients' descriptions of their experiences to complement and illustrate research-based explanations. In addition, we highlight and explore controversial topics in depth, including the following:

- Should culture-specific approaches in therapy be used in treating racial/ethnic minority populations? (Chapter 2)
- Are there disorders (culture-bound syndromes) unique to a particular culture? (Chapter 3)
- Is the fear of spiders due to disgust or perceived danger? (Chapter 4)
- Do women have higher rates of anxiety and depressive disorders? (Chapters 4 and 10)
- Was Sybil a genuine case of dissociative identity disorder? (Chapter 5)
- Do ethnic minorities and women receive inferior medical treatment? (Chapter 6)
- What are the effects of club drugs? (Chapter 8)
- Can people be addicted to sex? (Chapter 9)
- Do individuals with schizophrenia in developing countries have a better prognosis than those in developed countries? (Chapter 11)
- Can social psychological factors be a cause of schizophrenia? (Chapter 11)
- Should websites advocating anorexia nervosa be shut down? (Chapter 14)
- Should therapists maintain confidentiality with AIDS clients? (Chapter 15)

We clarify complex material by providing students with case descriptions, real life situations, and research findings. Examples of this approach can be seen in our discussions of the phenomenon of delusions and our careful examination of the various factors that affect clients with mood disorders. Our goal is to encourage students to think critically rather than merely assimilate a collection of facts and theories. As a result, we hope that students will develop an appreciation of the study of abnormal behavior. In addition to updating the book's coverage, its look, and its special features, we have maintained a streamlined organization of the book, as described next.

Organization of the Text

Chapters 1 through 3 provide a context for viewing abnormal behavior and treatment by introducing students to definitions of abnormal behavior, historical perspectives, and the research process involved in its study (Chapter 1), models used in the study of psychopathology and psychotherapeutic interventions (Chapter 2), and methods of assessment and classification (Chapter 3). These chapters provide the different models or perspectives upon which the etiology of the mental disorders can be viewed.

The bulk of the text, Chapters 4 through 14, presents the major disorders covered in DSM-IV-TR. In each chapter, symptoms are presented first, followed by diagnosis, theoretical perspectives, etiology, and treatment. Our enhanced disorders charts have been integrated to include not only the definitions of disorders but also their prevalence, onset, and course. At a glance, students are able to gain an important overview of the disorders. Highlights of the coverage in this part of the book include an entire chapter devoted to Eating Disorders (Chapter 14). A separate chapter was deemed important because eating disorders are becoming more prevalent in our society, especially among younger people. Research now links it to situational factors, biological proclivity, and other interlocking mental disorders. The fact that the majority of those who suffer from eating disorders are women is also a powerful statement of how the images society portrays to them may result in unhealthy behaviors. Discussions of treatment approaches are included in each of the chapters on disorders, allowing students some closure in covering particular disorders. Chapter 15 covers the issues and controversies surrounding topics such as the insanity defense, patients' rights, confidentiality, and mental health practices in general.

Teaching and Learning Support Package

This text is supported by a rich set of supplementary materials designed to enhance the teaching and learning experience.

For Instructors

- *Instructor's Resource Manual:* The *IRM* includes an extended chapter outline, learning objectives, discussion topics, classroom exercises, handouts, and list of supplementary reading and multimedia resources.

- *Test Bank:* The *Test Bank*, available in print or within a testing software program, features an extensive set of multiple-choice questions and essay questions with sample answers. Three types of objective questions are provided: factual, conceptual, and applied, and all answers are keyed to learning objectives, text pages, and question type, for easier test creation.

- **PowerPoint slides:** This updated set of PowerPoint slides has been specifically designed to help professors prepare their classroom lectures. For each chapter, slides feature lecture ideas, tables, and illustrations to help highlight the major topics in abnormal psychology.

- *HM ClassPrep CD-ROM with HMTesting:* This combined CD includes both the Computerized Test Bank and the HM ClassPrep CD. Our HMTesting program offers delivery of test questions in an easy-to-use interface, compatible with both MAC and WIN platforms. The HM ClassPrep instructor CD-ROM provides one location for all text-specific preparation materials that instructors might want to have available electronically. It contains PowerPoint lecture outlines and art from the textbook, as well as electronic versions of the *Instructors Resource Manual* and word files for the test bank.

- **Instructor website:** Instructors can access the useful and innovative teaching tools, activities, and other resources that support *Essentials of Understanding Abnormal Behavior* by logging onto our website at http://psychology.college.hmco.com/instructors.

- *Abnormal Psychology Lecture Starter Video:* Created especially for this textbook, this video offers approximately 60 minutes of brief video clips perfectly suited for classroom use.

For Students

- *Study Guide:* The *Study Guide* provides a complete review of the chapter with chapter outlines, learning objectives, fill-in-the-blank review of key terms, and multiple-choice questions. Answers to test questions include an explanation for both the correct answer and incorrect answer.

- *Student website:* Students can access the useful and innovative learning tools, activities, and resources that support *Essentials of Understanding Abnormal Behavior* by logging onto our website at http://psychology.college.hmco.com/students.

- *Casebook for Abnormal Psychology:* Written by Clark Clipson, California School of Professional Psychology, and Jocelyn Steer, San Diego Family Institute. Each of the 16 cases represents a major psychological disorder. After a detailed history of each case, critical-thinking questions prompt students to formulate hypotheses and interpretations based on the client's symptoms, family and medical background, and relevant information. The case proceeds with sections on assessment, case conceptualization, diagnosis, and treatment outlook. A final set of thought-provoking questions for discussion and writing concludes each case.

■ *Abnormal Psychology in Context: Voices and Perspectives:* Written by David Sattler, College of Charleston; Virginia Shabatay, Palomar College; and Geoffrey Kramer, Grand Valley State University. This unique supplementary text features 40 cases that include first-person accounts and narratives written by individuals who live with a psychological disorder and by therapists, relatives, and others who have direct experience with someone suffering from a disorder. These vivid and engaging narratives are accompanied by critical-thinking questions and a psychological concept guide that indicates which key terms and concepts are highlighted by each reading.

Acknowledgments

We continue to appreciate the feedback by reviewers and colleagues. The following individuals helped us prepare the basis of the *Essentials* edition by sharing with us valuable insights, opinions, and recommendations.

Kim L. Krinsky, *Georgia Perimeter College*

George-Harold Jennings, *Drew University*

Jerry L. Fryrear, *University of Houston, Clear Lake*

Theresa A. Wadkins, *University of Nebraska, Kearney*

Robert Hoff, *Mercyhurst College*

Sherry Davis Molock, *George Washington University*

David C. Schwebel, *University of Iowa*

Mark A. Kunkel, *School University of West Georgia*

We also wish to thank Eva Schepeler from the University of California, Davis. We acknowledge the continuing support and high quality of work by Houghton Mifflin personnel including Senior Sponsoring Editor Kerry Baruth, Marketing Manager Jane Potter, Development Editor Laura Hildebrand, and Senior Production Editor Aileen Mason. We also thank text designer and art editor Jean Hammond, photo editor Martha Shethar, copyeditor Elaine Lauble Kehoe, proofreader Robin Hogan, and indexer Kay Schlembach. Special thanks go to Diane Sue for her assistance in revising major portions of the childhood chapter.

D. S.
D. W. S.
S. S.

About the Authors

David Sue is Professor of Psychology at Western Washington University, where he is an associate of the Center for Cross-Cultural Research and has served as the Director of both the Psychology Counseling Clinic and the Mental Health Counseling Program. He and his wife are currently writing a book *Counseling and Psychotherapy in a Diverse Society*. He received his Ph.D. in Clinical Psychology from Washington State University. His research interests revolve around issues in cross-cultural counseling. He, his wife, and their three children enjoy tennis, hiking, and snowshoeing.

Derald Wing Sue is Professor of Psychology and Education in the Department of Counseling and Clinical Psychology at Teachers College, Columbia University. He has written extensively in the field of counseling psychology and multicultural counseling/therapy and is author of a best-selling book, *Counseling the Culturally Diverse: Theory and Practice*. Dr. Sue has served as president of the Society of Counseling Psychology and the Society for the Psychological Study of Ethnic Minority Issues. He received his doctorate from the University of Oregon and is married and the father of two children. Friends describe him as addicted to exercise and the Internet.

Stanley Sue is Distinguished Professor of Psychology and Asian American Studies at the University of California, Davis. He received his Ph.D. from UCLA and served on the psychology faculty for ten years at the University of Washington and for fifteen years at UCLA. His research interests lie in the areas of clinical-community psychology and ethnicity and mental health. His hobbies include working on computers, which has resulted in an addiction to the Internet, and jogging with his wife.

Essentials of

Understanding Abnormal Behavior

FOCUS QUESTIONS

- What is abnormal psychology?
- What criteria are used to determine normal or abnormal behaviors?
- How common are mental disorders?
- How have the explanations of abnormal behavior changed over time?
- Are mental disorders due primarily to biological or to psychological factors?
- What are some contemporary trends in abnormal psychology?
- What characteristics of the scientific method make it useful in studying abnormal behavior?
- What are some research methods used to ask and answer questions about psychopathology?
- What ethical issues are raised in research?

1 *Abnormal Behavior*

I had just finished all my doctoral course work and was beginning an internship on a psychiatric ward. Along with a group of other trainees, I was being given a tour of the ward facilities by the supervising psychologist. Sitting to my immediate right in a semicircle was a group of about twenty patients and the head psychiatrist, who was conducting a ward meeting. I recall making eye contact with one particular patient: Chung, a Chinese male, of short, stocky build. His eyes followed me throughout the orientation session, making me feel quite self-conscious. I assumed Chung was interested in me because I was probably one of the few Asian American mental health professionals he had ever seen. As we approached the nurse's station, I heard a low guttural growl and caught a quick movement of a fast-approaching figure on my right. Chung had launched himself toward me. He struck me with his left shoulder, driving me against the glass partition. I collapsed on the floor, completely stunned, as he stood over me, appearing equally surprised at what he had done. We stared at each other for what felt like hours before the attending psychiatrist and nurses gently but firmly pulled Chung away. Although I was in no way injured (except for a few bruises on my forearm and a deflated ego), I was baffled by what had happened. No amount of reading and course work could have prepared me for such an experience. My head filled with questions: What was wrong with Chung? Why did he attack me? Was he dangerous? Did the fact that both of us were of Chinese ancestry play a role in his reaction to me? What disorder did he suffer from? What type of therapy was he receiving?

In a sense, the purpose of this book, *Essentials of Understanding Abnormal Behavior,* is to help you answer such questions. To do this, however, we must first examine some basic aspects of the study of abnormal behavior, including some of its history and emerging changes in the field.

The Concerns of Abnormal Psychology

abnormal psychology The scientific study whose objectives are to describe, explain, predict, and treat behaviors that are considered strange or unusual.

psychodiagnosis An attempt to describe, assess, and systematically draw inferences about an individual's psychological disorder.

therapy A program of systematic intervention whose purpose is to modify a client's behavioral, affective (emotional), or cognitive state.

Abnormal psychology is the scientific study whose objectives are to describe, explain, predict, and treat behaviors that are considered strange or unusual. Its subject matter ranges from the bizarre and spectacular to the more commonplace—from the violent homicides and "perverted" sexual acts that are widely reported by the news media to such less sensational (but more prevalent) behaviors as exam anxiety, stuttering, depression, and ulcers.

We are most likely to be able to help individuals who are suffering from mental disorders when we can make an accurate **psychodiagnosis**, an attempt to describe, assess, and systematically draw inferences about an individual's psychological disorder. Information derived from clinical observations, psychological tests, reports from family and friends, and the person's psychological history may be used. The psychologist attempts to identify the causes of disorders in order to design a program of treatment. Abnormal behavior may be controlled through **therapy**, which is a program of systematic intervention whose purpose is to modify a client's behavioral, emotional, and/or cognitive state.

3

Table 1.1   The Mental Health Professions

Clinical psychology   Clinical psychology is the professional field concerned with the study, assessment, treatment, and prevention of abnormal behavior in disturbed individuals. Clinical psychologists must hold a Ph.D. degree from a university or a Psy.D. (doctor of psychology) degree, a more practitioner-oriented degree granted by several institutions.

School psychology   School psychology is the field of study concerned with the processes of cognitive and emotional development of students in educational settings. Thus it focuses on the processes of learning, remembering, and thinking and on human development as it applies to the educational process. School psychologists may hold either a master's or a doctoral degree.

Psychiatric social work   Those entering psychiatric social work are trained in a school of social work, usually in a graduate program leading to a master's degree or a D.S.W. (doctor of social work). They work in family counseling services or community agencies, where they specialize in intake (assessment and screening of clients), take psychiatric histories, and deal with other agencies.

Counseling psychology   To a great extent, a description of clinical psychology applies to counseling psychology as well. Whereas clinical psychologists are trained to work specifically with a disturbed client population, counseling psychologists are usually more immediately concerned with the study of life problems in relatively normal people.

Psychiatry   Psychiatrists hold an M.D. degree. Their education includes the four years of medical school required for that degree, along with an additional three or four years of training in psychiatry.

Psychoanalysis   Psychoanalysis has been associated with medicine and psychiatry because its founder, Sigmund Freud, and his major disciples were physicians. Most psychoanalysts hold either the M.D. or the Ph.D. degree. In addition, psychoanalysts receive intensive training in the theory and practice of psychoanalysis at an institute devoted to the field.

Marriage and family counseling   Marriage and family counselors have varied professional backgrounds, but their training usually includes a master's degree in counseling and many hours of supervised clinical experience.

In the past, mental health services were controlled primarily by psychiatrists, psychologists, and psychiatric social workers. The list of acceptable (licensed) providers in different fields has expanded rapidly. In 1968 there were 12,000 clinical psychologists in the United States; today there are more than 40,000. As Figure 1.1 illustrates, nearly 300,000 professional therapists now practice in the United States (see also Table 1.1). It has been observed that there are more professional therapists than librarians, firefighters, or mail carriers and that there are twice as many therapists as dentists and pharmacists.

Defining Abnormal Behavior

Implicit in our discussion is the one overriding concern of abnormal psychology: abnormal behavior itself. But what exactly is abnormal behavior, and how do psychologists recognize it? We can define **abnormal behavior** as behavior that departs from some norm and that harms the affected individual or others (see Figure 1.2).

Deviance

As a criterion for abnormality, deviance is generally related to our understanding of how often or how rarely a condition occurs. Statistical criteria equate normality with those behaviors that occur most frequently in the population. Abnormality is therefore defined in terms of those behaviors that occur least frequently. Bizarre or unusual behavior is an abnormal deviation from an accepted standard of behavior (such as an

abnormal behavior Behavior that departs from some norm and that harms the affected individual or others.

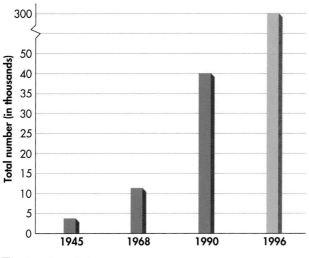

Clinical psychologists

All mental health professionals

Figure 1.1 Number of Professional Therapists in the United States   From 1945 to 1968 the number of clinical psychologists in the United States more than tripled; from that time until today, it quadrupled. Clinical psychologists represent only a small portion of mental health professionals, whose numbers now approach nearly three hundred thousand. Professional therapists include psychiatrists, social workers, counseling psychologists, marriage and family counselors, and others. *Source:* Data from Zilbergeld (1983); Cummings (1995).

antisocial act) or a false perception of reality (such as a hallucination). This criterion is extremely subjective; it depends on the individual being diagnosed, on the diagnostician, and on the particular culture.

Certain sexual behaviors, delinquency, and homicide are examples of acts that our society considers abnormal. But social norms are far from static, and behavioral standards cannot be considered absolute. Changes in our attitudes toward human sexuality provide a prime example. During the Victorian era, women wore six to eight undergarments to make sure that every part of the body from the neck down was covered. Exposing an ankle was roughly equivalent to wearing a topless bathing suit today. Taboos against publicly recognizing sexuality dictated that words be chosen carefully to avoid any sexual connotation. Victorians said "limb" instead of "leg" because the word *leg* was considered too erotic. People who did not adhere to these strict codes of conduct were considered immoral or even perverted.

Many American magazines and films now openly exhibit the naked human body, and topless and bottomless nightclub entertainment is hardly newsworthy. Various sex acts are explicitly portrayed in NC-17-rated movies. Women are freer to question traditional sex roles and to act more assertively in initiating sex. Such changes in behavior make it difficult to subscribe to absolute standards of normality.

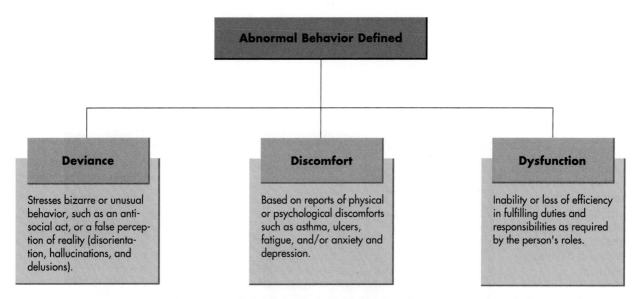

Figure 1.2 Abnormal Behavior Defined   There are numerous definitions of abnormal behavior that have been used by mental health professionals. Some of the most current and widely used ones are briefly described here.

Nevertheless, some behaviors can usually be judged abnormal in most situations. Among these are severe disorientation, hallucinations, and delusions. *Disorientation* is confusion with regard to identity, place, or time. People who are disoriented may not know who they are, where they are, or what historical era they are living in. *Hallucinations* are false impressions—either pleasant or unpleasant—that involve the senses. People who have hallucinations may hear, feel, or see things that are not really there, such as voices accusing them of vile deeds, insects crawling on their bodies, or monstrous apparitions. *Delusions* are false beliefs steadfastly held by the individual despite contradictory objective evidence. A *delusion of grandeur* is a belief that one is an exalted personage, such as Jesus Christ or Joan of Arc; a *delusion of persecution* is a belief that one is controlled by others or is the victim of a conspiracy.

Chung, in the opening case study in this chapter, suffered from delusions of persecution. He believed that his home country of Taiwan was engaged in a space war with the People's Republic of China and that "the enemy" had planted electrodes in his head during one of his ECT sessions so that his thoughts could be read. Because China was able to read his mind and extract valuable data about Taiwan's battle plans, Chung believed that he had been ordered to commit suicide for the sake of his country. His several suicide attempts were the result of these distorted beliefs.

Interestingly, Chung's attack on one of the authors arose from his belief that the author was a spy from China, getting ready to implant a more powerful mind-reading device in Chung's head. (He was due for electroconvulsive shock therapy that afternoon.) In many respects, Chung's delusions seem to incorporate realistic aspects of his life: the intern was Chinese; China and Taiwan have historically been countries at odds with each other; and the ECT process involved attaching electrodes to Chung's head and body. In the patient's belief system, these facts were misconstrued and transformed into an image of a spy from China who would soon implant powerful electronic devices to read Chung's thoughts.

Discomfort

Most people who seek the help of therapists are suffering physical or psychological discomfort. Many physical reactions stem from a strong psychological component; among them are disorders such as asthma, hypertension, and ulcers, as well as physi-

Determining What's Abnormal By most people's standards, the full-body tattoo of this man would probably be considered unusual at best and bizarre at worst. Yet despite the way his body appears, this person may be very functional in his work and personal life. This leads to an important question: What constitutes abnormal behavior and how do we recognize it?

cal symptoms such as fatigue, nausea, pain, and heart palpitations. Discomfort can also be manifested in extreme or prolonged emotional reactions, of which anxiety and depression are the most prevalent and common. Of course, it is normal for a person to feel depressed after suffering a loss or a disappointment. But if the reaction is so intense, exaggerated, and prolonged that it interferes with the person's capacity to function adequately, it is likely to be considered abnormal.

Dysfunction

Dysfunctions in a person's biological, mental, and emotional states are often manifested in role performance. One way to assess dysfunction is to compare an individual's performance with the requirements of a role. In everyday life, people are expected to fulfill various roles—as students or teachers, as workers and caretakers, as parents, lovers, and marital partners. Emotional problems sometimes interfere with the performance of these roles, and the resulting role dysfunction may be used as an indicator of abnormality.

Another related way to assess dysfunction is to compare the individual's performance with his or her potential. An individual with an IQ score of 150 who is failing in school can be labeled inefficient. (The label *underachiever* is often hung on students who possess high intelligence but obtain poor grades in school.) Similarly, a productive worker who suddenly becomes unproductive may be experiencing emotional stress. The major weakness of this approach is that it is difficult to accurately assess potential.

Cultural Considerations in Abnormality

All behaviors, whether normal or abnormal, originate from a cultural context. Psychologists are increasingly recognizing that this is an inescapable conclusion and that culture plays a major role in our understanding of human behavior (American Psychological Association, 2003). For our purposes, culture is "shared learned behavior which is transmitted from one generation to another for purposes of individual and societal growth, adjustment, and adaptation: culture is represented externally as artifacts, roles, and institutions, and it is represented internally as values, beliefs, attitudes, epistemology, consciousness and biological functioning" (Marsella, 1988, pp. 8–9). Three important points should be emphasized:

1. Culture is not synonymous with *race* or *ethnic group*. Jewish, Polish, Irish, and Italian Americans represent diverse ethnic groups whose individual members may share a common racial classification. Yet their cultural contexts may differ substantially from one another. Likewise, an Irish American and an Italian American, despite their different ethnic heritages, may share the same cultural context. And even within the same ethnic group, small groups of individuals may develop and transmit shared behavior patterns that in essence constitute a form of culture.

2. Every society or group that shares and transmits behaviors to its members possesses a culture. European Americans, African Americans, Latino/Hispanic Americans, Asian Americans/Pacific Islanders, Native Americans, and other social groups within the United States all have cultures.

3. Culture is a powerful determinant of worldviews (Sue & Sue, 2003). It affects how we define normal and abnormal behaviors and how we treat disorders encountered by members of that culture. Even racial or ethnic groups that possess many similarities may have quite different cultural constellations.

Cultural Relativism   Cultural differences often lead to misunderstandings and misinterpretations. In a society that values technological conveniences and clothing that comes from the runways of modern fashion, the lifestyles and cultural values of others may be perceived as strange. The Amish, for example, continue to rely on traditional modes of transportation (horse and buggy). And women in both the Amish and Islamic cultures wear simple, concealing clothing; in their circumstances, dressing in any other way would be considered deviant.

cultural universality The belief that the origin, process, and manifestation of disorders are equally applicable across cultures.

cultural relativism The belief that what is judged to be normal or abnormal may vary from one culture to another.

These three points give rise to a major problem: one group's definition of mental illness may not be shared by another. This contradicts the traditional view of abnormal psychology, which is based on **cultural universality**—the assumption that a fixed set of mental disorders exists whose obvious manifestations cut across cultures (Kim & Berry, 1993). Early research supported the belief that certain mental disorders occurred worldwide, had similar processes, and were more alike than dissimilar (Howard, 1992). From this belief flowed the corresponding belief that a disorder such as depression is similar in origin, process, and manifestation in all societies, whether Asia, Africa, or Latin America. As a result, no modifications in diagnosis and treatment need be made; Western concepts of normality and abnormality can be considered universal and equally applicable across cultures.

In contrast to the traditional view of cultural universality has been **cultural relativism,** the belief that lifestyles, cultural values, and worldviews affect the expression and determination of deviant behavior. This concept arose from the anthropological tradition and emphasized the importance of culture and diversity in the manifestation of abnormal symptoms. For example, a body of research supports the conclusion that acting-out behaviors associated with mental disorders are much more frequent in the United States than in Asia and that even Asian Americans in the United States are less likely to express symptoms via acting out (Chun et al., 1998; Hong & Domokos-Cheng Ham, 2001). Researchers have proposed that Asian cultural values (restraint of feelings, emphasis on self-control, and need for subtlety in approaching problems) all contribute to this restraint. Proponents of cultural relativism also point out that cultures vary in what they consider to be normal or abnormal behavior. In some societies and cultural groups, hallucinating (having false sensory impressions) is considered normal in specific situations. Yet in the United States, hallucinating is generally perceived to be a manifestation of a disorder.

Which view is correct? Should the criteria used to determine normality and abnormality be based on cultural universality or on cultural relativism? Few mental health professionals today embrace the extreme of either position, although most gravitate toward one or the other. Proponents of cultural universality focus on the disorder and minimize cultural factors, and proponents of cultural relativism focus on the culture and on how the disorder is manifested within it. Both views have validity. It is naive to believe that no disorders cut across different cultures and share universal characteristics. For example, even though hallucinating may be viewed as normal in some cultures, proponents of cultural universality argue that it still represents a breakdown in biological-cognitive processes. Likewise, it is equally naive to believe that the relative frequencies and manner of symptom formation for various disorders do not reflect dominant cultural values and the lifestyles of a society.

A third point to consider is that some common disorders, such as depression, are manifested similarly in different cultures.

A more fruitful approach to studying multicultural criteria of abnormality is to explore two questions:

- What is universal in human behavior that is also relevant to understanding psychopathology?
- What is the relationship between cultural norms, values, and attitudes and the incidence and manifestation of behavior disorders?

These are important questions that we hope you will ask as we continue our journey into the field of abnormal psychology.

Sociopolitical Considerations in Abnormality

All the criteria we have discussed have shortcomings. Many of these deficiencies are related to sociopolitical implications and have been well articulated by Thomas Szasz (1987). In a radical departure from conventional beliefs, he has asserted that mental illness is a myth, a fictional creation by society used to control and change people. According to Szasz, people may suffer from "problems in living," not from "mental illness." His argument stems from three beliefs: that abnormal behavior is so labeled because it is different, not necessarily because it is a reflection of "illness"; that unusual belief systems are not necessarily wrong; and that abnormal behavior is frequently a reflection of something wrong with society rather than with the individual. Individuals are labeled "mentally ill" because their behaviors violate the social order and their beliefs challenge the prevailing wisdom of the times. Szasz finds the concept of mental illness to be dangerous and a form of social control used by those in power. Hitler branded Jews as abnormal. Political dissidents in many countries, including both China and the former Soviet Union, have often been cast as mentally ill. And the history of slavery indicates that African Americans who tried to escape their white masters were often labeled as suffering from *drapetomania,* defined as a sickness that makes the person desire freedom.

Few mental health professionals would take the extreme position advocated by Szasz, but his arguments highlight an important area of concern. Those who diagnose behavior as abnormal must be sensitive not only to such variables as psychological orientation but also to individual value systems, societal norms and values, and potential sociopolitical ramifications.

The Frequency and Burden of Mental Disorders

prevalence The percentage of people in a population who have a disorder at a given point in time.

lifetime prevalence The total proportion of people in a population who have ever had a disorder in their lives.

incidence Onset or occurrence of a given disorder over some period of time.

A student once asked one of the authors, "How crazy is this nation?" This question, put more scientifically, has occupied psychologists for some time. Psychiatric epidemiology has attempted to answer this question by distinguishing between three concepts: (1) **prevalence,** the percentage of people in a population who suffer from a disorder at a given point in time; (2) **lifetime prevalence,** the total proportion of people in the population who have ever had a disorder in their lives; and (3) **incidence,** the onset or occurrence of a given disorder over some period of time. From this information, they are able to find out how frequently or infrequently various disturbances occur in the population with respect to ethnicity, gender, and age and whether current mental health practices are sufficient and effective.

Current Research into the Epidemiology of Mental Disorders

In one major study performed in 1950 (Srole et al., 1962), 1,500 New Yorkers were interviewed and rated on their psychological health. The results were startling: approximately 25 percent of those interviewed showed severe impairment, about 55 percent were mildly impaired, and only 20 percent (one in five) were rated unimpaired.

Perhaps the most thorough and comprehensive study of the incidence of mental disorders in the U.S. adult population (eighteen years and older) was conducted by the National Institute of Mental Health (NIMH, 1985; also Eaton et al., 1984; Freedman, 1984; Myers et al., 1984; Regier et al., 1988; Regier et al., 1993; Robins et al., 1984; Robins, Locke, & Regier, 1991). The NIMH epidemiological study included data collected from approximately 20,000 persons in three major cities: New Haven, Baltimore, and St. Louis.

Approximately 29 to 38 percent of the sample reported that they experienced at least one mental disorder. Schizophrenia, often one of the most severe mental disturbances, affects 1 percent of the population, or approximately 2.5 million Americans. Figure 1.3 presents one-year and lifetime-prevalence rates of various mental disorders as percentages of the total U.S. population.

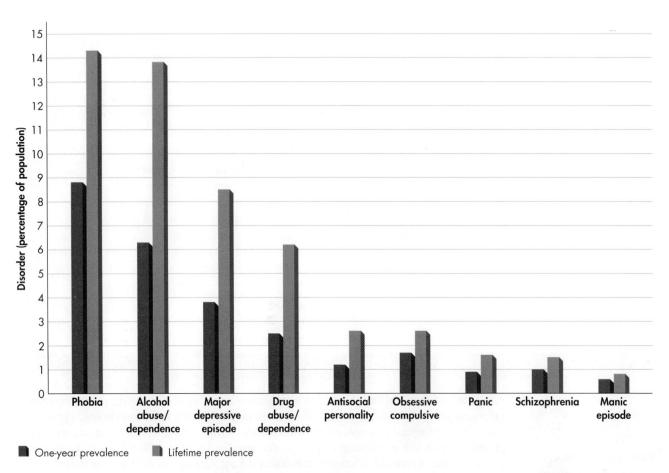

■ One-year prevalence   ■ Lifetime prevalence

Figure 1.3 Rates of Various Mental Disorders   This figure shows the one-year and lifetime prevalence of mental disorders as percentages of the population. It is clear that the most common mental disorders in the United States are phobias, followed by alcohol-related problems, anxiety, and depressive episodes. *Source:* Data from Robins & Regier (1991).

Incidence of Abnormal Behavior By all appearances, this photo seems to depict a well-functioning group of college graduates from many facets of life. Yet studies reveal that approximately one in three persons suffers from at least one mental disorder.

Researchers also found that, although men and women were equally likely to suffer from mental disorders, they differ in the kinds of disorders they experience. For example, alcohol abuse or dependence occurs in 24 percent of men but in only 4 percent of women; drug abuse is more likely to occur in men; and depression and anxiety are more likely to occur in women. Age was also an important factor. Alcoholism and depression are most prominent in the twenty-five- to forty-four-year-old age group; drug dependence in the eighteen- to twenty-four-year-old age group; and cognitive impairment in people age sixty-five and older. Phobias, however, were equally represented at all ages. Figure 1.4 summarizes the rates of psychiatric disorders in various demographic categories. Some of the findings are not surprising—for example, common sense might cause us to guess that financially dependent or less educated Americans would have higher rates of disorders. The relationship of disorders to other characteristics is more obscure and sometimes downright baffling: how would you explain the fact that the lowest percentages of disorders are found for people sixty-five or older or that rural dwellers have a lower rate of disorders than their urban counterparts? Such findings require critical analyses.

The cost and burden of mental disorders to our nation is indeed a major source of concern. The recognition of this problem was the impetus for *Achieving the Promise: Transforming Mental Health Care in America* (President's New Freedom Commission on Mental Health, 2003) and *Mental Health: A Report of the Surgeon General* (DHHS, 1999), comprehensive reports on the state of mental health in our nation. The conclusions were very troubling: (1) at least one in five Americans suffers from a mental illness; (2) we continue to lack adequate knowledge and information regarding the causes, treatment, and prevention of mental disorders; (3) the major obstacle to mental health progress is "stigma"; (4) collectively, mental disorders account for more than 15 percent of the overall burden of disease from all causes; and (5) mental illness and mental health must become part of a public health policy.

To indicate the profound impact mental disorders have on our health and productivity, the measure of disease burden, Disability Adjusted Life Years (DALYs), compares a disease (mental illness) across many different disease conditions (DHHS, 1999). DALYs record lost years of healthy life regardless of whether the years were lost to premature death or some form of disability. Mental illness ranks higher than cancer

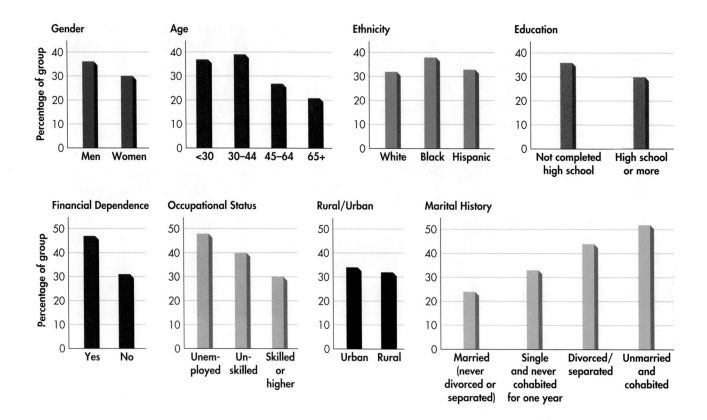

Figure 1.4 **Rates of Psychiatric Disorders in Particular Groups**   Research indicates that psychiatric disorders are present in about one-third of the U.S. population. The bar graphs in this figure illustrate the extent to which any psychiatric disorder is found in combination with other characteristics of the population, such as gender, age, ethnicity, and marital status. *Source:* Data from Robins & Regier (1991).

and all other malignant diseases. More frightening, however, is the point strongly made in the surgeon general's report: that many people suffer from "mental health problems" that do not meet the criteria for a mental disorder. These problems, the report observes, may be equally debilitating unless adequately treated.

These epidemiological findings are troubling, to say the least. Clearly, mental disturbances are widespread, and many persons are currently suffering from them. What is more troubling is that two-thirds of all people suffering from a diagnosable mental disorder are not receiving or seeking mental health services (Kessler et al., 1994; Regier et al., 1993). Yet spending on mental health services has declined over 54 percent, from $154/person in 1988 to $69/person in 1998, and the period from 1988 to 1997 saw mental health care benefits slashed 670 percent more than general health care benefits (Reed et al., 2001).

Historical Perspectives on Abnormal Behavior

Most ideas about abnormal behavior are firmly rooted in the system of beliefs that operate in a given society at a given time. Much of this history section is based on discussions of deviant behavior by Alexander and Selesnick (1966), Hunter and

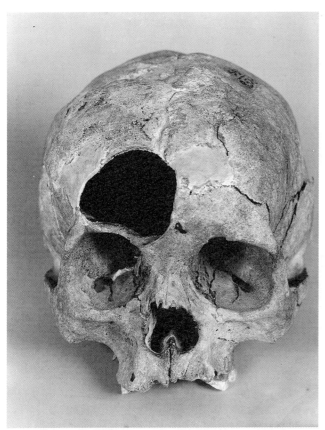

An Early Surgical Treatment   There are two theories about trephining. The most widely accepted postulates that trephining was a form of surgery that enabled an evil spirit to leave the body. The other theory rejects this idea, proposing instead that the holes were actually the result of wounds.

trephining An ancient surgical technique in which part of the skull was chipped away to provide an opening through which evil spirits could escape.

exorcism Ritual in which prayer, noise, emetics, and extreme measures such as flogging and starvation were used to cast evil spirits out of an afflicted person's body.

brain pathology Dysfunction or disease of the brain.

Macalpine (1963), Neugebauer (1979), Spanos (1978), and Zilboorg and Henry (1941). We must be aware, however, that our journey is necessarily culture bound and that other civilizations (non-Western) have histories of their own.

Prehistoric and Ancient Beliefs

Prehistoric societies some half a million years ago did not distinguish sharply between mental and physical disorders. Abnormal behaviors, from simple headaches to convulsive attacks, were attributed to evil spirits that inhabited or controlled the afflicted person's body. According to historians, these ancient peoples attributed many forms of illness to demonic possession, sorcery, or the behest of an offended ancestral spirit. Within this system of belief, called *demonology,* the victim was usually held at least partly responsible for the misfortune.

It has been suggested that Stone Age cave dwellers may have treated behavior disorders with a surgical method called **trephining,** in which part of the skull was chipped away to provide an opening through which the evil spirit could escape. People may have believed that when the evil spirit left, the person would return to his or her normal state. Surprisingly, some trephined skulls have been found to have healed over, indicating that some patients survived this extremely crude operation. Another treatment method used by the early Greeks, Chinese, Hebrews, and Egyptians was exorcism. In an **exorcism,** elaborate prayers, noises, emetics (drugs that induce vomiting), and extreme measures such as flogging and starvation were used to cast evil spirits out of an afflicted person's body.

Naturalistic Explanations (Greco-Roman Thought)

With the flowering of Greek civilization and its continuation into the era of Roman rule (500 B.C.–A.D. 500), naturalistic explanations gradually became distinct from supernatural ones. Early thinkers, such as Hippocrates (460–370 B.C.), a physician who is often called the father of medicine, actively questioned prevailing superstitious beliefs and proposed much more rational and scientific explanations for mental disorders. He believed that, because the brain was the central organ of intellectual activity, deviant behavior was caused by **brain pathology**—that is, a dysfunction or disease of the brain. He also considered heredity and environment important factors in psychopathology. Hippocrates classified mental illnesses into three categories—mania, melancholia, and phrenitis (brain fever)—and for each category gave detailed clinical descriptions of such disorders as paranoia, alcoholic delirium, and epilepsy. Many of his descriptions of symptoms are still used today—eloquent testimony to his keen powers of observation.

Other thinkers who contributed to the organic explanation of behavior were the philosopher Plato and the Greek physician Galen, who practiced in Rome. Plato

Casting Out the Cause of Abnormality   During the Middle Ages, people suffering from mental disorders were often perceived as being victims of a demonic possession. The most prevalent form of treatment was exorcism, usually conducted by religious leaders who used prayers, incantations, and sometimes torturous physical techniques to cast the evil spirit from the bodies of the afflicted.

(429–347 B.C.) carried on the thinking of Hippocrates; he insisted that the mentally disturbed were the responsibility of the family and should not be punished for their behavior. Galen (A.D. 129–199) made major contributions through his scientific examination of the nervous system and his explanation of the role of the brain and central nervous system in mental functioning. His greatest contribution may have been his codification of all European medical knowledge from Hippocrates' time to his own.

Reversion to Supernatural Explanations (the Middle Ages)

With the collapse of the Roman Empire and the rise of Christianity, rational and scientific thought gave way to a reemphasis on the supernatural. Religious dogma included the beliefs that nature was a reflection of divine will and beyond human reason and that earthly life was a prelude to the "true" life (after death). Scientific inquiry—attempts to understand, classify, explain, and control nature—was less important than accepting nature as a manifestation of God's will.

During this period, treatment of the mentally ill sometimes consisted of torturous exorcistic procedures that were seen as appropriate ways to combat Satan and eject him from the possessed person's body. Prayers, curses, obscene epithets, and the sprinkling of holy water—as well as such drastic and painful "therapy" as flogging, starving, and immersion in hot water—were used to drive out the devil. The humane treatments that Hippocrates had advocated centuries earlier were challenged severely. A time of trouble for everyone, the Dark Ages were especially bleak for the mentally ill.

Belief in the power of the supernatural became so prevalent and intense that it frequently affected whole populations. Beginning in Italy early in the thirteenth century, large numbers of people were affected by various forms of **mass madness,** or group hysteria, in which a great many people exhibit similar symptoms that have no apparent physical cause. One of the better known manifestations of this disorder was *tarantism,* a dance mania characterized by wild raving, jumping, dancing, and convulsions. The hysteria was most prevalent during the height of the summer and was attributed to the sting of a tarantula. A victim would leap up and run out into the

mass madness Group hysteria, in which large numbers of people exhibit similar symptoms that have no apparent cause.

street or marketplace, jumping and raving, to be joined by others who believed that they had also been bitten. The mania soon spread throughout the rest of Europe, where it became known as Saint Vitus' Dance.

How can these phenomena be explained? Stress and fear are often associated with outbreaks of mass hysteria. During the thirteenth century, for example, there was enormous social unrest. The bubonic plague had decimated one-third the population of Europe. War, famine, and pestilence were rampant, and the social order of the times was crumbling.

People whose actions were interpreted as peculiar were often suspected of witchcraft. It was acceptable to use torture to obtain confessions from suspected witches, and many victims confessed because they preferred death to prolonged agony. Thousands of innocent men, women, and even children were beheaded, burned alive, or mutilated.

Witch hunts occurred both in colonial America and in Europe. The witchcraft trials of 1692 in Salem, Massachusetts, were infamous. Authorities there acted on statements taken from children who may have been influenced by the sensational stories told by an old West Indian servant. Several hundred people were accused, many were imprisoned and tortured, and twenty were killed. It has been estimated that some 20,000 people (mainly women) were killed as witches in Scotland alone and that more than 100,000 throughout Europe were executed as witches from the middle of the fifteenth century to the end of the seventeenth century. It would seem reasonable to assume that the mentally ill would be especially prone to being perceived as witches. Indeed, most psychiatric historians argue that mental disorders were at the roots of witchcraft persecutions (Alexander & Selesnick, 1966; Deutsch, 1949; Zilboorg & Henry, 1941). Spanos (1978), however, in a comprehensive critical analysis, concluded that very little support could be found to indicate that accused witches were mentally ill.

The Rise of Humanism (the Renaissance)

A resurgence of rational and scientific inquiry during the Renaissance (fourteenth through sixteenth centuries) led to great advances in science and **humanism,** a philosophical movement that emphasizes human welfare and the worth and uniqueness of the individual. Until this time, most asylums were at best custodial centers in which the mentally disturbed were chained, caged, starved, whipped, and even exhibited to the public for a small fee, much like animals in a zoo. But the new way of thinking held that if people were "mentally ill" and not possessed, then they should be treated as though they were sick. A number of new methods for treating the mentally ill reflected this humanistic spirit.

In 1563 Johann Weyer (1515–1588), a German physician, published a revolutionary book that challenged the foundation of ideas about witchcraft. Weyer asserted that many people who were tortured, imprisoned, and burned as witches were mentally disturbed, not possessed by demons. The emotional agonies he was made to endure for committing this heresy are well documented. His book was severely criticized and banned by both church and state, but it proved to be a forerunner of the humanitarian perspective on mental illness. Others eventually followed his lead.

The Reform Movement (Eighteenth and Nineteenth Centuries)

In France, Philippe Pinel (1745–1826), a physician, was put in charge of La Bicêtre, a hospital for insane men in Paris. Pinel instituted what came to be known as the **moral treatment movement**—a shift to more humane treatment of the mentally disturbed. He ordered that inmates' chains be removed, replaced dungeons with sunny rooms, encouraged exercise outdoors on hospital grounds, and treated patients with kindness

humanism Philosophical movement that emphasizes human welfare and the worth and uniqueness of the individual.

moral treatment movement A shift to more humane treatment of the mentally disturbed; its initiation is generally attributed to Philippe Pinel.

Dorothea Dix (1802–1887)
During a time when women were discouraged from political participation, Dorothea Dix, a New England schoolteacher, worked tirelessly as a social reformer to improve the deplorable conditions in which the mentally ill were forced to live.

and reason. Surprising many disbelievers, the freed patients did not become violent; instead, this humane treatment seemed to foster recovery and improve behavior. Pinel later instituted similar, equally successful, reforms at La Salpêtrière, a large mental hospital for women in Paris.

In England William Tuke (1732–1822), a prominent Quaker tea merchant, established a retreat at York for the "moral treatment" of mental patients. At this pleasant country estate, the patients worked, prayed, rested, and talked out their problems—all in an atmosphere of kindness quite unlike that of the lunatic asylums of the time.

In the United States, three individuals—Benjamin Rush, Dorothea Dix, and Clifford Beers—made important contributions to the moral treatment movement. Benjamin Rush (1745–1813), widely acclaimed as the father of U.S. psychiatry, attempted to train physicians to treat mental patients and to introduce more humane treatment policies into mental hospitals. He insisted that patients be accorded respect and dignity and that they be gainfully employed while hospitalized, an idea that anticipated the modern concept of work therapy. Yet Rush was not unaffected by the established practices and beliefs of his times: his theories were influenced by astrology, and his remedies included bloodletting and purgatives.

Dorothea Dix (1802–1887), a New England schoolteacher, was the preeminent American social reformer of the nineteenth century. While teaching Sunday school to female prisoners, she became familiar with the deplorable conditions in which jailed mental patients were forced to live. (Prisons and poorhouses were commonly used to incarcerate these patients.) For the next forty years, Dix worked tirelessly for the mentally ill. She campaigned for reform legislation and funds to establish suitable mental hospitals and asylums. She raised millions of dollars, established more than thirty modern mental hospitals, and greatly improved conditions in countless others. But the struggle for reform was far from over. Although the large hospitals that replaced jails and poorhouses had better physical facilities, the humanistic, personal concern of the moral treatment movement was lacking.

That movement was given further impetus in 1908 with the publication of *A Mind That Found Itself,* a book by Clifford Beers (1876–1943) about his own mental collapse. His book describes the terrible treatment he and other patients experienced in three mental institutions, where they were beaten, choked, spat on, and restrained with straitjackets. His vivid account aroused great public sympathy and attracted the interest and support of the psychiatric establishment, including such eminent figures as psychologist-philosopher William James.

It would be naive to believe that these reforms have totally eliminated inhumane treatment of the mentally disturbed. Books such as Mary Jane Ward's *The Snake Pit* (1946) and films such as Frederick Wiseman's *Titicut Follies* (1967) continue to document harsh treatment of mental patients. Even the severest critic of the mental health system, however, would have to admit that conditions and treatment for the mentally ill have improved in this century.

▶ CHECKPOINT REVIEW

abnormal behavior *(p. 4)*

abnormal psychology *(p. 3)*

brain pathology *(p. 13)*

cultural relativism *(p. 8)*

What is abnormal psychology?
■ Abnormal psychology is the field that attempts to describe, explain, predict, and treat behaviors that are considered strange or unusual.

What criteria are used to determine normal or abnormal behaviors?
■ Clinicians use three major criteria: deviance, discomfort, and dysfunction.

cultur‚
exorci
hum‚
incid
life
ma
m

t
the
trephining *(p. 13)*

w common are mental disorders?
■ Mental health problems are widespread in the United States, and the human and economic costs are enormous.

ow have the explanations of abnormal behavior changed over time?
■ Ancient peoples believed in demonology and attributed abnormal behaviors to evil spirits that inhabited the victim's body. Treatments consisted of trephining, exorcism, and bodily assaults.
■ Rational and scientific explanations of abnormality emerged during the Greco-Roman era. Especially influential was the thinking of Hippocrates, who believed that abnormal behavior was due to organic, or biological, causes, such as a dysfunction or disease of the brain. Treatment became more humane.
■ With the collapse of the Roman Empire and the increased influence of the church and its emphasis on divine will and the hereafter, rationalist thought was suppressed, and belief in the supernatural again flourished. During the Middle Ages, famine, pestilence, and dynastic wars caused enormous social upheaval. Forms of mass hysteria affected groups of people. In the fifteenth century, some of the men, women, and children killed in church-endorsed witch hunts were people we would today call mentally ill.
■ The Renaissance brought a return to rational and scientific inquiry, along with a heightened interest in humanitarian methods of treating the mentally ill. The eighteenth and nineteenth centuries were a period characterized by reform movements.

Causes: Early Viewpoints

Paralleling the rise of humanism in the treatment of mental illness was an inquiry into its causes. Two schools of thought emerged. The *organic,* or *biological, viewpoint* holds that mental disorders are the result of physiological damage or disease; the *psychological viewpoint* stresses an emotional basis for mental illness. It is important to note that most people were not extreme adherents of one or the other. Rather, they tended to combine elements of both, predating the biopsychosocial model widely used today.

The Biological Viewpoint

Hippocrates' suggestion of an organic explanation for abnormal behavior was ignored during the Middle Ages but revived after the Renaissance. Not until the nineteenth century, however, did the organic, or **biological view**—the belief that mental disorders have a physical or physiological basis—become important. The ideas of Wilhelm Griesinger (1817–1868), a German psychiatrist who believed that all mental disorders had physiological causes, received considerable attention. Emil Kraepelin (1856–1926), a follower of Griesinger, observed that certain symptoms tend to occur regularly in clusters, called **syndromes.** Kraepelin believed that each cluster of symptoms represented a mental disorder with its own unique—and clearly specifiable—cause, course, and outcome. He attributed all disorders to one of four organic causes: metabolic disturbance, endocrine difficulty, brain disease, or heredity. In his *Textbook of Psychiatry* (1883/1923), Kraepelin outlined a system for classifying mental illnesses on the basis of their organic causes. That system was the original basis for the diagnostic categories in the *Diagnostic and Statistical Manual of Mental Disorders* (DSM), the classification system of the American Psychiatric Association. The biological viewpoint gained even greater strength with the discovery of the organic basis of *general paresis,* a progressively degenerative and irreversible physical and mental disorder (*paresis* is syphilis of the brain).

biological view The belief that mental disorders have a physical or physiological basis.

syndrome A cluster of symptoms that tend to occur together and that are believed to represent a particular disorder with its own unique cause, course, and outcome.

The Psychological Viewpoint

Some scientists noted, however, that certain types of emotional disorders were not associated with any organic disease in the patient. Such observations led to the **psychological view** that stressed psychological factors rather than biological factors as the cause of many disorders. For example, the inability to attain personal goals and resolve interpersonal conflicts could lead to intense feelings of frustration, depression, failure, and anger and to consequent disturbed behavior.

The idea that psychological processes could produce mental and physical disturbances began to gain credence among several physicians who were using hypnosis. Among them was the Viennese doctor Josef Breuer (1842–1925). After one of his female patients, while in a trance, spoke quite freely about her past traumatic experiences, Breuer discovered that many of her symptoms abated or disappeared. He achieved even greater success when the patient recalled previously forgotten memories and relived their emotional aspects. This latter technique became known as the **cathartic method,** a therapeutic use of verbal expression to release pent-up emotional conflicts. It foreshadowed psychoanalysis, whose founder, Sigmund Freud (1856–1939), was a colleague of Breuer's. Freud's theories have had a great and lasting influence in the field of abnormal psychology.

Whereas psychoanalysis offered an intrapsychic explanation of abnormal behavior, another viewpoint that emerged during the latter part of this period was more firmly rooted in laboratory science: *behaviorism.* The behavioristic perspective stressed the importance of directly observable behaviors and the conditions or stimuli that evoked, reinforced, and extinguished them. Behaviorism not only offered an alternative explanation of the development of both normal and abnormal behavior but also demonstrated a high degree of success in treating maladaptive behaviors.

▶ Contemporary Trends in Abnormal Psychology

Earlier, we made the statement that our current explanations of abnormal behavior have been heavily influenced by the beliefs of the past. Much has changed, however, in our understanding and treatment of psychopathological disorders. Twentieth-century views of abnormality continue to evolve in the twenty-first century as they incorporate the effects of several major events and trends in the field, two of which are the drug revolution in psychiatry and the influence of multicultural psychology.

The Drug Revolution

Many mental health professionals consider the introduction of psychiatric drugs in the 1950s as one of the great medical advances in the twentieth century (Lickey & Gordon, 1991; Nemeroff, 1998). Although some might find such a statement excessive, it is difficult to overemphasize the impact that drug therapy has had. It started in 1949 when an Australian psychiatrist, John F. J. Cade, reported on his successful experiments with lithium in radically calming manic patients who had been hospitalized for years. Several years later, French psychiatrists Jean Delay and Pierre Deniker discovered that the drug chlorpromazine (brand name, Thorazine) was extremely effective in treating agitated schizophrenics. Within a matter of years, drugs were developed to treat disorders such as depression, schizophrenia, phobias, obsessive-compulsive disorders, and anxiety. Large classes of drugs were developed for depression (antidepressant drugs), anxiety (antianxiety drugs), and grossly impaired thinking (antipsychotic drugs).

These drugs were considered revolutionary because they rapidly and dramatically decreased or eliminated troublesome symptoms experienced by patients. As a result,

psychological view The belief or theory that mental disorders are caused by psychological and emotional factors, rather than organic or biological factors.

cathartic method The therapeutic use of verbal expression to release pent-up unconscious conflicts.

multicultural psychology A field of psychology that stresses the importance of culture, race, ethnicity, gender, age, socioeconomic class, and other similar factors in its efforts to understand and treat abnormal behavior.

other forms of therapy became available to the mentally ill, who were now more able to focus their attention on their therapy. Their stays in mental hospitals were shortened and were more cost effective than prolonged hospitalizations. In addition, they were allowed to return home while receiving treatment.

The new drug therapies were credited with the depopulation of mental hospitals, often referred to as *deinstitutionalization*. This decline can be attributed not to a decrease in new admissions but rather to shorter stays and earlier releases (Lickey & Gordon, 1991; Manderscheid & Sonnenschein, 1992; NIMH, 1995). To handle the large number of patients returning to the community, outpatient treatment became the primary mode of service for the severely disturbed. In addition to changing the way therapy was dispensed, the introduction of psychiatric drugs revived strong belief in the biological bases of mental disorders.

Diversity and Multicultural Psychology

We are fast becoming a multicultural, multiracial, and multilingual society (see Figure 1.5). The 2000 U.S. Census reveals that within several decades, racial and ethnic minorities will become a numerical majority (Sue, 2003). These changes have been referred to as "the diversification of the United States" or, literally, the "changing complexion of society." Much of this change is fueled by two major trends in the United States: the increased immigration of visible racial and ethnic minorities and the differential birth rates among the various racial and ethnic groups in our society. In 1990, 76 percent of the population was composed of white Americans; in the year 2000, their numbers had declined to 69 percent of the population.

Diversity has had a major impact on the mental health profession, creating a new field of study called **multicultural psychology**. As we saw earlier in this chapter, the multicultural approach stresses the importance of culture, race, ethnicity, gender, age, socioeconomic class, and other similar factors in its effort to understand and treat abnormal behavior. There is now recognition that mental health professionals need to (1) increase their cultural sensitivity, (2) acquire knowledge of the worldviews and lifestyles of a culturally diverse population, and (3) develop culturally relevant therapy approaches in working with different groups (APA, 2003; Sue et al., 1998). Although issues of race, culture, ethnicity, and gender have traditionally been ignored or distorted in the mental health literature, these forces are now increasingly recognized as powerful influences on many aspects of normal and abnormal human development (Sue & Sue, 2003).

Four primary dimensions related to cultural diversity—social conditioning, cultural values and influence, sociopolitical influences, and bias in diagnosis—seem to explain how cultural forces exert their influence.

First, how we are raised, what values are instilled in us, and how we are expected to behave in fulfilling our roles seem to have a major effect on the type of disorder we are most likely to exhibit. Traditionally, in our culture men have been raised to fulfill the masculine role, to be independent, assertive, courageous, active, unsentimental, and objective. Women, in contrast, have been raised to be

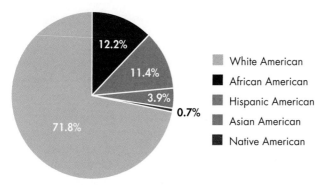

White American

■ African American

■ Hispanic American

■ Asian American

■ Native American

12.2%

11.4%

3.9%

0.7%

71.8%

Figure 1.5 Census 2000 Racial/Ethnic Composition of the United States   The rapid demographic transformation of the United States is illustrated in the fact that minorities now constitute an increasing proportion of the population. Several major trends are evident. First, within several decades, people of color will constitute a numerical majority. Second, the population of Hispanic Americans nearly equals that of African Americans and will soon surpass them. Because the 2000 Census now allows citizens to claim more than one racial category, the accuracy of counts have been made more difficult. There is little doubt, however, that mental health providers will increasingly be coming into contact with client groups who differ from them in race, ethnicity, and culture.

Mental Health and Society

Cultural Bias in Research

In the past, "mentally healthy" African Americans were described as interested in servitude and being faithful to their masters.

In "Diseases and peculiarities of the Negro race," Dr. Samuel Cartwright (1967) in the early 1800s described two mental disorders known specifically among slaves:

Drapetomania was a mental disorder with one symptom: the condition caused slaves to run away. Cartwright stated that with proper medical treatment (ministering to their needs, protecting them from abuse, and keeping them in servitude), the Negro would "become spell-bound and can not run away."

Dysaesthesia Aethiopica (or as called by slave owners, "Rascality"). The symptoms included destroying property, arguing, and creating disturbances with the overseers "without cause or motive." Cartwright argues that the condition was not due to slavery itself but exposure to "too much liberty."

Researchers have become more sophisticated in dealing with ethnic differences, but there are still indications that ethnic bias may exist in the diagnosis of mental disorders. African Americans are more likely to receive a diagnosis of schizophrenia than European Americans (Trierweiler et al., 2000). Researchers (Iwamasa, Larrabee, & Merritt, 2000) wanted to determine whether college students exhibit preconceived ideas when asked to assign personality disorder characteristics to different ethnic groups. The diagnostic criteria for the different personality disorders

were individually printed on 3 × 5 cards. The participants were told that the characteristics listed were those that people "sometimes have" and that they were to put each card in the box of the group they believed it described most often. The boxes were labeled "African American," "Asian American," "European American," "Latino," and "Native American." The participants were cautioned not to sort by "popular stereotypes" but according to their own beliefs.

The following personality disorders were disproportionately assigned to the following groups: antisocial and paranoid to African Americans; schizoid to Asian Americans; and schizotypal to Native Americans. Latinos did not receive a disproportionate assignment. One-fourth of the participants were African American. One ethnic difference was found. Although African Americans assigned antisocial personality characteristics equally to their own group and to European Americans, the latter were more likely to assign those characteristics to African Americans. These results can be interpreted several ways. First, a strong ethnic diagnostic bias exists that cannot be eliminated by instructions not to apply stereotypes. Second, personality disorders may actually be distributed differently among ethnic groups. A third point to consider is the possibility that the criteria for personality disorders may contain characteristics that are "culturally appropriate" rather than pathological in some ethnic groups. How might you determine which, if any, of these interpretations are accurate?

dependent, helpful, fragile, self-abnegating, conforming, empathetic, and emotional. Some mental health professionals believe that, as a result, women are more likely to internalize their conflicts (resulting in anxiety and depression), whereas men are more likely to externalize and act out (resulting in drug or alcohol abuse and dependence). Although gender roles have begun to change, their effects continue to be widely felt.

Second, mental health professionals now recognize that types of mental disorders differ from country to country and that major differences in cultural traditions among various racial and ethnic minority groups in the United States may influence their susceptibility to certain emotional disorders. Among Hispanic/Latino Americans and Asian Americans, experiencing physical complaints is a common and culturally accepted means of expressing psychological and emotional stress (Lopez, 1989; Uba, 1994). People with these cultural backgrounds believe that physical problems cause emotional disturbances and that the emotional disturbances will disappear as soon as appropriate treatment for the physical illness is instituted.

Third, in response to a history of prejudice, discrimination, and racism, many minorities have adopted various behaviors (in particular, behaviors toward whites) that have proved important for survival in a racist society (Ridley, 1995; Sue & Sue, 2003). Mental health professionals may define these behaviors as abnormal and deviant, yet from the minority group perspective, such behaviors may function as healthy survival mechanisms. We are pointing out that certain behaviors and characteristics need to be evaluated not only by an absolute standard but also by the sociopolitical context in which they arise.

Fourth, epidemiological studies reporting the distribution and types of mental disorders that occur in the population may be prone to bias on the part of the clinician and researcher. The mental health professional is not immune to inheriting the prejudicial attitudes, biases, and stereotypes of the larger society. Even the most enlightened and well-intentioned mental health professional may be influenced by biased attitudes about race, gender, and social class. Cultural bias has a long history as it relates to the research of racial minorities (see the Mental Health and Society box, "Cultural Bias in Research").

It is clear that one of the most powerful emerging trends in the mental health field is in increased interest, appreciation, and respect for multicultural psychology. Understanding abnormal behavior requires a realistic appraisal of the cultural context in which behavior occurs and an understanding of how culture influences the manifestations of abnormality.

The Scientific Method in Clinical Research

Our historical journey into the past suggests that mistaken notions about abnormality can lead to great human suffering. The principles of scientific inquiry and research allow us to guard against incorrect beliefs and to provide the foundations of accurate information. The **scientific method** is a mode of inquiry that provides for the systematic collection of data through controlled observation and for the testing of hypotheses. A **hypothesis** is a conjectural statement that usually describes a relationship between two variables. Different theories, whether supernatural or naturalistic, may result in different hypotheses about the same phenomenon. A **theory** is a group of principles and hypotheses that together explain some aspect of a particular area of inquiry. For example, hypothesized reasons for eating disorders have included biological or neurochemical causes, fear of sexual maturity, societal demands for thinness in women, and pathological family relationships. Each of these hypotheses reflects a different theory.

Characteristics of Clinical Research

Clinical research can proceed only when the relationship expressed in a hypothesis is clearly and systematically stated and when the variables of concern are measurable and defined. We need to define clearly what we are studying and to make sure that the variables are measured with reliable and valid instruments. Clinical research relies on these characteristics—the potential for self-correction, the hypothesizing of relationships, the use of operational definitions, and the consideration of reliability and validity.

Perhaps the unique and most general characteristic of the scientific method is its *potential for self-correction.* Under ideal conditions, data and conclusions are freely exchanged, and experiments are replicable (reproducible), so that all are subject to discussion, testing, verification, and modification. The knowledge developed under these conditions is as free as possible from the scientist's personal beliefs, perceptions, biases, values, attitudes, and emotions.

Another characteristic of the scientific method is that it attempts to identify and explain (*hypothesize*) the relationship between variables. Examples of hypotheses are statements such as: "Some seasonal forms of depression may be due to decreases in

scientific method A method of inquiry that provides for the systematic collection of data through controlled observation and for the testing of hypotheses.

hypothesis A conjectural statement, usually describing a relationship between two variables.

theory A group of principles and hypotheses that together explain some aspect of a particular area of inquiry.

Controlled Observation
The systematic collection of data through controlled observations is the hallmark of the scientific method. Although this child's behavior can be precisely measured and recorded in a laboratory setting, how likely is he to behave in a similar manner in school or at home?

light"; "Autism [a severe disorder beginning in childhood] is a result of poor parenting"; and "Eating disorders are a result of specific family interaction patterns."

Operational definitions are definitions of the variables that are being studied. For example, an operational definition of depression could be (1) a score representing some pattern of responses to a self-report questionnaire on a depression inventory, (2) a rating assigned by an observer using a depression checklist, or (3) a laboratory identification of specific neurochemical changes. Operational definitions are important because they force an experimenter to clearly define what he or she means by the variable.

The scientific method requires that the measures we use be reliable or consistent. *Reliability* refers to the degree to which a measure or procedure will yield the same results repeatedly. Consider, for example, an individual who has been diagnosed, by means of a questionnaire, as having an antisocial personality. If the questionnaire is reliable, the individual should receive the same diagnosis after taking the questionnaire again.

Even if consistent results are obtained, questions can arise over the *validity* of a measure. Does the testing instrument really measure what it was developed to measure? If we claim to have developed a test that identifies multiple personality disorder, we have to demonstrate that it can accomplish this task.

operational definitions Definitions of the variables under study.

experiment A technique of scientific inquiry in which a prediction—an experimental hypothesis—is made about two variables; the independent variable is then manipulated in a controlled situation, and changes in the dependent variable are measured.

experimental hypothesis A prediction concerning how an independent variable affects a dependent variable in an experiment.

▶ Experiments

independent variable A variable or condition that an experimenter manipulates to determine its effect on a dependent variable.

dependent variable A variable that is expected to change when an independent variable is manipulated in a psychological experiment.

The **experiment** is perhaps the best tool for testing cause-and-effect relationships. In its simplest form, the experiment involves formulating an **experimental hypothesis,** which is a prediction concerning how an **independent variable** (the possible cause) affects a **dependent variable** (the factor acted on). The experimenter also attempts to control extraneous or *confounding variables* (factors other than the independent variable that may affect the dependent variable). For example, expectancies of both the research participants and the researchers may influence the outcome of a study. Participants in a study may try to "help" the researcher succeed and, in so doing, may nullify the results of the study (Anderson & Strupp, 1996).

"MR. HARRIS, YOU'RE A HYPOCHONDRIAC,...TAKE THESE TWO PLACEBOS AND CALL ME IN THE MORNING!"

Experiments often make use of experimental and control groups. An *experimental group* is the group that is subjected to the independent variable. A *control group* is a group that is similar in every way to the experimental group except for the manipulation of the independent variable. Suppose you wanted to see whether violent films were more likely to elicit aggression in viewers than family-oriented (nonviolent) ones. Using an experimental design, you could assign participants to one of two groups: the experimental group (violent films) or the control group (nonviolent). The assignment, however, would be on a random basis to guard against preexisting differences among participants that might affect the results. *Random assignment* ensures that all participants have an equal probability of being assigned to either the experimental or the control group. So, if the violent-film group showed higher aggression than the control group, we have greater faith that a cause-and-effect relationship between exposure to violent films and increased aggression can be imputed.

The results of a study may be challenged for other reasons. For example, what if the participants in the experimental group became more aggressive not because of the film exposure but because they knew the hypothesis and/or expected to become more aggressive from watching violent films? Some researchers have found that if participants expect a particular outcome, this expectancy—rather than specific treatment—is responsible for the outcome.

Controlling participant expectancies is crucial to good experimental investigations. Thus experimenters rely on procedures such as *blind studies* (in which participants are prevented from being aware of the treatment they are receiving) and *placebo control groups* (which induce an expectancy without the treatment) in order to control for extraneous variables that might inadvertently affect the outcome.

Experimenter expectations can also influence diagnosis and the outcome of a study. To control for experimenter expectations, the researcher may use a *blind design*, in which the assistant carrying out the study is unaware of the purpose of the study. A method to reduce the impact of both experimenter and participant expectations is the *double-blind design*. In this procedure, neither the individual working directly with the participant nor the participant is aware of the experimental conditions.

Correlational Studies

A **correlation** is the extent to which changes in one variable are accompanied by increases or decreases in a second variable. The variables in a correlation, unlike those in an experiment, are not manipulated. Instead, a statistical analysis is performed to determine whether increases in one variable are accompanied by increases or decreases in the other. The relationship is expressed as a statistically derived *correlation coefficient*, symbolized by r, which has a numerical value between –1 and +1. In a positive correlation, an increase in one variable is accompanied by an increase in the other. When an increase in one variable is accompanied by a decrease in the other variable, it is a negative correlation. The greater the value of r, positive or negative, the stronger is the relationship. (See Figure 1.6 for examples of correlations.)

Figure 1.6 Possible Correlation Between Two Variables   The more closely the data points approximate a straight line, the greater the magnitude of the correlation coefficient r. The slope of the regression line rising from left to right in example (a) indicates a perfect positive correlation between two variables, whereas example (b) reveals a perfect negative correlation. Example (c) shows a lower positive correlation. Example (d) shows no relationship whatsoever.

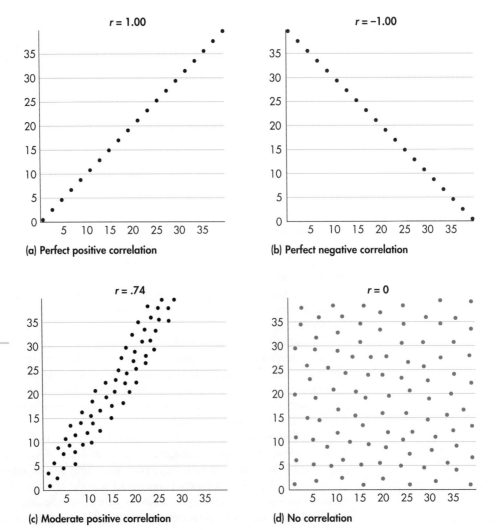

(a) Perfect positive correlation

(b) Perfect negative correlation

(c) Moderate positive correlation

(d) No correlation

Correlations indicate the degree to which two variables are related but not the reasons for the relationship. They do not tell us about a cause-and-effect relationship. If, for example, X and Y are positively related and both increase, we do not know whether X caused Y or whether Y caused X. Further, it may be that a third variable, Z, caused both X and Y to increase or decrease. For example, it has been observed the number of violent crimes (X) is positively correlated with the number of churches (Y) in the community. Does an increase in violent crimes (X) cause creation of more churches (Y), or does having more churches (Y) result in a greater number of violent acts (X)? What is the possibility that with increased size of a community (Z), one would naturally expect both more crime and more churches?

▶ Analogue Studies

Ethical, moral, or legal standards may prevent researchers from devising certain studies on mental disorders or on the effect of treatment. In other cases, studying real-life situations is not feasible because researchers would have a difficult time controlling all the variables. In such cases, researchers may resort to an **analogue study**—an investigation that attempts to replicate or simulate, under controlled conditions, a situation that occurs in real life (Noble & McConkey, 1995). The advantage of this type of investigation is that it allows us to study a phenomenon using experimental designs that are not possible with correlational studies. For example, to study the possible effects of a new form of treatment on patients with anxiety disorders, the researcher may use students who have high test anxiety rather than patients with anxiety disorders.

▶ Single-Participant Studies

Most scientists advocate the study of large groups of people to uncover the basic principles that govern behavior. This approach, called the *nomothetic orientation*, is concerned with formulating general laws or principles while deemphasizing individual variations or differences. Experiments and correlational studies are nomothetic. Other scientists advocate the in-depth study of one person. This approach, exemplified by the single-participant study, has been called the *idiographic orientation*. There has been much debate over which method is more fruitful in studying psychopathology.

Although the idiographic method has many limitations, especially its lack of generality, it has proved very valuable in applied clinical work. Furthermore, the argument over which method is more fruitful is not productive because both approaches are needed to study abnormal behavior. The nomothetic approach seems appropriate for laboratory scientists, whereas the idiographic approach seems appropriate for their clinical counterparts, the psychotherapists, who daily face the pressures of treating disturbed individuals.

There are two types of single-participant studies: the case study and the single-participant experiment. Both techniques may be used to examine a rare or an unusual phenomenon, to demonstrate a novel diagnostic or treatment procedure, to test an assumption, to generate future hypotheses on which to base controlled research, and to collect comprehensive information for a better understanding of the individual.

correlation The extent to which variations in one variable are accompanied by increases or decreases in a second variable.

analogue study An investigation that attempts to replicate or simulate, under controlled conditions, a situation that occurs in real life.

Only the single-participant experiment, however, can determine cause-and-effect relationships.

In psychology, a **case study** is an intensive study of one individual that relies on clinical data, such as observations, psychological tests, and historical and biographical information. A case study thus lacks the control and objectivity of many other methods and cannot be used to demonstrate cause-and-effect relationships. It can serve as the primary source of data in cases in which systematic experimental procedures are not feasible.

The **single-participant experiment** differs from the case study in that the former is actually an experiment in which some aspect of the person's own behavior is used as a control or baseline for comparison with future behaviors. To determine the effectiveness of a treatment, for example, the experimenter begins by plotting a baseline to show the frequency of a behavior before intervention. Then the treatment is introduced, and the person's behavior is observed. If the behavior changes, the treatment is withdrawn. If, after the withdrawal of treatment, the person's behavior again resembles that observed during the baseline condition, we can be fairly certain that the treatment was responsible for the behavior changes observed earlier. In the final step, the treatment is reinstated.

In a second type of single-participant experiment (multiple baseline), baselines are obtained on two or more behaviors. The same intervention is introduced with each. If the behaviors change only with the intervention, confidence is increased that the intervention caused the changed behavior.

Biological Research Strategies

More and more research is being performed in the biological area on the causes and treatment of mental disorders. In the year 2000, for example, the Human Genome Project was able to identify the entire 3.1-billion nucleotide basis of human DNA. The focus of future research will turn away from identifying genes to understanding how they affect behavior. For most forms of psychopathology, this approach will be most helpful in early identification rather than in genetic engineering, as multiple genes are involved in complex traits. Other biologically based research includes **genetic linkage studies** that attempt to determine whether a disorder follows a genetic pattern and identifying **biological markers** (biological indicators of a disorder that may or may not be causal) for specific disorders.

Ethical Issues in Research

case study Intensive study of one individual that relies on observation, psychological tests, and historical and biographical data.

single-participant experiment An experiment performed on a single individual in which some aspect of the person's own behavior is used as a control or baseline for comparison with future behaviors.

Although research is primarily a scientific endeavor, it also raises ethical issues. There is no question that to understand psychopathology and to devise effective treatment, experimenters occasionally may have to devise investigations that cause pain and involve deception. To study human behavior, pain may be inflicted (for example, surgical implants may cause pain, or shocks may be used to induce stress), and deception is sometimes necessary to conceal the true nature of a study. The research must be consistent with certain principles of conduct, however, and must be designed to protect participants, as well as to enable researchers to contribute to the long-term welfare of human beings (and other animals).

The American Psychological Association's (1992) guidelines state that participants should be fully informed of the procedures and risks involved in the research

MenfaL HeaLfh and and sociefy

"I Have It, Too": The Medical Student Syndrome

Medical students probably caught it first. As they read about physical disorders and listened to lecturers describing illnesses, some students began to imagine that they themselves had one disorder or another. "Diarrhea? Fatigue? Trouble sleeping? That's me!" In this way, a cluster of symptoms—no matter how mild or how briefly experienced—can lead some people to suspect that they are very sick.

Students who take a course that examines psychopathology may be equally prone to believe that they have a mental disorder that is described in their text. It is possible, of course, that some students do suffer from a disorder and would benefit from counseling or therapy. Most, however, are merely experiencing an exaggerated sense of their susceptibility to disorders. It has been found that one of every five individuals responded "yes" to the question, "Have you ever felt that you were going to have a nervous breakdown?" Of course, most of those people never suffered an actual breakdown.

Two influences in particular may make us susceptible to these imagined disorders. One is the universality of the human experience. All of us have experienced misfortunes in life. We can all remember and relate to feelings of anxiety, unhappiness, guilt, lack of self-confidence, and even thoughts of suicide. In most cases, however, these feelings are normal reactions to stressful situations, not symptoms of disease. Depression following the loss of a loved one or anxiety before giving a speech to a large audience may be perfectly normal and appropriate. Another influence is our tendency to compare our own functioning with our perceptions of how other people are functioning. The outward behaviors of fellow students may lead us to conclude that they experience few difficulties in life, are self-assured and confident, and are invulnerable to mental disturbance. If we were privy to their inner thoughts and feelings, however, we might be surprised to find that they share our apprehension and insecurities.

If you see yourself anywhere in the pages of this book, we hope you will take the time to discuss your feelings with a friend or with one of your professors. You may be responding to pressures that you have not encountered before—a heavy course load, for example—and to which you have not yet adjusted. Other people can help point out these pressures to you. If your discussion supports your suspicion that you have a problem, however, then by all means consider getting help from your campus counseling and/or health clinic.

and should give their consent to participate. Researchers may use deception only when alternative means are not possible, and participants should be free to withdraw from a study at any time. Participants must be treated with dignity, and research procedures must minimize pain, discomfort, and embarrassment. If undesirable consequences to participants are found, the researcher has the responsibility to detect the extent of these consequences and to remedy them. Finally, unless otherwise agreed on in advance, information obtained from participants is confidential.

▶ Some Closing Thoughts

genetic linkage studies Studies that attempt to determine whether a disorder follows a genetic pattern.
biological markers Biological indicators of a disorder that may or may not be causal.

As you can see, the study of abnormal psychology is not only complex but also heavily influenced by the tenor of the times. As we begin our journey into attempts to explain the causes of certain disorders, we encourage you not to become rigidly locked into one system of belief. Research offers us the tools to act as a counterbalance to our incorrect beliefs and biases. Further, no one explanation is equally applicable to all situations, problems, and populations. Most psychologists now believe that mental illness probably springs not only from a combination of biological and psychological factors but also from societal and environmental influences. The realization that biological, psychological, and sociocultural factors must all be considered in explaining and treating mental disorders has been termed the **biopsychosocial approach.** It would be a serious oversight to neglect the powerful impact on mental health of family upbringing and influence, the stresses of modern society (unemployment, poverty, loss of a loved one, adapting to technological change, and so on), experiences of oppression (prejudice, discrimination, stereotyping), effects of natural disasters (earthquakes, floods, hurricanes), and human-made conflicts such as wars.

Finally, we close this chapter with a word of caution. To be human is to encounter difficulties and problems in life. A course in abnormal psychology dwells on human problems—many of them familiar. As a result, we may be prone to the "medical student syndrome": reading about a disorder may lead us to suspect that we have the disorder or that a friend or relative has it when indeed that is not the case. (See the Mental Health and Society box, "I Have It, Too!") This reaction to the study of abnormal behavior is a common one, and one we must all guard against.

biopsychosocial approach The belief that biological, psychological, and social factors must all be considered in explaining and treating mental disorders.

▷ CHECKPOINT REVIEW

analogue study *(p. 25)*
biological markers *(p. 26)*
biological view *(p. 17)*
biopsychosocial approach *(p. 28)*
case study *(p. 26)*
cathartic method *(p. 18)*
correlation *(p. 24)*
dependent variable *(p. 22)*
experiment *(p. 22)*
experimental hypothesis *(p. 22)*
genetic linkage studies *(p. 26)*
hypothesis *(p. 21)*
independent variable *(p. 22)*
multicultural psychology *(p. 19)*
operational definitions *(p. 22)*
psychological view *(p. 18)*
scientific method *(p. 21)*
single-participant experiment *(p. 26)*
syndrome *(p. 17)*
theory *(p. 21)*

Are mental disorders due primarily to biological or to psychological factors?
- In the nineteenth and twentieth centuries, major medical breakthroughs fostered a belief in the biological roots of mental illness. Scientists believed that they would eventually find organic causes for all mental disorders.
- The treatment of hysteria corroborated the belief that psychological processes could also produce emotional disturbances.

What are some contemporary trends in abnormal psychology?
- Two trends have had a major influence in the mental health professions: (1) the drug revolution in psychiatry, which not only allowed many of the more severely disturbed to be treated outside of a hospital setting but also lent credence to the biological viewpoint; and (2) increasing diversity in the United States, leading to reliance on multicultural psychology.

What characteristics of the scientific method make it useful in studying abnormal behavior?
- Our beliefs about the causes of and treatments for mental disorders are often inaccurate and need to be evaluated. The scientific method provides both for the systematic and controlled collection of data through controlled observation and for the testing of hypotheses.
- Characteristics such as the potential for self-correction, the testing of hypotheses, the use of operational definitions, and a consideration of reliability and validity make the scientific method helpful in studying abnormal behavior.

What are some research methods used to ask and answer questions about psychopathology?
- The experiment is the most powerful research tool we have for determining and testing cause-and-effect relationships. In its simplest form, an experiment involves an experimental hypothesis, an independent variable, and a dependent variable.
- Correlation studies measure the degree to which two variables are related. These techniques provide less precision, control, and generality than experiments, and they cannot be taken to imply cause-and-effect relationships.

■ Analogue studies allow us to replicate or simulate, under controlled conditions, a situation that occurs in real life. It is used when ethical, moral, or legal factors prevent us from using more experimental methods.

■ Single-participant studies study one individual in depth. Two types of single-participant techniques are the case study and the single-participant experiment. The case study is especially appropriate when a phenomenon is so rare that it is impractical to try to study more than a few instances. Single-participant experiments differ from case studies in that cause-and-effect relationships can be determined. They rely on experimental procedures; some aspect of the person's own behavior is taken as a control or baseline for comparison with future behaviors.

■ Biological research strategies allow us to search for genetic factors involved in psychological disorders or to identify biological markers or indicators of a disorder.

What ethical issues are raised in research?

■ Like other tools, the scientific method is subject to misuse and misunderstanding, both of which can give rise to moral and ethical concerns. Such concerns have led the American Psychological Association to develop guidelines for ethical conduct and to establish ways for dealing with violations within the mental health professions.

FOCUS QUESTIONS

- How much of mental disorder can be explained through our biological makeup?

- How important are early childhood experiences and unconscious motivations in determining our mental health?

- What is the role of learning in the development of behavior disorders?

- How powerful are thoughts in causing mental disorders, and can positive thinking be used to combat irrational beliefs?

- Don't we all have within ourselves the ability to move toward health and away from disorders?

- What role does the family play in making us "sick" or "healthy"?

- How do race and culture affect psychopathology formulations?

- How do we reconcile individual and group differences with human commonalities in explaining abnormal behavior?

2 Abnormal Behavior: Models and Treatments

In the chapter "Abnormal Behavior," we described how the rise of humanism influenced society's attitude toward mental disorders. As rational thought replaced superstition in the eighteenth and nineteenth centuries, the mentally disturbed were increasingly regarded as unfortunate human beings who deserved respectful and humane treatment, not as monsters inhabited by the devil. As a result, two different schools of thought arose: (1) mental disorders are caused primarily by biological problems, and (2) abnormal behavior is essentially psychosocial, rooted not in cells and tissues but in the invisible complexities of the human mind or in environmental forces.

To help in understanding explanations of abnormal behavior, let's begin by clarifying two terms that you will encounter frequently. The first is **psychopathology,** which clinical psychologists use as a synonym for abnormal behavior. The second is **model,** a term that requires a more elaborate explanation.

Models in the Study of Psychopathology

A *model* is an analogy used by scientists to describe a phenomenon or process that they cannot directly observe. In using an analogy, the scientist borrows terms, concepts, or principles from one field and applies them to another, as when a physician describes the eye as a camera. When psychologists refer to their "patients" or speak of deviant behavior as "mental illness," they are borrowing the terminology of medicine and applying a *medical model* of abnormal behavior.

Most theorists realize that the models they construct will be limited and will not correspond in every respect to the phenomena they are studying. Because of the complexity of human behavior and because of our relatively shallow understanding of it, psychologists do not expect to develop the definitive model. Rather, they use the models to visualize psychopathology as if it truly worked in the manner described by the models (see Figure 2.1).

To aid us in understanding and applying the various models of abnormality, we present the case of Steven V. Each model in the following sections will provide a thumbnail sketch of Steve's situation as it might be seen by a clinician conceptualizing his condition and recommending treatment.

psychopathology Clinical term meaning abnormal behavior.

model An analogy used by scientists, usually to describe or explain a phenomenon or process that they cannot directly observe.

Steven V., a twenty-one-year-old college student, had been suffering from a crippling and severe bout of depression. Steve's friend, Linda, had recently broken off her relationship with him. Steve had a long psychiatric history and had been hospitalized twice for depression when he was in high school. In the past, he had been given such labels as *schizoid personality disorder, schizophrenia (paranoid type),* and *bipolar mood disorder.*

Steve was born in a suburb of San Francisco, California, the only child of an extremely wealthy couple. His father, who is of Scottish descent, was a prominent businessman who worked long hours and traveled frequently. On those rare occasions when he was at home, Mr. V. was often preoccupied with business matters and held himself quite aloof from his son. The few interactions they had were characterized by his constant ridicule and criticism of Steve. Mr. V. was greatly disappointed that his son seemed so timid, weak, and withdrawn. Although Steve was extremely bright and did well in school, Mr. V. felt that he lacked the "toughness" needed to survive and prosper

31

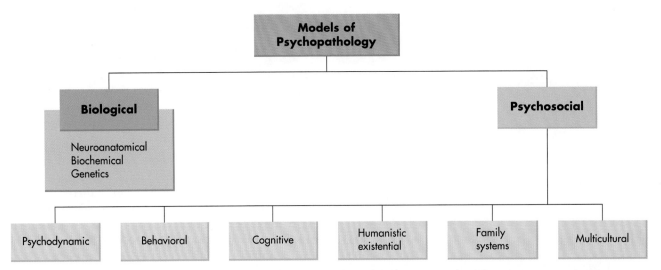

Figure 2.1 **The Major Models of Psychopathology**   Attempts to explain abnormal behavior have resulted in more than a hundred explanations. The major models of psycholopathology, however, are displayed here.

in today's world. Once, when Steve was about ten years old, he came home from school with a bloody nose and bruised face, crying and complaining of being picked on by his schoolmates. His father showed no sympathy but instead berated Steve for losing the fight. In his father's presence, Steve usually felt worthless, humiliated, and fearful of doing or saying the wrong thing.

Mrs. V. was very active in civic and social affairs, and she, too, spent relatively little time with her son. Although she treated Steve more warmly and lovingly than his father did, she seldom came to Steve's defense when Mr. V. bullied him. She generally allowed her husband to make family decisions. In reality, Mrs. V. was quite lonely. She felt abandoned by Mr. V. and harbored a deep resentment toward him, which she was too frightened to express.

When Steve was a child, his mother had been quite affectionate. She had often allowed Steve to sleep with her when her husband was away on business trips. She usually dressed minimally on these occasions and was very demonstrative—holding, stroking, and kissing Steve. This behavior had continued until Steve was twelve, when his mother abruptly refused to let Steve into her bed. The sudden withdrawal of this privilege had confused and angered Steve, who was not certain what he had done wrong. He knew, though, that his mother had been quite upset when she awoke one night to find him masturbating next to her.

Most of the time, Steve's parents seemed to live separately from each other and from their son. Steve was raised, in effect, by a full-time maid. He rarely had playmates of his own age. His birthdays were celebrated with a cake and candles, but the only celebrants were Steve and his mother. By age ten, Steve had learned to keep himself occupied by playing "mind games," letting his imagination carry him off on flights of fantasy. He frequently imagined himself as a powerful figure—Superman or Batman. His fantasies were often extremely violent, and his foes were vanquished only after much blood had been spilled.

As Steve grew older, his fantasies and heroes became increasingly menacing and evil. When he was fifteen, he obtained a pornographic videotape that he viewed repeatedly on a video player in his room. Often, Steve would masturbate as he watched scenes of women being sexually violated. The more violent the acts against women, the more aroused he became. He was addicted to the *Nightmare on Elm Street* films, in which the villain, Freddie Kreuger, disemboweled or slashed his victims to death with his razor-sharp glove. Steve now recalls that he spent much of his spare time between the ages of fifteen and seventeen watching X-rated videotapes or violent movies, his favorite being *The Texas Chainsaw Massacre,* in which a madman saws and hacks women to pieces. Steve always identified with the character perpetrating the outrage; at times, he imagined his parents as the victims.

At about age sixteen, Steve became convinced that external forces were controlling his mind and behavior and were drawing him into his fantasies. He was often filled with guilt and anxiety after one of his mind games. Although he was strongly attracted to his fantasy world, he also felt that something was wrong with it and with him. After seeing the movie *The Exorcist,* he became convinced that he was possessed by the devil.

Biological Models

Steven V. is a biological being, and his mental disorders are caused by some form of biological malfunctioning. Environmental influences are important but probably secondary to the manifestation of psychopathology. His problems are possibly due to a genetic predisposition to mental disorders, to an imbalance of brain chemistry, or, perhaps, to structural abnormalities in his neurological makeup. The most effective way to treat this disorder is through drug therapy or some variation of somatic intervention.

Modern biological explanations of normal and abnormal behavior continue to share certain assumptions: (1) the things that make people who they are—their physical features, susceptibility to diseases, temperaments, and ways of dealing with stress—are embedded in the genetic material of their cells; (2) human thoughts, emotions, and behaviors are associated with nerve cell activities of the brain and spinal cord; (3) a change in thoughts, emotions, or behaviors will be associated with a change in activity or structure (or both) of the brain; (4) mental disorders are highly correlated with some form of brain dysfunction; and (5) mental disorders can be treated by drugs or somatic intervention (Cottone, 1992; DHHS, 1999; Strohman, 2001).

Biological models have been heavily influenced by the neurosciences, a group of subfields that focus on brain structure, function, and disorder. Understanding biological explanations of human behavior requires knowledge about the structure and function of the central nervous system (composed of the brain and spinal cord). Especially important is knowledge about how the brain is organized, how it works, and, particularly, the chemical reactions that enhance or diminish normal brain actions.

The Human Brain

The brain is composed of billions of **neurons,** or nerve cells, that transmit messages throughout the body. The brain is responsible for three very important and highly complicated functions. It receives information from the outside world, it uses the information to decide on a course of action, and it implements decisions by commanding muscles to move and glands to secrete. Weighing approximately three pounds, this relatively small organ continues to amaze and mystify biological researchers.

The brain is separated into two hemispheres. A disturbance in either one (such as from a tumor or through electrical stimulation with electrodes) may produce specific sensory or motor effects. Each hemisphere controls the opposite side of the body. For

neurons Nerve cells that transmit messages throughout the body.

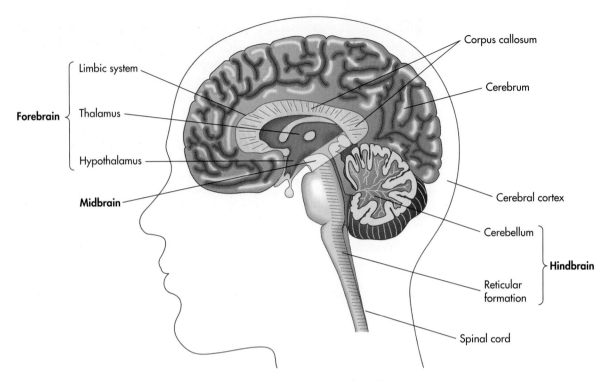

Figure 2.2 The Internal Structure of the Brain A cross-sectional view of the brain reveals the forebrain, midbrain, and hindbrain. Some of the important brain structures are identified within each of the divisions.

example, paralysis on the left side of the body indicates a dysfunction in the right hemisphere. In addition, the right hemisphere is associated with visual-spatial abilities and emotional behavior. The left hemisphere controls the language functions for nearly all right-handed people and for most left-handed ones.

Viewed in cross section, the brain has three parts: forebrain, midbrain, and hindbrain. Although each part is vital for functioning and survival, the forebrain is probably the most relevant to a discussion of abnormality.

The Forebrain The *forebrain* probably controls all the higher mental functions associated with human consciousness, learning, speech, thought, and memory. Within the forebrain are the thalamus, hypothalamus, reticular activating system, limbic system, and cerebrum (see Figure 2.2). The specific functions of these structures are still being debated, but we can discuss their more general functions with some confidence.

The thalamus appears to serve as a "relay station," transmitting nerve impulses from one part of the brain to another. The *hypothalamus* ("under the thalamus") regulates bodily drives, such as hunger, thirst, and sex, and body conditions, such as temperature and hormone balance. The *limbic system* is involved in experiencing and expressing emotions and motivation—pleasure, fear, aggressiveness, sexual arousal, and pain. The largest structure in the brain is the *cerebrum,* with its most visible part, the *cerebral cortex,* covering the midbrain and thalamus.

The Midbrain and Hindbrain The midbrain and hindbrain also have distinct functions.

- The *midbrain* is involved in vision and hearing and—along with the hindbrain—in the control of sleep, alertness, and pain. Mental health professionals are especially interested in the midbrain's role in manufacturing chemicals—serotonin, norepinephrine, and dopamine—that have been implicated in certain mental disorders.

- The *hindbrain* also manufactures serotonin. The hindbrain appears to control functions such as heart rate, sleep, and respiration. The *reticular formation,* a network of nerve fibers that controls bodily states such as sleep, alertness, and attention, starts in the hindbrain and threads its way into the midbrain.

Because the brain controls all aspects of human functioning, it is not difficult to conclude that damage or interruption of normal brain function and activity could lead to observable mental disorders. There are, of course, many biological causes for psychological disorders. Damage to the nervous system is one: As Fritz Schaudinn, a German zoologist, demonstrated in 1905, general paresis results from brain damage caused by parasitic microorganisms. Tumors, strokes, excessive intake of alcohol or drugs, and external trauma (such as a blow to the head) have also been linked to cognitive, emotional, and behavioral disorders. Two specific biological sources—body chemistry and heredity—have given rise to important biological theories of psychopathology.

Biochemical Theories

The basic premise of the biochemical theories is that chemical imbalances underlie mental disorders. This premise relies on the fact that most physiological and mental processes, from sleeping and digestion to reading and thinking, involve chemical actions within the body. Support for the biochemical theories has been found in research into anxiety disorders, mood disorders, Alzheimer's disease, autism, dyslexia, and schizophrenia (Carey & DiLalla, 1994; Lickey & Gordon, 1991; Plomin, Owen, & McGuffin, 1994). Some researchers have even claimed that our gene pool affects such characteristics as alienation, leadership, career choice, risk aversion, religious conviction, and pessimism (Colt & Hollister, 1998). To see how biochemical imbalances in the brain can result in abnormal behavior, we need to understand how messages in the brain are transmitted from nerve cell to nerve cell.

Nerve cells (neurons) vary in function throughout the brain and may appear different, but they all share certain characteristics. Each neuron possesses a cell membrane that separates it from the outside environment and regulates the chemical contents within it. On one end of the cell body are **dendrites,** numerous short rootlike structures whose function is to receive signals from other neurons. At the other end is an **axon,** a much longer extension that sends signals to other neurons, some a considerable distance away. Under an electron microscope, dendrites can be distinguished by their many short branches.

Messages travel through the brain by electrical impulses via neurons: an incoming message is received by a neuron's dendrites and is sent down the axon to bulblike swellings called *axon terminals,* usually located near dendrites of another neuron. Note that neurons do not touch one another. A minute gap (the **synapse**) exists between the axon of the sending neuron and the dendrites of the receiving neuron (see Figure 2.3). The electrical impulse crosses the synapse when the axon releases chemical substances called **neurotransmitters.** When the neurotransmitters reach the dendrites of the receiving neuron, they attach themselves to receptors and bind with them if their "shapes" correspond (see Figure 2.4). The binding of transmitters to receptors in the neuron triggers either a synaptic excitation (encouragement to produce other nerve

dendrites Rootlike structures that are attached to the body of the neuron and that receive signals from other neurons.

axon A long, thin extension at the end of neuron that sends signals to other neurons.

synapse A minute gap between the axon of the sending neuron and the dendrites of the receiving neuron.

neurotransmitters Chemical substances that are released by the axons of sending neurons and that are involved in the transmission of neural impulses to the dendrites of receiving neurons.

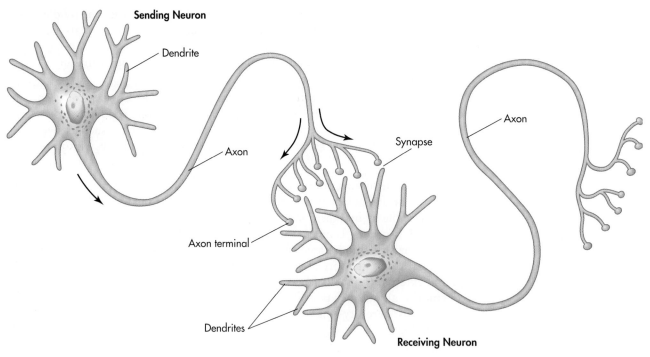

Sending Neuron

Dendrite

Axon

Synapse

Axon

Axon terminal

Dendrites

Receiving Neuron

Figure 2.3 Synaptic Transmission   Messages travel via electrical impulses from one neuron to another. The impulse crosses the synapse in the form of chemicals called *neurotransmitters.* Note that the axon terminals and the receiving dendrites do not touch.

impulses) or synaptic inhibition (a state preventing production of nerve impulses). The human body has many different chemical transmitters, and their effects on neurons vary (see Table 2.1). An imbalance of certain neurotransmitters in the brain is believed to be implicated in mental disorders. Research into biochemical mechanisms holds great promise for our understanding and treatment of mental disorders.

Genetic Explanations

Research strongly indicates that genetic makeup plays an important role in the development of certain abnormal conditions. For instance, animals can inherit "nervousness"; this finding was made some thirty-eight years ago through the breeding of generations of dogs that were either fearful or friendly (Murphree & Dykman, 1965). There is evidence that autonomic nervous system (ANS) reactivity may be inherited in human beings, as well; that is, a person may be born with an ANS that makes an unusually strong response to stimuli (Andreasen, 1984; Baker & Clark, 1990). Other studies (Carey & DiLalla, 1994; Cloninger et al., 1986; Gatz, 1990; Plomin, Owen, & McGuffin, 1994) implicate heredity as a causal factor in alcoholism, schizophrenia, and depression.

Biological inheritance is transmitted by genes. A person's genetic makeup is called his or her **genotype.** Interaction between the genotype and the environment results in the person's **phenotype,** or observable physical and behavioral characteristics. At times, however, it is difficult to determine whether genotype or environment is exerting a stronger influence. For example, characteristics such as eye color are determined solely by genotype—by the coding in one's genes. But other physical characteristics, such as

genotype A person's genetic makeup.
phenotype The observable results of the interaction of a person's genotype and the environment.

electroconvulsive therapy (ECT) The application of electric voltage to the brain to induce convulsions; used to reduce depression; also called *electroshock therapy.*

psychosurgery Brain surgery performed for the purpose of correcting a severe mental disorder.

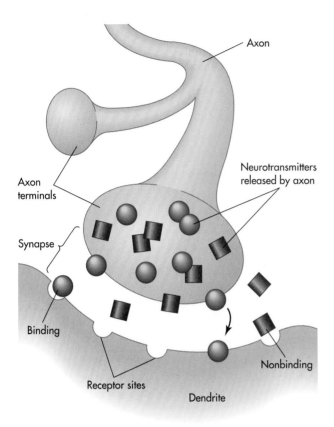

Figure 2.4 Neurotransmitter Binding
Neurotransmitters are released into the synapse and travel to the receiving dendrite. Each transmitter has a specific shape that corresponds to a receptor site. Like a jigsaw puzzle, binding occurs if the transmitter fits into the receptor site.

height, are determined partly by the genetic code and partly by environmental factors.

Biology-Based Treatment Techniques

Biologically based treatments are all intended to affect the biological makeup of the individual. **Electroconvulsive therapy (ECT)**, for example, is the application of electric voltage to the brain to induce convulsions. The patient lies on a padded bed or couch and is first injected with a muscle relaxant to minimize the chance of self-injury during the later convulsions. Then 65 to 140 volts of electricity are applied to the temporal region of the patient's skull, through electrodes, for 0.1 to 0.5 seconds. Convulsions occur, followed by coma. On regaining consciousness, the patient is often confused and suffers a memory loss for events immediately before and after the ECT. Evidence suggests that the treatment is particularly useful for endogenous cases of depression—those in which some internal cause can be determined (Klerman et al., 1994). But how ECT acts to improve depression is still unclear, although some speculate that it somehow alters brain chemistry.

During the 1940s and 1950s, **psychosurgery**—brain surgery performed for the purpose of correcting a severe mental disorder—became increasingly popular. The treatment was used most often with patients suffering from schizophrenia and severe depression, although many who had personality and anxiety disorders also underwent psychosurgery. Critics of psychosurgical procedures have raised both scientific and ethical objections. In the case of lobotomies, for example, initial reports of results were enthusiastic, but later evalua-

Table 2.1	Major Neurotransmitters and Their Effects
Neurotransmitter	**Source and Function**
Acetylcholine (ACH)	One of the most widespread neurotransmitters. Occurs in systems that control the muscles and in circuits related to attention and memory. Reduction in levels associated with Alzheimer's disease.
Dopamine	Concentrated in small areas of the brain, one of which is involved in the control of the muscles. In excess, dopamine can cause hallucinations. Associated with schizophrenia.
Endorphins	Found in the brain and spinal cord. Suppresses pain.
Gamma amino-butyric acid (GABA)	Widely distributed in the brain. Works against other neurotransmitters, particularly dopamine.
Norepinephrine	Occurs widely in the central nervous system. Regulates moods and may increase arousal and alertness. Often associated with mood disorders and eating disorders.
Serotonin	Occurs in the brain. Works more or less in opposition to norepinephrine, suppressing activity and causing sleep. Linked with anxiety disorders, mood disorders, and eating disorders.

Table 2.2 Drugs Most Commonly Used in Drug Therapy

Category	Generic Name	Brand Name	Examples of Clinical Use
Antianxiety	alprazolam	Xanax	Anxiety
	meprobamate	Miltown and Equanil	
	chlordiazepoxide	Librium	
	diazepam	Valium	
Antipsychotic drugs	chlorpromazine	Thorazine	Schizophrenia, psychosis
	trifluoperazine	Stelazine	
	fluphenazine	Prolixin	
	haloperidol	Haldol	
	clozapine	Clozaril	
Antidepressants	phenelzine	Nardil	Depression, anxiety
	tranylcypromine	Parnate	
	imipramine	Tofranil	
	doxepin	Sinequan	
	amitriptyline	Elavil	
	fluoxetine	Prozac	
	paroxetine	Paxil	
	sertraline	Zoloft	
Antimanic drugs	lithium carbonate	Eskalith	Mania
	carbamazapine	Tegretol	
Stimulants	methylphenadate	Ritalin	Attention deficit/hyperactivity disorder

tions indicated that the patient's improvement or lack of improvement was independent of the psychosurgical treatment. In addition, serious negative and irreversible side effects were frequently observed (Valenstein, 1986). On the whole, restriction and regulation of its use seems wise.

Psychopharmacology is the study of the effects of drugs on the mind and on behavior; it is also known as *medication* or *drug therapy*. The use of medications has generally replaced shock treatment and psychosurgery for treating serious behavior disorders. Since the 1950s medication has been a major factor in allowing the early discharge of hospitalized mental patients and permitting them to function in the community. Medication is now widely used throughout the United States: more mental patients receive drug therapy than receive all other forms of therapy combined. Table 2.2 lists the generic and brand names of the drugs most frequently prescribed to treat psychological disorders.

Antianxiety drugs (minor tranquilizers) are often prescribed to relieve anxiety, nervousness, and tension. Some of the better known are Librium and Valium. Because of its selective ability to diminish anxiety and leave adaptive behavior intact, Valium has been widely prescribed in the past. Antianxiety drugs have gained in popularity among the general public, and they are widely used in relieving psychological problems. These drugs can be addictive and can impair psychomotor skills; discontinuing them after prolonged usage at high doses can result in withdrawal symptoms (DHHS, 1999). But

psychopharmacology The study of the effects of drugs on the mind and on behavior; also known as *medication* and *drug therapy.*

they are considered safer than barbiturates, and there is little doubt that they effectively reduce anxiety and the behavioral symptoms of anxiety disorder.

Antipsychotic drugs (or major tranquilizers) are used to control hallucinations and distorted thinking of highly agitated patients and patients with schizophrenia. Several experimental studies have demonstrated the efficacy of antipsychotic drugs in treating schizophrenia (Klerman et al., 1994). A review of many large-scale controlled studies indicates that the beneficial effects of Thorazine, Stelazine, Prolixin, and other antipsychotic drugs have allowed institutions to release thousands of chronic "incurable" mental patients throughout the country (Lickey & Gordon, 1991; Wender & Klein, 1981).

Antidepressant drugs are used to relieve depression and are believed to work by correcting an imbalance of neurotransmitters in the brain. Some of these medications that are commonly known to the public are Prozac, Paxil, and Zoloft. *Antimanic drugs* such as lithium are mood-controlling medications that have been very effective in treating bipolar disorders, especially mania (Klerman et al., 1994). About 70 to 80 percent of manic states can be controlled by lithium, and it also controls depressive episodes. How lithium works remains highly speculative.

Criticisms of Biological Models

The biological model of abnormal behavior has some major shortcomings if it is viewed as the sole explanation for mental disorders. First, it does not adequately account for abnormal behavior for which no biological *etiology,* or cause, can be found. Some mental disorders, such as bipolar and unipolar psychotic mood states and schizophrenia, may have primary biological causes, but strong evidence exists that phobias, eating disorders, and others have a predominantly social cause.

Second, the biological model implicitly assumes a correspondence between organic dysfunction and mental dysfunction, with only a minimal impact from environmental, social, or cultural influences. But rarely are the equations of human behavior so uncomplicated. Increasingly, mental health research has focused on the **diathesis-stress theory,** originally proposed by Meehl (1962) and developed further by Rosenthal (1970). The diathesis-stress theory holds that it is not a particular abnormality that is inherited but rather *a predisposition to develop illness* (diathesis). Certain environmental forces, called *stressors,* may activate the predisposition, resulting in a disorder. Alternatively, in a benign and supportive environment, the abnormality may never materialize.

▶ Psychodynamic Models

> At the core of Steve's problems are his early childhood experiences and his inability to confront his own intense feelings of hostility toward his father and his unresolved sexual longing toward his mother. I believe that Steve did not receive the love and care a child needs to develop into a healthy adult. He was neglected, understimulated, and left on his own. Therapy should be aimed at uncovering Steve's unconscious conflicts, letting him relive his early childhood traumas, and helping him to attain insight into his motivations and fears.

diathesis-stress theory The theory that a predisposition to develop a mental illness—not the mental illness itself—is inherited and that this predisposition may or may not be activated by environmental forces.

psychodynamic models Models based on the view that adult disorders arise from traumas or anxieties originally experienced in childhood but later repressed because they are too threatening for the adult to face.

Psychodynamic models of abnormal behavior view disorders in adults as the result of childhood traumas or anxieties. They hold that many of these childhood-based anxieties operate unconsciously; because they are too threatening for the adult to face, they are repressed through mental defense mechanisms. As a result, people exhibit symptoms they are unable to understand. To eliminate the symptoms, the therapist must make the patient aware of these unconscious anxieties or conflicts.

Sigmund Freud   Freud began his career as a neurologist. He became increasingly intrigued with the relationship between illness and mental processes and ultimately developed psychoanalysis, a therapy in which unconscious conflicts are aired so that the patient can become aware of and understand his or her problems.

The early development of psychodynamic theory is generally credited to Sigmund Freud (1938, 1949), a Viennese neurologist who gave up his practice to enter psychiatry. During his clinical work, Freud became convinced that powerful mental processes could remain hidden from consciousness and could cause abnormal behaviors. **Psychoanalysis** is the process of using treatment techniques that seek to cure abnormal behaviors through airing and understanding unconscious dynamics. Freud believed that the therapist's role was to help the patient achieve insight into these unconscious processes.

Personality Structure

Freud believed that personality is composed of three major components—the *id,* the *ego,* and the *superego*—and that all behavior is a product of their interaction. The *id* is the original component of the personality; it is present at birth, and from it the ego and superego eventually develop. The id operates from the **pleasure principle**—the impulsive, pleasure-seeking aspect of our being—and it seeks immediate gratification of instinctual needs, regardless of moral or realistic concerns.

In contrast, the *ego* represents the realistic and rational part of the mind. It comes into existence because the human personality must be able to cope with the external world if it is to survive. The ego is influenced by the **reality principle**—an awareness of the demands of the environment and of the need to adjust behavior to meet these demands. The ego's decisions are dictated by realistic considerations rather than by moral judgments.

Moral judgments and moralistic considerations are the domain of the *superego;* they often represent society's ideals or values as interpreted by our parents. The superego is composed of the *conscience,* which instills guilt feelings about engaging in immoral or unethical behavior, and the ego *ideal,* which rewards altruistic or moral behavior with feelings of pride.

psychoanalysis Therapy based on the Freudian view that unconscious conflicts must be aired and understood by the patient if abnormal behavior is to be eliminated.

pleasure principle Usually associated with the id in Freudian theory; the impulsive, pleasure-seeking aspect of our being that seeks immediate gratification of instinctual needs regardless of moral or realistic concerns.

reality principle Usually associated with the ego in Freudian theory; an awareness of the demands of the environment and of the need to adjust behavior to meet these demands.

The energy system from which the personality operates occurs through the interplay of *instincts.* Instincts give rise to our thoughts and actions and fuel their expression. Freud emphasized *sex* and *aggression* as the dominant human instincts, because he recognized that the society in which he lived placed strong prohibitions on these drives and that, as a result, people were taught to inhibit them. A profound need to express one's instincts is often frightening and can lead a person to deny the existence of such instincts. Indeed, Freud felt that even though most impulses are hidden from one's consciousness, they nonetheless determine human actions.

Psychosexual Stages

According to psychodynamic theory, human personality develops through a sequence of five **psychosexual stages,** each of which brings a unique challenge. If unfavorable circumstances prevail, the personality may be drastically affected. Because Freud stressed the importance of early childhood experiences, he saw the human personality

Psychosexual Stages　During the oral stage, the first stage of psychosexual development, the infant not only receives nourishment but also derives pleasure from sucking and being close to its mother. Later, during the anal stage, toilet training can be a time of intense emotional conflict between parent and child or it can be a time of cooperation.

as largely determined in the first five years of life—during the *oral* (first year of life), *anal* (around the second year of life), and *phallic* (beginning around the third or fourth years of life) stages. The last two psychosexual stages are the *latency* (approximately six to twelve years of age) and *genital* (beginning in puberty) stages.

The importance of each psychosexual stage for later development lies in whether fixation occurs during that stage. (*Fixation* is the arresting of emotional development at a particular psychosexual stage.) If the infant is traumatized (harmed) in some way during the oral stage, for example, some of the infant's instinctual energy becomes trapped at that stage. Consequently, the personality of that person as an adult will retain strong features of the oral stage. Passivity, helplessness, obesity, chronic smoking, and alcoholism may all be characteristics of an oral personality. According to the psychodynamic model, each stage is characterized by distinct traits and, should fixation occur, by distinct conflicts.

Freud believed that a person who could transcend the various stages without fixation would develop into a normal, healthy individual. Heterosexual interests, stability, vocational planning, marriage, and other social activities would become a person's prime concern during the genital stage.

Defense Mechanisms

Neurotic behavior develops from the threat of overwhelming anxiety, which may lead to full-scale panic. To forestall this panic, the ego often resorts to defense mechanisms, such as those listed in Table 2.3. **Defense mechanisms** share three characteristics:

psychosexual stages In psychoanalytic theory, the sequence of stages—oral, anal, phallic, latency, and genital—through which human personality develops.

defense mechanisms In psychoanalytic theory, ego-protection strategies that shelter the individual from anxiety, that operate unconsciously, and that distort reality.

Table 2.3 Defense Mechanisms	

Repression   The blocking of forbidden or dangerous desires and thoughts to keep them from entering one's consciousness; according to Freud, the most basic defense mechanism. *Example:* A soldier who witnesses the horrible death of his friend in combat may force the event out of consciousness because it symbolizes his own mortality.

Reaction formation   Repression of dangerous impulses, followed by converting them to their direct opposite. *Example:* A woman who gives birth to an unwanted child may become an extremely overprotective mother who is afraid to let the child out of her sight and who showers the child with superficial attention.

Projection   Ridding oneself of threatening desires or thoughts by attributing them to others. *Example:* A worker may mask unpleasant feelings of inadequacy by blaming his poor performance on the incompetence of fellow workers or on a conspiracy in which enemies are disrupting his life.

Rationalization   Explaining one's behavior by giving well-thought-out and socially acceptable reasons that do not happen to be the real ones. *Example:* A student may explain flunking a test as follows: "I'm not interested in the course and don't really need it to graduate. Besides, I find the teacher extremely dull."

Displacement   Directing an emotion, such as hostility or anxiety, toward a substitute target. *Example:* A meek clerk who is constantly belittled by her boss, builds up tremendous resentment and snaps at her family members instead of at her boss, who might fire her.

Undoing   A symbolic attempt, often ritualistic or repetitive, to right a wrong or negate some disapproved thought, impulse, or act. *Example:* In Shakespeare's play, Lady Macbeth goads her husband into slaying the king and then tries to cleanse herself of sin by constantly going through the motions of washing her hands.

Regression   A retreat to an earlier developmental level—according to Freud, the person's most fixated stage—that demands less mature responses and aspirations. *Example:* A dignified college president drinks too much and sings old school songs at a reunion with college classmates.

they protect the individual from anxiety, they operate unconsciously, and they distort reality.

All individuals use some strategies to reduce anxiety. Defense mechanisms are considered maladaptive, however, when they are overused—that is, when they become the predominant means of coping with stress and when they interfere with one's ability to handle life's everyday demands. The difference is one of degree, not of kind.

Psychodynamic Therapy

Psychoanalytic therapy, or psychoanalysis, seeks to overcome defenses so that repressed material can be uncovered, the client can achieve insight into his or her inner motivations and desires, and unresolved childhood conflicts can be controlled. Psychoanalysts traditionally use four methods to achieve their therapeutic goals: (1) free association and dream analysis, (2) analysis of resistance, (3) transference, and (4) interpretation.

In **free association,** the patient says whatever comes to mind, regardless of how illogical or embarrassing it may seem, for the purpose of revealing the contents of his or her unconscious. Psychoanalysts believe that the material that surfaces in this process is determined by the patient's psychic makeup and that it can provide some understanding of the patient's conflicts, unconscious processes, and personality dynamics. Simply asking patients to talk about their conflicts is fruitless, because they have repressed the most important material from their consciousness. Instead, reports of dreams, feelings, thoughts, and fantasies reflect a patient's psychodynamics; the therapist's tasks are to encourage continuous free association of thoughts and to interpret the results.

Similarly, *dream analysis* is a very important therapeutic tool that depends on psychoanalytic interpretation of hidden meanings in dreams. Freud is often credited with referring to dreams as "the royal road to the unconscious." According to psychoana-

free association A psychoanalytic method that involves the patient saying whatever comes to mind, regardless of how illogical or embarrassing it may seem, for the purpose of revealing the contents of the patient's unconscious.

lytic theory, when people sleep, defenses and inhibitions of the ego weaken, allowing unacceptable motives and feelings to surface. This material comes out in the disguised and symbolic form of a dream. The portion we remember is called the *manifest content,* and the deeper, unacceptable impulse is the *latent content.* The therapist's job is to uncover the disguised symbolic meanings and let the patient achieve insight into the anxiety-provoking implications.

Analysis of resistance is another technique used in therapy. Throughout the course of psychoanalytic therapy, the patient's unconscious may try to impede the analysis, in a process known as **resistance,** by preventing the exposure of repressed material. In free association, for example, the patient may suddenly change the subject, lose the train of thought, go blank, or become silent. Such resistance may also show up in a patient's late arrival or failure to keep an appointment. A trained analyst is alert to telltale signs of resistance because they indicate that a sensitive area is being approached.

When a patient begins to perceive, or behave toward, the analyst as though the analyst were an important person in the patient's past, the process of transference is occurring. In **transference,** the patient reenacts early conflicts by carrying over and applying to the analyst feelings and attitudes that the patient had toward significant others—primarily parents—in the past. These feelings and attitudes then become accessible to understanding. They may be positive, involving feelings of love for the analyst, or negative, involving feelings of anger and hostility.

Through *interpretation*—the explanation of a patient's free associations, reports of dreams, and the like—a sensitive analyst can help the patient gain insight (both intellectual and emotional) into his or her repressed conflicts. By pointing out the symbolic attributes of a transference relationship or by noting the peculiar timing of symptoms, the analyst can direct the patient toward conscious control of unconscious conflicts.

Post-Freudian Perspectives

Freud's psychoanalytic approach attracted many followers. Some of Freud's disciples, however, came to disagree with his insistence that the sex instinct is the major determinant of behavior. Many of his most gifted adherents broke away from him and formulated coherent psychological models of their own. The major differences between the various post-Freudian theories and psychoanalysis lie in the emphasis that the former placed on ego autonomy and past interpersonal relations (object relations).

Among the ego-autonomy theorists were people such as Anna Freud, Heinz Hartmann, and Erik Erikson, who believed that cognitive processes of the ego were often constructive, creative, and productive, independent from the id. Likewise, object relations theorists such as Melanie Klein, Margaret Mahler, Otto Kernberg, and Heinz Kohut stressed the importance of interpersonal relationships and the child's separation from the mother as important in one's psychological growth.

Criticisms of Psychodynamic Models

Psychodynamic theory has had a tremendous impact on the field of psychology, but three major criticisms are often leveled at it (Joseph, 1991). First, Freud's observations about human behavior were often made under uncontrolled conditions. For example, he relied heavily on case studies and on his own self-analysis as a basis for formulating theory. His patients, from whom he drew conclusions about universal aspects of personality dynamics and behavior, tended to represent a narrow spectrum of one society. A second criticism of psychoanalysis is that it cannot be applied to a wide range of disturbed people. Among them are individuals who have speech disturbances or are inarticulate (talking is important in therapy); people who have urgent, immediate problems (classical psychoanalysis requires much time); and people who are very young or old. Third, psychodynamic formulations are very difficult to investigate in a scientific manner because they are so ambiguous and loosely formulated.

resistance During psychoanalysis, the process in which the patient unconsciously attempts to impede the analysis by preventing the exposure of repressed material; tactics include silence, late arrival, failure to keep appointments, and others.

transference During psychotherapy, a process in which the patient reenacts early conflicts by carrying over and applying to the therapist feelings and attitudes that the patient had toward significant others (primarily parents) in the past.

►► CHECKPOINT REVIEW

How much of mental disorder can be explained through our biological makeup?

■ Biological models cite various organic causes of psychopathology:
- Damage to the nervous system.
- Biochemical imbalances. Several types of psychological disturbances have been found to respond to drugs. In addition, a good deal of biochemical research has focused on identifying the role of neurotransmitters in abnormal behavior.
- Hereditary predisposition. Researchers have found correlations between genetic inheritance and certain psychopathologies.
- Mental health research increasingly focuses on the diathesis-stress theory—the idea that a predisposition to a disorder, not the disorder itself, may be inherited.

How important are early childhood experiences and unconscious motivations in determining our mental health?

■ Psychodynamic models emphasize childhood experiences and the role of the unconscious in determining adult behavior.

■ Sigmund Freud, the founder of psychoanalysis, believed that personality has three components: the id, which represents the impulsive, selfish, pleasure-seeking part of the person; the ego, which represents the rational part; and the superego, which represents society's values and ideals. Each component checks and balances the others.

■ Instincts, the energy system from which the personality operates, manifest themselves in various ways during the five psychosexual stages: oral, anal, phallic, latency, and genital. Each of these life stages poses unique challenges that, if not adequately resolved, can result in maladaptive adult behaviors.

■ Post-Freudians accept basic psychodynamic tenets but differ from traditional strict Freudian theorists along several dimensions: ego autonomy, the influence of social forces, and the importance of object relations.

◄◄ Behavioral Models

> The roots of Steve's problems can be traced to his behavioral repertoire. Many of the behaviors he has learned are inappropriate, and his repertoire lacks useful, productive behaviors. He has had little practice in social relationships, lacks good role models, and has difficulty distinguishing between appropriate and inappropriate behavior. When Steve discusses or acts out these beliefs, he garners much attention from his parents, peers, and onlookers (perhaps a form of reinforcement). In sum, I recommend behavioral therapy that includes modeling and role playing to enhance Steve's social skills and a program to eliminate or control his delusional thoughts.

The **behavioral models** of psychopathology are concerned with the role of learning in abnormal behavior. The differences among them lie mainly in their explanations of how learning occurs. Although some models appear to disagree, they generally tend to complement one another. The three learning models discussed here—classical conditioning, operant conditioning, and observational learning—are usually applied to different types of behavior.

The Classical Conditioning Model

Early in the twentieth century, Ivan Pavlov (1849–1936), a Russian physiologist, discovered a process known as **classical conditioning,** in which responses to new stimuli are learned through association. This process involves involuntary responses (such as

behavioral models Theories of psychopathology that are concerned with the role of learning in abnormal behavior.

classical conditioning A principle of learning in which involuntary responses to stimuli are learned through association.

Stimulus:	UCS (food)	UCS & CS (food & bell)	CS (bell alone)
Response:	UCR (salivation)	UCR (salivation)	CR (conditioned salivation)

Figure 2.5 A Basic Classical Conditioning Process   Dogs normally salivate when food is provided (left drawing). With his laboratory dogs, Ivan Pavlov paired the ringing of a bell with the presentation of food (middle drawing). Eventually, the dogs would salivate to the ringing of the bell alone, when no food was near (right drawing).

reflexes, emotional reactions, and sexual arousal), which are controlled by the autonomic nervous system. Pavlov's discovery was accidental. He was measuring dogs' salivation as part of a study of their digestive processes when he noticed that the dogs began to salivate at the sight of an assistant carrying their food. This response puzzled Pavlov and led to his formulation of classical conditioning. He reasoned that food is an **unconditioned stimulus (UCS)**, which, in the mouth, automatically elicits salivation; this salivation is an unlearned or **unconditioned response (UCR)** to the food. Pavlov then presented a previously *neutral* stimulus (one, such as the sound of a bell, that does not initially elicit salivation) to the dogs just before presenting the food. He found that, after a number of repetitions, the sound of the bell alone elicited salivation. This learning process is based on association: the neutral stimulus (the bell) acquires some of the properties of the unconditioned stimulus (the food) when they are repeatedly paired. When the bell alone can provoke the salivation, it becomes a **conditioned stimulus (CS)**. The salivation elicited by the bell is a **conditioned response (CR)**—a learned response to a previously neutral stimulus. Each time the conditioned stimulus is paired with the unconditioned stimulus, the conditioned response is said to be *reinforced*, or strengthened. Pavlov's conditioning process is illustrated in Figure 2.5.

In a classic and often-cited experiment, John B. Watson (Watson & Rayner, 1920), using classical conditioning principles, was able to demonstrate that the acquisition of a phobia (an exaggerated, seemingly illogical fear of a particular object or class of objects) could be explained by classical conditioning. Classical conditioning has provided explanations not only for the acquisition of phobias but also for certain unusual sexual attractions and other extreme emotional reactions.

The Operant Conditioning Model

An **operant behavior** is a voluntary and controllable behavior, such as walking or thinking, that "operates" on an individual's environment. In an extremely warm room, for example, you would have difficulty consciously controlling your sweating—"willing" your body not to perspire. You could, however, simply walk out of the uncomfortably warm room—an operant behavior. Most human behavior is operant in nature.

unconditioned stimulus (UCS) In classical conditioning, the stimulus that elicits an unconditioned response.

unconditioned response (UCR) In classical conditioning, the unlearned response made to an unconditioned stimulus.

conditioned stimulus (CS) In classical conditioning, a previously neutral stimulus that has acquired some of the properties of another stimulus with which it has been paired.

conditioned response (CR) In classical conditioning, the learned response made to a previously neutral stimulus that has acquired some of the properties of another stimulus with which it has been paired.

operant behavior A voluntary and controllable behavior that "operates" on an individual's environment.

B.F. Skinner   Skinner was a leader in the field of behaviorism. His research and work in operant conditioning started a revolution in applying the principles of learning to the psychology of human behavior. He was also a social philosopher, and many of his ideas fueled debate about the nature of the human condition. These ideas were expressed in his books, *Walden II* and *Beyond Freedom and Dignity*.

operant conditioning A theory of learning that applies primarily to voluntary behaviors and that holds that these behaviors are controlled by the consequences that follow them.

observational learning theory A theory of learning that holds that an individual can acquire behaviors simply by watching other people perform them.

modeling The process of learning by observing models and later imitating them; also known as *vicarious conditioning*.

systematic desensitization A form of counterconditioning aimed at reducing anxiety by overcoming it with an antagonistic response.

Operant conditioning differs from classical conditioning primarily in two ways. First, classical conditioning is linked to the development of involuntary behaviors, such as fear responses, whereas operant conditioning is related to voluntary behaviors. Second, behaviors based on *classical* conditioning are controlled by stimuli, or events *preceding* the response: salivation occurs only when it is preceded by a UCS (food in the mouth) or a CS (the thought of a sizzling, juicy steak covered with mushrooms, for example). In **operant conditioning,** however, behaviors are controlled by reinforcers—consequences that influence the frequency or magnitude of the event they follow. Positive consequences increase the likelihood and frequency of a response. But when the consequences are negative, the behavior is less likely to be repeated. For example, a student is likely to raise his or her hand in class often if the teacher recognizes the student, smiles, and seems genuinely interested in the student's comments.

Studies have demonstrated a relationship between environmental reinforcers and certain abnormal behaviors. For example, parents may unwittingly reinforce a child's self-injurious behaviors by showing greater attention and concern whenever such responses occur. Although positive reinforcement can account for some forms of self-injurious or other undesirable behaviors, in some instances other variables seem more important. *Negative reinforcement* (the removal of an aversive stimulus), for example, can also strengthen and maintain unhealthy behaviors. Consider a student who has enrolled in a class in which the instructor requires oral reports. The thought of doing an oral presentation in front of a class produces aversive feelings in the student, such as anxiety, sweating, an upset stomach, and trembling. To stop the unpleasant reaction, the student switches to another section in which the instructor does not require oral presentations. The student's behavior is reinforced by escape from aversive feelings, and such avoidance responses to situations involving "stage fright" will increase in frequency.

The Observational Learning Model

The traditional behavioral theories of learning—classical conditioning and operant conditioning—require that the individual actually perform behaviors to learn them. **Observational learning theory** suggests that an individual can acquire new behaviors simply by watching other people perform them (Bandura, 1969; Bandura & Walters, 1963). The process of learning by observing models (and later imitating them) is called *vicarious conditioning* or **modeling.** Direct and tangible reinforcement (such as giving praise or other rewards) for imitation of the model is not necessary, although reinforcers are necessary to maintain behaviors learned in this manner. Observational learning can involve both respondent and operant behaviors, and its discovery has had such an impact in psychology that it has been proposed as a third form of learning.

Learning by Observing Observational learning is based on the theory that behavior can be learned by observing it. Although much has been made of the relationship between violence and aggression viewed on television and in movies, observational learning can have positive benefits as well.

In explaining psychopathology, the assumption is that exposure to disturbed models is likely to produce disturbed behaviors. For example, when monkeys watched other monkeys respond with fear to an unfamiliar object, they learned to respond in a similar manner (Cook, Hodes, & Lang, 1986).

Behavioral Therapies

Treatments based on classical conditioning, operant conditioning, and observational learning have gained widespread popularity (DHHS, 1999; Norcross & Freedheim, 1992). Behavior therapists typically use a variety of techniques, but we confine our discussion to a limited number. They all, however, rely on the principles of learning to devise treatment strategies.

Systematic desensitization relies on classical conditioning principles to treat anxiety (Wolpe, 1973). This technique reduces anxiety to a feared situation by eliciting an alternative response that is incompatible with anxiety. For example, if a woman is afraid of flying in a jet plane, her anxiety response could be reduced by training her to relax while in airplanes. Two other techniques that use the classical conditioning principles of extinction are flooding and implosion (Levis, 1985; Stampfl & Levis, 1967). The two are very similar. **Flooding** attempts to extinguish fear by placing the client in a real-life anxiety-provoking situation at full intensity. **Implosion** attempts to extinguish fear by having the client imagine the anxiety-provoking situation at full intensity. The difference between systematic desensitization and flooding and implosion lies in the speed with which the fearful situation is introduced to the client. Systematic desensitization introduces it more slowly. Flooding and implosion require the client to immediately confront the feared situation in its full intensity. The belief is that the client's fears will be extinguished if he or she is not allowed to avoid or escape the situation. In flooding, for example, a client who is afraid of heights may be taken to the top of a tall building, mountain, or bridge and physically prevented from leaving. Some studies have indicated that flooding effectively eliminates specific fears such as phobias (Foa & Kozak, 1986). In implosion therapy, the client is forced to imagine a feared situation.

Aversive conditioning is a widely used classical conditioning technique in which an undesirable behavior is paired with an unpleasant stimulus to suppress the undesirable behavior. For example, aversive conditioning has been used to modify the smoking behaviors of heavy smokers. In the rapid-smoking technique, smokers who are trying to quit are asked to puff cigarettes at a fast rate (perhaps a puff every six or seven seconds). Puffing at this rate usually brings on nausea, so the nausea from puffing is associated with smoking behaviors. After repeated pairings, many smokers find cigarette smoke aversive and are more motivated to quit (Glasgow & Lichtenstein, 1987).

flooding A behavioral treatment that attempts to extinguish fear by placing the client in continued *in vivo* (actual) or imagined anxiety-provoking situations; a form of exposure therapy.

implosion A behavioral treatment that attempts to extinguish a fear by having the client imagine the anxiety-provoking situation at full intensity.

aversive conditioning A classical conditioning technique in which an undesirable behavior is paired with an unpleasant stimulus to suppress the undesirable behavior.

Behavior modification using operant methods have also flourished, and many ingenious programs have been developed. Treatment programs that reward patients with tokens for appropriate behaviors are known as **token economies.** The tokens may be exchanged for hospital privileges, food, or weekend passes. The goal is to modify patient behaviors using a secondary reinforcer (the tokens). In much the same way, money operates as a secondary reinforcer for people who work.

When more benign methods are ineffective, punishment is sometimes used in treating children with autism and schizophrenia. In an early study, Lovaas (1977; Lovaas, Schaeffer, & Simmons, 1965) used electric shock as a punishment for the purpose of modifying children's behaviors. A floor gridded with metal tape was constructed so that a painful but not physically damaging shock could be administered to their bare feet. By turning the shock on and off, the experimenters were able to condition desired behaviors in the children. Affectionate responses, such as kissing and hugging, were developed, and tantrum behaviors were eliminated—all via the use of shock as an aversive stimulus.

Criticisms of the Behavioral Models

Behavioral approaches to psychopathology have had a tremendous impact in the areas of etiology and treatment, and they are a strong force in psychology today. The contributions of behaviorist perspectives include: (1) questioning the adequacy of the biological model of psychological disorders, (2) stressing the importance of external influences on behavior, (3) requiring strict adherence to scientific methods, and (4) encouraging continuing evaluation of the techniques employed by psychologists. These features endow behaviorism with a degree of effectiveness and accountability that is lacking in the insight-oriented perspectives.

Opponents of the behavioral orientation point out that it often neglects or places a low importance on the inner determinants of behavior. They criticize the behaviorists' extension to human beings of results obtained from animal studies. Some also charge that because of its lack of attention to human values in relation to behavior, the behaviorist perspective is mechanistic, viewing people as "empty organisms." And some critics complain that behaviorists are not open-minded and that they tend to dismiss out of hand the advances and data accumulated by other approaches to therapy. Criticism that behavioral approaches ignore the person's inner life is less applicable to proponents of modeling.

Cognitive Models

> Steve is a "thinking being." The psychological problems he is experiencing derive from two main cognitive sources: his irrational thoughts or belief system about himself and others and his distorted thought processes, which lead him to misinterpret events. Steve needs to recognize the role that thinking and belief systems play in his problems. He must learn to identify self-statements, belief systems, or assumptions that are irrational and maladaptive and to respond to them by rationally disputing them.

token economy A treatment program, based on principles of operant conditioning, that rewards patients for appropriate behaviors with tokens, which can then be exchanged for hospital privileges, food, or weekend passes.

cognitive model A principle of learning that holds that conscious thought mediates, or modifies, an individual's emotional state and/or behavior in response to a stimulus.

Cognitive models are based on the assumption that conscious thought mediates, or modifies, an individual's emotional state and/or behavior in response to a stimulus. According to these models, people actually create their own problems (and symptoms) by the way they interpret events and situations. For example, one person who fails to be hired for a job may become severely depressed, blaming himself for the failure.

Another might become only mildly irritated, believing that failure to get the job had nothing to do with personal inadequacy. How does it happen that events (not being hired for a job) are identical for both people but the responses are very different? To explain this phenomenon, we have to look at *mediating processes*—the thoughts, perceptions, and self-evaluations that determine our reactions and behaviors.

Cognitive theories argue that modifying thoughts and feelings is essential to changing behavior. How people label a situation and how they interpret events profoundly affect their emotional reactions and behaviors. Cognitive psychologists usually search for the causes of psychopathology in one of two processes: in actual irrational and maladaptive assumptions and thoughts or in distortions of the actual thought process. Almost all cognitive theorists stress heavily that disturbed individuals have both irrational and maladaptive thoughts (Beck, 1997; Ellis, 1997; Meichenbaum, 1993). Clients often engage in an almost rigid, inflexible, and automatic interpretation of events they have experienced. These negative thoughts seem to "just happen" as if by reflex, even in the face of objective contrary evidence.

In working with his clients, Beck (1997) concluded that cognitive content is organized in a hierarchy along three levels. At the first level are our most accessible and least stable cognitions, the voluntary thoughts that we have the greatest ability to control and summon at will. Clients suffering from an anxiety disorder, for example, are readily able to describe their symptoms and to offer superficial causes and solutions for them. Most people do not, however, have such ready access to the second level of cognitions, the automatic thoughts that occur spontaneously. The cognitions at this second level are triggered by circumstances and intercede between an event or stimulus and the individual's emotional and behavioral reactions. A student who must make an oral presentation in class may think, "everyone will see I'm nervous." Such thoughts are given credibility without being challenged and usually derive from the third level of cognitions: underlying assumptions about ourselves and the world around us. For example, the belief that one is a failure and an ineffectual person in all aspects of life moderates interpretation of all events. These assumptions are quite stable and almost always outside of the person's awareness.

Ellis (1997) believes that psychological problems are produced by irrational thought patterns that stem from the individual's belief system. Unpleasant emotional responses that lead to anger, unhappiness, depression, fear, and anxiety result from one's *thoughts* about an event rather than from the *event itself*. These irrational thoughts have been conditioned through early childhood, but we also add to the difficulty by reinstilling these false beliefs in ourselves through autosuggestion and self-repetition. Ellis hypothesized that irrational thinking operates from dogmatic, absolutist "shoulds," "musts," and "oughts." Some examples are self-statements such as "I must be loved by my mother or father," "I ought to be able to succeed in everything," and "If I don't get what I want, it will be awful." Cynically, Ellis has referred to the many "musts" that cause human misery as "musturbatory activities."

Although being accepted and loved by everyone is desirable, it is an unrealistic and irrational idea, and as such it creates dysfunctional feelings and behaviors. Consider a student who becomes depressed after an unsuccessful date. An appropriate emotional response in such an unsuccessful dating situation might be frustration and temporary disappointment. A more severe depression will develop only if the student adds irrational thoughts, such as "Because this person turned me down, I am worthless. . . . I will never succeed with anyone of the opposite sex. . . . I am a total failure."

The study of cognitions as a cause of psychopathology has led many therapists to concentrate on the *process* (as opposed to the *content*) of thinking that characterizes both normal and abnormal individuals. Ellis (1962, 1997) believed that human beings are born with the potential for both rational and irrational thinking. Ellis described the process by which an individual acquires irrational thoughts through interactions with significant others, and he called it the *A-B-C theory of personality. A* is an event, a

Table 2.4 Beck's Six Types of Faulty Thinking	
Arbitrary inference Drawing conclusions about oneself or the world without sufficient and relevant information. *Example:* A man not hired by a potential employer perceives himself as "totally worthless" and believes he probably will never find employment of any sort.	**Magnification and exaggeration** The process of overestimating the significance of negative events. *Example:* A runner experiences shortness of breath and interprets it as a major health problem, possibly even an indication of imminent death.
Personalization Relating external events to one another when no objective basis for such a connection is apparent. *Example:* A student who raises his hand in class and is not called on by the professor believes that the instructor dislikes or is biased against him.	**Polarized thinking** An "all-or-nothing," "good or bad," and "either-or" approach to viewing the world. *Example:* At one extreme, a woman who perceives herself as "perfect" and immune from making mistakes; at the other extreme, a woman who believes she is totally incompetent.
Overgeneralization Holding extreme beliefs on the basis of a single incident and applying it to a different or dissimilar and inappropriate situation. *Example:* A depressed woman who has relationship problems with her boss may believe she is a failure in all other types of relationships.	**Selective abstraction** Drawing conclusions from very isolated details and events without considering the larger context or picture. *Example:* A student who receives a C on an exam becomes depressed and stops attending classes even though he has A's and B's in his other courses. The student measures his worth by failures, errors, and weaknesses rather than by successes or strengths.

fact, or the individual's behavior or attitude. *C* is the person's emotional or behavioral reaction. The activating event *A* never causes the emotional or behavioral consequence *C*. Instead, *B*, the person's beliefs about *A*, causes *C*.

Think back to the two job hunters. Job hunter 1, whose activating event *A* was being turned down for the position, may think to himself (irrational beliefs *B*), "How awful to be rejected! I must be worthless. I'm no good." Thus he may become depressed and withdraw (emotional and behavioral consequence *C*). Job hunter 2, on the other hand, reacts to the activating event *A* by saying (rational beliefs *B*), "How unfortunate to get rejected. It's frustrating and irritating. I'll have to try harder" (healthy consequence *C*). The two sets of assumptions and expectations are very different. Job hunter 1 blamed himself and was overcome with feelings of worthlessness; job hunter 2 recognized that not every person is right for every job (or vice versa) and left the situation with self-esteem intact. Job hunter 1 interprets the rejection as "awful and catastrophic" and, as a result, reacts with depression and may cease looking for a job. Job hunter 2 does not interpret the rejection personally, reacts with mild irritation and annoyance, and redoubles his efforts to seek employment.

Although the cognitive model proposed by Ellis applies to both rational and irrational thinking, interest has focused on identifying the types of cognitive distortions that lead to abnormal functioning. Aaron Beck has proposed six types of faulty thinking, which are described in Table 2.4.

Cognitive Approaches to Therapy

Most cognitive approaches share several elements. First, cognitive restructuring is used to change a client's irrational, self-defeating, and distorted thoughts and attitudes to more rational, positive, and appropriate ones. Second, skills training is used to help clients learn to manage and overcome stress. Third, problem solving provides clients with strategies for dealing with specific problems in living.

These techniques have been summarized by Beck and Weishaar (1989):

Cognitive therapy consists of highly specific learning experiences designed to teach patients (1) to monitor their negative, automatic thoughts (cognitions); (2) to recognize the connections between cognition, affect, and behavior; (3) to examine the evidence for and against distorted automatic thoughts; (4) to substitute more reality-oriented interpretations for these biased cognitions; and (5) to learn to identify and alter the beliefs that predispose them to distort their experiences. (p. 308)

Criticisms of the Cognitive Models

Cognitive theories have been attacked by more humanistically oriented psychologists, who believe that human behavior is more than thoughts and beliefs (Corey, 2001). They object to the mechanistic manner by which human beings are reduced to the sum of their cognitive parts. Do thoughts and beliefs really cause disturbances, or do the disturbances themselves distort thinking?

Criticisms have also been leveled at the therapeutic approach taken by cognitive therapists. The nature of the approach makes the therapist a teacher, expert, and authority figure. The therapist is quite direct and confrontational in identifying and attacking irrational beliefs and processes. In such interactions, clients can readily be intimidated into acquiescing to the therapist's power and authority. Thus the therapist may misidentify the client's disorder, and the client may be hesitant to challenge the therapist's beliefs.

Although more evaluative research must be conducted before the cognitive learning approach can be evaluated, this approach, with its emphasis on the powerful influence of internal mediating processes, seems to offer an exciting new direction for behaviorists. It is clear that psychology has undergone a "revolution" in that cognitive and behavioral approaches have been integrated into mainstream psychological thought.

Humanistic and Existential Approaches

> Steve is a flesh-and-blood person, alive, organic, and moving, with thoughts, feelings, and emotions. It appears that he is feeling trapped, immobilized, and lonely and that he is externalizing his problems. In this way, Steve may be evading responsibility for making his own choices and may be protecting himself by staying in the safe, known environment of his "illness." Steve needs to realize that he is responsible for his own actions, that he cannot find his identity in others, and that his life is not predetermined.

Although the humanistic and existential perspectives represent many schools of thought, they nevertheless share a set of assumptions that distinguishes them from other approaches or viewpoints. The first is that an individual's reality is a product of that person's unique experiences and perceptions of the world. Moreover, that individual's subjective universe—how he or she construes events—is more important than the events themselves. Hence, to understand why a person behaves as he or she does, the psychologist must reconstruct the world from that individual's vantage point.

Humanistic and existential theorists stress that individuals have the ability to make free choices and are responsible for their own decisions. The "wholeness" or integrity of the person is of utmost importance. Understanding and helping people does not come about through reducing them to a set of formulas or explaining their actions simply by measuring responses to certain stimuli. People are not machines, nor are they passive subjects to internal and external forces. They have the ability to become what they want to be, to fulfill their capacities, and to lead the lives best suited to them.

The Humanistic Perspective

One of the major contributions of the **humanistic perspective** is its positive view of the individual. Carl Rogers (1902–1987) is perhaps the best known of the humanistic psychologists. Rogers's theory of personality (1959) reflects his concern with human welfare and his deep conviction that humanity is basically "good," forward moving, and trustworthy. Instead of concentrating exclusively on behavior disorders, the humanistic approach is concerned with helping people *actualize* their potential and with bettering the state of humanity. It is based on the idea that people are motivated not only to satisfy their biological needs (for food, warmth, and sex) but also to cultivate, maintain, and enhance the self. The *self* is one's image of oneself, the part one refers to as "I" or "me."

The quintessence of this view is the concept of **self-actualization**—which is an inherent tendency to strive toward the realization of one's full potential. As one psychologist has pointed out, the actualizing tendency can be viewed as fulfilling a grand design or a genetic blueprint (Maddi, 1972). This thrust of life that pushes people forward is manifested in such qualities as curiosity, creativity, and joy of discovery. According to Rogers (1961), this inherent force is common to all living organisms (Maslow, 1954; Rogers, 1959). How one views the self, how others relate to the self, and what values are attached to the self all contribute to one's **self-concept**—the individual's assessment of his or her own value and worth.

Rogers believed that if people were left unencumbered by societal restrictions and were allowed to grow and develop freely, the result would be self-actualized, fully functioning people. In such a case, the self-concept and the actualizing tendency would be considered congruent.

However, society frequently imposes *conditions of worth* on its members, standards by which people determine whether they have worth. That is, significant others (such as parents, peers, friends, and spouse) in a person's life accept some but not all of that person's actions, feelings, and attitudes. The person's self-concept becomes defined as having worth only when others approve. But this reliance on others forces the individual to develop a distorted self-concept that is inconsistent with his or her self-actualizing potential, inhibiting that person from being self-actualized. A state of disharmony or *incongruence* is said to exist between the person's inherent potential and his or her self-concept (as determined by significant others). According to Rogers, this state of incongruence forms the basis of abnormal behavior.

Rogers believed that fully functioning people have been *allowed to grow* toward their potential. The environmental condition most suitable for this growth is called *unconditional positive regard* (Rogers, 1951). In essence, people who are significant figures in someone's life value and respect that person *as a person*. Giving unconditional positive regard is valuing and loving that person regardless of his or her behavior. People may disapprove of someone's actions, but they still respect, love, and care for that someone. The assumption that humans need unconditional positive regard has many implications for child rearing and psychotherapy. For parents, it means creating an open and accepting environment for the child. For the therapist, it means fostering conditions that will allow clients to grow and fulfill their potential; this approach has become known as *nondirective* or **person-centered therapy.**

Person-Centered Therapy

Carl Rogers emphasized that therapists' attitudes are more important than specific counseling techniques. The therapist needs to have a strong positive regard for the client's ability to deal constructively with all aspects of life. The more willing the thera-

humanistic perspective The optimistic viewpoint that people are born with the ability to fulfill their potential and that abnormal behavior results from disharmony between the person's potential and his or her self-concept.

self-actualization An inherent tendency to strive toward the realization of one's full potential.

self-concept An individual's assessment of his or her own value and worth.

person-centered therapy A humanistic therapy that emphasizes the therapist's attitudes in the therapeutic relationship rather than the precise techniques to be used in therapy.

Carl Rogers (1902–1987) Rogers believed that people need both positive regard from others and positive self-regard. According to Rogers, when positive regard is given unconditionally, a person can develop freely and become self-actualized.

pist is to rely on the client's strengths and potential, the more likely it is that the client will discover such strengths and potential. The therapist cannot help the client by explaining the client's behavior or by prescribing actions to follow. Therapeutic techniques involve expressing and communicating respect, understanding, and acceptance.

The way a person-centered therapist most commonly communicates understanding of a client's subjective world is through *reflecting feelings*. In "saying back" to the client what he or she understood the client to say, the therapist provides a "mirror" for the client. The client can then actively evaluate thoughts and feelings with less distortion. Even in very strained situations, the person-centered therapist relies on reflection of feelings and on acceptance in working with the client.

The Existential Perspective

The **existential approach** is really not a systematized school of thought but a set of attitudes. It shares with humanistic psychology an emphasis on individual uniqueness, a quest for meaning in life and for freedom and responsibility, a phenomenological approach (understanding the person's subjective world of experience) to understanding the person, and a belief that the individual has positive attributes that will eventually be expressed unless they are distorted by the environment.

The existential and humanistic approaches differ in several dimensions: on (1) Existentialism is less optimistic than humanism and focuses on the irrationality, difficulties, and suffering all humans encounter in life. (2) Humanists attempt to understand the subjective world of their clients through empathy, whereas existentialists believe that the individual must be viewed within the context of the human condition. (3) Humanism stresses individual responsibility for what he or she becomes in this life, whereas existentialists stress not only individual responsibility but also responsibility to others.

Criticisms of the Humanistic and Existential Approaches

Criticisms of the humanistic and existential approaches point to their "fuzzy," ambiguous, and nebulous nature and to the restricted population in which these approaches can be applied. Although these phenomenological approaches have been extremely creative in describing the human condition, they have been less successful in constructing theory. Moreover, they are not suited to scientific or experimental investigation. The emphasis on subjective understanding rather than prediction and control, on intuition and empathy rather than objective investigation, and on the individual rather than the more general category all tend to hinder empirical study.

Another major criticism leveled at the humanistic and existential approaches is that they do not work well with severely disturbed clients. They seem to be most effective with intelligent, well-educated, and relatively "normal" individuals who may be suffering adjustment difficulties.

existential approach A set of attitudes that has many commonalities with humanism but is less optimistic, focusing on (1) human alienation in an increasingly technological and impersonal world, (2) the individual in the context of the human condition, and (3) responsibility to others, as well as to oneself.

◢ CHECKPOINT REVIEW

aversive conditioning *(p. 47)*

behavioral models *(p. 44)*

classical conditioning *(p. 44)*

cognitive model *(p. 48)*

conditioned response (CR) *(p. 45)*

conditioned stimulus (CS) *(p. 45)*

existential approach *(p. 53)*

flooding *(p. 47)*

humanistic perspective *(p. 52)*

implosion *(p. 47)*

modeling *(p. 46)*

observational learning theory
  (p. 46)

operant behavior *(p. 45)*

operant conditioning *(p. 46)*

person-centered therapy *(p. 52)*

self-actualization *(p. 52)*

self-concept *(p. 52)*

systematic desensitization *(p. 47)*

token economy *(p. 48)*

unconditioned response (UCR)
  (p. 45)

unconditioned stimulus (UCS)
  (p. 45)

What is the role of learning in the development of behavior disorders?
- Behavioral models focus on the role of learning in abnormal behavior.
- The traditional behavioral models of psychopathology hold that abnormal behaviors are acquired through association (classical conditioning) or reinforcement (operant conditioning).
- Negative emotional responses such as anxiety can be learned through classical conditioning: a formerly neutral stimulus evokes a negative response after it has been presented along with a stimulus that already evokes that response.
- Negative voluntary behaviors may be learned through operant conditioning if those behaviors are reinforced (rewarded) when they occur.
- In observational learning, a person learns behaviors, which can be quite complex, by observing them in other people and then imitating, or modeling, those behaviors. Pathological behavior results when the imitated behavior is inappropriate or inappropriately applied.

How powerful are thoughts in causing mental disorders, and can positive thinking be used to combat irrational beliefs?
- According to the cognitive model, perceptions of events are mediated by thoughts and feelings, and the perception may have a greater influence on behavior than the event itself.

Don't we all have within ourselves the ability to move toward health and away from disorders?
- The humanistic perspective actually represents many perspectives and shares many basic assumptions with the existential perspective. Both view an individual's reality as a product of personal perception and experience. Both see people as capable of making free choices and fulfilling their potential. Both emphasize the whole person and the individual's ability to fulfill his or her capacities.
- The best known humanistic formulation is Carl Rogers's person-centered approach, which has as a strong tenet the belief that humanity is basically good. Rogers believed that people are motivated not only to meet their biological needs but also to grow and to enhance the self, to become actualized or fulfilled. If the actualizing tendency is thwarted, behavior disorders may result.
- Although the existential perspective shares similarities with its humanistic counterpart, it is generally less optimistic, focusing on the irrational, human alienation, and the search for meaning. It stresses that the individual has a responsibility not only to oneself but also to others.

◢ The Family Systems Model

Steve's problem is not an isolated phenomenon. It resides in the family system, which should be the primary unit of treatment. Although Steve is manifesting the disorders, his father and mother are also suffering, and their pathological symptoms are reflected in Steve. Attempts to help Steve must therefore focus on the entire family. It is obvious that the relationships between Steve and his father, between Steve and his mother, and between his father and his mother are unhealthy. As long as Steve is the "identified patient" and is seen as "the problem," Mr. and Mrs. V. can continue in their mutual self-deception that all is well between them. I recommend that Steve's entire family be included in a program of therapy.

Almost all of the theories of psychopathology discussed so far in this chapter have focused on the individual. In contrast, the **family systems model** emphasizes the family's influence on individual behavior. This viewpoint holds that all members of a family are enmeshed in a network of interdependent roles, statuses, values, and norms. The behavior of one member directly affects the entire family system. Correspondingly, people typically behave in ways that reflect family influences.

We can identify three distinct characteristics of the family systems approach (Corey, 2001; Goldenberg & Goldenberg, 1995). First, personality development is ruled largely by the attributes of the family, especially by the way parents behave toward and around their children. Second, abnormal behavior in the individual is usually a reflection or "symptom" of unhealthy family dynamics and, more specifically, of poor communication among family members. Third, the therapist must focus on the family system, not solely on the individual, and must strive to involve the entire family in therapy. As a result, the locus of disorder is seen to reside not within the individual but within the family system.

The family system model has spawned a number of approaches to treatment. Most, however, focus on lack of and/or distorted communications, unbalanced power relationships, and unhealthy family alliances among family members. The primary role of therapists is to actively intervene in the family process and aid members in developing healthy ways of responding to one another.

Criticisms of the Family Systems Model

There is no denying that we are social creatures, and by concentrating on this aspect of human behavior, the family systems approach has added an important social dimension to our understanding of abnormal behavior. In fact, much evidence shows that unhealthy family relationships can contribute to the development of disorders. But the family systems model is subject to a number of criticisms. For one thing, the definition of *family* used by these models may be culture bound. For example, the use of the nuclear family is in marked contrast to the way that many racial/ethnic minorities operate, within the extended family system. Further, exclusive emphasis on the family systems model may have particularly unpleasant consequences. Too often, psychologists have pointed an accusing finger at the parents of children who suffer from certain disorders, despite an abundance of evidence that parental influence may not be a factor in those disorders. The parents are then burdened with unnecessary guilt over a situation they could not have otherwise controlled.

Models of Diversity and Psychopathology

family systems model A model of psychopathology that emphasizes the family's influence on individual behavior.

Steven V. is not only a biological, feeling, behaving, thinking, and social being but also a cultural being. The cultural context in which his problems arise must be considered in understanding Steve's dilemma. He is a European American of Scottish descent, born to an extremely wealthy family in the upper socioeconomic class. He is a male, raised in a cultural context that values individual achievement. All of these characteristics mean that many of his experiences are likely to be very different from those of a person who is a member of a minority group, who is economically indigent, or who is female. One might argue, for example, that Steve's father values American individualistic competitiveness and achievement in the extreme. He has succeeded by his own efforts, but, unfortunately, his success has come at the emotional cost of his family. To truly

> understand Steve, we must recognize that the many multicultural variables—race, culture, ethnicity, gender, religion, sexual orientation, and so on—are powerful factors. As such, they influence the types of social-psychological stressors Steve is likely to experience, the ways he will manifest disorders, and the types of therapeutic approaches most likely to be effective.

The cry for the development of multicultural models of psychology has been fueled by a rapid increase in racial and ethnic minority populations in the United States and by a renewed interest in indigenous psychologies (psychologies developed in other countries; Kim & Berry, 1993). Multicultural psychology, however, encompasses more than the study of issues related to racial and ethnic minorities; it also focuses on issues concerning sexual orientation, religious preference, socioeconomic status, gender, physical disabilities, and other such factors (Sue, 2001). In the following discussion, however, we use racial and ethnic minority groups to illustrate the major premises of the multicultural models. To avoid misunderstanding and potential stereotyping, we urge you to read the Mental Health and Society feature, "Problems in Using Racial and Ethnic Group References," carefully before you continue with this topic.

Multicultural Models of Psychopathology

Early attempts to explain differences between various minority groups and their white counterparts tended to adopt one of two models. The first, the inferiority model, contends that racial and ethnic minorities are inferior in some respect to the majority population. For example, this model attributes low academic achievement and higher unemployment rates among African Americans and Latinos to low intelligence (heredity). The second model—the deprivations or deficit model—explained differences as the result of "cultural deprivation." It implied that minority groups lacked the "right" culture. Both models have been severely criticized as inaccurate, biased, and unsupported in the scientific literature (Samuda, 1998).

During the late 1980s and early 1990s, a new and conceptually different model emerged in the literature. Often referred to as the "multicultural model" (Johnson, 1990; White & Parham, 1990), the "culturally different model" (Sue & Sue, 1999), the "culturally pluralistic model," or the "culturally diverse model" (Ponterotto & Casas, 1991; Sue & Sue, 2003), the new model emphasizes that to be culturally different does not equal deviancy, pathology, or inferiority. The model recognizes that each culture has strengths and limitations and that differences are inevitable. Behaviors are to be evaluated from the perspective of a group's value system, as well as by other standards used in determining normality and abnormality.

The multicultural model makes an explicit assumption that all theories of human development arise from a particular cultural context (Sue & Sue, 1999; White & Parham, 1990). Thus many traditional European American models of psychopathology are culture bound, evaluating and viewing events and processes from a worldview not experienced or shared by other cultural groups. For example, individualism and autonomy are highly valued in the United States and are equated with healthy functioning. Most European American children are raised to become increasingly independent, to be able to make decisions on their own, and to "stand on their own two feet." In contrast, many traditional Asians and Asian Americans place an equally high value on "collectivity," in which the psychosocial unit of identity is the family, not the individual (Sue, 1995). Similarly, whereas European Americans fear the loss of "individuality," members of traditional Asian groups fear the loss of "belonging."

Given such different experiences and values, unenlightened mental health professionals may make biased assumptions about human behavior—assumptions that may influence their judgments of normality and abnormality among various racial and eth-

MENTAL HEALTH AND AND SOCIETY

Problems in Using Racial and Ethnic Group References

African American, American Indian, Asian American, and *Hispanic American* have emerged as commonly used terms to refer to four recognized racial and ethnic minority groups in the United States. These terms, however, are not without controversy, nor are they universally accepted by those who are classified as belonging to the groups (Atkinson, Morten, & Sue, 1998). Because we will refer to racial and ethnic groups throughout our text, we want to avoid potential confusion by clarifying some problematic issues.

1. *Terms may be accepted in some regions but not in others, and some generations will prefer one over the other.* For example, we use the term *Hispanic* to refer to individuals with ancestry from Mexico, Puerto Rico, Cuba, El Salvador, the Dominican Republic, and other Latin American countries. Some individuals, however, prefer to be called *Latinos* or *La Raza* (the race). Some younger, ethnically conscious Hispanics with roots in Mexico may refer to themselves as *Chicanos,* a statement indicating racial pride and consciousness. Many older Mexican Americans, however, consider *Chicanos* to be an insulting reference associated with the uneducated and exploited farm hands of the Southwest.

   Those individuals who trace their ancestry to Africa may prefer the term *black* to *African American.* The latter term links identification to country of origin, whereas *black* is a much more political statement of identity arising from the late 1960s. Likewise, many older individuals of Asian ancestry prefer the term *Oriental,* whereas younger members prefer *Asian American,* which for them reflects a self-identification process rather than an identity imposed by the larger society.

2. *Racial/ethnic references can create problems by failing to acknowledge ethnic and cultural differences within a group, thereby submerging many groups under one label.* The term *Asian American,* for example, technically encompasses between twenty-nine and thirty-two distinct identifiable Asian subgroups (Chinese, Japanese, Korean, Filipino, Vietnamese, Asian Indian, Laotian, Cambodian, etc.)—each with its own culture, language, customs, and traditions. The same can be said of the label *Hispanic American* as well (Mexican American, Puerto Rican American, Cuban American, etc.).

3. *An increasing number of people have mixed ancestry, and many of them prefer not to be identified with one specific racial or ethnic group* (Root, 1996). For the first time in history, the number of biracial babies is increasing at a faster rate than the number of monoracial babies (U.S. Bureau of the Census, 1992). People of mixed ancestry may prefer to be known as *biracial, biethnic, bicultural, multiethnic,* or some other term. A whole new vocabulary associated with this phenomenon is increasingly finding its way into the social science literature, including, for example, *Afroasian,* meaning people of African and Asian heritage; *Eurasian,* people of mixed white European and Asian ancestry; and *Mestiza,* people of Indian and Spanish ancestry. Indeed, in recognition of the increasing number of "mixed racial heritage" persons, the U.S. Census in the year 2000 allowed individuals to mark off more than one racial and ethnic descriptor. With 63 racial categories and the fact that "Hispanics" can be of any race, the dimension Hispanic and non-Hispanic makes for the possibility of 126 different racial/ethnic groups!

4. *Reference to* European American, white, Caucasian American, *and* Anglo *is also filled with controversy. Anglo* is perhaps least appropriate, because it technically refers to people of English descent (or, more distantly, of Germanic descent). People who trace their ancestry to Italy, France, and the Iberian peninsula may object to being called *Anglo American.* Our experience has been that many *whites* in our society also react quite negatively to that term; they prefer to refer to themselves as *Irish American, Jewish American, Italian American,* and so on. The terms *white* and *European American* are, however, gaining wider usage, the latter in part because of the emerging trend of identifying the region or country of ancestry for Americans.

In this text, we use the four terms *African American, American Indian, Asian American,* and *Hispanic American,* and we do so for the following reasons:

These terms are labels created and used by government reporting agencies, such as the U.S. Office of Management and Budget and the U.S. Census Bureau.

Such terms are necessary for purposes of discussing group differences and organizing our discussion around multicultural and diversity variables.

Reference to any group is necessarily fraught with hazards involving overgeneralization.

We are aware that such groupings are oversimplifications, and we apologize to readers who find any of them offensive.

Multicultural Perspectives   Multicultural models of human behavior regard race, culture, and ethnicity as central to the understanding of normality and abnormality. As diversification in the United States has increased, multicultural psychology has become increasingly important and has raised our awareness of different assumptions of healthy human development. In China, children are taught to value group harmony over individual competitiveness. In contrast, in the United States, individual efforts are valued and often encouraged, which may have influenced this woman to build her own house. Still, racial and ethnic minorities in the United States often possess a more collectivistic source of identity.

nic minorities. For example, a mental health professional who does not understand that Asian Americans value a collectivistic identity might see them as overly dependent, immature, and unable to make decisions on their own. Likewise, such a person might perceive "restraint of strong feelings"—a valued characteristic among some Asian groups—as evidence of being "inhibited," "unable to express emotions," or "repressed."

Culturally Diverse Populations and Psychotherapy

The multicultural model suggests that European American perspectives of pathology place too much emphasis on locating the problems within the person (intrapsychic). Although these perspectives do not deny that problems may originate outside the individual, they are likely to consider external or system forces equally important for all individuals, regardless of social or ethnic group (Sue & Sue, 2003). In contrast, the multicultural model suggests that problems are often located in the social system rather than within the person. Minority group members, for example, may have to deal with greater and more unique stressors than those of their white counterparts. Racism, bias, discrimination, economic hardships, and culture conflicts are just a few of the sociopolitical realities with which racial and ethnic minorities must contend. As a result, the role of therapist may be better served by ameliorating oppressive or detrimental social conditions than by attempting therapy aimed at changing the individual. Appropriate individual therapy may, however, be directed at teaching clients self-help skills and strategies focused on influencing their immediate social situations.

The Surgeon General's Report on Mental Health (DHHS, 1999) makes it explicitly clear that using European American standards to judge normality and abnormality is fraught with dangers; that it may result in denying appropriate treatment to minority groups; that it may oppress rather than help culturally different clients; and that it is important for mental health practitioners to recognize and respond to cultural concerns of African Americans, Asian Americans/Pacific Islanders, Latino or Hispanic Americans, and Native Americans (Ridley, 1995).

Criticisms of the Multicultural Model

In many respects, the multicultural model operates from a relativistic framework, that is, one in which normal and abnormal behavior must be evaluated from a cultural perspective. The reasoning is that behavior that is considered disordered in one context—seeing a vision of a dead relative, for example—might not be considered disordered in another time or place. As indicated in DSM-IV (American Psychiatric Association, 1994), some religious practices and beliefs consider it normal to hear or see a deceased relative during bereavement. In addition, certain groups, including some American Indian and Hispanic/Latino groups, may perceive "hallucinations" not as being disordered but actually as positive events.

Some critics of the multicultural model argue that "a disorder is a disorder," regardless of the cultural context in which it is considered. For example, a person suffering from schizophrenia and actively hallucinating is evidencing a malfunctioning of the senses (seeing, hearing, or feeling things that are not there) and a lack of contact with reality. Regardless of whether the *person* judges the occurrence to be desirable or undesirable, it nevertheless represents a disorder (biological dysfunction), according to this viewpoint.

Another criticism leveled at the multicultural model is the lack of empirical validation concerning many of its concepts and assumptions. The field of multicultural counseling and therapy, for example, has been accused of not being solidly grounded in research (Ponterotto & Casas, 1991). Most of the underlying concepts of the multicultural model are based on conceptual critiques or formulations that have not been subjected to formal scientific testing. The field generally relies heavily on case studies, ethnographic analyses, and investigations of a more qualitative type.

Multicultural psychologists respond to such criticisms by noting that they are based on a Western worldview that emphasizes precision and empirical definitions. They point out that there is more than one way to ask and answer questions about the human condition.

An Integrative Approach to Models of Psychopathology

Table 2.5 compares the models of psychopathology discussed in this chapter. (You can also review the models by applying them to the hypothetical case of Bill in the Mental Health and Society feature, "Applying the Models of Psychopathology.") Each model—whether biological, psychodynamic, behavioral, cognitive, existential-humanistic, family systems, or multicultural—represents different views of pathology. Each details a different perspective from which to interpret reality, the nature of people, the origin of disorders, the standards for judging normality and abnormality, and the therapeutic cure. Biological models focus on genetic, neuroanatomical, or biochemical explanations; psychodynamic models stress unconscious forces, the historical past, and the need for insight; cognitive-behavioral models assert that behaviors and cognitions are learned and that maladaptive ones can be unlearned; existential-humanistic approaches stress the need for growth, attaining one's potential, self-actualization, and autonomy; family systems theories promote wider family dynamics in structure and communications that affect human development; and the multicultural models focus on how cultural context affects the manifestation of mental disorders.

Table 2.5   A Comparison of the Most Influential Models of Psychopathology

Perspective	Biological	Psychodynamic	Behavioral
Motivation for behavior	State of biological integrity and health	Unconscious influences	External influences
Basis for assessment	Medical tests, self-reports, and observable behaviors	Incorrect data, oral self-reports	Observable, objective data, overt behaviors
Theoretical foundation	Animal and human research, case studies, and other research methods	Case studies, correctional methods	Animal research, case studies, experimental methods
Source of abnormal behavior	Biological trauma, heredity, biochemical imbalances	Internal: early childhood experiences	External: learning maladaptive responses or not acquiring appropriate responses
Treatment	Biological interventions (drugs, ECT, surgery, diet)	Dream analysis, free association, transference; locating unconscious conflict from early childhood; resolving the problem and reintegrating the personality	Direct modification of the problem behavior; analysis of the environmental factors controlling the behavior and alteration of the contingencies

Cognitive	Humanistic	Existential	Family Systems	Multicultural
Interaction of external and cognitive influences	Self-actualization	Capacity for self-awareness; freedom to decide one's fate; search for meaning in a meaningless world	Interaction with significant others	Cultural values and norms (race, culture, ethnicity, socioeconomic status, gender, sexual orientation, religious preference, physical disabilities, and so on)
Self-statements, alterations in overt behaviors	Subjective data, oral self-reports	Subjective data, oral self-reports, experiential encounter	Observation of family dynamics	Study of group norms and behaviors; understanding of societal values and interplay of minority and dominant group relations
Human research, case studies, experimental methods	Case studies, correlational and experimental methods	An approach to understanding the human condition rather than a firm theoretical model	Case studies, social psychological studies, experimental methods	Study of cultural groups; data from anthropology, sociology, and political science
Internal: learned pattern of irrational or negative self statements	Internal: incongruence between self and experiences	Failure to actualize human potential; avoidance of choice and responsibility	External: faulty family interactions (family pathology and inconsistent communication patterns)	Culture conflicts and oppression
Understanding relationship between self-statements and problem behavior; modification of internal dialogue	Nondirective reflection, no interpretation; providing unconditional positive regard; increasing congruence between self and experience	Provide conditions for maximizing self-awareness and growth, to enable clients to be free and responsible	Family therapy involving strategies aimed at treating the entire family, not just the identified patient	Understanding of minority group experiences; social system intervention

MENTAL HEALTH AND SOCIETY

Applying the Models of Psychopathology

A useful learning exercise to evaluate your mastery of the various models is to apply them to a case study. We invite you to try your hand at explaining the behavior of Bill, a hypothetical client. Table 2.5 summarizes the various models, and the following hints will help you to begin this exercise:

- Consider what each theory proposes as the basis for the development of a mental disorder.

- Consider the type of data that each perspective considers most important.

- Compare and contrast the models.

- Because there are eight models represented, you might wish to do a comparison only between selected models (psychoanalytic, humanistic, and behavioral, for example).

As you attempt to explain Bill's behavior, notice how your adoption of a particular framework influences the types of data you consider important. Is it possible that all the models hold some semblance of truth? Are their positions necessarily contradictory? Is it possible to integrate them into a unified explanation of Bill? (Again, you might wish to consult Table 2.5.)

Bill was born in Indiana to extremely religious parents who raised him in a rather strict moralistic manner. His father, a Baptist minister, often told Bill and his two sisters to "keep your mind clean, heart pure, and body in control." He forbade Bill's sisters to date at all while they lived at home. Bill's own social life and contacts were extremely limited, and he recalls how anxious he became around girls.

Bill's memories of his father always included feelings of fear and intimidation. No one in the family dared disagree with the father openly, lest they be punished and ridiculed. The father appeared to be hardest on Bill's two sisters, especially when they expressed any interest in boys. The arguments and conflicts between father and daughters were often loud and extreme, disrupting the typical quietness of the home. Although it was never spoken of, Bill was aware that one of his sisters suffered from depression, as did his mother; his sister had twice attempted suicide.

Bill's recollections of his mother were unclear, except that she was always sick with what his father referred to as "the dark cloud," which seemed to visit her periodically. His relationships with his sisters, who were several years older, were uncomfortable. When Bill was a young child, they had teased him mercilessly, and when he reached adolescence, they seemed to take sadistic delight in arousing his raging hormones by flaunting their partially exposed bodies. The result was that Bill became obsessed with having sex with one of his sisters, and he tended to masturbate compul-

sively. Throughout his adolescence and early adulthood, he was tortured by feelings of guilt and believed himself to be, as his father put it, "an unclean and damned sinner."

By all external standards, Bill was a quiet, obedient, and well-behaved child. He did well in school, attended Sunday school without fail, never argued or spoke against his parents, and seldom ventured outside of the home. Although Bill did exceptionally well in high school—obtaining nearly straight A's—some of his teachers were concerned about his introverted behavior and occasional bouts of depression. When they brought Bill's depression to the attention of his father, however, Mr. M. seemed unconcerned and dismissed it as no reason to worry. Indeed, Mr. M. complimented Bill on his good grades and unobtrusive behavior, rewarding him occasionally with small privileges, such as a larger portion of dessert or the choice of a television program. To some degree of awareness, Bill felt that his worth as a person was dependent only on "getting good grades" and "staying out of trouble."

As a young child, Bill had exhibited excellent artistic potential, and his teachers tried to encourage him in that direction. In elementary school he had won several awards for his drawings, and teachers frequently asked him to paint murals in their classrooms or to draw and design flyers and posters for school events. His artistic interests continued into high school, where his art instructor entered one of Bill's drawings in a state contest. His entry won first prize. Unfortunately, Mr. M. discouraged Bill from his interests and talents and told him that "God calls you in another direction." Attempting to please his father, Bill became less involved in art during his junior and senior years and concentrated more on math and the sciences. He did exceptionally well in these subjects, obtaining nearly straight A's at the finish of his high school years.

When Bill entered college, his prime objective was to remain a straight-A student. Although he had originally loved the excitement of learning, achieving, and mastering new knowledge, he now became cautious and obsessed with "safety"; he was fearful of upsetting his father. As his string of perfect grades became longer and longer, safety (not risking a B grade) became more and more important. He began to choose safe and easy topics for essays, to enroll in very easy courses, and to take incompletes or withdrawals when courses appeared tough.

Toward the end of his sophomore year, Bill suffered a mental breakdown characterized by pessimism and hopelessness. He became very depressed and was subsequently hospitalized after he tried to take his own life.

Each model has devout supporters who, in turn, are influenced by the model they support. But even though theory building and the testing of hypotheses are critical to psychology as a science, it seems evident that we can best understand abnormal behavior only by integrating the various approaches. These models of psychopathology are describing the same phenomena, but from different vantage points. Some models emphasize *feeling* (humanistic-existential), others *thinking* (cognitive), still others *behavior* (behavioral) or *social aspects* (family systems). A truly comprehensive model of human behavior, normal and abnormal, must address the possibility that people are all of these—*feeling, thinking, behaving,* and *social persons*—and probably much more: biological, cultural, spiritual, and political ones as well.

▷ CHECKPOINT REVIEW

family systems model *(p. 55)*

What role does the family play in making us "sick" or "healthy"?

- The family systems model asserts that family interactions guide an individual's development.
- Abnormal behavior is viewed as the result of distortion or faulty communication or unbalanced structural relationships within the family. Therapeutic techniques generally focus on the family as a whole rather than on one disturbed individual.

How do race and culture affect psychopathology formulations?

- Increases in racial and ethnic minority populations have corresponded with a renewed interest in multicultural models of psychology.
- Proponents of this approach believe that race, culture, ethnicity, gender, sexual orientation, religious preference, socioeconomic status, physical disabilities, and other variables are powerful influences in determining how specific cultural groups manifest disorders, how mental health professionals perceive disorders, and how disorders should be treated.
- Cultural differences have been perceived in three ways: (1) the inferiority model, in which differences are attributed to the interplay of undesirable elements in a person's biological makeup; (2) the deprivations or deficit model, in which differences in traits or behaviors are blamed on not having the "right culture"; and (3) the multicultural model, in which differences do not necessarily equate with deviance.

How do we reconcile individual and group differences with human commonalities in explaining abnormal behavior?

- Models of abnormal pathology may represent different perspectives on the same phenomena. An integrative approach recognizes that we are not only feeling, behaving, and thinking beings but also social and cultural ones.

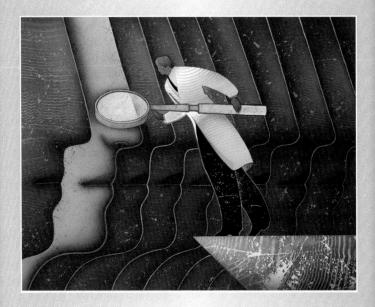

FOCUS QUESTIONS

- In attempting to make an accurate evaluation or assessment of a person's mental health, what kinds of standards must tests or evaluation procedures meet?

- What kinds of tools do clinicians employ in evaluating the mental health of people?

- How are mental health problems categorized or classified?

3 *Assessment and Classification of Abnormal Behavior*

Finding the nature and rate of mental disorders, the factors that cause or affect mental disorders, and an effective means of treating and preventing disorders are some of the most important tasks in the mental health field. To accomplish these tasks, therapists must collect information on the well-being of individuals and organize information about a person's condition. Among the assessment tools available to clinicians are observations, conversations and interviews, a variety of psychological and neurological tests, and the reports of the patient and his or her relatives and friends. When the data gathered from all sources are combined and analyzed, a therapist can gain a good picture of the patient's behavior and mental state.

The evaluation of the information leads to a psychodiagnosis, which involves describing and drawing inferences about an individual's psychological state. Psychodiagnosis is often an early step in the treatment process. For many psychotherapists, it is the basis on which a program of therapy is first formulated.

▶ Reliability and Validity

To be useful, assessment tools and classification systems must demonstrate both reliability and validity. **Reliability** is the degree to which a procedure or test—such as an evaluation tool or classification scheme—will yield the same results repeatedly under the same circumstances. There are several types of reliability (Robinson, Shaver, & Wrightsman, 1991).

Test-retest reliability determines whether a measure yields the same results when given to the same individual at two different points in time. For example, if we administer a measure of anxiety to an individual in the morning and then readminister the measure later in the day, the measure is reliable if the results show consistency or stability (that is, the results are the same) from one point in time to another.

A measure is considered reliable if it has *internal consistency*—that is, if various parts of the measure yield similar results. For example, if responses to different items on a measure of anxiety are not related to one another, the items may be measuring things other than anxiety.

Finally, *interrater reliability* refers to the consistency of responses when different judges or raters administer the measure. The extent to which the different raters agree is a measure of interrater reliability.

Validity is the extent to which a test or procedure actually performs the function it was designed to perform. If a measure that is intended to assess depression instead assesses anxiety, the measure demonstrates poor validity for depression. As in the case of reliability, there are several ways to determine validity.

Predictive validity refers to the ability of a test or measure to predict or foretell how a person will behave, respond, or perform. In general, psychological assessment is weaker at predicting what people will do than at describing what people are like (Weiner, 2003).

Criterion-related validity determines whether a measure is related to the phenomenon in question. Assume, for example, that we devise a measure that is intended to

reliability The degree to which a procedure or test will yield the same results repeatedly, under the same circumstances.

validity The extent to which a test or procedure actually performs the function it was designed to perform.

65

tell us whether persons recovering from alcoholism are likely to return to drinking. If we find that those who score high on the measure start drinking again and that those who score low do not, then the measure is valid.

Construct validity is actually a series of tasks with one common theme: all are designed to test whether a measure is related to certain phenomena that are empirically or theoretically thought to be related to that measure. Let us say that a researcher has developed a questionnaire to measure anxiety. To determine construct validity, the researcher should show that the questionnaire is correlated with other measures, such as existing tests of anxiety.

Finally, *content validity* refers to the degree to which a measure is representative of the phenomenon being measured. For example, we know that depression involves cognitive, emotional, behavioral, and physiological features. If a self-report measure of depression contains items that assess only cognitive features, such as items indicating pessimism, then the measure has poor content validity because it fails to assess three of the four known components of the disorder.

CHECKPOINT REVIEW

reliability *(p. 65)*
validity *(p. 65)*

In attempting to make an accurate evaluation or assessment of a person's mental health, what kinds of standards must tests or evaluation procedures meet?

- Assessment and classification of disorders are essential in the mental health field.
- In developing assessment tools and useful classification schemes, researchers and clinicians have been concerned with issues regarding:
  - reliability (the degree to which a procedure or test yields the same results repeatedly, under the same circumstances)
  - validity (the extent to which a test or procedure actually performs the function it was designed to perform).

The Assessment of Abnormal Behavior

Assessment is the process of gathering information and drawing conclusions about the traits, skills, abilities, emotional functioning, and psychological problems of the individual, generally for use in developing a diagnosis. Four principal means of assessment are available to clinicians: observations, interviews, psychological tests and inventories, and neurological tests. In general, clinicians should conduct assessments using multiple methods and tests in order to get more accurate information about clients (Kendall, Holmbeck, & Verduin, 2004).

Observations

Observations of overt behavior provide the most basic method of assessing abnormal behavior; indeed, behavioral observation is the most basic tool in all of science. *Controlled* (or *analogue*) *observations* are often made in a laboratory, clinic, or other contrived setting, and clients may be given instructions, stimuli, or tasks that allow the observers to evaluate responses to specific situations (Haynes, 2001). *Naturalistic observations*, which are much more characteristic of the clinician's work, are made in a natural setting—a schoolroom, an office, a hospital ward, or a home—rather than in a laboratory. Although we focus our discussion primarily on observing a client alone, interpersonal interactions, such as those between client and family, also offer important insights for determining the factors that produce and maintain disturbed behaviors (Guerin & Chabot, 1992; Norton & Hope, 2001).

Observations of behavior are usually made in conjunction with an interview, although verbal interaction is not necessary. A trained clinical psychologist watches for external signs or cues and expressive behaviors that may have diagnostic significance.

assessment With regard to psychopathology, the process of gathering information and drawing conclusions about the traits, skills, abilities, emotional functioning, and psychological problems of an individual.

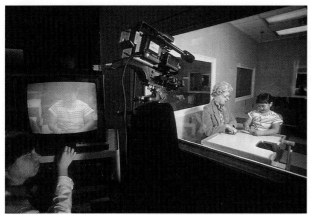 

Naturalistic vs. Controlled Observations   Naturalistic observations are made in settings that occur naturally in one's environment. Controlled observations, on the other hand, are made in a laboratory or in a contrived setting that allows researchers or clinicians to regulate many of the events that occur. Both of these photos depict controlled observation. The photo on the left shows the researcher taping responses of a six-year-old girl to certain stimuli. The researcher is seated at a video monitor behind a one-way mirror. The photo on the right shows a testing room. Note the reflection on the one-way mirror in the upper left corner.

The client's general mode of dress (neat, conventional, sloppy, flashy), significant scars or tattoos, and even choice of jewelry may be correlated with personality traits or, perhaps, with disorder. Likewise, other expressive behaviors, such as posture, facial expression, language and verbal patterns, handwriting, and self-expression through graphic art may all reveal certain characteristics of the client's life. Here is an example of some typical observations.

> Margaret was a thirty-seven-year-old patient with depression who was seen by one of the authors in a hospital psychiatric ward. She had recently been admitted for treatment. It was obvious from even a casual glance that Margaret had not taken care of herself for weeks. Her face and hands were dirty. Her long hair, which had originally been done up in a bun, had shaken partially loose on one side of her head and now hung down her left shoulder. Her beat-up tennis shoes were only halfway on her stockingless feet. Her unkempt and disheveled appearance and her stooped body posture would lead one to believe she was much older than her actual age.
>
> When first interviewed, Margaret sat as though she did not have the strength to straighten her body. She avoided eye contact with the interviewer and stared at the floor. When asked questions, she usually responded in short phrases: "Yes," "No," "I don't know," "I don't care." There were long pauses between the questions and her answers. Each response seemingly took great effort on her part.

Interviews

The clinical interview is a time-honored means of psychological assessment. It lets the therapist observe the client and collect data about the person's life situation and personality. Verbal and nonverbal behaviors, as well as the content (what the client is saying) and process (how the client is communicating—with anxiety, hesitation, or anger) of communications, are important to analyze (Reiser, 1988).

Depending on the particular disciplinary training of the interviewer, the interview's frame of reference and its emphasis may vary considerably. (This variability has been a source of inconsistency and error in the assessment of clients.) Psychiatrists, being trained in medicine, may be much more interested in biological or physical variables.

Social workers may be more concerned with life history data and the socioeconomic environment of the client. Clinical psychologists may be most interested in establishing rapport with clients as a form of therapy.

Likewise, variations in therapeutic orientation within the discipline of psychology can affect the interview. Because of their strong belief in the unconscious origin of behavior, psychoanalysts may be more interested in psychodynamic processes than in the surface content of the client's words. They are also more likely to pay particular attention to life history variables and dreams. Behaviorists are more likely to concentrate on current environmental conditions related to the client's behavior. In practice, however, mental health practitioners with different therapeutic orientations can also exhibit a great deal of similarity in psychotherapeutic style.

More recently, computer programs have become available for administering clinical interviews (and also IQ tests, personality inventories, and projective tests). These programs may also interpret responses of clients or other persons, such as applicants for jobs. The computers are programmed, for example, to simulate a structured clinical interview. Individuals who are being assessed sit before a keyboard and answer questions shown on the computer screen.

Standardization and Structure Standard administration means that common rules or procedures must be strictly followed. The same procedures are used from interview to interview. Interviews can vary in the degree to which they are structured, the manner in which they are conducted, and the degree of freedom of response on the part of the client. In some interviews, the client is given considerable freedom about what to say and when to say it. The clinician does little to interfere with conversation or to direct its flow. Psychoanalysts, who use free association, and humanistic Rogerian therapists, who carry on nondirective, person-centered therapy, tend to conduct highly unstructured interviews. Behaviorists tend to use more structured interviews.

The most highly structured interview is the *formal standardized interview*, in which questions are usually arranged as a checklist, complete with scales for rating answers. The interviewer uses the checklist to ask each interviewee the same set of questions, so that errors are minimized. Although structured interviews often do not permit interviewers to probe interviewee's responses in depth, they have the advantage of allowing consistent data to be collected across interviewees and they are less subject to interviewers' biases (Hill & Lambert, 2004).

A less structured but also widely used interview procedure is the *mental status examination*. The intent of this examination is to determine in a general way a client's cognitive, psychological, and behavioral functioning by means of questions, observations, and tasks posed to the client (Othmer & Othmer, 1994). The clinician considers the appropriateness and quality of the client's responses (behaviors, speech, emotions, intellectual functioning) and then attempts to render provisional evaluations of the diagnosis, prognosis, client dynamics, and treatment issues.

Errors In the field of mental health, straightforward questions do not always yield usable or accurate information. Believing personal information to be private, patients may refuse to reveal it, may distort it, or may lie about themselves. Furthermore, many patients may be unable to articulate their inner thoughts and feelings. An interview should therefore be considered a measurement device that is fallible and subject to error (Wiens, 1983).

psychological tests and inventories A variety of standardized test instruments used to assess personality, maladaptive behavior, development of social skills, intellectual abilities, vocational interests, and cognitive impairment.

Psychological Tests and Inventories

Psychological tests and inventories are standardized instruments that have been used to assess personality, maladaptive behavior, development of social skills, intellectual abilities, vocational interests, and cognitive impairment. Tests have also been developed for the purpose of understanding personality dynamics and conflicts. They vary in form (that is, they may be oral or written and may be administered to groups or to individuals), structure, degree of objectivity, and content. To varying degrees (less so in the case of projective personality tests), they share two characteristics that involve standard administration and use of a standardization sample (i.e., the group of people who have taken the test and whose performance can be used as the standard or norm). First, they provide a standard situation in which certain kinds of responses are elicited. The same instructions are given to all persons who take the same test, the same scoring is applied, and similar environmental conditions are maintained to ensure that the responses are due to each test taker's unique attributes rather than to differences in situations. Second, by comparing an individual test taker's responses with norms, established by the standardization sample, the therapist can make inferences about the underlying traits of the person. For instance, the test taker may answer "yes" to questions such as "Is someone trying to control your mind?" more frequently than is the norm. The therapist might infer that this pattern of response is similar to that of individuals diagnosed with paranoia.

Projective Personality Tests   In a **projective personality test**, the test taker is presented with ambiguous stimuli, such as inkblots, pictures, or incomplete sentences, and asked to respond to them in some way. The stimuli are generally novel, and the test is relatively unstructured. Conventional or stereotyped patterns of response usually do not fit the stimuli. The person must "project" his or her attitudes, motives, and other personality characteristics into the situation. The nature of the appraisal is generally well disguised: participants are often unaware of the true nature or purpose of the test and usually do not recognize the significance of their responses. Based largely on a psychoanalytic perspective, projective tests presumably tap into the individual's unconscious needs and motivations or dynamics of perception and motivation (Meyer et al., 2003).

Swiss psychiatrist Hermann Rorschach devised the *Rorschach technique* for personality appraisal in 1921. A Rorschach test consists of ten cards that display symmetrical inkblot designs. The cards are presented one at a time to participants, who are asked (1) what they see in the blots and (2) what characteristics of the blots make them see that. Inkblots are considered appropriate stimuli because they are ambiguous, are nonthreatening, and do not elicit learned responses.

What people see in the blots, whether they attend to large areas or to details, whether they respond to color, and whether their perceptions suggest movement are all assumed to be symbolic of inner promptings, motivations, and conflicts. Test takers react in a personal and "unlearned" fashion because there are no right or wrong answers. The psychologist then interprets the individual's reactions. Both the basic premise of the Rorschach test and the psychologist's interpretation of the symbolism within the patient's responses are strongly psychoanalytic. For example, seeing eyes or buttocks may imply paranoid tendencies; fierce animals may imply aggressive tendencies; blood may imply strong uncontrolled emotions; food may imply dependency needs; and masks may imply avoidance of personal exposure (Klopfer & Davidson, 1962). The single most important rationale for using the Rorschach and other projective tests is that they presumably provide information about personality dynamics that are outside the conscious awareness of the test takers (Clarkin, Hurt, & Mattis, 1999).

The *Thematic Apperception Test (TAT)* was first developed by Henry Murray in 1935 (Murray & Morgan, 1938). It consists of thirty picture cards, each typically depicting two human figures. Their poses and actions are vague and ambiguous enough to be open to different interpretations. Some cards are designated for specific age levels or for a single gender, and some are appropriate for all groups. Like the Rorschach technique, the TAT relies on projection to tap underlying motives, drives, and personality processes. Most clinicians agree, however, that the TAT is best when it is used to uncover aspects of interpersonal relationships.

projective personality test A personality assessment technique in which the test taker is presented with ambiguous stimuli and is asked to respond to them in some way.

The Rorschach Technique   Devised by Swiss psychiatrist Hermann Rorschach in 1921, the Rorschach technique uses a number of cards, each showing a symmetrical inkblot design similar to the one shown here. The earlier cards in the set are in black and white; the later cards are more colorful. A client's responses to the inkblots are interpreted according to assessment guidelines and can be compared by the therapist to the responses that other clients have made.

Generally, twenty TAT cards are shown to the participant, one at a time, with instructions to tell a story about each picture. Typically, the tester says, "I am going to show you some pictures. Tell me a story about what is going on in each one, what led up to it, and what its outcome will be." The entire story is recorded verbatim. There is usually no limit on time or the length of the stories.

A trained clinician interprets the participant's responses, either subjectively or by using a formal scoring system. Both interpretations usually take into account the style of the story (length, organization, and so on); recurring themes, such as retribution, failure, parental domination, aggression, and sexual concerns; the outcome of the story in relationship to the plot; primary and secondary identification (the choice of hero or secondary person of importance); and the handling of authority figures and sexual relationships. The purpose is to gain insight into the individual's conflicts and worries, as well as clues about his or her core personality structure (Woike & McAdams, 2001).

Other types of projective tests include sentence-completion and draw-a-person tests. In the *sentence-completion test,* the participant is given a list of partial sentences and is asked to complete each of them. Typical partial sentences are "My ambition . . .," "My mother was always . . .," and "I can remember . . ." Clinicians try to interpret the meaning of the individual's responses. In *draw-a-person tests,* such as the Machover D-A-P (Machover, 1949), the participant is actually asked to draw a person. Then he or she may be asked to draw a person of the opposite sex. Finally, the participant may be instructed to make up a story about the characters that were drawn or to describe the first character's background. Many clinicians analyze these drawings for size, position, detail, and so on, assuming that the drawings provide diagnostic clues. The analysis and interpretation of responses to projective tests are subject to wide variation. Clinicians given the same data frequently disagree with one another about scoring. Much of this disparity is caused by differences in clinicians' orientations, skills, and personal styles. But the demonstrably low

The Thematic Apperception Test   In the Thematic Apperception Test, clients tell a story about each of a series of pictures they are shown. These pictures—often depicting one, two, or three people doing something—are less ambiguous than Rorschach inkblots.

reliability and validity of these instruments means that they should be used with caution and in conjunction with other assessment measures (Weiss, 1988). And even when projective tests exhibit reliability, they may still have low validity. For example, many clinicians agree that certain specific responses to the Rorschach inkblots indicate repressed anger. The fact that many clinicians agree makes the test reliable, but those specific responses could indicate something other than repressed anger. In a major review of the research evidence, Lilienfeld, Wood, and Garb (2000) concluded that the reliability and validity of the Rorschach are problematic. Although some indicators in the Rorschach can identify a narrow range of disorders in a valid fashion, there are also some serious shortcomings in using it to diagnose disorders. In general, projective tests may yield important information when they are interpreted by clinicians who are highly skilled and insightful in their use. Because many projective tests are subjectively interpreted by clinicians in accordance with their intuition, however, overall validity of the tests is low. Exner's (1990) work in developing norms and in using empirical research in the Rorschach scoring system has been a major step in reducing subjectivity problems.

Self-Report Inventories   Unlike projective tests, **self-report inventories** require test takers to answer specific written questions or to select specific responses from a list of alternatives—usually self-descriptive statements. Participants are asked to either agree or disagree with the statement or to indicate the extent of their agreement or disagreement. Because a predetermined score is assigned to each possible answer, human judgmental factors in scoring and interpretation are minimized. In addition, participants' responses and scores can be compared readily with a standardization sample.

Perhaps the most widely used self-report personality inventory is the Minnesota Multiphasic Personality Inventory, or MMPI (Hathaway & McKinley, 1943). The MMPI-2, developed by Butcher and colleagues (see Butcher, 1990; Graham, 1990; Greene, 1991), consists of 567 statements; participants are asked to indicate whether each statement is true or false as it applies to them. There is also a "cannot say" alternative, but clients are strongly discouraged from using this category because too many such responses can invalidate the test.

The test taker's MMPI-2 results are rated on ten clinical scales and a number of validity scales. The ten clinical scales were originally constructed by analyzing the responses of diagnosed psychiatric patients (and the responses of normal participants) to the 567 test items. These analyses allowed researchers to determine what kinds of responses each of the various types of psychiatric patients usually made, in contrast to those of normal individuals. The validity scales, which assess degrees of candor, confusion, falsification, and so forth on the part of the respondent, help the clinician detect potential faking or special circumstances that may affect the outcome of other scales (Bagby et al., 1997). Figure 3.1 shows possible responses to ten sample MMPI-2 items and the kinds of responses that contribute to a high rating on the ten MMPI clinical scales.

self-report inventories An assessment tool that requires test takers to answer specific written questions or to select specific responses from a list of alternatives.

SAMPLE ITEMS

TEN MMPI CLINICAL SCALES WITH SIMPLIFIED DESCRIPTIONS

Scale	I like mechanics magazines.	I have a good appetite.	I wake up fresh and rested most mornings.	I think I would like the work of a librarian.	I am easily awakened by noise.	I like to read newspaper articles on crime.	My hands and feet are usually warm enough.	My daily life is full of things that keep me interested.	I am about as able to work as I ever was.	There seems to be a lump in my throat much of the time.
1. **Hypochondriasis (Hs)**—Individuals showing excessive worry about health with reports of obscure pains.		NO	NO				NO		NO	
2. **Depression (D)**—People suffering from chronic depression, feelings of uselessness, and inability to face the future.		NO			YES			NO	NO	
3. **Hysteria (Hy)**—Individuals who react to stress by developing physical symptoms (paralysis, cramps, headaches, etc.)		NO	NO			NO	NO	NO	NO	YES
4. **Psychopathic Deviate (Pd)**—People who show irresponsibility, disregard social conventions, and lack deep emotional responses.								NO		
5. **Masculinity-Femininity (Mf)**—People tending to identify with the opposite sex rather than their own.	NO			YES						
6. **Paranoia (Pa)**—People who are suspicious, sensitive, and feel persecuted.										
7. **Psychasthenia (Pt)**—People troubled with fears (phobias) and compulsive tendencies.			NO						NO	YES
8. **Schizophrenia (Sc)**—People with bizarre and unusual thoughts or behavior.								NO		
9. **Hypomania (Ma)**—People who are physically and mentally overactive and who shift rapidly in ideas and actions.										
10. **Social Introversion (Si)**—People who tend to withdraw from social contacts and responsibilities.										

Note: Item 5 illustrates a male's response.

Figure 3.1   The Ten MMPI-2 Clinical Scales and Sample MMPI-2 Test Items   Shown here are the MMPI-2 clinical scales and a few of the items that appear on them. As an example, answering "no" or "false" (rather than "yes" or "true") to the item "I have a good appetite" would result in a higher scale score for hypochondriasis, depression, and hysteria. *Source:* Adapted from Dahlstrom & Welsh (1965). These items from the original MMPI remain unchanged in the MMPI-2.

Whereas the MMPI-2 assesses a number of different personality characteristics, as well as mental disorders, of a person (Clarkin et al., 1999), some self-report inventories or questionnaires focus on only certain kinds of personality traits or emotional problems, such as depression or anxiety. For example, the *Beck Depression Inventory* (BDI) is composed of twenty-one items that measure various aspects of depression, such as mood, appetite, functioning at work, suicidal thinking, and sleeping patterns (Beck et al., 1961).

Intelligence Tests Intelligence testing has two primary diagnostic functions and one secondary function. The first primary function is to obtain an estimate of a person's current level of cognitive functioning, called the *intelligence quotient (IQ)*. An IQ score indicates an individual's level of performance relative to that of other people of the same age. As such, an IQ score is an important aid in predicting school performance and detecting mental retardation. (Through statistical procedures, IQ test results are converted into numbers, with 100 representing the mean, or average, score. An IQ score of about 130 indicates performance exceeding that of 95 percent of all same-age peers.) The second diagnostic function of intelligence testing is assessing intellectual deterioration in psychotic disorders. As a secondary function, an individually administered intelligence test may yield additional useful data for the clinician. The therapist may find important observations of how the person approached the task (systematic versus disorganized), handled failure (depression, frustration, or anger), and persisted in (or gave up) the task.

The two most widely used intelligence tests are the Wechsler Scales (Wechsler, 1981) and the Stanford-Binet Scales (Terman & Merrill, 1960; Thorndike, Hagen, & Sattler, 1986). The *Wechsler Adult Intelligence Scale* (the *WAIS* and its revised version, *WAIS-III*) is administered to persons age sixteen and older. Two other forms are appropriate for children ages six to sixteen (the *Wechsler Intelligence Scale for Children,* or *WISC-III*) and four to six (the *Wechsler Preschool and Primary Scale of Intelligence,* or *WPPSI-III*). The WAIS-III consists of six verbal and five performance scales, which yield verbal and performance IQ scores. These scores are combined to present a total IQ score. The WAIS consists of four factors: Verbal Comprehension, Perceptual Organization, Working Memory, and Processing Speed (Saklofske, Hildebrand, & Gorsuch, 2000). In contrast to the Wechsler, the *Stanford-Binet Intelligence Scale* is used only with children age two and older.

The use of IQ tests has been criticized on four major grounds. First, some investigators believe that IQ tests have been popularized as a means of measuring innate intelligence, when in truth the tests largely reflect cultural and social factors (Garcia, 1981; Williams, 1974). Thus IQ differences found between racial or ethnic groups are attributable to these factors rather than to innate or genetic differences. Second, the predictive validity of IQ tests has been criticized. That is, do IQ test scores accurately predict the future behaviors or achievements of different cultural groups? Third, investigators often disagree over criterion variables (in essence, what is actually being predicted by IQ tests). For example, is it better for IQ tests to predict future success in one's career or grades subsequently received in school? Fourth, some researchers have questioned whether our current conceptions of IQ tests and intelligence are adequate. A number of researchers have proposed that intelligence is a multidimensional attribute. E. H. Taylor (1990) stated that an important aspect of intelligence, and one that cannot be adequately assessed using IQ tests, is social intelligence or competency. Social skills may be important in such areas as problem solving, adaptation to life, social knowledge, and the ability to use resources effectively. As can be seen, IQ tests have generated quite a bit of controversy, and the arguments over the validity and usefulness of IQ testing may never fully subside.

Figure 3.2 The Nine Bender Designs The figures presented to participants are shown on the left. The distorted figures drawn by participants, shown on the right, are possibly indicative of organicity (brain damage). *Source:* Bender (1938).

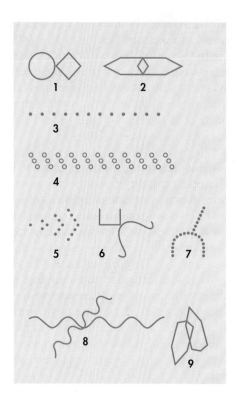
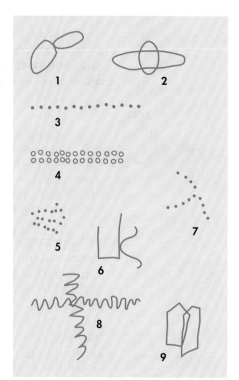

The Kaufman Assessment Battery for Children (K-ABC) An increasingly popular means of evaluating the intelligence and achievement of children ages two and one-half to twelve and one-half years is the *Kaufman Assessment Battery for Children (K-ABC)*. Based on theories of mental processing developed by neuropsychologists and cognitive psychologists, the K-ABC is intended for use with both the general population and special populations. For example, the assessment battery has been used with children who have hearing or speech impairments and with those who have learning disabilities. Because of its reliance on visual stimuli, the K-ABC is unsuitable for individuals with visual impairments (Kaufman, Kamphaus, & Kaufman, 1985).

The K-ABC can be used with exceptional children and members of ethnic minority groups. Its applicability to diverse groups has been attributed to measures that (1) are less culturally dependent than those found on traditional tests and (2) focus on the process used to solve problems rather than on the specific content of test items. A short form of the K-ABC is available that requires only fifteen to thirty minutes to complete (Kamphaus, Petoskey, & Rowe, 2000).

Tests for Cognitive Impairment Clinical psychologists, especially those who work in hospital settings, are concerned with detecting and assessing **organicity** (an older term referring to damage or deterioration in the central nervous system), or cognitive impairments due to brain damage. Such damage can have profound effects both physically (e.g., motor behavior) and psychologically (memory, attention, thinking, emotions, etc.; Gass, 2002).

One of the routine means of assessing cognitive impairment is the *Bender-Gestalt Visual-Motor Test* (Bender, 1938), shown in Figure 3.2. Nine geometric designs, each drawn in black on a piece of white cardboard, are presented one at a time to the test taker, who is asked to copy them on a piece of paper. Certain errors in the copies are

organicity Damage or deterioration in the central nervous system.

characteristic of neurological impairment. Among these are rotation of figures, perseveration (continuation of a pattern to an exceptional degree), fragmentation, oversimplification, inability to copy angles, and reversals.

The *Halstead-Reitan Neuropsychological Test Battery,* developed by Reitan from the earlier work of Halstead, has been used successfully to differentiate patients with brain damage from those without brain damage and to provide valuable information about the type and location of the damage (Boll, 1983). The full battery consists of eleven tests, although several are often omitted. Clients are presented with a series of tasks that assess sensorimotor, cognitive, and perceptual functioning, including abstract concept formation, memory and attention, and auditory perception. The full battery takes more than six hours to administer, so it is a relatively expensive and time-consuming assessment tool. Versions of the Halstead-Reitan Battery are available for children age five and older (Nussbaum & Bigler, 1989), and normative data for children have been collected. Reliability and validity of the tests are well established (Clarkin et al., 1999).

A less costly test for cognitive impairment is the *Luria-Nebraska Neuropsychological Battery,* which requires about two hours to administer and is more standardized in content, administration, and scoring than is the Halstead-Reitan Battery. Developed by C. J. Golden and colleagues (1981), this battery includes twelve scales that assess motor functions, rhythm, tactile functions, visual functions, receptive and expressive speech, memory, writing, intellectual processes, and other functions. Validation data indicate that the battery is highly successful in screening for brain damage and quite accurate in pinpointing damaged areas (Anastasi, 1982). A children's version has been developed (Golden, 1989).

Neuropsychological tests are widely used (Camara, Nathan, & Puente, 2000) and are effective and valid in evaluating cognitive impairment due to brain damage. In fact, they are far more accurate than evaluations made simply through interviews or informal observations (Kubiszyn et al., 2000).

Neurological Tests

In addition to psychological tests, a variety of neurological medical procedures are available for diagnosing cognitive impairments due to brain damage or abnormal brain functioning. For example, x-ray studies can often detect brain tumors. A more sophisticated procedure, *computerized axial tomography (CAT) scan,* repeatedly scans different areas of the brain with beams of x-rays and, with the assistance of a computer, produces a three-dimensional image of the structure of the brain. That image can provide a detailed view of brain deterioration or abnormality. In addition to the study of brain damage, CAT scans have been used to study brain tissue abnormalities among patients diagnosed with schizophrenia, affective disorders, Alzheimer's disease, and alcoholism (Coffman, 1989).

The *positron emission tomography (PET) scan* enables study of the physiological and biochemical processes of the brain, rather than the anatomical structures seen in the CAT scan. In PET scans, a radioactive substance is injected into the patient's bloodstream. The scanner detects the substance as it is metabolized in the brain, yielding information about brain functioning. PET scans, like CAT scans, have been used to study a variety of mental disorders and brain diseases. Characteristic metabolic patterns have been observed in many of these disorders (Holcomb et al., 1989).

An older and more widely used means of examining the brain is the *electroencephalograph (EEG).* Electrodes attached to the skull record electrical activity (brain waves), and abnormalities in the activity can provide information about the presence of tumors or other brain conditions.

CAT Scans   Neurological tests, such as CAT scans, PET scans, and MRIs, have dramatically improved our ability to study the brain and to assess brain damage. Shown here on the left is a normal CAT scan; on the right, a CAT scan showing the enlarged ventricles (butterfly shape in the center) of an individual suffering from senile dementia.

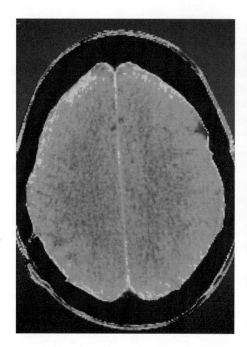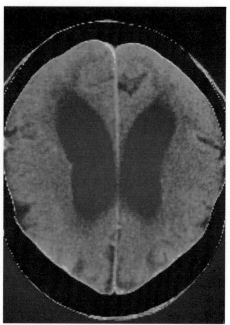

A final technique, *magnetic resonance imaging (MRI)*, creates a magnetic field around the patient and uses radio waves to detect abnormalities. MRIs can produce an amazingly clear "picture" of the brain and its tissues. Because of these superior pictures, which are reminiscent of postmortem brain slices, MRIs may eventually supplant CAT scans; some lesions are seen better using the MRI (Andreasen, 1989; Morihisa et al., 1999). In functional magnetic resonance imaging (fMRI), both the structures and also those changes that occur in specific brain functions can be observed. It provides high-resolution, noninvasive views of neural activity detected by a blood-oxygen-level-dependent signal.

These neurological techniques, coupled with psychological tests, are increasing diagnostic accuracy and understanding of brain functioning and disorders. Some researchers predict that in the future such techniques will allow therapists to make more precise diagnoses and to pinpoint precise areas of the brain affected by disorders such as Alzheimer's and Huntington's diseases (Matarazzo, 1992).

The Ethics of Assessment

Over the years, a strong antitesting movement has developed in the United States. Issues such as the confidentiality of client records, invasion of privacy, client welfare, cultural bias, and unethical practices have increasingly been raised (Bersoff, 1981; Weiner, 1995). In assessing and treating emotionally disturbed people, clinical psychologists must often ask embarrassing questions or use tests that may be construed as inva-

PET Scans   This PET scan reveals increased brain activity as a function of visual stimulation. The areas in red show the most intense stimulation, and as you can see, the more complex the information being processed, the more active the brain is.

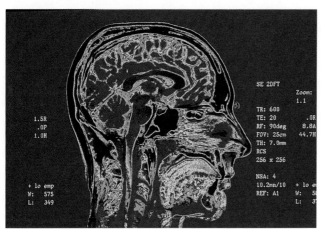

Magnetic Resonance Imaging (MRI)   In magnetic resonance imaging, a magnetic field is created around the patient, and radio waves are then used to produce amazingly detailed pictures of the brain.

sions of privacy. In many cases, a clinician may not know beforehand whether the test results will prove beneficial to the client. Yet to exclude testing because it may offend clients or place them in an uncomfortable position could ultimately deprive those clients of the test's long-range benefits.

Psychological testing has ethical, legal, and societal implications that go beyond the field of psychology. Psychologists should be aware of these implications and should guard against the misuse of test results. They should also carefully weigh the consequences of permitting such considerations to interfere with devising, improving, and applying tests that will benefit their patients. The mental health professions and the general public are increasingly aware of the need to guard against possible abuses and to continually refine and improve classification systems and assessment procedures. However, contrary to popular beliefs, psychological tests have been found to be as valid as medical tests in detecting conditions (Meyer et al., 2001).

A final problem relating to the use of psychological tests or assessment procedures addresses their ability to assess the status of individuals from different cultures. Evidence exists that biases often occur in the assessment of individuals from different cultures and that therapists of different ethnicities evaluate the same client behaviors differently (Okazaki & Sue, 1995). In one study (Li-Repac, 1980), five Chinese American and five European American male therapists rated Chinese American and European American male clients who appeared on a videotaped interview. The therapists evaluated clients of other ethnicities more negatively than they evaluated clients of their own ethnicities. European American therapists rated Chinese American clients as anxious, awkward, confused, and nervous, whereas Chinese American therapists perceived the same clients as alert, ambitious, adaptable, honest, and friendly. Chinese American therapists deemed their European American clients active, aggressive, rebellious, and outspoken, whereas European American therapists viewed these people as affectionate, adventurous, sincere, and easygoing. In addition, European American therapists rated Chinese American clients as being more depressed, more inhibited, less socially poised, and having a lower capacity for interpersonal relationships than did Chinese American therapists. Similarly, Chinese American therapists rated European American clients as more severely disturbed than did European American therapists.

These findings suggest that judgments about psychological functioning depend at least in part on whether therapists are of the same ethnic background as their clients. Because tests or procedures may not be normed, standardized, or widely used on individuals from different cultural groups, or because cultural biases may intrude on judgments, clinicians should consider the issues discussed in the Mental Health and Society feature, "Can We Accurately Assess the Status of Members of Different Cultural Groups?" New assessment strategies are also needed to overcome problems in the evaluation of people from different cultures. One researcher (Dana, 1998) has suggested implementing a number of cultural competency skills in the assessment process: ensuring the use of an appropriate language (by having bilingual clinicians or interpreters), noting culture-specific behaviors on the part of clients, determining clients' cultural orientations, and drawing implications for etiology, course, and prognosis of disorders.

mental health and society

Can We Accurately Assess the Status of Members of Different Cultural Groups?

We often have a difficult time evaluating the behaviors of people from other cultures. Cultural groups differ in many aspects, including dietary practices, type of clothing, religious rituals, and social interactions. How do we decide whether an individual from a different culture is behaving in a certain way because of a mental disorder or because of cultural practices? What signs or clues indicate that someone is truly mentally and emotionally disturbed? Can we use assessment measures standardized in the United States with people from other countries?

These questions are only a sampling of the kinds of issues clinicians must consider when trying to assess members of ethnic minority groups or individuals from different cultures. Brislin (1993) has identified several major problems, including the equivalence of concepts and scales.

First, certain concepts may not be equivalent across cultures. For instance, Americans living in the United States and the Baganda living in East Africa have different concepts of intelligent behavior. In the United States, one indicator of intelligence is quickness in mental reasoning; among the Baganda, slow, deliberate thought is considered a mark of intelligence. Obviously, tests of intelligence devised in the two cultures would differ. Individuals taking the tests could be considered intelligent on one culture's measure but not on the other.

Second, scores on assessment instruments may not really be equivalent in cross-cultural research. For example, many universities use the Scholastic Aptitude Test (SAT), which has a verbal and a quantitative component, as a criterion for admissions. Do the test scores mean the same thing for different groups in terms of assessing academic potential, achievements, and ability to succeed? SAT scores do tend to be moderately successful predictors of subsequent university grades. Sue and Abe (1988), however, found that the SAT score's ability to predict success varies according to ethnicity and the components of the SAT. Whereas the SAT verbal component was a good predictor of university grades for white American students, the SAT quantitative portion was a good predictor of grades for Asian American students. Thus Asian American and white American students with the same overall SAT scores may receive very different grades in individual courses. In every phase of testing, including test construction, test administration, and test interpretation, cultural factors are important to consider (Dana, 2000).

Third, the manner in which symptoms are expressed may vary from culture to culture, and certain cultural groups may have disturbances that are specific to those groups (Griffith, Gonzalez, & Blue, 1999). For example, culture-bound syndromes in DSM-IV-TR refer to syndromes that are often found in one cultural group but not in others.

▶ CHECKPOINT REVIEW

assessment *(p. 66)*

organicity *(p. 74)*

projective personality test *(p. 69)*

psychological tests and inventories *(p. 68)*

self-report inventories *(p. 71)*

What kinds of tools do clinicians employ in evaluating the mental health of people?
- Clinicians primarily use four methods of assessment: observations, interviews, psychological tests and inventories, and neurological tests.
- Observations of external signs and expressive behaviors are often made during an interview and can have diagnostic significance.
- Interviews, the oldest form of psychological assessment, involve a face-to-face conversation, after which the interviewer differentially weighs and interprets verbal information obtained from the interviewee.
- Psychological tests and inventories provide a more formalized means of obtaining information.
- Most testing situations share two characteristics: a standard situation in which certain responses are elicited and the measurement and use of the responses to infer underlying traits.
- In personality testing, projective techniques, in which the stimuli are ambiguous, or self-report inventories, in which the stimuli are much more structured, may be used.
- Two of the most widely used projective techniques are the Rorschach inkblot technique and the Thematic Apperception Test (TAT).

- Unlike projective tests, self-report personality inventories, such as the MMPI-2, supply the test taker with a list of alternatives from which to select an answer. Intelligence tests can be used to obtain an estimate of a person's current level of cognitive functioning and to assess intellectual deterioration.
- Behavioral observations of how a person takes the test provide additional information about personality attributes.
- The WAIS, Stanford-Binet, and Bender-Gestalt tests can be used to assess brain damage. The Halstead-Reitan and Luria-Nebraska test batteries specifically assess brain dysfunction.
- Neurological medical procedures, including x-rays, CAT and PET scans, EEG, and MRI, have added highly important and sophisticated means of detecting brain damage.

The Classification of Abnormal Behavior

The goal of having a **classification system** for abnormal behaviors is to provide distinct categories, indicators, and nomenclature for different patterns of behavior, thought processes, and emotional disturbances. Thus the pattern of behavior classified as *paranoid schizophrenia* should be clearly different from the pattern named *borderline personality*. At the same time, the categories should be constructed in such a way as to accommodate wide variation in these patterns. That is, the clinician should be able to categorize paranoid schizophrenic behavior as such, even when the patient does not show the "perfect" or "textbook" paranoid schizophrenic pattern.

Problems with Early Diagnostic Classification Systems

As discussed in the chapter "Abnormal Behavior," Emil Kraepelin, toward the end of the nineteenth century, devised the first effective classification scheme for mental disorders. Kraepelin held the biological view of psychopathology, and his system had a distinctly biogenic slant. Classification was based on the patient's symptoms, as it was in medicine. It was hoped that disorders (similar groups of symptoms) would have a common **etiology** (cause or origin), would require similar treatments, would respond to those treatments similarly, and would progress similarly if left untreated.

Many of these same expectations were held for the *Diagnostic and Statistical Manual of Mental Disorders* (DSM-I), the classification scheme that was intended to define and categorize mental disorders (Clarkin & Levy, 2004) that was first published by the American Psychiatric Association in 1952. These expectations, however, were not realized in DSM-I. The DSM was revised in 1968 (DSM-II), 1980 (DSM-III), 1987 (DSM-III-R), 1994 (DSM-IV), and 2000 (DSM-IV-TR). Each revision was made to increase the reliability, validity, and usefulness of the classification scheme. As mentioned previously, reliability and validity are crucial to any diagnostic scheme and, in fact, to any scientific construct.

The Current System: DSM-IV-TR

In 2000, the DSM-IV-TR (Text Revision) was published. DSM-IV-TR recommends that clinicians examine and evaluate the individual's mental state with regard to five factors or dimensions (called axes in the manual). Axes I, II, and III address the individual's present mental and medical condition. Axes IV and V provide additional information about the person's life situation and functioning. Together, the five axes are intended to provide comprehensive and useful information.

Axis I—Clinical syndromes and other conditions that may be a focus of clinical attention Any mental disorder listed in the manual (except those included on Axis II) is indicated on Axis I. If an individual has more than one mental disorder, they are all listed. The principal disorder is listed first.

classification system With regard to psychopathology, a system of distinct categories, indicators, and nomenclature for different patterns of behavior, thought processes, and emotional disturbances.

etiology The causes or origins of a disorder.

Axis II—Personality disorders and mental retardation Personality disorders, as well as prominent maladaptive personality features, are listed on Axis II. Personality disorders may be present either alone or in combination with a mental disorder from Axis I. If more than one personality disorder is present, they are all listed. Also included on Axis II is mental retardation.

Axis III—General medical conditions Listed on Axis III are any medical conditions that are potentially relevant to understanding and treating the person.

Axis IV—Psychosocial and environmental problems These problems may affect the diagnosis, treatment, and **prognosis** (i.e., the prediction of the future course) of a disorder. For example, a client may be experiencing the death of a family member, social isolation, homelessness, extreme poverty, and inadequate health services. The clinician lists these problems if they have been present during the year preceding the current evaluation or if they occurred before the previous year and clearly contribute to the disorder or have become a focus of treatment. The clinician has various categories in which to classify the types of problems.

Axis V—Global assessment of functioning The clinician provides a rating of the psychological, social, and occupational functioning of the person. Normally, the rating is made for the level of functioning at the time of the evaluation. The clinician uses a 100-point scale, in which 1 indicates severe impairment in functioning (for example, the individual is in persistent danger of severely hurting him- or herself or others or is unable to maintain minimal personal hygiene), and 100 refers to superior functioning with no symptoms.

The disorders (categories) for Axes I and II that are included in DSM-IV-TR are shown on the inside covers of this book. The Mental Health and Society feature, "An Example of Classification Using DSM-IV-TR," provides an example of the classifications that result from the five-axis evaluation.

It should be noted that many individuals who have one mental disorder also suffer from another. For example, an individual who is diagnosed with depression may also have a second disorder such as substance abuse. **Comorbidity** is the term for this co-occurrence of different disorders. One large-scale survey (Kessler et al., 1994) found that the rate of comorbidity is high—79 percent of those with one disorder also had another disorder. One possible explanation is that factors involved in one disorder, such as stress, may actually influence the development of other disorders (Krueger et al., 1998).

Figure 3.3 shows the prevalence rate (the percentage of the population with the disorder) of certain disorders, as determined by the largest epidemiological investigation (the study of the rate and distribution of disorders) ever conducted in the United States (Robins, Locke, & Regier, 1991).

Finally, DSM-IV-TR puts far more emphasis on cross-cultural assessment issues than previous versions of DSM did. It has an introductory section that places diagnosis within a cultural context. It provides a description of pertinent culture, age, and gender features for each disorder, and it supplies guidelines for addressing the cultural background of the client and the context for evaluating the client. DSM-IV-TR also contains an outline of *culture-bound syndromes,* disorders unique to a particular cultural group. These improvements make DSM-IV-TR far more culturally sensitive than were the previous editions.

Evaluation of the DSM Classification System

Further research is needed to determine the reliability and validity of DSM-IV-TR in relation to different populations and to study the social and research consequences of its use. Because research findings helped shape DSM-IV-TR, reliability and validity are stronger than in the previous versions (Brown et al., 2001; Williams, 1999). In general,

prognosis A prediction of the future course of a particular disorder.
comorbidity The co-occurrence of different disorders.

MENTAL HEALTH AND SOCIETY

An Example of Classification Using DSM-IV-TR

The client

Mark was a fifty-six-year-old machine operator who was referred for treatment by his supervisor. The supervisor noted that Mark's performance at work had deteriorated during the past four months. Mark was frequently absent from work, had difficulty getting along with others, and often had a strong odor of liquor on his breath after his lunch break. The supervisor knew Mark was a heavy drinker and suspected that Mark's performance was affected by alcohol consumption. In truth, Mark could not stay away from drinking. He consumed alcohol every day; during weekends, he averaged about 16 ounces of Scotch per day. Although he had been a heavy drinker for thirty years, his consumption had increased after his wife divorced him six months previously. She claimed she could no longer tolerate his drinking, extreme jealousy, and unwarranted suspicions concerning her marital fidelity.

Co-workers avoided Mark because he was a cold, unemotional person who distrusted others.

During interviews with the therapist, Mark revealed very little about himself. He blamed others for his drinking problems: if his wife had been faithful or if others were not out to get him, he would drink less. Mark appeared to overreact to any perceived criticisms of himself. A medical examina-

tion revealed that Mark was developing cirrhosis of the liver as a result of his chronic and heavy drinking.

The evaluation

Mark's heavy use of alcohol, which interfered with his functioning, resulted in an alcohol abuse diagnosis on Axis I. Mark also exhibited a personality disorder, which was diagnosed as paranoid personality on Axis II because of his suspiciousness, hypervigilance, and other behaviors. Cirrhosis of the liver was noted on Axis III. The clinician noted Mark's divorce and difficulties in his job on Axis IV. Finally, Mark was given a 54 on the Global Assessment of Functioning scale (GAF), used in Axis V to rate his current level of functioning, mainly because he was exhibiting moderate difficulty at work and in his social relationships. Mark's diagnosis, then, was as follows:

Axis I—Clinical syndrome: alcohol abuse

Axis II—Personality disorder: paranoid personality

Axis III—Physical disorder: cirrhosis

Axis IV—Psychosocial and environmental problems: (1) Problems with primary support group (divorce), (2) occupational problems

Axis V—Current GAF, 54

---

with the greater precision in specifying the criteria for making a diagnosis and with the increased role of research findings in defining disorders, reliability of diagnosis of disorders is higher in DSM-IV-TR than in earlier versions of DSM. However, increased reliability may not mean increased validity. As one critic (Sarbin, 1997) observes, sixteenth-century witch hunters developed explicit and reliable criteria (such as bodily abnormalities) for determining whether a person is a witch. Nevertheless, the diagnosis ("witch") had no validity.

Most objections to DSM have been about the system in general, and many are applicable to DSM-IV-TR. For example, some clinicians and researchers believe that DSM has a strong medical orientation, even though more than one-half of the disorders listed are not attributable to known or presumed organic causes and should not be considered biological in nature (Nelson-Gray, 1991; Schacht, 1985; Schacht & Nathan, 1977). Some psychologists see the medical emphasis in DSM in part as a response to psychiatrists' need to define abnormality more strongly within their profession. A survey of psychotherapists who are psychologists rather than psychiatrists indicated little enthusiasm for DSM (Smith & Kraft, 1983). Most of those respondents rejected the notion that mental disorders form a subset of medical disorders. They preferred a social and interpersonal, rather than a medical, approach to mental disorder. However, no such alternative to DSM enjoys widespread use at present. Still others (Hayes et al., 1996; Krueger et al., 1998) have also

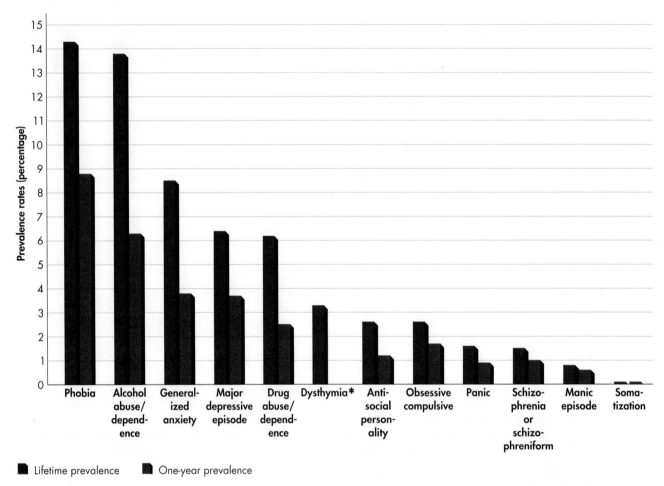

Lifetime prevalence   One-year prevalence

*One-year prevalence not ascertained.

Figure 3.3 Lifetime and One-Year Prevalence Rates for Mental Disorders, as Percentage of U.S. Population   As this graph shows, anxiety, alcohol abuse, and depressive disorders are among the most common. *Source:* Data from Robins, Locke, & Regier (1991).

suggested that the mental health field develop a system in which disorders are viewed as continuous or dimensional in nature. There is evidence that in some disorders, such as depression, the distinction between major and less severe mood states is a matter of degree rather than kind (Ruscio & Ruscio, 2000).

Other psychologists question the usefulness of the DSM classification scheme for research. One critique (Sarbin, 1997) observes that the procedures leading up to the development of DSM-IV-TR primarily involved committees negotiating the nomenclature rather than the use of scientifically derived data. Some categories were created out of compromises between conflicting views or were rooted in practical considerations, such as ease of application and acceptability to practitioners. Thus DSM-IV-TR is atheoretical—it lacks a scientific theory for its classification of disorders (Follette & Houts, 1996).

The debates over the usefulness of the DSM system have been valuable in suggesting new research directions, in increasing the role of research in developing the system, and in stimulating the examination of conceptual, methodological, philosophical, and clinical assumptions in the classification of mental disorders. Future research, particularly research that examines the construct validity of DSM, is essential to evaluating the usefulness of the system.

The Risks of Labeling A number of problems can occur when a diagnosis is used more as a convenient label. For one thing, if others know about the diagnosis, they may see everything the individual does as due to the disorder.

She's being treated for melodrama.

Objections to Classification and Labeling

Classification schemes can be of immense aid in categorizing disorders and in communicating information about them and conducting research on them. They have nevertheless been criticized on the grounds that classification schemes foster belief in an erroneous all-or-nothing quality of psychopathology. To place a diagnostic label on someone categorizes that person as "abnormal" and implies that he or she is qualitatively different from normal. Many psychologists now perceive that, for many disorders, the differences between normal and abnormal are differences of degree, not of kind (Persons, 1986). Many good arguments can be made for using alternatives to a categorical system, such as scores indicating the degree to which symptoms and traits are characteristic of a person (Clarkin & Levy, 2004).

▷ CHECKPOINT REVIEW

classification system (p. 79)
comorbidity (p. 80)
etiology (p. 79)
prognosis (p. 80)

How are mental health problems categorized or classified?

■ The first edition of DSM was based to a large extent on the biological model of mental illness and assumed that people who were classified in a psychodiagnostic category would show similar symptoms that stemmed from a common cause, that should be treated in a certain manner, that would respond similarly, and that would have similar prognoses. Critics questioned the reliability and validity of earlier versions of DSM.

■ The current DSM-IV-TR contains detailed diagnostic criteria; research findings and expert judgments were used to help construct this latest version. As a result, its reliability appears to be higher than that of the previous manuals. Furthermore, data are collected on five axes so that much more information about the patient is systematically examined.

■ General objections to classification are based primarily on the problems involved in labeling and the loss of information about a person when that person is labeled or categorized.

■ A number of ethical questions have been raised about classifying and assessing people through tests. These include questions about confidentiality, privacy, and cultural bias. Concerned with these issues, psychologists have sought to improve classification and assessment procedures and to define the appropriate conditions for testing and diagnosis. In spite of the problems and criticisms, classification and assessment are necessary to psychological research and practice.

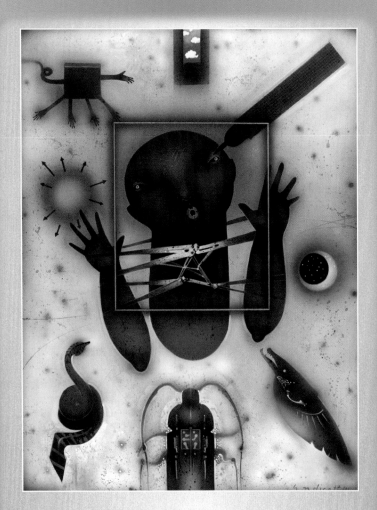

FOCUS QUESTIONS

- What are the different ways anxiety can be expressed, and under what conditions does it become so overwhelming that a panic attack occurs?

- In two anxiety disorders, the source of the fear cannot be clearly identified. What causes these reactions, and how can they be treated?

- Some people are housebound with fear, and others are afraid of public speaking or harmless insects. How do these irrational fears develop, and what is the best way of treating them?

- Intrusive thoughts, such as the desire to shout in a church, or behaviors that one is compelled to perform over and over again, such as checking to determine if the door is locked, are relatively common. When do they become a disorder, and how do you eliminate them?

- A large minority of individuals will face a traumatic incident sometime in their lives. Under what conditions will the trauma lead to a stress disorder such as PTSD, and how are these disorders best treated?

4 Anxiety Disorders

The disorders discussed in this chapter are all characterized by **anxiety,** or feelings of fear and apprehension. These disorders can produce seemingly illogical—and often restrictive—patterns of behavior, as illustrated in the following examples:

> A woman reports, "For me, a panic attack is almost a violent experience. I feel disconnected with reality.... I feel like I'm losing control.... My heart pounds really hard, I feel like I can't get my breath, and there's an overwhelming feeling that things are crashing in on me." (National Institute of Mental Health [NIMH], 2000, p. 2)

> Jane was a twelve-year-old Caucasian girl who presented for treatment with a five-year history of severe obsessions and compulsions. Obsessions centered around fear of contamination, fear that harm would come to her family, and fear that saying certain words (such as *never* and *goodbye*) would make her family disappear. Compulsions included washing rituals, avoidance of contaminants, elaborate praying rituals, and saying goodbye with an invented word. In addition, Jane called her mother at work approximately six times a day to check on her safety. (Piacentini et al., 1994, p. 283)

Anxiety is a fundamental human emotion that was recognized as long as five thousand years ago. Everyone has experienced it, and we will continue to experience it throughout our lives. Many observers regard anxiety as a basic condition of modern existence. Yet "reasonable doses" of anxiety act as a safeguard to keep us from ignoring danger, and anxiety appears to have an adaptive function. Something would be wrong if an individual did not feel some anxiety in facing day-to-day stressors. For example, many persons report anxiety in terms of overload at home, work, or school; family demands; financial concerns; and interpersonal conflicts. When facing these stressors, individuals who do not have a disorder are likely to handle the situation by facing it. They use strategies such as relaxation and problem solving to reduce stress. For others, however, overwhelming anxiety can disrupt social or occupational functioning or produce significant distress. When this occurs, the individual may develop one of the **anxiety disorders,** in which debilitating, irrational, or unrealistic anxiety is the prominent feature. The anxiety disorders do not involve a loss of contact with reality. Although people who have these disorders are aware of the illogical and self-defeating nature of some of their behaviors, they seem incapable of controlling them. In severe cases, the disturbed individuals may spend great amounts of time dealing with their debilitating fears, to no avail. This preoccupation may, in turn, lead to emotional stress and turmoil, maladaptive behaviors, and disruptions in interpersonal relationships.

In this chapter, we discuss five major groups of anxiety disorders—panic disorder, generalized anxiety disorder, phobias, obsessive-compulsive disorder, and acute and posttraumatic stress disorders. These are shown in the disorders chart in Figure 4.1, along with comparative data on the prevalence, onset, and course of some anxiety disorders. It is estimated that more than 19 million adults in the United States suffer from anxiety disorders (NIMH, 2000).

anxiety Feelings of fear and apprehension.

anxiety disorders A group of disorders that are primarily characterized by extreme, unrealistic, or debilitating anxiety. The anxiety itself is the major disturbance, and it may nearly always be present or manifested only in particular situations.

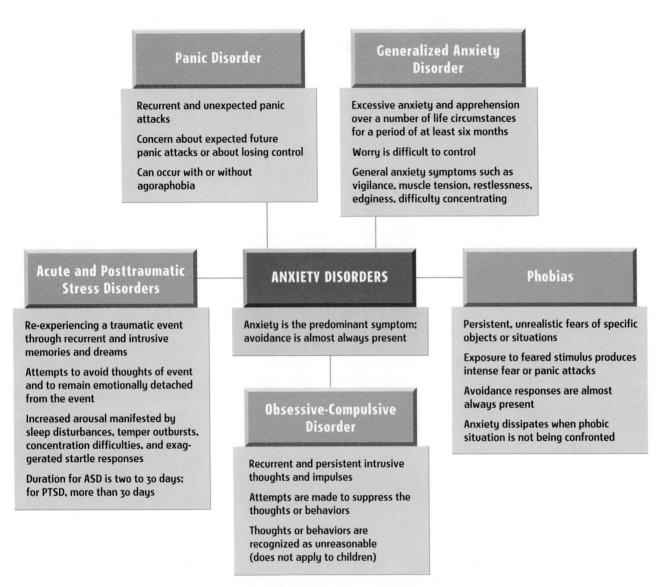

Figure 4.1 **Disorders Chart: Anxiety Disorders** *Source:* Based on data from American Psychiatric Association (2000); NIMH (1999); Stein (2001).

In each of the anxiety disorders, the person can experience *panic attacks,* which involve intense fear accompanied by symptoms such as a pounding heart, trembling, shortness of breath, or fear of losing control or dying. DSM-IV-TR recognizes three types of panic attacks: (1) situationally bound—those that occur before or during exposure to the feared stimulus; (2) situationally predisposed—those that occur usually but not always in the presence of the feared stimulus; and (3) unexpected or uncued— those that occur "spontaneously" and without warning. Persons with obsessive-compulsive disorder and social and specific phobias generally report that their panic attacks are triggered by specific situations (situationally bound). What has generated much controversy and research is the question of unexpected or "spontaneous" panic attacks. Why do some persons experience panic when no identifiable fearful stimulus is present? To gain insight into this question, we begin our discussion with a closer look at panic disorder. Individuals with panic disorder can have both unexpected and situation-specific panic attacks.

ANXIETY DISORDERS	Lifetime Prevalence	Gender and Cultural Factors	Age of Onset	Course
Panic Disorder	2–3%	May involve intense fear of the supernatural in some cultures. 2–3 times more common in females.	Late adolescence and mid-30s	Chronic; waxes and wanes
Generalized Anxiety Disorder	5%	Up to 2 times more prevalent in females. May be overdiagnosed in children.	Usually childhood or adolescence	Chronic; fluctuating; worsens during stress; over 2/3 have a comorbid disorder
Agoraphobia	Unknown; in clinical samples 95% met criteria for panic disorder or specific phobia	Far more prevalent in females.	20s to 40s	Little known
Social Phobias	3–13%; may depend on threshold used in study	More common in women. In certain Asian cultures may involve fear of offending others.	Mid-teens	Often continuous
Specific Phobia	7–13%	Approximately 2 times more common in females but depends on type of phobia. Fear of magic or spirits present in many cultures and only if reaction is excessive in context of culture would the diagnosis be considered.	Childhood or early adolescence but depends on type of phobia	Phobias that persist into childhood (about 20%) remit infrequently
Obsessive-Compulsive Disorder	1–2.5% depending on assessment tool	Equally common in males and females; less prevalent among African Americans, Asian Americans, and Hispanic Americans than White Americans.	Usually adolescence or early adulthood	Majority have chronic waxing and waning course
Post-Traumatic Stress Disorder	8%; elevated rates are found among refugees	More common in females, and in survivors of rape, military combat, and captivity.	Any age	Symptoms usually occur within 3 months after trauma, but may be delayed for some; approximately 50% recover within 3 months
Acute Stress Disorder	Currently not known; from 14–33% for specific traumas	Uncertain; probably more common in females.	Any age	Time limited to one month; if persists longer may meet criteria for PTSD

Figure 4.1 Disorders Chart: Anxiety Disorders (continued)

The predominant characteristic of both panic disorder and generalized anxiety disorder is unfocused, or *free-floating,* anxiety. That is, the affected individual is fearful and apprehensive but often does not know exactly what he or she is afraid of. Patients with panic disorder suffer episodes of intense fear accompanied by bodily sensations of heart palpitations, dyspnea (shortness of breath), and faintness, along with thoughts of dying, losing control, or going crazy. Individuals with generalized anxiety disorder tend to have milder anxiety-evoking thoughts dealing with themes such as misfortune, financial concerns, academic and social performance, and rejection. This disorder is often described as "chronic pathological worry."

Panic Disorder

Anxiety itself is the major disturbance in **panic disorder,** which is characterized by severe and frightening episodes of apprehension and feelings of impending doom. These episodes are described as horrible and can last from a few minutes to several hours. According to DSM-IV-TR, a diagnosis of panic disorder includes recurrent unexpected panic attacks and at least one month of apprehension over having another attack or worrying about the consequences of an attack. Individuals with panic disorder report intense panic attacks alternating with periods of lower level anxiety, during which they may be apprehensive about having another panic attack. One twenty-six-year-old Web designer described an episode this way: "It happened so suddenly. Without warning I felt like I had been swept up in a tornado! . . . my pulse was pounding, my palms were drenched with sweat, and my throat was closing up, leaving me gasping for air. I felt paralyzed with fear, convinced I was going to die" (Kusek, 2001, p. 182). The attacks are especially feared because they often occur unpredictably. Some people also develop *agoraphobia,* or anxiety about leaving the home, which is caused by fear of having an attack in a public place. Individuals with panic disorder often have comorbid (co-occurring) disorders involving other anxiety conditions or mood disturbances.

The *lifetime prevalence rate* (the proportion of individuals who have ever had the disorder) for panic disorder is approximately 3.5 percent, and it is two times more common in women (Kessler et al., 1994; NIMH, 1999). Women are also more likely than men to suffer a recurrence of panic symptoms after the remission of the disorder (Yonkers et al., 1998). Homosexual and bisexual men are nearly five times as likely to meet the criteria for panic disorder as heterosexual men (Cochran, Sullivan, & Mays, 2003). The prevalence rate for Mexican Americans is somewhat lower than for the general population. One-third to one-half of individuals diagnosed with a panic disorder also have agoraphobia (American Psychiatric Association, 2000a).

Although panic disorder is diagnosed in only a small percentage of individuals, panic attacks appear to be fairly common. Among college students, one-fourth to one-third reported having had a panic attack during a one-year period (Asmundson & Norton, 1993; Brown & Cash, 1990). Women are more likely to report panic symptoms. Nearly 45 percent of college women in one study had had one panic attack or more within the previous year (Whittal, Suchday, & Goetsch, 1994). Similarly, 43 percent of adolescents in another sample reported having had a panic attack (King et al., 1993). Most of these panic attacks are associated with an identifiable stimulus. Few people who have panic attacks will develop a panic disorder.

Generalized Anxiety Disorder

Generalized anxiety disorder (GAD) is characterized by persistent high levels of anxiety and excessive worry over many life circumstances. These concerns are accompanied by physiological responses such as heart palpitations, muscle tension, restlessness,

panic disorder Anxiety disorder characterized by severe and frightening episodes of apprehension and feelings of impending doom.

generalized anxiety disorder (GAD) Disorder characterized by persistent high levels of anxiety and excessive worry over many life circumstances.

The Scream, **by Edward Munch**   This painting depicts some of the symptoms that accompany anxiety. The swirling colors of the background evoke a feeling of uncontrollable disorder that cannot be escaped. The subject, clutching his head, seems terrorized by something, which must be in his own mind, for the scene is otherwise peaceful. *Copyright 2005 the Munch Museum/the Munch-Ellingsen Group/Artist Rights Society (ARS) NY*

trembling, sleep difficulties, poor concentration, and persistent apprehension and nervousness. Afflicted people are easily startled and are continually "on edge." Most will present their problem as somatic complaints, and "about 90 percent of those with GAD will say 'yes' to the question 'During the past 4 weeks, have you been bothered by feeling worried, tense, or anxious most of the time'" (Ballenger et al., 2000, p. 53). More than two-thirds of patients with GAD have comorbid (co-occurring) disorders, such as depression, substance abuse, or phobia. Of those with GAD only, 28 percent indicated that the symptoms interfered with life activities versus 51 percent of those with GAD and a comorbid condition (Stein, 2001).

Individuals with GAD, in contrast to those with panic disorder, are as likely to worry over minor events as over major events. Children with GAD reported concern over taking tests, doing schoolwork, being alone, hearing noises, being teased, experiencing personal harm, and going to hospitals. Somatic symptoms, such as headaches, stomachaches, and muscle tension, often accompanied their worries (Eisen & Silverman, 1998). Physiological reactions associated with GAD tend to be less severe than those that accompany panic disorder but tend to be more persistent (Gross & Eifert, 1990). Generalized anxiety disorder appears to be a cognitive problem involving excessive worry or apprehension. Individuals with GAD appear to have a lower threshold for uncertainty (Ladouceur et al., 2000).

To meet DSM-IV-TR's criteria for a diagnosis of generalized anxiety disorder, symptoms must be present for six months. In medical settings around the world, GAD is the most frequently diagnosed anxiety disorder (Goldberg, 1996; Stein, 2001). The disorder is chronic, and it produces social and functional impairment. Fewer than half of the individuals suffering from it seek treatment (Rickels & Schweizer, 1997). The lifetime prevalence rate for GAD is about 5.0 percent of the adult population, with women twice as likely to receive this diagnosis as men (NIMH, 2000). Especially at risk are lesbian and bisexual women, who are four times as likely to suffer from GAD as heterosexual women (Cochran et al., 2003).

Etiology of Panic Disorder and Generalized Anxiety Disorder

In our discussions of the causes and origins of mental disorders in this chapter and ensuing chapters, we must distinguish among the viewpoints that derive from the various models of psychopathology. Here we examine the etiology of unfocused anxiety disorders from the psychodynamic, behavioral, and biological perspectives. Research has been directed toward explaining the reason for unexpected panic attacks.

Psychodynamic Perspective   The psychodynamic view stresses the importance of internal conflicts (rather than external stimuli) in the origin of panic disorder and GAD. The problem originates from unconscious sexual and aggressive impulses that are seeking expression. When the forbidden impulse threatens to disturb the ego's integrity by becoming conscious, an intense anxiety reaction occurs. Because this conflict is unconscious, the individual does not know the source of the anxiety.

Figure 4.2 Positive Feedback Loop Between Cognitions and Somatic Symptoms Leading to Panic Attacks

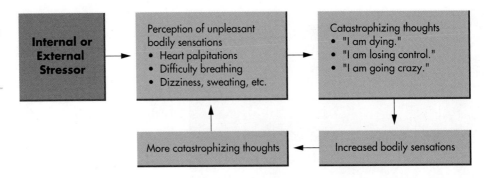

A person's defense against unfocused anxiety is generally considered poorly organized and less effective than defenses mounted against other anxiety disorders. In a phobia, for example, the conflict between id impulses and ego is displaced onto a specific external stimulus that can be controlled simply through avoidance. But the person with generalized anxiety disorder has only one defense—to try to repress the impulses. When that defense weakens, panic attacks may occur.

Cognitive Behavioral Perspective   The cognitive-behavioral model attributes panic attacks to the individual's interpretation of unpleasant bodily sensations as indicators of an impending disaster. People with panic disorder appear to have an overly active degree of bodily vigilance, along with intense fear of and worry about bodily sensations. They are likely to make "catastrophic" misinterpretations of bodily symptoms, interpreting heart palpitations, sweaty palms, and shortness of breath as indicators of an impending heart attack, suffocation, or death. The feedback loop between bodily sensations and thoughts results in increasingly higher levels of anxiety (Bakker et al., 2002; Clark, 1996; Ehlers, 1993). In other words, after an external or internal stressor, a person may become aware of a bodily sensation, such as a racing heart. Anxiety develops when the person interprets the sensation as a signal of a dreadful event. This belief then produces even greater physical reactions. Figure 4.2 illustrates this pattern. If the positive feedback loop continues, a panic attack may follow. Overconcern about physiological sensations such as heartbeat, trembling, and shortness of breath is related to panic attacks in adolescents (Weems et al., 2002). Cognitions (e.g., thoughts of dying, passing out, or looking foolish) preceding or accompanying panic attacks have been reported (Rapee, 1995; Schmidt, Lerew, & Trakowski, 1997; Whittal & Goetsch, 1995).

The search for cognitive factors, although promising, leaves some questions unanswered. First, although most individuals report that their panic attacks are accompanied by cognitions, a substantial percentage report that they are not aware of any thoughts during these episodes. Second, it is unclear why individuals with GAD and panic disorder are so prone to having thoughts of catastrophe. It must be remembered that the cognitive approach does not preclude the possible impact of biological factors in the cause of panic disorders.

Biological Perspective   Research on the biological factors involved in GAD and panic disorders has focused on neural structures and on neurochemical responses to stressful stimuli (Brawman-Mintzer et al., 1997). Anxiety involves a number of interacting subsystems that include cognitive, physiological, affective, and behavioral components. Changes in one can lead to changes in the others (Ladouceur, Dugas, et al., 2000). For example, the amygdala plays a central role in emotions, interacts with the hippocampus and medial prefrontal cortex, and also has connections to the thalamus, hypothalamus, and other brainstem sites. Fear may result in the overactivity of these

Learning to Use Coping Strategies For those who suffer from generalized anxiety disorder, identifying anxiety-evoking thoughts and developing coping strategies to deal with them is an important part of effective therapy.

systems. These connections allow one to speculate about why medications and psychotherapy may both be effective in treating anxiety disorders. Each may operate on different levels of the brain. Cognitive approaches may reduce arousal by deconditioning fear at the hippocampus, which will strengthen the ability of the medial prefrontal cortex to inhibit the amygdala. Medication may directly influence or decrease activity in the amygdala and other brainstem structures (Gorman et al., 2000; see Figure 4.3).

Genetic studies offer researchers another avenue in their search for a biological mechanism, although current studies have not eliminated the possible influence of environmental factors from their findings. Nevertheless, several studies seem to support a genetic influence for panic disorder. Higher concordance rates (percentages of relatives sharing the same disorder) for panic disorder have been found for monozygotic (MZ; identical) twins versus dizygotic (DZ; fraternal) twins (Kendler et al., 1992). Their estimate of the degree of heritability for agoraphobia and panic disorder due to genetic factors was about 35 percent, which is a modest contribution. There also appears to be a small but significant heritability factor in GAD (Brawman-Mintzer et al., 1997; Gorman, 2001; Kendler et al., 1992).

Treatment of Panic Disorder and Generalized Anxiety Disorder

The treatments of choice for GAD and panic disorder are medications such as antidepressants and antianxiety medications (Ballenger et al., 2000), although the newer antidepressants (selective serotonin reuptake inhibitors, or SSRIs) are recommended over antianxiety medications for the treatment of panic disorder (Bruce et al., 2003). Cognitive-behavioral psychotherapies have also been effective in treating these disorders (Borkovec & Ruscio, 2001; Ladouceur, Dugas, et al., 2000).

Biochemical Treatment Evaluating the efficacy of medical treatment for panic disorder can be difficult, given placebo response rates as high as 75 percent in clinical trials (American Psychiatric Association, 1998). Benzodiazepines have been successful in treating GAD, but these drugs can lead to tolerance and dependence (Nutt, 2001). They are not recommended for those who have a history of substance abuse, and, because of their sedating effect, they have been associated with an increase in falls and hip fractures in the elderly (Gorman, 2001). Because GAD is a chronic condition, antidepressants rather than benzodiazepines are the medications of choice (Davidson, 2001; Rabatin & Keltz, 2002).

The most frequently recommended medications are the SSRIs (Paxil, Prozac, and Zoloft), which have the fewest side effects. Side effects associated with antidepressants include possible weight gain and sexual dysfunction. It usually takes four to eight weeks for the medications to become fully effective, and some patients may initially have more panic attacks than usual during the first few weeks. Relapse rates

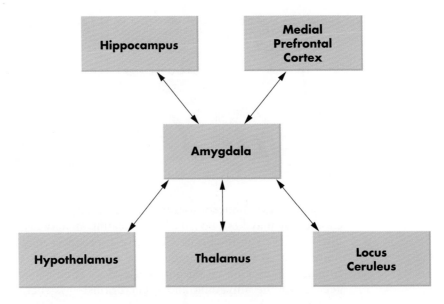

Figure 4.3 Neuroanatomical Basis of Panic and Other Anxiety Reactions
The fear network in the brain is centered in the amygdala and interacts with
the hippocampus and the medial prefrontal cortex. Projections from the
amygdala to the hypothalamic and brainstem sites are associated with
conditioned fear responses. Medication that influences the serotonin system
desensitizes the fear network from the level of the amygdala through
projections to the hypothalamus and brainstem. Cognitive behavioral
therapy or other psychotherapies reduce contextual fear and cognitive
misattributions at the level of the prefrontal cortex and the hippocampus.
Source: From Gorman et al. (2000).

after cessation of drug therapy appear to be quite high (Biondi et al., 2003; Gorman,
2001).

Behavioral Treatment Cognitive behavioral treatments, both in individual therapy
(Bakker et al., 2002; Barlow et al., 2000; Otto, Pollack, & Sabatino, 1996) and in
group therapy (Penava et al., 1998), have been successful in treating panic disorder. A
follow-up study of behavioral treatments involving exposure (exposing clients to fearful stimuli) for panic disorder (Fava et al., 1995) found promising remission rates: 96
percent remained in remission for at least two years; 78 percent for at least five years;
and 67 percent for at least seven years. How do clients feel about therapy that
involves exposure to anxiety-provoking situations? Most rated it as not well liked but
very useful—a sort of "bitter medicine" (Cox, Fergus, & Swinson, 1994). In general,
cognitive behavioral treatments for panic disorders involve the following steps
(American Psychiatric Association, 1998; Öst & Westling, 1995; Taylor et al., 1996):
(1) educating the client about panic disorder and symptoms, (2) training the client in
muscle-relaxation techniques, (3) reducing the client's alarm about panic symptoms
by inducing the symptoms in "safe" circumstances, (4) helping to change the client's
catastrophizing thoughts, and (5) helping the client learn to identify stressors and to
use relaxation and cognitive strategies to deal with them. Cognitive behavioral therapy appears to be successful in treating GAD, as well. It is the only consistently vali-
dated treatment for the disorder (Ballenger et al., 2000). The treatment strategies generally involve the following steps (Dugas & Ladouceur, 2000; Eisen & Silverman,
1998): (1) identifying and modifying the worrisome thoughts; (2) discriminating

between worries about situations that are amenable to problem solving and those that are not; (3) evaluating beliefs concerning worry; (4) discussing the evidence for and against the distorted beliefs; (4) decatastrophizing worrisome thoughts; (5) developing self-control skills to monitor and challenge irrational thoughts and substitute more positive, coping thoughts; and (6) using muscle relaxation to deal with somatic symptoms.

▶ CHECKPOINT REVIEW

anxiety *(p. 85)*

anxiety disorders *(p. 85)*

generalized anxiety disorder (GAD) *(p. 88)*

panic disorder *(p. 88)*

What are the different ways anxiety can be expressed, and under what conditions does it become so overwhelming that a panic attack occurs?

■ Anxiety is an emotion we all experience. It appears in our cognitions or thoughts, in our behaviors, and in our physiological or biological reactions.

■ When the anxiety becomes intense, panic attacks involving extreme fear may develop. In some cases, these attacks will occur almost invariably when exposed to a specific stimulus (situationally bound); others will usually occur in certain circumstances (situationally predisposed).

■ Panic attacks that seem to occur "out of the blue" (unexpected) have been the most difficult to explain.

■ Panic attacks are relatively common and not always associated with an anxiety or any other disorder.

In two anxiety disorders, the source of the fear cannot be clearly identified. What causes these reactions, and how can they be treated?

■ Panic disorder and generalized anxiety disorder (GAD) are characterized by direct and unfocused anxiety.

■ Panic disorder is marked by episodes of extreme anxiety and feelings of impending doom.

■ Generalized anxiety disorder involves chronically high levels of anxiety and excessive worry that is present for six months or more.

■ Psychoanalysts believe that symptoms of these disorders appear without warning because they stem from internal conflicts that remain in the person's unconscious.

■ Cognitive behavioral theorists emphasize cognitions and conditioning in the development of these disorders. According to the biological perspective, a specific biological dysfunction may predispose some people to panic disorder.

■ Drug therapy, behavioral therapies, and psychodynamic therapies have been used to treat these disorders.

▶ Phobias

phobia A strong, persistent, and unwarranted fear of some specific object or situation.

The word *phobia* comes from the Greek word that means "fear." A **phobia** is a strong, persistent, and unwarranted fear of a specific object or situation. An individual with a phobia often experiences extreme anxiety or panic attacks when he or she encounters the phobic stimulus. Attempts to avoid the object or situation notably interfere with the individual's life. Adults with this disorder realize that their fear is excessive, though children may not. Most people with a phobia have other anxiety, mood, or substance use disorders (Hofmann, Lehman, & Barlow, 1997). Nearly anything can become the focus of intense fear. Some people may even have a fear of phobias, called *phobophobia* (see Table 4.1). Phobias are the most common mental disorder in the United States. DSM-IV-TR includes three subcategories of phobias: agoraphobia, the social phobias, and the specific phobias.

Table 4.1 Phobias and Their Objects	
Acrophobia: fear of heights	**Microphobia:** fear of germs
Agoraphobia: fear of open spaces	**Monophobia:** fear of being alone
Ailurophobia: fear of cats	**Mysophobia:** fear of contamination or germs
Algophobia: fear of pain	**Nyctophobia:** fear of the dark
Arachnophobia: fear of spiders	**Ochlophobia:** fear of crowds
Astrapophobia: fear of storms, thunder, and lightning	**Pathophobia:** fear of disease
Aviophobia: fear of airplanes	**Phobophobia:** fear of phobias
Brontophobia: fear of thunder	**Pyrophobia:** fear of fire
Claustrophobia: fear of closed spaces	**Syphilophobia:** fear of syphilis
Dementophobia: fear of insanity	**Topophobia:** fear of performing
Genitophobia: fear of genitals	**Xenophobia:** fear of strangers
Hematophobia: fear of blood	**Zoophobia:** fear of animals or some particular animal

Agoraphobia

Agoraphobia is an intense fear of being in public places where escape or help may not be readily available. It arises from a fear that panic-like symptoms will occur and incapacitate the person or cause him or her to behave in an embarrassing manner, such as fainting, losing control over bodily functions, or displaying excessive fear in public. Anxiety over showing these symptoms can prevent people from leaving their homes. If the individual has a history of unexpected panic attacks, a more appropriate diagnosis might be panic disorder with agoraphobia. Some researchers (Goisman et al., 1995) believe that agoraphobia should be considered a variant of, or a secondary response to, panic disorder, not a separate entity. In support of this perspective, it was found that over 95 percent of individuals who seek help in clinics for agoraphobia have either a current diagnosis or a history of panic disorder (American Psychiatric Association, 2000a).

Social Phobias

A **social phobia** is an intense, excessive fear of being scrutinized in one or more social or performance situations. An individual with a social phobia avoids or endures these situations, which can lead to intense anxiety reactions or panic attacks. The person's reaction stems from the fear that, when in the company of others, he or she will perform one or more activities in a way that is embarrassing or humiliating (Bruch, Fallon, & Heimberg, 2003). There is no such anxiety when the person engages in any of these activities in private. Examples of fearful thoughts by patients with social anxiety during social situations are: "I'll shake constantly," "I'll look anxious," "I'll blush and people will think I'm anxious," and "I'll look very tense and people will stare at me" (Wells & Papageorgiou, 1999). The most common fears in social phobia involve public speaking and meeting new people (American Psychiatric Association, 2000a). The following case example describes a typical fear:

agoraphobia An intense fear of being in public places where escape or help may not be readily available; in extreme cases, a fear of leaving one's home.

social phobia An intense, excessive fear of being scrutinized in one or more social situations.

> In any social situation, I felt fear. I would be anxious before I even left the house, and it would escalate as I got closer to a college class, a party or whatever. When I would walk into a room full of people, I'd turn red and it would feel like everybody's eyes were on me. I was embarrassed to stand off in a corner by myself, but I couldn't think of anything to say.... It was humiliating.... I couldn't wait to get out. (NIMH, 2000, p. 5)

Mental Health and Society

Anxiety Disorders from a Cross-Cultural Perspective

Determining the prevalence of disorders in different countries is problematic. Diagnosis of such disorders usually relies on systems such as DSM-IV-TR, which were developed in Western countries, and the forms and patterns of abnormal behavior in non-Western cultures may not fit specifically within the DSM-IV-TR categories. For example, the American Psychiatric Association (2000a) describes a number of culture-bound syndromes that are not "universal" but are limited to specific cultures. Taijin Kyofusho, for instance, is a culturally distinctive phobia found in Japan. It is somewhat similar to social phobia as described in DSM-IV-TR. However, instead of a fear involving social or performance situations, Taijin Kyofusho is a fear of offending or embarrassing others, a concept consistent with Japanese cultural emphasis on maintaining interpersonal harmony. Individuals with this disorder are fearful that their appearance, facial expression, eye contact, body parts, or odor are offensive to others (Suzuki et al., 2003). In one study of suburban high school students in Japan, 0.8 percent of boys and 0.2 percent of girls had a phobia involving their body odor; 0.3 percent of boys and 0.2 percent of girls were fearful of offending others with eye contact (Yasumatsu, 1993). Even though rare, Taijin Kyofusho is considered to be a cultural syndrome and is included in the Japanese diagnostic system for mental disorders.

Although questions remain about the validity of using Western-devised diagnostic instruments with other cultures, some cross-cultural research on anxiety disorders has been accomplished. In one study of five European cities (Weiller et al., 1998), the most prevalent anxiety disorder was generalized anxiety disorder (GAD), with an average current prevalence rate of 8.5 percent. GAD prevalence rates were higher in Paris and Berlin than in Mainz (Germany), Manchester (United Kingdom), and Groningen (Netherlands; Weiller et al., 1998). Similar symptom patterns emerged in a ten-country cross-national epidemiological study of panic disorders (Weissman et al., 1997). Prevalence rates for panic disorder ranged from 1.4 percent in Edmonton, Canada, to 2.9 percent in Florence, Italy. (The prevalence rate was only 0.4 percent in Taiwan, but all rates of mental disorder in that country are low.)

In all countries, women were more likely to be diagnosed with panic disorder, but there was a large difference in the sex ratio from country to country, ranging from nearly six times more women than men in Korea to only 1.3 times in Puerto Rico. In another study (Davey et al., 1998), college students in seven Western and Asian countries responded similarly in their ratings of fear of animals. However, students in Hong Kong and Japan scored significantly higher mean fear ratings than in the other countries. In all seven countries, however, women indicated more fear of animals than did males.

Although cross-cultural investigations on anxiety disorders are useful, it is difficult to determine the meaning of differences. Taiwan's levels of reported mental disorders are very low compared with those of other countries. These low levels could reflect a social stigma attached to admitting having mental symptoms, or it could result from differences in the ways questions are interpreted or understood. Whatever the explanation, interpretation of such findings remains problematic so long as cross-cultural studies apply Western diagnostic categories to other cultural groups. The very system of classification may obscure important culturally specific mental disorders.

People with social phobias, like those with other phobias, usually realize that their behavior and fears are irrational, but this understanding does not reduce the distress they feel. In a given year, about 3.7 percent of adults have social phobia. Women are twice as likely as men to have this disorder; however, more men seek treatment (NIMH, 1999). Social phobias tend to begin during adolescence, and they appear to be more common in families who use shame as a method of control and who stress the importance of the opinions of others (Bruch & Heimberg, 1994). These child-rearing practices are common in Asian families, and social evaluative fears are more prevalent in Chinese children and adolescents than in Western comparison groups (Dong, Yang, & Ollendick, 1994). Culture can also influence the ways in which anxiety disorders are expressed. The Mental Health and Society feature, "Anxiety Disorders from a Cross-Cultural Perspective," discusses this issue.

Specific Phobias   The extreme fear of spiders is a specific phobia. An individual with this fear may believe that the spider is malevolent and has targeted him or her for attack.

Specific Phobias

A **specific phobia** is an extreme fear of a specific object (such as snakes) or situation (such as being in an enclosed place). Exposure to the stimulus nearly always produces intense anxiety or a panic attack. The specific phobias provide a catchall category for irrational fears that cannot be classified as either agoraphobia or social phobias. The only similarity among the various specific phobias is the existence of an irrational fear. To produce some organizational framework, DSM-IV-TR divides specific phobias into five types:

1. Animal (such as spiders or snakes).
2. Natural environmental (such as earthquakes, thunder, water).
3. Blood/injections or injury; individuals with this type of phobia, as opposed to other phobias, are likely to have a history of fainting in the phobic situation.
4. Situational (includes fear of traveling in cars, planes, and elevators and fear of heights, tunnels, and bridges).
5. Other (phobic avoidance of situations that may lead to choking, vomiting, or contracting an illness).

The following is a report of a fairly common specific phobia in a twenty-six-year-old public relations executive:

> If I see a spider in my house, I get out! I start shaking, and I feel like I'm going to throw up. I get so scared, I have to bolt across the street to drag my neighbor over to get rid of the spider. Even after I know it's gone, I obsess for hours. I check between my sheets 10 times before getting in bed, and I'm so creeped out that I won't get up and go to the bathroom at night, even if my bladder feels like it's about to burst. (Kusek, 2001, p. 183)

Specific phobias are about twice as prevalent in women as in men (see Figure 4.1) and are rarely incapacitating. The degree to which they interfere with daily life depends on how easy it is to avoid the feared object or situation. These phobias often begin during childhood. In a study of 370 patients with phobias (Öst, 1987, 1992), retrospective data revealed that animal phobias tended to have the earliest onset age (seven years), followed by blood phobia (nine years), dental phobia (twelve years), and claustrophobia (twenty years). Figure 4.4 illustrates ages at which different phobias typically begin.

The most common childhood fears are of spiders, the dark, frightening movies, and being teased (Muris, Merckelbach, & Collaris, 1997). Most of these fears do not persist into adulthood (Poulton et al., 1997). Among a sample of 160 primary school children, 17.6 percent met the criteria for a specific phobia (Muris & Merckelbach, 2000).

Blood phobias differ from other phobias in being associated with a unique physiological response—fainting in the phobic situation. Fainting appears to result from an initial increase in autonomic arousal followed by a sudden drop in blood pressure and heart rate. Nearly 70 percent of those with blood phobias report a history of fainting in the feared situation (Antony, Brown, & Barlow, 1997). Many are severely handicapped by the phobia. They may avoid medical examinations, caring for an injured child, or shopping at the meat counter in supermarkets (Hellstrom, Fellenius, & Öst, 1996).

Etiology of Phobias

How do such strong and "irrational" fears develop? Both psychological and biological explanations have been proposed. In this section, we examine the psychodynamic,

specific phobia An extreme fear of a specific object or situation; a phobia that is not classified as either agoraphobia or a social phobia.

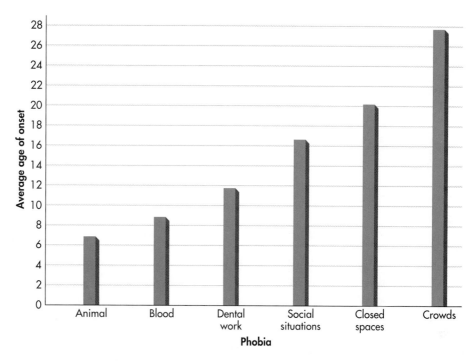

Figure 4.4　Phobia Onset　This graph illustrates the average ages at which 370 patients said their phobias began. Animal phobias began during childhood, whereas the onset of agoraphobia did not occur until the individuals were in their late twenties. What do you feel accounts for the differences reported in the age of onset? *Source:* Data from Öst (1987, 1992).

behavioral, and biological views of the etiology of phobias. Although these perspectives are discussed separately, it is plausible that phobias may result from an interaction of biological, cognitive, and environmental factors.

Psychodynamic Perspective　According to the psychodynamic viewpoint, phobias are "expressions of wishes, fears and fantasies that are unacceptable to the patient" (Barber & Luborsky, 1991, p. 469). These unconscious conflicts are displaced (or shifted) from their original internal source to an external object or situation. The phobia is less threatening to the person than recognition of the underlying unconscious impulse. A fear of knives, for example, may represent castration fears produced by an unresolved Oedipus complex or aggressive conflicts. People with agoraphobia may develop their fear of leaving home because they unconsciously fear that they may act out unacceptable sexual desires. The presence of a friend or spouse lowers anxiety because it provides some protection against the agoraphobic impulses. In this sense, phobias represent a compromise between the ego and the impulses that seek gratification. The person blocks from consciousness the real source of anxiety and is able to avoid the dangerous impulse that the phobia represents.

Therapists in the psychodynamic tradition believe that the level of phobic fear is an indicator of the strength of the underlying conflict. This perspective, presented by Freud in 1909, was based on his analysis of a fear of horses displayed by a five-year-old boy named Hans (Freud, 1909/1959). Freud believed that the horse phobia represented a displaced fear arising from the Oedipus complex that involved the boy's incestuous attraction to his mother, hostility toward his father because of the father's sexual privileges, and castration fear (fear of retribution by his father). Freud became convinced that these unconscious elements were responsible for the phobia.

"You know, Burkhart, if you're so damn afraid of the flu maybe you should just stay home."

Source: © The New Yorker Collection 2000, Robert Mankoff from cartoonbank.com. All rights reserved.

Behavioral Perspective   Behaviorists have examined three possible processes—classical conditioning, modeling, and cognitive-negative information—in their attempts to explain the etiology of phobias (King, Eleonora, & Ollendick, 1998). The specific process by which phobias develop may depend on the type of fear. Children report that animal fears, medical fears, and fear of failure or criticism develop from conditioning experiences, whereas fears of the unknown, danger, and death arise from information they have received from the environment (Muris et al., 1997).

Classical Conditioning Perspective   The view that phobias are conditioned responses is based primarily on Watson's conditioning experiment with an infant, Little Albert. Watson was able to produce a fear response to a white rat (not initially feared) in the infant by pairing it with a loud sound (Watson & Rayner, 2000). Thus Watson believed that fears can result through classical conditioning or association.

Most children with severe phobias report conditioning experiences as the cause (King, Clowes-Hollins, & Ollendick, 1997; King et al., 1998). Similarly, more clients attributed their phobias to direct (classical) conditioning experiences than to any other factor (Öst, 1987; Öst & Hugdahl, 1981). Öst and Hugdahl (1981) found that people with agoraphobia were most likely to attribute their disorder to direct conditioning experiences; the next most likely were those with claustrophobia and dental phobia.

In general, retrospective reports seem to indicate that conditioning experiences play a role in the development of phobias for most clients seeking therapy and that this process may be more important for some types of phobias than for others. However, a substantial percentage of surveyed patients report something other than a direct conditioning experience as the "key" to their phobias. Also, the classical conditioning perspective does not explain why only some people exposed to potential conditioning experiences actually develop phobias.

Observational Learning and Negative Information Perspective   Emotional conditioning can be developed through observational learning, or modeling. A fear or phobia in children can result from the observation of fright displayed by a parent or friend or in media such as television or the movies. In a clinical example involving modeling, several people who had seen the horror film *The Exorcist* had to be treated for a variety of anxiety reactions (Bozzuto, 1975).

To determine the influence of negative information on the acquisition of nighttime fears in children, researchers asked them questions such as, "Did you see frightening things on television about . . . ?" (Muris et al., 2001). The most common fears included concern with intruders, imaginary creatures, frightening dreams, animals, and frightening thoughts. Most (73.3 percent) of the children attributed their fears to negative information acquired largely from television. However, the study involved fears; it is not clear whether negative information is sufficient to produce a phobia.

Cognitive-Behavioral Perspective   Why do individuals with spider phobia react with such terror at the sight of a spider? Some researchers believe cognitive distortions and catastrophic thoughts may contribute to strong fears (Teachman & Woody, 2003).

For example, people with spider phobia believe that spiders single them out for attack and that they will move rapidly and aggressively toward them (Riskind, Moore, & Bowley, 1995). Others report thoughts that the spider "will attack me" or "will take revenge" (Mulkens, de Jong, & Merckelbach, 1996). Similar negative thoughts, such as "I will be trapped," "I will suffocate," or "I will lose control," have been reported by individuals with claustrophobia. Removal of these thoughts was associated with dramatic decreases in the patients' fear (Shafran, Booth, & Rachman, 1993). Such studies seem to indicate that cognitions involving catastrophic or distorted thinking may be causal or contributing factors for phobias.

Biological Perspective   Some researchers (Kendler, Myers, & Prescott, 2002; Muris et al., 2001) believe that biological factors such as genetics or biological preparedness may explain why the origins of some fears or phobias cannot be identified. Studies on male and female twin pairs have supported a moderate to modest contribution from common genetic factors for all phobia subtypes (Hettema et al., 2003; Kendler et al., 2001) and the degree of influence may vary among the different subtypes (Kendler et al., 1992). However, evidence for the direct genetic transmission resulting in a specific type of phobia is not strong.

A different biological approach to the development of fear reactions involves the concept of *preparedness* (Poulton et al., 2000; Seligman, 1971). Proponents of this position argue that fears do not develop randomly. In particular, they believe that it is easier for human beings to learn fears to which we are physiologically predisposed. Such quickly aroused (or "prepared") fears may have been necessary to the survival of pretechnological humanity (Poulton et al., 2001). Other researchers (Davey et al., 1998; deJong, Vorage, & van den Hout, 2000) believe that the preparedness theory based on fear is incomplete and that human phobias that concern animals such as spiders and rats (normally physically harmless) are due instead to the emotional response of disgust. These researchers attribute the anxiety aroused as due to an inherent fear of disease or contamination associated with these animals, not to a threat of physical danger.

To test out this hypothesis, Mulkens and colleagues (1996) had women with and without spider phobias indicate their willingness to eat a cookie. An assistant of the researchers then guided a "medium sized" spider (*Tegenaria Atrica*) across the cookie. An associate then removed the spider from the room. The researchers reasoned that if disgust is a factor, those with a spider phobia should be more reluctant to eat the "contaminated" cookie. Fear should not be a factor, because the spider was removed. Results supported the idea of disgust: only 25 percent of women with spider phobia eventually ate some of the cookie, compared with 70 percent of the control group participants. Other studies, however, indicate that fear may be more important than disgust in spider phobia (Thorpe & Salkovskis, 1998; Sawchuk et al., 2000). It is possible that some animals evoke both fear and disgust, whereas others evoke only one emotion.

Although the combination of classical conditioning and prepared learning is a promising area for further research, it is difficult to believe that most phobias stem from prepared fears. Many simply do not fit into the prepared-fear model. It would be difficult, for example, to explain the survival value of social phobias such as the fear of using public restrooms and of eating in public, of agoraphobia, and of many specific phobias. In addition, prepared fears appear to have variable age of onset and are among the easiest to eliminate.

Treatment of Phobias

Specific and social phobias have been successfully treated by both behavioral methods and medication. In some studies the two types of treatments have been combined.

Biochemical Treatments Biochemical treatments are predicated on the view that anxiety disorders involve neurobiological abnormalities that can be normalized with medication. In general, antidepressants can help reduce not only the extreme fear but also the depression that often accompanies anxiety disorders. In treating phobias, a number of medications appear to be effective. For agoraphobia, there is "clear evidence of clinical efficacy" for benzodiazepines (antianxiety medications), tricyclic antidepressants, and SSRIs. For social phobia, both benzodiazepines and SSRIs have shown "preliminary evidence of efficacy," and benzodiazepines have been used with some success in treating specific phobias (Lader & Bond, 1998). As with most medications, side or negative effects can occur. Benzodiazepines can produce dependence and withdrawal symptoms. SSRIs can result in diminished libido and decreased sexual arousal and functioning. Some antidepressants can result in weight gain, dry mouth, memory impairment, and other anticholinergic effects. The phobia symptoms often recur if the patient stops taking the medications (Sundel & Sundel, 1998).

Behavioral Treatments Phobias have been successfully treated with a variety of behavioral approaches. These approaches can include: exposure (gradually introducing the individual to the feared situation or object until the fear dissipates); desensitization (similar to exposure but with an additional response, such as relaxation, to help combat anxiety); modeling (demonstration of another person's successful interactions with the feared object or situation); cognitive restructuring (identifying irrational or anxiety-arousing thoughts associated with the phobia and changing them); and skills training (learning skills necessary to function in the phobic situation). Some behavioral programs rely primarily on one approach; others combine several techniques (Velting, Setzer, & Albano, 2004).

Exposure Therapy In **exposure therapy,** the patient is introduced (most often gradually, but sometimes rapidly) to increasingly difficult encounters with the feared situation. For example, in agoraphobia, which involves the fear of leaving the house, the therapist may first ask the patient only to visualize or imagine the anxiety-evoking situation. After completing this task, the person would be asked to actually take walks outside the home with the therapist until the fear has been eliminated. Exposure therapy has also been used successfully to treat specific phobias (Mystkowski et al., 2003).

Exposure therapies employing computer technology ("virtual reality therapy") have recently been developed. These therapies involve computer-generated three-dimensional images that immerse the participant in a realistic setting (Maltby et al., 2002). These images are viewed through a helmet with video monitors. One thirty-seven-year-old woman with a severe spider phobia that had lasted for twenty years was treated with virtual reality therapy (Carlin, Hoffman, & Weghorst, 1997). Encountering a spider or spider web would produce panic. She washed and vacuumed her car each day and fumigated it with pesticides to eliminate spiders. While driving her car, she wore "spider gloves" to sweep out any spider webs observed. To prevent spiders from entering her bedroom, she sealed the windows with duct tape. When the woman first began the sessions, her body shook uncontrollably. After twelve sessions, her twenty-year-long spider phobia was completely eliminated. In fact, when Mary now spots a spider in her home, she responds by saying, "I'm sorry, you came to the wrong house!" and squashes it (Salyer, 1997, p. C2).

exposure therapy A therapy technique in which the patient is introduced to encounters (can be gradual or rapid) with the feared situation.

Cognitive Strategies In this approach, unrealistic thoughts are altered, as they are believed to be responsible for phobias. Individuals with social phobias, for example, tend to be intensely self-focused and fearful that others will see them as anxious,

Modeling Therapy   Watching a fear-producing act being performed successfully (such as the man handling the snake) can help people overcome their own fear. Modeling therapy has proven effective in treating both specific and social phobias. How does modeling work in eliminating fears?

incompetent, or weak. Their own self-criticism is the basis for their phobias (Harvey et al., 2000; Hofman, 2000). Cognitive strategies can help "normalize" social anxiety by encouraging patients to interpret emotional and physical tension as "normal anxiety" and by helping them redirect their attention from themselves to others in similar social situations. This approach has been successful in treating individuals with public-speaking phobia (Furman et al., 2002; Woody, Chambless, & Glass, 1997).

Systematic desensitization uses muscle relaxation to treat specific and social phobias. Wolpe (1958, 1973), who introduced the treatment, taught patients a relaxation response that is incompatible with fear. Relaxation is then repeatedly paired with visualizations of the feared stimulus. This procedure was adopted for Mr. B., who had a fear of urinating in restrooms when others were present. He was trained in muscle relaxation and, while relaxed, learned to urinate under the following conditions: no one in the bathroom, therapist in the stall, therapist washing hands, therapist at adjacent urinal, therapist waiting behind client. These conditions were arranged in ascending difficulty. The easier items were practiced first until Mr. B.'s anxiety was sufficiently reduced. Over a period of seventeen weeks, the anxiety diminished completely, and the gains were maintained in a follow-up at seven and one-half months (McCracken & Larkin, 1991). Systematic desensitization has been shown to be effective with both specific and social phobias (deJong et al., 2000).

Modeling therapy procedures—which include filmed modeling, live modeling, and participant modeling—have also been highly effective in treating certain phobias. When modeling is used as therapy, the person with the phobia observes a model in the act of coping with, or responding appropriately in, the fear-producing situation (Ollendick & King, 1998). Some researchers believe that modeling is a unique therapeutic approach in its own right, whereas others believe that it is a type of exposure treatment.

systematic desensitization A behavioral therapy technique in which relaxation is used to eliminate the anxiety associated with phobias and other fear-evoking situations.

modeling therapy A therapeutic approach to phobias in which the person with the phobia observes a model in the act of coping with, or responding appropriately in, the fear-producing situation.

▶ CHECKPOINT REVIEW

agoraphobia *(p. 94)*

exposure therapy *(p. 100)*

modeling therapy *(p. 101)*

phobia *(p. 93)*

social phobia *(p. 94)*

specific phobia *(p. 96)*

systematic desensitization *(p. 101)*

Some people are housebound with fear, and others are afraid of public speaking or harmless insects. How do these irrational fears develop, and what is the best way of treating them?

■ Phobias are strong fears that exceed the demands of the situation.

■ Agoraphobia is an intense fear of being in public places; it can keep afflicted people from leaving home because attempts to do so may produce panic attacks.

■ Social phobias are irrational fears about situations in which the person can be observed by others. The anxiety generally stems from the possibility of appearing foolish or making mistakes in public.

■ Specific phobias include all the irrational fears that are not classed as social phobias or agoraphobia. Commonly feared objects in specific phobias include small animals, heights, and the dark.

■ In the psychodynamic view, phobias represent unconscious conflicts that are displaced onto an external object or situation.

■ Behavioral explanations include the classical conditioning view, in which phobias are acquired through an association between some aversive event and a stimulus; through conditioning by observational learning; through thoughts that are distorted and frightening; and through operant conditioning by reinforcement for fear behaviors.

■ Biological explanations are based on studies of the influence of genetic, biochemical, and neurological factors or on the idea that humans are biologically prepared to develop certain fears.

■ The most effective treatments for phobias seem to be biochemical (via antidepressants) and behavioral (via exposure and flooding, systematic desensitization, modeling, and graduated exposure).

▶ Obsessive-Compulsive Disorder

Obsessive-compulsive disorder (OCD) is characterized by **obsessions** (intrusive, repetitive thoughts or images that produce anxiety) or **compulsions** (the need to perform acts or to dwell on thoughts to reduce anxiety). Although obsessions and compulsions can occur separately, they frequently occur together (Freeston & Ladouceur, 1997), as in the following case involving a forty-five-year-old-woman:

> [W]hen I left any room in the house, or entered a room, I would have to touch a light switch, and I would have to touch a doorknob. If I could do something the first time …, and I did it perfectly—if it felt right to me—then I could go on to the next thing, move out of the room, or go to the next ritual. If it didn't feel right, then I would have to do it again. But I couldn't do it just 1 more time because then that would be 2 times, and 2 wasn't my good number, 5 was. So, automatically, if I didn't do it right the first time, I had to do it 5 times. If I didn't get it right in 5 times, then I would have to do it 25 times. So you can see why I ended up in my bed for the next 8 months. Because it was so out of control, it could take me an hour just to get out of my bedroom and into the bathroom…. The reason I do these kinds of rituals and obsessing is that I have a fear that someone is going to die. This is not rational thinking to me. I know I can't prevent somebody from dying by putting 5 ice cubes in a glass instead of 4. (Jenike, 2001, p. 2122)

obsessive-compulsive disorder (OCD) Disorder characterized by intrusive and repetitive thoughts or images, or by the need to perform acts or dwell on thoughts to reduce anxiety.

obsession An intrusive and repetitive thought or image that produces anxiety.

compulsion The need to perform acts or to dwell on thoughts to reduce anxiety.

The woman was hospitalized for depression and did not realize that she had OCD until she saw a television program describing the disorder. She was treated with medication and cognitive behavioral therapy.

Obsessive-compulsive disorder was once thought to be relatively rare. Individuals with the disorder are reluctant to talk about their symptoms. Screening questions such

Figure 4.5 Common Obsessions and Compulsions About half of the patients reported both obsessions and compulsions. Twenty-five percent believed that their symptoms were reasonable. How would a therapist work with a patient who believed that his or her symptoms were appropriate? *Source:* Data from Foa & Kozak (1995).

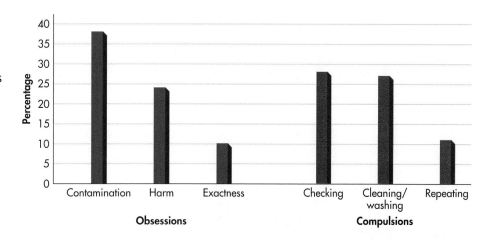

as: "Do you have repetitive thoughts that make you anxious and that you cannot get rid of regardless of how hard you try?" "Do you keep things extremely clean or wash your hands frequently?" And "Do you check things to excess?" (Jenike, 2004, p. 260) have improved the likelihood of diagnosis. In epidemiological studies of obsessive-compulsive disorder, the lifetime prevalence rate for the disorder is estimated to be 2.5 percent (American Psychiatric Association, 2000a). The disorder is about equally common in males and females but is less common in African Americans and Mexican Americans (Zhang & Snowden, 1999). See Figure 4.5 for some of the more common obsessions and compulsions.

Obsessions

As mentioned earlier, an obsession is an intrusive and repetitive anxiety-arousing thought or image. The person may realize that the thought is irrational, but he or she cannot keep it from arising over and over again. One successful woman in her mid-twenties was tormented by thoughts of hurting children, even though she adores them, and of couples copulating on the altar during Mass (Wen, 2001). Obsessions common to adults involve bodily wastes or secretions, dirt or germs, and environmental contamination (George et al., 1993). Among a sample of children and adolescents, the most common obsessions involved dirt or germs, disease and death, or danger to self or loved ones (Swedo et al., 1989). Do "normal" people have intrusive, unacceptable thoughts and impulses? Several studies (Edwards & Dickerson, 1987; Freeston & Ladouceur, 1993; Ladouceur, Freeston, et al., 2000) have found that more than 80 percent of normal samples report the existence of unpleasant intrusive thoughts and impulses. Apparently, a considerable majority of the "normal" population has obsessive symptoms. However, obsessions reported by patients lasted longer, were more intense, produced more discomfort, and were more difficult to dismiss than they were among those without the disorder (Rachman & DeSilva, 1987).

Compulsions

A compulsion is the need to perform acts or to dwell on mental acts repetitively. Distress or anxiety occurs if the behavior is not performed or if it is not done "correctly." Compulsions are often, but not always, associated with obsessions. Mild forms include behaviors such as refusing to walk under a ladder or step on cracks in sidewalks, throwing salt over one's shoulder, and knocking on wood. The three most common compulsions among a sample of children and adolescents (Swedo et al., 1989) involved excessive or ritualized washing, repeating rituals (such as going in and out of a door and getting up and down from a chair), and checking behaviors (doors and appliances).

Compulsions are also a common phenomenon in nonclinical populations. In one study of 150 undergraduates, nearly 55 percent acknowledged that they "have rituals

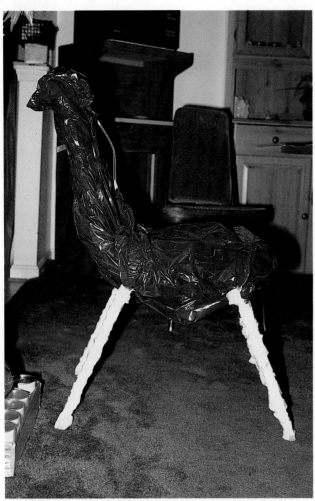

Contamination Obsession   The individual who wrapped this chair had an obsessive fear of dust that reached psychotic proportions. What kinds of thoughts about dust can produce such anxiety?

or feel compelled to carry out certain behaviors in certain circumstances" (Muris, Merckelbach, & Clavan, 1997). The students reported having one or more of the following compulsions: checking (26.8 percent); washing, cleaning, or ordering items (15.9 percent); magical protective acts, such as saying particular numbers or touching a lucky object (10.5 percent); and avoiding particular objects (6.1 percent). A continuum appears to exist between "normal" rituals and "pathological" compulsions; in individuals with obsessive-compulsive disorder, the compulsions are more frequent and of greater intensity, and they produce more discomfort if not performed.

Etiology of Obsessive-Compulsive Disorder

The causes of obsessive-compulsive disorder remain speculative, although increased attention has recently been paid to biological explanations. We examine the cause of this disorder from the perspectives of the psychodynamic, behavioral, and biological models.

Psychodynamic Perspective   In the psychodynamic perspective, obsessive-compulsive behaviors are attempts to fend off anal sadistic (antisocial), anal libidinous (pleasurable soiling), and genital (masturbatory) impulses (Burgy, 2001). For example, Freud (1949) believed that obsessions represent the substitution or replacement of an original conflict, usually sexual in nature, with an associated idea that is less threatening. He found support for his notion in the case histories of some of his patients. One patient, a girl, had disturbing obsessions about stealing or counterfeiting money; these thoughts were absurd and untrue. During analysis, Freud discovered that these obsessions reflected anxiety that stemmed from guilt about masturbation. When the patient was kept under constant observation, which prevented her from masturbating, the obsessional thoughts (or, perhaps, the reports of the thoughts) ceased.

Behavioral and Cognitive Perspectives   Proponents of the behavioral perspective maintain that obsessive-compulsive behaviors develop because they reduce anxiety. A distracting thought or action recurs more often if it reduces anxiety. For example, many college students may develop mild forms of compulsive behavior during final examinations. During this stressful and anxiety-filled time, students may find themselves engaging in escape activities such as daydreaming, straightening up their rooms, or eating five or more times a day, all of which serve to shield them from thoughts of the upcoming tests. If the stress lasts a long time, a compulsive behavior may develop.

Researchers have also attempted to determine the cognitive factors that lead to severe doubts associated with compulsive behavior. It seems that patients with OCD do not trust their own memories and judgment and make futile attempts to determine whether they actually performed the behaviors or performed them "correctly." The uncertainly leads to the rituals, and doubts may occur even in the face of unambiguous evidence. An "OC checker may turn the key in the lock over and over again without being able to convince himself or herself that the door has in fact been locked, even

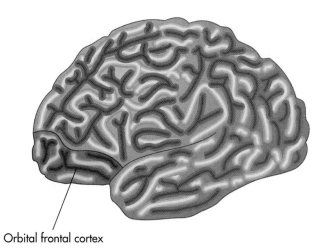

Orbital frontal cortex

Figure 4.6 Orbital Frontal Cortex   Untreated patients with obsessive-compulsive disorder show a high metabolism rate in this area of the brain. This rate is reduced to "normal" levels by certain medications, which also produce a reduction in obsessive-compulsive symptoms. What would it mean if similar results are found with psychotherapy?

though he or she can plainly see that the key is in the proper position, hear it engaging, and feel the lock snapping" (Dar et al., 2000, p. 673). Individuals with OCD may have a disconfirmatory bias—that is, they generate a search for evidence that undermines their confidence. The person checking the lock may develop thoughts of all the factors that may have prevented the door from staying locked (Rassin et al., 2000).

Biological Perspective   Biological explanations of obsessive-compulsive behaviors are based on data relating to brain structure, genetic studies, and biochemical abnormalities. Positron emission tomography (PET) has enabled us to observe metabolic reactions in the brain. These reactions have been found to differ among people with obsessive-compulsive disorder, severe depression, or no evidence of psychiatric disorders. Those with obsessive-compulsive disorder show increased metabolic activity in the frontal lobe of the left hemisphere. Perhaps this area of the brain, the orbital frontal cortex, is associated with obsessive-compulsive behaviors (Blier et al., 2000; see also Figure 4.6). Heightened glucose metabolism in the frontal lobes has also been found in individuals with obsessive-compulsive disorder. Of special interest is the fact that when these individuals were given fluoxetine (a medication that increases the activity level of serotonin), the cerebral blood flow to the frontal lobes was decreased to values found in individuals without the disorder. Associated with this change was a reported reduction in OCD symptoms in patients (Hoehn-Saric et al., 1991). Interestingly, exposure therapy also appears to produce normalized brain changes in patients with OCD (Stein, 2002).

Some researchers (Bellodi et al., 2001; Comings & Comings, 1987) believe that obsessive-compulsive disorder is the result of genetic factors. Family and twin studies offer some support for this theory. First-degree relatives of individuals with obsessive-compulsive disorder are more likely to have an anxiety disorder than are first-degree relatives of psychiatrically normal controls (Black et al., 1992). It may be that an "overreactive tendency" or vulnerability to developing an anxiety disorder may be inherited and that the actual development of an obsessive-compulsive disorder may depend on life events or personality factors.

Treatment of Obsessive-Compulsive Disorder

The primary modes of treatment for obsessive-compulsive disorder are either biological or behavioral in nature. Behavioral therapies have been used successfully for many years, but treatment with medication has recently enjoyed increased attention. Cultural aspects of treatment must also be considered. In treating two African American women with OCD, Williams, Chambless, and Steketee (1998) found that each woman believed that she was the only black person to have this problem (neither had contact with the other). Their sense of isolation was increased when they found that the local OCD support group had no black members. Both declined to join the group. Although both women improved with cognitive behavior therapy, the therapists, who were European Americans, were concerned about the possible impact of therapist-client racial match. They stress the need to be sensitive to special issues involved in therapy with ethnic minorities and point out that African Americans with OCD have been underrepresented in clinical outcome studies.

Biological Treatments Because obsessive-compulsive disorder is classified as an anxiety disorder, minor tranquilizers were thought to be helpful. However, these drugs have not proven capable of decreasing to any extent the frequency of patients' obsessive thoughts or compulsive rituals. In contrast, fluoxetine and clomipramine (antidepressants), which increase the serotonin levels in the brain, are successful in treating patients with obsessive-compulsive disorder (Lydiard, 1996; Pigott, 1996; Tollefson et al., 1994). However, only 65 percent of persons with obsessive-compulsive disorder respond to these medications, and often the relief is only partial (30% to 60% improvement in symptoms; Hurley et al., 2002). Many clients also report adverse side-effect reactions to medications and drop out of treatment (Clomipramine Collaborative Study Group, 1991). In addition, there is a rapid return of symptoms, and relapse occurs within months, after stopping the medication (Jenike, 2001; Stanley & Turner, 1995).

Behavioral Treatments The treatment of choice for obsessive-compulsive disorder is the combination of exposure and response prevention (Abramowitz, Foa, & Franklin, 2003). Exposure is a technique that involves actual or imagined *exposure* to the fear-arousing situations; it can be performed at high-anxiety level (**flooding**) or with more gradual exposure. The steps generally involve (Franklin et al., 2000): (1) educating the clients about OCD and the rationale for exposure and response prevention; (2) development of an exposure hierarchy (from moderately fearful to most feared situations); (3) exposure to feared situations until anxiety has diminished; and (4) refraining from rituals (response prevention). Follow-up studies that range from one to six years indicate that from 55 to 79 percent of individuals treated with behavior therapy maintain their improvement (Stanley & Turner, 1995).

◀ Acute and Posttraumatic Stress Disorders

> A fifty-year-old man noticed smoke coming from the hood of his car as he was driving on the freeway. He became more frightened when he observed flames coming out near his windshield. He quickly stopped the car and tried to get out. However, the onboard computer was malfunctioning, and the automatic door locks were locking and unlocking at high frequency. In desperation, he managed to flip the handle just as the door unlocked. As he ran from the car, the gas tank exploded. (Green, 2003)

flooding A behavioral treatment that attempts to extinguish fear by placing the client in continued *in vivo* (actual) or imagined high anxiety-provoking situations; a form of exposure therapy.

acute stress disorder (ASD) Exposure to a traumatic stressor that results in dissociation, reliving the experience, and attempts to avoid reminders of the events and that lasts for more than two and less than thirty days.

posttraumatic stress disorder (PTSD) An anxiety disorder that lasts for more than thirty days; develops in response to a specific extreme stressor; characterized by intrusive memories of the traumatic event, emotional withdrawal, and heightened autonomic arousal.

Acute and posttraumatic stress disorders are anxiety disorders that develop in response to an extreme psychological or physical trauma. The reaction to the event must involve intense fear and evoke feelings of helplessness or horror. Many individuals who experienced or witnessed the horror of the September 11, 2001, terrorist attacks on the World Trade Center and the Pentagon also developed one of the stress disorders. Although stress disorders have many similarities to other anxiety disorders, they also have some unique symptoms, such as detachment from others, restricted range of affect, nightmares, and loss of interest in activities.

Acute stress disorder (ASD) develops after exposure to a traumatic stressor and results in dissociation, reliving the experience, and attempts to avoid reminders of the event; this disorder lasts for more than two and fewer than thirty days and occurs within four weeks of exposure to the stressor. **Posttraumatic stress disorder (PTSD)** lasts for more than thirty days, develops in response to a specific extreme stressor, and is characterized by intrusive memories of the traumatic event, emotional withdrawal,

Table 4.2   Lifetime Prevalence Exposure to Stressors by Gender and PTSD Risk

Trauma	Lifetime Prevalence (%)		PTSD Risk	
	Male	*Female*	*Male*	*Female*
Life-threatening accident	25.0	13.8	6.3	8.8
Natural disaster	18.9	15.2	3.7	5.4
Threatened with weapon	19.0	6.8	1.9	32.6
Physical attack	11.1	6.9	1.8	21.3
Rape	0.7	9.2	65.0	45.9

Note: Some traumas are more likely to result in PTSD than others. Significant gender differences were found in reactions to "being threatened with a weapon" or "physical attack." What accounts for the differences in risk for developing PTSD among the specific traumas and for the gender differences? *Source:* From Ballenger et al. (2000).

and heightened autonomic arousal. The events that trigger these disorders may involve a threat to one's life or to a spouse or family member. A large minority of individuals will face a traumatic event in their lives, and up to 25 percent will develop ASD or PTSD. Some types of traumas are more likely to produce ASD or PTSD (Hidalgo & Davidson, 2000; Kubany et al., 2004; see Table 4.2 for PTSD prevalence associated with specific stressors).

Diagnosis of Acute and Posttraumatic Stress Disorders

The diagnostic criteria for acute stress disorder (ASD) and posttraumatic stress disorder (PTSD) are similar. Both require exposure to an extreme stressor. They differ primarily in onset (ASD, within four weeks, and PTSD, at any time) and duration (ASD, two to twenty-eight days, and PTSD, longer than one month). An individual with an initial diagnosis of ASD is likely to receive a diagnosis of PTSD if the symptoms persist for more than four weeks (Classen et al., 1998). Because of the high degree of overlap in symptoms between ASD and PTSD, some researchers question whether they actually represent distinct diagnoses (Brewin, Andrews, & Rose, 2003; Harvey & Bryant, 2002).

DSM-IV-TR Criteria   In addition to having experienced an event involving fear, helplessness, or horror, the following additional symptoms are necessary for the diagnosis. We examine them in more detail.

1. *Reexperiencing the event in disturbing dreams or intrusive memories.* One woman who had been forced to play Russian roulette described flashbacks and nightmares of the event: "Different scenes came back, replays of exactly what happened, only the time is drawn out. . . . It seems to take forever for the gun to reach my head" (Hudson et al., 1991, p. 572).

2. *Emotional numbing, or avoiding stimuli associated with the trauma.* As a defense against intrusive thoughts, people may withdraw emotionally and may avoid anything that might remind them of the events. One twenty-five-year-old woman who had been raped described her response this way: "I spoke about the rape as though it was something that happened to someone else . . . there was just no feeling. (NIMH, 2000, p. 4).

3. *Heightened autonomic arousal.* This reaction can include symptoms such as sleep disturbance, hypervigilance, and loss of control over aggression. Combat veterans with PTSD show an exaggerated startle response (Orr et al., 1995).

One Possible Cause for Anxiety Disorders   A 15-year-old student at Santana High School in California opened fire, killing two fellow students and wounding 13 others. The horror and fear felt by the students can lead to the development of acute stress or post traumatic stress disorder.

In the National Comorbidity Survey, the lifetime prevalence of PTSD for Americans between the ages fifteen and fifty-four was 8 percent, with about twice as many women as men receiving the diagnosis (Kessler et al., 1995).

In both ASD and PTSD, the acute reactions can be considered normative responses to an overwhelming and traumatic stimulus. Symptoms such as numbing, detachment, depersonalization, and dissociation can help the individual minimize awareness of traumatic memories and subsequently alleviate discomfort (Harvey, Bryant, & Dang, 1998). Most victims show a marked decrease in symptoms with time (Shalev et al., 1998). For example, among the 29.8 percent of children who developed severe or very severe PTSD symptoms after Hurricane Andrew, only 12.5 percent still had the disorder after ten months (LaGreca et al., 1996).

Etiology and Treatment of Acute and Posttraumatic Stress Disorders

The development of acute or posttraumatic stress disorder appears to depend on the nature of the traumatic event, on a reaction involving intense fear and horror, and on vulnerability factors such as a past psychiatric history. This latter component probably plays a larger role with some traumatic events, whereas in others, the nature of the specific traumas may predominate, such as in the case of rape or torture.

The degree of trauma is one variable in developing PTSD, but the person's own coping style and the presence of a supportive recovery environment can reduce its effects. Attempts to identify predisposing factors have produced mixed results and may depend on the specific population or trauma being studied. In one study, patients with PTSD had significantly fewer premorbid predisposing factors related to their disorder than individuals with agoraphobia (McKenzie, Marks, & Liness, 2001). However, other studies have reported the importance of preexisting conditions, such as family or past history of mental illness and prior trauma (Green, 2003; Ozer et al., 2003).

PTSD and Battered Women   Women who have been battered or have suffered sexual assaults often report high rates of acute stress or posttraumatic disorder. Here a group of women in a battered women's shelter are participating in a group counseling session.

Behavioral Perspective   Because a traumatic event precipitates the disorder, several researchers (Orr et al., 1995; Yehuda & McFarlane, 1995) believe that classical conditioning is involved. People who have PTSD often show reactions to stimuli present at the time of the trauma (darkness, time of day, smell of diesel fuel, propeller noises, and so on). According to this perspective, the reason extinction does not occur is that the individual avoids thinking about the situation.

Exposure to the cues associated with the trauma appears to be effective in treating PTSD (Basoglu, Livanou, & Salcioglu, 2003; Foa, 2000; Taylor et al., 2003). The process of exposure may involve asking the person to re-create the traumatic event in imagination. In one study of victims of sexual assault (Foa et al., 1999), the women were asked to repeatedly imagine and describe the assault "as if it were happening now." They verbalized the details of the assault, as well as their thoughts and emotions regarding the incident. Their descriptions were recorded, and this process was repeated for about an hour. The women were then instructed to listen to the recordings once a day and, when doing so, to "imagine that the assault is happening now." This process allowed extinction to occur.

Biological Perspective and Treatment   There is some evidence that PTSD is not a biologically normative stress response but one in which a number of neural and biological systems are sensitized, resulting in hypersensitivity to stimuli that recall or are associated with the traumatic event. The normal fear response involves the amygdala, the part of the brain that is the major interface between sensory experiences such as trauma and the neurochemical and neuroanatomical circuitry of fear. The amygdala has connections with the reticularis pontis caudalis, which initiates the startle response. The signal to the sympathetic nervous system produces increases in heart rate and blood pressure. Additional responses occur from the hypothalamus and adrenal glands, which release different hormones. Once the stressor is removed, responding returns to the base level. People with PTSD continue to demonstrate enhanced startle

Treating PTSD Veterans are attending a group counseling session at the VA Center in Fort Lauderdale, Florida. This session was held on March 25, 2003. Events such as the tension and conflict with Iraq often result in an increase in the number of veterans seeking help.

responses even to neutral cues. Why this is so is unclear. The nature of the alteration of the neurobiology of PTSD is still being investigated. The changes in sensitivity of the neural and biological systems may not be permanent, as over half of those with PTSD recover (Yehuda, 2000).

Tricyclic antidepressants and SSRIs have been successfully utilized in treating both ASD and PTSD. These medications alter serotonin levels, acting at the level of the amygdala and its connections, and desensitize the fear network. Depending on the specific medication, 50 percent to 85 percent report that they are "very or much improved" in symptom relief, although from 17 percent to 62 percent of those on placebos also report the same degree of improvement (Davidson, 2000). SSRIs (Zoloft, Paxil, Prozac) are the treatment of choice for ASD and PTSD (Ballenger et al., 2000). However, they are associated with side effects such as insomnia, diarrhea, nausea, fatigue, and depressed appetite. Because of this, discontinuation rates are twice as high as those of behavioral treatments (Davidson, 2000; Foa, 2000).

▶ CHECKPOINT REVIEW

acute stress disorder (ASD) *(p. 106)*

compulsion *(p. 102)*

flooding *(p. 106)*

obsession *(p. 102)*

obsessive-compulsive disorder (OCD) *(p. 102)*

posttraumatic stress disorder (PTSD) *(p. 106)*

Intrusive thoughts, such as the desire to shout in a church, or behaviors that one is compelled to perform over and over again, such as checking to determine if the door is locked, are relatively common. When do they become a disorder, and how do you eliminate them?

■ Obsessive-compulsive disorder involves thoughts or actions that are involuntary, intrusive, repetitive, and uncontrollable. Most persons with obsessive-compulsive disorder are aware that their distressing behaviors are irrational.

■ Obsessions (which involve thoughts or images) and compulsions (which involve actions or thoughts) may occur together or separately. The behaviors have to cause marked distress or significantly interfere with life activities before the diagnosis is given.

- Freud believed that this disorder represented the substitution of a threatening unconscious conflict with a conscious behavior or thought that was less threatening.
- According to the anxiety-reduction hypothesis, a behavioral explanation, obsessions and compulsions develop because they reduce anxiety.
- Proponents of the cognitive perspective suggest that the disorder stems from a style of thinking that is characterized by severe doubts and a disconfirmatory bias that prevents individuals from trusting their own judgment.
- Positron emission tomography has opened new avenues of research for those using the biological approach.
- The most commonly used biological treatments involve the use of antidepressants such as fluoxetine and clomipramine.
- The treatment of choice is a combination of flooding and response prevention, sometimes combined with cognitive therapy.

A large minority of individuals will face a traumatic incident sometime in their lives. Under what conditions will the trauma lead to a stress disorder such as PTSD, and how are these disorders best treated?

- Posttraumatic and acute stress disorders involve exposure to a traumatic event, resulting in intrusive memories of the occurrence, attempts to forget or repress the memories, emotional withdrawal, and increased arousal.
- Exposure to extreme stress will result in a strong emotional reaction in most people. A diagnosis of a stress disorder is given only when symptoms of distress are clinically significant and last for at least two days for ASD or one month for PTSD.
- Classical conditioning, cognitive approaches, and biological principles have been used to both explain and treat the condition.

FOCUS QUESTIONS

- What are dissociations? What forms can they take? How are they caused, and how are they treated?
- When do physical complaints become a type of disorder? What are the causes and treatments of these conditions?

5 Dissociative Disorders and Somatoform Disorders

The following two cases illustrate characteristics found in the **dissociative disorders**—mental disorders in which a person's identity, memory, and consciousness are altered or disrupted.

> Sam McNulty was found by the police sitting in a motel room in Houston two days after being reported missing. He had disappeared after just getting married and reported that he did not know who he is and had no memory of his life. Psychiatrists believe that McNulty is suffering from psychogenic fugue. (Lezon, 2002)

> A woman came in for therapy because of several puzzling events. She had been told that she had been dancing and flirting in a bar, an event that she could not remember and that was against her moral standards. She had also awakened in a hospital after an overdose and had not remembered being suicidal. Under hypnosis, thirteen different personalities were revealed. (M. K. Shapiro, 1991)

In this chapter, we examine these disorders and the **somatoform disorders,** which involve physical symptoms or complaints that have no physiological basis. Both groups of disorders occur because of some psychological conflict or need.

The symptoms of the dissociative disorders and the somatoform disorders, such as memory disturbance or physical impairment, generally become known through self-reports. Thus the possibility of faking must be considered. Wadlh El-Hage, a defendant on charges of being a conspirator with Osama bin Laden in the attacks on the U.S. Embassies in Kenya and Tanzania, claimed that he suffered from a loss of memory. The court-appointed experts voiced the opinion that the defendant was "malingering and faking the symptoms of amnesia" (Weiser, 2000). In addition to the possibility of faking, other questions have been raised about several of the dissociative disorders. For example, some researchers are concerned about the sudden increases in reports of multiple personalities and dissociative amnesia. They believe that counselors and therapists or clients may be inadvertently "creating" these disorders.

Physical complaints from individuals with somatoform disorders are also difficult to evaluate when no biological basis seems to exist for the physical symptoms. Yet the fact remains that in genuine cases of dissociative and somatoform disorders, the symptoms are produced "involuntarily" or unconsciously. Affected individuals actually are puzzled by their memory loss or behavioral changes and genuinely suffer from their physical symptoms or disability. This situation leads to a paradox: a person *does* suffer memory disturbance in psychogenic (of psychological or emotional origin) amnesia, yet that memory must exist somewhere in the neurons and synapses of the brain. Similarly, a person *does* "lose" his or her sight in hysterical blindness, yet physiologically the eyes are perfectly capable of seeing. What exactly happens in these cases? The dissociative and somatoform disorders are among the most puzzling of all disorders.

dissociative disorders Mental disorders in which a person's identity, memory, or consciousness is altered or disrupted; include dissociative amnesia, dissociative fugue, dissociative identity disorder (multiple-personality disorder), and depersonalization disorder.

somatoform disorders Mental disorders that involve physical symptoms or complaints that have no physiological basis; include somatization disorder, conversion disorder, pain disorder, hypochondriasis, and body dysmorphic disorder.

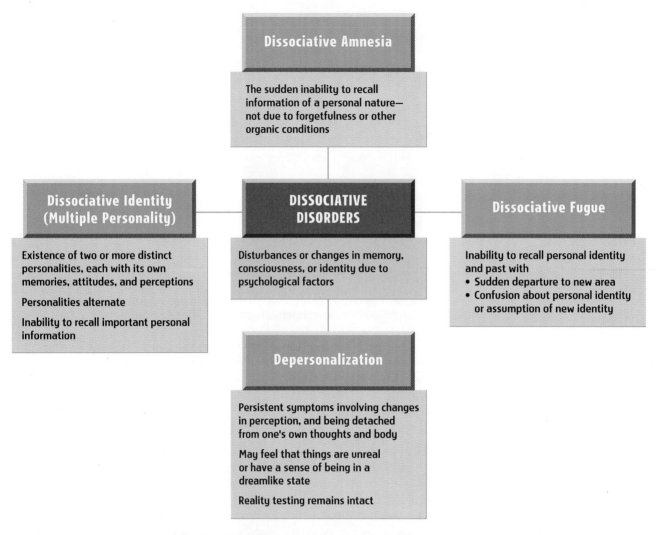

Figure 5.1 **Disorders Chart: Dissociative Disorders** *Source:* Data from American Psychiatric Association (2000a).

Dissociative Disorders

The dissociative disorders—*dissociative amnesia, dissociative fugue, dissociative identity disorder (multiple personality),* and *depersonalization disorder*—are charted in Figure 5.1. Each disorder involves some sort of dissociation, or separation, of a part of the person's consciousness, memory, or identity. Figure 5.1 also summarizes the prevalence rates, age of onset, and course of dissociative disorders.

Dissociative Amnesia

Dissociative amnesia is the partial or total loss of important personal information, sometimes occurring suddenly after a stressful or traumatic event. The disturbed person may be unable to recall information such as his or her name, address, friends, and relatives, but he or she does remember the necessities of daily life—how to read, write, and drive. Individuals with this disorder often score high on tests measuring hypnotizability and may also report depression, anxiety, and trance states (American Psychiatric Association, 2000a).

dissociative amnesia A dissociative disorder characterized by the partial or total loss of important personal information, sometimes occurring suddenly after a stressful or traumatic event.

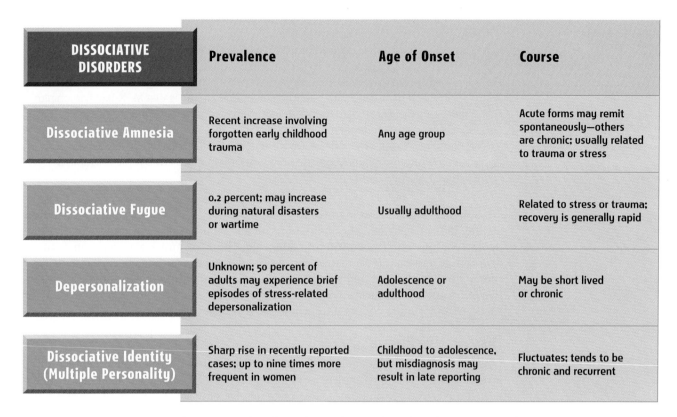

DISSOCIATIVE DISORDERS	Prevalence	Age of Onset	Course
Dissociative Amnesia	Recent increase involving forgotten early childhood trauma	Any age group	Acute forms may remit spontaneously—others are chronic; usually related to trauma or stress
Dissociative Fugue	0.2 percent; may increase during natural disasters or wartime	Usually adulthood	Related to stress or trauma; recovery is generally rapid
Depersonalization	Unknown; 50 percent of adults may experience brief episodes of stress-related depersonalization	Adolescence or adulthood	May be short lived or chronic
Dissociative Identity (Multiple Personality)	Sharp rise in recently reported cases; up to nine times more frequent in women	Childhood to adolescence, but misdiagnosis may result in late reporting	Fluctuates; tends to be chronic and recurrent

Figure 5.1 **Disorders Chart: Dissociative Disorders (continued)**

There are five types of dissociative amnesia—localized, selective, generalized, systematized, and continuous—and they vary in terms of the degree and type of memory that is lost. The most common, **localized amnesia,** is a failure to recall all the events that happened in a specific short period, often centered on some highly painful or disturbing event. The following cases are typical of localized amnesia.

> A thirty-eight-year-old mother had no memory of being molested by her father until she underwent therapy at the age of thirty-three.

> An eighteen-year-old woman who survived a dramatic fire claimed not to remember it or the death of her child and husband in the fire. She claimed her relatives were lying about the fire. She became extremely agitated and emotional several hours later, when her memory abruptly returned.

Selective amnesia is an inability to remember certain details of an incident. For example, a man remembered having an automobile accident but could not recall that his child had died in the crash. Selective amnesia is often claimed by people accused of violent criminal offenses (Mendlowicz et al., 2002). Many murderers report that they remember arguments but do not remember killing anyone. According to one estimate, about 70 percent of criminals who say they have amnesia of the crime are feigning (Merryman, 1997).

Generalized amnesia is an inability to remember anything about one's past life. The following cases illustrate some of the psychological events associated with generalized amnesia:

localized amnesia The most common type of amnesia; an inability to recall all the events that happened during a specific period, often centered on some highly painful or disturbing event.

selective amnesia An inability to remember certain details of an incident.

generalized amnesia An inability to remember anything about one's past life.

> Mr. X. was brought to the admission ward of a psychiatric hospital at the end of February 1988....He could not give any information about himself apart from vague recollections from the immediate past. He had no money or identification on him on admission....He mainly expressed concern that he might have left a wife who might be looking for him. ...We contacted the pastor of the church mentioned in the leaflet Mr. X. had had on him on admission. The pastor led us to a woman who recognized and identified Mr. X....He suddenly remembered that his wife had died and that he had promised her he would kill himself as he felt he could not live without her....He explained in his own words: "I must have lost my memory because otherwise I might have killed myself." (Domb & Beaman, 1991, pp. 424–425)

Systematized amnesia involves the loss of memory for only selected types of information. Patients may lose the ability to recall all memories of their families or of a particular person. Finally, **continuous amnesia**, the fifth and least common form of dissociative amnesia, is an inability to recall any events that have occurred between a specific time in the past and the present time. The individual remains alert and attentive but forgets each successive event after it occurs. This cognitive problem may be transient and is more common in people age fifty and over (Sadovsky, 1998).

Dissociative Fugue

Dissociative fugue (also called *fugue state*) is confusion over personal identity (often involving the partial or complete assumption of a new identity), accompanied by unexpected travel away from home. Most cases involve only short periods away from home and an incomplete change of identity. However, there are exceptions:

> Jane Dee Williams says she remembers nothing before the day in May 1985 when she was found wandering and disoriented in an Aurora, Colorado, shopping mall, wearing a green coat and carrying a Toyota key, a copy of *Watership Down,* two green pens, and a notebook—but having no clue as to who she was. She went to Aurora police for help and ended up at the Colorado Mental Health Institute at Fort Logan with a diagnosis of psychogenic fugue. Jane Dee Williams was actually Jody Roberts, who had disappeared five days earlier from her home and job as a reporter in Tacoma. She was treated and released without recovering her memory. During the next twelve years she remained missing and amnesic. During that time she married and had two sets of twins. In 1997, a tip to the police from someone who recognized Roberts from photographs led to her discovery. She had no memory of her biological family (Merryman, 1997, A8). Although most people with dissociative fugue recover their memories, after two years Jane Dee Williams still could not remember her childhood. (Kremer, 1999)

As with dissociative amnesia, recovery from fugue state is often abrupt and complete, although the gradual return of bits of information has also occurred.

Depersonalization Disorder

Depersonalization disorder is perhaps the most common dissociative disorder. It is characterized by feelings of unreality concerning the self and the environment. This diagnosis is given only when the feelings of unreality and detachment cause major impairment in social or occupational functioning (Lambert et al., 2001). At one time or another, most young adults have experienced some symptoms typical of depersonalization disorder: perceptions that the body is distorted or that the environment has somehow changed, feelings of living out a dream, or feelings of detachment. In a sample of thirty individuals with depersonalization disorder, the illness started in mid-adolescence, with a waxing and waning of symptoms. Among these individuals, the disorder followed a chronic course and was resistant to treatment. One woman

systematized amnesia The loss of memory for only selected types of information, such as all members of one's family.

continuous amnesia An inability to recall any events that have occurred between a specific time in the past and the present time; the least common form of psychogenic amnesia.

dissociative fugue Confusion over personal identity accompanied by unexpected travel away from home; also called *fugue state*.

depersonalization disorder A dissociative disorder in which feelings of unreality concerning the self or the environment cause major impairment in social or occupational functioning.

dissociative identity disorder (DID) A dissociative disorder in which two or more relatively independent personalities appear to exist in one person; formerly known as *multiple-personality disorder*.

described her symptoms this way: "It is as if the real me is taken out and put on a shelf and stored somewhere inside of me. Whatever makes me me is not there" (Simeon et al., 1997, p. 1110). The condition tends to be chronic and is often accompanied by mood and anxiety disorders (Simeon et al., 2000). Like other dissociative disorders, depersonalization can be precipitated by physical or psychological stress (Simeon et al., 2001). See the Mental Health and Society feature "Culture and Somatoform and Dissociative Disorders," for culture-specific forms of dissociation or somatoform disorders.

Dissociative Identity Disorder (Multiple-Personality Disorder)

Dissociative identity disorder (DID), formerly known as *multiple-personality disorder,* is a dramatic condition in which two or more relatively independent personalities appear to exist in one person. The relationships among the personalities are often complex. Only one personality is evident at any one time, and the alternation of personalities usually produces periods of amnesia in the personality that has been displaced. However, one or several personalities may be aware of the existence of the others. The personalities usually differ from one another and sometimes are direct opposites, as the following cases illustrate.

Fugue State, Delusion, or Both? In the film *Nurse Betty,* Renee Zellweger witnesses the killing of her husband and develops amnesia about the event and her identity. She then develops an identity based on her favorite soap opera and leaves for Los Angeles in search of a fictional character on the show. How would you diagnose her condition?

Depersonalization Disorder An individual may feel like an automaton—mechanical and robotlike—when suffering from depersonalization disorder. This painting, "The Subway" (ca. 1950), by George Tooker, captures this feeling.

mental health and society

Culture and Somatoform and Dissociative Disorders

A fifty-six-year-old South American man requested an evaluation and treatment. He had the firm belief that his penis was retracting and entering his abdomen, and he was reacting with a great deal of anxiety. He attempted to pull on his penis to prevent the retraction. This procedure had been effective with a previous episode that occurred when he was nineteen. An evaluation of his mental state ruled out other psychiatric diagnoses such as obsessive-compulsive disorder or schizophrenia (Hallak, Crippa, & Zuardi, 2000).

Dibuk ak Suut, a Malaysian woman, goes into a trance-like state in which she will follow commands and blurt out offensive phrases and may mimic the actions of people around her. She displays profuse sweating and increased heart rate but claims to have no memory of what she did or said. This behavior is set off by being startled or suddenly frightened (Osbourne, 2001).

The symptoms of the first case fit the description of *koro*, a culture-bound syndrome listed in DSM-IV-TR that has been reported primarily in South and East Asia. The symptoms involve an intense fear that the penis or, in a woman, the labia, nipples, or breasts are receding into the body. Koro may be related to body dysmorphic disorder, but it differs in that koro is usually of brief duration and is responsive to positive reassurances. In the second case, the woman is displaying symptoms related to *latah*, a condition found in Malaysia and many other parts of the world that involves mimicking or following the instructions or behaviors of others and dissociation or trancelike states. Other culture-bound disorders may be related to either somatoform or dissociative disorders:

Brain fag Somatic symptoms involving a "fatigued" brain, neck or head pain, or blurring of vision due to difficult coursework or classes. It is found primarily in West Africa among high school and college students.

Dhat A term used in India to describe hypochondriacal concerns and severe anxiety over the discharge of semen. The condition produces feelings of weakness or exhaustion.

Nervios Commonly found in Hispanics residing in the United States and Latin America. The symptoms can include "brain aches," stomach disturbances, anxiety symptoms, and dizziness. Patterns of symptoms can resemble somatoform, anxiety, dissociative, or depressive disorders.

Pibloktoq A dissociative-like episode accompanied by extreme excitement that may be followed by convulsions and coma. Generally found in Inuit communities. The victim may perform aggressive and dangerous acts and report amnesia after the episode.

Zar A condition found in Middle Eastern or North African societies that involves the experience of being possessed by a spirit. The person may engage in bizarre behaviors that may include shouting or hitting his or her head against the wall. During this period the individual is in a dissociative state.

Culture-bound syndromes are interesting because they point to the existence of a pattern of symptoms that are associated primarily with specific societies or groups. These "disorders" do not fit easily into the DSM-IV-TR classification nor into many of the biological and psychological models for dissociative and somatoform disorders. What does it mean when disorders are discovered that do not fit into Western-developed classification systems? Would we assume that the etiology and treatment would be similar to those developed for somatoform and dissociative disorders?

"Little Judy" is a young child who laughs and giggles. "Gravelly Voice" is a man who speaks with a raspy voice. The "one who walks in darkness" is blind and trips over furniture. "Big Judy" is articulate, competent, and funny. These are four of the forty-four personalities that exist within Judy Castelli. She was initially diagnosed with schizophrenia but later told that dissociative identity disorder was the appropriate diagnosis. She has become a lay expert on mental health issues, a singer, a musician, an inventor, and an artist whose work appeared on the February 2000 cover of the American Psychological Association *Monitor*. (Woliver, 2000)

Dissociative identity disorder is much more prevalent in women, and reports of childhood physical or sexual abuse, depression, and anxiety are common (Boon & Draijer, 1993; Coons, 1994; Mulder et al., 1998; see Figure 5.2). Dissociative identity

Dissociative Identity Disorder Judy Castelli stands beside her stained glass artwork. The people in the art have no faces but are connected and touching each other. She considers her artistic endeavors a creative outlet for her continuing struggle with multiple personalities.

disorder appears to originate during childhood, with most reporting their first alternate personality before the age of twelve (Richardson, 1998). In contrast to other diagnostic groups, females with dissociative identity disorder report more alterations in consciousness, have a history of trance states and sleepwalking, and have very high levels of substance abuse and suicidal impulses (Scroppo et al., 1998).

Diagnostic Controversy We noted earlier that dissociative identity disorder is among the less common dissociative disorders, but there is some question about how rare it really is. Before the case of Sybil (a patient who appeared to have sixteen different personalities) became popularized in a movie and book in the 1970s, there were fewer than two hundred reported cases of multiple personality worldwide. Now there are about six thousand new cases reported each year (Milstone, 1997). Some clinicians believe that dissociative identity disorder is relatively common but that the condition is underreported because of misdiagnosis. Others believe that the increased prevalence of DID is due to questionable assessment and therapeutic techniques. For example, the following questions have been used to determine whether some type of dissociation is occurring in children (M. K. Shapiro, 1991):

"Do you ever kinda space out, and lose track of what's going on around you?" (decreased awareness of the environment)

"Do you have any problems with forgetting things?" (amnesia)

"Does it ever happen that time goes by, and then you can't really remember what you were doing during that time?" (fugue state)

"Does it ever seem like things aren't real, like everything is just a dream?" (feelings of unreality)

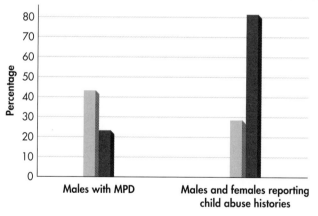

Between 1800 and 1965

1980s

Figure 5.2 Comparison of Characteristics of Reported Cases of Dissociative Identity Disorder (Multiple-Personality Disorder) This graph illustrates characteristics of multiple-personality disorder (MPD) cases reported in the 1980s versus those reported between 1800 and 1965. What could account for these differences? *Source:* Data from Goff & Simms (1993).

Cross-Cultural Factors and Dissociation Dissociative trance states can be entered voluntarily as part of certain cultural or religious practices, as demonstrated by this woman in Brazil. Can the study of such phenomena in another culture shed light on the process of dissociation in Western societies?

> "Does it ever happen that you do things that surprise you, and afterward you stop and say to yourself, 'Why did I do that?'"

However, many children, adolescents, and adults may answer "yes" to questions such as these without having a dissociative disorder.

In a survey of psychologists (Cormier & Thelen, 1998), most believed dissociative identity disorder to be a rare but valid diagnosis. About half believed that they had encountered a client with the disorder, but one-third believed that some clients were feigning it. Some believed that the "condition" was produced by a therapist (iatrogenic) through the use of suggestive techniques such as hypnosis. In a survey of board-certified American psychiatrists (Pope et al., 1999), only one-third felt that dissociative disorders should be included in DSM-IV without reservation; more believed that they should be included only as a "proposed diagnosis."

With the exception of the Netherlands and Turkey, dissociative identity or multiple-personality disorder is rarely diagnosed outside the United States and Canada (Merskey, 1995; Tutkun et al., 1998). One prominent psychiatrist indicated that in forty years of practice he had encountered only one "doubtful case" of the disorder and wondered why he and his colleagues had seen so few cases of multiple-personality disorder (Chodoff, 1987). The psychiatrists who treated "Eve," another well-known case that became popularized in a movie, received tens of thousands of referrals and found only one genuine case of multiple personality (Thigpen & Cleckley, 1984). Whether the increase in cases of dissociative identity disorder represents more accurate diagnosis, false positives, an artifact, or an actual increase in the incidence of the disorder is still being debated.

Etiology of Dissociative Disorders

We next examine the causes of dissociative disorders from the psychodynamic and learning perspectives, and we also examine the possible influence of the clinician. It is important to realize that none of these approaches provides completely satisfactory explanations. As we indicated earlier, the dissociative disorders are not well understood.

Psychodynamic Perspective Psychodynamic theory views the dissociative disorders as a result of the person's use of repression to block from consciousness unpleasant or traumatic events (Richardson, 1998). When complete repression of these impulses is not possible because of the strength of the impulses or the weakness of the ego, dissociation or separation of certain mental processes may occur. In dissociative amnesia and fugue, for example, large parts of the individual's personal identity are no longer available to conscious awareness. This process protects the individual from painful memories or conflicts (Paley, 1988).

> A twenty-seven-year-old man found lying in the middle of a busy intersection was brought to a hospital. He appeared agitated and said, "I wanted to get run over." He claimed not to know his personal identity or anything about his past. He only remembered being brought to the hospital by the police. The inability to remember was highly distressful to him. Psychological tests using the TAT (Thematic Apperception Test) and the Rorschach inkblot test revealed primarily anxiety-arousing, violent, and sexual themes. The clinician hypothesized that a violent incident involving sex might underlie the amnesia. Under hypnosis the patient's memory returned, and he remembered being sexually assaulted. He had repressed the painful experience. (Kaszniak et al., 1988)

The dissociation process is carried to an extreme in dissociative identity disorder. Here, the splits in mental processes become so extreme that more or less independent identities are formed, each with its own unique set of memories. Conflicts within the personality structure are responsible for this process. Equally strong and opposing personality components (stemming from the superego and the id) render the ego incapable of controlling all incompatible elements. A compromise solution is then reached in which the different parts of the personality are alternately allowed expression and repressed. Because intense anxiety and disorganization would occur if these personality factions were allowed to coexist, each is sealed off from the others.

Most people with dissociative identity disorder report a history of physical or sexual abuse during childhood (Boon & Draijer, 1993; Fagan & McMahon, 1984; Richardson, 1998). Besides traumatic childhood events, the person must have the capacity to dissociate—or separate—certain memories or mental processes. A person's susceptibility to hypnotism may be a characteristic of the dissociation process, and, in fact, people who have multiple personalities appear to be very receptive to hypnotic suggestion. Some researchers believe that pathological dissociation is a result of the interaction between auto- or self-hypnosis and acute traumatic stress (Butler et al., 1996). People with this disorder might escape unpleasant experiences through self-hypnosis—by entering a hypnotic state. According to Kluft (1987), the four factors necessary in the development of multiple personalities are:

1. The capacity to dissociate (whether this is produced by traumatic events or is innate is not known).
2. Exposure to overwhelming stress, such as physical or sexual abuse.
3. Encapsulating or walling off the experience.
4. Developing different memory systems.

If a supportive environment is not available or if the personality is not resilient, multiple personality results from these factors (Irwin, 1998; also see Figure 5.3).

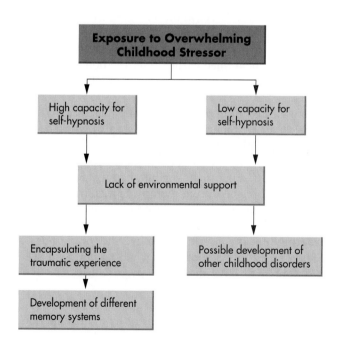

Figure 5.3 Psychodynamic Model for Dissociative Identity Disorder Note the importance of the capacity for self-hypnosis in the development of dissociative identity disorder. *Source:* Adapted from Kluft (1987), and Loewenstein (1994).

Behavioral Perspective Behavioral theorists suggest that the avoidance of stress by indirect means is the main factor to consider in explaining dissociative disorders. For example, patients with dissociative amnesia and fugue are often ill-equipped to handle emotional conflicts. Their way of fleeing stressful situations is either to forget them or to block out the disturbing thoughts. These people typically have much to gain and little to lose from their dissociative symptoms. The causes of dissociative identity disorders may be found in social learning theory. One of the current approaches is the sociocognitive model of DID, developed by Spanos (1994) and further elaborated by Scott Lilienfeld et al. (1999). In this perspective, the disorder is conceptualized as:

> [A] syndrome that consists of rule-governed and goal-directed experiences and displays of multiple role enactments that have been created, legitimized, and maintained by social reinforcement. Patients with DID synthesize these role enactments by drawing on a wide variety of sources of information, including the print and broadcast media, cues provided by therapists, personal experiences, and observations of individuals who have enacted multiple identities. (Lilienfeld et al., 1999, p. 507)

According to this model, patients learn the behaviors through a variety of means and produce these roles according to the demands of the situation. The "personalities" are displayed spontaneously and without conscious deception. Support for this perspective comes from the large increases in DID seen after this disorder was portrayed in the mass media and from the possibility that procedures used to investigate the disorder may actually produce the condition.

As noted earlier, *iatrogenic* refers to an unintended effect of therapy—a condition or disorder produced by a physician or therapist through such mechanisms as selective attention, suggestion, reinforcement, and expectations that are placed on the client. Could some or even most cases of dissociative identity disorder be the result of these factors? A number of researchers and clinicians say yes. They believe that many of the "cases" of multiple personalities and of dissociative amnesia have unwittingly been produced by therapists, self-help books, and the mass media (Aldridge-Morris, 1989; Chodoff, 1987; Goff & Simms, 1993; Loftus, Garry, & Feldman, 1994; Merskey, 1995; Ofshe, 1992; Weissberg, 1993). As mentioned earlier, after the book and movie on Sybil, a woman with multiple personalities, were publicized, the number of cases of DID reported increased dramatically.

The authenticity of this well-known case of multiple personality has recently been questioned (Borch-Jacobsen, 1997). Herbert Spiegel, a hypnotist, also worked with Sybil and used her to demonstrate hypnotic phenomena in his classes. He described her as a "Grade 5" or "hypnotic virtuoso," something found in only 5 percent of the population. Sybil told Spiegel that her psychiatrist, Cornelia Wilbur, had wanted her to be "Helen," a name given to a feeling she expressed during therapy. Spiegel later came to believe that Wilbur had been using a technique in which different memories or emotions were converted into "personalities." Sybil also wrote a letter denying that she had multiple personalities and stating that the "extreme things" she told about her mother were not true. Recently, audiotapes of sessions between Wilbur and Sybil were found, and they indicate that Wilbur may have described personalities for Sybil (Associated Press, 1998).

Although iatrogenic influences can be found in any disorder, dissociative disorders may be especially vulnerable, in part because of the high levels of hypnotizability and suggestibility found in people with dissociative disorders. As Goff (1993) states, it is "no coincidence that the field of [multiple-personality disorder] studies in the United States largely originated among practitioners of hypnosis" (p. 604). Hypnosis and other memory-retrieval methods may create rather than uncover personalities in suggestible clients. Although some cases of dissociative identity disorder probably are

mental health and society

"Suspect" Techniques to Treat Dissociative Identity Disorder

Bennett Braun, who founded the International Society for the Study of Dissociation and who has trained many therapists to work with dissociative identity disorder, was brought up on charges by the Illinois Department of Professional Regulation. The charges stemmed from a former patient's claims that Braun used inappropriate techniques in therapy with her. The former patient, Patricia Burgess, claimed that Braun inappropriately used hypnotic and psychotic drugs, hypnosis, and leather strap restraints to stimulate "abuse" memories. Under repressed-memory therapy, Burgess became convinced that she possessed three hundred personalities, was a high priestess in a satanic cult, ate meatloaf made of human flesh, and sexually abused her children. Burgess later began to question her "memories." In November 1997, she won a $10.6 million lawsuit, alleging inappropriate treatment and emotional harm to both her and her children. The lawsuit named Braun, the hospital he is affiliated with, and another psychiatrist (Associated Press, 1998). In a similar case, Elizabeth Gale was recently awarded $7.5 million dollars in damages (Dardick, 2004). In Braun's defense, Marlene Hunter, currently president of the association he founded, described Braun as a dedicated psychiatrist who "has done the best he could according to what he thought was right at the time" (p. A12). Bennett Braun lost his license to practice for two years and was placed on probation for an additional five years. While on probation he will have to submit the judgment against him to prospective employers and will not be allowed to treat patients diagnosed with dissociative identity disorder. His former patient, Pat Burgess, said she was satisfied with the decision (Bloomberg, 2000).

Such lawsuits create a quandary for mental health practitioners. Many feel intimidated by the threat of legal action if they attempt to treat adult survivors of childhood sexual abuse, especially those cases involving recovered memories. However, discounting the memories of patients may represent further abuse and condone the actions of the perpetrators. But for those who take on such cases, the risks are high. In 1994, about 16 percent of all claims made against clinicians involved repressed memories ("Repressed memory claims," 1995). Especially worrisome is the use of certain techniques such as hypnosis, as they may produce inaccurate "memories," resulting in legal action by either the client or family members (Benedict & Donaldson, 1996). One risk analysis (Knapp & VandeCreek, 1996) indicates that liability risks are greatest when therapists employ nonexperimentally supported techniques, such as trance work, body memories, or age regression, in cases of recovered memories. Encouraging the client to confront the "perpetrator" also increases malpractice risks.

What's your opinion?

In the case of "repressed memories," should therapeutic techniques be restricted, and should clients be told that some techniques are experimental and may produce inaccurate information? Under what conditions, if any, should a therapist express doubt about information "remembered" by a client? Given the high prevalence of child sexual abuse and the indefinite nature of "repressed" memories, how should clinicians proceed if a client claims to remember early memories of abuse?

therapist produced, we do not know to what extent iatrogenic influences can account for this disorder.

Treatment of Dissociative Disorders

A variety of treatments for the dissociative disorders have been developed, including supportive counseling and the use of hypnosis and personality reconstruction. Currently, there are no specific medications for treatment of the dissociative disorders. Instead, medications are prescribed to treat the anxiety or depression that may accompany dissociative disorders. The Mental Health and Society feature, "'Suspect' Techniques to Treat Dissociative Identity Disorder," discusses some controversial practices.

Dissociative Amnesia and Dissociative Fugue The symptoms of dissociative amnesia and fugue tend to remit, or abate, spontaneously. Moreover, patients typically

A Famous Case of Dissociative Identity Disorder   Chris Sizemore, whose experiences with dissociative identity inspired the book and movie *The Three Faces of Eve,* is an artist today and no longer shows any signs of her former disorder. She is working as an advocate for the mentally ill. How do recovered individuals with DID reconcile having had different identities?

complain of psychological symptoms other than the amnesia, perhaps because the amnesia interferes only minimally with their day-to-day functioning. As a result, therapeutic intervention is often not directed specifically toward the amnesia. Instead, therapists provide supportive counseling for clients with amnesia.

It has been noted, however, that depression is often associated with the fugue state and that stress is often associated with both fugue and dissociative amnesia. A reasonable therapeutic approach is then to treat these dissociative disorders indirectly by alleviating the depression (with antidepressants or cognitive behavior therapy) and the stress (through stress-management techniques).

Depersonalization Disorder   Depersonalization disorder is also subject to spontaneous remission, but at a much slower rate than that of dissociative amnesia and fugue. Treatment generally concentrates on alleviating the feelings of anxiety or depression or the fear of going insane. Occasionally a behavioral approach has been tried. For example, behavior therapy was successfully used to treat depersonalization disorder in a fifteen-year-old girl who had blackouts that she described as "floating in and out." These episodes were associated with headaches and feelings of detachment, but neurological and physical examinations revealed no biological cause. Treatment involved getting increased attention from her family and reinforcement from them when the frequency of blackouts was reduced, training in appropriate responses to stressful situations, and self-reinforcement (Dollinger, 1983).

Dissociative Identity Disorder   The mental health literature contains more information on the treatment of dissociative identity disorder than on the other three dissociative disorders combined. Treatment for this disorder is not always successful. Chris Sizemore (who was the inspiration for *The Three Faces of Eve*) developed additional personalities after therapy but has now recovered. She is a writer, lecturer, and artist.

Sybil also recovered—she became a college art professor and died in Lexington, Kentucky, in 1998 at the age of seventy-five (Miller & Kantrowitz, 1999). A two-year follow-up study of fifty-four patients with dissociative identity disorder showed somewhat optimistic results. Most showed improvement, especially those who had been able to integrate their separate personalities during therapy (Ellason & Ross, 1997).

Although working through the traumatic material is important in treating dissociative identity disorder, there is growing recognition that "remembered" events may be inaccurate, and there is a greater emphasis on helping patients develop new coping skills (Kluft, 1996). In the past, much attention was placed on bringing forth and studying the different personalities. There is now increasing focus on the behavioral problems exhibited by individuals with this disorder. Even as they acknowledge the possibility of false memories involving child abuse or cult involvement, therapists are shifting attention from the accuracy of the memories to helping the individuals work through emotional issues. In the area of *treatment,* the emphasis is on using research-based methods and approaches to achieve quick resolution of acute symptoms. This problem-focused therapy holds patients responsible for their own behaviors and involves the whole person rather than the separate personalities. The goal is to improve functioning early in treatment rather than waiting for personality integration (Mungadze, 1997). Greater effort has also been made to incorporate cognitive behavior strategies in treatment, even among psychodynamically oriented therapists (Fine, 1999; Shusta, 1999).

▶ CHECKPOINT REVIEW

continuous amnesia *(p. 116)*

depersonalization disorder *(p. 116)*

dissociative amnesia *(p. 114)*

dissociative disorders *(p. 113)*

dissociative fugue *(p. 116)*

dissociative identity disorder (DID) *(p. 117)*

generalized amnesia *(p. 115)*

localized amnesia *(p. 115)*

selective amnesia *(p. 115)*

somatoform disorders *(p. 113)*

systematized amnesia *(p. 116)*

What are dissociations? What forms can they take? How are they caused, and how are they treated?

- Dissociation involves a disruption in consciousness, memory, identity, or perception and may be transient or chronic.
- Dissociative amnesia and dissociative fugue involve a selective form of forgetting in which the person loses memory of information that is of personal significance.
- Depersonalization disorder is characterized by feelings of unreality—distorted perceptions of oneself and one's environment.
- Multiple personality involves the alternation of two or more relatively independent personalities in one individual.
- Psychoanalytic perspectives on the etiology of dissociative disorders attribute them to the repression of certain impulses that are seeking expression.
- Behavioral explanations suggest role enactment, reinforcement, and responding to the expectations of the situation.
- Dissociative amnesia and dissociative fugue tend to be short-lived and to remit spontaneously; behavioral therapy has also been used successfully.
- Dissociative identity disorder has most often been treated with a combination of psychotherapy and hypnosis, as well as with behavioral and family therapies. In most cases, the therapist attempts to fuse the several personalities.

▶ Somatoform Disorders

The somatoform disorders, charted in Figure 5.4, involve complaints of physical symptoms that closely mimic authentic medical conditions. Although no actual physiological basis exists for the complaints, the symptoms are not considered voluntary or under conscious control. The patient believes that the symptoms are real and are indications of a physical problem. The somatoform disorders include somatization disorder, conversion disorder, pain disorder, hypochondriasis, and body dysmorphic

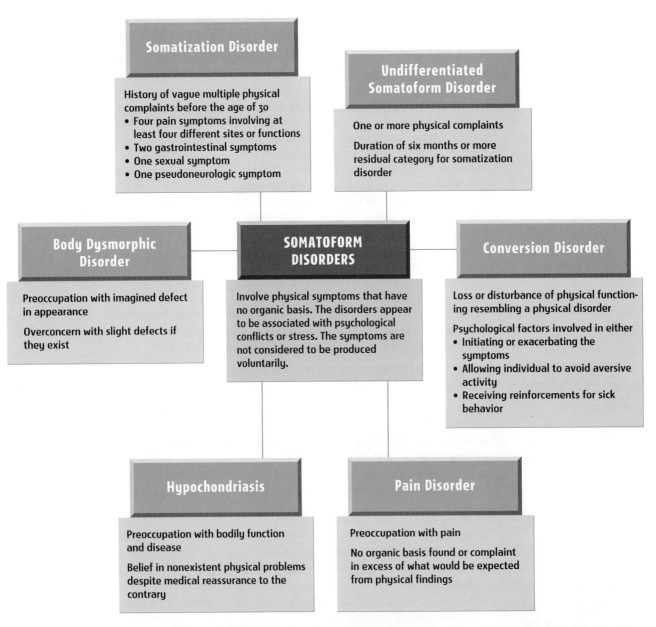

Figure 5.4 Disorders Chart: Somatoform Disorders *Sources:* Data from Phillips, McElroy, et al. (1993); Swartz et al. (1991); American Psychiatric Association (2000a).

disorder. Common comorbid disorders include mood disorder, personality disorder, and substance use disorder (Smith, Clarke, et al., 2000; Noyes et al., 2001). Figure 5.4 summarizes the prevalence, onset, and course of somatoform disorders, and Table 5.1 presents some of the differences between these disorders.

Depending on the particular primary care setting, from 10 to 50 percent of all patients report physically unexplained symptoms (Allen et al., 2001; Shaibani & Sabbagh, 1998; Smith, Clarke, et al., 2000). However, determining whether the proper diagnosis for these individuals is somatoform disorder can be difficult. As Peveler (1998) points out, "Somatoform disorder diagnoses are still mostly diagnoses of exclusion, rather than constructs with clinical utility" (p. 94). In some cases, physical or

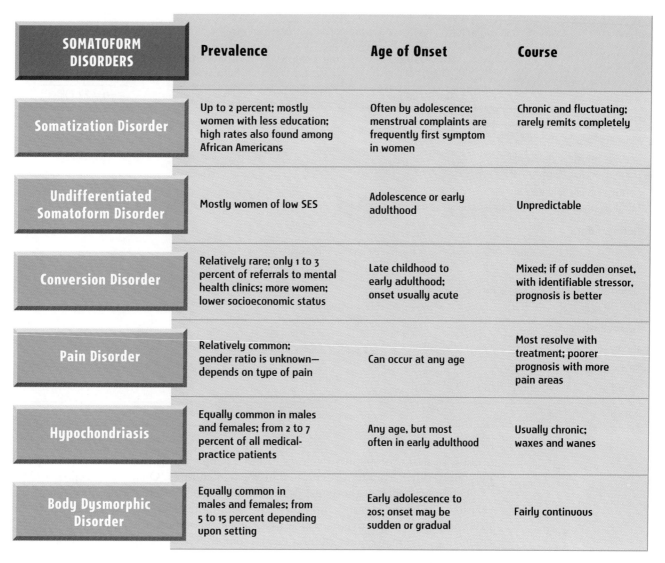

SOMATOFORM DISORDERS	Prevalence	Age of Onset	Course
Somatization Disorder	Up to 2 percent; mostly women with less education; high rates also found among African Americans	Often by adolescence; menstrual complaints are frequently first symptom in women	Chronic and fluctuating; rarely remits completely
Undifferentiated Somatoform Disorder	Mostly women of low SES	Adolescence or early adulthood	Unpredictable
Conversion Disorder	Relatively rare; only 1 to 3 percent of referrals to mental health clinics; more women; lower socioeconomic status	Late childhood to early adulthood; onset usually acute	Mixed; if of sudden onset, with identifiable stressor, prognosis is better
Pain Disorder	Relatively common; gender ratio is unknown— depends on type of pain	Can occur at any age	Most resolve with treatment; poorer prognosis with more pain areas
Hypochondriasis	Equally common in males and females; from 2 to 7 percent of all medical-practice patients	Any age, but most often in early adulthood	Usually chronic; waxes and wanes
Body Dysmorphic Disorder	Equally common in males and females; from 5 to 15 percent depending upon setting	Early adolescence to 20s; onset may be sudden or gradual	Fairly continuous

Figure 5.4 **Disorders Chart: Somatoform Disorders (continued)**

neurological factors that explain the symptoms have later been discovered (Moser et al. 1998).

Before we discuss the somatoform disorders individually, we should note that they are wholly different from either **malingering**—faking a disorder to achieve some goal, such as an insurance settlement—or the factitious disorders. **Factitious disorders** are mental disorders in which the symptoms of physical or mental illnesses are deliberately induced or simulated with no apparent incentive (see the Mental Health and Society feature, "Factitious Disorders"). In contrast to both of these conditions, individuals with somatoform disorders believe that a physical condition actually exists.

Cultural factors can influence the frequency, expression, and interpretation of somatic symptoms. Physical complaints often occur in reaction to stress among Asian Americans (Sue & Sue, 1999). In fact, Asian Indian children who were referred for psychiatric services had three times as many somatoform disorders as their counterparts in a control sample of white children (Jawed, 1991). Among some African

malingering Faking a disorder to achieve some goal, such as an insurance settlement.

factitious disorders Disorders in which symptoms of physical or mental illnesses are deliberately induced or simulated with no apparent incentive.

Table 5.1   Variables That Distinguish Subgroups of Confirmed Somatoform Disorder (*n* = 127)

Variable	Conversion Disorder *n* = 30 (%)	Somatization Disorder *n* = 10 (%)	Somatoform Pain Disorder *n* = 60 (%)	Hypochondriasis *n* = 27 (%)
Demographic data				
Married	39.3	30.0	65.0	61.5
Serious physical illness in patient—past 12 months	57.7	90.0	74.6	50.0
Serious physical illness in family—past 12 months	36.0	12.5	13.6	4.3
Referral data				
Referred for strange behavior	33.3	20.0	10.0	11.5
Referred for pain	6.7	30.0	68.3	26.9
Referred for diagnosis—suspected psychological component	83.3	80.0	43.3	65.4
Intervention				
Increase physical activity	41.4	10.0	18.6	3.7
Anxiolytics recommendation	3.3	0	31.7	7.7
Antidepressant recommendation	20.0	50.0	51.7	26.9

Source: From Smith et al. (2000).

groups, somatic complaints (feelings of heat, peppery and crawling sensations, and numbness) differ from those expressed in Western cultures (Ohaeri & Odejide, 1994).

Differences such as those just described may reflect different cultural views of the relationship between mind and body. The dominant view in Western culture is the *psychosomatic* perspective, in which psychological conflicts are expressed in physical complaints. But many other cultures have a *somatopsychic* perspective, in which physical problems produce psychological and emotional symptoms. Although we probably believe that our psychosomatic view is the "correct" one, the somatopsychic view may be the dominant perspective in most cultures. As G. M. White (1982) claimed, "It is rather the more psychological and psychosomatic mode of reasoning found in Western cultures which appears unusual among the world's popular and traditional system of belief" (p. 1520). Physical complaints expressed by persons of ethnic minorities may have to be interpreted differently than similar complaints made by members of the majority culture.

Somatization Disorder

somatization disorder A somatoform disorder in which the person chronically complains of a number of bodily symptoms that have no physiological basis; complaints include at least four symptoms in different sites, two gastrointestinal symptoms, one sexual symptom, and one pseudoneurological symptom.

An individual with **somatization disorder** chronically complains of bodily symptoms that have no physical basis. According to DSM-IV-TR, the following are necessary for a diagnosis of somatization disorder:

- A history of complaints that involve at least four pain symptoms in different sites, such as the back, head, and extremities.
- Two gastrointestinal symptoms, such as nausea, diarrhea, and bloating.
- One sexual symptom, such as sexual indifference, irregular menses, or erectile dysfunction.

MenTaL HeaLth and society

Factitious Disorders

A most remarkable type of mental disorder is illustrated in the following cases:

> In a two-year period, four women presented for HIV-related care, claiming that they were HIV-seropositive, but repeated serologic testing revealed no evidence of HIV infection. In all cases, the women were either quite angry or appeared surprised when told they did not have HIV infection. A common denominator in all four women was a history of prolonged sexual, physical, or emotional abuse. Three of the four had been to other physicians, changing doctors as soon as the absence of HIV infection was established. (Mileno et al., 2001, p. 263)

> A hidden camera at a children's hospital captured the image of a mother suffocating the baby she had brought in for treatment of breathing problems. In another case, a child was brought in for treatment of ulcerations on his back; hospital staff discovered the mother had been rubbing oven cleaner on his skin. A "sick" infant had been fed laxatives for nearly four months (Wartik, 1994). In each of these cases, no apparent incentive was found other than the attention the parent received from the hospital staff who cared for the child's "illness."

These cases illustrate a group of mental disorders, termed *factitious disorders* in DSM-IV-TR, in which people voluntarily simulate physical or mental conditions or voluntarily induce an actual physical condition. The criteria include: (1) intentional production or feigning of physical or psychological symptoms; (2) the only apparent motivation

for the behavior is to assume the sick role or to be a patient; and (3) the purpose of this behavior is not for external incentives such as economic gain, avoiding legal responsibilities, and so forth. This practice differs from *malingering*, which involves simulating a disorder to achieve some goal—such as feigning sickness to collect insurance. The goals usually are apparent, and the individual can "turn off" the symptoms whenever they are no longer useful. In factitious disorders, the purpose of the simulated or induced illness is much less apparent, complex psychological variables are assumed to be involved, and the individual is usually unaware of the motivation for the behaviors. The individual displays a compulsive quality in the need to simulate illness. Signs of a factitious disorder may include: long unexplained illnesses with multiple surgical or complex treatments, "remarkable willingness" to undergo painful or dangerous treatments, tendency to anger if the illness is questioned, and the involvement of multiple doctors (Flaherty et al., 2001).

In a study of 93 patients diagnosed with factitious disorder (Krahn, Li, & O'Connor, 2003), the following results were found. Nearly three-fourths were women, of whom 47 percent were health care workers who had the knowledge to report plausible illnesses. However, only 11.5 percent of men had a medical background. Immediate confrontation did not appear to be effective with most patients.

If an individual deliberately feigns or induces an illness in another person, the diagnosis is *factitious disorder by proxy*. In the preceding cases, the mothers produced symptoms in their children to indirectly assume the sick role. Because this diagnostic category is somewhat new, little information is available on prevalence, age of onset, or familial pattern.

- One pseudoneurological symptom, such as conversion symptoms, amnesia, or breathing difficulties.

If the individual does not fully meet these criteria but has at least one physical complaint of six months' duration, he or she would be given a diagnosis of **undifferentiated somatoform disorder.** The following case illustrates several of the characteristics involved in these disorders.

undifferentiated somatoform disorder At least one physical complaint with no physical basis that has lasted for six months or more.

> Cheryl was a thirty-eight-year-old, separated Italian American woman who was raising her ten-year-old daughter without much support....Cheryl suffered from vertigo and had a history of neck pain and other vague somatic complaints, as well as a history of

> several abusive relationships and unresolved grief about the loss of her mother.... Cheryl and Melanie described in rich detail an elaborate system of cues that Melanie had learned to respond to by comforting her mother, providing remedies such as back rubs and hot compresses or taking over activities such as grocery shopping if her mother felt dizzy in the store. (McDaniel & Speice, 2001)

The problem was treated by having Cheryl and Melanie identify "non-helpful behaviors" that may reinforce the symptoms and those that are useful in adapting to problem situations. Helpful behaviors were reinforced, but not those that encouraged helplessness.

People who have somatization disorder tend to constantly "shop around" for doctors and often have unnecessary operations. Psychiatric interviews typically reveal psychological conflicts that may be involved in the disorder. Anxiety and depression and other psychiatric disorders are common complications of somatization disorder (Allen et al., 2001; Stern, Murphy, & Bass, 1993).

Although physical complaints are common, the diagnosis of somatization disorder (or *hysteria*, as it was formerly called) is relatively rare, with an overall prevalence rate of 2 percent (see Figure 5.4). It is much more prevalent in females and African Americans and twice as likely among those with less than a high school education (Swartz et al., 1991). In a cross-cultural study on the prevalence of somatization disorder in fourteen countries, it was found to be relatively rare (average frequency of 0.9 percent). The highest frequency of somatic complaints was found in the cities of Rio de Janeiro, Santiago, Berlin, and Paris; the lowest were in Taiwan, Ibadân, Manchester, Nagasaki, and Verona (Gureje et al., 1997).

Conversion Disorder

Conversion disorder is one of the more puzzling disorders. The term *conversion neurosis* comes from Freud, who believed that an unconscious sexual or aggressive conflict was "converted" into a physical problem. An individual with **conversion disorder** will complain of physical problems or impairments of sensory or motor functions controlled by the voluntary nervous system—such as paralysis, loss of feeling, and impairment in sight or hearing—all suggesting a neurological disorder but with no underlying organic cause. In rare cases, complaints may also include memory loss or "cognitive or intellectual impairment" that resembles dementia but is reversible (Liberini et al., 1993). The symptoms are not consciously faked as are those in factitious disorder, nor are they due to malingering. A person with conversion disorder actually believes that there is a genuine physical problem that produces notable distress or impairment. Psychological factors are considered important in conversion disorder, in either the initiation or exacerbation of the problem, as illustrated in the following case:

conversion disorder A somatoform disorder in which patients complain of physical problems or impairments of sensory or motor functions controlled by the voluntary nervous system, all suggesting a neurological disorder, but for which no underlying physical cause can be found.

pain disorder A somatoform disorder characterized by reports of severe pain that has no physiological or neurological basis, is greatly in excess of that expected with an existing condition, or lingers long after a physical injury has healed.

> A forty-four-year-old woman was admitted to a psychiatric hospital from a neurology ward with "pseudoseizures" and "functional hemiplegia" (paralysis of one side of the body). She was wheelchair-bound and lived in a specially adapted council bungalow with a female friend. She described a disrupted childhood with a physically abusive, alcoholic father. She had two stormy and violent marriages.... Although reluctant to accept a psychological origin of her symptoms, she agreed to undergo hypnosis. Under hypnosis, she walked and moved her paralyzed limbs normally. She received psychotherapy, exploring her childhood and relationship difficulties. Within six months she was using her right upper limb normally and walking with a frame. (Singh & Lee, 1997, pp. 426–427)

The most common conversion symptoms seen in neurological clinics involve psychogenic pain, disturbances of stance and gait, sensory symptoms, dizziness, and

Conversion Disorder
Although there is nothing physically wrong with the eyes of this Cambodian woman, she claims to be blind. It is thought that trauma suffered in Cambodian prison camps due to the brutality of the Khmer Rouge produced such horror that her eyesight "shut down" psychologically. Hysterical blindness is a very rare conversion disorder in the United States but is quite high among Cambodian refugees. Approximately 150 individuals (mostly women) from a Cambodian community of 85,000 people in Long Beach, California, suffer from this disorder.

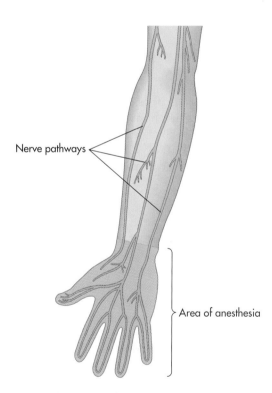

Figure 5.5 Glove Anesthesia   In glove anesthesia, the lack of feeling covers the hand in a glovelike shape. It does not correspond to the distribution of nerve pathways. This discrepancy leads to a diagnosis of conversion disorder.

Nerve pathways

Area of anesthesia

psychogenic seizures (Rechlin, Loew, & Joraschky, 1997). The occurrence of symptoms is often related to stress. Nearly 75 percent of respondents in one sample reported that their conversion symptoms developed after they had experienced a stressor. A man became "paralyzed" after finding his wife in bed with another man. One woman developed a speech disturbance after disclosing childhood sexual abuse (Singh & Lee, 1997). In a ten-year follow-up study of individuals diagnosed with conversion disorder, symptoms persisted in about 40 percent of the cases (Mace & Trimble, 1996). Sudden onset, shorter duration of symptoms, and a good premorbid (preillness) personality are associated with a positive outcome (Crimlisk et al., 1998; Singh & Lee, 1997).

It is often difficult to distinguish between actual physical disorders and conversion reactions. Some symptoms, such as glove anesthesia (the loss of feeling in the hand, ending in a straight line at the wrist), are easily diagnosed as conversion disorder because the area of sensory loss does not correspond to the distribution of nerves in the body (see Figure 5.5). Other symptoms may require extensive neurological and physical examinations to rule out a true medical disorder before a diagnosis of conversion disorder can be made. Discriminating between people who are faking and those with conversion disorder is difficult.

Pain Disorder

Pain disorder is characterized by reports of severe pain that may (1) have no physiological or neurological basis, (2) be greatly in excess of that expected with an existing physical

Figure 5.6 Physical Complaints: A Comparison of Individuals with Pain Disorder Versus Healthy Controls Individuals with somatoform disorders have numerous physical complaints. This graph illustrates the percentage of complaints expressed by a group of individuals with pain disorders. *Source:* Data from Bacon et al. (1994).

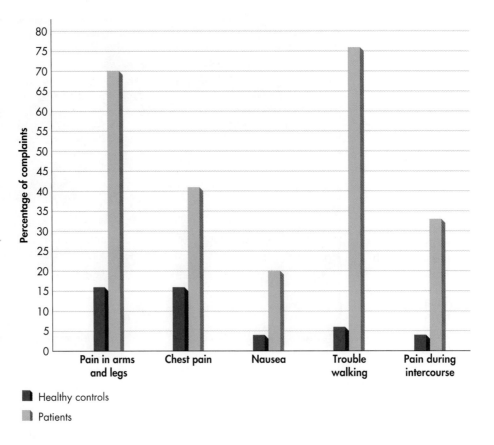

■ Healthy controls

▨ Patients

condition, or (3) linger long after a physical injury has healed. As with the other somatoform disorders, psychological conflicts are involved. People who have pain disorder make frequent visits to physicians and may become drug or medication abusers. Most individuals with pain disorder have numerous physical complaints (see Figure 5.6). Compared with individuals who have an organic basis for their pain, those with psychogenic pain are vague in their description of the experience and are less able to clearly localize the area of pain (Adler et al., 1997). Unexplained physical pain involving the abdomen, headaches, and limbs are present in a considerable number of young children (Hunfeld et al., 2002).

Hypochondriasis

The primary characteristic of **hypochondriasis** is a persistent preoccupation with one's health and physical condition, even in the face of physical evaluations that reveal no organic problems. The disorder is a complex phenomenon that includes a fear of having a disease, fear of death or illness, a tendency toward self-observation, and oversensitivity to bodily sensations (Kellner, Hernandez, & Pathak, 1992; Leibbrand, Hiller, & Fichter, 2000). People with this disorder are hypersensitive to bodily functioning and processes. They regard symptoms such as chest pain or headaches as evidence of an underlying disease, and they seek repeated reassurance from medical professionals, friends, and family members. An estimated 4 to 9 percent of general medical patients have this disorder (Barsky, Wyshak, & Klerman, 1992; American Psychiatric Association, 2000a).

hypochondriasis A somatoform disorder characterized by persistent preoccupation with one's health and physical condition, even in the face of physical evaluations that reveal no organic problems.

body dysmorphic disorder (BDD) A somatoform disorder that involves preoccupation with an imagined physical defect in a normal-appearing person, or an excessive concern with a slight physical defect.

Mr. X is a sixty-eight-year-old Chinese man who reported sleep disturbances, loss of appetite, dizziness, and a sensation of tightness around his chest. Several episodes of chest pain led to admission and medical evaluation at the local hospital. All results, including tests for ischemic heart disease, were normal. He was referred to psychiatric consultation. Because traditional Chinese views of medicine recognize an interconnection between mind and body, the psychiatrist accepted and showed interest in the somatic symptoms, such as their onset, duration, and exacerbating and relieving factors. Medication was provided as a supportive treatment. Later the man was able to tell the psychiatrists that his physical symptoms became worse when his wife aggravated him. He reported that they argued frequently over decisions. Suggestions were made on how to improve communication, and the couple decided to take turns making decisions. Physical complaints decreased as the communication improved. (Yeung & Deguang, 2002)

In his review of hypochondriacs, Kellner (1985) found several predisposing factors. These factors included a history of physical illness, parental attention to somatic symptoms, low pain threshold, or greater sensitivity to somatic cues. Hypochondriasis, therefore, might develop in predisposed people when the following occur: an anxiety or stress-arousing event, the perception of somatic symptoms, and the fear that sensations reflect a disease process, resulting in even greater attention to somatic cues.

Body Dysmorphic Disorder

According to DSM-IV-TR, **body dysmorphic disorder** (BDD) involves a preoccupation with some imagined defect in appearance in a normal-appearing person or an excessive concern over a slight physical defect. The preoccupation produces marked clinical distress and may be underdiagnosed because many of those with the disorder feel too embarrassed to talk about the problem (Grant, Kim, & Crow, 2001).

The patient is a twenty-four-year-old Caucasian male in his senior year of college. He presented at intake by stating, "I've got a physical deformity (small hands) and it makes me very uncomfortable, especially around women with hands bigger than mine. I see my deformity as a sign of weakness; it's like I'm a cripple."...He spent considerable time researching hand sizes for different populations and stated at intake that his middle finger is one and one-fourth inches smaller than the average size for a male in the United States....He also reported being concerned that women might believe small hands are indicative of having a small penis. (Schmidt & Harrington, 1995, pp. 162–163)

Imagining Defects   This individual with body dysmorphic disorder is preoccupied with an imagined "defect" in his appearance. What leads to such an inaccurate belief?

Concern commonly focuses on bodily features such as excessive hair or lack of hair and the size or shape of the nose, face, or eyes (see Figure 5.7). In DSM IV-TR, body build or muscularity has been added as an area of body preoccupation in BDD. Individuals with BDD often engage in frequent mirror checking, regard their "defect" with embarrassment and loathing, and are concerned that others may be looking at or thinking about their defect. People with body dysmorphic disorder show evidence of emotional problems, have a minimal degree of "disfigurement," and make frequent requests for additional operations despite the outcome of previous treatment. The degree of insight they have about their condition ranges from good to absent (Phillips et al., 2001). As with the other somatoform disorders, individuals with body dysmorphic disorder

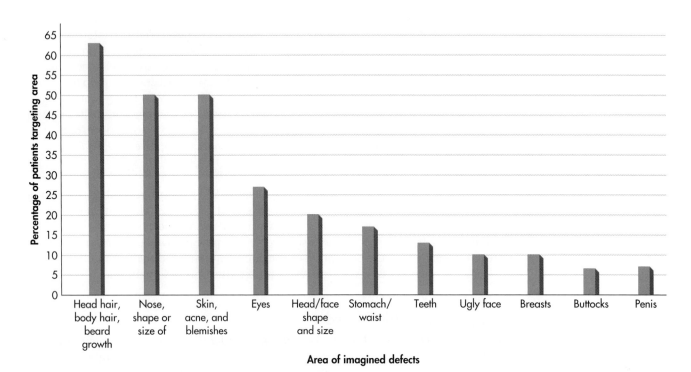

Figure 5.7 Imagined Defects in Patients with Body Dysmorphic Disorder   This graph illustrates the percentage of thirty patients who targeted different areas of their body as having "defects." Many of the patients selected more than one body region. *Source:* From Phillips, McElroy, et al. (1993).

seek medical attention—often from dermatologists or plastic surgeons. They are also likely to undergo multiple medical procedures (Schmidt & Harrington, 1995). Persons with body dysmorphic disorder often suffer from functional impairment. They may avoid social activities, work, and school and may become housebound and suicidal (Schmidt & Harrington, 1995). They are also likely to have a mood disorder or social phobia (Otto et al., 2001). Some body builders who show a pathological preoccupation with their muscularity may also suffer from body dysmorphic disorder. Researchers identified a subgroup of body builders who scored high in body dissatisfaction, had low self-esteem, and mistakenly believed they were "small" even though they were large and very muscular (Choi et al., 2002; O'Sullivan & Tiggermann, 1997). Some questions that may indicate the presence of BDD follow (the more a person agrees with these statements, the more likely he or she is to have characteristics of this disorder):

1. Do you believe that there is a "defect" in a part of your body or appearance?
2. Do you spend considerable time checking this "defect"?
3. Do you attempt to hide or cover up this "defect" or remedy it by exercising, dieting, or seeking surgery?
4. Does this belief cause you significant distress, embarrassment, or torment?
5. Does the "flaw" interfere with your ability to function at school, at social events, or at work?
6. Do friends or family members tell you that there is nothing wrong or that the "defect" is minor?

The preoccupation with the imagined defect in body dysmorphic disorder is very similar to characteristics found in obsessive-compulsive disorder. Some researchers

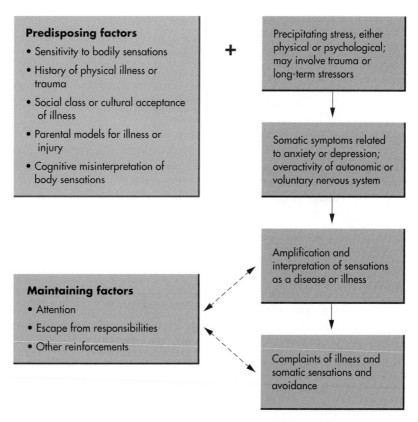

Figure 5.8 Diathesis-Stress Model for Somatoform Disorders   This chart illustrates a diathesis-stress model for somatoform disorder that considers a number of predisposing factors, stressors, and maintaining variables. *Source:* Adapted from Kellner (1985); Gramling et al. (1996).

believe the disorders are related to one another or are variants of the same disorder (Neziroglu & Yaryura-Tobias, 1997; Saxena et al., 2001).

Etiology of Somatoform Disorders

Most etiological theories tend to focus on what they consider to be the "primary" cause of somatoform disorders. Diathesis-stress models, however, point to multiple contributing factors. For example, Barsky and Wyshak (1990) believe that a predisposition either may develop through learning or may be "hard-wired" into the central nervous system. They believe the predisposition involves (1) hypervigilance or exaggerated focus on bodily sensation, (2) increased sensitivity to weak bodily sensations, and (3) a disposition to react to somatic sensations with alarm. The predisposition becomes a fully developed disorder only when a trauma or stressor occurs that the individual cannot deal with. An even broader diathesis-stress model, shown in Figure 5.8, includes other variables, such as social and cultural components, personality, and maintaining factors (Gramling, Clawson, & McDonald, 1996; Kellner, 1985).

Psychodynamic Perspective   In psychodynamic theory, somatic symptoms are seen as a defense against the awareness of unconscious emotional issues (Dworkin, VonKorff, & LeResche, 1990). Sigmund Freud believed that hysterical reactions (biological complaints of pain, illness, or loss of physical function) were caused by the repression of some type of conflict, usually sexual in nature. To protect the individual from intense anxiety, this conflict is converted into some physical symptom (Breuer & Freud, 1895/1957). For example, in the case of a thirty-one-year-old woman who developed visual problems, therapy revealed that the woman had, as a child, witnessed her parents engaging in sexual intercourse. The severe anxiety associated with this traumatic scene was later converted into visual difficulties (Grinker & Robbins, 1954).

The psychodynamic view suggests that two mechanisms produce and then sustain somatoform symptoms. The first provides a *primary gain* for the person by protecting him or her from the anxiety associated with the unacceptable desire or conflict through physical symptoms. This focus on the body keeps the patient from an awareness of the underlying conflict (Simon & VonKorff, 1991). Then a *secondary gain* accrues when the person's dependency needs are fulfilled through attention and sympathy. Consider the case of an eighty-two-year-old man who reported the sudden onset of diffuse right abdominal pain in March 1977. No abnormal signs were found at that time. In August 1977, he was rehospitalized for the same complaint. Again nothing physical was found. In an analysis of the case, Weddington (1979) noted that the patient's symptom first developed near the twelfth anniversary of his wife's death. His second hospitalization took place near the anniversary of his mother's death, which had occurred when he was twelve. Weddington hypothesized that the painful memories were converted to a physical symptom and that the care and attention bestowed by the hospital staff fulfilled the patient's dependency needs.

Behavioral Perspective Behavioral theorists have stressed the importance of reinforcement, modeling, cognitive styles, or a combination of these in the development of somatoform disorders. Some contend that people with somatoform disorders assume the "sick role" because it is reinforcing and because it allows them to escape unpleasant circumstances or avoid responsibilities (Schwartz, Slater, & Birchler, 1994).

Fordyce (1982, 1988) analyzed psychogenic pain from the operant perspective. He pointed out that the only available data concerning the pain (or any other somatoform symptoms) are the subjective reports from the afflicted people. Physicians and nurses are trained to be attentive and responsive to reports of pain. Medication is given quickly to relieve suffering. In addition, exercise and physical therapy programs are set up so that exertion continues only until pain or fatigue is felt. These practices serve to reinforce reports of pain. The importance of reinforcement was shown in a study of male pain patients. Men with supportive wives (attentive to pain cues) reported significantly greater pain when their wives were present than when the wives were absent. The reverse was true of patients whose wives were nonsupportive: reports of pain were greater when their wives were absent (Williamson, Robinson, & Melamed, 1997).

Parental modeling and reinforcement of illness behaviors may also be influential in determining people's current reactions to illness. Individuals with somatoform disorders showed a background of parental models or family members with chronic physical illnesses (Smith, Clarke, et al., 2000), and they were also more likely to report having missed school for health reasons and having had childhood illnesses (Barsky et al., 1995).

The most recent views of somatoform disorders stress the importance of cognitive factors. Individuals with hypochondriasis appear to take a threat-confirming strategy, especially as it applies to health concerns, and any perception of threat activates a "better safe than sorry" orientation. Because of this, individuals with these disorders are prone to making unrealistic interpretations of bodily sensations and to overestimating the dangerousness of bodily symptoms and the probability of negative health effects (Haenen et al., 2000). Believing such sensations to be abnormal then leads to a preoccupation that one has a serious disease. Thus common bodily sensations are amplified or misinterpreted.

Biological Perspective Some physical complaints may have more than a merely imaginary basis. Researchers have found that hypochondriac patients were more sensitive to bodily sensations than other people (Barsky et al., 1993). They were better at estimating their heart rates when exposed to short films than were individuals with phobias (Tyrer, Lee, & Alexander, 1980). In a test involving a physical stressor (foot placed in cold water), individuals with hypochondriasis demonstrated greater increases in heart rate, displayed a greater drop in temperature in the immersed limb, rated the experience as more unpleasant, and terminated the task more frequently relative to a control group (Gramling et al., 1996). College students who are predisposed to attending to somatic symptoms rate the sensations they experience more negatively than those who attend less to bodily symptoms (Ahles, Cassens, & Stalling, 1987). Innate factors may account for greater sensitivity to pain and bodily functions.

Treatment of Somatoform Disorders

Somatoform disorders have been treated with psychodynamic approaches, cognitive and operant techniques, and family therapy. The behavioral approaches have received the greatest amount of attention.

Psychodynamic Treatment The earliest treatment for somatoform disorders was psychoanalysis and the use of hypnosis. Freud believed that the crucial element in treating hysterical patients with psychoanalysis was to help them *relive* the actual feelings associated with the repressed traumatic event—and not simply to help them remember the details of the experience. Once the emotions connected with the traumatic situation were experienced, the symptoms would disappear.

Although Freud eventually dropped hypnosis from his psychoanalytic repertoire, many of his disciples continued to find it beneficial, and variations of it became known as *hypnotherapy*. Bliss (1984) was a modern advocate of hypnotherapy as treatment for somatization disorder and conversion symptoms. Bliss argued that people afflicted with a somatoform disorder engage in involuntary self-hypnosis as a defense, in much the same way that patients with multiple-personality disorders do. Hypnotherapy involves bringing repressed conflicts to consciousness, mastering these traumas, and developing coping skills that are more adaptive than self-hypnosis.

Behavioral Treatment Individuals with hypochondriasis have been treated with a variety of approaches, including cognitive strategies, exposure, and response prevention (Looper & Kirmayer, 2002). The approach generally involves explaining the role of selective perception in the development of illness fears and modifying the misinterpretation of bodily sensations, extinction, and nonreinforcement of complaints of bodily symptoms. For example, in one study, seventeen patients were forced to confront their health fears by visiting hospitals, reading literature about their feared illness, and writing down extensive information about the illness. Some were asked to try to "bring forth a heart attack." Reassurance seeking was banned, and relatives were taught not to reinforce the behavior. If a patient said, "My heart has a pain. I think it might be a heart attack," relatives were instructed to ignore the statements. Under this program, the patients improved significantly. However, seven of the patients were found to still have concerns about illness or disease at a five-year follow-up (Warwick & Marks, 1988).

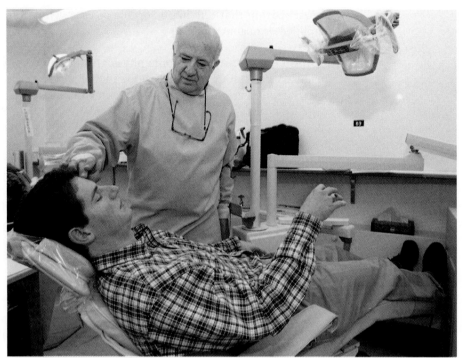

Hypnosis as Therapy or Assessment Tool   Hypnosis is used by Dr. Clarke during teeth extractions and root canals. What happens to an individual under hypnosis is still not understood. Some practitioners continue to use hypnosis to assess and treat somatoform disorders, based on the belief that these disorders may be induced by self-hypnosis. What kind of research evidence supports this orientation, and what questions do you have regarding this approach?

Cognitive behavioral strategies for noncardiac chest pain that involve relaxation training and correcting cognitive distortions have been effective in reducing somatic complaints and improving mood and anxiety symptoms (Looper & Kirmayer, 2002). Case studies indicate that systematic desensitization, exposure, and cognitive therapy are promising approaches in the treatment of body dysmorphic disorder (Neziroglu & Yaryura-Tobias, 1997; Rosen, Reiter, & Orosan, 1995).

Biological Treatment Antidepressant medications have been prescribed for the somatoform disorders, primarily somatization and somatoform pain disorders. In addition, interventions involving an increase in physical activity have been recommended for conversion disorders (Smith, Clarke, et al., 2000). SSRIs such as fluvoxamine have proven useful in improving nearly two-thirds of individuals with body dysmorphic disorder (Phillips et al., 2001).

▷ CHECKPOINT REVIEW

body dysmorphic disorder (BDD) *(p. 133)*

conversion disorder *(p. 130)*

factitious disorders *(p. 127)*

hypochondriasis *(p. 132)*

When do physical complaints become a type of disorder? What are the causes and treatments of these conditions?

■ Somatoform disorders involve complaints about physical symptoms that mimic actual medical conditions but that have no apparent organic basis. Instead, psychological factors are directly involved in the initiation and exacerbation of the problem.

malingering *(p. 127)*

pain disorder *(p. 131)*

somatization disorder *(p. 128)*

undifferentiated somatoform
    disorder *(p. 129)*

■ Somatization disorder is characterized by chronic multiple complaints and early onset.

■ Conversion disorder involves such problems as the loss of sight, paralysis, or another physical impairment that has no organic cause.

■ Pain disorder is a condition in which reported severe pain has a psychological rather than a physical basis. Hypochondriasis involves a persistent preoccupation with bodily functioning and disease.

■ Body dysmorphic disorder is preoccupation with an imagined bodily defect in a normal-appearing individual.

■ The psychoanalytic perspective holds that somatoform disorders are caused by the repression of sexual conflicts and their conversion into physical symptoms.

■ Behavioral theorists contend that the role of "being sick" is reinforcing and allows the individual to escape from unpleasant circumstances or avoid responsibilities.

■ Psychogenic pain is often reinforced by the external environment.

■ Psychoanalytic treatment emphasizes reliving the emotions associated with the repressed traumatic event.

■ Other treatment approaches involve reinforcing only "healthy" behaviors rather than the pain or disability. If possible, treatment is administered within the family system.

FOCUS QUESTIONS

- What are psychophysiological disorders, and how do they differ from conversion disorders?
- What kinds of stressors affect physical health, and why doesn't everyone develop an illness when exposed to them?
- How do stressors (both physical and psychosocial) affect the immune system? How do factors such as personality and mood states influence the course of an illness such as AIDS or cancer?
- What is the evidence that illnesses such as coronary heart disease, hypertension, headaches, and asthma are affected by emotional states, and how are the emotions involved?
- What are possible causes of psychophysiological disorders?
- What methods have been developed to treat the psychophysiological disorders?

6 *Psychological Factors Affecting Medical Conditions*

On November 7, 1991, basketball star Magic Johnson announced to the world that he had tested positive for HIV. More than 12 years later, Johnson remains in good health ("Magic Johnson," 2002). One individual who contracted HIV believes that psychological states are associated with longevity. "I feel it all goes back to my attitude.... I won't let this make me ill. I've watched quite a number of friends go from being relatively healthy to sick and dead in very short periods of time. In every case, they all bought into the idea that you have to die from AIDS if you have HIV. I just simply don't agree with that." (Associated Press, 1994)

Why is it that some individuals who are HIV positive succumb and develop AIDS (acquired immune deficiency syndrome) rapidly, whereas others, such as Magic Johnson, are able to resist the disease? It is possible that one's attitude may be related to survival. However, alternative explanations may be that some individuals are carrying a less virulent strain of HIV or that they have a genetically superior immune system. Such factors must be eliminated before we can assess the importance of a positive attitude in delaying the appearance of AIDS.

But in some cases, attitudes do appear to influence the course of an illness. What other biological effects might attitudes have? Can people "worry or scare themselves to death"? Medical evidence suggests that they can. Stress and anxiety appear to have at least some role in what is called the **sudden death syndrome**—unexpected, abrupt death that often seems to have no specific physical basis.

Sudden death is the leading cause of death in industrialized countries. Each year, about half a million people in the United States wake up feeling fine but collapse and die later in the day. Rates of sudden death are highest among African Americans and lowest among Hispanic Americans (Gillum, 1997). Some people who die this way are discovered to have coronary heart disease, such as narrowing of the arteries or evidence of past heart attacks, but many who succumb have normal hearts and cardiac vessels (Wren, 2002). Sudden death may involve the physiological changes that occur with stress, such as heart arrhythmias (Carels et al., 2003); faster blood clotting, which increases the risk of blockage of the coronary arteries; and blood pressure increases, which may tear loose fat deposits (Evans, 1997; Merz, 1997).

Certainly, the sudden death syndrome is an extreme example of the power of anxiety and stress to affect physiological processes. (See the Mental Health and Society feature, "The Hmong Sudden Death Syndrome," for another example of a similar phenomenon.) Most researchers now acknowledge that attitudes and emotional states can have an impact on physical well-being. In keeping with this perspective, DSM-IV-TR (American Psychiatric Association, 2000a) places medical conditions in which there are psychological influences under the heading "Psychological Factors Affecting Medical Condition." For the purpose of brevity, we use the term **psychophysiological disorder** to describe any physical disorder that has a strong psychological basis or component.

sudden death syndrome
Unexpected abrupt death that seems to have no specific physical basis.

psychophysiological disorder Any physical disorder that has a strong psychological basis or component.

141

MentaL HeaLth and society

The Hmong Sudden Death Syndrome

Vang Xiong is a former Hmong (Laotian) soldier who, with his wife and child, resettled in Chicago in 1980. The change from his familiar rural surroundings and farm life to an unfamiliar urban area must have produced a severe culture shock. In addition, Vang vividly remembered seeing people killed during his escape from Laos, and he expressed feelings of guilt about having to leave his brothers and sisters behind in that country. He reported having problems almost immediately.

[He] could not sleep the first night in the apartment, nor the second, nor the third. After three nights of sleeping very little, Vang came to see his resettlement worker, a bilingual Hmong man named Moua Lee. Vang told Moua that the first night he woke suddenly, short of breath, from a dream in which a cat was sitting on his chest. The second night, the room suddenly grew darker, and a figure, like a large black dog, came to his bed and sat on his chest. He could not push the dog off, and he grew quickly and dangerously short of breath. The third night, a tall, white-skinned female spirit came into his bedroom from the kitchen and lay on top of him. Her weight made it increasingly difficult for him to breathe, and as he grew frantic and tried to call out he could manage but a whisper. He attempted to turn onto his side, but found he was pinned down. After fifteen

minutes, the spirit left him, and he awoke, screaming. (Tobin & Friedman, 1983, p. 440)

As of 1993, 150 cases of sudden death among South-east Asian refugees had been reported. Almost all were men, with the possible exception of one or two women; most occurred within the first two years of residence in the United States. Autopsies produced no identifiable cause for the deaths. Some cases of sudden unexplained deaths have also been reported in Asian countries. Although the number of cases is declining, these deaths remain a most puzzling phenomenon (Gib Parrish, Centers for Disease Control, personal communication, 1993). All the reports were the same: a person in apparently good health went to sleep and died in his or her sleep. Often, the victim displayed labored breathing, screams, and frantic movements just before death. Some consider the deaths to represent an extreme and very specific example of the impact of psychological stress on physical health.

Vang was one of the lucky victims of the syndrome—he survived it. He went for treatment to a Hmong woman, Mrs. Thor, who is a highly respected shaman in Chicago's Hmong community. She interpreted his problem as being caused by unhappy spirits and performed the ceremonies that are required to release them. After that, Vang reported, he had no more problems with nightmares or with his breathing during sleep.

► Characteristics of Psychophysiological Disorders

The psychophysiological disorders should not be confused with the conversion disorders discussed in the chapter "Dissociative Disorders and Somatoform Disorders." The conversion disorders do involve reported physical symptoms, such as loss of feeling, blindness, and paralysis, but they do not involve any actual physical disorder or process. They are considered essentially psychological in nature. By contrast, most psychophysiological disorders involve tissue damage (such as coronary heart disease) or physiological dysfunction (as in asthma or migraine headaches). Both medical treatment and psychotherapy are usually required.

A DSM-IV-TR diagnosis of psychological factors affecting medical condition requires both the presence of a medical condition and the presence of one of the following:

- A temporal relationship between psychological factors and the onset of, exacerbation of, or delay in recovery from a medical condition.

- A psychological factor that interferes with treatment.

- Psychological factors that constitute additional health-risk factors in the individual.

stressor An external event or situation that places a physical or psychological demand on a person.

stress An internal response to a stressor.

Psychological factors can influence physical processes in three ways (Stone et al., 2000; White & Moorey, 1997). First, they can directly produce physiological changes in the immune system through the release of neurohormones (catecholamines, corticosteroids, and endorphins) or neurotransmitters. In individuals with irritable bowel syndrome, for example, emotional changes can produce spasms in the colon motility. Second, psychological conditions such as depression can influence behaviors that affect health. An individual who is depressed or is facing stress may sleep and exercise less, eat less healthy foods, and consume more caffeine, alcohol, or cigarettes. These behaviors may in turn increase the individual's susceptibility to disease or may prolong an existing illness. Third, an individual's beliefs about the causes, symptoms, duration, and curability of the disease may determine whether the person seeks help and follows the program for treatment. Patients who strongly believe that an illness is controllable or treatable often recover more quickly than others who believe otherwise (Weinman & Petrie, 1997). Thus psychological factors can affect illness in many different ways.

In this chapter, we first consider three models that help explain the impact of stress on physical health. Second, we examine the evidence that suggests a connection between stress and some ways in which decreased immunological function can contribute to the onset and course of cancer. Third, we discuss several of the more prevalent psychophysiological disorders: coronary heart disease, hypertension (high blood pressure), headaches, and asthma.

◀▶ Models for Understanding Stress

A **stressor** is an external event or situation that places a physical or psychological demand on a person. **Stress** is an internal response to a stressor. But something that disturbs one person doesn't necessarily disturb someone else, and two people who react to the same stressor may do so in different ways. Many people who are exposed to stressors, even traumatic ones, eventually get on with their lives. Other people show intense and somewhat long-lasting psychological symptoms.

This section discusses three stress models—the general adaptation, the life-change, and the transaction models—each of which seeks to explain how stressors, both large and small, can influence physical condition and illness and why some people have the ability to cope more easily with stress.

Flying after September 11   Situations producing uncertainty and fear are likely to be stressful. Here on September 13, 2001, passengers wait to check in for the first flights out of Los Angeles International Airport after the September 11 terrorist attacks. But the amount of stress needed to negatively affect an individual physically varies from person to person. In fact, some people seem to deal efficiently with a great deal of stress, whereas others find it difficult to cope with even small amounts. Why do some people become ill when facing stressors while others do not?

The General Adaptation Model

Being alive means that you are constantly exposed to stressors: relationship problems, illness, marriage, divorce, the death of someone you love, job seeking, aging, retiring, even schoolwork. Most people can cope with the stressors they encounter, provided those stressors are not excessively severe and do not "gang up" on the individual. But when someone is confronted with excessive external demands, coping behaviors may fail, and he or she may resort to inappropriate means of dealing with them. The result may be psychophysiological symptoms, apathy, anxiety, panic, depression, violence, and even death.

Hans Selye (1956, 1982) proposed a helpful model for understanding the body's physical reaction to biological

Life Change and Stress Changes such as leaving home to enter school, adjusting to a roommate, preparing for papers and exams, leaving your old network of friends, and eating dorm or self-prepared food can function as stressors. Why is it that some people will develop an illness as a reaction to the changes?

stressors. He put forth a three-stage model, which he called the **general adaptation syndrome (GAS),** for understanding the body's physical and psychological reaction to biological stressors. The stages are alarm, resistance, and exhaustion. Selye describes the *alarm stage* as a "call to arms" of the body's defenses when it is invaded or assaulted biologically. During this first stage, the body reacts immediately to the assault, with rapid heartbeat, loss of muscle tone, and decreased temperature and blood pressure. A rebound reaction follows as the adrenal cortex enlarges and the adrenal glands secrete corticoid hormones.

If exposure to the stressor continues, the *adaptation* or *resistance stage* follows. Now the body mobilizes itself to defend, destroy, or coexist with the injury or disease. The symptoms of illness may disappear. With HIV, for example, the immune system reacts by producing nearly a billion lymphocytes a day to combat the virus. Over time, the immune system gradually weakens and is overcome (Ho et al., 1995). The decrease in the body's resistance increases its susceptibility to other infections or illnesses. If the stressor continues to tax the body's finite resistive resources, the symptoms may reappear as exhaustion sets in (therefore the name *exhaustion stage*). If stress continues unabated, death may result.

For years scientists were skeptical about the supposed effects of stress on the body and dismissed any relationship between the two as folklore. We now know, however, that stress affects the immune system, heart function, hormone levels, nervous system, and metabolic rates. Bodily "wear and tear" owing to stress can contribute to diseases such as hypertension, chronic pain, heart attacks, cancer, and the common cold.

The Life-Change Model

As several researchers (deJong, Timmerman, & Emmelkamp, 1996; Holmes & Holmes, 1970; Rahe, 1994) have noted, events that lead to stress reactions need not be of crisis proportions. Seemingly small, everyday events can also create stress, and any life changes, even positive ones, can have a detrimental impact on health. These researchers' work led to the formulation of the **life-change model,** which assumes that all changes in a person's life—large or small, desirable or undesirable—can act as stressors and that the accumulation of small changes can be as powerful as a major stressor. Consider the following case:

general adaptation syndrome (GAS) A three-stage model for understanding the body's physical and psychological reactions to biological stressors.

life-change model An explanation of stress that assumes that all changes in a person's life—large or small, desirable or undesirable—can act as stressors and that the accumulation of small changes can be as powerful as one major stressor.

transaction model of stress Explanation of stress that states that stress resides neither in the person alone nor in the situation alone, but rather in a transaction between the two.

> Janet M., a college freshman, had always been a top-notch student in her small-town high school and had been valedictorian of her graduating class. Her social life was in high gear from the moment she arrived on the Berkeley campus. Yet Janet was suffering. It started with a cold that she seemed unable to shake. During her first quarter, she was hospitalized once with the "flu" and then three weeks later for "exhaustion." In high school Janet appeared vivacious, outgoing, and relaxed; at Berkeley she became increasingly tense, anxious, and depressed.

Table 6.1   Sample Stressors Generated and Ranked by College Undergraduates

Item	Severity	Frequency
Death of family member or friend	3.97	1.89
Had lots of tests	3.62	4.39
Finals week	3.62	3.64
Breaking up a relationship	3.45	2.21
Property stolen	3.41	1.96
Having roommate conflicts	3.10	2.68
Lack of money	3.07	3.36
Arguments with friends	2.97	2.43
Trying to decide on a major	2.79	3.25
Sat through boring class	1.66	4.07

Note: Event severity was rated on a 4-point scale, ranging from "none" to "a lot." Event frequency was rated on a 5-point scale, ranging from "never" to "always."
Source: Data from Crandall, Preisler, & Aussprung (1992).

In Janet's case, all the classic symptoms of stress were present. No single stressor was responsible; rather, a series of life changes had a cumulative impact. Janet moved from a conservative small-town environment to a liberal campus, changed from being the top student in her high school to being a slightly above average student at Berkeley, lived in a dormitory with a roommate rather than her private room at home, worked part-time to support herself, left her boyfriend and high school friends behind, and had to adjust to dorm food rather than home-cooked meals.

Although each of these changes may seem small, their cumulative impact was anything but insignificant. And what happened to Janet is seen, to various degrees, among many students entering college. Going to college is a major life change. Most students can cope with the demands, but others need direct help dealing with stress. See Table 6.1 for ratings of stressors among U.S. undergraduates.

Negative or Positive Stress—It Makes a Difference
Research has found that undesirable life changes, such as loss of a spouse, are more likely to produce anxiety, depression, and physical symptoms in people than are positive life changes, such as moving to a new house in a better neighborhood.

The Transaction Model

The general adaptation syndrome model is concerned with the process by which the body reacts to stressors, and the life-change model is concerned with external events that cause stress as a response. But neither model considers the person's subjective interpretation of stressful events or life changes. Several processes intervene between the stressor and the development of stress. In particular, the thoughts and interpretations we have about impending threats (stressors), the emotions we attach to them, and the actions we take to avoid them can either increase or decrease the impact of stressors (Levenstein et al., 1993).

In his classic book *Psychological Stress and the Coping Process* (1966), Richard Lazarus formulated a **transaction model of stress.** He noted that stress resides neither in the person alone nor in the situation alone, but rather in a transaction between the two. An example can illustrate this point:

> On the morning of August 16, 2004, Mrs. Mavis C. discovered a small lump on her left breast. She immediately contacted her doctor and made an appointment to see him. After examining her, the physician stated that the lump could be either a cyst or a tumor and recommended a biopsy. The results revealed that the tumor was malignant.
> Mrs. C. accepted the news with some trepidation but went about her life with minimal disruption. When she was questioned about the way in which she was handling the situation, she replied that there was no denying that this was a serious problem and that there was great ambiguity about the prognosis but that people are successfully treated for cancer. She planned to undergo treatment and would not give up.

Unlike Mrs. C., many patients would have been horrified at even the thought of having cancer. They might have viewed the news that the tumor was malignant as a catastrophe and focused on thoughts of dying, abandoning all hope. This reaction differs from Mrs. C.'s, who coped with the stressor through internal processes. The impact of stressors can be reduced or magnified depending on the way the situation is interpreted. People who can adapt cognitively may reduce susceptibility to illness or limit its course. They may make efforts to alter health-impairing habits and to adhere to treatment guidelines, whereas those who view the illness with a sense of hopelessness may give up (Shnek et al., 2001).

One dominant theme threads its way through each of the models discussed: no one factor is enough to cause illness. Rather, illness results from a complex interaction of psychosocial, physiological, and cognitive influences.

Stress and the Immune System

We have already suggested a relationship between stress and illness. How do emotional and psychological states influence the disease process? Consider the following case:

> Anne was an unhappy and passive individual who always acceded to the wishes and demands of her husband. She had difficulty expressing strong emotions, especially anger, and often repressed her feelings. She had few friends and, other than her husband, had no one to talk to. She was also depressed and felt a pervasive sense of hopelessness. During a routine physical exam, her doctor discovered a lump in her breast. The results of a biopsy revealed that the tumor was malignant.

Could Anne's personality or emotional state have contributed to the formation or the growth of the malignant tumor? If so, how? Could she now alter the course of her disease by changing her emotional state? That such questions are being asked represents a profound change in the way in which physical illness is now being conceptualized.

The view that diseases, other than traditional psychophysiological disorders, are strictly organic appears too simplistic. Many theorists (such as Cohen et al., 1998; Cohen & Rodriguez, 1995; White & Moorey, 1997) now believe that most diseases are caused by an interaction of social, psychological, and biological factors (see Figure 6.1). This relationship has been found in many diseases. For example, chronic stress may create greater susceptibility to disease. Cohen and his associates (1998) had 276 volunteers complete a life-stressor interview, after which they were evaluated to determine whether they were ill. Those who were healthy were then quarantined and given nasal drops containing cold viruses to determine whether they would develop a cold within five days. Of this group, 84 percent became infected with the virus, but only 40 percent developed cold symptoms. Participants with acute stressful life events lasting less than one month tended not to develop a cold. In contrast, those who suffered severe stress for one or more months were much more likely to develop colds.

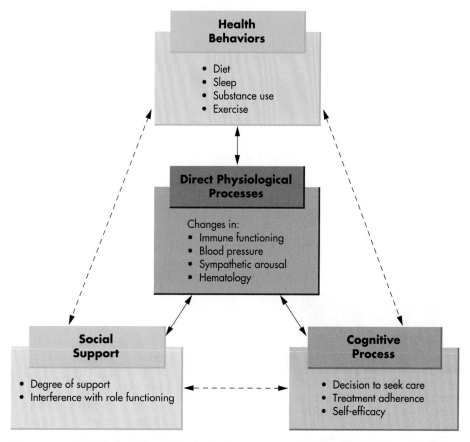

Figure 6.1 Ways in Which Psychological or Emotional States Can Affect the Illness Process   Emotional or psychological states can influence the disease process from a number of different pathways. Although these are presented separately, they also interact with one another. Changes in health behaviors, health care practices, or social support can also affect one another, as well as produce changes in physiological processes. *Source:* Cohen & Rodriguez (1995); Stone et al. (2000).

The cognitive or emotional state of an individual can influence the course or severity of a disease through the following pathways: (1) biological—there may be a direct physiological reaction (blood pressure, heart rate, etc.) or changes in immune functioning following a stressor; (2) behavioral—the individual may respond either by engaging in poor health practices and not adhering to treatment or by altering his or her lifestyle in a positive manner; (3) cognitive—thoughts of hopelessness or optimism could have an impact on health decisions; (4) social—the stressor or emotional state could cause a deterioration or an increase in the social support system. Each pathway has received some experimental support in the progression of a disease (see Figure 6.1). Research has tended to focus on only one of the pathways, whereas several may be involved. For example, the biological process of depression may directly produce a deterioration of the immune system, but poorer immune functioning could also be due to behavioral characteristics associated with depression, such as not eating appropriately or a lack of exercise. Following treatment guidelines can also influence the course of a disease. In one study, nearly one-third of individuals with HIV had missed medication doses. Rates of adherence were related to levels of depression, self-efficacy, social support, and side effects of medication (Catz et al., 2000). As you can see, immune functioning can be influenced through different pathways.

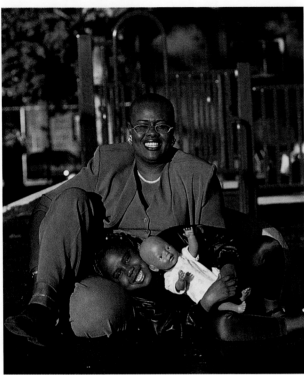

Coping with Stress The evidence supporting the importance of psychosocial stressors on the development and progress of AIDS may be mixed, but the reality for Michelle Lopez and her daughter, Raven, is clear. Five years ago, when Raven was diagnosed HIV-positive, Michelle was homeless and using drugs. Since then Michelle has quit drugs and found an apartment and a job educating women and children about AIDS. Both she and Raven are enrolled in a clinical trial to test a new drug for AIDS, and Raven is now symptom free.

The Immune System

We know that stress is related to illness, but what is the precise relationship between the two? How does stress affect health? Stress itself does not appear to cause infections, but it may decrease the immune system's efficiency, thereby increasing a person's susceptibility to disease (Koh, 1998; Luecken et al., 1997). This connection has received the greatest amount of attention.

The white blood cells in the immune system help maintain health by recognizing and destroying pathogens such as bacteria, viruses, fungi, and tumors. In an intact system, more than 1,000 billion white blood cells are based in the lymph system or circulate through the bloodstream (Cohen & Herbert, 1996; Kiecolt-Glaser & Glaser, 1993). As mentioned earlier, stress produces physiological changes in the body. Part of the stress response involves the release of several neurohormones that impair immune functioning. Because of the weakening in defenses, infections and diseases are more likely to develop or worsen.

Impaired immunological functioning has been associated with a variety of social and psychological stressors (Pike et al., 1997; Ursano, 1997; Vedhara & Nott, 1996). The spouses of dementia victims showed lower immune functioning than was found among controls, and spouses who reported lower levels of social support showed the greatest drop (Kiecolt-Glaser et al., 1991). Divorced or separated men tend to have poorer immunological functioning than their married counterparts. Happily married men tend to have stronger immune systems than men who are experiencing marital problems (Kiecolt-Glaser et al., 1987). And abrasive marital interactions between long-married men and women are associated with immunological changes (Kiecolt-Glaser et al., 1997). The quality of social relationships may affect our vulnerability to illnesses.

Although our discussion has focused on the direct impact of stress on the immune system, indirect pathways must also be considered. For example, the health care practices of an individual who is depressed or facing many different stressors may deterio-

Under Attack This highly magnified photo shows the surface of a T-cell that is infected with the HIV virus. T-cells function as a part of the immune response to viruses and infections. In this case it is being compromised. Some believe that one's attitude can influence the susceptibility of components of the immune system such as T-cells, whereas others disagree.

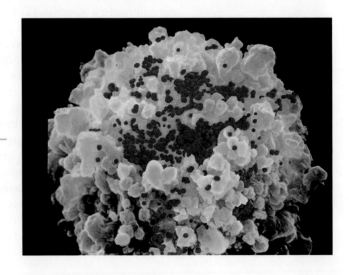

Control and Stress   Although these assembly-line workers at Apple Computer would seem to have low-stress jobs, they may be highly vulnerable to stress-related illnesses. What seems to be most important is the perception of control over your work. How could you increase the feeling of control in assembly-line work?

hardiness A concept developed by Kobasa and Maddi that refers to a person's ability to deal well with stress.

rate (getting less sleep, eating less-nutritious meals, consuming more alcohol, and paying less attention to physical care). Such changes can also decrease immune functioning (Heckman et al., 2004). Research that attempts to link changes in immune functioning directly with stressors or psychological states must control for such variables.

Mediating the Effects of Stressors

As we have seen, not everyone who faces stressful events develops an illness. In this section, we explore some of the intervening factors that can mediate the effects of a stressor.

Helplessness or Control   A direct relationship between control and the immune system has been found in several studies. In one study, ten participants were placed in two stressful situations involving noise. In the first situation, participants could control the noise level by pressing buttons in a simple sequence. In the other, participants could not control the noise level. Blood samples were obtained and analyzed after each session. The level of epinephrine (a hormone released during stress) in the uncontrollable-stress situation was significantly higher than that found in the controllable-stress situation. The participants also reported a greater sense of helplessness, higher tension, anxiety, and depression while in the uncontrollable-stress situation (Breier et al., 1987). Although changes in physical functioning occur with stress, can we show experimentally that lack of control is related to disease?

One study that attempted to do so directly measured the effect of the ability to "control" on immune functioning in rats injected with cancer cells. The rats were assigned to one of three groups: (1) a controllable-shock group (pressing a bar would end the shock), (2) a yoked-control group (rats in this group would receive the same pattern of shocks as in the escapable condition but would have no control over the shocks), or (3) a no-shock control group. Sixty-five percent of the rats in the controllable-shock group rejected the cancer cells, as opposed to only 27 percent in the yoked-control group and 55 percent in the no-shock control group. The inability to control a stressor seems to decrease immune system efficiency (Laudenslager et al., 1983; Visintainer, Volpicelli, & Seligman, 1982).

Hardiness: Personality Characteristics and Mood State   Maddi (1972) believes that "hardy" people are more resistant to illnesses. In a classic study, Kobasa and her colleagues (1979) conducted large-scale research on highly stressed executives in various occupations, seeking to identify the traits that distinguish those who handle stress well from those who do not. They found that high-stress executives who reported few illnesses showed three kinds of hardiness, or ability to deal well with stress. In their attitudes toward life, these stress-resistant executives showed an *openness to change*, a feeling of *involvement* or *commitment*, and a *sense of control* over their lives. The most important protective factor that was correlated with health was attitude toward change (or *challenge*). Those who are open to change seem likely to interpret events to their advantage and to reduce their levels of stress. Although the idea that **hardiness**

Mood and Cancer   Though research evidence is still mixed, many people believe that emotions can affect the onset and course of serious diseases such as cancer. In an effort to show emotional support for Sarah DeCristoforo, when she returned to school after receiving chemotherapy, her teacher and two friends shaved their heads.

may buffer the impact of stressors makes sense, the construct has been difficult to define and assess.

Self-Efficacy and Optimism   Another cognitive variable that appears to have an impact on illness is the belief in one's ability to take action to attain goals or to effect change. An individual with high self-efficacy may engage in more health-related activities when an illness occurs, whereas low self-efficacy would result in feelings of hopelessness. Self-efficacy has been related to recovery from orthopedic surgery; the stronger the belief in the ability to recover by participating in rehabilitation, the more successful the outcome (Waldrop et al., 2001). Similar findings were reported for individuals suffering from degenerative disk disease and low-back problems (Kaivanto et al., 1995; Lackner, Carosella, & Feuerstein, 1996). Individuals with high self-efficacy are more likely to follow treatment guidelines, to exercise, and to follow a healthier diet, thereby shortening the recovery period. Optimism, another cognitive state, also appears to mediate the impact of a disease. Optimism or even illusory positive beliefs about serious illnesses may improve psychological and possibly mental health.

Personality, Mood States, and Cancer

Are certain emotions or personality characteristics involved in either the cause or the course of cancers? A number of researchers (Colon et al., 1991; Greer, 1991; Phillips, Todd, & Wagner, 1993; Temoshok & Dreher, 1992) believe that certain emotional states—such as depression, hopelessness, or anger—or specific personality styles can cause or influence the course of cancer. Demonstrating such a link would have important implications in treatment and prevention. Over 1,660,000 individuals succumbed to cancer in 2001 (American Cancer Society, 2003). About 8 million Americans are currently living with cancer or are cancer survivors.

Greer (1991) believes that a "fighting spirit" can increase survival time in cancer patients. It is possible that stressful emotions can impair cellular functions, such as DNA repair, and could contribute to cancer, whereas positive emotions improve immune functioning. However, the emotional state or self esteem of an individual may also affect the course of cancer by producing altered health habits or adherence to treatment (Baum & Posluszny, 1999; Helgeson, Snyder, & Seltman, 2004). Some early researchers (Bahnson, 1981; Simonton, Mathews-Simonton, & Creighton, 1978) argued that negative emotions and the inability to form lasting relationships increase an individual's chances of developing cancer. Such research led to the hypothesis that positive emotional states would enhance immune functioning. See the Mental Health and Society feature, "Can Laughter or Humor Influence the Course of a Disease?," for the possible impact of a positive emotion such as humor on the disease process.

Several problems exist in research investigating the relationship between moods and personality on cancer. First, *cancer* is a general name for a variety of disease processes, each of which may have a varying susceptibility to emotions. Second, cancer develops over a relatively long period of time. Determining a temporal relationship between its occurrence and a specific mood or personality is not possible. Third, most studies examining the relationship between psychological variables and cancer have

mental health and society

Can Laughter or Humor Influence the Course of a Disease?

It's hard not to feel a laugh bubbling to the surface at the sight of a grown man—a psychotherapist, no less—standing before a group of his sober-minded peers, holding a teddy bear that tells knock-knock jokes when you press its paw. Hard not to laugh when he talks about building a concept of personal "mindfoolness." Hard not to resist a smirk as he hands out finger traps, those venerable props from kidhood in which you stick one finger in each end and can't pull them out no matter how hard you tug (McGuire, 1999, p.1).

Clown noses, whoopee cushions, the antics of the Three Stooges can produce laughter. Can humor reduce the severity of a physical illness or even be curative? Norman Cousins, who suffered from rheumatoid disease, described how he recovered his health through laughter. He claimed that ten minutes of laughter would provide two hours of pain relief (Cousins, 1979). In 1999, Patch Adams, a physician whose use of humor with his patients was made into a movie, received an award for "excellence in the field of therapeutic humor" at the American Association of Therapeutic Humor. The president of the association, Steven Sultanoff, believes that humor can reduce the risk of coronary heart disease by producing beneficial physiological changes in the body.

How might humor influence the disease process? Several routes are possible. (1) Humor may have a direct impact on physiological functioning. (2) Humor may influence people's beliefs about the ability to carry out health-promoting behaviors and give them greater confidence that their actions can relieve the illness. (3) Humor may serve as a buffer between exposure to stressors and the development of negative states, such as depression, which have been found to be related to the development or severity of physical conditions. (4) Humor may make an individual more likely to receive social support from friends and family. In two reviews of studies on the relationship between humor, laughter, and physical health (Martin, 2001; Salovey et al., 2000), limited support was found. There does appear to be an increase in immune functioning after exposure to humorous videotapes versus tapes that are neutral or sad. Humor can also increase the self-efficacy of individuals and reduce the impact of negative events. The relationship between humor and social support has not received adequate attention. A major problem in this area has been an accepted definition of humor. How would you determine what is funny?

been retrospective—that is, personality or mood states were assessed after the cancer was diagnosed. The discovery that one has a life-threatening disease can produce a variety of emotions. People who receive the life-threatening diagnosis of cancer may respond with depression, anxiety, and confusion. Thus, instead of being a cause, negative emotions may be a result of the knowledge of having a life-threatening disease. Fourth, although it has been shown that injected malignant cells are more likely to grow in stressed versus unstressed mice, the findings do not address the development of "spontaneous" cancers. Would the stressed mice be more likely to develop cancer anyway, without being injected with malignant cells?

▶ CHECKPOINT REVIEW

general adaptation syndrome (GAS) *(p. 144)*

hardiness *(p. 149)*

life-change model *(p. 144)*

psychophysiological disorder *(p. 141)*

stress *(p. 143)*

stressor *(p. 143)*

sudden death syndrome *(p. 141)*

transaction model of stress *(p. 145)*

What are psychophysiological disorders, and how do they differ from conversion disorders?
- Psychophysiological disorders are any physical disorders that:
  - demonstrate a temporal relationship between psychological factors and the course of a physical illness.
  - interfere with treatment.
  - constitute additional health risk factors.
- They are different from conversion disorders in that actual physical processes or conditions are involved.

What kinds of stressors affect physical health, and why doesn't everyone develop an illness when exposed to them?
- Stressors may be large or relatively weak.
- Several models have been created to explain the development of physical illness.

- The general adaptation model describes the body's reaction when exposed to stressors.
- If the stressors are long lasting, the body's defenses may be overwhelmed, and a disease will develop.
- The life-change model is based on the view that any changes, even positive ones, can produce illness if there are too many of them.
- Neither model explains why some people will not develop an illness even though they may be exposed to stressors.
- The transaction model emphasizes the subjective interpretation of stressors by an individual.
- The development of a disease is dependent on the way stressors are viewed.

How do stressors (both physical and psychosocial) affect the immune system? How do factors such as personality and mood states influence the course of an illness such as AIDS or cancer?

- Immunological functioning seems to be affected by physical and psychological stress, both short term and long term.
- A variety of factors, such as anxiety, divorce, and bereavement, can produce poor immunological responses. The causal direction of this relationship is unclear.
- Some research supports the suggestion that psychological stress can influence the initiation and course of certain infectious diseases through changes in immune functioning.
- Other research, particularly that focusing on AIDS, offers only limited support.
- Although stress decreases the ability of animals to reject injected cancer cells, whether psychological variables can influence the development of cancer in human beings is not known.
- Personality or mood states may also affect the course of a disease through changes in immune functioning, health habits, or amount of social support.
- *Cancer* is a term describing a variety of disease processes, which may vary in their susceptibility to emotions. Most studies are short term and retrospective, and they do not address the development of spontaneous cancer.

Psychological Involvement in Specific Physical Disorders

Although the study of the impact of psychological factors on immune function is fairly recent, the mind-body connection between some physical disorders has been extensively studied. In many instances, a relationship has been found between psychological or social factors and the origin and exacerbation of these conditions.

Coronary Heart Disease

Coronary heart disease (CHD) is a narrowing of the arteries in or to the heart, resulting in the restriction or partial blockage of the flow of blood and oxygen to the heart. Symptoms of CHD may include chest pain (*angina pectoris*), heart attack, or, in severe cases, cardiac arrest. In a longitudinal study, depression seems to be a risk factor for cardiac mortality, both in individuals who had or did not have cardiac disease at the beginning of the study. The risk was twice as high for those with major than with minor depression, although any depression was associated with increased mortality (Penninx et al., 2001; see Figure 6.2). For women, estrogen appears to offer some protection: women tend to develop coronary heart disease about ten years later than men do. However, because of the aging of the U.S. population, the number of women dying from coronary heart disease is now approaching that of men, and more women than men now die of cardiovascular disease each year (Torpy, 2002; Wenger, 1997).

One study (Legato, 1996) found that the fatality rate for women within the first year of a heart attack (44 percent) is higher than that for men (27 percent). The

coronary heart disease (CHD) A narrowing of the arteries in or near the heart, resulting in the restriction or partial blockage of the flow of blood and oxygen to the heart.

(a) Without cardiac disease

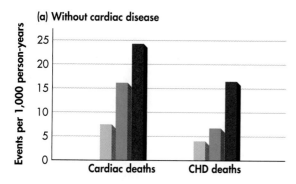

(b) With cardiac disease

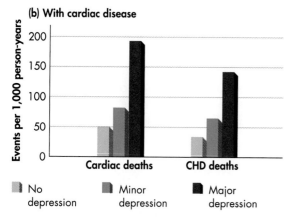

■ No depression   ■ Minor depression   ■ Major depression

Figure 6.2 Cardiac Death and Cardiac Heart Disease (CHD) Death Rates per 1,000 Person-Years by Depression Status   Data represent (a) individuals without cardiac disease and (b) individuals with cardiac disease. The presence of depression, especially major depression, is associated with cardiac deaths in both conditions. *Source:* From Penninx et al. (2001).

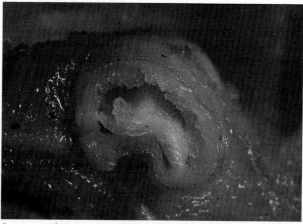

Stress and Coronary Heart Disease   Stress may produce physiological changes that promote plaque buildup on the wall of the coronary artery, contributing to coronary heart disease. In this picture, the artery is almost entirely blocked.

Mental Health and Society feature, "Does Bias Exist in Medical Treatment?" discusses some of the findings on coronary heart disease and women and other related studies. Studies suggest that psychological and social variables may be contributory factors that produce certain pathogenic physiological changes. Psychosocial factors can directly affect physiological processes that influence blood coagulation and increases in blood pressure, thereby increasing the thickness of artery walls and contributing to CHD (Harenstam, Theorell, & Kaijser, 2000). Some evidence also exists that high levels of anxiety may be related to incidents of fatal heart attacks. In a thirty-two-year prospective study on 2,280 men with and without coronary heart disease, those with anxiety symptoms, as measured by a five-item questionnaire, were more than three times more likely to eventually die of sudden cardiac arrest. (See Table 6.2 for questions used in the anxiety questionnaire.) It is possible that anxiety may hasten the development of coronary heart disease and may produce coronary spasms or

Table 6.2	**Anxiety Questionnaire Items that Correlated with Eventual Onset of Fatal Heart Attacks**

Participants who checked yes for two or more of these questions were more than three times more likely to develop fatal coronary heart disease than were those who answered no.

■ Do strange people or places make you afraid?

■ Are you considered a nervous person?

■ Are you constantly keyed up and jittery?

■ Do you often become suddenly scared for no good reason?

■ Do you often break out in a cold sweat?

Source: Kawachi et al. (1994).

Mental Health and Society

Does Bias Exist in Medical Treatment?

If someone close to you becomes seriously ill, will his or her treatment be influenced by his or her gender or ethnic group? Use your critical thinking skills to find the answer to that question. As you consider the following findings, attempt to develop several possible explanations for the facts in each one. Consider factors such as personality, gender and ethnic differences, biological differences, and social variables, including bias. Which findings may indicate bias, and which might be better explained by other factors? After you reach your conclusion, think about what you could do to change each of these situations.

- Six months after a heart attack, women are twice as likely to die as men are (25.8 percent vs. 10.8 percent), even when the comparisons are adjusted to control for other disorders and age (Marrugat et al., 1998).

- Men are more likely to receive thrombolytic therapy (clot-dissolving medication) than women are (41.3 percent vs. 23.9 percent) and are more likely to receive an early coronary angiograph to determine the extent of artery blockage (Marrugat et al., 1998).

- After experiencing symptoms of a heart attack, women reach a hospital approximately one hour later than their male counterparts. Additionally, following their arrival in the emergency room, women are transferred to a coronary care unit about two hours later than men are (Marrugat et al., 1998).

- An examination of 440 advertisements in medical journals revealed that advertisements for cardiovascular medications portrayed significantly more males than females (Leppard, Ogletree, & Wallen, 1993).

- In 1989, a National Institutes of Health Panel (NIH, 1989) could not make a firm recommendation for reducing cholesterol levels in women to prevent coronary arterial disease—data on women were insufficient to reach any conclusion.

- Few studies on women and HIV and AIDS exist, even though there is preliminary evidence that treatment guidelines based on research on males may not be completely applicable to females.

- Among individuals with injuries to their limbs, rates of amputation were higher and arterial vascularization (reopening arteries) procedures were performed less often for black patients than for white patients, even when all were covered by Medicare (Guadagnoli et al., 1995).

- In one study (Ayanian et al., 1993) of a national sample of 27,485 Medicare enrollees who underwent coronary angiography (x-rays of blood vessels to the heart), white men and women were significantly more likely (57 and 50 percent, respectively) to receive a revascularization procedure than were black men and women (40 and 34 percent, respectively).

ventricular arrhythmias that lead to fatal cardiac arrest (Kawachi et al., 1994). Among older women, depression was significantly related to cardiovascular disease (Wassertheil-Smoller et al., 2004).

Friedman and Rosenman (1974) identified a behavior pattern, called *Type A behavior,* that they believed was associated with increased risk of heart attack. The pattern involves aggressiveness, competitiveness, hostility, time pressure, and constant striving for achievement. Although evidence initially suggested that the Type A personality was related to coronary heart disease, recent research suggests something different. Several researchers (Mann & James, 1998; Julkunen, Idanpaan-Heikkila, & Saarinen, 1993) reviewed the characteristics of the Type A personality that might be related to CHD and found that the only significant risk factors were irritability and hostility. The current emphasis is on the anger-hostility-aggression (AHA) syndrome in CHD (Richards, Alvarenga, & Hof, 2000).

Several possibilities exist that may explain the relationship between hostility and coronary heart disease. First, hostility may increase the hostile person's cardiovascular responsivity and physiology, subsequently increasing his or her risk of developing CHD. At least one study (Miller et al., 1998) supports this view. In that study, individuals who scored high on hostility showed exaggerated cardiovascular reactivity to a

Stress and Hypertension   On September 11, 2001, hijacked United Airlines 175 from Boston crashed into the World Trade Center. Many survivors recounted the terror they felt during the attack and their fight for survival. Onlookers were also horrified to see people jump to their deaths; many people barely escaped the collapsing building. The survivors and observers went through a traumatic event that produced severe physiological reactions. What was happening to them physiologically?

stressor (verbal harassment) compared with participants who were low on hostility. Thus hostility may lead to damaging physiological responses. The experience of strong anger in young healthy males when they were frustrated or treated unfairly was related to elevations in serum cholesterol and low-density lipoproteins, both of which have been found to increase the risk of developing CHD (Richards et al., 2000).

A second possibility is that hostile individuals may have health-damaging lifestyles. They may sleep less, have less healthy diets, exercise less, or smoke and consume alcohol excessively. One sample of individuals with high hostility ratings consumed more salt than did those with low hostility ratings (Miller et al., 1998). A third possibility is that hostility could be an individual's reaction to having a particular disease rather than being a causal factor. Patient groups with serious diseases other than coronary heart disease have also scored higher on hostility (Ranchor et al., 1997).

A final area of concern is that much of the research on hostility and CHD has been done on men. There is some evidence that hostility measures do not correlate with cardiovascular reactivity in women in the same way that they do in men. Whereas high hostility is associated with higher resting blood pressure in men, women high in hostility show a lower resting blood pressure than men do (Davidson, Hall, & MacGregor, 1997). Because of socialization differences, hostility may have different health implications for men and women.

Stress and Hypertension

On October 19, 1987, the stock market drastically dropped 508 points. By chance, a forty-eight-year-old stockbroker was wearing a device measuring stress in the work environment on that day. The instrument measured his pulse every fifteen minutes. At the beginning of the day, his pulse was sixty-four beats per minute and his blood pressure was 132 over 87 (both rates within the normal range). As stock prices fell dramatically, the man's physiological system surged in the other direction. His heart rate increased to eighty-four beats per minute, and his blood pressure hit a dangerous 181 over 105. His pulse was "pumping adrenaline, flooding his arteries, and maybe slowly killing himself in the process." (Tierney, 1988)

These events illustrate the impact of a stressor on blood pressure, the measurement of the force of blood against the walls of the arteries and veins. We all experience a transient physiological response to stressors, but in some people, it develops

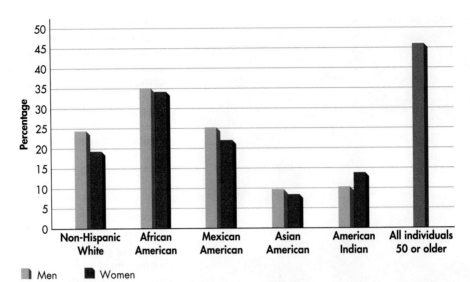

■ Men ■ Women

Figure 6.3 Gender and Ethnic Differences in Hypertension Among U.S. Adults The highest prevalence (percentage) of chronic high blood pressure occurs most frequently among African Americans and among all individuals over the age of fifty. Women tend to score somewhat lower than other groups. Biological, lifestyle, and psychological factors have been implicated in the gender and ethnic differences in hypertension. *Source:* Data from Burt et al. (1995) and American Heart Association (1998).

into a chronic condition called **essential hypertension,** or high blood pressure of 140 (systolic, or blood pressure when the heart is contracting) over 90 (diastolic, or blood pressure when the heart is at rest) or higher. Systolic blood pressure appears to be a better predictor of cardiovascular problems than diastolic blood pressure (Mallik, 2001). Essential hypertension is found in about 23 percent of the U. S. adult population. It is most prevalent in the African American population and the aged. More than three-fourths of women and two-thirds of men over the age of seventy-five have hypertension (National Center for Health Statistics, 2001b). In older individuals, the disorder is often the result of the loss of elasticity in the aorta and large arteries. In other cases, no specific physiological cause can be determined. Figure 6.3 shows some gender and ethnic comparisons of hypertension among adults. Chronic hypertension may lead to arteriosclerosis (narrowing of arteries) and to increased risk of strokes and heart attacks (Everson et al., 1999; National Center for Health Statistics, 2001b).

A number of studies suggest that stressors, emotional states, and hypertension may be related. Individuals placed under stress experience significant increases in blood pressure (Smith, Ruiz, & Uchino, 2000; Uchino & Garvey, 1997). Individuals with high blood pressure have exhibited exaggerated reactions to a stressor, compared with their counterparts in control groups with normal or borderline high blood pressure (Tuomisto, 1997). Hypertensive individuals with depression were more than twice as likely as nondepressed individuals to develop heart failure (8.1 percent vs. 3.2 percent) during a five-year follow-up (Abramson et al., 2001).

Gender may also be a factor in the development of hypertension. In a study by Lai and Linden (1992), men and women were evaluated on emotional expressiveness and classified as either "anger in" (suppressing anger) or "anger out" (expressing anger). They were then exposed to verbal harassment and either allowed to release their anger or inhibited from doing so. Men displayed greater cardiovascular reactivity to the harassment than did women. The opportunity to release anger facilitated heart

essential hypertension Chronic high blood pressure, usually with no known biological cause; the most common disease in the United States.

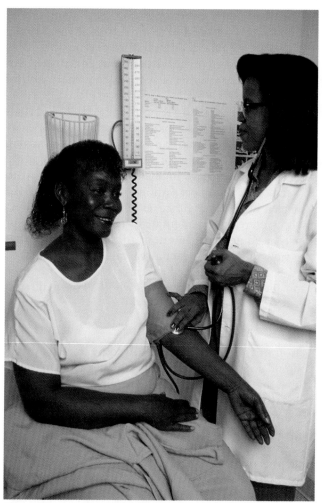

Ethnicity and Hypertension   African Americans have much higher rates of hypertension than their white counterparts, whereas Asian Americans and American Indians have much lower rates. What factors may account for the large between-group differences?

rate and diastolic recovery in men but not in women. Women with "anger in" tendencies showed better systolic recovery than women with "anger out" tendencies, regardless of whether they had an opportunity to express anger. Holding in anger did not produce the strong negative physiological reactions in women that it did in men. The researchers hypothesized that these differences in recovery patterns may be due to the differential socialization of males and females.

Ethnic differences have also been found. African Americans have higher mean blood pressure levels and higher rates of hypertension than their white counterparts. Over a seven-year period, black youths in one study showed consistently greater systolic and diastolic blood pressure than their white counterparts (Murphy et al., 1995). Such findings have been taken as evidence of possible genetic influences on the incidence of hypertension in the two groups, possibly manifested as differences in sympathetic nervous system activity.

Although genetic and other biological factors may explain the high rate of hypertension in African Americans, another line of research supports a psychological explanation. In one study, African Americans who reported taking no action against personally experienced discrimination had higher blood pressure than those who reported that they challenged discriminatory situations (Krieger & Sidney, 1996). In another study, African Americans who watched videotapes or imagined depictions of social situations involving racism showed increases in heart rate and blood pressure (Fang & Myers, 2001; Jones et al., 1996). Thus exposure to discrimination may increase the prevalence of hypertension (Troxel et al., 2003).

Data on hypertension in other ethnic groups is very limited. Hispanic Americans have rates of hypertension similar to those of the non-Hispanic white population (American Heart Association, 1998). Surveyed groups of Asian Americans have lower rates of hypertension than are found in the general population (Kang et al., 1997). Information is very sparse on the prevalence of hypertension among Pacific Islanders, American Indians, or Alaskan natives. Among the Navajo, 23 percent of men and 14 percent of women had hypertension (Mendlein et al., 1997).

Migraine, Tension, and Cluster Headaches

A forty-two-year-old woman described her headache as a throbbing that pulsed with every heartbeat and occurred during every menstrual period. The pain was accompanied by visual effects, such as sparklers flashing across her visual field. The symptoms would last for up to three days. (Adler & Rogers, 1999)

Headaches are among the most common psychophysiological complaints, accounting for more than 18 million visits to medical practitioners each year (Jones, 1995). The pain of a headache can vary in intensity from dull to excruciating. It is unclear whether the different forms of headaches (migraine, tension, and cluster) are produced by different psychophysiological mechanisms or whether they merely differ in severity.

A number of conditions have been associated with the onset of headaches, including stress, negative emotions, sexual harassment, poor body posture, eyestrain, exercise, too much or too little sleep, sexual intercourse, exposure to smoke or strong odors, the weather, temperature changes, and changes in altitude (Goldenhar et al., 1998; Ohayon, 2004; Levin, 2002; Silberstein, 1998). In one experiment, Martin and Seneviratne (1997) attempted to verify that food deprivation and negative emotions can precipitate headaches. For nineteen hours, they either withheld food from thirty-eight women and eighteen men who suffered from migraine or tension headaches or exposed them to a stressor that produced negative emotions (difficult-to-solve anagrams). The findings supported the view that the two conditions can induce headaches. Individuals who had been deprived of food or subjected to stress reported both more headaches and headaches of greater intensity than individuals who had been allowed to eat or were not exposed to stress.

Migraine Headaches   Constriction of cranial arteries, followed by dilation of the cerebral blood vessels resulting in moderate to severe pain, are the distinguishing features of **migraine headache.** Anything that affects the size of these blood vessels, which are connected to sensitive nerves, can produce a headache. Thus certain chemicals, such as sodium nitrate (found in hot dogs), monosodium glutamate, and tyramine (found in red wines), can produce headaches by distending blood vessels in certain people. Pain from a migraine headache may be mild, moderate, or severe. It may last from a few hours to several days and is often accompanied by nausea and vomiting. Depending on which part of the brain is affected most, the person may show various neurological symptoms, such as distortion of vision, numbness of parts of the body, or speech and coordination problems. When the blood vessels then become distended to compensate for the diminished blood supply, severe pain occurs. About 28 million Americans, most of them young adult women, suffer from migraine headaches (Marquardt, 2000). A nationwide survey (Stewart et al., 1992) revealed that migraine headaches were common not only among women but also among people with lower incomes. They are less common among African Americans than among white Americans. Although stress is a factor, sufferers may be congenitally predisposed to migraines (Marquardt, 2001).

Tension Headaches   **Tension headaches** were once thought to be produced by prolonged contraction of the scalp and neck muscles, resulting in vascular constriction and steady pain. Some studies, however, have found a lack of correspondence between reports of pain and muscle tension among people who have tension headaches. Many people showed no detectable muscle tension but still reported headaches (Martin, 1993). More women than men get this type of headache, and whites had a higher prevalence of tension headaches than did African Americans. Interestingly, reported headaches were higher among individuals with more education, and headaches peaked in those with graduate school education (Schwartz et al., 1998). Tension headaches are generally not as severe as migraine headaches, and they can usually be relieved with aspirin or other analgesics.

migraine headache Severe headache characterized by constriction of cranial arteries, followed by dilation of the cerebral blood vessels, resulting in moderate to severe pain.

tension headache A headache thought to be produced by prolonged contraction of the scalp and neck muscles, resulting in vascular constriction.

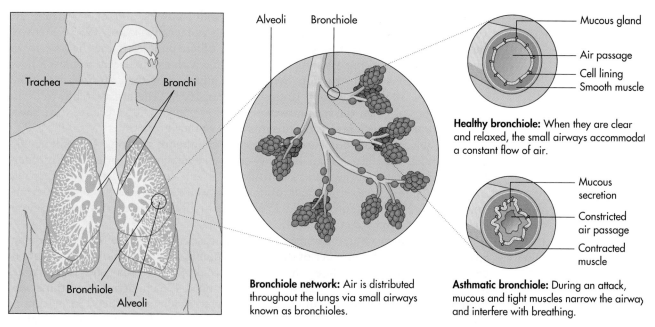

Healthy bronchiole: When they are clear and relaxed, the small airways accommodate a constant flow of air.

Bronchiole network: Air is distributed throughout the lungs via small airways known as bronchioles.

Asthmatic bronchiole: During an attack, mucous and tight muscles narrow the airway and interfere with breathing.

When the respiratory system is working properly, the air we breathe passes in and out of the lungs through a network of airways (above, left). But for people with asthma, even a minor irritant will set off an immune response that can shut down the airways.

Figure 6.4 An Asthma Attack Asthma attacks and deaths have increased dramatically during the past fifteen years. *Source:* Cowley & Underwood (1997, p. 61).

Cluster Headaches **Cluster headaches** are excruciating stabbing or burning sensations located in the eye or cheek. Episodic cluster headaches occur in cycles, and incapacitating attacks can happen up to ten times a day (Jones, 1996). Each attack may last from fifteen minutes to three hours before ending abruptly. Along with the headache, the individual may experience eye tearing or a stuffy nose on the same side of the head on which the pain is felt (Silberstein, 1998). In attempting to alleviate the pain, an individual may pace relentlessly and rub his or her head. The cycles may last from several days to months, followed by pain-free periods. In chronic cluster headaches, no more than one week passes without a headache. Only about 10 to 20 percent of cluster headaches are of the chronic type. Cluster headaches do not appear to run in families and, in contrast to other headaches, are more common in men (Silberstein, 1998).

Asthma

Asthma is a chronic inflammatory disease of the airways in the lungs. Bronchiospasms, excessive mucus secretions, and edema (fluid accumulation) constrict the airways, making it difficult to completely empty the lungs and therefore reducing the amount of air that can be inhaled (see Figure 6.4). The symptoms range from mild and infrequent to severe daily wheezing with the need to seek emergency care. In severe asthma attacks, respiratory failure can occur. The prevalence rate has increased sharply throughout the world, primarily among the more affluent and developed countries (Woodruff & Fahy, 2001). In the United States, asthma has increased dramatically in the past fifteen years. It now afflicts up to 15 million individuals, accounting for more

cluster headache Excruciating headache that produces stabbing or burning sensations in an eye or cheek.

asthma A chronic inflammatory disease of the airways in the lungs, in which the airways become constricted, making it difficult to empty the lungs and therefore reducing the amount of air that can be inhaled.

than 5,400 deaths a year (National Center for Health Statistics, 2001a). The death rate from asthma has risen disproportionately among women (Rollason, 1995). Many of the deaths may occur because the individual or others underestimate the severity of attacks and delay seeking assistance. Many people with asthma seem to have a poor perception of air flow obstruction. Some fail to notice when their air flow is reduced by as much as 50 percent (Stout, Kotses, & Creer, 1997). The disease tends to occur mainly in persons under the age of seventeen, and as many as 80 percent of them show substantial or complete remission of symptoms as they grow older (Mrazek, 1993). Asthma is the most common chronic disease of childhood, affecting 4.8 million children (Girard et al., 1998). Ethnic minority children living in inner cities are disproportionately represented in the increased incidence. In one study involving 654 Hispanic American children between the ages of nine and twelve, nearly 28 percent had symptoms of asthma (Christensen et al., 1996). The highest prevalence is found among Puerto Ricans (Burchard et al., 2004).

The recent increase in the number of asthma cases in the United States is puzzling. Suspicion grows that a number of different pollutants (cigarette smoke, air pollution, pet hair and dander, indoor molds, and cockroaches) may be responsible. Rosenstreich, Eggleston, and Kattan (1997) examined 476 children with asthma who lived in inner cities. They found that 23 percent were allergic to pets, 35 percent to dust mites, and 37 percent to cockroaches. Allergy to cockroaches had the highest association with emergency room treatment, hospitalization, and school absences in these children. Although pollutants may be responsible for the increase in asthma cases, psychological factors seem to be important in producing attacks (Chen et al., 2003). After the September 11, 2003, attack, about 27 percent of Manhattan residents with asthma reported severe asthma symptoms (Centers for Disease Control and Prevention, 2002). Children who have parents with asthma are more likely to develop this condition if their family environment is characterized as being negative than are children who have asthmatic parents who did not provide poor or conflictual parenting (McCarthy, 2002). Emotional arousal has been found to be associated with decreased size of the airways of the lung (Isenberg, Lehrer, & Hochron, 1992) or feelings of breathlessness in individuals with asthma (Rietveld, Everaerd, & van Beest, 2000).

Perspectives on Etiology

As we mentioned earlier, psychologists are becoming increasingly aware that single-cause models of psychophysiological illness are inadequate. Illness results from interactions at the cellular, organismic, interpersonal, group, and environmental levels (Drossman, 1998). However, different theoretical perspectives have offered a variety of insights in attempting to answer the following questions. Why does stress produce a physical disorder in some people but not in others? If a disorder does develop in someone experiencing emotional duress, what determines what the psychophysiological illness will be? Innate, developmental, and acquired characteristics certainly interact, but the nature and contribution of each are not well understood. In this section we discuss different perspectives on cause—none of which adequately accounts for all the factors involved.

Psychodynamic Perspective Psychoanalysts have developed several formulations to explain physical disorders associated with psychological factors. According to these formulations, each type of psychophysiological disorder is produced by a specific unconscious conflict.

Alexander (1950) believed that an early unresolved childhood conflict produces an emotional response that is reactivated in adulthood. For example, the inhibition of aggressive feelings may produce hypertension or other cardiovascular disorders. According to this hypothesis, aggression and dependency needs are the basis for most of the psychophysiological disorders. The expression of dependency needs increases activity of the parasympathetic division of the autonomic nervous system. Chronic activation of this division produces such disorders as diarrhea and colitis. If feelings of anger predominate, the energy-expending sympathetic nervous system is activated, which may result in hypertension, migraine headaches, or arthritis.

Although Alexander's theory is impressive in breadth and specificity, his propositions have not been experimentally supported. However, the idea that certain emotions or personality dynamics are related to specific disorders has received some support (Mann & James, 1998; Martin & Seneviratne, 1997; Ranchor et al., 1997; Schulz et al., 1996; Spiro et al., 1995).

Biological Perspective Some evidence points to a genetic base for the development of psychophysiological disorders. For example, migraine headaches appear to run in families and to have a genetic component (Silberstein, 1998). Additionally, African Americans as a group are at risk for hypertension. A modest significant correlation on cardiovascular reactivity has been found between monozygotic twins. Presumably a greater reactivity could contribute to the development of hypertension and coronary heart disease. Children with one asthmatic parent have a 20 percent chance of developing asthma. The probability increases to 50 percent with two asthmatic parents. (Mrazek, 1993).

The Behavioral Perspective As noted, classical conditioning may be involved in the psychophysiological disorders. The conditioning of neutral stimuli can elicit or activate a physiological response through generalization, as discussed in the chapter "Assessment and Classification of Abnormal Behavior." The greater the number of stimuli that can produce a specific physical reaction, the greater the probability that a chronic condition will develop.

Psychophysiological reactions can generalize to such stimuli as words, thoughts, and odors (Rietveld, Van Beest, & Everaerd, 2000). Such generalizations may increase the probability of developing asthma or other disorders. In a review of twenty studies involving 427 persons with asthma, more than one-third of the persons with asthma were found to be "reactors," that is, they showed significant bronchial effects following suggestion that they were being exposed to substances to which they were allergic when in fact they were exposed only to neutral solutions (Isenberg et al., 1992).

Sociocultural Perspectives Conflicts with cultural expectations appear also to result in physiological symptoms. Samoans, for example, have a culture that stresses rigid control of behaviors, including strict discipline for children, control of anger for females, and suppression of emotions in adults. Steele and McGarvey (1997) hypothesized that the Samoan traditional pattern in which women were expected to suppress their emotions could conflict with the expanded roles expected by modern young women, resulting in increases in blood pressure. In support of their hypothesis, the investigators found an interesting contrast: higher blood pressure was related to an inhibition of anger in young women but to an outward expression of anger in older women. Thus conflicting cultural gender expectations can influence physiological responses.

Maintaining Tradition and Reducing Risk—It Works for Some   Japanese Americans who maintain traditional lifestyles have a lower rate of coronary heart disease than those who have acculturated. The difference does not appear to be due to diet or other investigated risk factors. What reasons can you come up with to explain the findings?

Cultural factors are also implicated in a study of Japanese persons living in Japan, Hawaii, and California, in which researchers found the highest mortality rate from coronary heart disease among those living in California and the lowest among those living in Japan. In trying to decide what was responsible for the variation in mortality rates, the researchers compared Japanese immigrants who had maintained a traditional lifestyle with those who had acculturated (adopted the habits and attitudes prevalent in their new home). The CHD rate for acculturated Japanese individuals was five times greater than that for those who had retained their traditional values (Marmot & Syme, 1976). Perhaps breaking close social and community ties, which is part of the acculturation process, promoted a greater vulnerability to the disease.

Treatment of Psychophysiological Disorders

behavioral medicine A number of disciplines that study social, psychological, and lifestyle influences on health.

Treatment programs for psychophysiological disorders generally consist of both medical treatment for the physical symptoms and conditions and psychological therapy to eliminate stress and anxiety. **Behavioral medicine** comprises a number of disciplines that study social, psychological, and lifestyle influences on health. This combined approach provides a wide array of approaches to these disorders, with mainly positive results. Two of the dominant psychological approaches are stress management and anxiety management programs, which usually include either relaxation training or biofeedback. The concept of combined therapies is illustrated in the following case:

> Jerry R. is a thirty-three-year-old male who has always taken pride in the vigor with which he attacks everything he does. He worries about keeping slim, so he exercises at a health spa three nights a week. He was shocked to discover, during a routine physical exam, that he has borderline high blood pressure.
>
> His physician recommended that he take steps to lower his blood pressure by reducing his intake of salt, caffeine, and alcohol. Because coronary heart disease runs in Jerry's family, the physician also recommended that Jerry decrease his cholesterol intake by reducing the amount of eggs, saturated fats, and whole milk in his diet. He commended Jerry for having given up smoking five months previously.
>
> Finally, Jerry was urged to become active in a stress management program geared toward lowering his blood pressure and preventing coronary heart disease. Although the effectiveness of these programs is somewhat controversial, Jerry's physician believes Jerry has more to gain than to lose by participating in a course of biofeedback and relaxation training.

The success of combined treatment programs suggests that the psychological approach to the treatment of certain physical disorders is more than a passing fad. Relaxation training, biofeedback, and cognitive-behavioral interventions are emerging as the primary stress management techniques of behavioral medicine. They are used in treating all the psychophysiological disorders described in this chapter.

Relaxation and Biofeedback

Relaxation training involves having an individual acquire the ability to relax the muscles of the body through a set of muscle relaxation exercises. This procedure reduces feelings of tension and anxiety. In **biofeedback training,** the client is taught to *voluntarily* control some physiological function, such as heart rate or blood pressure. During training, the client receives second-by-second information (feedback) regarding the activity of the organ or function of interest. For someone attempting to lower high blood pressure, for example, the feedback might be actual blood pressure readings, which might be presented visually on a screen or as some auditory signal transmitted through a set of headphones. The biofeedback device enables the patient to learn his or her own idiosyncratic method for controlling the particular physiological function. Eventually the patient learns to use that method without benefit of the feedback device.

relaxation training A therapeutic technique in which the person acquires the ability to relax the muscles of the body in almost any circumstances.

biofeedback training A therapeutic technique in which the person is taught to voluntarily control a particular physiological function, such as heart rate or blood pressure.

> A twenty-three-year-old male patient was found to have a resting heart rate that varied between 95 and 120 beats per minute. He reported that his symptoms first appeared during his last year in high school, when his episodes of tachycardia were associated with apprehension over exams. The patient came into treatment concerned that his high heart rate might lead to a serious cardiac condition.
>
> The treatment consisted of eight sessions of biofeedback training. The patient's heart rate was monitored, and he was provided with both a visual and an auditory feedback signal. After the treatment period, his heart rate had stabilized and was within normal limits. One year later, his heart rate averaged 73 beats per minute. The patient reported that he had learned to control his heart rate during stressful situations such as job interviews, both relaxing and concentrating on reducing the heart rate. (Janssen, 1983)

Controlling Physiological Responses In biofeedback training, clients can get instant-to-instant information about their heart rate, blood pressure, muscle tension, temperature, and other physical functions. Interestingly, after the training, clients can often effect changes in these autonomic areas, but they are uncertain as to how they do it.

Cognitive-Behavioral Interventions

Because hostility is associated with hypertension, cognitive-behavioral programs have been developed to reduce the expression of this emotion. In one study, individuals with hypertension participated in a six-week anger management program (Larkin & Zayfert, 1996). When initially exposed to confrontational role-playing situations, they experienced sharp rises in blood pressure. The participants learned to relax by using muscle relaxation techniques and to change their thoughts about confrontational situations. They also received assertiveness training to learn appropriate ways of expressing disagreements. After the various types of training, their blood pressure was significantly reduced when they again participated in confrontational role-playing scenes.

Cognitive strategies to improve coping skills and to manage stress have also been effective in improving both physiological functioning and psychological distress in HIV seropositive men (Cruess et al., 2000). Among patients with asthma, engaging in three sessions of writing about a trauma ("write about the most stressful experience in your life") significantly improved lung function compared with those patients who wrote only about time management (Stone et al., 2000).

Although much is known about the psychophysiological disorders, a great deal is still to be learned. Psychologists in behavioral medicine are seeking to decrease a person's vulnerability to physical problems by suggesting changes in lifestyle, attitudes, and perceptions. Attention is also directed toward altering the course of an illness after it has occurred. The field of behavioral medicine will continue to receive greater attention from psychologists. We are only beginning to understand the relationship between psychological factors and physical illnesses.

CHECKPOINT REVIEW

asthma *(p. 159)*
behavioral medicine *(p. 162)*
biofeedback training *(p. 163)*
cluster headache *(p. 159)*
coronary heart disease (CHD) *(p. 152)*
essential hypertension *(p. 156)*
migraine headache *(p. 158)*
relaxation training *(p. 163)*
tension headache *(p. 158)*

What is the evidence that illnesses such as coronary heart disease, hypertension, headaches, and asthma are affected by emotional states, and how are the emotions involved?
- The incidence of CHD is influenced by social factors, personality, and lifestyle, as well as by such risk factors as smoking, obesity, inactivity, hypertension, and cholesterol levels.
- Hypertension is related to the emotions and how they are expressed, especially anger. There are gender and ethnic differences in the prevalence of hypertension.
- Migraine headaches involve the constriction and then the dilation of blood vessels in the brain.
- Tension headaches are thought to be caused by contraction of the neck and scalp muscles, which results in vascular constriction. These headaches can also occur in the absence of detectable tension.

- Cluster headaches are excruciating and occur on one side of the head near the eye.
- The onset of headaches may be preceded by emotional stress.
- Asthma attacks result from constriction of the airways in the lungs. Breathing is extremely difficult during the attacks, and acute anxiety may worsen the situation. In most cases, physical and psychological causes interact.

What are possible causes of psychophysiological disorders?

- Etiological theories must be able to explain why some people develop a physical disorder under stress, whereas others do not, and what determines which psychophysiological illness develops.
- None of the traditional perspectives does this in a satisfactory way.
- According to the psychodynamic perspective, the particular illness that is manifested depends on the stage of psychosexual development and the type of unresolved unconscious conflict involved.
- Biological explanations focus on genetic influences and inherited reactivity.
- The behavioral perspective emphasizes the importance of classical and operant conditioning in acquiring or maintaining these disorders.

What methods have been developed to treat the psychophysiological disorders?

- Behavioral medicine combines a number of approaches to psychophysiological disorders.
- These disorders are treated through stress management or anxiety management programs, combined with medical treatment for physical symptoms or conditions.
- Relaxation training and biofeedback training, which help the client learn to control muscular or organic functioning, are usually a part of such programs.
- Cognitive-behavioral interventions, which involve changing anxiety-arousing thoughts, have also been useful.

FOCUS QUESTIONS

- What kinds of personality patterns are associated with mental disorders?
- Why do some people have a callous disregard for others and lack guilt and anxiety?

7 *Personality Disorders*

Personality refers to traits, attitudes, and behaviors that characterize an individual. We often view a person as being shy, happy-go-lucky, friendly, or hostile. These characterizations describe the person's personality pattern. Sometimes, the patterns are extreme and maladaptive. In this chapter, different DSM-IV-TR personality disorders are examined.

The Personality Disorders

Personality disorders are characterized by inflexible, long-standing, and maladaptive personality traits that cause significant functional impairment or subjective distress for the individual. In addition to personal and social difficulties, people with these disorders also display temperamental deficiencies or aberrations, rigidity in dealing with life problems, and defective perceptions of self and others.

In spite of all these difficulties, people with personality disorders often function well enough to get along without aid from others. Thus people with these disorders rarely seek help from mental health professionals, and those who do enter treatment often terminate prematurely (Clarkin & Levy, 2004). For all these reasons, the incidence of personality disorders has been difficult to ascertain. Available statistics indicate that personality disorders account for 5 to 15 percent of admissions to hospitals and outpatient clinics. The overall lifetime prevalence of personality disorders is 10 to 13 percent, which indicates that the disorders are relatively common in the general population (Phillips & Gunderson, 1999; Weissman, 1993).

Gender distribution varies from one personality disorder to another. Men are more likely than women to be diagnosed as having paranoid, obsessive-compulsive, and antisocial personality disorders, whereas women more often receive diagnoses of borderline, dependent, or histrionic personality disorders (Reich, 1987; Widiger & Spitzer, 1991). The existence of gender differences in the diagnosis of certain personality disorders is widely accepted. The question being debated is whether these differences are attributable to biases in making diagnoses or to actual gender variations in disorders (Widiger & Coker, 2002).

Gender bias in the diagnostic system occurs when diagnostic categories are not valid and when they have a different impact on men and women. Note that the mere fact that men and women have different prevalence rates for a particular disorder is not sufficient to prove gender bias. Rates may differ because of actual biological conditions (for example, a genetic predisposition) or social conditions (stressors) that affect one gender more than another. In order to call the diagnostic system itself biased, we must be able to attribute the differences to errors or problems in the categories, diagnostic criteria, or procedures in making a diagnosis. At this point, there is disagreement on how to interpret many of the diagnostic differences found.

Similar issues arise in relation to culture and ethnicity. Not surprisingly, one's culture shapes habits, customs, values, and personality characteristics, so that expressions of personality in one culture may differ from those in another culture. Asians, for example, are more likely to exhibit shyness and collectivism, whereas Americans are more likely to show assertiveness and individualism. Japanese and Asian Indians

personality disorder A disorder characterized by inflexible and maladaptive personality traits that cause significant functional impairment or subjective distress for the individual.

167

Linking Symptoms with Personality Disorders Symptoms such as chronic distrust and suspiciousness must be evaluated within the context of an individual's life before making a judgment as to whether the symptoms the person is experiencing are indicative of paranoid personality. These undocumented immigrants applying for amnesty at an Immigration and Naturalization Service office may be distrustful and suspicious, but understandably so. What criteria would you use to distinguish between paranoid personality disorder and normal variations of distrust and suspiciousness?

display the overt dependent behaviors characteristic of dependent personality more than Americans or Europeans display them (Bornstein, 1997). Does this mean that people in Japan and India are more likely to have this personality disorder? More likely, the high incidence of these behaviors reflects the influence of other factors, one of which may be cultural bias in the classification system. Anyone making judgments about personality functioning and disturbance must consider the individual's cultural, ethnic, and social background (American Psychiatric Association, 2000a).

The signs of a personality disorder usually become evident during adolescence. In some cases, a person with a personality disorder may have had a similar childhood disorder. For example, it is common to find that a person diagnosed as having schizoid personality disorder was previously diagnosed as having schizoid disorder of childhood. When the features of certain childhood disorders persist into adulthood (that is, beyond age eighteen), the diagnosis may be changed to a personality disorder.

In the diagnostic scheme of DSM-IV-TR, personality disorders are recorded on Axis II. A person may receive diagnoses on both Axis I and Axis II. For example, a person with a personality disorder may also be diagnosed with schizophrenia or alcohol dependency (Axis I disorders). Usually, people with personality disorders are hospitalized only when a second, superimposed disorder so impairs social functioning that they require inpatient care. In fact, the treatment outcome for people with an Axis I disorder who also have a personality disorder is worse than for those who have an Axis I disorder alone (Clarkin & Levy, 2004; Benjamin & Karpiak, 2002). The rationale for having two axes for mental disorders is that Axis II disorders generally begin in childhood or adolescence and persist in a stable form into adulthood. Axis I disorders usually fail to show these characteristics.

As Figure 7.1 illustrates, DSM-IV-TR lists ten specific personality disorders and groups them into three clusters, depending on whether they are characterized by odd or eccentric behaviors; dramatic, emotional, or erratic behaviors; or anxious or fearful behaviors. The clustering of these disorders is based more on descriptive similarities than on similarities in etiology (Phillips & Gunderson, 1999). Clustering and categorizing the disorders also mask dimensional aspects. That is, the task of categorizing can conceal differences in the degree to which people possess certain characteristics. In any event, we begin by discussing each of the ten personality disorders rather briefly. Then we focus on one of them—*antisocial personality disorder*—in more detail, primarily because more information is available for this disorder.

Disorders Characterized by Odd or Eccentric Behaviors

Three personality disorders are included in this cluster: paranoid personality, schizoid personality, and schizotypal personality.

Paranoid Personality Disorder   People with **paranoid personality disorder** show unwarranted suspiciousness, hypersensitivity, and reluctance to trust others. They interpret others' motives as being malevolent, question their loyalty or trustworthiness, persistently bear grudges, or are suspicious of the fidelity of their spouses. They may demonstrate restricted affect (that is, aloofness and lack of emotion), and they tend to be rigid andpreoccupied with unfounded beliefs that stem from their suspicions and sensitivity. These beliefs are extremely resistant to change. Many persons with this disorder fail to go for treatment because of their guardedness and mistrust (Meissner, 2001).

Certain groups, such as refugees and members of minority groups, may display guarded or defensive behaviors not because of a disorder but because of their minority group status or their unfamiliarity with the majority society. To avoid misinterpreting the clinical significance of such behaviors, clinicians assessing members of these groups must do so cautiously.

DSM-IV-TR estimates the prevalence of paranoid personality disorder to be about 0.5 to 2.5 percent of the population, and probably somewhat higher among males (see Figure 7.1). Here is an example of paranoid personality disorder:

> Ralph and Ann married after knowing each other for two months. The first year of their marriage was relatively happy, although Ralph tended to be domineering and very protective of his wife. Ann had always known that Ralph was a jealous person who demanded a great deal of attention. She was initially pleased that her husband was concerned about how other men looked at her; she felt that it showed Ralph really cared for her. It soon became clear, however, that his jealousy was excessive. One day when she came home from shopping later than usual, Ralph exploded. He demanded an explanation but did not accept Ann's, which was that she stopped to talk with a neighbor. Ralph told her that he wanted her to be home when he returned from work—always. Believing him to be in a bad mood, Ann said nothing. Later, she found out that Ralph had called the neighbor to confirm her story.
>
> The situation progressively worsened. Ralph began to leave work early to be with his wife. He said that business was slow and that they could spend more time together. Whenever the phone rang, Ralph insisted on answering it himself. Wrong numbers and male callers took on special significance for him; he felt they must be trying to call Ann. Ann found it difficult to discuss the matter with Ralph. He was always quick to take the offensive, and he expressed very little sympathy or understanding toward her.
>
> Ralph's suspicions regarding his wife's fidelity were obviously unjustified. Nothing that Ann did implicated her with other men. Yet Ralph persisted in his pathological jealousy and suspiciousness, and he took the offensive when she suggested that he was wrong in distrusting her. This behavior pattern, along with Ralph's absence of warmth and tenderness, indicates paranoid personality disorder.
>
> Follow-up: After several weeks of treatment, Ann began to feel stronger in her relationship with Ralph. During one confrontation, in which Ralph objected to her seeing the therapist, Ann asserted that she would continue the treatment. She said that she had always been faithful to him and that his jealousy was driving them apart. In a rare moment, Ralph broke down and started crying. He said that he needed her and begged her not to leave him. At this time, Ralph and Ann are each seeing a counselor for marital therapy.

paranoid personality disorder
A personality disorder characterized by unwarranted suspiciousness, hypersensitivity, and a reluctance to confide in others.

Some psychodynamic explanations propose that persons with paranoid personality disorder engage in the defense mechanism of projection, denying their unacceptable impulses and attributing them to others ("I am not hostile; they are"). Vaillant (1994) has shown that paranoid personality is associated with projection to a striking degree.

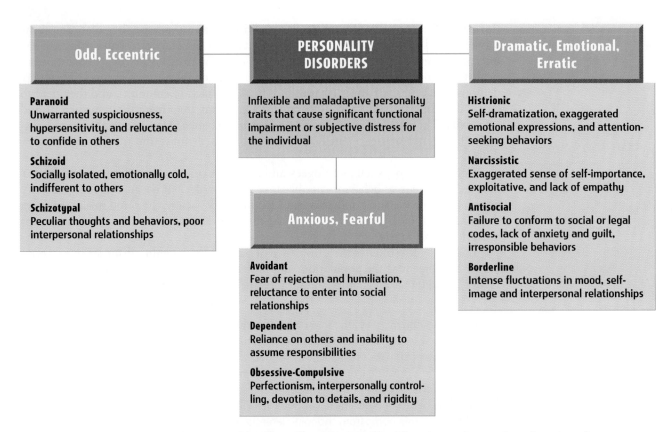

Figure 7.1 **Disorders Chart: Personality Disorders** *Source:* Based on American Psychiatric Association (2000), Corbitt & Widiger (1995), Marmar (1988), and Weissman (1993). Prevalence figures and gender differences have varied from study to study, and investigators may disagree on the rates.

Schizoid Personality Disorder **Schizoid personality disorder** is marked primarily by social isolation, emotional coldness, and indifference to others. People with this disorder have a long history of impairment of social functioning. They are often described as being reclusive and withdrawn (Siever, 1981). Many live alone in apartments or furnished rooms and engage in solitary recreational activities such as watching television, reading, or taking walks. They tend to neither desire nor enjoy close relationships; they have few activities that provide pleasure. Because of a lack of capacity or desire to form social relationships, people with schizoid disorder are perceived by others as peculiar and aloof and therefore inadequate as dating or marital partners. The disorder appears to be uncommon, and slightly more males are diagnosed with it, according to DSM-IV-TR. Members of different cultures vary in their social behaviors, and diagnosticians must consider the cultural background of individuals who show schizoid symptoms.

People with schizoid disorder may have to relate to others in the workplace and similar situations, but these relationships are superficial and frequently awkward. In such situations, people with this disorder tend to comply with the requests or feelings of others, perhaps in an attempt to avoid extensive involvement, conflicts, and expressions of hostility. They tend to prefer a hermit-like existence (Stone, 2001). Social isolation can be found even in their marital relationships. Spitzer et al. (1981) describe the case of a man who had married primarily to please his parents. After a while, his wife literally forced him to see a therapist because he was unaffectionate, lacked interest in

schizoid personality disorder
A personality disorder characterized by social isolation, emotional coldness, and indifference to others.

PERSONALITY DISORDERS	Prevalence (%)	Gender Differences	Age of Onset*	Course**
Paranoid	0.5 – 2.5	Higher in males	—	—
Schizoid	0.2 – 0.3	Higher in males	—	—
Schizotypal	2.5 – 3.0	Higher in males	—	—
Histrionic	0.7 – 3.0	None	—	—
Narcissistic	0.3 – 1.0	Higher in males	—	—
Antisocial	2.0	Higher in males	—	—
Borderline	1.0 – 2.0	Higher in females	—	—
Avoidant	0.3 – 1.0	None	—	—
Dependent	1.9 – 2.5	Unclear	—	—
Obsessive-Compulsive	1.0 – 1.9	Higher in males	—	—

* In all of the personality disorders, early symptoms appear in childhood or adolescence.
** Personality disorders tend to be stable and to endure over time, although symptoms of antisocial and borderline personality disorders tend to remit with age.

Figure 7.1 Disorders Chart: Personality Disorders (continued)

sex, and was unwilling to participate in family activities. He was as emotionally unresponsive to members of his family as he was to his colleagues at work.

Schizotypal Personality Disorder   People who have **schizotypal personality disorder** manifest peculiar thoughts and behaviors and have poor interpersonal relationships. Many believe they possess magical thinking abilities or special powers ("I can predict what people will say before they say it"), and some are subject to recurrent illusions ("I feel that my dead father is watching me"). Speech oddities, such as frequent digression or vagueness in conversation, are often present. The disorder occurs in approximately 3 percent of the population (American Psychiatric Association, 2000a), more frequently among men than women. Again, the evaluation of individuals must take into account their cultural milieu. Superstitious beliefs, delusions, and hallucinations may be condoned or encouraged in certain religious ceremonies or other cultures.

The peculiarities seen in schizotypal personality disorder stem from distortions or difficulties in cognition (Siever, 1981). That is, these people seem to have problems in thinking and perceiving. People with this disorder often show social isolation, hypersensitivity, and inappropriate affect (emotions). They seem to lack pleasure from social interactions (Blanchard et al., 2000).

The prevailing belief is that the disorder is defined primarily by cognitive distortions, however, and that affective and interpersonal problems are secondary. Research has demonstrated some cognitive processing abnormalities in individuals with this disorder that help to explain many of the symptoms (Stone, 2001).

The man described in the following case was diagnosed as having schizotypal personality disorder:

> A forty-one-year-old man was referred to a community mental health center's activities program for help in improving his social skills. He had a lifelong pattern of social isolation, with no real friends, and spent long hours worrying that his angry thoughts about his older brother would cause his brother harm. On interview the patient was distant and somewhat distrustful. He described in elaborate and often irrelevant detail his rather uneventful and routine daily life.... For two days he had studied the washing instructions on a new pair of jeans—Did "Wash before wearing" mean that the jeans were to be washed before wearing the first time, or did they need, for some reason, to be washed each time before they were worn? ... He asked the interviewer whether, if he joined the program, he would be required to participate in groups. He said that groups made him very nervous because he felt that if he revealed too much personal information, such as the amount of money that he had in the bank, people would take advantage of him or manipulate him for their own benefit. (Spitzer et al., 1994, pp. 289–290)

The man's symptoms included absence of close friends, magical thinking (worrying that his thoughts might harm his brother), being distant in the interview, and social anxiety. They are associated with schizotypal personality disorder. As is true of schizoid personality disorder, many characteristics of schizotypal personality disorder resemble those of schizophrenia, although in less serious form. For example, people with schizophrenia exhibit problems in personality characteristics, psychophysiological responses, and information processing—deficits that have also been observed among persons with schizotypal personality disorder (Grove et al., 1991; Lenzenweger, 2001; Lenzenweger, Cornblatt, & Putnick, 1991). Some evidence is consistent with a genetic interpretation of the link between the two disorders. Kendler (1988) found a higher risk of schizotypal personality disorder among relatives of people diagnosed with schizophrenia than among members of a control group. In general, family, twin, and adoption studies support the genetic relationship between schizophrenia and schizotypal personality disorder.

schizotypal personality disorder
A personality disorder characterized by peculiar thoughts and behaviors and by poor interpersonal relationships.

Histrionic Behavior
One criterion of histrionic personality disorder is attention seeking. The person receiving the tongue piercing to display a tongue ring may be interested in getting the attention of others. To warrant a diagnosis, however, the individual would also need to show a number of additional characteristics, such as self-dramatization, exaggerated expression of emotions, shallowness, and egocentricity. Can you think of any cultures in which attention seeking is discouraged?

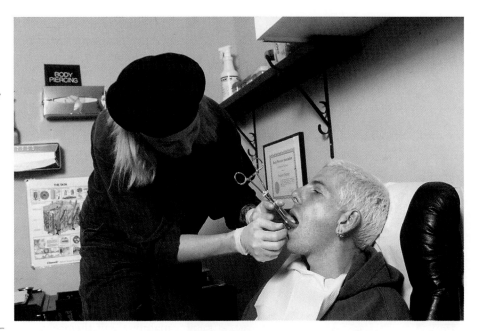

Disorders Characterized by Dramatic, Emotional, or Erratic Behaviors

The group of disorders characterized by dramatic, emotional, or erratic behaviors includes four personality disorders: histrionic, narcissistic, antisocial, and borderline.

Histrionic Personality Disorder People with **histrionic personality disorder** engage in self-dramatization, exaggerated expression of emotions, and attention-seeking behaviors. The desire for attention may lead to flamboyant acts or flirtatious behaviors (Phillips & Gunderson, 1999). Despite superficial warmth and charm, the histrionic person is typically shallow and egocentric. Individuals from different cultures vary in the extent to which they display their emotions, but the histrionic person goes well beyond cultural norms. In the United States, about 1 to 3 percent of the population may have this disorder. Gender differences are not evident (Corbitt & Widiger, 1995). Histrionic behaviors were evident in a woman client seen by one of the authors:

> The woman was a thirty-three-year-old real estate agent who entered treatment for problems involving severe depression. Her boyfriend had recently told her that she was a self-centered and phony person. He found out that she had been dating other men, despite their understanding that neither would go out with others. The woman claimed that she never considered "going out with other men" as actual dating. Once their relationship was broken, her boyfriend refused to communicate with her. The woman then angrily called the boyfriend's employer and told him that unless the boyfriend contacted her, she would commit suicide. He never did call, but instead of attempting suicide, she decided to seek psychotherapy.
>
> The woman was attractively dressed for her first therapy session. She wore a tight and clinging sweater. Several times during the session she raised her arms, supposedly to fix her hair, in a very seductive manner. Her conversation was animated and intense. When she was describing the breakup with her boyfriend, she was tearful. Later, she raged over the boyfriend's failure to call her and, at one point, called him a "son of a bitch." Near the end of the session, she seemed upbeat and cheerful, commenting that the best therapy might be for the therapist to arrange a date for her.

histrionic personality disorder
A personality disorder characterized by self-dramatization, the exaggerated expression of emotions, and attention-seeking behaviors.

Narcissistic Behavior Blanche Dubois, a character in the film *A Streetcar Named Desire,* illustrates many of the symptoms of narcissistic personality disorder, including an exaggerated sense of self-importance, an excessive need for admiration, and an inability to accept criticism or rejection. Do you think that narcissistic personality disorder is increasing among young people?

narcissistic personality disorder
A personality disorder characterized by an exaggerated sense of self-importance, an exploitative attitude, and a lack of empathy.

None of the behaviors exhibited by this client alone warrants a diagnosis of histrionic personality disorder. In combination, however, her self-dramatization, incessant drawing of attention to herself via seductive movements, angry outbursts, manipulative suicidal gesture, and lack of genuineness point to this disorder. Both biological factors, such as autonomic or emotional excitability, and environmental factors, such as parental reinforcement of a child's attention-seeking behaviors and the existence of histrionic parental models, may be important influences in the development of histrionic personality disorder (Millon & Everly, 1985).

Narcissistic Personality Disorder The clinical characteristics of **narcissistic personality disorder** are an exaggerated sense of self-importance, an exploitative attitude, and a lack of empathy. People with this disorder require attention and admiration and have difficulty accepting personal criticism. In conversations, they talk mainly about themselves and show a lack of interest in others. Many have fantasies about power or influence, and they constantly overestimate their talents and importance. Individuals diagnosed with this disorder show reflective responses and idealization involving unlimited success, a sense of entitlement, and a sense of self-importance (Hilsenroth et al., 1997). Owing to their sense of self-importance, people with narcissistic personality disorder expect to be the superior participants in all relationships. For example, they may be impatient and irate if others arrive late for a meeting but may frequently be late themselves and think nothing of it.

One narcissistic client reported, "I was denied promotion to chief executive by my board of directors, although my work was good, because they felt I had poor relations with my employees. When I complained to my wife, she agreed with the board, saying my relations with her and the children were equally bad. I don't understand. I know I'm more competent than all these people" (Masterson, 1981, p. ix). The client was depressed and angry about not being promoted and about the suggestion that he had difficulty in forming social relationships. His wife's confirmation of his problems further enraged him. During therapy, he was competitive and sought to devalue the observations of the therapist. Many persons with this disorder exhibit arrogance and grandiosity (Groopman & Cooper, 2001).

In a study that evaluated the kinds of defense mechanisms used by individuals with different personality disorders, narcissistic personality disorder was strongly associated with the use of dissociation as a defense mechanism (Vaillant, 1994). People with this disorder may use denial and dissociation to ward off feelings of inferiority developed from early childhood (Kernberg, 1975; Marmar, 1988), and they may attempt to maintain their inflated self-concept by devaluing others (Kernberg, 1975).

Narcissistic traits are common among adolescents and do not necessarily imply that a teenager has the disorder (American Psychiatric Association, 2000a). The prevalence of narcissistic personality disorder is about 1 percent, although some studies have

Borderline Personality Disorder   In the film *Fatal Attraction,* the character Alex Forrest exhibits many traits of borderline personality disorder: impulsiveness, marked fluctuations in mood, chronic feelings of emptiness, and unstable and intense interpersonal relationships. Why do women receive this diagnosis far more frequently than do men?

found lower rates. More males than females are given the diagnosis.

Antisocial Personality Disorder Chronic antisocial behavioral patterns, such as a failure to conform to social or legal codes, a lack of anxiety and guilt, and irresponsible behaviors, indicate **antisocial personality disorder.** People with this disorder show little guilt for their wrongdoing, which may include lying, using other people, and aggressive sexual acts. Their relationships with others are superficial and fleeting and involve little loyalty. Antisocial personality disorder, which is far more prevalent among men than among women, is discussed in greater detail later in this chapter.

Borderline Personality Disorder **Borderline personality disorder** is characterized by intense fluctuations in mood, self-image, and interpersonal relationships. Persons with this disorder are impulsive, have chronic feelings of emptiness, and form unstable and intense interpersonal relationships. They may be quite friendly one day and quite hostile the next. Many report the presence of malevolent others—people who were hostile or physically violent—during their early childhoods (Nigg et al., 1992). Many exhibit recurrent suicidal behaviors or gestures (Yen et al., 2003), and the probability of suicide is higher than average among those who have this disorder (Duberstein & Conwell, 1997). Although no single feature defines borderline personality disorder, its essence can be captured in the capriciousness of behaviors and the lability of moods (Millon & Everly, 1985).

According to DSM-IV-TR, the prevalence is about 2 percent of the population, with females three times more likely than males to receive the diagnosis. This is the most commonly diagnosed personality disorder in both inpatient and outpatient settings (Trull, 1995). Some researchers believe that the prevalence of the disorder is increasing because our society makes it difficult for people to maintain stable relationships and a sense of identity.

The following example illustrates some of the many facets of borderline personality disorder.

Bryan was a twenty-three-year-old graduate student majoring in sociology at a prestigious university. He was active in student government and was viewed as charismatic, articulate, and sociable. When he met other students for the first time, he could often persuade them to participate in the campus activities that interested him. Women were quite attracted to him because of his charm and self-disclosing nature. They described him as exciting, intense, and different from other men. Bryan could form close relationships with others very quickly.

Bryan could not, however, maintain his social relationships. Sometimes he would have a brief but intense affair with a woman and then abruptly and angrily ask himself what he ever saw in her. At other times, the woman would reject him after a few dates,

antisocial personality disorder
A personality disorder characterized by a failure to conform to social and legal codes, by a lack of anxiety and guilt, and by irresponsible behaviors.

borderline personality disorder
A personality disorder characterized by intense fluctuations in mood, self-image, and interpersonal relationships.

because she thought Bryan was moody, self-centered, and demanding. He often called his friends after midnight because he felt lonesome, empty, and bored and wanted to talk. Several times he threatened to commit suicide. He gave little thought to the inconvenience he was causing. Once he organized a group of students to protest the inadequate student parking the university provided. The morning of the planned protest demonstration, he announced that he no longer supported the effort. He said he was not in the right mood for the protest, much to the consternation of his followers, who had spent weeks preparing for the event. Bryan's intense but brief relationships, the marked and continual shifts in moods, and boredom with others in spite of his need for social contacts all point to borderline personality.

Masterson (1981) believes that many clients with borderline personality disorder lack purposefulness. For example, one of his clients reported, "I have such a poor self-image and so little confidence in myself that I can't decide what I want, and when I do decide, I have even more difficulty doing it" (p. ix). Masterson sees this lack as a deficiency in the borderline-personality-affected person's emotional investment in the self—a lack of directedness in long-term goals.

People who have borderline personality disorder may exhibit psychotic symptoms, such as auditory hallucinations (for example, hearing imaginary voices that tell them to commit suicide), but the symptoms are usually transient. They also usually have an ego-dystonic reaction to their hallucinations (Spitzer et al., 1981). That is, they recognize their imaginary voices or other hallucinations as being unacceptable, alien, and distressful. By contrast, a person with a psychotic disorder may not realize that his or her hallucinations are pathological. Some researchers (Trull, 1995; Trull et al., 1997) have found that individuals with borderline personality characteristics are more likely to show dysfunctional moods, interpersonal problems, poor coping, and cognitive distortions than are people without borderline personality characteristics.

Although diverse models have been used to conceptualize borderline personality disorder, most of the literature comes from those with psychodynamic perspectives. For example, Kernberg (1976) proposed the concept of object splitting—that people with borderline personality disorder perceive others as all good or all bad at different times. This split results in emotional fluctuations toward others.

Another perspective looks at the disorder from a social learning viewpoint. One view (Millon, 1981) is that borderline personality is caused by a faulty self-identity, which affects the development of consistent goals and accomplishments. As a result, persons with this disorder have difficulty coping with their own emotions and with life in general. They then develop a conflict between the need to depend on others and the need to assert themselves. A similar model (Sable, 1997) views the conflict as a desire for proximity and attachment versus a dread and avoidance of engagement, but it attributes the conflict to traumatic attachment experiences that occurred early in life, not to a faulty self-identity. A third possibility is that the fluctuations in emotions or dysfunctions in emotional regulation are at the core of the disorder (Linehan, 1987). An interesting aspect of this approach is the idea that biological factors may be responsible for the emotional dysregulation among individuals with borderline personality disorder.

Cognitive-oriented approaches have also been used. Westen (1991) defined two core aspects of borderline personality: difficulties in regulating emotions and unstable and intense interpersonal relationships. According to this approach, these two aspects are affected by distorted or inaccurate attributions (explanations for others' behaviors or attitudes). Westen's cognitive-behavioral therapy for borderline personality disorders therefore attempts to change the way clients think about and approach interpersonal situations. Another cognitive theorist, Beck, assumed that an individual's basic assumptions (that is, thoughts) play a central role in influencing perceptions, interpretations, and behavioral and emotional responses (Beck, Freeman, and Associates, 1990). Individuals with borderline personality disorder seem to have three basic assumptions: (1) "The world is dangerous and malevolent," (2) "I am powerless and vulnerable," and (3) "I am inherently unacceptable." Believing in these assumptions, individuals with this disorder become fearful, vigilant, guarded, and defensive. For these reasons, they are difficult to treat. Regardless of therapeutic approach, most individual psychotherapies end with the borderline patient's dropping out of treatment (Gunderson & Links, 2001). Finally, Linehan (1993) has developed dialectical behavior therapy for clients with borderline personality disorder. Patients are taught skills including emotional regulation, distress tolerance, and interpersonal effectiveness (Benjamin & Karpiak, 2002). This treatment has been found to decrease dropping out, improve treatment outcomes, and reduce suicidal behaviors. In fact, studies have indicated that behavior therapy that includes dialectical treatment has been effective in borderline personality disorders (Emmelkamp, 2004).

These diverse theoretical perspectives on this disorder reflect the strong interest in borderline personality. In contrast to the theoretical contributions, empirical research is sparse. Some investigators have found that individuals with the disorder have a history of chaotic family environments, including physical and sexual abuse (Clarkin, Marziali, & Munroe-Blum, 1991; Phillips & Gunderson, 1999) and family history of mood and substance-use disorders (Morey & Zanarini, 2000). Such family experiences may affect perceptions of self and others. Benjamin and Wonderlich (1994) found in one study that individuals with borderline personality disorder viewed their mothers and others in their environment as more hostile than did a comparable group of people with mood disorders.

Again, mood changes, intense and unstable interpersonal relationships, identity problems, and other characteristics associated with borderline personality disorder can be observed in all persons to a greater or lesser extent. In fact, although borderline personality disorder is associated with relationship dysfunctions and problems, so are other personality disorders (Daley, Burge, & Hammen, 2000). As is the case with other personality disorders, diagnosis is difficult, and formulations about the causes of the disorder must rely on what we know about personality development in general.

Disorders Characterized by Anxious or Fearful Behaviors

Another cluster of personality disorders is characterized by anxious or fearful behaviors. This category includes the avoidant, dependent, and obsessive-compulsive personality disorders.

Avoidant Personality Disorder   The essential features of **avoidant personality disorder** are a fear of rejection and humiliation and a reluctance to enter into social relationships. Persons with this disorder tend to have low self-esteem and to avoid social relationships without a guarantee of uncritical acceptance by others. Unlike persons with schizoid personalities, who avoid others because they lack interest, and unlike persons who are shy because of their cultural background, people with avoidant personality disorder do not desire to be alone. On the contrary, they crave affection and an active social life. They want—but fear—social contacts, and this ambivalence may be reflected in different ways. For example, many people with this disorder engage in intellectual pursuits, wear fine clothes, or are active in the artistic community (Millon, 1981). Their need for contact and relationships is often woven into their activities. Thus an avoidant person may write poems expressing the plight of the lonely or the need for human intimacy. A primary defense mechanism is fantasy, whereby wishes are fulfilled to an excessive degree in the person's imagination (Millon & Everly, 1985).

avoidant personality disorder
A personality disorder characterized by a fear of rejection and humiliation and a reluctance to enter into social relationships.

Avoidant personality disorder occurs in less than 1 percent of the population, and no gender differences are apparent (American Psychiatric Association, 2000a). People with this disorder are caught in a vicious cycle: because they are preoccupied with rejection, they are constantly alert to signs of derogation or ridicule. This concern leads to many perceived instances of rejection, which cause them to avoid others. Their social skills may then become deficient and invite criticism from others. In other words, their very fear of criticism may lead to criticism. People with avoidant personality disorder often feel depressed, anxious, angry at themselves, inferior, and inadequate.

> Jenny L., an unmarried twenty-seven-year-old bank teller, shows several features of avoidant personality disorder. Although she functions adequately at work, Jenny is extremely shy, sensitive, and quiet with fellow employees. She perceives others as being insensitive and gross. If the bank manager jokes with other tellers, she feels that the manager prefers them to her.
>
> Jenny has very few hobbies. A great deal of her time is spent watching television and eating chocolates. (As a result, she is about forty pounds overweight.) Television romances are her favorite programs; after watching one, she tends to daydream about having an intense romantic relationship. Jenny L. eventually sought treatment for her depression and loneliness.

Some researchers believe that avoidant personality disorder is on a continuum with the Axis I disorder social phobia, whereas others see it as a distinct disorder that simply has features in common with social phobia (Sutherland, 2001). Little research has been conducted on the etiology of avoidant personality disorder. One suggestion (Marmar, 1988) is that a complex interaction of early childhood environmental experiences and innate temperament produce the disorder. Parental rejection and censure, reinforced by rejecting peers, have been proposed as factors in the disorder (Phillips & Gunderson, 1999).

Dependent Personality Disorder People who rely on others and are unwilling to assume responsibility show **dependent personality disorder.** These people lack self-confidence, and they subordinate their needs to those of the people on whom they depend. Nevertheless, casual observers may fail to recognize or may misinterpret their dependency and inability to make decisions. Friends may perceive dependent personalities as understanding and tolerant, without realizing that they are fearful of taking the initiative because they are afraid of disrupting the relationship. In addition, a dependent personality may allow his or her spouse to be dominant or abusive for fear that the spouse will otherwise leave. Beck and associates (1990) believe that the dependency is not simply a matter of being passive and unassertive, problems that can be treated with assertiveness training. Rather, dependent personalities have two deeply ingrained assumptions that affect their thoughts, perceptions, and behaviors. First, they see themselves as inherently inadequate and unable to cope. Second, they conclude that their course of action should be to find someone who can take care of them. Depression, helplessness, and suppressed anger are often present in dependent personality disorder.

The individual's environment must be considered before rendering a diagnosis of dependent personality disorder. The socializing process that trains people to be independent, assertive, and individual rather than group oriented is not equally valued in all cultures. Nor do all people manifest dependency all the time in the cultures that do value it. Some individuals, such as hospitalized patients, typically develop some degree of dependency during confinement.

dependent personality disorder
A personality disorder characterized by reliance on others and an unwillingness to assume responsibility.

The prevalence of this disorder is about 2.5 percent. The prevalence by gender is unclear. Bornstein (1997) finds evidence that it is found more often among men than among women, but Corbitt and Widiger (1995) believe there are no gender differences in this disorder. The following case illustrates a dependent personality disorder that cannot be attributed to cultural or situational factors.

> Jim was fifty-six, a single man who was living with his seventy-eight-year-old widowed mother. When his mother was recently hospitalized for cancer, Jim decided to see a therapist. He was distraught and depressed over his mother's condition. Jim indicated that he did not know what to do. His mother had always taken care of him, and, in his view, she always knew best. Even when he was young, his mother had "worn the pants" in the family. The only time that he was away from his family was during his six years of military service. He was wounded in the Korean War, was returned to the United States, and spent a few months in a Veterans Administration hospital. He then went to live with his mother. Because of his service-connected injury, Jim was unable to work full time. His mother welcomed him home, and she structured all his activities.
>
> At one point, Jim met and fell in love with a woman, but his mother disapproved of her. During a confrontation between the mother and Jim's woman friend, each demanded that Jim make a commitment to her. This was quite traumatic for Jim. His mother finally grabbed him and yelled that he must tell the other woman to go. Jim tearfully told the woman that he was sorry but she must go, and the woman angrily left.
>
> While Jim was relating his story, it was clear to the therapist that Jim harbored some anger toward his mother, though he overtly denied any feelings of hostility. Also clear were his dependency and his inability to take responsibility. His life had always been structured, first by his mother and then by the military. His mother's illness meant that his structured world might crumble.

People clearly differ in the degree to which they are dependent or submissive. How dependency is explained varies according to theoretical perspective. From the psychodynamic perspective, the disorder is a result of maternal deprivation, which causes fixation at the oral stage of development (Marmar, 1988). Behavioral learning theorists believe that a family or social environment that rewards dependent behaviors and punishes independence may promote dependency. Some cognitive theorists attribute dependent personality disorder to the development of distorted beliefs about one's inadequacies and helplessness that discourage independence. Research findings (Bornstein, 1997) show that dependency is associated with overprotective, authoritarian parenting styles. Presumably, these parenting styles prevent the child from developing a sense of autonomy and self-efficacy. In general, dependent personality disorder is successfully treated more often than other personality disorders, such as borderline or antisocial personality disorder (Perry, 2001).

Obsessive-Compulsive Personality Disorder The characteristics of **obsessive-compulsive personality disorder** are perfectionism, a tendency to be interpersonally controlling, devotion to details, and rigidity. Again, these traits are found in many normal people. Unlike normal people, however, individuals with obsessive-compulsive personality disorder show marked impairment in occupational or social functioning. Their relationships with others may be quite stiff, formal, and distant (McCullough & Maltsberger, 2001). Further, the extent of the character rigidity is greater among people who have this disorder (Weintraub, 1981). Unlike obsessive-compulsive disorder, in which there are specific recurrent thoughts or repetitive behaviors (see the

obsessive-compulsive personality disorder A personality disorder characterized by perfectionism, a tendency to be interpersonally controlling, devotion to details, and rigidity.

chapter "Anxiety Disorders"), obsessive-compulsive personality disorder involves general traits of perfectionism, inflexibility, and attention to details.

The preoccupation with details, rules, and possible errors leads to indecision and an inability to see "the big picture." There is an overconcern with being in control, not only over the details of their lives but also over their emotions and other people (Phillips & Gunderson, 1999). Coworkers may find the individual with this disorder too demanding, inflexible, miserly, and perfectionistic. He or she may actually be ineffective on the job, despite long hours of devotion, as in the following case.

> Cecil, a third-year medical student, was referred for therapy by his graduate adviser. The adviser told the therapist that Cecil was in danger of being expelled from medical school because of his inability to get along with patients and with other students. Cecil often berated patients for failing to follow his advice. In one instance, he told a patient with a lung condition to stop smoking. When the patient indicated he was unable to stop, Cecil angrily told the patient to go for medical treatment elsewhere—that the medical center had no place for such a "weak-willed fool." Cecil's relationships with others were similarly strained. He considered many members of the faculty to be "incompetent old deadwood," and he characterized fellow graduate students as "partygoers."
>
> The graduate adviser told the therapist that Cecil had not been expelled only because several faculty members thought that he was brilliant. Cecil studied and worked sixteen hours a day. He was extremely well read and had an extensive knowledge of medical disorders. Although he was always able to provide a careful and detailed analysis of a patient's condition, it took him a great deal of time to do so. His diagnoses tended to cover every disorder that each patient could conceivably have, on the basis of all possible combinations of symptoms.

Obsessive-compulsive personality disorder occurs in about 1 percent of the population and is about twice as prevalent among males as females, according to DSM-IV-TR. Cognitive-behavioral therapy, as well as supportive forms of psychotherapy, have helped some clients (Barber et al., 1997; Beck et al., 1990).

▷ CHECKPOINT REVIEW

antisocial personality disorder (p. 175)

avoidant personality disorder (p. 177)

borderline personality disorder (p. 175)

dependent personality disorder (p. 178)

histrionic personality disorder (p. 173)

narcissistic personality disorder (p. 174)

obsessive-compulsive personality disorder (p. 179)

paranoid personality disorder (p. 169)

personality disorders (p. 167)

schizoid personality disorder (p. 170)

schizotypal personality disorder (p. 172)

What kinds of personality patterns are associated with mental disorders?
- The personality disorders include a diversity of behavioral patterns in people who are typically perceived as being odd or eccentric; dramatic, emotional, and erratic; or anxious and fearful.
- DSM-IV-TR lists ten specific personality disorders; each causes notable impairment of social or occupational functioning or subjective distress for the person. They are usually manifested in adolescence, continue into adulthood, and involve disturbances in personality characteristics.
- Because personality is at the core of the disorders, etiological explanations focus on factors that influence personality, such as heredity, family environment, self-identity, and others.

◄ Antisocial Personality Disorder

We turn now to the etiology and treatment of antisocial personality disorder, which we lightly touched on earlier in this chapter. Research on the other personality disorders has been quite limited. By discussing antisocial personality disorder at greater length, we hope to give you a broader view and an appreciation of the wide range of explanatory views that can be proposed for the personality disorders in general.

The following case presents an example of antisocial personality disorder:

> Roy W. was an eighteen-year-old high school senior who was referred by juvenile court for diagnosis and evaluation. He was arrested for stealing an automobile, something he had done on several other occasions. The court agreed with Roy's mother that he needed evaluation and perhaps psychotherapy.
>
> During his interview with the psychologist, Roy was articulate, relaxed, and even witty. He said that stealing was wrong but that none of the cars he stole was ever damaged. The last theft occurred because he needed transportation to a beer party (which was located only a mile from his home) and his leg was sore from playing basketball. When the psychologist asked Roy how he got along with young women, he grinned and said that he was very outgoing and could easily "hustle" them. He then related the following incident:
>
> "About three months ago, I was pulling out of the school parking lot real fast and accidentally sideswiped this other car. The girl who was driving it started to scream at me. God, there was only a small dent on her fender! Anyway, we exchanged names and addresses and I apologized for the accident. When I filled out the accident report later, I said that it was her car that pulled out from the other side and hit my car. How do you like that? Anyway, when she heard about my claim that it was her fault, she had her old man call me. He said that his daughter had witnesses to the accident and that I could be arrested. Bull, he was just trying to bluff me. But I gave him a sob story—about how my parents were ready to get a divorce, how poor we were, and the trouble I would get into if they found out about the accident. I apologized for lying and told him I could fix the dent. Luckily he never checked with my folks for the real story. Anyway, I went over to look at the girl's car. I really didn't have any idea of how to fix that old heap so I said I had to wait a couple of weeks to get some tools for the repair job.
>
> "Meanwhile, I started to talk to the girl. Gave her my sob story, told her how nice I thought her folks and home were. We started to date and I took her out three times. Then one night I laid her. The crummy thing was that she told her folks about it. Can you imagine that? Anyway, her old man called and told me never to get near his precious little thing again. She's actually a slut.
>
> "At least I didn't have to fix her old heap. I know I shouldn't lie but can you blame me? People make such a big thing out of nothing."

The irresponsibility, disregard for others, and disregard for societal rules and morals evident in this interview indicated to the psychologist that Roy has antisocial personality disorder. Historically, the terms *moral insanity, moral imbecility, moral defect,* and *psychopathic inferiority* have been attached to this condition. An early nineteenth-century British psychiatrist, J. C. Prichard (1837), described it this way:

> The moral and active principles of the mind are strongly perverted or depraved; the power of self-government is lost or greatly impaired; and the individual is found to be incapable, not of talking or reasoning upon any subject proposed to him. . . . but of conducting himself with decency and propriety in the business of life. (p. 15)

Antisocial Personality Disorder   Criminal behavior, irritability, aggressiveness, impulsivity, lack of remorse, and deceitfulness are all characteristics of antisocial personality disorder. Serial murderer Ted Bundy exhibited many of these characteristics. He is shown here in front of television cameras after his indictment for the murders of two Florida State University women. Bundy was executed for his crimes in 1989.

Prichard believed that the disorder was reflected not in a loss of intellectual skills but in gross violations of moral and ethical standards.

The diagnosis of antisocial personality (also referred to as *sociopathic* or *psychopathic* personality) has now lost some of its original moral overtones. Nevertheless, people with antisocial personalities do show a disregard for conventional societal rules and morals.

Cleckley's (1976) classic description of the disorder included the following characteristics:

1. *Superficial charm and good intelligence.* Persons with antisocial personalities are often capable in social activities and adept at manipulating others.

2. *Shallow emotions and lack of empathy, guilt, or remorse.* Absent are genuine feelings of love and loyalty toward others and of concern over the detrimental consequences of their behaviors.

3. *Behaviors indicative of little life plan or order.* The actions of antisocial personalities are not well planned and are often difficult to understand or predict.

4. *Failure to learn from experiences and absence of anxiety.* Although the behaviors may be punished, people with antisocial personality disorder may repeat the same behaviors, and they frequently show little anxiety.

5. *Unreliability, insincerity, and untruthfulness.* Persons with antisocial personalities are irresponsible and may lie or feign emotions to callously manipulate others; their social relationships are usually unstable and short-lived.

Some of these characteristics are apparent in Roy's case. For example, he felt no guilt for his actions or for manipulating the young woman and her family. In fact, he was quite proud of his ability to seduce her and avoid responsibility for the automobile repair. The ease with which Roy related his story to the psychologist demonstrated his lack of concern for those who were hurt by his behaviors. Roy showed no anxiety during the interview.

DSM-IV-TR criteria for the disorder differ somewhat from Cleckley's description, which is based on clinical observations of various cases. For example, DSM-IV-TR criteria do not include lack of anxiety, shallow emotions, failure to learn from past experiences, and superficial charm. They do include a history before age fifteen of failing to conform to social norms with respect to lawful behaviors, irritability and aggressiveness, impulsivity, lack of remorse, and deceitfulness. For the diagnosis to be made, the individual must be at least eighteen years old. DSM-IV-TR criteria, however, fail to convey the conceptual sense of the disorder that was conveyed in Cleckley's original description.

In the United States, the incidence of antisocial personality disorder is estimated to be about 2 percent overall; rates differ by gender, at 3 percent for men and less than 1 percent for women (American Psychiatric Association, 2000a). Overall estimates vary from study to study, however, which may be due to differences in sampling, diagnostic, and methodological procedures. Goodwin and Guze (1984) found that antisocial personality is fairly common. It is much more frequent in urban environments than in rural ones, and in lower socioeconomic groups than in higher ones. Rates of antisocial personality disorder appear comparable among whites, African Americans, and Latino Americans (Robins, Tipp, & Przybeck, 1991). Although African Americans had a

Behavior Patterns, Context, and Diagnosis   Individuals who engage in social protest or civil disobedience are rarely regarded as having antisocial personality disorder. Although some may break the law, the other features of antisocial personality disorder—chronic lack of remorse and deceitfulness, for example—are usually absent. In this photo, a group of students demonstrates at an anti-war parade. Are social protests, as well as antisocial personality disorders, more common among young adults than older adults?

higher rate of incarceration for crimes, their rate of antisocial personality disorder was no different from those of the other groups.

The behavior patterns associated with antisocial personality disorder are different and distinct from behaviors involving social protest or criminal lifestyles. People who engage in civil disobedience or violate the conventions of society or its laws as a form of protest are not as a rule persons with antisocial personalities. Such people can be quite capable of forming meaningful interpersonal relationships and of experiencing guilt. They may perceive their violations of rules and norms as acts performed for the greater good. Similarly, engaging in delinquent or adult criminal behavior is not a necessary or sufficient condition for diagnosing antisocial personality. Although many convicted criminals have been found to have antisocial characteristics, many others do not. They may come from a subculture that encourages and reinforces criminal activity; hence in perpetrating such acts they are adhering to group mores and codes of conduct. As mentioned earlier, DSM-IV-TR criteria tend to emphasize criminality, but the appropriateness of this emphasis is being questioned.

Explanations of Antisocial Personality Disorder

People with antisocial personality disorder are apparently unable to learn from past experience. They continue to engage in antisocial behaviors despite criticism and scorn from others, the disruption of close personal relationships, and frequent encounters with legal authorities. They often sincerely promise to change their lives and make amends, only to return to antisocial behavior soon after. A variety of theories emphasize the inability of persons with antisocial personalities to learn appropriate social and ethical behaviors. The reasons given for this defect, however, are quite diverse.

Theories of the etiology of this disorder vary with theoretical orientation and with the theorist's definition of *antisocial personality*. We examine a number of the most frequently cited constructs from the psychodynamic, family and socialization, biological, and anxiety-arousal-behavioral perspectives.

Psychodynamic Perspective   According to one psychodynamic approach, the psychopath's absence of guilt and frequent violation of moral and ethical standards are the result of faulty superego development (Fenichel, 1945). Id impulses are more likely to be expressed when the weakened superego cannot exert very much influence. People exhibiting antisocial behavior patterns presumably did not adequately identify with their parents. Frustration, rejection, or inconsistent discipline resulted in fixation at an early stage of development.

Family and Socialization Perspectives   Some early theorists believed that relationships within the family—the primary agent of socialization—are paramount in the development of antisocial patterns (McCord & McCord, 1964). In a review of factors that predict delinquency and antisocial behaviors in children, Loeber (1990) found that a family's socioeconomic status was a weak predictor, whereas other family characteristics, such as poor parental supervision and involvement, were good predictors. Rejection or deprivation by one or both parents may mean that the child has little opportunity to learn socially appropriate behaviors or that the value of people as socially reinforcing agents is diminished. There is also evidence that family structure, predictability of expectations, and dependability of family roles are related to lower antisocial tendencies (Tolan et al., 1997). Parental separation or absence and assaultive or inconsistent parenting are related to antisocial personality (Phillips & Gunderson, 1999). Children may have been traumatized or subjected to a hostile environment during the parental separation (Vaillant & Perry, 1985), or the hostility in such families may result in interpersonal hostility among the children (Millon & Everly, 1985). Such situations may lead to little satisfaction in close or meaningful relationships with others. Individuals with this disorder do show a significant amount of misperception about people in general (Widom, 1976). The inability to perceive another's viewpoint can create problems in personal interactions.

People with antisocial personality disorder can learn and use social skills very effectively (Ullmann & Krasner, 1975), as shown in their adeptness at manipulation, lying, and cheating and their ease at being charming and sociable. The difficulty is that, in many areas of learning, these individuals do not pay attention to social stimuli, and their schedules of reinforcement differ from those of most other people. Perhaps this relatively diminished attention stems from inconsistent reinforcement from parents or inadequate feedback for behaviors.

Genetic Influences   Throughout history, many people have speculated that some individuals are "born to raise hell." These speculations are difficult to test because of the problems involved in distinguishing between the influences of environment and heredity on behavior. For example, antisocial personality disorder is five times more common among first-degree biological relatives of males and ten times more common among first-degree biological relatives of females with this disorder than among the general population (American Psychiatric Association, 1987, 2000a). These findings can be used to support either an environmental or a genetic hypothesis. Within the past decade, however, some interesting research has been conducted on genetic influences in antisocial personality disorder.

One strategy has been to compare concordance rates for identical, or monozygotic (MZ), twins with those for fraternal, or dizygotic (DZ), twins. Most studies show that MZ twins do tend to have a higher concordance rate than DZ twins for antisocial tendencies, delinquency, and criminality (Mednick & Christiansen, 1977); this finding tends to support a genetic basis for these behavior patterns.

Another strategy for studying genetic influence is to note the rate of antisocial personality disorder among adopted people with antisocial biological parents. Because many of these adoptees were separated from their biological parents early in life, learning antisocial behaviors from those parents would have been difficult. Results have generally shown that adoptees whose biological parents exhibited antisocial behaviors have a higher rate of antisocial characteristics than that found among adoptees whose biological parents did not exhibit antisocial behaviors (Cadoret & Cain, 1981).

Do adoptive parents of antisocial individuals show more antisocial patterns than biological parents? If so, this would be evidence of environmental influence. Research results show, however, that the rate of criminality or antisocial tendencies is higher among the biological parents than among the adoptive parents of such individuals (Hutchings & Mednick, 1977; Mednick & Kandel, 1988; Schulsinger, 1972). Again the evidence suggests that antisocial personality patterns are influenced by heredity (Goodwin & Guze, 1984).

Although this body of evidence seems to show a strong causal pattern, it should be examined carefully, for several reasons. The first reason is that many of the studies fail to clearly distinguish between antisocial personalities and criminals; as we noted earlier, they may draw research participants only from criminal populations. Truly representative samples of people with antisocial personality disorder should be investigated.

The second reason for caution is that evidence supporting a genetic basis for antisocial tendencies does not preclude the environment as a factor. Antisocial personality is undoubtedly caused by environmental, as well as genetic, influences (Slutske et al., 1997). One way to try to sort out genetic and environmental influences is to study family members who vary in genetic relatedness and who share or do not share environmental factors. One such study (O'Connor et al., 1998) investigated these variations with MZ twins, DZ twins, full siblings, half siblings, and unrelated siblings. Heredity accounted for 56 percent of the variance in antisocial behavior, and shared environmental experiences (for example, those that are common to both siblings) explained about 25 percent of the variance.

The third reason for caution is that studies indicating that genetic factors are important do not provide much insight into how antisocial personality is inherited. What exactly is transmitted genetically? Rutter (1997) suggests that genetic factors do not influence crime and antisocial behavior directly but rather that they affect the probability that such behavior will occur. Hence there may be no specific "gene for crime."

Central Nervous System Abnormality Some early investigators suggested that people with antisocial personalities tend to have abnormal brain wave activity (Hill & Watterson, 1942; Knott et al., 1953). In these studies, the measurement of the brain waves, or electroencephalograms (EEGs), of psychopaths were sometimes found to be similar to those of normal young children or to have some EEG abnormalities. However, there simply is not enough evidence to support such a view. Many persons diagnosed with antisocial personality disorder do not show EEG abnormalities, and individuals who do not have the disorder may also exhibit theta-wave activity (Milstein, 1988). In addition, the EEG is an imprecise diagnostic device, and abnormal brain wave activity in people with antisocial personalities may simply be correlated with, rather than a cause of, disturbed behavior. For example, these individuals could simply be less anxious or more bored than other people, which may account for the slow-wave EEGs.

Autonomic Nervous System Abnormalities Other interesting research points to the involvement of the autonomic nervous system (ANS) in the prominent features of antisocial personality disorder: the inability to learn from experience, the absence of anxiety, and the tendency to engage in thrill-seeking behaviors. Two lines of investigation can be identified, both based on the assumption that people with antisocial personality disorder have ANS deficiencies or abnormalities. The first is based on the premise that ANS abnormalities make antisocial personalities less susceptible to anxiety and therefore less likely to learn from their experiences in situations in which aversive stimuli (or punishment) are involved (see Lykken, 1982). The second line of research focuses on the premise that ANS abnormalities could keep antisocial people emotionally underaroused (see Hare, 1968). To achieve an optimal level of arousal or to avoid boredom, underaroused individuals might seek excitement and thrills and fail to conform to conventional behavioral standards. The two premises—lack of anxiety and underarousal—may, of course, be related, because underarousal could include underaroused anxiety.

Fearlessness or Lack of Anxiety   Lykken (1982) maintained that because of genetic predisposition, people vary in their levels of fearlessness. Antisocial personality develops because of fearlessness or low anxiety levels. People who have high levels of fear avoid risks, stress, and strong stimulation; relatively fearless people seek thrills and adventures. Fearlessness is associated with heroes (such as those who volunteer for dangerous military action or who risk their lives to save others), as well as with individuals with antisocial personalities who may engage in risky criminal activities or impulsively violate norms and rules.

Arousal, Sensation-Seeking, and Behavioral Perspectives   These studies by Lykken and others suggest that individuals with antisocial personalities may have deficiencies in learning because of lower anxiety. Another line of research proposes that antisocial personalities simply have lower levels of ANS reactivity and are underaroused. According to this view, the sensitivity of individuals' reticular cortical systems varies, although there is an optimal level for each person. The system regulates the tonic level of arousal in the cortex, so that some people have high and some have low levels of arousal. Those with low sensitivity need more stimulation to reach an optimal level of arousal (Goma, Perez, & Torrubia, 1988). If psychopaths are underaroused, it may take a more intense stimulus to elicit a reaction in them than in nonpsychopaths. A study by Hare (1968) focused on the intensity of the stimulus needed to elicit a reaction in psychopaths and in nonpsychopaths. The study assessed the resting state reactivity and the stress-produced reactivity of primary psychopaths (those lacking anxiety and guilt), secondary psychopaths (those exhibiting antisocial behaviors but expressing guilt over them), and nonpsychopaths using cardiac, galvanic skin response, and respiratory measures. Hare found that psychopaths required a more intense stimulus, in both the resting state and in response to stressors, than did nonpsychopaths. The lowered levels of reactivity may cause psychopaths to perform impulsive, stimulus-seeking behaviors to avoid boredom (Quay, 1965).

Zuckerman (1996) believes that a trait he calls *impulsive unsocialized sensation seeking* can help explain not only antisocial personality disorder but also other disorders. Those with this trait want to seek adventures and thrills, are disinhibited, and are susceptible to boredom. Psychopaths, particularly primary psychopaths, score high for this trait. Similarly, Farley (1986) proposed that people vary in their degree of thrill-seeking behaviors. At one end of the thrill-seeking continuum are the "Big T's"—the risk takers and adventurers who seek excitement and stimulation. Because of their low levels of CNS or ANS arousal, Big T's need stimulation to maintain an optimal level of arousal. On the other end of the continuum are "Little t's"—people with high arousal who seek low levels of stimulation to calm their hyped-up nervous systems. In contrast to Big T's, Little t's prefer certainty, predictability, low risk, familiarity, clarity, simplicity, low conflict, and low intensity.

Farley speculated that Big T characteristics can lead to either constructive or destructive behaviors, which can occur in either mental or physical domains. In the con-

Sensation Seeking and Antisocial Personality   Lykken theorized that people with low anxiety levels are often thrill seekers. The difference between the psychopath who takes risks and the adventurer may largely be a matter of whether the thrill-seeking behaviors are channeled into destructive or constructive acts. Are there gender differences in thrill-seeking behaviors? If so, what can account for the gender differences?

structive-mental domain, Big T's include artists, scientists, and entertainers, who channel their thrill-seeking tendencies into creative mental contributions. In the destructive-mental domain, criminal masterminds, schemers, and con artists are Big T's whose actions in society are harmful. In the constructive-physical domain, Big T's become adventurers and physical risk takers. Their destructive-physical-domain counterparts are violent delinquents and criminals whose Big T characteristics result in antisocial, destructive behaviors. Farley (1986) reported that juvenile delinquents are more likely than nondelinquents to be Big T's. In a study of delinquents in prison, Big T's were more likely than Little t's to fight, disobey supervisors, and attempt to escape. Farley believes that we need to direct stimulation-hungry Big T's into constructive, rather than destructive, mental and physical activities.

Other researchers have found evidence of underarousal, as well as lowered levels of anxiety, among those with antisocial personality disorder. If learning deficiencies among individuals with antisocial personality disorder are caused by the absence of anxiety and by lowered autonomic reactivity, is it possible to improve their learning by increasing their anxiety or arousal ability? To test this idea, researchers designed two conditions in which psychopaths, a mixed group, and nonpsychopaths would perform an avoidance learning task, with electric shock as the unconditioned stimulus. Under one condition, participants were injected with adrenaline, which presumably increases arousal; under the other, they were injected with a placebo. Psychopaths receiving the placebo made more errors in avoiding the shocks than did nonpsychopaths; psychopaths receiving adrenaline, however, tended to perform better than nonpsychopaths. These findings imply that psychopaths do not react to the same amount of anxiety as do nonpsychopaths and that their learning improves when their anxiety is increased (Schachter & Latané, 1964).

The *kind* of punishment used in avoidance learning is also an important consideration in evaluating psychopaths' learning deficiencies (Schmauk, 1970). Whereas psychopaths may show learning deficits when faced with physical (electric shock) or social (verbal feedback) punishments, they learn as well as nonpsychopaths when the punishment is monetary loss.

The *certainty* of punishment may also influence the responsiveness of those with antisocial personality disorder to punishment. Psychopaths and nonpsychopaths do not seem to differ in responding when punishment is a near certainty (Siegel, 1978). When the probability of punishment is highly uncertain, however, psychopaths do not suppress their behaviors. Threats of punishment by themselves do not seem to be sufficient to discourage psychopaths.

Normal people respond to physical, social, or material punishment, and they are influenced by uncertain, as well as certain, punishment. The work of Schmauk and Siegel suggested that psychopaths do not respond to the same range of aversive conditions.

Reid (1981) viewed the disorder as a heterogeneous condition with many causes. Familial, biological, social, and developmental factors may converge and provide a coherent picture in explaining the disorder.

Treatment of Antisocial Personality Disorder

As you have seen, evidence is growing that low anxiety and low autonomic reactivity characterize individuals with antisocial personality disorder. But we still do not know whether these characteristics are products of inherited temperament, of an acquired congenital defect, or of social and environmental experiences during childhood. The theory that psychopaths have developed a defense against anxiety is intriguing, but the factors behind the development of such a defense have not been pinpointed. Because people with antisocial personality disorder feel little anxiety, they are poorly motivated to change themselves; they are also unlikely to see their behaviors as "bad" and may try to manipulate or "con" therapists. Thus traditional treatment approaches, which require the genuine cooperation of the client, may be ineffective for antisocial personality disorder. Few treatment outcome studies have been conducted for this disorder (Simon, 1998). In some studies, drugs with tranquilizing effects (phenothiazines and Dilantin) have been helpful in reducing antisocial behavior (Meyer & Osborne, 1982). People with antisocial personality disorder, however, are not likely to follow through with self-medication. Moreover, drug treatment is effective in only a few cases, and it can result in side effects such as blurred vision, lethargy, and neurological disorders.

It may be that successful treatment can occur only in a setting in which behavior can be controlled (Vaillant, 1975). That is, treatment programs may need to provide enough control so that those with antisocial personalities cannot avoid confronting their inability to form close and intimate relationships and the effect of their behaviors on others. Such control is sometimes possible for psychopaths who are imprisoned for crimes or who, for one reason or another, are hospitalized. Intensive group therapy may then be initiated to help clients with antisocial personalities in the required confrontation.

Some behavior modification programs have been tried, especially with delinquents who behave in antisocial ways. The most useful treatments are skill based and behavioral (Meloy, 2001). Money and tokens that can be used to purchase items have been used as rewards for young people who show appropriate behaviors (discussion of personal problems, good study habits, punctuality, and prosocial and nondisruptive behaviors). This use of material rewards has been fairly effective in changing antisocial behaviors (Van Evra, 1983). Once the young people leave the treatment programs, however, they are likely to revert to antisocial behavior unless their families and peers help them maintain the appropriate behaviors.

Cognitive approaches have also been used. Because individuals with antisocial personalities may be influenced by dysfunctional beliefs about themselves, the world, and the future, they vary in their abilities to anticipate and act on possible negative outcomes of their behaviors. Beck and colleagues (1990) have advocated that the therapist build rapport with the client, attempting to guide the patient away from thinking only in terms of self-interest and immediate gratification and toward higher levels of thinking. These higher levels would include, for example, recognizing the effects of one's behaviors on others and developing a sense of responsibility.

Kazdin (1987) noted that, because current treatment programs do not seem very effective, new strategies must be used. These strategies should focus on antisocial youths who seem amenable to treatment, and treatment programs should broaden the base of intervention to involve not only the young clients but also their families and peers. Farley (1986) believes that because people with antisocial personality disorder may seek thrills (Big T's), they may respond to intervention programs that provide the physical and mental stimulation they need. Longitudinal studies show that the prevalence of this disorder diminishes with age as these individuals become more aware of the social and interpersonal maladaptiveness of their social behaviors (Phillips & Gunderson, 1999).

▷ CHECKPOINT REVIEW

Why do some people have a callous disregard for others and lack guilt and anxiety?

- The main characteristics of antisocial (or psychopathic) personality are selfishness, irresponsibility, lack of guilt and anxiety, failure to learn from experience, superficiality, and impulsiveness.
- People with antisocial personalities frequently violate the rules, conventions, or laws of society.
- Most explanations of antisocial personality attribute its development to family and socialization factors, heredity, or autonomic nervous system abnormalities that result in lowered anxiety or underarousal.
- Traditional treatment approaches are not particularly effective with antisocial personalities.

FOCUS QUESTIONS

■ What are substance-use disorders?

■ Why do people become addicted to drugs?

■ How can we successfully help people to overcome
  substance abuse and addiction?

8 *Substance-Related Disorders*

Throughout history, people have swallowed, sniffed, smoked, or otherwise taken into their bodies a variety of chemical substances for the purpose of altering their moods, levels of consciousness, or behaviors. The widespread use of drugs in our society today is readily apparent in our vast consumption of alcohol, tobacco, coffee, medically prescribed tranquilizers, and illegal drugs such as cocaine, marijuana, and heroin. Compared with other societies, our society is generally permissive with regard to the use of these substances. As indicated in Figure 8.1, many people have tried substances, especially alcohol, at some time in their lives. The substances or drugs are psychoactive in that they alter moods, thought processes, or other psychological states.

Our society becomes less permissive and more concerned when a person's ingestion of drugs results in

- Impairment of social or occupational functioning.
- An inability to abstain from using the drug despite its harmful effects on the body.
- The user's becoming a danger to others.
- Criminal activities, such as the sale of illegal drugs or robbery, to support a drug habit.

The first two of these problems are directly involved in **substance-related disorders**, which result from the use of psychoactive substances that affect the central nervous system, causing significant social, occupational, psychological, or physical problems, and that sometimes result in abuse or dependence. The other two problems arise in connection with such use.

substance-related disorders
Disorders resulting from the use of psychoactive substances that affect the central nervous system, causing significant social, occupational, psychological, or physical problems, and that sometimes result in abuse or dependence.

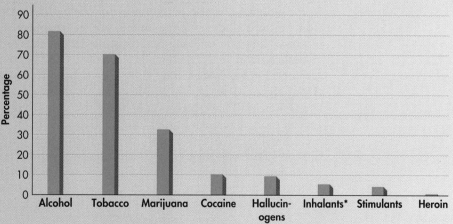

*Substances that are inhaled, such as glue.

Figure 8.1 Percentage of Persons Who Reported Using Specific Substances at Any Time During Their Lives (Age 12 and Over)   As you can see, the vast majority of Americans have used psychoactive substances, particularly alcohol and tobacco.
Source: Data from Office of National Drug Control Policy (1998).

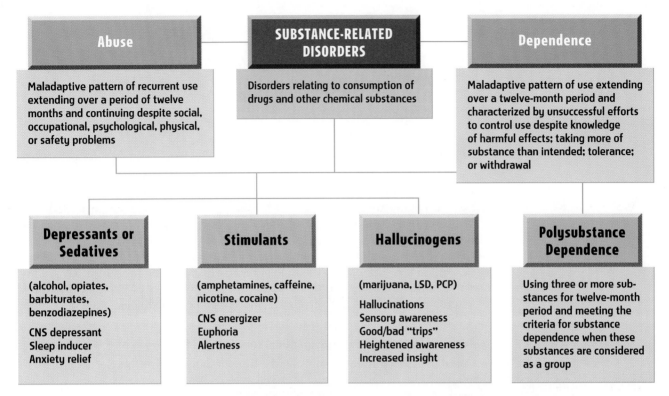

Figure 8.2 Disorders Chart: Substance-Related Disorders   *Source:* Data from American Psychiatric Association (2000a).

Yet another concern is that use of one substance may lead to use of other substances. In a longitudinal study of drug use among youths, Ellickson, Hays, and Bell (1992) found that involvement with "legal" drugs such as alcohol and cigarettes tended to precede the use of illicit drugs such as marijuana and "hard" drugs. Furthermore, alcohol or drug-related disorders are often part of a dual diagnosis, that is, the individual is also diagnosed with some other mental disorder, such as depression, antisocial personality, mania, or schizophrenia (Emmelkamp, 2004). For instance, cigarette smoking and nicotine dependence are associated with depression (Windle & Windle, 2001). Finally, as many as half of people with severe mental disorders develop alcohol or other substance abuse problems at some point in their lives (U.S. Surgeon General, 1999). Although a number of explanations (biological as well as psychosocial) have been proposed for this comorbidity or dual diagnosis (the presence of more than one disorder), the cause is unknown.

DSM-IV-TR (American Psychiatric Association, 2000a) divides substance-related disorders into two categories: (1) substance-use disorders that involve dependence and abuse and (2) substance-induced disorders, such as withdrawal and substance-induced delirium. The discussion in this chapter focuses primarily on the substance-use disorders represented in Figure 8.2. Substance-induced cognitive disorders are discussed in the Chapter "Cognitive Disorders."

DSM-IV-TR differentiates the substance-use disorders in two ways: (1) by the actual substance used and (2) by whether the disorder pattern is that of substance abuse or substance dependence. Regardless of the substance involved, the general characteristics of the abuse or dependence are the same. **Substance abuse** is a maladaptive pattern of recurrent use that extends over a period of twelve months, that leads to

substance abuse Maladaptive pattern of recurrent use that extends over a period of twelve months; leads to notable impairment or distress; and continues despite social, occupational, psychological, physical, or safety problems.

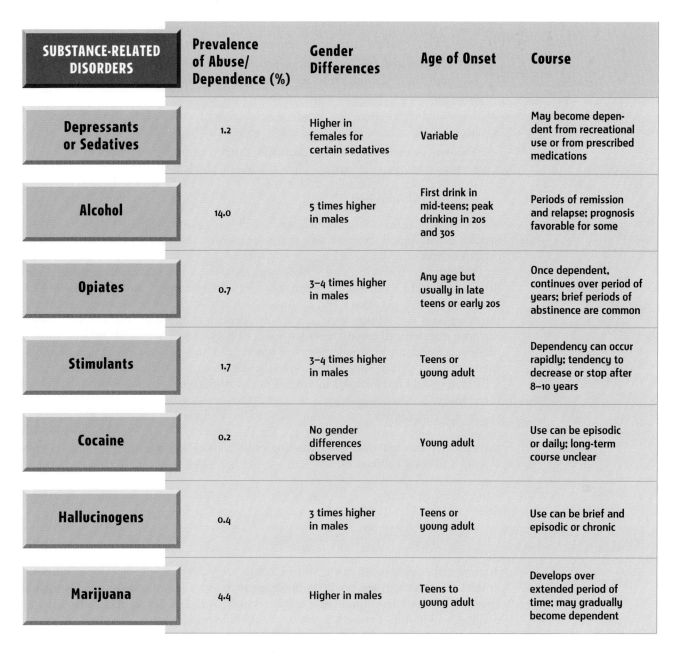

Figure 8.2 Disorders Chart: Substance-Related Disorders (continued)

notable impairment or distress, and that continues despite social, occupational, psychological, physical, or safety problems. The abuse may cause legal problems or jeopardize the safety of the user or others (such as driving while intoxicated). It may impair the user's ability to maintain meaningful social relationships or fulfill major role obligations at work, school, or home. And need for the substance may lead to a preoccupation with its acquisition and use.

To make the diagnosis of **substance dependence**, a therapist must find that the client exhibits several of the following symptoms over a twelve-month period:

substance dependence Maladaptive pattern of use extending over a twelve-month period and characterized by unsuccessful efforts to control use, despite knowledge of harmful effects; taking more of substance than intended; tolerance; or withdrawal.

1. The user is unable to cut down or control use of the substance, despite knowledge of its harmful physical, psychological, or interpersonal effects.

2. The user takes increasingly larger amounts of the substance or continues to use it over a longer period than he or she intended.

3. The user devotes considerable time to activities necessary to obtain the substance, even though those activities mean that important social, occupational, and recreational activities must be sacrificed.

4. The user exhibits evidence of **tolerance**: increasing doses of the substance are necessary to achieve the desired effect, such as a "high."

5. The user shows evidence of **withdrawal**: distress or impairment in social, occupational, or other areas of functioning or physical or emotional symptoms such as shaking, irritability, and inability to concentrate after reducing or ceasing intake of the substance.

In diagnosing substance dependence, the clinician also specifies whether the dependence is physiological; evidence of either tolerance or withdrawal indicates physiological dependence.

Although intoxication and withdrawal are considered substance-induced disorders, and therefore outside the primary topic of this chapter, we discuss them here because they are necessary for an understanding of the substance-use disorders. **Intoxication** is a condition in which a substance affecting the central nervous system has been ingested and certain maladaptive behaviors or psychological changes, such as belligerence and impaired judgment and functioning, are evident. The effects of intoxication and withdrawal vary according to the substance, but they generally cause significant distress or impairment in social, occupational, or other important areas of functioning.

In this chapter, we first examine substance-use disorders, including the effects of the abuse of alcohol and various drugs. We also examine the degree to which different theories may increase our understanding of the causes and treatment of the abuse of alcohol and other substances.

Substance-Use Disorders

tolerance Condition in which increasing doses of a substance are necessary to achieve the desired effect.

withdrawal Condition characterized by distress or impairment in social, occupational, or other areas of functioning or by physical or emotional symptoms such as shaking, irritability, and inability to concentrate after reducing or ceasing intake of a substance.

intoxication Condition in which a substance affecting the central nervous system has been ingested and certain maladaptive behaviors or psychological changes, such as belligerence and impaired functioning, are evident.

A number of substances can result in abuse, dependence, intoxication, and withdrawal. Among them are prescription drugs such as Valium; legal substances such as alcohol and cigarettes; and illegal substances such as LSD (lysergic acid diethylamine), cocaine, and heroin. Figure 8.2 shows the lifetime prevalence of various drug abuse/dependent disorders found in the Epidemiologic Catchment Area (ECA) study (Anthony & Helzer, 1991)—the most comprehensive survey ever conducted of the mental health of adult Americans. Alcohol and substance abuse is the second leading cause of disability in the United States, Canada, and Western Europe, ahead of physical diseases and second only to mental illness (President's New Freedom Commission on Mental Health, 2003).

Substance-related disorders are most prevalent among youths and young adults. In terms of drug abuse/dependence (not including alcohol), the ECA study found the adult lifetime prevalence for controlled substances to be 6.2 percent (Anthony & Helzer, 1991). Abuse/dependence was greatest for marijuana. Note that a person may abuse or be dependent on more than one drug. It is anticipated that abuse will increase among the elderly, as the baby boomers age (U.S. Surgeon General, 1999).

Each of the drugs discussed in this chapter can create an abuse or dependence disorder. Many are also associated with legal problems, because their use is expressly prohibited except under strict medical supervision. We discuss general categories of

Table 8.1   Characteristics of Various Psychoactive Substances

Drugs	Short-Term Effects*	Potential for Dependency
Sedatives		
Alcohol	Central nervous system (CNS) depressant, loss of inhibitions	Moderate
Narcotics (codeine, morphine, heroin, opium, methadone)	CNS depressant, pain relief	High
Barbiturates (amytal, nembutal, seconal)	CNS depressant, sleep inducer	Moderate to high
Benzodiazepines (Valium)	CNS depressant, anxiety relief	Low
Stimulants		
Amphetamines (Benzedrine, Dexedrine, Methedrine)	CNS energizer, euphoria	High
Caffeine	CNS energizer, alertness	Low
Nicotine	CNS energizer	High
Cocaine and crack	CNS energizer, euphoria	High
Hallucinogens		
Marijuana, hashish	Relaxant, euphoria	Moderate
LSD	Hallucinatory agent	Low
PCP	Hallucinatory agent	Moderate

*Specific effects often depend on the quality and dosage of the drug, as well as on the experience, expectancy, personality, and situation of the person using the drug.

substances—depressants, stimulants, and hallucinogens—which contain many specific drugs, such as alcohol, narcotics, barbiturates, benzodiazepines, amphetamines, caffeine, nicotine, cocaine and crack, marijuana, LSD, and phencyclidine (PCP). Table 8.1 lists these substances, their effects, and their potential for dependency. In practice, some substances are not easily classified because they may have multiple effects.

Depressants or Sedatives

Depressants or *sedatives* cause generalized depression of the central nervous system and a slowing down of responses. People taking such substances feel calm and relaxed. They may also become sociable and open because of lowered interpersonal inhibitions. Let us examine in more detail one of the most widely used depressants—alcohol—and then discuss other depressants, such as narcotics, barbiturates, and benzodiazepines.

Alcohol-Use Disorders Alcohol abuse and alcohol dependence are, of course, substance abuse and dependence in which the substance is alcohol. People who have either of these alcohol-related disorders are popularly referred to as **alcoholics,** and their disorder as **alcoholism.** Drinking problems can be exhibited in two major ways. First, the person may need to use alcohol daily to function; that is, he or she may be unable to abstain. Second, the person may be able to abstain from consuming alcohol for certain periods of time but unable to control or moderate intake once he or she resumes drinking. This person is a "binge" drinker. Both patterns of drinking can result in

depressant Substance that causes generalized depression of the central nervous system and a slowing down of responses; a sedative.

alcoholic Person who abuses alcohol and is dependent on it.

alcoholism Substance-related disorder characterized by abuse of, or dependency on, alcohol, which is a depressant.

deteriorating relationships, job loss, family conflicts, and violent behavior while intoxicated. The following case is typical.

> Jim was a fifty-four-year-old alcoholic. He was well educated, having received a bachelor's degree in engineering and a master's degree in management. Until recently, he was employed as a middle manager in an aerospace firm. Because of federal defense industry budget cuts and because of his absenteeism from work caused by drinking, Jim lost his job. He decided to enter treatment.
>
> His drinking history was long. Jim clearly recalled the first time that he drank. At age fifteen, he attended a party at his friend's house. Alcohol was freely served. Jim took a drink, and despite the fact that alcohol "tasted so bad," he forced himself to continue drinking. Indeed, he became drunk and had a terrible hangover the next day. He swore that he would never drink again, but two weeks later he drank again at his friend's house. Over the next several years, Jim acquired the ability to consume large amounts of alcohol and was proud of his drinking capacity. At social gatherings, he was uninhibited and the "life of the party." His drinking continued during college, but it was confined primarily to his fraternity weekend parties. He was considered a very heavy drinker in the fraternity, but the drinking did not seem to affect his academic performance. He frequently drove his car during weekend binges, however, and was once caught and convicted of drunken driving.
>
> After graduate school, he got married and took a position in an aerospace firm. Katie, Jim's wife, also drank, but never as heavily as Jim. Although his drinking had been largely confined to weekends, Jim started drinking throughout the week. He attributed his increased drinking to pressures at work, company-sponsored receptions in which alcohol was served, and a desire to feel "free and comfortable" in front of company executives during the receptions. Over time, Jim was unable to complete work assignments on time and was frequently absent from work because of his drinking. The drinking continued despite frequent arguments with Katie over his drinking and a physician's warning, after a routine physical examination, that alcohol had probably caused the abnormal results of Jim's liver-functioning tests. He could not control his alcohol consumption.

Problem drinking can develop in many different ways and can begin at almost any age. However, Jim's history is typical in several respects. First, as is true of most people, he initially found the taste of alcohol unpleasant, and, after his first bout of drunkenness, he swore that he would never drink again. Nevertheless, Jim did return to drinking. Second, heavy drinking served a purpose: it reduced his anxiety, particularly at work. Third, consumption continued despite the obvious negative consequences. Fourth and finally, a preoccupation with alcohol consumption and the deterioration of social and occupational functioning are also characteristic of the problem drinker.

Alcohol Consumption in the United States People drink considerable amounts of alcohol in the United States. About 11 percent of adults consume one ounce or more of alcohol a day, 55 percent drink fewer than three alcoholic drinks a week, and 35 percent abstain completely (American Psychiatric Association, 1987). The per-person average annual consumption is 2.43 gallons of absolute alcohol (Franklin & Frances, 1999). Most of the alcohol is consumed by a small percentage of people; 50 percent of the total alcohol consumed is drunk by only 10 percent of drinkers. Heavy drinking is most common among those between eighteen and twenty-five years of age (National Institute on Drug Abuse, 1991). One national survey found that 20 percent of youths ages twelve to seventeen had used alcohol in the previous month (Office of National Drug Control Policy, 1998). Early use of alcohol has been found to be a strong predictor of progression into serious problem drinking (Nelson, Heath, & Kessler, 1998). Another study of adults revealed that 14 percent had been dependent on alcohol at

Patterns of Alcohol Consumption   Societies differ not only in the extent to which alcohol is consumed but also in the pattern of use. In many European countries, alcohol is freely used with meals throughout the day. Wine drinking is relatively high. Are rates of alcoholism likely to be higher in these countries?

some time in their lives and that approximately 7 percent had been dependent during the previous year (American Psychiatric Association, 2000a). Men drink two to five times as much as women, although gender differences in the use of alcohol are decreasing (Nelson et al., 1998). Jackson and colleagues (2001) examined the drinking habits of college students from their first year in college to six years later. Interestingly, they found that over time, many drank as frequently as before but reduced the amount consumed (e.g., not drinking to drunkenness). However, those with a history of family alcoholism did not show this reduction in amount consumed.

Alcohol consumption varies according to the cultural traditions of various societies. In Italy and some other countries, wine is a traditional accompaniment to meals, and individuals drink freely throughout the day. In most societies, females tend to consume less alcohol than do males, and in Asian countries, the male-to-female rate of consumption is particularly high. In general, drinking alcohol is less common in some Asian countries than in Europe or the United States. The low prevalence rates among Asians may be caused by a deficiency, in perhaps 50 percent of Japanese, Chinese, and Korean individuals, of the form of aldehyde dehydrogenase that eliminates low levels of the first breakdown product of alcohol, acetaldehyde. This leads to the accumulation of acetaldehyde, which accounts for dysphoria, a flushed face, and palpitations among many Asians (American Psychiatric Association, 2000a). Within the United States, alcohol consumption varies according to gender, ethnicity, and age. Rates for non-Hispanic whites are higher than those for either African Americans or Hispanic Americans. In all groups, males consume more alcohol than females (Office of National Drug Control Policy, 1998).

Problems associated with alcohol consumption in the United States are apparent in terms of social, medical, physical, and financial costs. Alcohol consumption and alcoholism are associated with serious health care costs; lowered productivity on the job; shortened life expectancy (by about ten to twelve years); and high rates of suicide, automobile accidents, spousal abuse, and divorce. One hundred thousand deaths per year are alcohol related (Franklin & Frances, 1999). Concern has also developed over the children of alcoholic parents, who are at risk for social maladjustment, self-deprecation, lower self-esteem, and alcoholism (Berkowitz & Perkins, 1988; Cooper & McCormack, 1992).

Fighting Mad   Mothers Against Drunk Driving (MADD) is an organization started by Candy Lightner, a mother whose daughter was killed by a drunk driver. MADD's goal is to prevent drunk people from driving and to assist the victims of drunk drivers and victims' families. Well over one-half million individuals are involved in MADD. Has MADD had a beneficial impact in reducing drinking and driving?

In view of the problems associated with alcohol use, why do people continue drinking? Particularly ironic is the fact that, like Jim in the earlier case, most people consuming alcoholic beverages for the first time find the taste unpleasant. To better understand this puzzle, let's consider the physiological and psychological effects of alcohol.

The Effects of Alcohol   Alcohol has both physiological and psychological effects, which can be further broken down into short-term and long-term effects. Once swallowed, alcohol is absorbed into the blood without digestion. When it reaches the brain, its short-term physiological effect is to depress central nervous system functioning. When the alcohol content in the bloodstream (the blood alcohol level) is about 0.1 percent (the equivalent of drinking 5 ounces of whiskey or 5 glasses of beer), muscular coordination is impaired. The drinker may have trouble walking a straight line or pronouncing certain words. At the 0.5 percent blood alcohol level, the person may lose consciousness or even die.

The short-term physiological effects of alcohol on a specific person are determined by the individual's body weight, the amount of food present in the stomach, the drinking rate over time, prior drinking experience, heredity, personality factors, and the individual's environment and culture. They often include feelings of happiness, loss of inhibitions (because alcohol depresses the inhibitory brain centers), poor judgment, and reduced concentration. Depending on the situation or context in which drinking occurs, other effects, such as negative moods and anger, may also be experienced. Reactions also depend on the expectancy that individuals have developed with respect to alcohol (Hull & Bond, 1986). Some people behave differently in the presence of others simply because of their perception that they have been drinking, not because of the effects of the alcohol (as, for example, when an individual has only a few sips of beer and begins to act hostile). Heavy and prolonged drinking often impairs sexual performance and produces a hangover. The long-term psychological effects of heavy drinking are more serious. Although there is no single type of alcoholic, Jellinek (1971) observed certain patterns in the course of individuals who develop alcohol dependence. Most people begin to drink in social situations. Because the alcohol relieves tension, the drinkers tend to drink more and to drink more frequently. Tolerance levels may increase over a period of months or years.

Because of stress, inability to adequately cope, or biological predisposition to alcoholism, some drinkers become preoccupied with thoughts of alcohol. They may worry about whether there will be enough alcohol at a party; they may try to drink inconspicuously or furtively. They begin to consume large amounts and may "gulp" their drinks. Such drinkers frequently feel guilty; they are somewhat aware that their drinking is excessive. Heavy, sustained drinking may lead to blackouts, periods of time for which drinkers have no memory of their activities.

The long-term physiological effects of alcohol consumption include an increase in tolerance as the person becomes used to alcohol, physical discomfort, anxiety, and hallucinations. Chronic alcoholism destroys brain cells and is often accompanied by poor nutritional habits and physical deterioration. Other direct or indirect consequences generally attributed to chronic alcoholism are liver diseases such as *cirrhosis,* in which an excessive amount of fibrous tissue develops and impedes the circulation of blood; heart failure; hemorrhages of capillaries, particularly those on the sides of the nose; and cancers of the mouth and throat. Alcohol consumption in pregnant women may affect their unborn children: children who suffer *fetal alcohol syndrome* are born mentally retarded and physically deformed. Interestingly, the moderate use of alcohol (one or two drinks a day) in adults has been associated in some studies with lowered risk of heart disease. The precise reasons for this effect are unknown.

Narcotics (Opiates) Like alcohol, the organic **narcotics**, which include opium and its derivatives morphine, heroin, and codeine, depress the central nervous system, act as sedatives to provide relief from pain, anxiety, and tension, and are addictive. Feelings of euphoria and well-being (and sometimes negative reactions such as nausea) often accompany narcotics use. Opium and its derivatives (especially heroin) result in dependency. Tolerance for narcotics builds rapidly, and withdrawal symptoms are severe. Opiates such as heroin are usually administered intravenously, causing puncture marks on the extremities of the body and spreading diseases such as AIDS, which can be transmitted through needle sharing (Smith & Landry, 1988). Twenty-five percent of AIDS cases involve persons who abuse intravenous drugs (Franklin & Frances, 1999).

About 0.7 percent of the adult population has shown opioid abuse or dependence at some time during their lives. The prevalence of addiction decreases with age, and males are more affected than females, by a ratio of 1.5:1 for opioids other than heroin (i.e., those available by prescription) and 3:1 for heroin. (American Psychiatric Association, 2000a).

Because dependency is likely to occur after repeated use, narcotics addicts are usually unable to maintain normal relationships with family and friends or to pursue legitimate careers. They live to obtain the drug through any possible means. Nonmedical use of narcotics is illegal, and many addicts have little choice but to turn to criminal activities to obtain the drug and to support their expensive habits.

Barbiturates Synthetic **barbiturates**, or "downers," are powerful depressants of the central nervous system and are commonly used to induce relaxation and sleep. Next to the narcotics, they represent the largest category of illegal drugs, and they are quite dangerous for several reasons. First, psychological and physical dependence can develop. Second, although their legal use is severely restricted, their widespread availability makes it difficult to control misuse or abuse. More than 1 million individuals—primarily middle-aged and older people—are now estimated to be barbiturate addicts. Third, users often experience harmful physical effects. Excessive use of either barbiturates or heroin can be fatal, but barbiturates are the more lethal. Constant heroin use increases the amount of the drug required for a lethal dosage. The lethal dosage of barbiturates does not increase with prolonged use, so accidental overdose and death can easily occur. And combining alcohol with barbiturates can be especially dangerous because alcohol compounds the depressant effects of the barbiturates, as it did in the following case.

narcotics Drugs such as opium and its derivatives—morphine, heroin, and codeine—which depress the central nervous system; act as sedatives to provide relief from pain, anxiety, and tension; and are addictive.

barbiturates Substances that are a powerful depressant of the central nervous system; commonly used to induce relaxation and sleep; and capable of inducing psychological and physical dependency.

> Kelly M., a seventeen-year-old girl from an upper-middle-class background, lived with her divorced mother. Kelly was hospitalized after her mother found her unconscious from an overdose of barbiturates consumed together with alcohol. She survived the overdose and later told the therapist that she had regularly used barbiturates for the previous year and a half. The overdose was apparently accidental and not suicidal.
>
> For several weeks following the overdose, Kelly openly discussed her use of barbiturates with the therapist. She had been introduced to the drugs by a boy in school who

told her they would help her relax. Kelly was apparently unhappy over her parents' divorce. She felt that her mother did not want her, especially because her mother spent a lot of time away from home building a real estate agency. And, although she enjoyed her occasional visits with her father, Kelly felt extremely uncomfortable in the presence of the woman who lived with him. The barbiturates helped her relax and relieved her tensions. Arguments with her mother would precipitate heavy use of the drugs. Eventually she became dependent on barbiturates and always spent her allowance to buy them. Her mother reported that she had no knowledge of her daughter's drug use. She did notice, though, that Kelly was increasingly isolated and sleepy.

The therapist informed Kelly of the dangers of barbiturates and of combining them with alcohol. Kelly agreed to undergo treatment, which included the gradual reduction of barbiturate use and psychotherapy with her mother.

Kelly's practice of *polysubstance use,* or the use of more than one chemical substance at the same time, can be extremely dangerous. For example, heavy smokers who consume a great deal of alcohol run an increased risk of esophageal cancer. Chemicals taken simultaneously may exhibit a synergistic effect, interacting to multiply one another's effects. For example, when a large dose of barbiturates is taken along with alcohol, death may occur because of a synergistic effect that depresses the central nervous system. Furthermore, one of the substances (such as alcohol) may reduce the person's judgment, resulting in excessive (or lethal) use of the other drug. Equally dangerous is the use of one drug to counteract the effect of another. For instance, a person who has taken a stimulant to feel euphoric may later take an excessive amount of a depressant (such as a barbiturate) in an attempt to get some sleep. The result can be an exceedingly harmful physiological reaction.

According to DSM-IV-TR, **polysubstance dependence** may be diagnosed if (1) a person has used at least three substances (not including nicotine and caffeine) for a period of twelve months and (2) during this period, the person meets the criteria for substance dependence for the substances considered as a group but not for any single specific substance.

Benzodiazepines One member of this category of drugs is Valium, which is one of the most widely prescribed drugs in the United States today. Like other sedatives, Valium is a central nervous system depressant; it is often used to reduce anxiety and muscle tension. People who take the drug seem less concerned with and less affected by their problems. Some side effects may occur, such as drowsiness, skin rash, nausea, and depression, but the greatest danger in using Valium is in abusing it. Life stressors are unavoidable, and many people use Valium as their sole means of dealing with stress; as tolerance develops, dependence on the drug may also grow. The female-to-male and white-to-African-American use ratios are about 3:1 (Franklin & Frances, 2000). Benzodiazepines are more likely to be prescribed for older adults, so that there is special concern for this population (U.S. Surgeon General, 1999).

Stimulants

A **stimulant** is a substance that is a central nervous system energizer and that produces elation, grandiosity, hyperactivity, agitation, and appetite suppression. Commonly used stimulants are the amphetamines, caffeine, nicotine, and cocaine and crack.

Amphetamines The **amphetamines**, also known as "uppers," speed up central nervous system activity and bestow on users increased alertness, energy, and sometimes feelings of euphoria and confidence. They increase the concentration of the neuro-

polysubstance dependence Substance dependence in which dependency is not based on the use of any single substance but on the repeated use of at least three groups of substances (not including caffeine and nicotine) for a period of twelve months.

stimulant Substance that is a central nervous system energizer, inducing elation, grandiosity, hyperactivity, agitation, and appetite suppression.

amphetamines Drugs that speed up central nervous system activity and produce increased alertness, energy, and, sometimes, feelings of euphoria and confidence; also called "uppers."

transmitter dopamine in synapses, which exposes the postsynaptic cells to high levels of dopamine. Increased concentration of dopamine may amplify nerve impulses in the brain that are associated with pleasure (Wise, 1988). Amphetamines inhibit appetite and sleep, and some are used as appetite suppressants or diet pills. These stimulants may be physically addictive and become habit forming with a rapid increase in tolerance. They are taken orally, intravenously, or nasally ("snorting"). "Speed freaks" inject amphetamines into their blood vessels and become extremely hyperactive and euphoric for days. Another immediate and powerful effect is obtained by smoking a pure, crystalline form ("ice") of the substance (American Psychiatric Association, 2000a). Assaultive, homicidal, and suicidal behaviors can occur during this time. Heavy doses may trigger delusions of persecution, similar to those seen among paranoid schizophrenics. Overdoses are fatal, and brain damage has been observed among chronic abusers.

About 2 percent of U.S. adults have suffered from amphetamine abuse or dependence at some time during their lives. It is more common among persons from lower socioeconomic groups and among men than women by a ratio of three or four to one (American Psychiatric Association, 2000a).

Caffeine *Caffeine* is a widely used legal stimulant ingested primarily in coffee, chocolate, tea, and cola drinks. The average American consumes approximately 200 milligrams (mg) of caffeine per day (Larson & Carey, 1998). Caffeine is considered intoxicating when, after the recent ingestion of 250 mg (about two cups of coffee) or more, a person shows several of the following symptoms: restlessness, nervousness, excitement, insomnia, flushed face, gastrointestinal disturbance, rambling speech, and cardiac arrhythmia. The consequences of caffeine intoxication are usually transitory and relatively minor. In some cases, however, the intoxication is chronic and seriously affects the gastrointestinal or circulatory system.

Nicotine *Nicotine* is another widely used legal stimulant, and dependence on it is most commonly associated with cigarette smoking. A U.S. surgeon general's report (U.S. Surgeon General, 1999) has indicated that cigarette smoking accounts for one-sixth of the deaths in the United States and is the single most preventable cause of death. The prevalence of smoking is decreasing slightly in most industrialized nations, but it is rising in developing areas. In 1996 a national survey of drug use reported that 72 percent of the adult population in the United States had used cigarettes at some time, with 32 percent reporting use in the prior year and 29 percent reporting use in the prior month. The survey also revealed substantial rates of use of smokeless tobacco, with 17 percent of the U.S. population acknowledging having used these products at some time and 5 percent reporting use in the prior month. Surveys of drug use in high school students indicate that tobacco use in the younger population is on the rise. In a 1997 survey of twelfth graders, 65 percent reported having used cigarettes at some time—an increase over the 1994 proportion of 62 percent. As it is estimated that between 80 percent and 90 percent of regular smokers are nicotine dependent, up to 25 percent of the U.S. population may be nicotine dependent (American Psychiatric Association, 2000a).

The following symptoms are characteristic of nicotine dependence:

- Attempts to stop or reduce tobacco use on a permanent basis have been unsuccessful.

- Attempts to stop smoking have led to withdrawal symptoms, such as a craving for tobacco, irritability, difficulty in concentrating, sleep difficulties, and restlessness.

- Tobacco use continues despite a serious physical disorder, such as emphysema, that the smoker knows is exacerbated by tobacco use.

A Not So Pretty Picture
Ad campaigns like this one by the American Cancer Society use fear appeals to encourage people to stop smoking or never start. Do you think these ad campaigns help to decrease smoking? How do these ads make you feel?

Cocaine and Crack   A great deal of publicity and concern have been devoted to the use of **cocaine,** a substance that is extracted from the coca plant and that induces feelings of euphoria and self-confidence in users. A number of professional athletes, film stars, political figures, and other notables use this drug regularly. Cocaine is a fashionable drug, especially among middle-class and upper-class professionals, and use is equally distributed between males and females. From 1 to 3 million cocaine abusers are in need of treatment, a number many times higher than the number of heroin addicts (Gawin, 1991).

Cocaine can be eaten, injected intravenously, or smoked, but it is usually "snorted" (inhaled). Eating it does not produce rapid effects, and intravenous use requires injection with a needle, which leaves needle marks and introduces the possibility of infection. When cocaine is inhaled into the nasal cavity, however, the person quickly feels euphoric, stimulated, and confident. Heart rate and blood pressure increase, and (according to users) fatigue and appetite are reduced. Users may become dependent on cocaine, sometimes after only a short period of time (American Psychiatric Association, 2000a). Although users do not show gross physiological withdrawal symptoms, Gawin (1991) noted that the distinction between psychological and physical addiction is difficult to make and that chronic abuse of cocaine can produce neurophysiological changes in the central nervous system. The constant desire for cocaine can impair social and occupational functioning, and the high cost of the substance can cause users to resort to crime to feed their habit. In addition, side effects can occur. Feelings of depression and gloom may be produced when a cocaine high wears off. Heavy users sometimes report weight loss, paranoia, nervousness, fatigue, and hallucinations. Because cocaine stimulates the sympathetic nervous system, premature ventricular heartbeats and death may occur.

Crack is a purified and potent form of cocaine produced by heating cocaine with ether ("freebasing"). Crack is sold as small, solid pieces or "rocks." When smoked, crack produces swift and marked euphoria, followed by depression. About 3 percent of young adults between the ages of eighteen and twenty-five reported having used crack during a twelve-month period (Office of National Drug Control Policy, 1998). Some young adults are heavily into "club drugs" as presented in the Mental Health and Society feature, "Club Drugs."

cocaine Substance extracted from the coca plant; induces feelings of euphoria and self-confidence in users.

MenTaL HeaLTh and socieTy

"Club Drugs"

"Club drugs" is a term that comes from the popular use of certain drugs at dance clubs and "raves." At these clubs, groups of young people dance to rapid, electronically synthesized music. As many as 70 percent of the attendees may be using drugs (McDowell, 2001). Among the commonly used club drugs are: Ecstasy or MDMA (methylenedioxymethamphetamine), LSD (d-lysergic acid diethylamide), GHB (gamma hydroxybutyrate), Ketamine, methamphetamine, and Roofies or Rohypnol (flunitrazepam). Of these six drugs, methamphetamine accounts for the largest number of emergency room visits (Clay, 2001). Many young people at raves take multiple substances, which may include alcohol, marijuana, and cocaine.

Two of the better known club drugs are Ecstasy and Rohypnol. Ecstasy is a synthetic type of amphetamine with stimulant properties. Although recreational use is illegal in the United States, its use has skyrocketed (McDowell, 2001).

It tends to induce feelings of well-being and connection with others and one's environment. After it is ingested, the effects of well-being may last for hours. The aftereffects may last for 24 hours or more, and users may experience lethargy, low motivation, and fatigue. Some experience severe effects, such as depression and anxiety, as well as physical changes in blood pressure, convulsions, and even death. Users tend not to increase use over time because highs usually diminish, whereas undesirable effects increase.

Roofies are short-acting benzodiazepines that interfere with short-term memory. It is known as the "date-rape" drug because unsuspecting individuals who are given the drug may feel uninhibited and not remember recent activities. It is a tasteless and odorless drug that dissolves easily in beverages. Because of psychological, cognitive, and biological dangers associated with their use, club drugs are considered unsafe.

Hallucinogens

Hallucinogens are substances that produce hallucinations, vivid sensory awareness, heightened alertness, or perceptions of increased insight. Their use does not typically lead to physical dependence (that is, to increased tolerance or withdrawal reaction), although psychological dependency may occur. Common hallucinogens are marijuana, LSD, and PCP.

Marijuana   The mildest and most commonly used hallucinogen is **marijuana,** also known as "pot" or "grass." Although DSM-IV-TR does not technically consider marijuana a hallucinogen, it does have many of the same effects as hallucinogens. This substance is generally smoked in a cigarette, or "joint." About 33 percent of the U.S. population (including youngsters) have used marijuana, although it is an illegal substance (Office of National Drug Control Policy, 1998).

The subjective effects of marijuana include feelings of euphoria, tranquility, and passivity. Once the drug has taken effect, subjective time passes slowly, and some users report increased sensory experiences, as well as mild perceptual distortions. Individual reactions vary according to prior experience with marijuana, expectancy of its effects, and the setting in which it is used. Simons and colleagues (1998) found that the enhancement of perceptual and cognitive experiences was an important motive in marijuana use.

Although much controversy has raged over the effects of marijuana, many states have now decriminalized the possession of small quantities of this substance. Marijuana has been helpful in treating some physical ailments, such as certain forms of glaucoma (an eye disorder), and in reducing the nausea of patients being treated with chemotherapy for cancer.

hallucinogen Substance that produces hallucinations, vivid sensory awareness, heightened alertness, or increased insight.

marijuana The mildest and most commonly used hallucinogen; also known as "pot" or "grass."

Lysergic Acid Diethylamide (LSD) LSD or "acid" gained notoriety as a hallucinogen in the mid-1960s. Praised by users as a potent psychedelic consciousness-expanding drug, LSD produces distortions of reality and hallucinations. "Good trips" are experiences of sharpened visual and auditory perception, heightened sensation, convictions that one has achieved profound philosophical insights, and feelings of ecstasy. "Bad trips" include fear and panic from distortions of sensory experiences, severe depression, marked confusion and disorientation, and delusions. Some users report "flashbacks," the recurrence of hallucinations or other sensations days or weeks after taking LSD. Fatigue, stress, or the use of another drug may trigger a "flashback."

Phencyclidine (PCP) Phencyclidine, also known as PCP, "angel dust," "crystal," "superweed," and "rocket fuel," has emerged as one of the most dangerous of the so-called street drugs. Originally developed for its pain-killing properties, PCP is a hallucinatory drug that causes perceptual distortions, euphoria, nausea, confusion, delusions, and violent psychotic behavior. Reactions to the drug are influenced by dosage, the individual user, and the circumstances in which it is taken. One thing is clear: PCP has in many cases caused aggressive behavior, violence, or death from the taker's recklessness or delusions of invincibility. The drug is illegal, but it is still widely used, often sprinkled on marijuana and smoked.

▷ CHECKPOINT REVIEW

alcoholic *(p. 195)*

alcoholism *(p. 195)*

amphetamines *(p. 200)*

barbiturates *(p. 199)*

cocaine *(p. 202)*

depressant *(p. 195)*

hallucinogen *(p. 203)*

intoxication *(p. 194)*

marijuana *(p. 203)*

narcotics *(p. 199)*

polysubstance dependence *(p. 200)*

stimulant *(p. 200)*

substance abuse *(p. 192)*

substance dependence *(p. 193)*

substance-related disorders *(p. 191)*

tolerance *(p. 194)*

withdrawal *(p. 194)*

What are substance-use disorders?

- Substance abuse is defined as a maladaptive pattern of recurrent use over a twelve-month period, during which the person is unable to reduce or cease intake of a harmful substance, despite knowledge that its use causes social, occupational, psychological, medical, or safety problems. Substance dependence is a more serious disorder, involving not only excessive use but also tolerance and withdrawal in many cases.
- Substance-use disorders vary according to age, gender, and ethnic group. Major categories of substances are depressants, stimulants, and hallucinogens.
- A large proportion of the U.S. population consumes alcohol, one of the depressants. Alcohol is associated with traffic accidents, absenteeism from work, accidents, violence, and family problems. The consumption of alcohol results in both long-term and short-term psychological and physiological effects.
- Other depressants, such as narcotics, barbiturates, and benzodiazepines, can also cause psychological, physiological, or legal problems.
- Other categories of psychoactive substances include stimulants and hallucinogens. Stimulants energize the central nervous system, often inducing elation, grandiosity, hyperactivity, agitation, and appetite suppression.
- Amphetamines and cocaine/crack cocaine, as well as widely used substances such as caffeine and nicotine, are considered stimulants.
- Abuse and dependency often occur after regular use of stimulants.
- Hallucinogens, another category of psychoactive substances, often produce hallucinations, altered states of consciousness, and perceptual distortions.
- Included in this category are marijuana, LSD, and PCP.
- Drug dependency is relatively rare, although abuse may occur.
- PCP in many cases causes delusions, perceptual distortions, and violent behaviors.

◁ Etiology of Substance-Use Disorders

Why do people abuse substances, despite the knowledge that alcohol and drugs can have devastating consequences in their lives? The answer to this question is complicated by the number of different kinds of substances that are used and the number of

Polysubstance Abuse   Using one psychoactive drug can be dangerous in itself, but mixing two or more chemical substances at the same time can be deadly. Each of these talented performers—Jim Morrison, Janis Joplin, John Belushi, and River Phoenix—died from polydrug use. How common is polydrug use?

factors that interact to account for the use of any one substance. Many theories have been proposed in the attempt to answer the question. Of these, the major types have been either biological in perspective (involving genetic or physiological factors) or psychological and cultural (involving psychodynamic, personality, sociocultural, or behavioral and cognitive factors). Both perspectives offer valid insights into addiction. The first focuses on dependence, or the bodily need for alcohol or drugs. The second attempts to explain how abuse patterns develop before actual dependence and why addicts who try to stop their habit may relapse and return to substance use. In the case of alcohol, for example, drinking behavior was traditionally believed to be the result of psychological factors, whereas the maintenance of heavy drinking resulted from physical dependence on alcohol. According to this viewpoint, one first drinks because of curiosity; because of exposure to drinking models such as parents, peers, or television characters; and because of the tension-reducing properties of alcohol. After prolonged consumption, however, the person becomes physically dependent and drinks heavily to satisfy bodily needs.

As these statements indicate, traditional theories often assumed that the acquisition and maintenance of substances were largely distinct processes in which psychological factors influenced acquisition and biological factors were responsible for maintenance. This assumption is overly simplistic. Both the acquisition and maintenance of drinking behavior are influenced by a complex interaction of psychological and physical factors.

Because of alcohol's widespread use, availability, and consequences to society, more research has been conducted on alcohol than on other substances. Most of our discussion therefore centers on alcohol, although we comment on the relevance of different theories to the use of substances other than alcohol.

Biological Explanations

Because alcohol affects metabolic processes and the central nervous system, investigators have explored the possibility that heredity or congenital factors increase susceptibility

Family Ties Today, Drew Barrymore's life seems filled with successes. But it hasn't always been so; in 1988, at the young age of thirteen, Drew entered rehabilitation to deal with her addiction to drugs and alcohol. Although it is difficult to separate out environmental and genetic influences in cases of alcohol and substance abuse, it is likely that both were operating in Drew's case. Not only did she experience the stress of being thrust into the limelight of an acting career at a very young age, but she also had a family history filled with problems of alcohol abuse—her grandfather, John Barrymore, drank himself to death, and her father had long abused both alcohol and drugs. Does this mean that drug abuse is inherited?

to addiction. The incidence of alcoholism is four times higher among male biological offspring of alcoholic fathers than among offspring of nonalcoholic fathers (Franklin & Frances, 1999). Because children share both genetic and environmental influences with their parents, researchers face the challenge of somehow separating the contributions of these two sets of factors. The role of in utero and neonatal influences must also be determined. Many investigators have attempted to isolate genetic and environmental factors through the use of adoption studies and twin studies.

Several studies have indicated that children whose biological parents were alcoholics but who were adopted and raised by nonrelatives are more likely to develop drinking problems than are adopted children whose biological parents were not alcoholics (Franklin & Frances, 1999; Goodwin, 1979; Kanas, 1988). In one study of alcohol abuse among adopted individuals, Cadoret and Wesner (1990) found clear-cut evidence of a genetic factor operating from biological parent to adopted child. However, they also found evidence of environmental influences: having an alcoholic in the adoptive home also increases the risk of alcohol problems in the adopted person.

Investigators studying the concordance rates for alcoholism among identical and fraternal twins have reported similar findings. Concordance rates indicate the likelihood that *both* twins have a disorder. Although identical twins have higher concordance rates, fraternal twins also have high rates (Rosenthal, 1971).

Collectively, these two sets of findings suggest that both heredity and environmental factors are important. Two types of alcoholism may exist: familial and nonfamilial (Goodwin, 1985). *Familial alcoholism* shows a family history of alcoholism, suggesting genetic predisposition. This type of alcoholism develops at an early age (usually by the late twenties), is severe, and is associated with an increased risk of alcoholism (but not other mental disorders) among blood relatives (Emmelkamp, 2004). Genetic factors appear to be important both for males and females (Slutske et al., 1998). *Nonfamilial alcoholism* does not show these characteristics and is presumably influenced more by environment.

Psychodynamic Explanations

A number of psychodynamic explanations have been proposed for alcoholism. Most hold that childhood traumas (such as an overprotecting mother, maternal neglect, or frustration of dependency needs), especially during the oral stage of development, result in the repression of painful conflicts involving dependency needs (Kanas, 1988). During stress or encounters with situations reminiscent of the original conflicts, symptoms such as anxiety, depression, and hostility begin to occur. Alcohol is seen as (1) releasing inhibitions and allowing the repressed conflicts to be expressed or (2) enabling people to obtain oral gratification and to satisfy dependency needs. Most of the psychoanalytic formulations are based on retrospective clinical case studies rather than empirical data, so their validity is open to question.

Explanations Based on Personality Characteristics

Some researchers believe that certain personality characteristics function as a predisposition, making people vulnerable to alcoholism. Alcoholism has been found to be associated with high activity level, emotionality, goal impersistence, and sociability. Causality cannot be determined from correlational data, but these characteristics may interact with one's social environment to increase the risk of alcoholism (Tarter & Vanyukov, 1994).

Life transitions or maturational events, such as changing from a student to a working-adult role, may also affect drinking patterns. In one study of the stability of alcohol consumption from college years and beyond (Gotham, Sher, & Wood, 1997), researchers identified young adults who drank heavily during their years in college and who significantly decreased their drinking after college. The investigators found that entering the work force full time, being male, and being less open to experiences were important predictors of the change in consumption.

In reviews of research on personality and alcoholism, Nathan (1988), Franklin and Frances (1999), and Sher and Trull (1994) have concluded that there is no single alcoholic personality. Nathan found only two personality characteristics—antisocial behavior and depression—associated with drinking problems. Particularly consistent is the relationship between a childhood or adolescent history of antisocial behavior (such as rejection of societal rules) and alcoholism. Nathan warned, however, that the role of personality characteristics, including antisocial tendencies and depression, as causal factors in alcoholism cannot be uncritically accepted. Many alcohol abusers do not show antisocial histories, and many antisocial people do not drink excessively. Furthermore, depression may well be a consequence rather than an antecedent of alcohol abuse (that is, problem drinking may cause people to feel depressed).

Sociocultural Explanations

Drinking varies according to sociocultural factors such as gender, age, socioeconomic status, ethnicity, religion, and country (American Psychiatric Association, 2000a). In terms of religious affiliation, heavier drinking is found among Catholics than among Protestants or Jews. Furthermore, drinking behavior varies from country to country. In wine-producing countries such as France and Italy, alcohol consumption is high (Goodwin, 1985). Relative to France and Italy, consumption is low in Israel and mainland China, with the United States being moderate in consumption. Among ethnic groups within the United States, American Indians and Irish Americans are far more likely to become alcoholics than are Americans of Italian, Hispanic, or Asian backgrounds (Sue & Nakamura, 1984). These findings suggest that cultural values play an important role in drinking patterns. The values affect not only the amount consumed and the occasions on which drinking takes place but also the given culture's tolerance of alcohol abuse.

Studies also indicate that both peer selection and peer socialization influence drug-use patterns. Frequency of alcohol and drug use reported by African American adolescents was significantly related to both peer pressure and peer drug use in one study (Farrell & White, 1998). In another study of adolescents who did not initially smoke, those who had more friends who smoked were subsequently more likely to smoke (Killen et al., 1997). Curran, Stice, and Chassin (1997) note that the association between peer use and one's own use of drugs appears to be a two-way street: a drug user tends to choose friends who are users, and friends who use drugs tend to influence one to take drugs.

As in the case of alcohol, use of other psychoactive substances varies widely, and these variations reflect sociocultural influences. For example, in the United States, lifetime prevalence of drug abuse and dependence is higher among white Americans than among African and Hispanic Americans, although white Americans have lower rates of alcoholism than do the other two groups (Robins & Regier, 1991). Similarly, although white Americans are less likely than African or Hispanic Americans to have used heroin during their lifetimes, they are more likely to have used hallucinogens and PCP (National Institute on Drug Abuse, 1991).

Behavioral Explanations

Early behavioral explanations for alcohol abuse and dependence were based on two assumptions: (1) alcohol temporarily reduces anxiety and tension, and (2) drinking behavior is learned.

Anxiety Reduction In a classic experiment, researchers induced an "experimental neurosis" in cats (Masserman et al., 1944). After the cats were trained to approach and eat food at a food box, they were given an aversive stimulus (an air blast to the face or an electric shock) whenever they approached the food. The cats stopped eating and exhibited "neurotic" symptoms—anxiety, psychophysiological disturbances, and peculiar behaviors. When the cats were given alcohol, however, their symptoms disappeared, and they started to eat. As the effects of the alcohol wore off, the symptoms began to reappear.

The experimenters also found that these cats now preferred "spiked" milk (milk mixed with alcohol) to milk alone. Once the stressful shocks were terminated and the fear responses extinguished, however, the cats no longer preferred spiked milk. Alcohol apparently reduced the cats' anxieties and was used as long as the anxieties were present. (Note that the cats were placed in an *approach-avoidance conflict*; that is, their desire to approach the food box and eat was in conflict with their desire to avoid the air blast or shock.)

Learned Expectations A group of researchers (Marlatt, Demming, & Reid, 1973; Smith et al., 1995) provided evidence that learned expectations also affect consumption. In the process, they challenged the notion that alcoholism is a disease in which drinking small amounts of alcohol leads, in an alcoholic, to involuntary consumption to the point of intoxication. In their study, alcoholics and social drinkers were recruited to participate in what was described as a "tasting experiment." Some of the research participants were led to believe that they had consumed alcohol (whether or not they really did) and others were led to believe that they had not consumed any alcoholic beverage (whether or not they really did) during the beverage tasting. The results suggested that alcoholism is not simply a disease in which a person loses control over drinking. Participants who were told that they would receive alcohol drank more than those who were told they would receive tonic, and those who actually consumed alcohol did not drink more than those who consumed tonic (Marlatt et al., 1973). The participants' expectancy had a stronger effect than the actual content of their drinks on how much they consumed. In fact, several people who were given tonic when they believed they were imbibing alcohol acted as though they were "tipsy" from the drinks!

Cognitive Influences The *tension-reducing model,* which assumes that alcohol reduces tension and anxiety and that the relief of tension reinforces the drinking

response, is difficult to test, and research with alcoholics has produced conflicting findings. In fact, prolonged drinking is often associated with increased anxiety and depression (McNamee, Mello, & Mendelson, 1968). Although alcoholics who have high
blood alcohol levels after drinking may show low muscular tension, they tend to
report a high degree of distress (Steffen, Nathan, & Taylor, 1974). Alcohol is a sedative that can reduce anxiety, and, ironically, it is possible that the knowledge that one
is drinking alcohol can increase one's level of anxiety (Polivy, Schueneman, & Carlson,
1976).

Other evidence supports the idea that the tension-reducing model is too simplistic.
Steele and Josephs (1988, 1990) found that alcohol can either increase or decrease
anxiety, depending on the ways alcohol affects perception and thought. When confronted with a stressful situation, people who drank alcohol in the experiment experienced anxiety reduction if they were allowed to engage in a distracting activity. When
faced with a stressor, however, those who drank and did not have a distracting activity
experienced an increase in anxiety. The investigators argued that the distracting activity allowed drinkers to divert attention from the stressor. Without the distraction,
drinkers' attention may have focused on the stressor, which served to magnify their
anxiety.

Both the expectancy and tension-reduction models have difficulty accounting for
the two phases of alcohol effects, in which blood alcohol levels initially rise and then
fall. Giancola and Zeichner (1997) found that increases in aggression tended to occur
during the ascending phase (when blood alcohol level is increasing) rather than the
descending phase (when blood alcohol level is decreasing) of blood alcohol levels. That
is, despite having similar blood alcohol levels, individuals exhibited more aggression
during the ascending rather than during the descending phase. The expectancy and
tension-reduction models have a problem explaining this two-phase effect because the
blood alcohol levels, tensions, and expectations are presumably similar regardless of
the phase. This research raises the possibility that the concepts of expectancy and tension reduction are too simple to explain the effects of alcohol.

Relapse: A Source of Evidence For persons attempting to abstain from using substances after addiction, relapse is common. Factors associated with relapse include
younger age at onset of drug use; more extensive involvement with substances; antisocial behavior; comorbid psychiatric disorder; less involvement in school or work; and
less support from drug-free family and peers (Walter, 2001). In terms of relapse,
Marlatt (1978) suggested that the type of stressor, the loss of a sense of personal control over situations, and the lack of alternative coping responses influence drinking and
resumption of drinking after abstinence.

Relapse is the resumption of drinking after a period of voluntary abstinence. A
fairly consistent relationship has been found between relapse and time elapsed since
last use of a substance for alcohol, heroin, tobacco, and other substances (Woody &
Cacciola, 1994). Risk of relapse is greatest during the first three months following
treatment, becoming less and less likely over time. By the end of three years, relapse is
unlikely. Negative emotional states (such as depression, interpersonal conflict, and anxiety) are highly associated with relapse (Cooney et al., 1997). They account for 53 percent of relapses among alcoholics trying to quit drinking (Hodgins, El-Guebaly, &
Armstrong, 1995). Negative emotional states tended to play a role in major relapse
(substantial use of the substance), whereas social pressure led to minor relapse (taking
just a beer). Negative physical states, urges and temptations, and positive emotional
states did not strongly predict relapse. Interestingly, there was a gender difference in
the states reported. Women were more likely than men to cite interpersonal conflict
and less likely to report emotional states such as depression. This suggests that women

may be more vulnerable to social influences than men are in the context of alcohol use and relapse.

Many researchers and clinicians formerly believed that addiction and relapse to other substances, such as heroin, could be best explained by biological factors such as physical dependence and the attempt to avoid withdrawal symptoms. However, we now know that drug use is a complex phenomenon and that explanatory models must also incorporate the roles of learning, expectancy, and situational factors. Consider heroin withdrawal, for example. Some have characterized heroin withdrawal reactions as no more agonizing than a bad case of the flu (Ausubel, 1961). Heroin addicts who enter a hospital and receive no heroin while hospitalized will stop having withdrawal symptoms in a week or two. Nevertheless, these statements about the addicts' physiological responses do not explain why the vast majority who have lost their bodily need for the drug resume heroin use after hospitalization. Further evidence of the influence of cognitive and behavioral factors comes from the behavior of Vietnam servicemen who were addicted to heroin. When they returned to the United States, many discontinued its use because they had easier access to alcohol and great difficulty in procuring heroin (Pilisuk, 1975).

In a study of marijuana and cocaine use among college students, Schafer and Brown (1991) showed the importance of expectancies. Their survey of positive and negative expectancies (for example, relaxation, social facilitation, and cognitive impairment) for the use of marijuana and cocaine showed that students who used these drugs also expected strong positive experiences. Such studies show that there are many factors that maintain drug use and drug dependence.

> ## ▷ CHECKPOINT REVIEW

Why do people become addicted to drugs?

■ There appears to be no single factor that can account for drug abuse or for dependence on other substances such as depressants, stimulants, and hallucinogens. In all likelihood, heredity and environmental factors are important.

■ With respect to alcoholism, some research has indicated that heredity, along with environmental factors, plays an important role.

■ Recent experiments have demonstrated the importance of cognitive factors in drinking behavior.

■ The tension-reducing hypothesis alone is inadequate to account for alcoholism because alcohol consumption sometimes results in increased feelings of depression or anxiety.

■ Drinking and alcoholism may be closely related to the type of stress anticipated, the perceived benefits of alcohol, the availability of alternative coping responses in a particular situation, and the drinker's genetic or physiological makeup.

■ For narcotic addiction, both physical and psychological factors are important.

■ Overall theories of addiction have been proposed that emphasize changes in motivation for drug use with chronic consumption, the positive and negative reinforcing effects of drugs, and cognitive factors in maintaining drug use.

▷ Intervention and Treatment of Substance-Use Disorders

detoxification Alcohol or drug treatment phase characterized by removal of the abusive substance; after that removal, the user is immediately or eventually prevented from consuming the substance.

Treatment of substance abusers and addicts depends on both the individual user and the type of drug being used. Most alcohol and drug treatment programs have two phases: first, the removal of the abusive substance and second, long-term maintenance without it. In the first phase, which is also referred to as **detoxification,** the user is immediately or eventually prevented from consuming the substance. The removal of the substance may trigger withdrawal symptoms that are opposite in effect to the reactions produced by the drug. For instance, a person who is physically addicted to a central nervous system depressant such as a barbiturate will experience drowsiness, decreased respiration, and reduced anxiety when taking the drug. When the depressant is withdrawn, the user experiences symptoms that resemble the effects of a stimulant—agitation, restlessness, increased respiration, and insomnia. Helping someone successfully cope during withdrawal has been a concern of many treatment strategies dealing with various drugs, particularly in treating heroin addicts. Sometimes, addicts are given medication to alleviate some of the withdrawal symptoms. For example, tranquilizers may be helpful to alcoholics experiencing withdrawal.

In the second phase, intervention programs attempt to prevent the person from returning to the substance (in some rare cases, controlling or limiting the use of the substance). These programs may be community programs, which include sending alcoholics or addicts to a hospital, residential treatment facility, or halfway house, where support and guidance are available in a community setting. Family therapy has consistently been successful in treating adolescent substance abusers (Sexton, Alexander, & Mease, 2004). Whatever the setting, the treatment approach may be chemical, cognitive or behavioral, or multimodal. In this section, we discuss these approaches to the treatment of various substance-use disorders and review their effectiveness. We also take a quick look at prevention programs.

Self-Help Groups

Alcoholics Anonymous (AA) is a self-help organization composed of alcoholics who want to stop drinking. Perhaps a million or more alcoholics worldwide participate in the AA program, which is completely voluntary. There are no fees, and the only membership requirement is the desire to stop drinking. AA assumes that once a person is an alcoholic, he or she is always an alcoholic—an assumption based on the disease model of alcoholism. Members must recognize that they can never drink again and must concentrate on abstinence, one day at a time. As a means of helping members abstain, each may be assigned a sponsor who provides individual support, attention, and help. Group meetings encourage fellowship, spiritual awareness, and public self-revelations about past wrongdoings because of alcohol.

Some people believe that membership in AA is one of the most effective treatments for alcoholism. A few studies with methodological limitations have found an association between AA attendance and positive treatment outcome (McCrady, 1994), although the success rate of AA is not as high as AA members claim it is (Brandsma, 1979). Approximately one-half of the alcoholics who stay in the organization are still abstinent after two years (Alford, 1980), but many drop out of the program and are not counted as failures. In one of the most rigorous studies of AA, Morgenstern et al. (1997) investigated the effects of affiliation with AA among individuals who had undergone treatment for alcoholism. Greater affiliation with AA did predict better treatment outcomes. However, the involvement with AA was associated with increased feelings of self-efficacy, active coping, and motivation to stop drinking, which were, in turn, predictors of outcome. Spinoffs of AA such as Al-Anon and Alateen have been helpful in providing support for adults and teenagers living with alcoholics (Kanas, 1988). There are similar self-help groups for drug abuse (Narcotics Anonymous), although they have not gained the widespread attention and participation seen in AA.

Pharmacological Approach

To keep addicts from using certain substances, some treatment programs dispense other chemical substances. For example, alcohol treatment programs may include the chemical *Antabuse* (disulfiram) to produce an aversion to alcohol. A person who

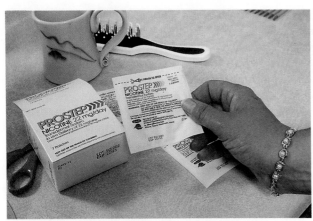

Kicking the Habit with Nicotine Replacement
Transdermal nicotine patches such as the ones shown are usually applied to the arm. They deliver nicotine, which is absorbed through the skin. The patches are intended to help smokers quit smoking by fulfilling the need for nicotine without the use of tobacco.

consumes alcohol one to two days after taking Antabuse suffers a severe reaction, including nausea, vomiting, and discomfort. Antabuse has the effect of blocking the progressive breakdown of alcohol so that excessive acetaldehyde accumulates in the body; acetaldehyde causes dysphoria (depression or distress). Most alcoholics will not consume alcohol after ingesting Antabuse. Those who do risk not only discomfort but also, in some cases, death.

While clients are taking Antabuse and are typically abstinent, as demonstrated in several studies (see Gallant, 2001), psychotherapy and other forms of treatment may be used to help them develop coping skills or alternative life patterns. The families of patients may also be encouraged to work at solving the problems created by the drinking. Knowing that alcohol consumption is unlikely during Antabuse treatment, families do not have to rely solely on the alcoholic's promise to stop drinking—a promise that alcoholics often make but are rarely able to keep.

The problem with Antabuse treatment is that alcoholic patients may stop taking the drug once they leave the hospital or are no longer being monitored. And some may drink anyway because they believe the effects of Antabuse have dissipated, because they have forgotten when they last took it, or because they are tempted to drink in spite of the Antabuse. Naltrexone has been used to reduce craving or the reinforcing effects of alcohol. The reduced craving appears specific to alcohol, not to just any drink (e.g., fruit juices), as found in a study by Rohsenow and colleagues (2000).

Pharmacological agents such as clonidine and naltrexone have allowed some heroin addicts to be detoxified as outpatients (Franklin & Frances, 2000). Chemical treatment may also be used to reduce the intensity of withdrawal symptoms in heroin addicts who are trying to break the drug habit. The drug methadone is prescribed to decrease the intensity of withdrawal symptoms. *Methadone* is a synthetic narcotic chemical that reduces the craving for heroin without producing euphoria (the "high"). It was originally believed that reformed heroin addicts could then quite easily discontinue the methadone at a later date. Although methadone initially seemed to be a simple solution to a major problem, it has an important drawback: it can itself become addicting.

It is clear that the use of chemical substances, such as Antabuse or methadone, has not had a dramatic impact in the treatment of addiction. Side effects and potential addiction to chemical treatments are major problems that have to be considered.

In smoking cessation programs, however, one tactic has been the use of nicotine replacement strategy, especially in the application of transdermal nicotine patches. A patch is applied to the arm, and the nicotine in the patch is absorbed through the skin. Researchers are also studying the effectiveness of directly inhaling nicotine.

Cognitive and Behavioral Approaches

aversion therapy Conditioning procedure in which the response to a stimulus is decreased by pairing the stimulus with an aversive stimulus.

Cognitive and behavioral therapists have devised several strategies for treating alcoholism and other substance-use disorders. **Aversion therapy,** which is based on classical conditioning principles, has been used for many years. Aversion therapy is a conditioning procedure in which the response to a stimulus is decreased by pairing the stimulus with an aversive stimulus. For example, alcoholics may be given painful electric shocks while drinking alcohol, or they may be given *emetics* (agents that induce vomiting) after smelling or tasting alcohol or when they get the urge to drink. After several sessions in which the emetic is used, alcoholics may vomit or feel nauseated when they smell, taste, or think about alcohol.

Imagery has been used as part of **covert sensitization,** an aversive conditioning technique in which the individual imagines a noxious stimulus in the presence of a behavior. Alcoholic patients, for example, are trained to imagine nausea and vomiting in the presence of alcoholic beverages (Cautela, 1966). Covert sensitization has also been used for drug addicts. One difficulty with this technique is the inability of some patients to generalize the treatment—that is, to pair the learned aversive reaction (nausea and vomiting) with the stimulus (taking a particular drug) outside the clinic or hospital setting.

Skills training has also been used in drug-cessation programs. These skills may involve techniques for refusing to give in to peer pressures or temptations, for resolving emotional conflicts or problems, and for more effective communication. Smith, Meyers, and Delaney (1998) found that skills training was effective in reducing alcohol consumption among homeless alcohol-dependent individuals. Bickel et al. (1997) found that **reinforcing abstinence** was effective for opioid-dependent individuals. The individuals received either reinforcement (such as vouchers for cash) for being abstinent, as measured by urinalysis, or standard forms of counseling used in methadone clinics. Results indicated that the behavioral method was more effective than the counseling method in promoting abstinence.

Behavioral Treatment for Cigarette Smoking

People who wish to end their addiction to cigarette smoking have used behavioral techniques almost exclusively. Most aversive procedures (such as covert sensitization and shock) have yielded rather disappointing results, but "rapid smoking" has achieved some positive outcomes. This technique requires the client to puff a cigarette once every six seconds, until he or she absolutely cannot continue any longer. Its purpose is to pair a highly aversive situation (the feeling of illness that results from extremely rapid smoking) with the act of smoking. This is expected to eliminate or reduce the person's desire to smoke. Although rapid smoking has been reasonably effective over both the short and the long term, it is somewhat controversial. Some early studies suggested that the technique may increase heart rate and blood pressure (Lichtenstein & Glasgow, 1977; Lichtenstein & Rodrigues, 1977). Other studies of smokers with cardiopulmonary disease who engaged in rapid smoking, however, showed that the treatment was effective and did not produce any cardiac complications (Hall et al., 1984).

Another treatment for cigarette smoking is *nicotine fading* (Foxx & Brown, 1979). In this method, the client attempts to withdraw gradually from nicotine by progressively smoking cigarette brands that contain less and less nicotine. When clients reach the stage at which they are smoking cigarettes that contain only 0.1 milligrams of nicotine, their reduced dependence should enable them to stop altogether (Lichtenstein & Danaher, 1976). However, some individuals who smoke low-nicotine cigarettes may simply inhale more deeply or smoke more rapidly, defeating the purpose of smoking low-nicotine cigarettes. A more familiar method is simply to smoke less and less—increasing the interval between cigarettes. Cinciripini and his colleagues (1995) found that systematically increasing the amount of time between using cigarettes was a more effective way of achieving abstinence one year later than were other methods, such as going "cold turkey" (abruptly ceasing smoking) or gradually reducing smoking without any fixed and systematic plan. The scheduled-interval method also appeared to be superior in decreasing tension and withdrawal symptoms. The investigators suggest

covert sensitization Aversive conditioning technique in which the individual imagines a noxious stimulus occurring in the presence of a behavior.

skills training Teaching skills for resisting peer pressures or temptations, resolving emotional conflicts or problems, or for more effective communication.

reinforcing abstinence Giving behavioral reinforcements for abstinence from substance use.

that individuals using this method could plan and bring to bear coping mechanisms to deal with urges to smoke.

In general, multicomponent behavioral therapy programs that incorporate relapse-prevention techniques appear to be very effective for quitting smoking (Compas et al., 1998). These programs combine behavioral strategies, such as relaxation and gradual reduction of nicotine intake, with relapse-prevention skills, such as learning how to refuse peer pressures to smoke. Because smoking cessation is related to body-weight increase (Klesges et al., 1997), some attention must also be paid to smokers' concerns over gaining weight after quitting smoking.

Other Cognitive-Behavioral Treatments   Relaxation and systematic desensitization may be useful in reducing anxiety. Almost any aversive conditioning procedure may be effective in treating alcoholism if there is also a focus on enhanced social functioning, resistance to stress, and reduction of anxiety (Nathan, 1976). Some programs incorporate social learning techniques.

Cognitive-behavioral treatments, based on analyses of why addicts experience relapse, have also been tried. Niaura and colleagues (1988) believe that certain cues are strongly associated with substance use (smoking while having coffee, drinking alcohol at a party, and so forth). They suggested that addicts be placed in these situations or in the presence of the cues and prevented from using the substance. In this way, the consumption response to these cues is extinguished. To prevent relapse, some treatment programs help addicts restructure their thoughts about the pleasant effects of drug use (Cooper, Russell, & George, 1988). Addicts are taught to substitute negative thoughts for positive ones when tempted to use the substance. For example, instead of focusing on the euphoria felt from taking cocaine, a person might be taught to say, "I feel an urge to take the substance, but I know that I will feel depressed later on, that many of my friends want me to stop taking it, and that I may get arrested."

The Controlled-Drinking Controversy   A great deal of debate has been generated by the suggestion that it is possible for alcoholics to control their intake and learn to become social drinkers. Proponents of controlled drinking assume that, under the right conditions, alcoholics can learn to limit their drinking to appropriate levels. The finding that alcoholics tend to gulp drinks rather than sip them (as social or moderate drinkers do), to consume straight rather than mixed drinks, and to drink many rather than a few drinks gave investigators clues to behaviors that require modification. Alcoholics were then trained to drink appropriately. In a setting resembling a bar, they were permitted to order and drink alcohol, but they were administered an aversive stimulus for each inappropriate behavior. For example, alcoholics who gulped drinks or ordered too many were given painful electric shocks.

There is evidence that controlled drinking may work for some alcohol abusers (Emmelkamp, 2004). However, one problem with this technique is that patients need to receive periodic retraining or to learn alternative responses to drinking. Otherwise, they tend to revert to their old patterns of consumption on leaving the treatment program (Marlatt, 1983). The major task is to discover the conditions under which controlled drinking or abstinence interventions work.

Opponents of controlled drinking generally believe that total abstinence should be the goal of treatment, that controlled drinking cannot be maintained over a period of time, and that alcoholism is a genetic-physiological problem. Furthermore, by trying to teach alcoholics that they can resume and control drinking, proponents are unwittingly contributing to the alcoholics' problems. There have even been questions about the validity of the findings in controlled drinking programs (see Pendery, Maltzman, & West, 1982).

Multimodal Treatment

In view of the many factors that maintain drug-use disorders, some treatment programs make systematic use of combinations of approaches. For example, alcoholics may be detoxified through Antabuse treatment and simultaneously receive behavioral training (via aversion therapy, biofeedback, or stress management), as well as other forms of therapy. In one outpatient treatment program, alcohol-dependent men were given standard care (life-skills training, relapse prevention and coping skills, after-care meetings, and counseling). A group of these men was randomly assigned to another condition, the contingency management group. In this group, the men were given the opportunity to win prizes (ranging from small gift certificates to larger gifts, such as a television) if they tested negative for alcohol consumption on a Breathalyzer. Those patients who had the combined treatment involving contingency management and standard care were more likely to be abstinent than patients who were exposed solely to standard care (Petry et al., 2000).

Other therapies may include combinations of Alcoholics Anonymous, educational training, family therapy, group therapy, and individual psychotherapy. Proponents of multimodal approaches recognize that no single kind of treatment is likely to be totally effective and that successful outcomes often require major changes in the lives of alcoholics. The combination of therapies that works best for a particular person in his or her particular circumstances is obviously the most effective treatment.

One recent multimodal project involved 600 youths being treated for marijuana use, the largest experiment ever conducted on outpatient adolescent treatment (Clay, 2001). The youths were exposed to a number of different treatments that included the adolescents, their families, schools, and other systems. Preliminary results showed dramatic changes in the adolescents' drug use. For example, the percentage of youths reporting no marijuana abuse or dependence in the previous month increased from 19 percent before treatment to 61 percent six months after treatment. Problems with the criminal justice system, their families, and schools also decreased.

Prevention Programs

Prevention programs have been initiated to discourage drug and alcohol use before it begins. Campaigns to educate the public about the detrimental consequences of substance use, to reestablish norms against drug use, and to give coping skills to others who are tempted by drug use are waged in the media. Other prevention programs take place in schools, places of worship, youth groups, and families.

Such programs are having some effect. For example, Marlatt and colleagues (1998) assigned heavy-drinking college students to a brief intervention group or to a no-intervention control group for three months of the first year of college. The intervention consisted of providing students with feedback on the extent of their drinking and on possible consequences, without confrontation or direct advice. The investigators conducted one-year and two-year follow-up assessments of drinking, which indicated that the intervention was successful. Students receiving the intervention reported lower alcohol consumption and fewer problems resulting from drinking, and the self-reports from students were consistent with those of friends of the students who were also asked to provide ratings of the students.

In another study, Dent and his colleagues (1995) evaluated the outcome of a junior high school smoking-prevention program. One group of students received training focused on (1) resistance to social influence (for example, resisting peer pressure to smoke), (2) information (such as correcting misperceptions of the social image of smokers), (3) the physical consequences of smoking, or (4) a combination of the three other approaches. A control group of students was not involved in the training program. The participants received three initial training sessions and a booster training session given a year later. Two years after the initial three sessions, the students exposed to the training were generally less likely to show increases in smoking or in trying smoking than were students not exposed to the training. The investigators warn that longer term success may depend on additional training in high school or at some other future time.

Because of the public's constant exposure to television, radio, and newspapers, some researchers have used these media as a means to prevent drug use, as noted earlier. Jason (1998) has found that media programs to prevent or reduce drug use and to maintain abstinence have been very successful.

Effectiveness of Treatment

Research evidence indicates that treatment programs are effective in reducing substance abuse and dependence (McLellan et al., 1994), although outcomes have been quite modest (Woody & Cacciola, 1994) and estimates vary from study to study. About one-third of alcoholic clients remain abstinent one year after treatment. Most opiate-dependent clients and heroin addicts are readdicted within the first year following treatment. The majority of treated smokers return to smoking within one year. Again, relapse occurs most frequently during the first several months of abstinence, and the type of substance is important to consider. Part of the problem in delivering effective treatment is that many individuals with substance-use disorders do not continue treatment (Stark, 1992). However, some individuals recover on their own, without treatment. Other individuals who relapse after treatment subsequently undergo treatment again and become abstinent or develop an ability to control their intake.

Interestingly, McLellan and his colleagues (1994) believe that treatment of substance abuse is effective and find that the same factors predict outcome regardless of the substance used. They examined the outcome of male and female clients in twenty-two inpatient and outpatient treatment programs for opiate, alcohol, and cocaine dependency. Outcome was assessed six months after treatment, and demographic background, severity of problems, and type of treatment were examined as predictors of outcome. Although a no-treatment control group was not available for comparison purposes, all groups showed significant and pervasive improvements in reduced substance use, family relations, and adjustment six months after treatment, and the same factors predicted outcomes regardless of the type of drug problem. The findings suggest that treatment can be helpful and that outcomes are governed by the same client and treatment factors. In a review of the treatment outcomes for adolescents, Williams and Chang (2000) found that treatment for substance abuse was generally beneficial, especially if the adolescents completed treatment and if parental and peer support for nonuse was available. Read, Kahler, and Stevenson (2001) conclude that there is probably no single "best" treatment for substance use disorders, although a number of different treatment approaches exist and are helpful. The task is to find the best combination of treatments for particular individuals with substance use disorders.

▷ CHECKPOINT REVIEW

aversion therapy *(p. 212)*

covert sensitization *(p. 213)*

detoxification *(p. 210)*

reinforcing abstinence *(p. 213)*

skills training *(p. 213)*

How can we successfully help people to overcome substance abuse and addiction?

- A variety of treatment approaches have been used, including detoxification, drug therapies, psychotherapy, and behavior modification.
- Multimodal approaches (the use of several treatment techniques) are probably the most effective.
- Many alcoholics are helped by treatment, and some achieve abstinence by themselves.
- The treatment prescribed for other drug users depends on the type of drug and on the user.
- Heroin addicts usually undergo detoxification followed by methadone maintenance and forms of treatment such as residential treatment programs, psychotherapy, cognitive or behavior therapy, and group therapy. Detoxification and occupational, recreational, and family therapies may be suggested for users of other drugs.

FOCUS QUESTIONS

- What are normal and abnormal sexual behaviors?
- What does the normal sexual response cycle tell us about sexual dysfunctions?
- What causes gender identity disorders?
- What are the paraphilias?

9 Sexual and Gender Identity Disorders

Sexual and gender identity disorders encompass a wide range of behaviors. Consider the following cases:

Joan R., a thirty-four-year-old woman, came for couples counseling at the urging of her live-in male friend. They had been in an intimate sexual relationship for four years and had intended to marry shortly. All through their relationship, Joan had kept a secret from her friend—she had never felt sexually aroused, did not enjoy having sex, and had never had an orgasm. Although she enjoyed physical contact such as cuddling and kissing and wanted to enjoy sex, she states "intercourse did nothing for me." Her male friend had suspected something was wrong because Joan found it increasingly difficult to "fake being aroused and excited." Her friend was very concerned that Joan was "frigid" and now doubted whether they should marry.

Roger recalls that, as a young child, he always seemed more interested in "girly things" and activities. He often believed he was a girl, played like a girl, and had no interest in boys' games. Roger often got in trouble for using the women's restroom (because he needed to sit while urinating), dressing in his sister's clothes, and wearing his mother's makeup. As he became older, Roger could not help believing that nature had played a cruel hoax on him, that he was a woman trapped in a man's body. After much counseling and exploration, Roger became "Rosie" via sex-reassignment surgery. Although Rosie eventually married, she regrets not being able to conceive a child.

From early childhood, Peter F., a forty-one-year-old man, had fantasies of being mistreated, humiliated, and beaten. He recalls how he would become sexually excited when envisioning such activities. As he grew older, he experienced difficulty achieving an orgasm unless he was able to experience pain from his sexual partners. He was obsessed with masochistic sexual acts, which made it difficult for him to concentrate on other matters. He had been married and divorced three times because of his proclivity for demanding that his wives engage in "sex games" that involved having them hurt him. These games involved being bound spread-eagled on his bed and tortured by whippings, biting his upper thighs, the sticking of pins into his legs, and other forms of torture. During these sessions, he could ejaculate.

These cases illustrate some of the disorders we present in this chapter. We discuss three large classes of DSM-IV-TR disorders: (1) sexual dysfunctions, which involve problems of inhibited sexual desire, arousal, and response (Joan R.'s problems), (2) gender-identity disorders, which involve an incongruity or conflict between one's anatomical sex and one's psychological feeling of being male or female (Roger/Rosie), and (3) paraphilias, which involve sexual urges and fantasies about situations, objects, or people that are not part of the usual arousal pattern leading to reciprocal and affectionate sexual activity (Peter F.'s activities).

Cultural Influences and Sexuality   Sexuality is influenced by how different cultures view it. Some societies have very rigid social, cultural, and religious taboos associated with exposure of the human body, whereas other societies are more open. Note the contrast between the Muslim and American teens shown here.

The Study of Human Sexuality

Because sexual behavior is such an important part of our lives and because so many taboos and myths surround it, people have great difficulty dealing with the topic in an open and direct manner. In addition, determining normal from abnormal sexual behavior becomes difficult when behavioral, legal, and cultural standards become involved (see the Mental Health and Society feature, "What Is 'Normal' Sexual Behavior?"). To some extent, Freud made the discussion of sexual topics more acceptable when he made sex (libido) an important part of psychoanalytic theory. His knowledge of sexual practices and behavior, however, was largely confined to his clinical cases and his speculations from the understanding of social mores.

Our contemporary understanding of human sexual physiology and sexual practices and customs is based on the works of Alfred Kinsey and his colleagues (Kinsey, Pomeroy, & Martin, 1948; Kinsey et al., 1953), of William Masters and Virginia Johnson in their seminal works *Human Sexual Response* (1966) and *Human Sexual Inadequacy* (1970), on the *Janus Report* (Janus & Janus, 1993), and on the work of other contemporary sex researchers. Although the nature of the subject matter and the means used to obtain the information proved controversial and provocative, these studies dispelled myths and provided explicit evidence of human sexual responsiveness, attitudes, and practices.

The Sexual Response Cycle

Explaining human sexual dysfunction requires an understanding of the normal sexual response cycle, which consists of four stages: appetitive (desire), arousal, orgasm, and resolution (see Figure 9.1).

1. The *appetitive phase* is characterized by the person's desire for sexual activity. The person begins to have thoughts or fantasies surrounding sex. He or she may begin to feel attracted to another person and to daydream increasingly about sex.

2. The *arousal phase* moves out of the appetitive phase when specific and direct—but not necessarily physical—sexual stimulation occurs. Heart rate, blood pressure, and respiration rate increase. In the male, blood flow increases in the penis,

Understanding Sexuality   Through their clinical research and well-known publications, *Human Sexual Response* (1966) and *Human Sexual Inadequacy* (1970), William Masters and Virginia Johnson, shown here, have done much to further understanding of and dispel myths about human sexuality.

resulting in an erection. In the female, the breasts swell, nipples become erect, blood engorges the genital region, and the clitoris expands. Vaginal lubrication reflexively occurs, and a sex flush may appear on the skin (usually later in this phase).

3. The *orgasm phase* is characterized by involuntary muscular contractions throughout the body and the eventual release of sexual tension. In the man, muscles at the base of the penis contract, propelling semen through the penis. In the woman, the outer third of the vagina contracts rhythmically. Following orgasm, men enter a refractory period during which they are unresponsive to sexual stimulation for a period of time. However, women are capable of multiple orgasms with continued stimulation.

4. The *resolution phase* is characterized by relaxation of the body after orgasm. Heart rate, blood pressure, and respiration return to normal.

Problems may occur in any of the four phases of the sexual response cycle, although they are rare in the resolution phase. If problems related to arousal, desire, or orgasm are recurrent and persistent, they may be diagnosed as dysfunctions.

Homosexuality

We debated at length whether to include the topic of homosexuality in this textbook. Although the American Psychiatric Association and the American Psychological Association no longer consider homosexuality to be a mental disorder, some individuals still harbor this belief. As recently as April 2003, Rick Santorum, chairman of

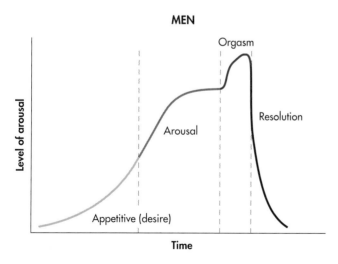

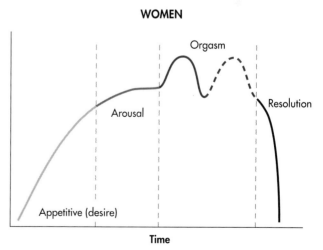

Figure 9.1 Human Sexual Response Cycle   The studies of Masters and Johnson reveal similar normal sexual response cycles for men and women. Note that women may experience more than one orgasm. Sexual disorders may occur at any of the phases, but seldom at the resolution phase.

mental health and society

What Is "Normal" Sexual Behavior?

It was an affair that shocked the country. Under investigation by Kenneth Starr and the Office of the Independent Counsel, former President Clinton admitted to a sixteen-month affair with a young female intern. The Starr Report, as it came to be known, provided excruciating and graphic descriptions of the sexual activity—including oral sex, phone sex, and use of a cigar—that took place between Clinton and Monica Lewinsky. The public discussions that ensued focused not only on legal and constitutional issues but also on whether the described sexual behaviors were normal or abnormal.

■ Is oral sex normal? Many consider oral sex offensive, but it is not an uncommon practice. One survey (Andersen & Cyranowski, 1995) indicates that 70 percent of sexually active college-age women have orally stimulated the genitals of their partners and that the same percentage have had their genitals orally stimulated in return.

■ Does Clinton's use of a "cigar" in sex play constitute perversion? Many men and women use sex toys (such as vibrators and dildos) and engage in sex games (phone sex, "talking dirty," and verbally creating sexual fantasies).

■ Is the former president oversexed, and is he a "sex addict"? DSM-IV-TR does not recognize the existence of a "sex addiction" disorder, nor does it classify "oversexed" as a sexual desire disorder. Sexual desire and frequency of sexual intercourse vary widely.

Slightly over 2 percent of married men and 1 percent of married women have intercourse more than once a day (Laumann et al., 1994; LoPiccolo & Friedman, 1988). By statistical standards, would these people be considered abnormal?

Of all the psychological or psychiatric disorders discussed in this text, sexual and gender identity disorders present the greatest difficulty for those attempting to distinguish between "abnormal" (maladaptive) behavior and non-harmful variances that reflect personal values and tastes markedly different from social norms. The definitions of normal sexual behavior vary widely and are influenced by both moral and legal judgments. For example, the laws of some states define oral-genital sex as a "crime against nature." This view is reflected in a California statute that was repealed as late as 1976:

Oral Sex Perversion—Any person participating in an act of copulating the mouth of one person with the sexual organ of another is punishable by incarceration in the state prison for a period not exceeding fifteen years, or by imprisonment in the county jail not to exceed one year.

It would be difficult today to justify the classification of oral sex as a "perversion." The pioneering work of Kinsey and colleagues revealed that oral sex is widespread, especially among the more highly educated part of the population (Kinsey et al., 1953). And, as noted earlier, surveys (Young, 1980; Andersen & Cyranowski, 1995) have found

the Republican Senate Caucus, compared homosexuality to incest, bigamy, and adultery; Trent Lott in 1998, then the U.S. Senate majority leader, described homosexuality as a disorder akin to alcoholism and kleptomania—a condition that should be treated (Mitchell, 1998). Jerry Falwell, on the Pat Robertson program, stated that the September 11, 2001, terrorist attack that took thousands of lives was punishment for the growing influence of gay and lesbian groups. It is clear from the tone of these statements that *homophobia*—the irrational fear of homosexuality—continues to be a major part of these objections.

Given the level of public misunderstanding and misinformation, we believe it is important to discuss briefly what homosexuality is not. Is homosexual behavior illegal? The answer is no. On July 26, 2003, the U.S. Supreme Court overruled *Bowers v. Hardwick* that had prohibited consensual sodomy. The court ruled that no state could demean gays by making their private sexual conduct a crime. The ruling represented a major civil rights victory for gays. Is homosexuality a mental disorder? The answer is no. The American Psychiatric Association did not include homosexuality in either DSM-III-R or DSM-IV-TR.

Mental Health and Society (continued)

that most sexually experienced college men and women have engaged in this behavior. As you can see, legal decisions on sexuality sometimes reflect past moods and morals or questionable and idiosyncratic views. Consider the 1943 ruling of the Minnesota Supreme Court in the case of *Dittrick v. Brown County*. The court upheld the conviction of a father of six as a sexual psychopath because he had an "uncontrollable craving for sexual intercourse with his wife." This "craving" amounted to three or four times a week. If he were tried today, Mr. Dittrick could base his defense on the views of some current researchers who believe that not having sex often *enough* indicates a sexual desire disorder.

Shifting perspectives on sexual conduct challenge legal definitions of normal and abnormal. One area currently being challenged involves relations between individuals of the same sex. In 1998, two men were arrested in Houston, Texas, for violating the state's 119-year-old law against sodomy. Six states consider consensual oral and anal sex between homosexual couples a crime even if it occurs in private ("Houston Case," 1998). In 2003, the U.S. Supreme Court struck down the Texas sodomy laws and declared that homosexual sexual acts could not be considered criminal ones.

Classification of normal and abnormal behavior becomes especially difficult when one compares Western and non-Western cultures or different time periods within a particular culture. For example, in ancient Greece, homosexuality was not only accepted but encouraged (Arndt, 1991). In many countries, sex with animals is fairly common among rural youths but is rare among urban boys. And in

many parts of Southeast Asia, individuals are afflicted by a disorder called "koro," characterized by a sudden and intense anxiety that the penis will recede into the body. Thus it is clear that definitions of sexual disorders are also strongly influenced by cultural norms and values.

If legal, moral, and statistical models fall short of the viable definition of normal sexual behavior that is needed, can we resolve the controversy by simply stating that sexual behavior is deviant if it is a threat to society, causes distress to participants, or impairs social or occupational functioning? Using this definition, there would be no objection to our considering incest and pedophilia as deviant behaviors; they include the elements of nonconsent, force, and victimization. But what about sexual arousal to an inanimate object (fetishism), or low sexual drive, or gender identity conflict? These conditions are not threats to society; they may not cause distress to people who experience them; and they may not result in impaired social or occupational functioning. They are deviant simply because they do not fall within "normal arousal and activity patterns." And they are considered deviant even though what constitutes a normal sexual pattern is the subject of controversy (Nevid et al., 1995).

In short, ambiguities surround all the classification systems. Nevertheless, the Merck Manual of Diagnosis and Therapy (Beers & Berkow, 1999) provides a three-phase process of judging whether something constitutes a sexual problem: (1) it is persistent and recurrent over a long period of time; (2) it causes personal distress; and (3) it negatively affects one's relationship with one's sexual partner.

Earlier versions of DSM classified homosexuality as sexual deviance because sexual behavior was considered normal only if it occurred between two consenting adults of opposite sexes. The changing view of homosexuality has been influenced by two main objections. First, many clinicians felt that heterosexual sexuality should not be the standard by which other sexual behaviors are judged. Second, many homosexual people argued that they are mentally healthy and that their sexual preference reflects a normal variant of sexual expression. Research supports these views. Studies on male and female homosexuals suggest that most accepted their sexual orientation and indicated no regrets at being homosexual (Bell, Weinberg, & Hammersmith, 1981; Gonsiorek, 1982; Laird & Green, 1996). In a move indicative of changing international views of homosexuality, the Chinese Psychological Association, as of 2001, no longer considers it an illness. This move is even more meaningful because China has always been very conservative toward sexual orientation matters, and its recognition that homosexuality is not an illness may mean that the estimated 30 million gays and lesbians in China may become increasingly visible.

It is also important to note that although the human sexual response cycle appears equally applicable for a homosexual population, the sexual issues may differ quite dramatically (Strong & DeVault, 1994). For example, problems among heterosexuals most often focus on sexual intercourse, whereas gay and lesbian sexual concerns focus on other behaviors (aversion toward anal eroticism and cunnilingus). Lesbians and gay men must also deal with societal or internalized homophobia, which often inhibits open expression of their affection toward one another. Finally, gay men are forced to deal with the association between sexual activity and HIV infection. These broader contextual issues may create diminished sexual desire, sexual aversion, and negative feelings toward sexual activity (Strong & DeVault, 1994).

In summary, the available studies (Bell & Weinberg, 1978; Green et al., 1986; Hu, Pattatucci, & Patterson, 1995; Laird & Green, 1996; Masters & Johnson, 1979; Strong & DeVault, 1994; Turner, 1995; Wilson, 1984) on homosexuals and heterosexuals lead to the following conclusions:

- There are no physiological differences in sexual arousal and response between homosexuals and heterosexuals.
- On measures of psychological disturbance, homosexuals and heterosexuals do not differ significantly from each other.
- Homosexuals do not suffer from gender identity confusion; rather, any gender conflicts they experience are due to societal intolerance to their lifestyles.
- Because of the societal context in which they live (homophobia, health concerns, and other such issues), sexual concerns of homosexuals may differ significantly from those of heterosexuals.
- Research suggests that homosexuality is not simply a lifestyle choice but is rather a naturally occurring phenomenon linked to a biological disposition.

Nothing more need be said. Homosexuality is not a psychological disorder.

Aging and Sexual Activity

It is important to understand how the aging process can affect sexuality. When women reach menopause, estrogen levels drop, and women may experience vaginal dryness and thinning of the vaginal wall. This may result in discomfort during sexual activity. Likewise, older men are at higher risk for prostate problems that may increase the risk of erectile dysfunction. Both sexes are also at higher risk for illnesses that affect sexual performance and interest (diabetes, high blood pressure, rheumatism, and heart disease). Hormone replacement therapy, Viagra, and other medical procedures may help minimize the effects of these organic problems on sexual activity. Nevertheless, our society continues to perpetuate the myth that aging is associated with sexual difficulties and unhappiness. A recent survey of 1,384 adults aged forty-five and older shed much light on the sexual behaviors and attitudes of a segment of the population (American Association of Retired Persons [AARP], 1999):

- Although most men and woman report that satisfying sex is important in their lives, they found relationships to be more important than sex.
- Sexual activity is affected by the "partner gap." Whereas 80 percent of those surveyed between the ages of forty-five and fifty-nine have partners, only 58 percent of men and 21 percent of women seventy-five and older do.
- Both men and women report that sexual activity declines with advancing age due to health problems; yet 64 percent of men and 68 percent of women with sexual partners report being satisfied with their sex lives.

A comprehensive survey (Janus & Janus, 1993) suggested that sexual activity and enjoyment among the older population remains surprisingly high. The Januses' survey

Sexual Behavior Among Seniors   Contrary to the belief that the elderly lose their sexual desire, studies reveal that sexual desire, activity, and enjoyment remain high in the older population.

found that (1) the sexual activity of people ages sixty-five and older declined little from that of their thirty- to forty-year-old counterparts, (2) their ability to reach orgasm and have sex diminished very little from their early years, and (3) their desire to continue a relatively active sex life was unchanged. These findings are supported by a recent poll of 1,292 Americans (534 men and 758 women) age sixty or older who reported that their interest in sex remains high, that over half engage in sexual activity at least once a month (see Figure 9.2), and that half rated their sexual activity to be physically better now than in their youth (National Council on the Aging, 1998).

Aside from sexual outlook and behavior, physiologically based changes in patterns of sexual arousal and orgasm have been found in people over age sixty-five (Masters & Johnson, 1966). For both men and women, sexual arousal takes longer. Erection and vaginal lubrication are slower to occur, and the urgency for orgasm is reduced. Both men and women are fully capable of sexual satisfaction if no physiological conditions interfere. Many elderly individuals felt that such changes allowed them to experience sex more fully. They reported that they had more time to spend on a seductive buildup, felt positively about their ability to experience unhurried sex-for-joy, and experienced more warmth and intimacy after the sex act (Janus & Janus, 1993).

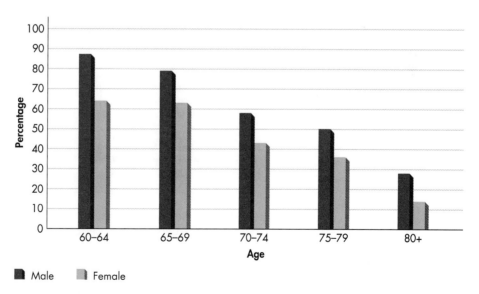

Figure 9.2 Percentages of Men and Women Remaining Sexually Active, Ages 60 and Older   Contrary to many myths about aging and reduced sexual activity, studies reveal that elderly people are surprisingly active. At all age levels, however, men continue to be more sexually active than women. What explanations might account for this difference?

Sexual Arousal Disorders

Problems involving feelings of sexual pleasure or physiological changes associated with sexual excitement

Male erectile disorder
Inability to attain or maintain an erection sufficient for sexual intercourse and/or psychological arousal during sexual activity

Female sexual arousal disorder
Inability to attain or maintain physiological response and/or psychological arousal during sexual activity

SEXUAL DYSFUNCTIONS

Persistent and recurrent problems in the appetitive, excitement, and orgasm phases of the sexual cycle. Dysfunctions are either psychological or psychophysiological in origin (never primarily physiological)

Sexual Desire Disorders

Problems during the appetitive phase

Hypoactive sexual desire disorder
Absent or low sexual interest or desire

Sexual aversion disorder
Avoidance of and aversion to sexual intercourse

Orgasmic Disorders

Problems with the orgasm phase of the sexual cycle

Female orgasmic disorder
Persistent delay or inability to achieve an orgasm after the excitement phase has been reached. The sexual activity must be adequate in focus, intensity, and duration

Male orgasmic disorder
Persistent delay or inability to achieve an orgasm after the excitement phase has been reached and the sexual activity has been adequate in focus, intensity, and duration. Usually restricted to the inability to reach orgasm introvaginally

Premature ejaculation
Ejaculation with minimal sexual stimulation before, during, or shortly after penetration

Sexual Pain Disorders

Dyspareunia
Genital pain in a man or woman that is not due to a lack of lubrication in the vagina. It occurs either before, during, or after sexual intercourse

Vaginismus
Involuntary spasm of the outer third of the vaginal wall that prevents or interferes with sexual intercourse

Figure 9.3   Disorders Chart: Sexual Dysfunctions   *Sources:* Data from American Psychiatric Association (2000a); Spector & Carey (1990); LoPiccolo (1995, 1997); Hooper (1998).

Sexual Dysfunctions

sexual dysfunction A disruption of any part of the normal sexual response cycle.

A **sexual dysfunction** is a disruption of any part of the normal sexual response cycle. Problems in sexual functioning, such as premature ejaculation, low sexual desire, and difficulties in achieving orgasm, are quite common in our society (Strong & DeVault,

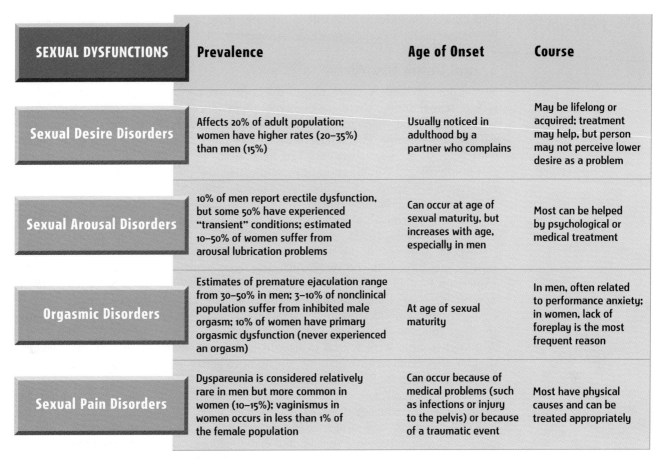

SEXUAL DYSFUNCTIONS	Prevalence	Age of Onset	Course
Sexual Desire Disorders	Affects 20% of adult population; women have higher rates (20–35%) than men (15%)	Usually noticed in adulthood by a partner who complains	May be lifelong or acquired; treatment may help, but person may not perceive lower desire as a problem
Sexual Arousal Disorders	10% of men report erectile dysfunction, but some 50% have experienced "transient" conditions; estimated 10–50% of women suffer from arousal lubrication problems	Can occur at age of sexual maturity, but increases with age, especially in men	Most can be helped by psychological or medical treatment
Orgasmic Disorders	Estimates of premature ejaculation range from 30–50% in men; 3–10% of nonclinical population suffer from inhibited male orgasm; 10% of women have primary orgasmic dysfunction (never experienced an orgasm)	At age of sexual maturity	In men, often related to performance anxiety; in women, lack of foreplay is the most frequent reason
Sexual Pain Disorders	Dyspareunia is considered relatively rare in men but more common in women (10–15%); vaginismus in women occurs in less than 1% of the female population	Can occur because of medical problems (such as infections or injury to the pelvis) or because of a traumatic event	Most have physical causes and can be treated appropriately

Figure 9.3 Disorders Chart: Sexual Dysfunctions (continued)

1994). For example, lifetime prevalence of sexual problems in young adults at some time in their lives is summarized in the following list (Haas & Haas, 1993):

Women
- Reduced libido: 40 percent
- Arousal difficulties: 60 percent
- Reaching orgasm too soon: 10 percent
- Inability to have orgasm: 35 percent
- Dyspareunia (pain): 15 percent

Men
- Reduced libido: 30 percent
- Arousal difficulties: 50 percent
- Reaching orgasm too soon: 15 percent
- Inability to have orgasm: 2 percent
- Dyspareunia: 5 percent

To be diagnosed as a dysfunction, the disruption must be recurrent and persistent. DSM-IV-TR also requires that such factors as frequency, chronicity, subjective distress, and effect on other areas of functioning be considered in the diagnosis. As indicated in Figure 9.3, the DSM-IV-TR categories for sexual dysfunctions are sexual desire disorders, sexual arousal disorders, orgasmic disorders, and sexual pain disorders. Prevalence of the sexual dysfunctions is summarized here as well.

Sexual Desire Disorders

Sexual desire disorders are related to the appetitive phase and are characterized by a lack of sexual desire. There are two types: *hypoactive sexual desire disorder,* characterized by little or no interest in sexual activities, either actual or fantasized, and *sexual aversion disorder,* characterized by an avoidance of and aversion to sexual intercourse. Both of these disorders can be lifelong or acquired and may be due to psychological or a combination of psychological and biological factors. Some people may report low sexual desire because of inexperience. Many of these people may not have learned to label or identify their own arousal levels, may not know how to increase their arousal, and may have a limited expectation for their ability to be aroused (LoPiccolo, 1995).

About 20 percent of the adult population (20 to 35 percent of women and 15 percent of men) are believed to be suffering from hypoactive sexual desire disorder (American Psychiatric Association, 1994; LoPiccolo, 1995; Rosen & Leiblum, 1995; Spector & Carey, 1990). Some clinicians estimate that 40 to 50 percent of all sexual dysfunctions involve deficits in desire (Stuart, Hammond, & Pett, 1987), and it is now the most common complaint of couples seeking sex therapy (Spector & Carey, 1990). Although people with sexual desire disorders are often capable of experiencing orgasm, they claim to have little interest in, or to derive no pleasure from, sexual activity (LoPiccolo, 1995; Rosen & Leiblum, 1995).

We do not really know what constitutes "normal" sexual desire, and we know little about what frequency of sexual fantasies or what activities are "normal." Kinsey and colleagues (1948) found tremendous variation in reported total sexual outlet, or release. One man reported that he had ejaculated only once in thirty years; another claimed to have averaged thirty orgasms per week for thirty years. After analyzing mean frequencies of orgasm from sex surveys, a group of researchers noted that "a total orgasmic outlet of less than once every two weeks is considered one marker of low desire . . . unless extenuating circumstances such as a lack of privacy occur" (Schover et al., 1982, p. 616).

However, using some average frequency of sexual activity does not seem appropriate for categorizing people as having inhibited sexual desire. One person may have a high sex drive but not engage in sexual activities; another may not have sexual interest or fantasies but may engage in frequent sexual behaviors for the sake of his or her partner (Rosen & Leiblum, 1987). Furthermore, using number of orgasms (through intercourse or masturbation) or desire for orgasms may introduce gender bias into the definition of "normal" sexual desire. The *Janus Report* indicated that, for all age groups, men masturbate and experience orgasms more than women do (Janus & Janus, 1993). Does this mean that women's sexual desire is less than that of men? Until we can decide on a normal range of sexual desire, we can hardly discover the causes of sexual desire disorders or develop treatment programs for them.

Sexual Arousal Disorders

Sexual arousal disorders are problems that occur during the excitement (arousal) phase and that relate to difficulties with feelings of sexual pleasure or with the physiological changes associated with sexual excitement. In men, inhibited sexual excitement takes the form of **male erectile disorder,** an inability to attain or maintain an erection sufficient for sexual intercourse and/or psychological arousal during sexual activity. The man may feel fully aroused, but he cannot finish the sex act. In the past, such a dysfunction has

sexual desire disorders Sexual dysfunctions that are related to the appetitive phase and are characterized by a lack of sexual desire.

sexual arousal disorders Problems occurring during the excitement (arousal) phase and relating to difficulties with feelings of sexual pleasure or with the physiological changes associated with sexual excitement.

male erectile disorder An inability to attain or maintain an erection sufficient for sexual intercourse.

"...WE'VE JUST GOTTA WORK ON THIS 'FASTER THAN A SPEEDING BULLET,' STUFF."

been attributed primarily to psychological reasons ("it's all in the head"). Masters and Johnson (1970), for example, estimated that only about 5 percent of erectile dysfunctions were due to physical conditions. Recent studies now indicate that from 30 percent (Segraves, Schoenberg, & Ivanoff, 1983) to as many as 70 percent (Hooper, 1998) of erectile dysfunctions are caused by some form of vascular insufficiency, such as diabetes, atherosclerosis, or traumatic groin injury, or by other physiological factors. A primary reason that DSM-IV-TR includes general medical conditions as a factor in sexual dysfunctions is that a man may also have a minor organic impairment that "makes his erection more vulnerable to being disrupted by psychological, biological, and sexual technique factors" (LoPiccolo & Stock, 1986).

Primary erectile dysfunction is the diagnosis for a man who has never been able to engage successfully in sexual intercourse. This difficulty often has a clear psychological origin, because many men with this dysfunction can get an erection and reach orgasm during masturbation and can show erection during the REM (rapid eye movement) phase of sleep. In *secondary erectile dysfunction,* the man has had at least one successful instance of sexual intercourse but is currently unable to achieve an erection and penetration in 25 percent or more of his sexual attempts (Masters & Johnson, 1970).

The prevalence rate of erectile dysfunction is difficult to determine because it is often unreported. Clinicians estimate that approximately 50 percent of men have experienced transient impotence (Feldman, Goldstein, et al., 1994). Prior to the introduction of the drug Viagra, the generally accepted figure of erectile dysfunction among men was between 10 million and 15 million (Leary, 1992). Current estimates of erectile problems place the figure at approximately 30 million (Hooper, 1998). Several factors may be contributing to this increase in the number of reported cases: (1) an increasing acceptance that the dysfunction may be caused by some physical condition and not by feelings of "psychological inadequacy"; (2) the availability of Viagra as a nonintrusive successful treatment; (3) an increasing willingness among men to talk about this problem; and (4) a greater acceptance of women's right to expect satisfaction in sexual

Table 9.1   Some Possible Physical Causes of Erectile Disorder and Dyspareunia

Erectile Disorder

- Alcoholism (neuropathy)
- Diabetes mellitus
- Arterial disease (e.g., Leriche syndrome)
- Renal failure
- Carcinomatosis
- Neurosyphilis
- Hypothalamo-pituitary dysfunction
- Liver failure
- Multiple sclerosis
- Many others

Dyspareunia

Female

- Failure of vaginal lubrication
- Failure of vasocongestion
- Failure of uterine elevation and vaginal ballooning during arousal
- Estrogen deficiency leading to atrophic vaginitis
- Radiotherapy for malignancy
- Vaginal infection (e.g., Trichomonas or herpes)
- Vaginal irritation (e.g., sensitivity to creams or deodorants)
- Abnormal tone of pelvic floor muscles
- Scarring after episiotomy or surgery
- Bartholin's gland cysts or abscess
- Rigid hymen, small introitus

Male

- Painful retraction of the foreskin
- Herpetic and other infections
- Asymmetrical erection due to fibrosis or Peyronie's disease
- Hypersensitivity of the glans penis

Source: Haas & Haas (1993).

relationships. As Table 9.1 indicates, there is now increasing recognition that physical factors play a significant role in sexual arousal disorders.

Female sexual arousal disorder is an inability to attain or maintain physiological response and/or psychological arousal during sexual activity. It is characterized by a lack of physical signs of excitement, such as vaginal lubrication or erection of the nipples, or complaints of a lack of pleasure during sexual interactions (American Psychiatric Association, 1994). As with other sexual dysfunctions, this disorder may be lifelong or acquired and is often the result of negative attitudes about sex or early sexual experiences. Receiving negative information about sex, having been sexually assaulted or molested, and having conflicts with a sexual partner can contribute to the disorder.

Estimates of this disorder vary widely, from 10 to 50 percent of the female population; accurate numbers are difficult to obtain because it is extremely difficult to distinguish this condition from other sexual disorders (Laumann et al., 1994; LoPiccolo, 1997). Indeed, female sexual arousal disorder is rarely diagnosed alone and usually is accompanied by or submerged with other desire or orgasmic disorders.

Orgasmic Disorders

An *orgasmic disorder* is an inability to achieve an orgasm after entering the excitement phase and receiving adequate sexual stimulation.

Female Orgasmic Disorder (Inhibited Female Orgasm)   A woman with **female orgasmic disorder,** or *inhibited female orgasm,* experiences persistent delay or inability to achieve an orgasm with stimulation that is "adequate in focus, intensity, and duration" after entering the excitement phase. Whether the lack of orgasm is categorized as a dysfunction or as a "normal variant" is left to the judgment of the clinician. Again, the criteria that define adequate functioning during sexual intercourse are quite controversial.

Inhibited female orgasm may be termed *primary,* to indicate that orgasm has never been experienced, or *secondary,* to show that orgasm has been experienced. Primary orgasmic dysfunction is considered relatively common in women: approximately 10 percent of all women have never achieved an orgasm (Rosen & Lieblum, 1995; Spector & Carey, 1990). This disorder is not equivalent to primary orgasmic dysfunction in males, who often can achieve orgasm through masturbation or by some other means.

female sexual arousal disorder
The inability to attain or maintain physiological response and/or psychological arousal during sexual activity.

Male Orgasmic Disorder (Inhibited Male Orgasm)   Male orgasmic disorder, or *inhibited male orgasm,* is the persistent delay or inability to achieve an orgasm after the excitement phase has been reached and sexual activity has been adequate in focus, intensity, and duration. The term is usually restricted to the inability to ejaculate within the vagina, even with full arousal and penile erection. As noted, men who have this dysfunction can usually ejaculate when masturbating. Inhibited orgasm in males is relatively rare, and little is known about it (Dekker, 1993). Treatment is often urged by the wife, who may want to conceive or who may feel (because of the husband's lack of orgasm) that she is unattractive.

Premature Ejaculation   The inability to satisfy a sexual partner is a source of anguish for many men. **Premature ejaculation** is ejaculation with minimal sexual stimulation before, during, or shortly after penetration. It is a relatively common problem, but sex researchers and therapists differ in their criteria for prematurity. Kilmann and Auerbach (1979) suggested that ejaculation less than five minutes after coital entry is a suitable criterion of prematurity. Masters and Johnson (1970) contended that a man who is unable to delay ejaculation long enough during sexual intercourse to produce an orgasm in the woman 50 percent of the time is a premature ejaculator. The difficulty with the latter definition is the possibility that a man may be "premature" with one partner but entirely adequate for another. From the perspective of males, however, surveys suggest that slightly more than one in three men admit to occasional premature ejaculation problems (Spector & Carey, 1990).

Sexual Pain Disorders

Sexual pain disorders can be manifested in both males and females in a condition termed **dyspareunia,** which is a recurrent or persistent pain in the genitals before, during, or after sexual intercourse. Dyspareunia is not caused exclusively by lack of lubrication or by **vaginismus,** which is an involuntary spasm of the outer third of the vaginal wall, preventing or interfering with sexual intercourse. The incidence of vaginismus is not known, but it is considered very rare. Several causal factors have been identified in vaginismus. Masters and Johnson (1970) found one or more of the following conditions among many women with this dysfunction: (1) a husband or partner who was impotent; (2) rigid religious beliefs about sex; (3) prior sexual trauma, such as rape; (4) prior homosexual identification; and (5) painful intercourse. A history of incestuous molestation is often found in women with this disorder (LoPiccolo & Stock, 1986).

DSM-IV-TR also recognizes the diagnoses of sexual dysfunction due to a general medical condition and substance-induced sexual dysfunction. For example, a man may suffer from an erectile disorder caused by a general medical condition, such as diabetes, as noted earlier, or by a substance-induced condition, such as alcohol abuse.

Etiology and Treatment of Sexual Dysfunctions

Sexual dysfunctions may be due to psychological factors alone or to a combination of psychological and biological factors. They may be mild and transient or lifelong and chronic.

Biological Factors and Medical Treatment   Lower levels of testosterone or higher levels of estrogens such as prolactin (or both) have been associated with lower sexual interest in both men and women and with erectile difficulties in men (Kresin, 1993; Spark, 1991). Drugs that suppress testosterone levels appear to decrease sexual desire in men (Schiavi & Segraves, 1995). Conversely, the administration of androgens is associated with reports of increased sexual desire in both men and women. However, the relationship between hormones and sexual behavior is complex and difficult to understand. Many people with sexual dysfunctions have normal testosterone levels (Spark, 1991).

Medications given to treat ulcers, glaucoma, allergies, and convulsions have also been found to affect the sex drive. Drugs such as hypertensive medication and alcohol

---

female orgasmic disorder A sexual dysfunction in which the woman experiences persistent delay or inability to achieve an orgasm with stimulation that is adequate in focus, intensity, and duration after entering the excitement phase; also known as *inhibited orgasm.*

male orgasmic disorder Persistent delay or inability to achieve an orgasm after the excitement phase has been reached and sexual activity has been adequate in focus, intensity, and duration; usually restricted to an inability to ejaculate within the vagina (also known as *inhibited male orgasm*).

premature ejaculation Ejaculation with minimal sexual stimulation before, during, or shortly after penetration.

dyspareunia Recurrent or persistent pain in the genitals before, during, or after sexual intercourse.

vaginismus Involuntary spasm of the outer third of the vaginal wall, preventing or interfering with sexual intercourse.

are also associated with sexual dysfunctions, as are illnesses and other physical conditions (Schiavi & Segraves, 1995; Schiavi, 1990). But again, not everyone who takes hypertensive drugs, consumes alcohol, or is ill has a sexual dysfunction. In some people, these factors may combine with a predisposing personal history or current stress to produce problems in sexual function. A complete physical workup—including a medical history, a physical exam, and a laboratory evaluation—is a necessary first step in assessment before treatment decisions are made.

For some, a lack of sexual desire may be physiological. One group of women reported no feelings of anxiety about, or aversion to, sexual intercourse. However, they showed significantly lower sexual arousal during exposure to erotic stimuli than did sexually active women, and no increase in responsiveness after participation in therapy (Wincze, Hoon, & Hoon, 1978). The researchers concluded that the absence of sexual arousal in these women is biological and that the appropriate treatment for this condition is unknown. Hypersensitivity to physical stimulation may also affect sexual functioning (Assalian, 1988). Men who ejaculate prematurely may have difficulty determining when ejaculation is inevitable once the sympathetic nervous system is triggered.

The amount of blood flowing into the genital area is also associated with orgasmic potential in women and erectile functioning in men. In women, masturbation training and Kegel exercises (tightening muscles in the vagina) may increase vascularization of labia, clitoris, and vagina. In men, vascular surgery to increase blood flow to the penis is successful when used appropriately. Unfortunately, if the problem is due to arteriosclerosis, which affects a number of the small blood vessels, vascular surgery meets with little success (LoPiccolo & Stock, 1986; Hooper, 1998).

If hormone replacement and sex therapy do not appear beneficial, men with organic erectile dysfunction may be treated with vacuum pumps, suppositories, or penile implants (Blakeslee, 1993). The penile prosthesis is an inflatable or semirigid device that, once inflated, produces an erection sufficient for intercourse and ejaculation. One study of men with penile implants found that 90 percent would choose it again (Steege, Stout, & Carson, 1986).

Another form of medical treatment for erectile problems is the injection of substances into the penis (Mohr & Beutler, 1990). Within a very short time the man will obtain a very stiff erection, which may last from one to four hours. Although men and their mates have reported general satisfaction with the method (Althof et al., 1987), it does have some side effects. There is often bruising of the penis and the development of nodules. Some men find the prolonged erection disturbing in the absence of sexual stimulation.

Viagra made headlines in 1998 as a "miracle cure" for the 30 million men suffering from erectile dysfunctions. According to the nonstop hype surrounding the drug, it can make aging baby boomers as virile as teenagers; increase fertility, libido, or orgasms; and offer sexual insurance even to normally functioning men. Former presidential candidate Robert Dole and his wife, Elizabeth, have also made sly pronouncements of its ability to improve their sex lives.

Viagra does not produce an automatic erection in the absence of sexual stimuli. If a man becomes aroused, the drug enables the body to follow through the sexual response cycle to completion. Urologists claim that for individuals with no sexual dysfunction, taking Viagra will not improve their erections; in other words, Viagra will not provide physiological help that will enable normally functioning men to improve their sexual functioning, nor will it lead to a stiffer erection. Viagra may aid sexual arousal and performance by stimulating men's expectations and fantasies; this psychological boost may then lead to subjective feelings of enhanced pleasure.

In 2003, GlaxoSmithKline & Bayer introduced Levitra, and its presence in the marketplace has quickly challenged Viagra as the preferred drug in the treatment of erectile disorders. Makers of Levitra claim that it works faster and longer than Viagra by improving the quality and duration of erections. Whether such claims will hold up under closer scrutiny remains to be seen.

Psychological Factors and Behavioral Therapy Psychological causes for sexual dysfunctions may include predisposing or historical factors, as well as more current problems and concerns.

Predisposing or Historical Factors Early experiences can interact with current problems to produce sexual dysfunctions. Traditional psychoanalysts have stressed the role of unconscious conflicts. For example, erectile difficulties and premature ejaculation represent male hostility to women due to unresolved early developmental conflicts involving the parents. Psychodynamic treatment is directed toward uncovering and resolving the unconscious hostility. The results of this approach have been disappointing (Kaplan, 1974; Kilmann & Auerbach, 1979). It seems plausible, however, that the attitudes that parents display toward sex and affection and toward each other can influence their children's attitudes. For example, women with sexual desire disorders rated their parents' attitudes toward sex more negatively than did women without sexual desire disorders (Stuart et al., 1987). Being raised in a strict religious environment is also associated with sexual dysfunctions in both men and women (Masters & Johnson, 1970). Traumatic sexual experiences involving incestuous molestations during childhood or adolescence or rape are also factors to consider (Burgess & Holmstrom, 1979; LoPiccolo & Stock, 1986).

Current Factors Current problems may interfere with sexual functioning. A relationship problem is often a contributing factor, even in the apparent absence of predisposing factors. In a study of fifty-nine women with sexual desire disorders, only eleven had had the problem before marriage; the other forty-eight developed it gradually after being married. The women voiced dissatisfaction about their relationships with their husbands, complaining that their spouses did not listen to them. Marital dissatisfaction may have caused them to lose their attraction toward their husbands (Leiblum & Rosen, 1991).

Situational or coital anxiety can interrupt sexual functioning in both men and women. A group of men with psychological erectile dysfunction reported anxieties over sexual overtures, including a fear of failing sexually, a fear of being seen as sexually inferior, and anxiety over the size of their genitals. These patients also reported marked increases in subjective anxiety and displayed somatic symptoms, such as sweating, trembling, muscle tension, and heart palpitations, when asked to imagine engaging in sexual intercourse (Cooper, 1969). In a sample of 275 college men, sexual pressure from a partner was associated with sexual dysfunction (Spencer & Zeiss, 1987). The men most affected were those who identified most heavily with the traditional masculine role.

Factors associated with orgasmic dysfunction in women include having a sexually inexperienced or dysfunctional partner; a crippling fear of performance failure, of never being able to attain orgasm, of pregnancy, or of venereal disease; an inability to accept the partner, either emotionally or physically; and misinformation or ignorance about sexuality or sexual techniques.

Therapy Many approaches have been used to treat sexual dysfunctions, including desensitization, graded exercises, masturbation, sex education training, and the modification of sexual expectations. Most general treatment approaches include the following components:

- *Education* The therapist replaces sexual myths and misconceptions with accurate information about sexual anatomy and functioning.
- *Anxiety reduction* The therapist uses procedures such as desensitization or graded approaches to keep anxiety at a minimum. The therapist explains that constantly "observing and evaluating" one's performance can interfere with sexual functioning.
- *Structured behavioral exercises* The therapist gives a series of graded tasks that gradually increase the amount of sexual interaction between the partners. Each partner takes turns touching and being touched over different parts of the body

except for the genital regions. Later the partners fondle the body and genital regions, without making demands for sexual arousal or orgasm. Successful sexual intercourse and orgasm is the final stage of the structured exercises.

■ *Communication training* The therapist teaches the partners appropriate ways of communicating their sexual wishes to each other and also teaches them conflict resolution skills.

Some specific nonmedical treatments for other dysfunctions are as follows:

1. *Female orgasmic dysfunction* The general approach just described has been successful in treating sexual arousal disorders in women and erectile disorders in men. Masturbation appears to be the most effective way for orgasmically dysfunctional women to have an orgasm. The procedure involves education about sexual anatomy, visual and tactile self-exploration, using sexual fantasies and images, and masturbation, both individually and with a partner.

2. *Premature ejaculation* In one technique, the partner stimulates the penis while it is outside the vagina until the man feels the sensation of impending ejaculation. At this point, the partner stops the stimulation for a short period of time and then continues it again. This pattern is repeated until the man can tolerate increasingly greater periods of stimulation before ejaculation (Semans, 1956). Masters and Johnson (1970) and Kaplan (1974) used a similar procedure, called the "squeeze technique." They reported a success rate of nearly 100 percent. The treatment is easily learned.

   Although the short-term success rate for treating premature ejaculation is very high, a follow-up study of men after six years of treatment found that relapses were very common (Hawton et al., 1986).

3. *Vaginismus* The results of treatment for vaginismus have been uniformly positive (Kaplan, 1974; LoPiccolo & Stock, 1986). The involuntary spasms or closure of the vaginal muscle can be deconditioned by first training the woman to relax, and by then inserting successively larger dilators while she is relaxed, until insertion of the penis can occur.

▷ CHECKPOINT REVIEW

dyspareunia *(p. 231)*

female orgasmic disorder *(p. 230)*

female sexual arousal disorder *(p. 230)*

male erectile disorder *(p. 228)*

male orgasmic disorder *(p. 230)*

premature ejaculation *(p. 231)*

sexual arousal disorders *(p. 228)*

sexual desire disorders *(p. 228)*

sexual dysfunction *(p. 226)*

vaginismus *(p. 231)*

What are normal and abnormal sexual behaviors?

■ One of the difficulties in diagnosing abnormal sexual behavior is measuring it against a standard of normal sexual behavior. No attempt to establish such criteria has been completely successful, but these attempts have produced a better understanding of the normal human sexual response cycle.

■ That cycle has four stages: the appetitive, arousal, orgasm, and resolution phases. Each may be characterized by problems, which may be diagnosed as disorders if they are recurrent and persistent.

■ Many myths and misunderstandings continue to surround homosexuality. The belief that homosexuality is deviant seems to relate more to homophobia than to scientific findings. DSM-IV-TR no longer considers homosexuality to be a psychological disorder.

■ Despite myths to the contrary, sexuality extends into old age. However, sexual dysfunction becomes increasingly prevalent with aging, and the frequency of sexual activity typically declines.

What does the normal sexual response cycle tell us about sexual dysfunctions?

■ Sexual dysfunctions are disruptions of the normal sexual response cycle. They are fairly common in the general population and may affect a person's ability to become sexually aroused or to engage in intercourse. Many result from fear or anxiety regarding sexual activities; the various treatment programs are generally successful.

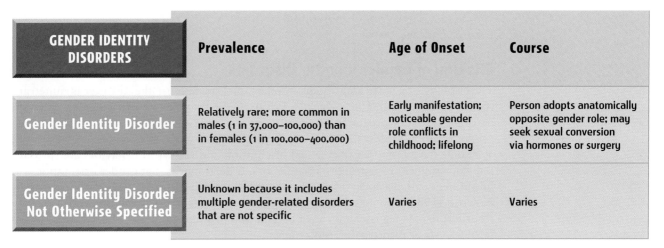

Figure 9.4 Disorders Chart: Gender Identity Disorders   *Sources:* Data from American Psychiatric Association (2000a); Arndt (1991); Laumann et al. (1994).

Gender Identity Disorders

In contrast to the sexual dysfunctions, which involve any disruption of the normal sexual response cycle, the **gender identity disorders** are characterized by conflict between a person's anatomical sex and his or her gender identity, or self-identification as male or female. These disorders, which are shown in Figure 9.4, are relatively rare, and they may appear in both adults and children.

In the specified category of gender identity disorder—often called **transsexualism**—the person experiences strong and persistent cross-gender identification and persistent discomfort with his or her anatomical sex, creating significant impairment in social, occupational, or other important areas of functioning. People with this disorder hold a lifelong conviction that nature has played a cruel hoax by placing them in a body of the wrong gender. This feeling produces a preoccupation with eliminating the "natural" physical and behavioral sexual characteristics and acquiring those of the opposite sex.

People with gender identity disorders tend to exhibit gender-role conflicts at an early age and to report transsexual feelings in childhood, some as early as two years (Beers & Berkow, 1999; Tsoi, 1993). Most children with gender identity conflicts do not develop gender identity disorders as adults. As a result, a diagnosis of this disorder should not be made until much later in life. Boys with this disorder are frequently labeled "sissies" by their male peers. They prefer playing with girls and generally avoid

gender identity disorder Disorder characterized by conflict between a person's anatomical sex and his or her gender identity, or self-identification as male or female.

transsexualism A strong and persistent cross-gender identification and persistent discomfort with one's anatomical sex, which cause significant impairment in social, occupational, or other areas of functioning.

the rough-and-tumble activities in which boys are traditionally encouraged to partici-pate. They are more likely than normal boys to play with "feminine" toys.

Girls with a gender identity disorder may insist that they have a penis or will grow one and may exhibit an avid interest in rough-and-tumble play. Female transsexuals report being labeled "tomboys" during their childhoods. Although it is not uncommon for girls to be considered tomboys, the strength, pervasiveness, and persistence of the cross-gender identification among those with a gender identity disorder are the distin-guishing features.

Transsexuals may report little interest in homosexual, heterosexual, or bisexual activities before the diagnosis of transsexualism (Blanchard, 1988). Those who are attracted to members of the same sex do not consider themselves to be homosexuals because they believe they actually *are* members of the opposite sex. Gender identity disorders are in no way related to homosexuality (Selvin, 1993).

Transsexualism is more common in males than in females. According to various estimates, the prevalence rate of the disorder ranges from 1 in 100,000 to 1 in 30,000 among males and from 1 in 400,000 to 1 in 100,000 among females (Arndt, 1991; Beers & Berkow, 1999).

Etiology of Gender Identity Disorders

The etiology of gender identity disorders is unclear. Because the disorder is quite rare (Green & Blanchard, 1995; Zucker, 1990), investigators have focused more attention on other sexual disorders. In all likelihood, a number of variables interact to produce gender identity disorders.

Some have proposed that sexual orientation and sex-typed behaviors are substan-tially determined by neurohormonal factors. It does appear that gender orientation can be influenced by a lack or excess of sex hormones. In a review of the research, Bancroft (1989) also noted other biological differences in persons with gender identity disorder: female transsexuals have been found in some studies to show raised testos-terone levels or menstrual irregularities.

Some researchers believe that gender identity is malleable. Because many transsexual children have normal hormone levels, their ability to adopt an opposite-sex orientation raises doubt that biology alone determines male-female behaviors (Hurtig & Rosenthal, 1987). In psychodynamic theory, all sexual deviations symbolically represent unconscious conflicts that began in early childhood (Meyers, 1991). The male or female child has a basic conflict between the wish for and the dread of maternal reengulfment (Meyer & Keith, 1991). The conflict results from a failure to deal successfully with separation-individuation phases of life, which creates a gender identity problem. Inability to resolve the Oedipus complex is important in gender identity disorder, according to this view.

Other researchers have hypothesized that childhood experiences via conditioning influence the development of gender identity disorders (Bernstein et al., 1981; Green, 1987). Factors thought to contribute to these disorders in boys include parental encouragement of feminine behavior, discouragement of the development of autonomy, excessive attention and overprotection by the mother, the absence of an older male as a model, a relatively powerless or absent father figure, a lack of exposure to male playmates, and encouragement to cross-dress (Marantz & Coates, 1991).

Treatment of Gender Identity Disorders

Most treatment programs for children identified as having a gender identity disorder include separate components for the child and for his or her parents. The child's treat-ment begins with sex education. The therapist highlights favorable aspects of the child's physical gender and discusses the child's reasons for avidly pursuing cross-gender activities. The therapist attempts to correct stereotypes regarding certain roles that are "accepted" for one gender and not for the other. Young boys are always assigned to male therapists, which facilitates positive male identification.

A Case of Sex Reassignment   Before sex-reassignment surgery, Renée Richards (right), a top-ranked tennis player and now coach, was Dr. Richard Raskin (left), a successful ophthalmologist.

Meanwhile, the child's parents receive instruction in the behavior modification practice of reinforcing appropriate gender behavior and extinguishing "inappropriate" behavior (Roberto, 1983). Some therapists help children deal with the peer-group ostracism that frequently occurs when a child exhibits strong cross-gender identities and behaviors (Zucker, 1990).

Some success has been reported for behavioral programs that incorporate strategies for modifying sex-typed behavior through modeling and rehearsal. The therapist demonstrates appropriate masculine behavior and mannerisms (modeling) in a number of different situations, and then patients practice (rehearse) their own versions of these behaviors. This is followed by a behavioral procedure that reinforces heterosexual fantasies: electric shock is applied whenever the person reports transsexual fantasies (Barlow, Abel, & Blanchard, 1979; Khanna, Desai, & Channabasavanna, 1987).

In spite of such gains with psychotherapy and behavioral procedures, sex-change operations are indicated for some transsexuals. Prior to surgery, patients may be required to pass the "real-life" test, in which they try to live as completely as possible as members of the opposite gender (Clemmensen, 1990). This requires changing names, clothing, roles, and so on. Almost all patients must deal with reactions from employers, coworkers, friends, and relatives. Successfully "passing" the test paves the way for actual surgical change.

Research suggests that sex-change operations for men and women can produce happier lives, especially in highly motivated and carefully screened transsexuals who have a stable work record and a network of social support (Beers & Berkow, 1999). In some cases, accompanying treatment includes teaching patients how to "pass" in public, using sex-role gestures and voice modulation. Most females who "changed" to males express satisfaction over the outcome of surgery, although males who "changed"

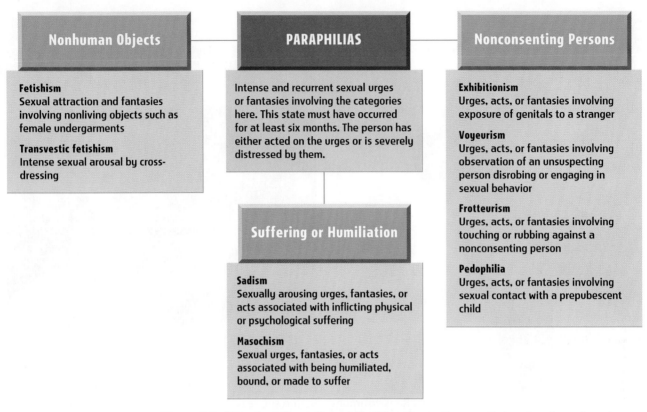

Figure 9.5 Disorders Chart: Paraphilia Disorders *Sources:* Data taken from American Psychiatric Association (2000a); Tsoi (1993); Kinsey et al. (1953); Spector & Carey (1990); Allgeier & Allgeier (1998).

to females are less likely to feel satisfied (Arndt, 1991). Perhaps adjusting to life as a man is easier than adjusting to life as a woman, or perhaps others may react less negatively to woman-to-man changes than man-to-woman changes.

Many transsexuals, however, remain depressed and suicidal after surgery (Hershkowitz & Dickes, 1978; Meyer & Peter, 1979). In one study (Kockott & Fahrner, 1987), more than one-half of the people who were offered sex-conversion surgery later changed their minds or became ambivalent about having the operations. Psychotherapy is typically recommended for patients who discover that their problems have not disappeared as a result of the operation (McCauley & Ehrhardt, 1984).

Paraphilias

paraphilias Sexual disorders of at least six months' duration in which the person has either acted on, or is severely distressed by, recurrent urges or fantasies involving nonhuman objects, nonconsenting persons, or suffering or humiliation.

Paraphilias are sexual disorders of at least six months' duration in which the person has either acted on or is severely distressed by recurrent urges or fantasies involving any of the following three categories (see Figure 9.5): (1) nonhuman objects, as in fetishism and transvestic fetishism; (2) nonconsenting others, as in exhibitionism, voyeurism, frotteurism (rubbing against others for sexual arousal), and pedophilia; and (3) real or simulated suffering or humiliation, as in sadism and masochism. A person who is highly distressed by paraphiliac urges or fantasies but has not acted on them would be diagnosed as having a mild case of the paraphilia. All of these acts are considered deviant because they are obligatory for sexual functioning (erection, for example, cannot occur without the stimulus).

PARAPHILIAS	Prevalence	Age of Onset	Course
Fetishism	Primarily a male disorder; rare in women; exact figures unavailable	Usually begins in adolescence	Causes of fetishism are difficult to pinpoint; conditioning and learning seem likely
Transvestic Fetishism	Exact figures difficult to obtain because cross-dressing often goes unreported and is acceptable in many societies	Begins as early as puberty	Cross-dressing is not usually associated with major psychiatric problems
Exhibitionism	Almost exclusively a male activity; exact figures lacking	Begins in teenage years, but the exhibitionist is most likely to be in his 20s	Most likely to have doubts about his masculinity; likes to shock; many have an erection during the act; most masturbate after the exposure
Voyeurism	Difficult to determine; most are men	Begins at the age of 15 and tends to be chronic	Voyeurs tend to be young and male; they become sexually aroused and may masturbate during or after the "peeping" episode
Frotteurism	Difficult to determine; most are men	Begins in adolescence or earlier	Usually decreases after age 25
Pedophilia	Primarily men; exact figures not available	Must be at least 16 years of age; contrary to the "dirty old man" image, pedophiles tend to be in their late 20s and 30s	Prefer children who are at least 5 years younger than they are and usually less than 13 years old; most are friends, relatives, or acquaintances of the victim; pedophiles often have very poor social skills
Sadism	Usually male, rates unknown, however, 22% of men and 12% of women in one study report some sexual arousal from sadistic stories	Begins in early childhood with sexual fantasies	While fantasies begin in childhood, sadistic acts usually develop in adulthood and can stay at the same level of cruelty or, more rarely, increase to problematic proportions
Masochism	Precise figures difficult to obtain; most information comes from questionnaires and/or sadomasochistic magazines	Males report first interests around 15 years and women at age 22	Not all suffering arouses; usually it must be produced in a specific way; classical conditioning strongly implicated as causal

Figure 9.5 **Disorders Chart: Paraphilia Disorders (continued)**

People in this category may possess multiple paraphilias (Abel & Osborn, 1992). In one study of sex offenders (Rosenfield, 1985), researchers found that nearly 50 percent had engaged in a variety of sexually deviant behaviors, averaging between three and four paraphilias, and had committed more than 500 deviant acts. For example, a substantial number of men who had committed incest had also molested nonrelatives, exposed themselves, raped adult women, and engaged in voyeurism and frotteurism. In most cultures, paraphilias seem to be much more prevalent in males than in females (Beers & Berkow, 1999). This finding has led some to speculate that biological reasons may account for the unequal distribution.

Paraphilias Involving Nonhuman Objects

Fetishism Fetishism comprises an extremely strong sexual attraction and fantasies involving inanimate objects such as female undergarments. The fetish is often used as a sexual stimulus during masturbation or sexual intercourse. The disorder is rare among women.

> Mr. M. met his wife at a local church. Some kissing and petting took place but never any other sexual contact. He had not masturbated before marriage. Although he and his wife loved each other very much, he was unable to have sexual intercourse with her because he could not obtain an erection. However, he had fantasies involving an apron and was able to get an erection while wearing an apron. His wife was described as upset over this discovery but was persuaded to accept it. The apron was kept hanging somewhere in the bedroom, and it allowed him to consummate the marriage. He remembers being forced to wear an apron by his mother during his childhood years. (Kohon, 1987)

Most males find the sight of female undergarments sexually arousing and stimulating; this does not constitute a fetish. An interest in such inanimate objects as panties, stockings, bras, and shoes becomes a sexual disorder when the person is often sexually aroused to the point of erection in the presence of the fetish item, needs this item for sexual arousal during intercourse, chooses sexual partners on the basis of their having the item, or collects these items (Jones, Shainberg, & Byer, 1977). In many cases, the fetish item is enough by itself for complete sexual satisfaction through masturbation, and the person does not seek contact with a partner. Common fetishes include aprons, shoes, undergarments, and leather or latex items. As a group, people diagnosed with fetishism are not dangerous, nor do they tend to commit serious crimes.

Transvestic Fetishism A diagnosis of fetishism is not made if the inanimate object is an article of clothing used only in cross-dressing. In such cases, the appropriate diagnosis would be **transvestic fetishism**—intense sexual arousal obtained through cross-dressing (wearing clothes appropriate to the opposite gender). This disorder should not be confused with *transsexualism,* which is a gender identity disorder in which one *identifies* with the opposite gender. Although some transsexuals and homosexuals cross-dress, most transvestites are exclusively heterosexual and married. Some research, however, suggests that transvestites may be fairly hostile and self-centered, with high levels of marital discord and a limited capacity for intimacy (Wise et al., 1991). Several aspects of transvestism are illustrated in the following case study:

> A twenty-six-year-old graduate student referred himself for treatment following an examination failure. He had been cross-dressing since the age of ten and attributed his exam failure to the excessive amount of time that he spent doing so (four times a week). When he was younger, his cross-dressing had taken the form of masturbating while wearing his mother's high-heeled shoes, but it had gradually expanded to the present stage, in which he dressed completely as a woman, masturbating in front of a mirror. At

fetishism Sexual attraction and fantasies involving inanimate objects, such as female undergarments.

transvestic fetishism Intense sexual arousal obtained through cross-dressing (wearing clothes appropriate to the opposite gender); not to be confused with transsexualism.

no time had he experienced a desire to obtain a sex-change operation. He had neither homosexual experiences nor homosexual fantasies. Heterosexual contact had been restricted to heavy petting with occasional girlfriends. (Lambley, 1974, p. 101)

Not Necessarily What You Might Think   The etiology and behavioral symptoms of gender identity disorder go far beyond enjoying dressing as the opposite sex; more important is persistent cross-gender identification and discomfort with one's own anatomical sex. As outlandish as some of Dennis Rodman's cross-dressing may seem, it's unlikely that gender identity disorder is the diagnosis for him.

Sexual arousal while cross-dressing is an important criterion in the diagnosis of transvestic fetishism. If arousal is not present or has disappeared over time, a more appropriate diagnosis may be gender identity disorder. This distinction, however, may be difficult to make. Some transsexuals show penile erections to descriptions of cross-dressing (Blanchard, Racansky, & Steiner, 1986). Whether sexual arousal occurs in cross-dressing, therefore, may not serve as a valid distinction between transsexualism and transvestic fetishism. If the cross-dressing occurs only during the course of a gender identity disorder, the person is not considered in the category of transvestic fetishism.

Paraphilias Involving Nonconsenting Persons

This category of disorders involves persistent and powerful sexual fantasies about unsuspecting strangers or acquaintances. The victims are nonconsenting in that they do not choose to be the objects of the attention or sexual behavior.

Exhibitionism   Exhibitionism is characterized by urges, acts, or fantasies of exposing one's genitals to a stranger, often with the intent of shocking the unsuspecting victim. Exhibitionism is relatively common. The exhibitionist is most often male and the victim female. Surveys of selected groups of young women in the United States have indicated that between one-third and one-half have been victims of exhibitionists (Cox & McMahon, 1978).

The main goal of the exhibitionist seems to be the sexual arousal he gets by exposing himself; most exhibitionists want no further contact. However, there may be two types of exhibitionists—those who engage in criminal behavior and those who do not. The former tend to be sociopathic and impulsive, and they may be more likely to show aggression (Forgac & Michaels, 1982; Forgac, Cassel, & Michaels, 1984).

Exhibitionists may expect to produce surprise, sexual arousal, or disgust in the victim. The act may involve exposing a limp penis or masturbating an erect penis. In a study of ninety-six exhibitionists, only 50 percent reported that they "almost always" or "always" had erections when exposing, although a large percentage of the men wanted the women to be impressed with the size of their penises. Fantasies about being watched and admired by female observers were common among exhibitionists. More than two-thirds reported that they would not have sex with the victim even if she were receptive (Langevin et al., 1979). Most exhibitionists are in their twenties—far from being the "dirty old men" of popular myth. Most are married. Their exhibiting has a compulsive quality to it, and they report that they feel a great deal of anxiety about the act.

exhibitionism   Disorder characterized by urges, acts, or fantasies about the exposure of one's genitals to strangers.

Voyeurism Voyeurism comprises urges, acts, or fantasies of observing an unsuspecting person disrobing or engaging in sexual activity. "Peeping," as voyeurism is sometimes termed, is considered deviant when it includes serious risk, is done in socially unacceptable circumstances, or is preferred to coitus. The typical voyeur is not interested in looking at his wife or girlfriend; about 95 percent of the cases of voyeurism involve strangers. Observation alone produces sexual arousal and excitement, and the voyeur often masturbates during this surreptitious activity.

The voyeur is like the exhibitionist in that sexual contact is not the goal; viewing an undressed body is the primary motive. However, a voyeur may also exhibit or use other indirect forms of sexual expression (American Psychiatric Association, 1994). Because the act is repetitive, arrest is predictable. Usually an accidental witness or a victim notifies the police. Potential rapists or burglars who behave suspiciously are often arrested as voyeurs.

Frotteurism Whereas physical contact is not the goal of voyeurism, contact is the primary motive in frotteurism. Frotteurism involves recurrent and intense sexual urges, acts, or fantasies of touching or rubbing against a nonconsenting person. The touching, not the coercive nature of the act, is the sexually exciting feature. As in the case of the other paraphilias, the diagnosis is made when the person has acted on the urges or is markedly distressed by them.

Pedophilia Pedophilia is a disorder in which an adult obtains erotic gratification through urges, acts, or fantasies of sexual contact with a prepubescent child. According to DSM-IV-TR, to be diagnosed with this disorder, the person must be at least sixteen years of age and at least five years older than the victim. Pedophiles may victimize their own children (incest), stepchildren, or those outside the family. Most pedophiles prefer girls, although a few choose prepubertal boys.

Sexual abuse of children is common. Between 20 and 30 percent of women report having had a childhood sexual encounter with an adult man. And, contrary to the popular view of the child molester as a stranger, most pedophiles are relatives, friends, or casual acquaintances of their victims (Morenz & Becker, 1995; Zverina et al., 1987).

In most cases of abuse, only one adult and one child are involved, but cases involving several adults or groups of children have been reported. For example, a fifty-four-year-old man, a person who had won a community award for his work with youths, was arrested for child molestation involving boys as young as ten years old. The man encouraged and photographed sexual acts between the boys, including mutual masturbation and oral and anal sex. He then would have sex with one of them (Burgess et al., 1984).

A study of 229 convicted child molesters (Erickson, Walbek, & Seely, 1988) revealed the following information. Nearly one-fourth of the victims were younger than six years of age. Another 25 percent were ages six to ten, and about 50 percent were ages eleven to thirteen. Fondling the child was the most common sexual behavior, followed by vaginal and oral-genital contact. Bribery was often used to gain the cooperation of the victims. Pedophiles have a relapse rate of approximately 35 percent, the highest among sex offenders (Erickson et al., 1987).

Child molesters tend to have profiles indicating passive-dependent personality, discomfort in social situations, impulsiveness, and alcoholism (Erickson et al., 1987). Compared with control group members, child molesters are deficient in social skills. They also display a significantly higher fear of negative evaluation (Overholser & Beck, 1986).

Some cases of child abuse are also incestuous. Incest is nearly universally taboo in human society. It involves sexual relations between people too closely related to marry (father-daughter/stepdaughter, brother-sister, etc.). The cases of incest most frequently

voyeurism Urges, acts, or fantasies involving observation of an unsuspecting person disrobing or engaging in sexual activity.

frotteurism Disorder characterized by recurrent and intense sexual urges, acts, or fantasies of touching or rubbing against a nonconsenting person.

pedophilia A disorder in which an adult obtains erotic gratification through urges, acts, or fantasies involving sexual contact with a prepubescent child.

incest Sexual relations between people too closely related to marry legally.

Tools of the Sadomasochistic Trade   Pain and humiliation are associated with sexual satisfaction in sadism and masochism. Sadism involves inflicting pain on others; masochism involves receiving pain. Instruments used in sadomasochistic activities include handcuffs, whips, chains, and sharp objects.

reported to law enforcement agencies are those between a father and his daughter or stepdaughter. This type of incestuous relationship generally begins when the daughter is between six and eleven years old, and it continues for at least two years (Stark, 1984). Unlike sex between siblings, father-daughter incest is always exploitative. The girl is especially vulnerable because she depends on her father for emotional support. As a result, the victims often feel guilty and powerless. Their problems continue into adulthood and are reflected in their high rates of drug abuse, sexual dysfunction, and psychiatric problems (Emslie & Rosenfeld, 1983; Gartner & Gartner, 1988).

Studies suggest that incestuous fathers are lower in intelligence than other fathers (Williams & Finkelhor, 1990) and often shy (Masters, Johnson, & Kolodny, 1992). Three types of incestuous fathers have been described (Herman & Hirschman, 1981). The first is a socially isolated man who is highly dependent on his family for interpersonal relationships; his emotional dependency gradually evolves (and expands) into a sexual relationship with his daughter. The second type of incestuous father has a psychopathic personality and is completely indiscriminate in choosing sexual partners. The third type has pedophilic tendencies and is sexually involved with several children, including his daughter. In addition, incest victims have reported family patterns in which the father is violent and the mother is unusually powerless. Williams and Finkelhor (1990) noted that some studies have shown that incestuous fathers were more likely than nonincestuous fathers to have experienced childhood sexual abuse themselves, although such abuse is absent in many cases. They also found that incestuous fathers tend to have difficulties in empathy, nurturance, caretaking, social skills, and masculine identification.

Paraphilias Involving Pain or Humiliation

Pain and humiliation do not appear to be related to normal sexual arousal. In sadism and masochism, however, they play a prominent role. **Sadism** is a form of paraphilia in which sexually arousing urges, fantasies, or acts are associated with inflicting physical or psychological suffering on others. The word *sadism* was coined from the name of the Marquis de Sade (1740–1814), a French nobleman who wrote extensively about the sexual pleasure he received by inflicting pain on women. The marquis himself was so cruel to his sexual victims that he was declared insane and jailed for twenty-seven years.

Masochism is a paraphilia in which sexual urges, fantasies, or acts are associated with being humiliated, bound, or made to suffer. The word *masochism* is derived from the name of a nineteenth-century Austrian novelist, Leopold von Sacher-Masoch, whose fictional characters obtained sexual satisfaction only when pain was inflicted on them.

Sadistic behavior may range from the pretended or fantasized infliction of pain through mild to severe cruelty toward partners to an extremely dangerous pathological form of sadism that may involve mutilation or murder. Because of their passive roles, masochists are not considered dangerous. For some sadists and masochists, coitus becomes unnecessary; pain or humiliation alone is sufficient to produce sexual pleasure. As with other paraphilias, DSM-IV-TR specifies that to receive the diagnosis the person must have acted on the urges or must be markedly distressed by them.

In a study of 178 sadomasochists (47 women and 131 men), most reported engaging in and enjoying both submissive and dominant roles. Only 16 percent were exclusively

sadism Form of paraphilia in which sexually arousing urges, fantasies, or acts are associated with inflicting physical or psychological suffering on others.

masochism A paraphilia in which sexual urges, fantasies, or acts are associated with being humiliated, bound, or made to suffer.

Table 9.2 Sadomasochistic Activities, Ranked by Selected Samples of Male and Female Participants

Activity	Male (%)	Female (%)
Spanking	79	80
Master-slave relationships	79	76
Oral sex	77	90
Bondage	67	88
Humiliation	65	61
Restraint	60	83
Anal sex	58	51
Pain	51	34
Whipping	47	39
Use of rubber or leather	42	42
Enemas	33	22
Torture	32	32
Golden showers (urination)	30	37

Note: These sadomasochistic sexual preferences were reported by both male and female respondents. Many more men express a preference for S&M activities, but women who do so are likely to engage in this form of sexual behavior more frequently and with many more partners.

Source: Data from Brewslow, Evans, & Langley (1986).

dominant or submissive. Many engaged in spanking, whipping, and bondage (see Table 9.2). Approximately 40 percent engaged in behaviors that caused minor pain using ice, hot wax, biting, or face slapping. Fewer than 18 percent engaged in more harmful procedures, such as burning or piercing. Nearly all respondents reported sadomasochistic (S&M) activities to be more satisfying than "straight" sex (Moser & Levitt, 1987). Most sadomasochists who have been studied report that they do not seek harm or injury but that they find the sensation of utter helplessness appealing (Baumeister, 1988). S&M activities are often carefully scripted and involve role playing and mutual consent by the participants (Weinberg, 1987). In addition, fantasies involving sexual abuse, rejection, and forced sex are not uncommon among both male and female college students (Sue, 1979). Most sadomasochistic behavior among college students involves very mild forms of pain (such as in biting or pinching) that are accepted in our society.

Some cases of sadomasochism appear to be the result of classical conditioning in which sexual arousal is associated with pain. One masochistic man reported that as a child he was often "caned" on the buttocks by a school headmaster as his "attractive" wife looked on (Money, 1987). He reported, "I got sexual feelings from around the age of twelve, especially if she was watching" (p. 273). He and some of his schoolmates later hired prostitutes to spank them. Later yet, he engaged in self-whipping.

In addition to the paraphilias covered here, DSM-IV-TR lists many others under the category of "not otherwise specified" paraphilias. They include *telephone scatalogia* (making obscene telephone calls) and sexual urges involving corpses *(necrophilia)*, animals *(zoophilia)*, or feces *(coprophilia)*.

Etiology and Treatment of Paraphilias

All etiological theories for the paraphilias must answer three questions (Finkelhor & Araji, 1986). (1) What produced the deviant arousal pattern? (2) Why doesn't the person develop a more appropriate outlet for his or her sexual drive? (3) Why is the behavior not deterred by normative and legal prohibitions? So far, biological, psychodynamic, and behavioral perspectives have provided only partial answers.

Earlier, we noted that investigators have attempted to find genetic, neurohormonal, and brain anomalies that might be associated with sexual disorders. Some of the research findings conflict; others need replication and confirmation (Nevid, Fichner-Rathus, & Rathus, 1995). In any event, researchers need to continue applying advanced technology in the study of the biological influences on sexual disorders. Even if biological factors are found to be important in the causes of these disorders, psychological factors are also likely to contribute in important ways.

Psychodynamic theorists believe that all sexual deviations symbolically represent unconscious conflicts that began in early childhood. The psychodynamic treatment of sexual deviations involves helping the patient understand the relationship between the deviation and the unconscious conflict that produced it. To treat the man whose fetish was wearing an apron before he could engage in sexual intercourse, the therapist used dream analysis and free association. These techniques helped the patient understand the "roots" of his behavior. The psychoanalyst helped the patient bring the conflicts into conscious awareness through interpretation. After this, the patient gained insight into his behavior and was able to work through his problem.

Learning theorists stress the importance of early conditioning experiences in the etiology of sexually deviant behaviors. One such conditioning experience is masturbating while engaged in sexually deviant fantasies, combined with inadequate social skills that hamper the development of normal sexual patterns. For example, one boy developed a fetish for women's panties at age twelve after he became sexually excited watching girls come down a slide with their underpants exposed. He began to masturbate to fantasies of girls with their panties showing and had this fetish for twenty-one years before seeking treatment (Kushner, 1965).

Learning approaches to treating sexual deviations have generally involved one or more of the following elements: (1) weakening or eliminating the sexually inappropriate behaviors through processes such as extinction or aversive conditioning; (2) acquiring or strengthening sexually appropriate behaviors; and (3) developing appropriate social skills.

▷ CHECKPOINT REVIEW

exhibitionism *(p. 241)*

fetishism *(p. 240)*

frotteurism *(p. 242)*

gender identity disorder *(p. 235)*

incest *(p. 242)*

masochism *(p. 243)*

paraphilias *(p. 238)*

pedophilia *(p. 242)*

sadism *(p. 243)*

transsexualism *(p. 235)*

transvestic fetishism *(p. 240)*

voyeurism *(p. 242)*

What causes gender identity disorders?

■ Specified gender identity disorder involves a strong and persistent cross-gender identification.

■ Transsexuals feel a severe psychological conflict between their sexual self-concepts and their genders. Some transsexuals seek sex-conversion surgery, although behavioral therapies are increasingly being used. Gender identity disorder can also occur in childhood.

■ Children with this problem identify with members of the opposite gender, deny their own physical attributes, and often cross-dress. Treatment generally includes the parents and is behavioral in nature.

■ Other disorders in this group are classified as gender identity disorder, not otherwise specified.

What are the paraphilias?

■ The paraphilias are of three types, characterized by (1) a preference for nonhuman objects for sexual arousal, (2) repetitive sexual activity with nonconsenting partners, or (3) the association of real or simulated suffering with sexual activity.

■ Suggested causes of the paraphilias are unconscious conflicts (the psychodynamic perspective) and conditioning, generally during childhood.

■ Biological factors such as hormonal or brain processes have also been studied, but the results have not been consistent enough to permit strong conclusions about the role of biological factors in the paraphilias.

■ Treatments are usually behavioral and are aimed at eliminating the deviant behavior while teaching more appropriate behaviors.

FOCUS QUESTIONS

- What are the symptoms of mood disorders?
- How are mood disorders classified in the APA diagnostic scheme?
- Why do people develop depression and mania?
- What kinds of treatment are available for people with mood disorders, and how effective are the therapies?
- What do we know about suicide?
- Why do people decide to end their lives?
- How can we intervene or prevent suicides?

10 Mood Disorders and Suicide

We have all felt depressed or elated at some time during our lives. The loss of a job or the death of a loved one may result in depression; good news may make us manic (for example, ecstatic, hyperactive, and brazen). This chapter first discusses mood disorders and then examines suicide. Although the vast majority of people with mood disorders do not commit suicide and although many suicides are not attributable to depression, we include suicide in this chapter on mood disorders because depression is implicated in many suicides.

Mood disorders are disturbances in emotions that cause subjective discomfort, hinder a person's ability to function, or both. Depression and mania are central to these disorders. **Depression** is characterized by intense sadness, feelings of futility and worthlessness, and withdrawal from others. **Mania** is characterized by elevated mood, expansiveness, or irritability, often resulting in hyperactivity.

The prevalence of depression has been found to be more than ten times higher than that of mania (Robins et al., 1991). Depression is quite prevalent in the general population and is much higher among women than men. Some 10 million Americans, and more than 100 million people worldwide, will experience clinical depression this year. Lifetime prevalence (the proportion of people who develop severe depression at some point in their lives) ranges from 10 to 25 percent for women and from 5 to 12 percent for men (American Psychiatric Association, 2000a). A large-scale study has found even higher overall lifetime prevalence rates for all mood disorders—reaching almost 15 percent for adult males and almost 24 percent for adult females. Among college students, one survey found that over half indicated that they had experienced depression, 9 percent had thought of suicide, and 1 percent had attempted suicide since the beginning of college (Furr et al., 2001). Depression shortens life expectancy and increases the risk of dying from heart disease by as much as threefold (President's New Freedom Commission on Mental Health, 2003).

Severe depression may afflict rich or poor, successful or unsuccessful, highly educated or uneducated. The following case illustrates one woman's experience:

> Amanda was a thirty-nine-year-old homemaker with three children, ages nine, eleven, and fourteen. Her husband, Jim, was the sales manager for an auto agency. For years, family life was stable, and no serious problems existed between family members. However, Jim began to notice that his wife was becoming more and more unhappy and depressed. She constantly said that her life lacked purpose.
>
> After a while, Amanda no longer bothered to keep the house clean, to cook, or to take care of the children. At first Jim thought she was merely in a "bad mood" and that it would pass, but as her lethargy deepened, he became increasingly worried. Amanda told him that she was tired, and that simple household chores took too much energy. She said that she still loved Jim and the children but no longer had strong feelings for anything. Life was no longer important, and she just wanted to be left alone. Nothing Jim said could bring her out of the depression or stop her from crying.

mood disorders Disturbances in emotions that cause subjective discomfort, hinder a person's ability to function, or both; depression and mania are central to these disorders.

depression An emotional state characterized by intense sadness, feelings of futility and worthlessness, and withdrawal from others.

mania An emotional state characterized by elevated mood, expansiveness, or irritability, often resulting in hyperactivity.

The Symptoms of Depression

Certain core characteristics are often seen among people with depression. These characteristics may be organized within the four psychological domains used to describe anxiety: the affective domain, the cognitive domain, the behavioral domain, and the physiological domain (see Table 10.1). The most striking *affective* symptom of depression is depressed mood, with feelings of sadness, dejection, and an excessive and prolonged mourning. Feelings of worthlessness and of having lost the joy of living are common.

To illustrate these affective characteristics, we present the following statements, made by a severely depressed patient who had markedly improved after treatment:

> It's hard to describe the state I was in several months ago. The depression was total—it was as if everything that happened to me passed through this filter, which colored all experiences. Nothing was exciting to me. I felt I was no good, completely worthless, and deserving of nothing. The people who tried to cheer me up were just living in a different world.

Certain thoughts and ideas, or *cognitive* symptoms, are clearly related to depressive reactions. For example, the person has profoundly pessimistic beliefs about the future. Disinterest, decreased energy, and loss of motivation make it difficult for the depressed person to cope with everyday situations. Self-accusations of incompetence and general self-denigration are common, as are thoughts of suicide. Depression may be reflected in a cognitive triad, which consists of negative views of the self, of the outside world, and of the future (Beck, 1974).

Behavioral symptoms, such as social withdrawal and lowered work productivity, may occur. This low energy level is one of the dominant behavioral symptoms of depression, and it has been found to distinguish depressed individuals from nondepressed individuals (Christensen & Duncan, 1995). The person may show lack of concern for personal cleanliness. A dull, masklike facial expression may become characteristic, and the person tends to move slowly and does not initiate new activities. Speech is similarly reduced and slow, and responses may be limited to short phrases. This slowing down of all bodily movements, expressive gestures, and spontaneous responses is called *psychomotor retardation*.

The following physiological and somatic and related symptoms frequently accompany depression:

1. *Loss of appetite and weight* The loss of appetite often stems from the person's disinterest in eating; food seems tasteless. In severe depression, weight loss can become life threatening. Some people, however, have increased appetite and gain weight.

2. *Constipation* The person may not have bowel movements for days at a time.

3. *Sleep disturbance* Difficulty in falling asleep, waking up early, waking up erratically during the night, insomnia, and nightmares leave the person exhausted and tired during the day. Some depressed people, however, show hypersomnia, or excessive sleep.

4. *Disruption of the normal menstrual cycle in women* The disruption is usually a lengthening of the cycle, and the woman may skip one or several periods. The volume of menstrual flow may decrease.

5. *Aversion to sexual activity* Many people report that their sexual arousal dramatically declines.

Culture influences the experience and expression of symptoms of depression. In some cultures, depression may be experienced largely in somatic or bodily complaints,

Table 10.1   Symptoms of Depression and Mania

Domain	Depression	Mania
Affective	Sadness, unhappiness, apathy, anxiety, brooding	Elation, grandiosity, irritability
Cognitive	Pessimism, guilt, inability to concentrate, negative thinking, loss of interest and motivation, suicidal thoughts	Flighty and pressured thoughts, lack of focus and attention, poor judgment
Behavioral	Low energy, neglect of personal appearance, crying, psychomotor retardation, agitation	Overactive, speech difficult to understand, talkative
Physiological	Poor or increased appetite, constipation, sleep disturbance, disruption of the menstrual cycle in women, loss of sex drive	High levels of arousal, decreased need for sleep

rather than in sadness or guilt. Complaints of "nerves" and headaches (in Latino and Mediterranean cultures), of weakness, tiredness, or "imbalance" (in Chinese and Asian cultures), of problems of the "heart" (in Middle Eastern cultures), or of being "heartbroken" (among Hopi) may reveal the depressive experience (American Psychiatric Association, 2000a).

The Symptoms of Mania

In mania, *affective* symptoms include elevated, expansive, or irritable mood (see Table 10.1). Social and occupational functioning is impaired, as shown in the following case:

> Alan was a forty-three-year-old unmarried computer programmer who had led a relatively quiet life until two weeks before, when he returned to work after a short absence for illness. Alan seemed to be in a particularly good mood. Others in the office noticed that he was unusually happy and energetic, greeting everyone at work. At first everyone was surprised and amused by his antics. But two colleagues working with him on a special project became increasingly irritated because Alan didn't put any time into their project. He just insisted that he would finish his part in a few days.
>
> On the day the manager had decided to tell Alan of his colleagues' concern, Alan behaved in a delirious, manic way. When he came to work, he immediately jumped onto a desk and yelled, "Listen, listen! We aren't working on the most important aspects of our data! I know, since I've debugged my mind. Erase, reprogram, you know what I mean!" Alan then spouted profanities and made obscene remarks to several of the secretaries. Onlookers thought that he must have taken drugs. The manager, who had been summoned, also couldn't calm him. His speech was so rapid and disjointed that it was difficult to understand him. Within hours, he was taken to a psychiatric hospital for observation.

People with mania, like Alan, show boundless energy, enthusiasm, and self-assertion. If frustrated, they may become profane and quite belligerent, as he did. Some of the *cognitive* symptoms of mania include flightiness, pressured thoughts, lack of focus and attention, and poor judgment. Speech is usually quite accelerated and pressured. Individuals with mania may change topics in midsentence or utter irrelevant and idiosyncratic phrases. In terms of *behavioral* symptoms, individuals with mania are often uninhibited, engaging impulsively in sexual activity or abusive discourse.

"BUT YOU MUST ADMIT HALLUCINATIONS ARE MORE INTERESTING THAN DEPRESSION."

People who suffer from serious forms of mania display more disruptive behaviors, including pronounced overactivity, grandiosity, and irritability. Their speech may be incoherent, and they do not tolerate criticisms or restraints imposed by others. In the more severe form of mania, the person is wildly excited, rants and raves (the stereotype of a wild "maniac"), and is constantly agitated and on the move. Hallucinations and delusions may appear. The most prominent *physiological* or somatic characteristic is a decreased need for sleep, accompanied by high levels of arousal.

▶ Classification of Mood Disorders

Mood disorders are largely divided into two major categories in DSM-IV-TR: depressive disorders (often referred to as *unipolar disorder*) and bipolar disorder. Once a depressive or manic episode occurs, the disorder is classified into both a category and a subcategory (see Figure 10.1). Let us examine the major categories and subcategories, as well as other aspects of the classification scheme.

Depressive Disorders

Depressive disorders in DSM-IV-TR include major depressive disorders, dysthymic disorder, and depressive disorders not otherwise specified. All of these disorder classifications include no history of a manic episode. People who experience a major depressive episode are given the diagnosis of **major depression.** Symptoms should have been present for at least two weeks and should represent a change from the individual's previous functioning. The symptoms of major depression include a depressed mood or a loss of interest or pleasure, weight loss or gain, sleep difficulties, fatigue, feelings of worthlessness, inability to concentrate, and recurrent thoughts of death. About one-half of those who experience a depressive episode eventually have another episode. In general, the earlier the age of onset, the more likely is a recurrence (Reus, 1988).

If a disorder is characterized by depressed mood but does not meet the criteria for major depression, dysthymic disorder may be diagnosed. In **dysthymic disorder,** the depressed mood is chronic and relatively continual. Typical symptoms include pessimism or guilt, loss of interest, poor appetite or overeating, low self-esteem, chronic fatigue, social withdrawal, or concentration difficulties. Unlike major depression, dysthymia may last for years, although the symptoms are often not as severe (Klein et al., 1998). Each year, about 10 percent of individuals with dysthymia go on to have a first major depressive episode. In dysthymia, the depressive symptoms are present most of the day and for more days than not during a two-year period (or, for children and adolescents, a one-year period). One study (Myers et al., 1984) found the prevalence of dysthymia to be higher among women than men. Overall, the lifetime prevalence is about 6 percent (American Psychiatric Association, 2000a).

Bipolar Disorders

The essential feature of **bipolar disorders** is the occurrence of one or more manic or hypomanic episodes; the term *bipolar* is used because the disorders are usually accompanied by one or more depressive episodes. Symptoms of manic episodes include abnor-

depressive disorders DSM-IV-TR category including major depressive disorders, dysthymic disorder, and depressive disorders not otherwise specified; also known as *unipolar disorders* because no mania is exhibited.

major depression A disorder in which a group of symptoms, such as depressed mood, loss of interest, sleep disturbances, feelings of worthlessness, and an inability to concentrate, are present for at least two weeks.

dysthymic disorder A disorder characterized by chronic and relatively continual depressed mood that does not meet the criteria for major depression.

bipolar disorder A category of mood disorders characterized by one or more manic or hypomanic episodes and, usually, by one or more depressive episodes.

mally and persistently elevated, expansive, or irritable moods lasting at least one week in the case of mania and four days in the case of hypomania. Grandiosity, decreased need for sleep, flight of ideas, distractibility, and impairment in occupational or social functioning are often observed in persons with the disorder.

As indicated in the disorders chart, bipolar disorders include subcategories that describe the nature of the disorder (e.g., bipolar I disorders include *single manic episode, most recent episode manic*, etc.). Persons in whom manic but not depressive episodes have occurred are extremely rare; in such cases, a depressive episode will presumably appear at some time. Interestingly, mood disorders, especially bipolar conditions, have occasionally been associated with artistic talent (Jamison, 1996). For example, Michelangelo, Van Gogh, Tchaikovsky, F. Scott Fitzgerald, Ernest Hemingway, and Walt Whitman experienced such disorders.

In contrast to the much higher lifetime prevalence rates for depressive disorders, the lifetime prevalence rates for bipolar I and II hover around 0.8 and 0.5 percent, respectively (Weissman et al., 1991). Unlike depression, there appear to be no major gender differences in the prevalence of bipolar disorders (Dubovsky & Buzan, 1999). Some people have hypomanic episodes and depressed moods that do not meet the criteria for major depressive episode. If the symptoms are present for at least two years, the individuals are diagnosed with **cyclothymic disorder.** (For children and adolescents, one year rather than two years is the criterion.) As in the case of dysthymia, cyclothymic disorder is a chronic and relatively continual mood disorder in which the person is never symptom free for more than two months. The risk that a person with cyclothymia will subsequently develop a bipolar disorder is 15 to 50 percent (American Psychiatric Association, 2000a).

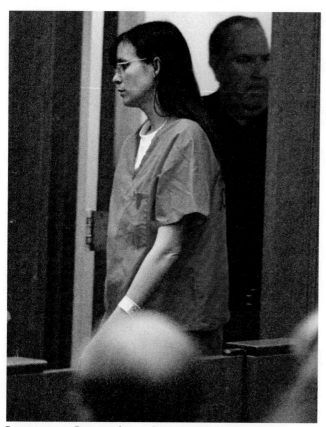

Postpartum Depression   Depression is sometimes associated with certain life events or changes. Specifiers are used to more precisely describe the mood disorder. One course specifier indicates whether the depression or mania in women occurs within four weeks of childbirth. If it does, the mood disorder has the specifier "postpartum onset." On June 20, 2001, Andrea Yates drowned her five children, ages 7 years to 6 months, in a bathtub. She had been suffering from postpartum depression since the birth of her 2 year old and had attempted suicide several times.

Symptom Features and Specifiers

To be more precise about the nature of the mood disorders, DSM-IV-TR has listed certain characteristics that may be associated with these disorders. They are important symptom features that may accompany the disorders but that are not criteria used to determine diagnosis. *Specifiers* may be used to more precisely describe the major depressive episode. Certain features, such as severity, presence or absence of psychotic symptoms, and remission status may be noted. Course specifiers indicate the cyclic, seasonal, postpartum, or longitudinal pattern of mood disorders. For example, in the *rapid cycling* type, which is applicable to bipolar disorders, the manic or depressive episodes have occurred four or more times during the previous twelve months. The episodes may also appear with periods of relative normality in between. One of the more interesting course specifiers involves a *seasonal pattern*. In seasonal affective disorder (SAD), serious cases of depression fluctuate according to the season, although the precise reasons for this fluctuation are unclear. Proposed explanations include the

cyclothymic disorder A chronic and relatively continual mood disorder characterized by hypomanic episodes and depressed moods that do not meet the criteria for major depressive episode.

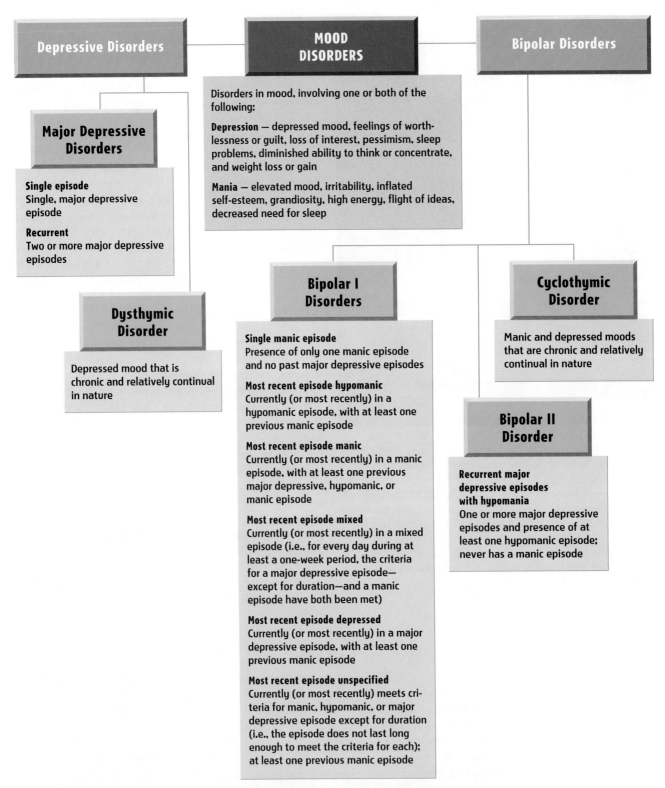

Depressive Disorders

MOOD DISORDERS

Bipolar Disorders

Disorders in mood, involving one or both of the following:

Depression — depressed mood, feelings of worthlessness or guilt, loss of interest, pessimism, sleep problems, diminished ability to think or concentrate, and weight loss or gain

Mania — elevated mood, irritability, inflated self-esteem, grandiosity, high energy, flight of ideas, decreased need for sleep

Major Depressive Disorders

Single episode
Single, major depressive episode

Recurrent
Two or more major depressive episodes

Dysthymic Disorder

Depressed mood that is chronic and relatively continual in nature

Bipolar I Disorders

Single manic episode
Presence of only one manic episode and no past major depressive episodes

Most recent episode hypomanic
Currently (or most recently) in a hypomanic episode, with at least one previous manic episode

Most recent episode manic
Currently (or most recently) in a manic episode, with at least one previous major depressive, hypomanic, or manic episode

Most recent episode mixed
Currently (or most recently) in a mixed episode (i.e., for every day during at least a one-week period, the criteria for a major depressive episode—except for duration—and a manic episode have both been met)

Most recent episode depressed
Currently (or most recently) in a major depressive episode, with at least one previous manic episode

Most recent episode unspecified
Currently (or most recently) meets criteria for manic, hypomanic, or major depressive episode except for duration (i.e., the episode does not last long enough to meet the criteria for each); at least one previous manic episode

Cyclothymic Disorder

Manic and depressed moods that are chronic and relatively continual in nature

Bipolar II Disorder

Recurrent major depressive episodes with hypomania
One or more major depressive episodes and presence of at least one hypomanic episode; never has a manic episode

Figure 10.1 Disorders Chart: Mood Disorders   *Source:* American Psychiatric Association (2000).

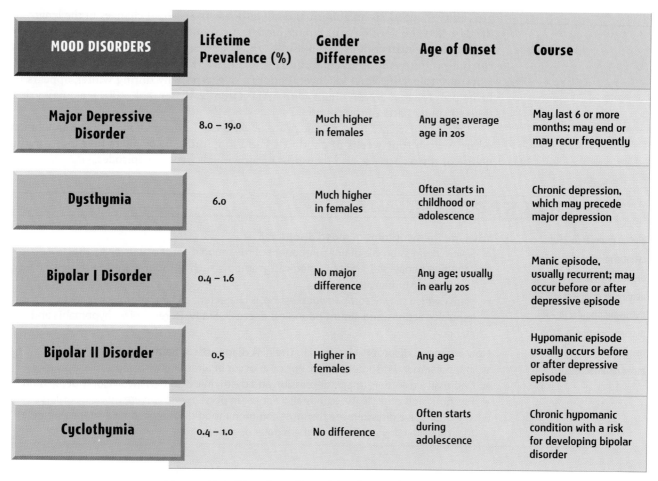

MOOD DISORDERS	Lifetime Prevalence (%)	Gender Differences	Age of Onset	Course
Major Depressive Disorder	8.0 – 19.0	Much higher in females	Any age; average age in 20s	May last 6 or more months; may end or may recur frequently
Dysthymia	6.0	Much higher in females	Often starts in childhood or adolescence	Chronic depression, which may precede major depression
Bipolar I Disorder	0.4 – 1.6	No major difference	Any age; usually in early 20s	Manic episode, usually recurrent; may occur before or after depressive episode
Bipolar II Disorder	0.5	Higher in females	Any age	Hypomanic episode usually occurs before or after depressive episode
Cyclothymia	0.4 – 1.0	No difference	Often starts during adolescence	Chronic hypomanic condition with a risk for developing bipolar disorder

Figure 10.1 Disorders Chart: Mood Disorders (continued)

Seasonal Patterns of Depression   In seasonal affective disorder (SAD), depressive symptoms vary with the seasons. One theory for this is that during winter, reduced daylight affects hormone levels, which in turn may induce depression. The man in this photo is receiving light therapy, which involves exposure to bright light. The treatment appears to be helpful in some cases of SAD.

possibility that SAD is an abnormal body response to seasonal changes in the length of the day, that the dark days of winter may bring about hormonal changes in the body that somehow affect depression levels, and that disruption of the body's circadian rhythm produces mood fluctuations (Lee et al., 1998). Interestingly, "light therapy" (exposure to bright light) for several hours a day, especially during winter, appears to be helpful for many individuals with SAD (Oren & Rosenthal, 2001), as may vacations to sunny parts of the country.

Other course specifiers include *postpartum onset* (if depression or mania in women occurs within four weeks of childbirth) and longitudinal specifiers that indicate the nature of the recurrence and the status of individuals between episodes.

▶ CHECKPOINT REVIEW

bipolar disorder *(p. 250)*
cyclothymic disorder *(p. 251)*
depression *(p. 247)*
depressive disorders *(p. 250)*
dysthymic disorder *(p. 250)*
major depression *(p. 250)*
mania *(p. 247)*
mood disorders *(p. 247)*

What are the symptoms of mood disorders?
- Severe depression is a major component of the mood disorders; it involves affective, cognitive, behavioral, and physiological symptoms, such as sadness, pessimism, low energy, and sleep disturbances.
- Mania, which may accompany depression, is characterized by elation, lack of focus, impulsive actions, and almost boundless energy. DSM-IV-TR recognizes hypomania and mania.

How are mood disorders classified in the APA diagnostic scheme?
- In bipolar mood disorders, manic episodes occur or alternate with depressive episodes.
- Depressive disorders (major depression and dysthymic disorder) involve only depression.
- Psychotic and other features may also appear in persons with severe mood disorders.
- The depressive disorders are the most common mood disorders; some evidence suggests that they are fairly distinct from the bipolar disorders.

▶ The Etiology of Mood Disorders

Little is known about what causes the extreme mood changes in the bipolar disorders. Some research findings raise the possibility that manic symptoms in bipolar disorder are manifestations of dysregulation in the brain activation system, which corresponds to neural pathways in the brain. In any case, much more is known about what causes unipolar depression than about what causes the bipolar disorders, and psychological-sociocultural perspectives focus primarily on depression rather than on mania. Biological factors appear to play a more prominent role in the etiology of bipolar disorders than in unipolar disorders. Another possibility is that the category of unipolar disorders is more heterogeneous and that some of these disorders are caused by internal conditions within the organism, whereas others are caused by external precipitating events. In any case, we focus our discussion of psychological or sociocultural explanations primarily on depression. The later section on biological explanations covers both unipolar and bipolar disorders, leading into treatment approaches based on those explanations.

Psychological or Sociocultural Approaches to Depression

Over the years, a number of different explanations have been proposed to account for depression. Some of the major theories discussed in this section are the psychodynamic, behavioral, cognitive, cognitive-learning, and sociocultural viewpoints.

Psychodynamic Explanations The psychodynamic explanation of depression focuses mainly on two concepts: separation and anger. Separation may occur when a

Loss as a Source of Depression   Mourning over the death of a loved one occurs in all cultures and societies, as illustrated by this Colombian father mourning the loss of his nine-year-old daughter, an earthquake victim, as her grandmother closes the casket. However, in most cultures, severe and incapacitating depression rarely continues after the first three months. If it does continue longer, then a depressive disorder may have developed. What other characteristics or symptoms would help one to distinguish between "normal" grief and a depressive disorder?

spouse, lover, child, parent, or significant other person dies or leaves for one reason or another. But depression cannot always be correlated with the immediate loss of a loved one, and for those instances, Freud used the construct of "symbolic loss." That is to say, the depressed person may perceive any form of rejection or reproach as symbolic of an earlier loss. For example, the withdrawal of affection or support or a rejection can induce depression.

Freud also believed that a person in depression fails to follow through the normal process of mourning, which he called "grief or mourning work." In this process, the mourner consciously recalls and expresses memories about the lost person in an attempt to undo the loss. In addition, the mourner is flooded with two strong sets of feelings: anger and guilt. The anger, which arises from the sense of being deserted, can be very strong. The mourner may also be flooded with guilt feelings about real or imagined sins committed against the lost person.

Psychodynamic explanations of depression have strongly emphasized the dynamics of anger. Many patients in depression have strong hostile or angry feelings, and some clinicians believe that getting clients to express their anger reduces their depression. Such a belief has led some to speculate that depression is really anger turned against the self (Freud, 1917). Freud suggested that, when a person experiences a loss (symbolic or otherwise), he or she may harbor feelings of resentment and hostility toward the lost person, in addition to feelings of love and affection. There have been relatively few empirical tests of psychodynamic ideas.

Behavioral Explanations Behaviorists may also see the separation or loss of a significant other as important in depression. However, behaviorists tend to see reduced reinforcement as the cause, rather than fixation or symbolic grief, which they view as untestable concepts. When a loved one is lost, an accustomed level of reinforcement (whether affection, companionship, pleasure, material goods, or services) is immediately withdrawn. The survivor can no longer obtain the support or encouragement of the lost person, and the survivor's level of activity (talking, expressing ideas, working, joking, engaging in sports, going out on the town) diminishes markedly in the absence of this reinforcement. Thus many behaviorists view depression as a product of inadequate or insufficient reinforcers in a person's life, leading to a reduced frequency of behavior that previously was positively reinforced (Lewinsohn, 1974; Wells, et al., 1996).

Sympathetic friends or relatives may try to help the depressed person. However, by being sympathetic, they may be reinforcing the person's current state of inactivity. (This reinforcement for a lower activity level is known as *secondary gain*.) Thus the depression continues to deepen, and the person disengages still further from the environment and further reduces the chance of obtaining positive reinforcement from normal activity.

Lewinsohn's model of depression is perhaps the most comprehensive behavioral explanation of depression (Lewinsohn, 1974; Lewinsohn et al., 1985). Along with the reinforcement view of depression, Lewinsohn suggested three sets of variables that may enhance or hinder a person's access to positive reinforcement.

The Reinforcement Factor   Learning theory suggests that depression may be a product of reduced reinforcement in a person's life, which may lead to reduced activity levels. Ironically, consolation and sympathy from others may sometimes serve to reinforce and maintain depressive behaviors. In such cases, should you withhold sympathy? Would this be beneficial?

1. *The number of events and activities that are potentially reinforcing to the person.* This number depends very much on individual differences and varies with the biological traits and experiential history of the person. For example, age, gender, or physical attributes may determine the availability of reinforcers. Handsome people are more likely to receive positive attention than are nondescript people.

2. *The availability of reinforcements in the environment.* Harsh environments, such as regimented institutions or remote isolated places, reduce reinforcements.

3. *The instrumental behavior of the individual.* The number of social skills a person can exercise to bring about reinforcement is important. People in depression lack social behaviors that can elicit positive reinforcements. They interact with fewer people, respond less, have very few positive reactions, and initiate less conversation. A low rate of positive reinforcement in any of these three situations can lead to depression.

Cognitive Explanations   Rather than low rates of positive reinforcement, cognitively oriented psychologists have proposed that the way people think can cause depression. In their view, depressed persons have negative thoughts and specific errors in thinking that result in pessimism, negative views of self, feelings of hopelessness, and depression (Emmelkamp, 2004). Such thoughts or beliefs are often exaggerated and irrational and are interpreted in a catastrophic manner (Ellis, 1989).

Beck (1976) proposed one major cognitive theory that views depression as a primary disturbance in *thinking* rather than a basic disturbance in *mood*. According to this theory, people in depression operate from a "primary triad" of negative self-views, present experiences, and future expectations.

Although the cognitive explanation of depression has merit, it seems too simple. At times, negative cognitions may be the result, rather than the cause, of depressed moods, as noted by Hammen (1985). That is, one may first feel depressed and then, as a result, have negative or pessimistic thoughts about the world.

Cognitive-Learning Approaches: Learned Helplessness and Attributional Style
Martin Seligman (1975; Nolen-Hoeksema, Girgus, & Seligman, 1992) proposed a unique and interesting view of depression based on cognitive-learning theory. The basic assumption of this approach is that both cognitions and feelings of helplessness are learned and that depression is **learned helplessness**—an acquired belief that one is helpless and unable to affect the outcomes in one's life. A person who sees that his or her actions continually have very little effect on the environment develops an expectation of being helpless. When this expectation is borne out in settings that may not be controllable, passivity and depression may result.

learned helplessness Acquiring the belief that one is helpless and unable to affect the outcomes in one's life.

A person's susceptibility to depression, then, depends on his or her experience with controlling the environment. In his study of helplessness, Seligman discovered strong parallels between the symptoms and causes of helplessness and those of depression. He also noticed similarities in cures; one could say that depression is cured when the person no longer believes he or she is helpless.

Attributional Style Seligman and his coworkers revised the model to include more cognitive elements (Abramson, Seligman, & Teasdale, 1978). The essential idea is that people who feel helpless make *causal attributions,* or speculations about why they are helpless. These attributions can be internal or external, stable or unstable, and global or specific. For instance, suppose that a student in a math course receives the same low grades regardless of how much he has studied. The student may attribute the low grades to internal or personal factors ("I don't do well in math because *I'm* scared of math") or to external factors ("The *teacher* doesn't like me, so I can't get a good grade"). The attribution can also be stable ("I'm the type of person who can never do well in math") or unstable ("My poor performance is due to my heavy workload"). Additionally, the attribution can be global or specific. A global attribution ("I'm a poor student") has broader implications for performance than a specific one ("I'm poor at math but good in other subjects"). Abramson and coworkers believe that a person whose attributions for helplessness are internal, stable, and global is likely to have more pervasive feelings of depression than someone whose attributions are external, unstable, and specific. Attributions have been found to be associated with many aspects of life.

Learned Helplessness and Depression   According to Seligman, feelings of helplessness can lead to depression. However, if people can learn to control their environment and believe in their ability to succeed, despite difficulties, they can overcome their feelings of helplessness and despair and begin to lead productive lives again. California Angels' pitcher Jim Abbott fought feelings of helplessness and won his battle with depression. In Seligman's theory, what can be done to alter feelings of helplessness?

Some people tend to have a pessimistic attributional style, explaining bad events (such as failure to pass an examination) in global, stable, and internal terms (such as believing that "I fail in many courses, it always happens to me, and I am stupid"). Attributional style is related to a number of characteristics. People who have pessimistic attributional styles receive lower grades in universities, perform worse as sales agents, and have poorer health (Seligman, 1987).

Helplessness theory and attributions may explain only a certain type of depression (Abramson, Metalsky, & Alloy, 1989; DeVellis & Blalock, 1992). Depression may be a heterogeneous disorder that can be caused by genetic, biochemical, or social factors.

Sociocultural Explanations Cross-cultural studies of mood disorders have found that prevalence rates and manifestation of symptoms vary considerably among different cultural groups and societies (Goodwin & Guze, 1984). For example, American Indians and Southeast Asians living in the United States appear to have higher rates of depression than are found among other Americans (Chung & Okazaki, 1991; Vega & Rumbaut, 1991). In China, Chinese patients with depression commonly present somatic (bodily) complaints rather than dysphoria (depression, anxiety, or restlessness), which indicates that the expression of symptoms for a particular disorder may differ from culture to culture (Kleinman, 1991). These findings suggest that factors such as culture, social experiences, and psychosocial stressors play an important role in mood disorders.

Stress and Depression   Conceptualizations of the role of stress in psychopathology in general and in depression in particular have typically proposed that stress is one of three broad factors that are important to consider: diathesis, stress, and resources or social supports. (See the discussion of stress in the chapter "Psychological Factors Affecting Medical Conditions.")

Diathesis refers to the fact that because of genetic or constitutional or social conditions, certain individuals may have a predisposition or vulnerability to developing depression (Monroe & Simons, 1991). Stress may act as a trigger to activate this predisposition, especially when individuals lack resources to adjust to the stress. Presumably, individuals with low predisposition (compared with those with high predisposition) require greater levels of stress to become depressed. The importance of stress in depression has been demonstrated (Stader & Hokanson, 1998).

Gender and Depression   Depression is far more common among women than among men regardless of region of the world, race and ethnicity, or social class (Strickland, 1992). Although women are more likely than men to be seen in treatment and to be diagnosed with depression, this may not mean that women are more prone to depression. Other explanations for this finding are noted in Table 10.2. First, women may simply be more likely than men to seek treatment when depressed; this tendency would make the reported depression rate for women higher, even if the actual male and female rates were equal. Second, women may be more willing to report their depression to other people. That is, the gender differences may occur in self-report behaviors rather than in actual depression rates. Third, diagnosticians or the diagnostic system may be biased toward finding depression among women (Caplan, 1995). And fourth, depression in men may take other forms and thus be given other diagnoses, such as substance dependency.

Some clinicians believe that these four possibilities account for only part of the gender difference in depression and that women really do have higher rates of depression (Radloff & Rae, 1981). Attempts to explain these differences have focused on physiological or social psychological factors.

Although biological factors, such as genetic or hormonal differences between the sexes, may account for the gender differences in depression, relatively little research has been conducted on these factors. Moreover, available findings are inconsistent with respect to hormonal changes and depression. This fact has led researchers to propose social or psychological factors, one of which is women's traditional gender role. Women have been encouraged to present themselves as attractive, sensitive to other people, and passive in relationships (Strickland, 1992).

In a review of different explanations for the gender differences in rates of depression, Nolen-Hoeksema (1987) concluded that none truly accounts for the observed differences. She hypothesized that the way a person responds to depressed moods contributes to the severity, chronicity, and recurrence of depressive episodes. In her view, women tend to ruminate and amplify their depressive moods, and men tend to dampen or find means to minimize dysphoria.

Biological Perspectives on Mood Disorders

Biological approaches to the causes of mood or affective disorders generally focus on genetic predisposition, physiological dysfunction, or combinations of the two.

Table 10.2 Explaining the Findings That Rates of Depression Are Higher Among Women Than Among Men

The Gender Differences Only Appear Real Because

- Women may be more likely to seek treatment.
- Women may be more willing to report their depression to other people.
- Diagnosticians or the diagnostic system may be gender biased.
- Men may exhibit depression in different ways and may be given other diagnoses.

The Gender Differences Are Real Because

- Genetic or hormonal differences between genders may account for higher depression levels among women.
- Women are subjected to gender roles that may be unfulfilling and that limit occupational opportunities.
- Gender roles may lead to feelings of helplessness.
- Traditional feminine roles may be less successful at eliciting positive reinforcement from others, compared with traditional male roles, which foster assertive and forceful behavior.

The Role of Heredity Mood disorders tend to run in families, and the same type of disorder is generally found among members of the same family (American Psychiatric Association, 2000a; Perris, 1966; Winokur, Clayton, & Reich, 1969). As we have noted in earlier chapters, one way to assess the role of heredity is to compare the incidence of disorders among the biological and adoptive families of people who were adopted early in life and who had the disorders. The results of such a comparison indicated that the incidence of mood disorders was higher among the biological families than among the adoptive families; the latter showed an incidence similar to that of the general population (American Psychiatric Association, 2000a).

Another way to study the possible genetic transmission of mood disorders is to compare identical and fraternal twins. Nine such studies of twins have been reported. The concordance rate (the probability of one twin having the same disorder as the other twin) for bipolar disorders was 72 percent for identical (monozygotic—MZ) twins and 14 percent for fraternal (dizygotic—DZ) twins. A study of MZ and DZ twins 75 years of age or older also revealed a higher concordance rate for depressive symptoms among MZ than among DZ twins (McGue & Christensen, 1997). The studies suggest that the genetic component is extremely important, although nongenetic factors also appear to be influential (Baron, 1991). By contrast, the concordance rate for unipolar mood disorders was only 40 percent for MZ twins and 11 percent for DZ twins (Goodwin & Guze, 1984).

Neurotransmitters and Mood Disorders

But how is heredity involved in the major mood disorders? A growing number of researchers believe that genetic factors influence the amounts of catecholamines—a group of substances, including norepinephrine, dopamine, and serotonin—which are found at specific sites in the brain. These substances, called neurotransmitters, help transmit nerve impulses from one neuron to another. They may mediate between active motor behavior and emotions. Nerve impulses are transmitted from neuron to neuron across *synapses,* which are small gaps between the axon (or transmitting end) of one neuron and the

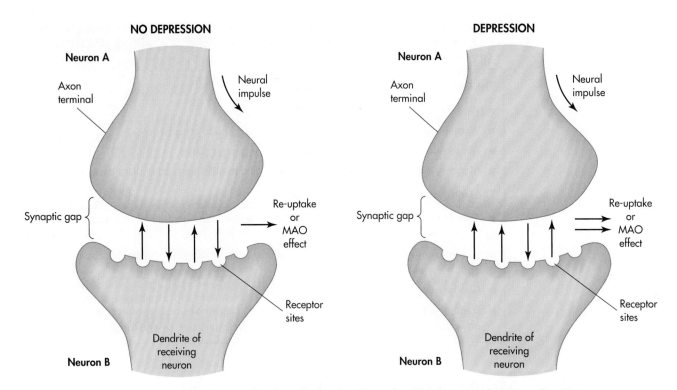

NO DEPRESSION

Neuron A

Axon terminal

Neural impulse

Synaptic gap

Re-uptake or MAO effect

Receptor sites

Dendrite of receiving neuron

Neuron B

DEPRESSION

Neuron A

Axon terminal

Neural impulse

Synaptic gap

Re-uptake or MAO effect

Receptor sites

Dendrite of receiving neuron

Neuron B

Figure 10.2 The Catecholamine Hypothesis: A Proposed Connection Between Neurotransmitters and Depression On the left is a representation of the production of neurotransmitter substances at a synapse between two neurons in the brain of a person with no depression. Some of the neurotransmitter is reabsorbed by the transmitting neuron in a process known as *reuptake*. Neurotransmitters are also broken down or chemically depleted by the enzyme monoamine oxidase (MAO), which is normally found in the body. In people with depression (right representation), either or both of these two processes may reduce neurotransmitters to a level that is insufficient for normal functioning.

dendrites (or receiving end) of a receptor neuron. In Figure 10.2, Neuron A is the transmitting neuron, and Neuron B is the receptor neuron. For a nerve impulse to travel from A to B, the axon at A must release a neurotransmitter into the synaptic gap, thereby stimulating B to fire, or transmit the impulse. According to the *catecholamine hypothesis*, depression is caused by a deficit of specific neurotransmitters at brain synapses; similarly, mania is presumed to be caused by an oversupply of these substances (Bunney et al., 1979).

As in other areas, most research has focused on the study of depression. Figure 10.2 illustrates two mechanisms, either of which could cause the amount of neurotransmitters in the synapses to be insufficient: (1) neurotransmitters are broken down or chemically depleted by the enzyme monoamine oxidase (MAO), which is normally found in the body; (2) neurotransmitters are reabsorbed by the releasing neuron in the process of *reuptake*.

Different lines of research offer support for the catecholamine hypothesis. One of these is studies of the effects of antidepressant medication on neurotransmitters and on mood changes. Antidepressant medications appear to increase the level of neurotransmitters. One group, the MAO inhibitors (MAOIs), blocks the effects of MAO in breaking down the neurotransmitters. Another group, the tricyclic drugs, blocks the reuptake of certain transmitter substances. Selective serotonin reuptake inhibitors such as fluoxetine (Prozac) seem to block the reuptake of serotonin in particular.

Some researchers have suggested that the level, or amount, of neurotransmitters present is not the primary factor. They noted that, to travel from one neuron to another, an electrical impulse must release neurotransmitters that stimulate the receiving neuron. The problem may not be the amount of neurotransmitter made available by the sending neuron but rather a dysfunction in the reception of the neurotransmitter by the receiving neuron (Sulser, 1979). Other researchers suggest that the catecholamine hypothesis may be simplistic. They note, for example, that drugs that raise the level of neurotransmitters in the synapse trigger such increases immediately, yet the alleviation of depressive symptoms may be delayed for several weeks after this increase. This delay may indicate that other factors, such as longer term membrane responses to changes in neurotransmitters, are also important in alleviating depression (Rivas-Vazquez & Blais, 1997). Thus the catecholamine hypothesis is probably too simplistic in explaining depression, although catecholamine impairment may be one of the manifestations or correlates of depression (U.S. Surgeon General, 1999).

One good way to think about mood disorders is to see them as a range of mood states resulting from an interaction between environmental and biological factors (U.S. Surgeon General, 1999). On one end of the range is mild sadness, then normal grief and the specific affective disorders, and, at the other end of the range, the major mood disorders. The causes of milder instances of depression (or, for that matter, mania) may tend to be more external. In mood disorders in the middle of the spectrum, both external and internal factors may be important. In severe disorders, including psychotic forms of the major mood disorders, endogenous factors may become more prominent.

▶▶ **CHECKPOINT REVIEW**

learned helplessness *(p. 256)*

neurotransmitters *(p. 259)*

Why do people develop depression and mania?

- Psychological theories of depression have been proposed by adherents of the psychodynamic, behavioral, cognitive, cognitive-learning, and sociocultural viewpoints, but each has certain weaknesses.
- Psychodynamic explanations focus on separation and anger.
- Behavioral explanations focus on reduced reinforcement following losses.
- Cognitive explanations see low self-esteem as an important factor.
- According to the learned helplessness theory of depression, susceptibility to depression depends on the person's experience with controlling the environment. The person's attributional style—speculations about why he or she is helpless—is also important.
- Sociocultural explanations have focused on cultural factors that influence the rates and symptoms of mood disorders and the role of stress and of social supports.
- Some people may be more vulnerable to depression, perhaps because of biological or psychosocial factors.
- Sociocultural factors have also been used to explain the higher observed rates of depression among women. They include gender role differences that make women more likely than men to amplify depressive symptoms.
- Genetic and biochemical research has demonstrated that heredity plays a role in depression and mania, probably by affecting neurotransmitter activity or levels in the brain.
- For example, according to the catecholamine hypothesis, a decrease in the amount of serotonin or norepinephrine causes depression. Sensitivity of neurotransmitter receptors may also be a factor.

▶▶ **The Treatment of Mood Disorders**

Biological approaches to the treatment of mood disorders are generally based on the catecholamine hypothesis. That is, treatment consists primarily of controlling the level

"More lithium."

of neurotransmitters at brain synapses. Psychological treatment also seems to offer promise for persons with depression.

Biomedical Treatments for Depressive Disorders

Biomedical treatments are interventions that alter the physical or biochemical state of the patient. They include the use of medication and electroconvulsive therapy.

Medication According to the U.S. Surgeon General (1999), antidepressant medications are effective across the full range of severity of depressive episodes, although effectiveness is greater with less severe depressive episodes. There are four kinds of antidepressant medication: tricyclic antidepressants (TCAs), heterocyclic antidepressants (HCAs), monoamine oxidase inhibitors (MAOIs), and selective serotonin reuptake inhibitors (SSRIs). Each medication is designed to heighten the level of a target neurotransmitter at the neuronal synapse. This heightening can be accomplished by (1) boosting the neurotransmitter's synthesis, (2) blocking its degradation, (3) preventing its reuptake from the synapse, or (4) mimicking its binding to postsynaptic receptors.

Many of the medications have side effects—the tricyclics, for example, may cause drowsiness, insomnia, agitation, fine tremors, blurred vision, dry mouth, and reduced sexual ability. MAOIs also have many side effects, including insomnia, irritability, dizziness, constipation, impotence, and serious adverse reactions to a substance found in cheese. Such side effects are a major drawback of the antidepressant drugs, and careful monitoring of the patient's reactions is thus absolutely necessary. Another drawback is that the antidepressant drugs are essentially ineffective during the first two weeks of use, which is a serious concern, particularly in cases in which suicide is a danger.

SSRIs block the reuptake of serotonin. The SSRIs include the drugs Prozac (fluoxetine hydrochloride), Paxil (paroxetine), and Zoloft (sertraline). They have become quite popular in the treatment of depression because they seem to have fewer side effects and to be at least as effective as the other tricyclics (U.S. Surgeon General, 1999). Sometimes effectiveness can be improved by the application of systematic procedures. The Texas Medication Algorithm Project is an evidence-based practice in which a flow chart is used to help clinicians make the best choice of medications. The systematic application of the procedures has been found to be more effective than treatment as usual for depression and bipolar disorders (President's New Freedom Commission on Mental Health, 2003).

Electroconvulsive Therapy Electroconvulsive therapy (ECT) is generally reserved for patients with severe unipolar depression who have not responded to antidepressant medications. It consists of applying a moderate electrical voltage to the person's brain for up to half a second. The patient's response to the voltage is a convulsion (seizure) lasting thirty to forty seconds, followed by a five- to thirty-minute coma.

Most patients with serious depression show at least a temporary improvement after about four ECT treatments (Campbell, 1981). The ECT mechanism is not

Mental Health and Society

I Am Suffering from Depression

Dr. Norman Endler, a prominent psychologist, stable family man, and chairman of the psychology department at York University, wrote:

> I honestly felt subhuman, lower than the lowest vermin. Furthermore, I was self-deprecatory and could not understand why anyone would want to associate with me, let alone love me....
>
> I was positive that I was a fraud and phony and that I didn't deserve my Ph.D. I didn't deserve to have tenure; I didn't deserve to be a full professor; I didn't deserve to be chairman of the psychology department. (Endler, 1982, pp. 45–48)

These comments are from a poignant and very explicit book in which Endler described his experiences with bipolar disorder and his reactions to treatment. Until the spring of 1977, Endler felt fine. He was at the height of his successful career. He was active in sports and was constantly on the move. In retrospect, Endler realized that he was showing evidence of hypomania as early as the fall of 1976, but not until the following April did he became aware that something was wrong. He had difficulty sleeping and had lost his sex drive. "I had gone from being a winner to feeling like a loser. Depression had turned it around for me. From being on top of the world in the fall, I suddenly felt useless, inept, sad, and anxious in the spring" (p. 11).

Endler sought treatment and was administered several drugs that did not prove effective. He was then given electroconvulsive therapy (ECT). Endler described his reaction to ECT, as well as the way the treatment was administered:

> I was asked to lie down on a cot and was wheeled into the ECT room proper. It was about eight o'clock. A needle was injected into my arm and I was told to count back from 100. I got about as far as 91. The next thing I knew I was in the recovery room and it was about eight-fifteen. I was slightly groggy and tired but not confused. (Endler, 1982, p. 81)

After about seven ECT sessions, his depression lifted dramatically: "My holiday of darkness was over and fall arrived with a bang!" (p. 83).

The next few months were free of depression, and Endler enjoyed everything he did. However, the mania and depression returned. Slowly, over the course of about two years, he improved with the aid of medication.

Endler concludes by offering some advice. First, when people think they are depressed, they should seek treatment immediately. Second, some combinations of treatments, such as psychotherapy, antidepressant drugs, and ECT, may be effective. Third, the person's family can have an important effect on recovery: when a family member has severe depression, existing family conflicts may become exacerbated. A supportive and understanding family can help a person survive this disorder.

Depression is a common pervasive illness affecting all social classes, but it is eminently treatable. A great deal of heartbreak can be avoided by early detection and treatment. There is nothing to be ashamed of. There is no stigma attached to having an affective disorder. It is unwise to try to hide it and not seek help. I lived to tell and to write about it. (Endler, 1982, pp. 167–169)

fully understood; it may operate on neurotransmitters at the synapses, as do antidepressants. One major advantage of ECT is that the response to treatment is relatively fast (Gangadhar, Kapur, & Kalyanasundaram, 1982). However, common side effects include headaches, confusion, and memory loss. And many patients are terrified of ECT. In about 1 of every 1,000 cases, serious medical complications occur (Goldman, 1988). The U.S. Surgeon General (U.S. Surgeon General, 1999) considers ECT as among those treatments that are effective for severe depression. Still, ECT is controversial, and critics have urged that it be banned as a form of treatment. The Mental Health and Society feature, "I Am Suffering from Depression," describes a case in which medication was used in combination with ECT to treat a bipolar affective disorder.

Overcoming Depression   Television correspondent Mike Wallace suffered for years with depression but leads a very productive life. Indeed, Wallace's insights into his mental disorder have resulted in numerous public service messages on the topic. Actress Carrie Fisher's battle with bipolar disorder became widely known when she published an autobiographical novel, *Postcards from the Edge.* Since then, with treatment and a great deal of support from family and friends, she has recovered to the point where she has been able to continue her writing career.

Psychotherapy and Behavioral Treatments for Depressive Disorders

A variety of psychological forms of treatment have been used for depression, such as psychoanalysis, behavior therapy, group psychotherapy, and family therapies—all with some success (Hirschfield & Shea, 1985; McDermut, Miller, & Brown, 2001).

Treatment strategies reflect the theoretical orientation of the therapists. For example, psychodynamic therapists attempt to have their clients gain insight into unconscious and unresolved feelings of separation or anger. To this end, the therapist interprets the client's free associations, reports of dreams, resistances, and transferences. Psychodynamic therapies of depression have not been rigorously studied, but some investigations suggest that brief dynamic therapy appears to be effective in reducing the depressive symptoms of patients (Gabbard, 2001).

In contrast to psychodynamic therapists, behavioral therapists may believe that reduced reinforcement is responsible for depression. They would attempt to teach clients to increase their exposure to pleasurable events and activities and to improve their social skills and interactions.

Two types of treatment—interpersonal psychotherapy and cognitive-behavioral therapy—have been intensively examined for their effectiveness in depressive disorders. There is evidence that the two treatments are effective (and in some studies, just as effective as antidepressant medications), particularly in the treatment of less severe cases of unipolar depression (Cardemil & Barber, 2001; Dubovsky & Buzan, 1999; President's New Freedom Commission on Mental Health, 2003).

Both psychotherapy and drug therapy are effective, and some evidence shows that antidepressant medications may be particularly advantageous with severe cases of depression (Lambert & Ogles, 2004). However, there appear to be advantages in combined treatments that involve medication and psychotherapy. Medication tends to produce rapid and reliable reductions in symptoms and to suppress relapse, whereas psychotherapy can enhance social functioning or reduce subsequent risk (Hollon & Fawcett, 2001).

Treatment for Bipolar Disorders

Although the forms of psychotherapy and behavior therapy used for depressive disorders are also used for bipolar disorders (e.g., MAOIs and SSRIs), drugs (especially lithium) are typically given to bipolar clients. Since it was introduced to the United States in 1969, lithium (in the form of lithium carbonate) has been the treatment of choice for bipolar and manic disorders. Response rates with lithium range from 60 percent to 80 percent in "classic" bipolar disorder (Delgado & Gelenberg, 2001).

Some initial positive results have been reported with anticonvulsant drugs such as carbamazepine, valproate, lamotrigine, and gabapentin in the treatment of bipolar disorders (Dubovsky & Buzan, 1999). Further testing of the effectiveness of these drugs is essential.

▷ CHECKPOINT REVIEW

What kinds of treatment are available for people with mood disorders, and how effective are the therapies?

- Biomedical approaches to treating depression focus on increasing the amounts of neurotransmitters that are available at brain synapses or that affect the sensitivity of postsynaptic receptors through either medication or electroconvulsive therapy.
- Different forms of psychological and behavioral treatments have been found to be effective with mood disorders, such as cognitive-behavioral treatment, which seeks to replace negative thoughts with more realistic (or positive) cognitions, and interpersonal therapy, which is a short-term treatment focused on interpersonal issues.
- The most effective treatment for bipolar and manic disorders is lithium, a drug that lowers the level of neurotransmitters at synapses by increasing the reuptake of norepinephrine, although other drugs are being tested for use in these disorders.

▷ Suicide

Cleopatra, Nirvana's Kurt Cobain, Bruno Bettelheim (psychiatrist), Ernest Hemingway, Adolf Hitler, Jim Jones (People's Temple leader), David Koresh (Branch Davidian sect leader), Marshal Herff Applewhite (leader of the cult Heaven's Gate), Marilyn Monroe, Freddie Prinze (comedian), King Saul, Samson, and Virginia Woolf.

What do these individuals have in common? As you may have guessed, they all committed **suicide**—the intentional, direct, and conscious taking of one's own life. Suicide is now recognized as a serious threat to public health. The World Health Organization (2002) found that suicide worldwide causes more deaths every year than homicide or war. Suicide is not only a tragic act; it is a baffling and confusing one as well. We can never be entirely certain why people knowingly and deliberately end their own lives. A single explanation is simplistic. Suicide has many causes, and people kill themselves for many different reasons. Depression is involved in more than half of attempted suicides (United States Public Health Service [USPHS], 1999) and is often related to unhappiness over a broken or unhappy love affair, marital discord, disputes

suicide The intentional, direct, and conscious taking of one's own life.

A Tragic Act   Although some suicidologists believe that there are commonalities among those who choose to die, it is also true that people take their lives for many different reasons. We can never be sure of the exact reasons for their suicides, but we do know that Ernest Hemingway (left) had become increasingly despondent over growing physical problems and that Kurt Cobain (right) was finding it difficult dealing with the fame and fortune of being lead singer in the popular group Nirvana.

with parents, and recent bereavements. Interestingly, patients seldom commit suicide while severely depressed. Such patients generally show motor retardation and low energy, which keep them from reaching the level of activity required for suicide. The danger period often comes after some treatment, when the depression begins to lift. It should be noted that although serious depression may lead to suicide, depression is neither necessary nor sufficient for suicide. Our discussion of suicide follows the course charted in Figure 10.3.

Suicide is not classified as a mental disorder in DSM-IV-TR, although the suicidal person usually has clear psychiatric symptoms. Many persons who suffer from depression, alcohol dependence, and schizophrenia exhibit suicidal thoughts or behavior. Suicide is the eighth leading cause of death for all Americans. Every year, there have been more deaths due to suicide than to homicide!

Study of Suicide

People who commit suicide—who complete their suicide attempts—can no longer inform us about their motives, frames of mind, and emotional states. We have only indirect information, such as case records and reports by others, to help us understand what led them to their tragic act. The systematic examination of existing information for the purpose of understanding and explaining a person's behavior before his or her death is called a **psychological autopsy** (Jacobs & Klein, 1993; Roberts, 1995). The psychological autopsy attempts to make psychological sense of a suicide or homicide by compiling and analyzing case histories of victims, recollec-

psychological autopsy The systematic examination of existing information for the purpose of understanding and explaining a person's behavior before his or her death.

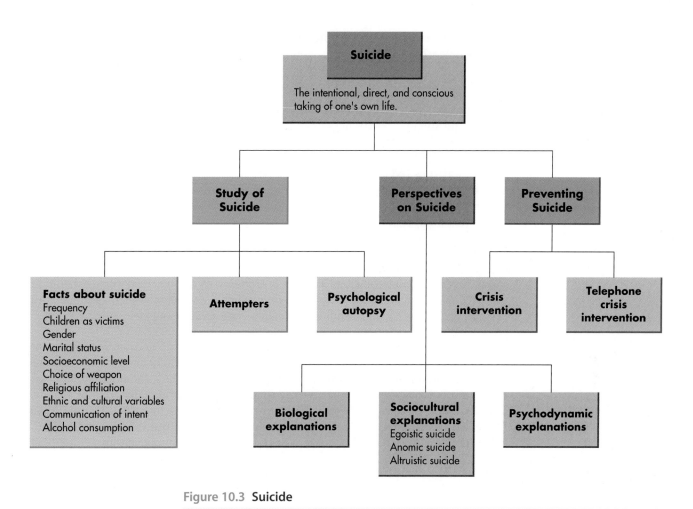

Figure 10.3 **Suicide**

tions of therapists, interviews with relatives and friends, information obtained from crisis phone calls, and messages left in suicide notes. Unfortunately, these sources are not always available or reliable. Only 12 to 34 percent of victims leave suicide notes (Black, 1993; Leenaars, 1992), and many people who commit suicide have never undergone psychotherapy (Fleer & Pasewark, 1982). Explanations from relatives or friends are often distorted because of the emotional impact of the loved one's death.

Another strategy involves studying those who survive a suicide attempt. The problem with this method is that it assumes that people who attempt suicide (attempters) are no different from those who succeed. Studies suggest that these two populations differ on many important dimensions (Diekstra, Kienhorst, & de Wilde, 1995; Furr et al., 2001; Lester, 1994). In general, attempters are more likely to be white females, housewives in their twenties and thirties, who are experiencing marital difficulties, and who attempt suicide with barbiturates. Those who succeed are likely to be white males, in their forties or older, who suffer from ill health or depression, and who shoot or hang themselves (Fremouw, Perczel, & Ellis, 1990).

Despite difficulties in compiling information, the psychological autopsy and the study of attempters continue to be used, not only because they represent the only limited avenues open to us but also because they serve a broad and important need. If psychologists can isolate the events and circumstances that lead to suicide and can identify the characteristics of potential suicide victims, they may be able to prevent other people from performing this irreversible act.

Facts About Suicide

No single explanation is sufficient to account for all types of suicide. In seeking to understand suicide, researchers have focused on events, characteristics, and demographic variables that recur in psychological autopsies and that are highly correlated with the act. Higher suicide rates are associated with divorce (National Center for Health Statistics [NCHS], 1988, 1994; USPHS, 1999) and with certain professions (psychiatry in particular). Alcohol is frequently implicated (Cornelius et al., 1995; Rogers, 1992), and men are more likely to kill themselves using firearms than by other means (Kushner, 1995; NCHS, 1988).

Frequency   Every twenty minutes or so, someone in the United States takes his or her own life. Approximately 31,000 persons kill themselves each year. Some evidence shows that the number of actual suicides is probably 25 to 30 percent higher than that recorded. Many deaths that are officially recorded as accidental—such as single-auto crashes, drownings, or falls from great heights—are actually suicides.

Children and Young People as Victims   Persons under age 25 account for 15 percent of all suicides in 1997. Recent reports suggest that about 12,000 children between the ages of five and fourteen are admitted to psychiatric hospitals for suicidal behavior every year, and it is believed that twenty times that number actually attempt suicide. Suicides among young people ages fifteen to twenty-four have increased by more than 40 percent in the past decade (50 percent for males and 12 percent for females); suicide is now the second leading cause of death for whites in this age group.

Gender   The completed suicide rate for men is about three to four times that for women, although recent findings suggest that many more women are now incurring a higher risk. Further, women are more likely to make attempts, but it appears that men are more successful because they use more lethal means.

Marital Status   The lowest incidence of suicide is found among people who are married and the highest among those who are divorced. The suicide rates for single and widowed or divorced men are about twice those for women of similar marital status.

Socioeconomic Level   Suicide is represented proportionately among all socioeconomic levels. Level of wealth does not seem to affect the suicide rate as much as do changes in that level. In the Great Depression of the 1930s, suicide was higher among the suddenly impoverished than among those who had always been poor.

Choice of Weapon   Over 60 percent of suicides are committed by firearms, and 70 percent of attempts are accounted for by drug overdose. Men most frequently choose firearms as the means of suicide; poisoning and asphyxiation via barbiturates are the preferred means for women. Among children younger than fifteen years, the most common suicide method tends to be jumping from buildings and running into traffic. Older children try hanging or drug overdoses. Younger children attempt suicide impulsively and thus use more readily available means.

Religious Affiliation   Religious affiliation is correlated with suicide rates. Although the U.S. rate is 12.2 per 100,000, in countries in which Catholic Church influences are strong—Latin America, Ireland, Spain, and Italy—the suicide rate is relatively low (less than 10 per 100,000). Islam, too, condemns suicide, and the suicide rates in Arab countries are correspondingly low.

Ethnic and Cultural Variables Suicide rates vary among ethnic minority groups in the United States. American Indian groups have the highest rate, followed by white Americans, Mexican Americans, African Americans, Japanese Americans, and Chinese Americans. American Indian youngsters have frighteningly high rates (26 per 100,000) as compared with white youths (14 per 100,000).

Communication of Intent More than two-thirds of the people who commit suicide communicate their intent to do so within three months of the fatal act. The belief that people who threaten suicide are not serious about it, or will not actually make such an attempt, is ill founded. It is estimated that 20 percent of persons who attempt suicide try again within one year and that 10 percent finally succeed. However, it has been estimated that fewer than 5 percent unequivocally wish to end their lives.

Alcohol Consumption One of the most consistently reported correlates of suicidal behavior is alcohol consumption (Flavin, Franklin, & Francis, 1990; Hirschfield & Davidson, 1989; Schuckit, 1994). As many as 60 percent of suicide attempters drink alcohol before the act, and autopsies of suicide victims suggest that 25 percent are legally intoxicated (Flavin, Franklin, & Frances, 1990; Suokas & Lonnqvist, 1995).

Perspectives on Suicide

Some clinicians believe that everyone, at one time or another, has wished to end his or her life. Fortunately, most of us do not act on such wishes, even during extreme distress. But why do some people do so? Even though suicide is closely linked to hopelessness and depression, and even though many theories of depression apply to suicide as well, the question cannot be answered easily. The French sociologist Emile Durkheim (1897/1951) believed that suicides may occur because one is alienated from society (egoistic suicide), unbalanced in relation to society (anomic suicide; e.g., because of sudden loss of wealth), or committing suicide for a greater good (altruistic suicide; e.g., an act of political protest). In the classical Freudian approach, self-destruction was seen as the result of hostility that is directed inward against the introjected love object (the loved one with whom the person has identified). Later, Freud posited the existence of *thanatos,* a death instinct that is antagonistic to the life instinct. Whatever one's perspective, it is clear that many different factors can be involved in suicide.

Preventing Suicide

In almost every case of suicide, there are hints that the act is about to occur. Suicide is irreversible, of course, so preventing it depends very much on early detection and successful intervention (Bongar, 1992; Cantor, 1991; Maltsberger, 1991). Mental health professionals involved in suicide prevention efforts operate under the assumption that potential victims are ambivalent about the act. That is, the wish to die is strong, but there is also a wish to live. Potential rescuers are trained to exert their efforts to preserve life. Part of their success in the prevention process is the ability to assess a client's suicide **lethality**—the probability that a person will choose to end his or her life.

Working with a potentially suicidal individual is a three-step process that involves (1) knowing what factors are highly correlated with suicide; (2) determining whether there is high, moderate, or low probability that the person will act on the suicide wish; and (3) implementing appropriate actions. People trained in working with suicidal clients often attempt to quantify the "seriousness" of each factor. For example, a person with a *clear suicidal plan* who has *the means* (e.g., a gun) to carry out a suicide threat is considered to be in a more lethal state than a recently *divorced* and *depressed* person.

lethality The probability that a person will choose to end his or her life.

Crisis Intervention Suicide prevention can occur at several levels, and the mental health profession has now begun to move in several coordinated directions to establish prevention efforts. At the clinical level, attempts are being made to educate staff at mental health institutions and even at schools to recognize conditions and symptoms that indicate potential suicides (Kneisel & Richards, 1988). For example, a single man older than fifty years of age who is suffering from a sudden acute onset of depression and expressing hopelessness should be recognized by mental health professionals as being at high risk.

When a psychiatric facility encounters someone who fits a particular risk profile for suicide, crisis intervention strategies will most likely be used to abort or ameliorate the processes that could lead to a suicide attempt. Crisis intervention is aimed at providing intensive short-term help to a patient in resolving an immediate life crisis. Unlike traditional psychotherapy, in which sessions are spaced out and treatment is provided on a more leisurely long-term basis, crisis intervention recognizes the immediacy of the patient's state of mind. The patient may be immediately hospitalized, given medical treatment, and seen by a psychiatric team for two to four hours every day until the person is stabilized and the immediate crisis has passed. In these sessions, the team is very active not only in working with the patient but also in taking charge of the person's personal, social, and professional life outside of the psychiatric facility. Many suicide intervention strategies have been developed through clinical work rather than research because the nature of suicide demands immediate action. Waiting for empirical studies is not a luxury the clinician can afford.

Telephone Crisis Intervention Suicide prevention centers typically operate twenty-four hours a day, seven days a week. Because most suicide contacts are by phone, a well-publicized telephone number is made available throughout the community for calls at any time of the day or night. Furthermore, many centers provide inpatient or outpatient crisis treatment. Those that lack such resources develop cooperative programs with other community mental health facilities. Most telephone hot lines are staffed by paraprofessionals. All workers have been exposed to crisis situations under supervision and have been trained in crisis intervention techniques such as the following:

1. *Maintain contact and establish a relationship.* The skilled worker who establishes a good relationship with the suicidal caller not only increases the caller's chances of working out an alternative solution but also can exert more influence. Thus it is important for the worker to show interest, concern, and self-assurance.

2. *Obtain necessary information.* The worker elicits demographic data and the caller's name and address. This information is very valuable in case an urgent need arises to locate the caller.

3. *Evaluate suicidal potential.* The staff person taking the call must quickly determine the seriousness of the caller's self-destructive intent. Most centers use lethality rating scales to help the worker determine suicide potential. These usually contain questions on age, gender, onset of symptoms, situational plight, prior suicidal behavior, and the communication abilities of the caller. Staffers also elicit other demographic and specific information that might provide clues to lethality.

4. *Clarify the nature of the stress and focal problem.* The worker must help callers to clarify the exact nature of their stress, to recognize that they may be under so much duress that their thinking may be confused and impaired, and to realize that there are other solutions besides suicide. Callers are often disoriented, so the worker must be specific to help bring them back to reality.

5. *Assess strengths and resources.* In working out a therapeutic plan, the worker can often mobilize a caller's strengths or available resources. In their agitation,

suicidal people tend to forget their own strengths. Their feelings of helplessness are so overwhelming that helping them recognize what they can do about a situation is important. The worker explores the caller's personal resources (family, friends, coworkers), professional resources (doctors, clergy, therapists, lawyers), and community resources (clinics, hospitals, social agencies).

6. *Recommend and initiate an action plan.* Besides being supportive, the worker is highly directive in recommending a course of action. Whether the recommendation entails immediately seeing the person, calling the person's family, or referring the person to a social agency the next day, the worker presents a plan of action and outlines it step by step.

This list implies a rigid sequence, but in fact both the approach and the order of the steps are adjusted to fit the needs of the individual caller.

Clearly, suicide and suicide prevention involve a number of important social and legal issues, as well as the personal value systems of clients and their families, mental health professionals, and those who devise and enforce our laws. And just as clearly, we need to know much more about the causes of suicide and the detection of people who are at high risk for suicide, as well as the most effective means of intervention. Life is precious, and we need to do everything possible, within reason, to protect it.

▶ CHECKPOINT REVIEW

lethality *(p. 269)*
psychological autopsy *(p. 266)*
suicide *(p. 265)*

What do we know about suicide?

■ Suicide is both a tragic and a puzzling act. In the past, it has often been kept hidden, and relatives and friends of the victim did not speak of it. Mental health professionals now realize that understanding the causes of suicide is extremely important.

Why do people decide to end their lives?

■ Many different factors are involved in suicide, and various theories have tried to explain suicide. Although depression is implicated in many suicides, only a small percentage of depressed persons commit suicide, and suicides can occur in the absence of depression.

How can we intervene or prevent suicides?

■ Perhaps the best way to prevent suicide is to recognize its signs and intervene before it occurs. People are more likely to commit suicide if they are older, male, have a history of attempts, describe in detail how the act will be accomplished, and give verbal hints that they are planning self-destruction.

■ Crisis intervention techniques, the services of suicide prevention centers, and telephone hot lines have been used successfully to treat clients who contemplate suicide. Intensive short-term therapy is used to stabilize the immediate crisis.

FOCUS QUESTIONS

- How have our views of schizophrenia changed over time?
- What kinds of symptoms are found in this disorder?
- How do the specific types of schizophrenia differ from one another?
- Is there much chance of recovery from schizophrenia?
- What causes schizophrenia?
- Is schizophrenia an inherited condition?
- What supports the view that schizophrenia is a result of brain abnormalities?
- Can psychological factors "cause" schizophrenia?
- What is the best etiological model for schizophrenia?
- What kinds of treatments are currently available, and are they effective?

11 Schizophrenia: Diagnosis and Etiology

Schizophrenia is a severely disabling disorder that has a profound impact both on the victim and on family members and friends. Jackie Powell (1998) presents a personal perspective of the impact on her childhood and adulthood by her mother's illness. In the following account, she discusses her reaction to her mother's return from hospitalization:

> I tried extremely hard not to be afraid of her, but I did not know this person who used to be my mother: The mother who made me laugh when we watched television together, the mother who listened to music and danced with my friends and me, the mother who combed my hair for school each day, and the mother who made sure I was safe at night did not return home.... She was able to verbalize her love for me, but her affect did not demonstrate affection: Something was missing.... Although my mother tried desperately to recuperate from each psychotic episode ... she became increasingly reclusive and paranoid.... As for my relationship as an adult with my mother, I would be lying to say that I do not think of her condition daily. I also grieve over the loss of my mother as I knew her before the first episode. For brief moments, my mother gets better and she is more aware of who I am as my own being. Sadly, I have to acknowledge the brevity of this connectiveness and merely treasure the moment. (Powell, 1998, pp. 176–177)

For the relatives of individuals with schizophrenia, the psychotic symptoms shown by their loved ones can be confusing, frightening, and heart wrenching. At times, reality becomes so distorted that affected people cannot trust their perceptions and thoughts.

Schizophrenia

Schizophrenia is a group of disorders characterized by severely impaired cognitive processes, personality disintegration, affective disturbances, and social withdrawal. People thus affected may lose contact with reality, may see or hear things that are not actually occurring, or may develop false beliefs about themselves or others. The lifetime prevalence rate of schizophrenia in the United States is about 1 percent, and it is found in males and females equally (NIMH, 2001). Although DSM-IV-TR presents schizophrenia as a distinct disorder, evidence suggests that it is a heterogeneous clinical syndrome with different etiologies and outcomes.

The age of onset for schizophrenia occurs earlier in males than in females. The gender ratio shifts by the mid-forties, when the percentage of women receiving this diagnosis is greater than that of men. This trend is especially pronounced in the mid-sixties and later (Castle & Murray, 1993; Howard et al., 2000). The reason for the gender differences in age of onset appears to be the presence of estrogen, which diminishes after menopause (Hafner et al., 1998; Hoff et al., 2001). The lifetime prevalence rate for schizophrenia is higher among African Americans (2.1 percent) and lower among Hispanic Americans (0.8 percent).

schizophrenia A group of disorders characterized by severely impaired cognitive processes, personality disintegration, affective disturbances, and social withdrawal.

273

Eugen Bleuler (1857–1939)
Bleuler was a Swiss psychiatrist who believed that the age of onset and the outcomes for schizophrenia were variable. He was the first to use the term *schizophrenia*.

History of the Diagnostic Category and DSM-IV-TR

In 1896 Emil Kraepelin recognized that symptoms such as hallucinations, delusions, and intellectual deterioration were characteristic of a particular disorder whose onset began at an early age. He called this disorder *dementia praecox* (insanity at an early age). Because he believed that the disorder involved some form of organic deterioration, its outcome was considered to be poor. People who recovered from dementia praecox were thought to have been misdiagnosed.

A Swiss psychiatrist, Eugen Bleuler (1911/1950), disagreed with Kraepelin's theory for several reasons. He did not believe that all or even most cases of schizophrenia developed at an early age. He argued that the outcome of schizophrenia did not always involve progressive deterioration and believed that dementia praecox represented a group of disorders that have different causes. Bleuler also theorized that environmental factors interacting with a genetic predisposition produced the disorder.

Bleuler's definition of schizophrenia was broader than Kraepelin's in that age of onset and the course of the disorder were more variable. DSM-I and DSM-II employed the broader definition of schizophrenia, which allowed more disorders to be incorporated in this category. However, several international studies (Cooper et al., 1972; World Health Organization, 1973) revealed that other countries used a stricter definition for schizophrenia. When patients diagnosed with schizophrenia in the United States were rediagnosed according to the international standards, approximately 50 percent were placed into other categories, such as mood disorders, personality disorders, or other psychotic disorders.

This discrepancy with other diagnostic systems forced researchers to reexamine the criteria used to define schizophrenia, and this reexamination resulted in changes in DSM-III and DSM-III-R. For example, in DSM-II, brief psychotic episodes were considered to represent acute forms of schizophrenia. With DSM-III-R, people who have "schizophrenic" episodes that last fewer than six months are now diagnosed as having either **brief psychotic disorder** (duration of at least one day but less than one month) or **schizophreniform disorder** (duration of at least one month but less than six months). If the symptoms last more than six months, the diagnosis of schizophrenia is often given. DSM-IV-TR (American Psychiatric Association, 2000a) continues to use the more restrictive duration requirement (See Table 11.1 for DSM-IV-TR criteria for schizophrenia).

Table 11.1   DSM-IV-TR Criteria for Schizophrenia

A. At least two of the following symptoms lasting for at least one month in the active phase (exception: only one symptom if it involves bizarre delusions or if hallucinations involve a running commentary on the person or two or more voices talking with each other).

  1. Delusions

  2. Hallucinations

  3. Disorganized speech (incoherence or frequent derailment)

  4. Grossly disorganized or catatonic behavior

  5. Negative symptoms (flat affect, avolition, alogia, or anhedonia)

B. During the course of the disturbance, functioning in one or more areas such as work, social relations, and self-care has deteriorated markedly from premorbid levels (in the case of a child or adolescent, failure to reach expected level of social or academic development).

C. Signs of the disorder must be present for at least six months.

D. Schizoaffective and mood disorders with psychotic features must be ruled out.

E. The disturbance is not substance-induced or caused by organic factors.

The Symptoms of Schizophrenia

Symptoms of schizophrenia include delusions, hallucinations, thought disorder (shifting and unrelated ideas that produce incoherent communication), and bizarre behavior. There appear to be three uncorrelated dimensions in schizophrenia (Andreasen et al., 1995; Arndt et al., 1995). The first two—*psychoticism*, represented by hallucinations and delusions, and *disorganization*, which includes disorganized speech and behavior, inappropriate affect, motoric disturbances, and disordered thought—are often described as **positive symptoms**. They appear to reflect an excess or dis-

"A Beautiful Mind" John Nash, a Princeton University professor whose struggles with schizophrenia were portrayed in a film, addresses a news conference on October 11, 1994, after winning the Nobel Prize for economics. He struggled with his psychotic symptoms and learned to ignore hallucinations. Even today, he occasionally hears voices.

tortion of normal functions. These symptoms are present during the active phase of the disorder and tend to dissipate with treatment. **Negative symptoms,** the third dimension, are associated with inferior premorbid (before the onset of illness) social functioning and carry a poorer prognosis. One such symptom is **flat affect**—little or no emotion in situations in which strong reactions are expected. Others include *alogia* (a lack of meaningful speech) and *avolition* (an inability to take goal oriented action). Positive symptoms may indicate a reversible condition, whereas negative symptoms may represent irreversible neuronal loss in a structurally abnormal brain (Roth et al., 2004).

Individuals with schizophrenia often become quite distressed and confused over their symptoms. One woman had terrifying hallucinations and delusions, which included seeing her nephew's head sitting on top of her VCR laughing at her and believing that flying saucers were beaming obscene words into her head and that she was being raped by the devil (Gerhardt, 1998). These terrors are privately experienced, and some unusual behaviors—such as shaving or cutting off one's hair, wearing unnecessary clothing, or drastically changing makeup—may represent an attempt to maintain identity or to deal with anxieties before a psychotic break (Campo et al., 1998).

Others may deal with the turmoil by withdrawing into themselves to obtain some peace. "I wait for time to go by. . . . I want calmness, to be with myself, then to evolve internally" (Corin, 1998, p. 139). Most display a feeling of personal failure and sense of inadequacy. "A normal woman will not go out with a guy who has been in a psychiatric hospital. . . . Will I end up alone, without a wife, without children, alone in the street?" (p. 142). The despair felt by an individual with schizophrenia takes a severe toll; up to 11 percent commit suicide (Wiersma et al., 1998).

Positive Symptoms

Positive symptoms represent distortions or excesses of normal functioning; with treatment, they diminish in intensity. These symptoms include delusions, hallucinations, disorganized communication and thought disturbances, and motor disturbances.

Delusions The disordered thinking of schizophrenics may be exhibited in **delusions,** which are false personal beliefs that are firmly and consistently held despite disconfirming evidence or logic. Delusions may begin with a sense of heightened awareness and anxiety, followed by the person's attempt to "make sense" of his or her fears, and finally by an initial sense of relief when the "new awareness" crystallizes (Kapur, 2003). However, this "awareness" can lead to frightening interpretations of the external world. Individuals with schizophrenia may become terrified that their inner world has been completely exposed and that others can see into their minds and even "hear" them engaging in activities such as reading a paper. They may believe that the entire world is audience to their most private thoughts and behaviors (Leferink, 1998). Delusions may vary from those that are plausible, such as being followed or spied on, to those that are bizarre (internal organs have been removed or thoughts are being placed in their minds).

Studies have suggested that delusions may differ in their strength and their effects on the person's life. An example of a delusion follows:

brief psychotic disorder Psychotic disorder that lasts no longer than one month.

schizophreniform disorder Psychotic disorder that lasts more than one month but less than six months.

positive symptoms Symptoms that are present during the active phase of schizophrenia and that tend to disappear with treatment; they may include hallucinations and delusions, as well as disorganized speech and behavior, inappropriate affect, and formal thought disorders.

negative symptoms In schizophrenia, symptoms that are associated with inferior premorbid social functioning and carry a poorer prognosis than positive symptoms; they include flat affect, poverty of speech, anhedonia, apathy, and avolition.

flat affect Little or no emotion in situations in which strong reactions are expected.

delusion A false belief that is firmly and consistently held despite disconfirming evidence or logic.

> Ms. A., an 83-year-old widow who had lived alone for fifteen years, complained that the occupant of an upstairs flat was excessively noisy and that he moved furniture around late at night to disturb her. Over a period of six months, she developed delusional persecutory ideas about this man. He wanted to frighten her from her home and had started to transmit "violet rays" through the ceiling to harm her and her ten-year-old female mongrel dog.... For protection, she placed her mattress under the kitchen table and slept there at night. She constructed what she called an "air raid shelter" for her dog from a small table and a pile of suitcases and insisted that the dog sleep in it. When I visited Ms. A. at her home, it was apparent that the dog's behavior had become so conditioned by that of its owner that upon hearing any sound from the flat upstairs, such as a door closing, it would immediately go to the kitchen and enter the shelter. (Howard, 1992, p. 414)

Individuals with schizophrenia may reach conclusions based on little information, a characteristic that may be related to the development of unusual beliefs. Delusional individuals appear to make errors during the stages of hypothesis formation and evaluation. They develop unlikely hypotheses and then overestimate the probability that the hypotheses are true, especially with information that is considered to be emotionally salient or threatening (McGuire et al., 2001).

People with schizophrenia may be trained to challenge their delusions. One fifty-one-year-old patient believed that she was the daughter of Princess Anne and under the age of twenty. Her therapist asked her to view her belief as only one possible interpretation of the facts. They discussed evidence for her belief, and the therapist presented the inconsistencies and irrationality involved, as well as alternative perspectives. After this procedure, the patient reported a large drop in the conviction of her beliefs, stating "I look 50 and I tire more quickly than I used to; I must be 50" (Lowe & Chadwick, 1990, p. 471). She agreed that she was probably older than Princess Anne and therefore could not be her daughter. Belief modification appears to be a helpful procedure for some individuals with schizophrenia, though there is some controversy surrounding this approach, as the Mental Health and Society feature, "Should We Challenge Delusions and Hallucinations?" illustrates.

Perceptual Distortion Those with schizophrenia often report **hallucinations,** which are sensory perceptions that are not directly attributable to environmental stimuli. They may claim to see people or objects, to hear voices, or to smell peculiar odors that are not really present.

Hallucinations may involve a single sensory modality or a combination of modalities: hearing (*auditory* hallucinations), seeing (*visual* hallucinations), smelling (*olfactory* hallucinations), feeling (*tactile* hallucinations), and tasting (*gustatory* hallucinations). Auditory hallucinations are the most common (Garrett & Silva, 2003) and can range from derogatory ("We will kill you if you walk the streets") to nonderogatory or encouraging ("That's right, B!" [Payne, 1992, p. 727]). The patients' interpretations of the auditory hallucinations determined the degree of distress felt (Morrison & Baker, 2000).

Delusions of Grandeur   Assuming the identity of another, powerful person can be a sign that an individual suffering from schizophrenia is experiencing delusions of grandeur.

hallucinations Sensory perceptions that are not directly attributable to environmental stimuli.

MenTaL HeaLTh and socieTy

Should We Challenge Delusions and Hallucinations?

The doctor asked of a patient who insisted that he was dead:"Look. Dead men don't bleed, right?"When the man agreed, the doctor pricked the man's finger and showed him the blood. The patient said, "What do you know, dead men do bleed after all." (Walkup, 1995, p. 323)

Clinicians have often been unsure about whether to challenge psychotic symptoms. Some believe that the delusions and hallucinations serve an adaptive function and that any attempt to change them would be useless or even dangerous. The previous example is supposed to illustrate the futility of using logic in treating people with schizophrenia. However, Walkup and other clinicians (Beck & Rector, 2000; Chadwick et al., 2000; Chadwick & Birchwood, 1994; Kuipers et al., 1997) have found that some clients respond well to challenges to their hallucinations and delusions.

The approach has two phases. In the first, hypothetical contradictions are used to assess how open the patients are to conflicting information. During this phase, patients are introduced to information that might contradict their beliefs, and it is here that their delusions are often weakened.

■ A woman, H.J., with auditory hallucinations was asked if her belief in the "voices" would change if it could be determined that they were coming from her. She agreed. She was given a set of industrial earmuffs, which she wore. She still reported hearing voices.

■ A woman believed that God was commanding her to kill. She was asked if her belief would be lessened if a priest informed her that God would not ask anyone to kill another person.

In the second phase the therapist issues a verbal challenge, asking clients to give evidence for their beliefs and to develop alternative interpretations. For example, one client claimed that voices were accurate in telling her when her spouse would return. The therapist asked how she might determine her husband's return if the voices were unable to foretell the future. Another patient who claimed he would be killed if he did not comply with auditory commands was told that he could resist the voices and would not die.

Alternative explanations are proposed for the hallucinations, such as the possibility that the voices are "self-talk" or thoughts. After cognitive behavioral treatment, most patients report a decrease in the strength of their beliefs in their psychotic symptoms. In H.J.'s case (presented earlier), her degree of certainty about her auditory hallucinations dropped from 100 percent to 20 percent. Although she still heard voices telling her she would die, she learned to disregard them and attributed them as "coming from her head."

Should we challenge psychotic symptoms? We are beginning to find that the development of active coping responses to symptoms in individuals with schizophrenia is better than "getting along with them" (Bak et al., 2003).

Disorganized Thought and Speech

Interviewer: ALL POLICE WORLD DISAPPEAR. ... WHAT HAPPENS?

Patient: WHEN WORLD c.e.l.l. c.e.l.l. GROW SPREAD SPREAD LATER YOU KNOW d.o.n.o.s.a.u.r. WALK SIDEWAYS MONKEY RISE UP SLOW (Thacker, 1994, p. 821).

Disordered thinking is a primary characteristic of schizophrenia, as illustrated in the preceding example. Interestingly, the response was obtained from a deaf individual with schizophrenia. Disturbances in thought and communication were demonstrated during the interview through the use of sign language. During communication, the individual may jump from one topic to another, speak in an unintelligible manner, or reply tangentially to questions. The **loosening of associations,** or *cognitive slippage,* is the continual shifting from topic to topic without any apparent logical or meaningful connection between thoughts. It may be shown by incoherent speech and bizarre and idiosyncratic responses, as indicated in the following example (Thomas, 1995).

Interviewer: "You just must be an emotional person, that's all."

Patient (1): "Well, not very much I mean, what if I were dead. It's a funeral age. Well I um. Now I had my toenails operated on. They got infected and I wasn't able to do it. But they wouldn't let me at my tools." (p. 289)

loosening of associations Continual shifting from topic to topic without any apparent logical or meaningful connection between thoughts.

Painting the Symptoms of Schizophrenia The inner turmoil and private fantasies of schizophrenics are often revealed in their artwork. The painting you see here was created in the 1930s by a psychiatric patient in a European hospital. It is part of the Prinzhorn collection. What do you think the painting represents?

The beginning phrase in the first sentence appears appropriate to the interviewer's comment. However, the reference to death is not. Slippage appears in the comments referring to a funeral age, having toenails operated on, and getting tools. None of these thoughts are related to the interviewer's observation. People with schizophrenia may also respond to words or phrases in a very concrete manner and demonstrate difficulty with abstractions. A saying such as "a rolling stone gathers no moss" might be interpreted as "moss can't grow on a rock that is rolling." Part of their communication problem appears to be an inability to inhibit contextually irrelevant information (Titone, Levy, & Holzman, 2000).

Disorganized Motoric Disturbances The symptoms of schizophrenia that involve motor functions can be quite bizarre. The person may show extreme activity levels (either unusually high or unusually low), peculiar body movements or postures, strange gestures and grimaces, or a combination of these. Like hallucinations, a patient's motoric behaviors may be related to his or her delusions. Some individuals with this disorder may display extremely high levels of motor activity, moving about quickly, swinging their arms wildly, talking rapidly and unendingly, or pacing constantly. At the other extreme, others hardly move at all, staring out into space (or perhaps into themselves) for long periods of time. The inactive patients also tend to show little interest in others, to respond only minimally, and to have few friends. During periods of withdrawal, they are frequently preoccupied with personal fantasies and daydreams.

The assumption and maintenance of an unusual (and often awkward) body position is characteristic of the *catatonic* type of schizophrenia (to be discussed shortly). A catatonic patient may stand for hours at a time, perhaps with one arm stretched out to the side, or may lie on the floor or sit awkwardly on a chair, staring, aware of what is going on around him or her, but not responding or moving. If a hospital attendant tries to change the patient's position, the patient may either resist stubbornly or may simply assume and maintain the new position.

Negative Symptoms

Negative symptoms have been associated with a poor prognosis and may be the result of structural abnormalities in the brain. Clinicians must be careful to distinguish between *primary symptoms* (symptoms that arise from the disease itself) and *secondary symptoms* (symptoms that may develop as a response to medication and institutionalization). It is the former that researchers are primarily interested in. You may recall from our earlier discussion that the negative symptoms include *avolition* (an inability to take action or become goal-oriented), *alogia* (a lack of meaningful speech), and *flat affect* (little or no emotion in situations in which strong reactions are expected; a delusional patient, for instance, might explain in detail how parts of his or her body are rotting away but show absolutely no concern or worry through voice tone or facial expression). However, flat affect may not be a symptom of the disorder but rather the result of institutionalization, depression, or antipsychotic medications (Lieberman, 1995). If negative symptoms are a result of medication, institutionalization, or a mood disorder, they must not be used in making the diagnosis of schizophrenia.

Associated Features and Mental Disorders

Several other characteristics are relatively common in individuals with schizophrenia. *Anhedonia* (an inability to feel pleasure) is often present (Herbener & Harrow, 2002). Social anhedonia, or the decreased ability to derive pleasure from interactions with others, is also observed in depression but appears to be an enduring characteristic of individuals with schizophrenia (Blanchard, Horan, & Brown, 2001). Another common associated symptom of schizophrenia is lack of insight. One woman with a Ph.D. could not understand the bizarre nature of her hallucinations and delusions, such as

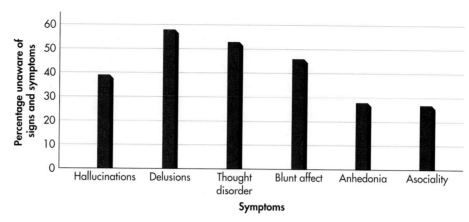

Figure 11.1 Lack of Awareness of Psychotic Symptoms in Patients with Schizophrenia
Most individuals with schizophrenia are unaware or only moderately aware that they
have symptoms of the disorder. The symptoms they were most unaware of having were
delusions, thought disorder, and blunt or flat affect. *Source:* Amador et al. (1994).

being controlled by the television station, having the mental power to make dogs bark,
and receiving brain waves from alien creatures (Payne, 1992). In one study (Amador et
al., 1994), more than 57 percent of the participants were either "unaware" or only
"moderately aware" of their symptoms (see Figure 11.1).

Cultural Issues

Culture may affect how disorders are responded to and how symptoms are manifested.
In Japan schizophrenia is highly stigmatized, partly because the condition is called
seishin-bunretsu-byou, which roughly translates as a split in mind or spirit. The term
conjures up an irreversible condition. Because of this connotation, the Japanese Society
of Psychiatry and Neurology is considering using a less negative term (Sugiura et al.,
2001). Symptom patterns may also differ. In Western countries, individuals with schizophrenia tend to show more depressive symptoms and report thought broadcasting
and insertion, whereas those in non-Western countries tend to report more visual and
directed auditory hallucinations (Jilek, 2001).

Ethnic group differences have also been found. Among those hospitalized for schizophrenia, Irish Americans tended to show less hostility and acting out but more fixed
delusions than did Italian Americans. Similarly, Japanese patients hospitalized for schizophrenia are often described as rigid, compulsive, withdrawn, and passive—symptoms that
reflect the Japanese cultural values of conformity within the community and reserve
within the family (Sue & Morishima, 1982). In a study of 273 patients with schizophrenia
admitted to hospitals and mental health centers in Missouri over a three-and-one-half-year
period, researchers found that African American patients exhibited more severe symptoms
than white patients: angry outbursts, impulsiveness, and strongly antisocial behavior. They
also showed greater disorientation and confusion and more severe hallucinatory behaviors
compared with white patients (Abebimpe et al., 1982). These research findings may be
interpreted as real differences in symptomology. However, they could also be produced by
diagnostic errors. As DSM-IV-TR notes, "There is some evidence that clinicians may have
a tendency to overdiagnose Schizophrenia in some ethnic groups. Studies conducted in the
United Kingdom and the United States suggest that Schizophrenia may be diagnosed more
often in individuals who are African American and Asian American than in other racial
groups" (American Psychiatric Association, 2000a, p. 307). It is not clear whether these
differences in rates are actual or if they represent clinician bias.

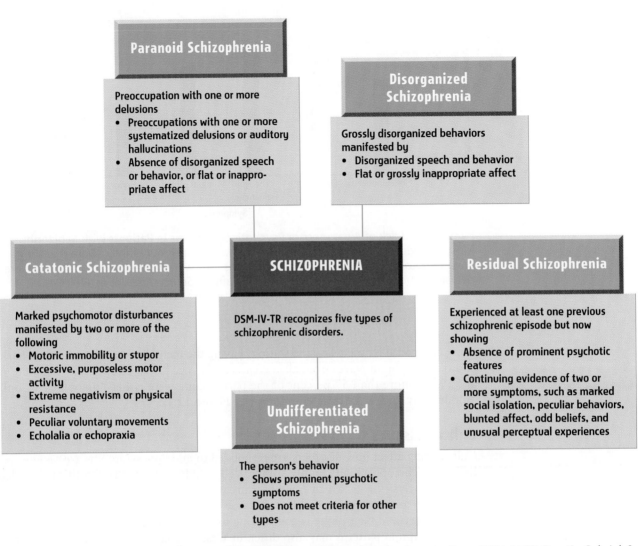

Paranoid Schizophrenia

Preoccupation with one or more delusions
• Preoccupations with one or more systematized delusions or auditory hallucinations
• Absence of disorganized speech or behavior, or flat or inappropriate affect

Disorganized Schizophrenia

Grossly disorganized behaviors manifested by
• Disorganized speech and behavior
• Flat or grossly inappropriate affect

Catatonic Schizophrenia

Marked psychomotor disturbances manifested by two or more of the following
• Motoric immobility or stupor
• Excessive, purposeless motor activity
• Extreme negativism or physical resistance
• Peculiar voluntary movements
• Echolalia or echopraxia

SCHIZOPHRENIA

DSM-IV-TR recognizes five types of schizophrenic disorders.

Residual Schizophrenia

Experienced at least one previous schizophrenic episode but now showing
• Absence of prominent psychotic features
• Continuing evidence of two or more symptoms, such as marked social isolation, peculiar behaviors, blunted affect, odd beliefs, and unusual perceptual experiences

Undifferentiated Schizophrenia

The person's behavior
• Shows prominent psychotic symptoms
• Does not meet criteria for other types

Figure 11.2 **Disorders Chart: Schizophrenia** *Sources:* From DSM-IV-TR; Beratis, Gabriel, & Hoidas (1994); Pfuhlmann & Stober (1997).

Types of Schizophrenia

Five types of schizophrenic disorders are traditionally recognized: paranoid, disorganized, catatonic, undifferentiated, and residual (see Figure 11.2).

Paranoid Schizophrenia

The most common form of schizophrenia is the paranoid type. **Paranoid schizophrenia** is characterized by one or more systematized delusions or auditory hallucinations and by the absence of such symptoms as disorganized speech and behavior or flat affect. Several studies have found that individuals with paranoid delusions externalize their problems (Kinderman & Bentall, 1996, 1997). Delusions of persecution are the most common symptom. The deluded individuals believe that others are plotting against them, are talking about them, or are out to harm them in some way. Interestingly, as compared with nonparanoid schizophrenic patients and control participants, paranoid

paranoid schizophrenia A schizophrenic disorder characterized by one or more systematized delusions or auditory hallucinations and the absence of such symptoms as disorganized speech and behavior or flat affect.

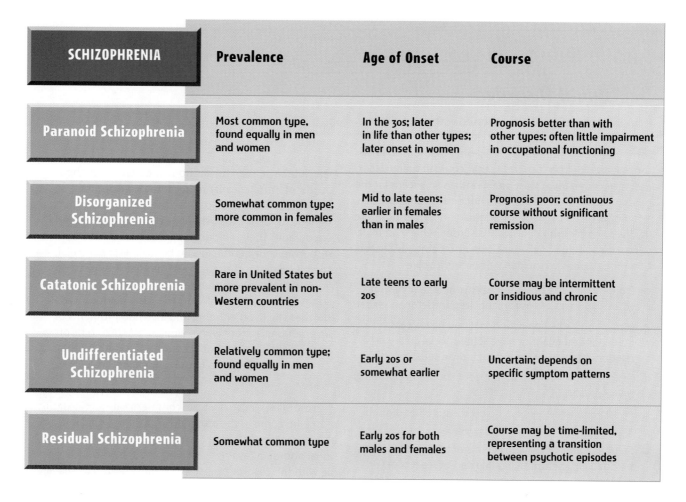

SCHIZOPHRENIA	Prevalence	Age of Onset	Course
Paranoid Schizophrenia	Most common type, found equally in men and women	In the 30s; later in life than other types; later onset in women	Prognosis better than with other types; often little impairment in occupational functioning
Disorganized Schizophrenia	Somewhat common type; more common in females	Mid to late teens; earlier in females than in males	Prognosis poor; continuous course without significant remission
Catatonic Schizophrenia	Rare in United States but more prevalent in non-Western countries	Late teens to early 20s	Course may be intermittent or insidious and chronic
Undifferentiated Schizophrenia	Relatively common type; found equally in men and women	Early 20s or somewhat earlier	Uncertain; depends on specific symptom patterns
Residual Schizophrenia	Somewhat common type	Early 20s for both males and females	Course may be time-limited, representing a transition between psychotic episodes

Figure 11.2 Disorders Chart: Schizophrenia (continued)

schizophrenic patients were more accurate in recognizing genuine nonverbal expressions of emotions (Davis & Gibson, 2000).

> Mr. A., a thirty-seven-year-old Mexican American Vietnam veteran previously treated at several Veterans Administration hospitals with the diagnosis of paranoid schizophrenia, came to the emergency room stating, "My life is in danger."...Mr. A. told a semicoherent story of international spy intrigue that was built around the release of soldiers still missing in action or held as prisoners of war in Vietnam. He believed he was hunted by Vietnamese agents....Mr. A. reported hearing the voices of the men from his company who died....He had become so disturbed by these beliefs and auditory hallucinations that he made suicidal efforts to escape the torment. (Glassman, Magulac, & Darko, 1987, pp. 658–659)

Individuals with paranoid schizophrenia may be prone to anger, as many feel persecuted. The prognosis for the paranoid type tends to be more positive than for other types of schizophrenia (Hill et al., 2001). A similar disorder, **delusional disorder,** is characterized by persistent, nonbizarre delusions that are not accompanied by other unusual or odd behaviors. It is not a form of schizophrenia, although it is often confused with paranoid schizophrenia. Delusional disorder is described in the Mental Health and Society feature, "Delusional Disorder."

delusional disorder A disorder characterized by persistent, nonbizarre delusions that are not accompanied by other unusual or odd behavior.

MenTaL HeaLTh and socieTy

Delusional Disorder

Delusional disorder is often confused with schizophrenia. In both, thought processes are disturbed. Nevertheless, some differences do exist. Delusional disorder involves "nonbizarre" beliefs (situations that could actually occur) that have lasted for at least one month. Also, except for the delusion, the person's behavior is not odd. In schizophrenia, additional disturbances in thoughts and perceptions are involved. People with delusional disorder behave normally when their delusional ideas are not being discussed. Common themes in delusional disorders involve

- *Erotomania*—the belief that someone is in love with you; usually the love is romanticized rather than sexual.

- *Grandiosity*—the conviction that you have great, unrecognized talent or have some special ability or relationship with an important individual.

- *Jealousy*—the conviction that your spouse or partner is being unfaithful.

- *Persecution*—the belief in being conspired or plotted against.

- *Somatic complaints*—convictions of having body odor, being malformed, or being infested by insects or parasites.

The following case illustrates some features of delusional disorders:

> Mr. A, a fifty-five-year-old single man, was remanded to the Regional Psychiatric Centre.... For over twenty-
> one years he had pursued a famous female entertainer.... He met the entertainer for the first time twenty-one years ago when she invited him to join her fan club. Since then he has bombarded her with thousands of phone calls, many letters and gifts.... Notwithstanding her public denials, he has maintained the belief that she loves him, approves and encourages their relationship.... Several things were responsible for 'reinforcing' his behaviour. In particular, she had never returned any of his letters or gifts. He implied that she communicated with him through her songs but would not elaborate.... His identical twin brother still lived at home and also had problems of an emotional nature with a woman. She had to resort to calling the police, but according to Mr. A's mother, "at least he knew when to quit." (Menzies et al., 1995, p. 530)

Erotomania occurs more commonly in females, but most who come to the attention of the law are males. Lack of feedback may play a role in the development of delusional disorder (Zayas & Grossberg, 1998). In a study of people with this disorder, most were characterized as socially isolated, and nearly half had a physical impairment such as deafness or visual problems (Holden, 1987). A decreased ability to obtain corrective feedback, combined with a pre-existing personality type that tends toward suspiciousness, may increase the susceptibility to developing delusional beliefs.

Disorganized Schizophrenia

Disorganized schizophrenia (formerly called *hebephrenic schizophrenia*) is characterized by grossly disorganized behaviors manifested in disorganized speech and behavior and flat or grossly inappropriate affect. Behaviors may begin at an early age. People with this disorder act in an absurd, incoherent, or very odd manner that conforms to the stereotype of "crazy" behavior. Their emotional responses to real-life situations are typically flat, but a silly smile and childish giggle may appear at inappropriate times. The hallucinations and delusions of patients with disorganized schizophrenia tend to shift from theme to theme rather than remain centered on a single idea, such as persecution or sin. Because of the severity of the disorder, many people affected with disorganized schizophrenia are unable to care for themselves and are institutionalized. People with this disorder usually exhibit extremely bizarre and seemingly childish behaviors, such as masturbating in public or fantasizing aloud.

disorganized schizophrenia A schizophrenic disorder characterized by grossly disorganized behaviors manifested by disorganized speech and behavior and flat or grossly inappropriate affect.

Characteristics of Disorganized Schizophrenia Grossly disorganized behavior in which an individual dresses or behaves in an unusual manner is displayed in some people with schizophrenia. Here, a hospitalized patient showers in her clothes. Would the woman understand that this behavior is odd?

Characteristics of Catatonic Schizophrenia Individuals with catatonic schizophrenia experience a variety of disturbances in motor activity. Those who are excited exhibit great agitation and hyperactivity; those who are withdrawn (like the woman shown in this picture) may exhibit extreme unresponsiveness or adopt strange postures.

Catatonic Schizophrenia

Marked disturbance in motor activity—either extreme excitement or motoric immobility—is the prime characteristic of **catatonic schizophrenia**. Diagnostic criteria include two or more of the following symptoms: motoric immobility or stupor; excessive, purposeless motor activity; extreme negativism (resisting direction) or physical resistance; peculiar voluntary posturing or movements; or echolalia (repetition of other people's speech) or echopraxia (repetition of other people's movements; American Psychiatric Association, 2000a). This disorder is quite rare but somewhat more prevalent in non-Western countries.

People with *excited catatonia* are agitated and hyperactive. They may talk and shout constantly, while moving or running until they drop from exhaustion. They sleep little and are continually "on the go." Their behavior can become dangerous, however, and violent acts are not uncommon. People in *withdrawn catatonia* are extremely unresponsive. They show prolonged periods of stupor and mutism, despite their awareness of all that is going on around them. Some may adopt and maintain strange postures and refuse to move or change position. Others exhibit a *waxy flexibility*, allowing themselves to be "arranged" in almost any position and then remaining in that position for

catatonic schizophrenia Rare schizophrenic disorder characterized by marked disturbance in motor activity—either extreme excitement or motoric immobility; symptoms may include motoric immobility or stupor; excessive purposeless motor activity; extreme negativism or physical resistance; peculiar voluntary movements; or echolalia or echopraxia.

long periods of time. During periods of extreme withdrawal, people with catatonic schizophrenia may not eat or control their bladder or bowel functions. Alternating periods of excited motor activity and withdrawal may occur in this disorder.

Undifferentiated and Residual Schizophrenia

Undifferentiated schizophrenia is diagnosed when the person's behavior shows prominent psychotic symptoms that do not meet the criteria for the paranoid, disorganized, or catatonic categories. These symptoms may include thought disturbances, delusions, hallucinations, incoherence, and severely impaired behavior. Sometimes undifferentiated schizophrenia turns out to be an early stage of another subtype.

The diagnosis of **residual schizophrenia** is reserved for people who have had at least one previous schizophrenic episode but who are now showing an absence of prominent psychotic features. There is continuing evidence of two or more symptoms, such as marked social isolation, peculiar behaviors, blunted affect, odd beliefs, or unusual perceptual experiences.

▶ CHECKPOINT REVIEW

brief psychotic disorder *(p. 274)*

catatonic schizophrenia *(p. 283)*

delusion *(p. 275)*

delusional disorder *(p. 281)*

disorganized schizophrenia *(p. 282)*

flat affect *(p. 275)*

hallucinations *(p. 276)*

loosening of associations *(p. 277)*

negative symptoms *(p. 275)*

paranoid schizophrenia *(p. 280)*

positive symptoms *(p. 274)*

residual schizophrenia *(p. 284)*

schizophrenia *(p. 273)*

schizophreniform disorder *(p. 274)*

undifferentiated schizophrenia *(p. 284)*

How have our views of schizophrenia changed over time?
- ■ Kraepelin believed that the onset of schizophrenia was early, a result of organic deterioration, the outcome of which is poor. Bleuler believed that both the age of onset and the course were variable.
- ■ DSM-I and II used Bleuler's broader definition. In DSM-III and through DSM-IV-TR, a stricter definition more in line with Kraepelin's view has been adopted.

What kinds of symptoms are found in this disorder?
- ■ Positive symptoms of schizophrenia include delusions; perceptual distortion, as in hallucinations; disorganized communications; and thought disturbances, including loosening of associations, attention problems, and disorganized motoric disturbances.
- ■ Negative symptoms in schizophrenia include avolition, alogia, anhedonia, and flat affect.

How do the specific types of schizophrenia differ from one another?
- ■ DSM-IV-TR distinguishes five types of schizophrenia:
  - • Paranoid schizophrenia is characterized by persecutory delusions or frequent auditory hallucinations.
  - • Disorganized schizophrenia is characterized by disorganized speech and behavior and inappropriate affect. Extreme social impairment and severe regressive behaviors are often seen.
  - • Catatonic schizophrenia's major feature is disturbance of motor activity. Patients show excessive excitement, agitation, and hyperactivity, or withdrawn behavior patterns.
  - • The undifferentiated type includes schizophrenic behavior that cannot be classified as one of the other types.
  - • Residual schizophrenia is a category for people who have had at least one episode of schizophrenia but are not now showing prominent symptoms. In addition, other severe disorders may include schizophrenic-like symptoms.

◀ The Course and Outcome of Schizophrenia

undifferentiated schizophrenia A schizophrenic disorder in which the person's behavior shows prominent psychotic symptoms that do not meet the criteria for paranoid, disorganized, or catatonic schizophrenia.

The typical course of schizophrenia consists of three phases: prodromal, active, and residual. The *prodromal phase* includes the onset and buildup of schizophrenic symptoms. Social withdrawal and isolation, peculiar behaviors, inappropriate affect, poor communication patterns, and neglect of personal grooming may become evident during this phase. Of eleven patients who were interviewed in one study (Campo et al.,

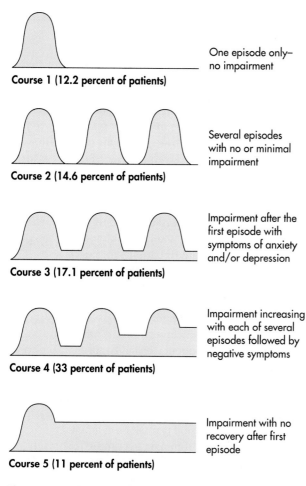

Course 1 (12.2 percent of patients)
One episode only–
no impairment

Course 2 (14.6 percent of patients)
Several episodes with no or minimal impairment

Course 3 (17.1 percent of patients)
Impairment after the first episode with symptoms of anxiety and/or depression

Course 4 (33 percent of patients)
Impairment increasing with each of several episodes followed by negative symptoms

Course 5 (11 percent of patients)
Impairment with no recovery after first episode

Figure 11.3 Some Different Courses Found in Schizophrenia This figure shows five of the many courses that schizophrenia may take. These courses were observed in individuals during a fifteen-year follow-up study. *Source:* Wiersma et al. (1998).

1998), nine indicated that they had drastically changed their appearances (cutting or changing hairstyles, wearing multiples of the same type of clothing) just before the onset of the schizophrenic episode.

Often, psychosocial stressors or excessive demands on an individual with schizophrenia in the prodromal phase result in the onset of prominent psychotic symptoms, or the *active phase* of schizophrenia. In this phase, the person shows the full-blown symptoms of schizophrenia, including severe disturbances in thinking, deterioration in social relationships, and flat or markedly inappropriate affect. At some later time, the person may enter the *residual phase,* in which the symptoms are no longer prominent. The severity of the symptoms declines, and the individual may show the milder impairment found in the prodromal phase.

What are the chances for recovery or improvement from schizophrenia? Kraepelin believed that the disorder follows a deteriorating course. He would have agreed with the following statement concerning the prognosis for schizophrenia: "Complete remission (i.e., a return to full premorbid functioning) is probably not common in this disorder" (American Psychiatric Association, 2000a, p. 309). The long-term outcome for people with schizophrenia may be more positive than that portrayed by Kraepelin and DSM-IV-TR. In a fifteen-year follow-up study of eighty-two individuals diagnosed with schizophrenia, a number of different courses were found (see Figure 11.3). More than 26 percent had complete remission of symptoms, although about half of this group had had more than one psychotic episode. About 50 percent had partial remission of symptoms that were either accompanied by anxiety and depression or negative symptoms, and 11 percent showed no recovery after the initial psychotic episode. Relapses occurred in two-thirds of this sample, after which about one of six showed no remission of symptoms (Wiersma et al., 1998). "Full recovery" for about half the individuals diagnosed with schizophrenia may take the form of time-limited remissions (Torgalsboen & Rund, 1998). For whatever reason, recovery rates appear higher in developing countries. (See the Mental Health and Society feature, "Schizophrenia in Developing Countries," for a discussion of this phenomenon.)

Etiology of Schizophrenia

residual schizophrenia A category of schizophrenic disorder reserved for people who have had at least one previous schizophrenic episode but are now showing an absence of prominent psychotic features and continuing evidence of two or more symptoms, such as marked social isolation, peculiar behaviors, blunted affect, odd beliefs, or unusual perceptual experiences.

A thirteen-year-old boy who was having behavioral and academic problems in school was taking part in a series of family therapy sessions. Family communication was negative in tone, with a great deal of blaming. Near the end of one session, the boy suddenly broke down and cried out, "I don't want to be like her." He was referring to his mother, who had been receiving treatment for schizophrenia and was taking antipsychotic medication. He had often been frightened by her bizarre behavior, and he was concerned that his friends would "find out" about her condition. But his greatest fear was that he would inherit the disorder. Sobbing, he turned to the therapist and asked, "Am I going to be crazy, too?"

mental health and society

Schizophrenia in Developing Countries

The following observation appears in DSM-IV-TR: "Individuals with schizophrenia in developing nations tend to have a more acute course and a better outcome than do individuals in industrialized nations" (p. 307). Do people in developing countries who have schizophrenia recover more quickly and fully than individuals in developed countries? If so, why? The World Health Organization examined these questions in a cross-cultural study (Sartorius et al., 1986). The study applied standardized and reliable sets of criteria and found similar prevalence rates for schizophrenia in ten different countries. However, a follow-up of 1,379 persons diagnosed with schizophrenia and described as "remarkably similar in their symptom profiles" in the nine countries revealed that patients in India, Colombia, and Nigeria showed more rapid and more complete recovery than those in London, Moscow, or Washington. Fifty-six percent of people diagnosed with this disorder in developing countries had only one schizophrenic episode, compared with 39 percent in developed countries. Severe chronic course was found in 40 percent of those from developed countries, compared with 24 percent in developing countries. Sartorius and colleagues hypothesized that some cultural factor might be responsible for the observed difference in outcome. Why should patients from developing countries who have less access to modern treatment recover so quickly? Some have speculated that in developing countries, recovered patients are quickly reintegrated into society. In India, for example, patients with schizophrenia are more likely to be living with their families and to be employed than are similar patients in England (Sharma et al., 1998). In fact, researchers in another study reported difficulty in interviewing recovered patients because they were working in the fields (Warner, 1986). Returning to work and being socially integrated may help prevent relapses.

Stevens (1987) believes that the higher recovery rate for schizophrenia found in developing countries is due to misdiagnosis. To support her view, she pointed out that in the WHO study, 36 percent of patients in Nigeria and 27 percent in India recovered in less than one month. She conjectured that the illnesses were in actuality either brief psychotic disorders or schizophreniform disorders and not schizophrenia. Although this explanation is certainly plausible, the WHO investigation had found an approximately equal frequency of schizophrenia among the different countries. If misdiagnosis did occur, it must mean that brief psychotic disorders and schizophreniform disorders are more prevalent in developing countries and that schizophrenia occurs less frequently in these countries. This possibility must be examined.

If we define schizophrenia as a "chronic" condition, how could we account for the fact that more than 50 percent of people diagnosed with schizophrenia in developing countries recover after one episode? If schizophrenia is a brain disorder, why is the outcome so different between developing and developed countries? If "culture" is responsible for the more positive outcome in developing countries, how does it influence the course of this disorder?

If you were the therapist, how would you respond? We are constantly exposed to news articles indicating that schizophrenia is produced by an "unfortunate" combination of genes or is due to physical problems in the brain. Does this mean that schizophrenia is only a biological disorder? Some evidence also exists that family communication patterns can influence relapse in individuals with schizophrenia. Can the way we interact in a family also precipitate a schizophrenic episode? If so, how? Researchers generally agree that this boy's chances of developing schizophrenia are greater than average. Why this is so is a subject of controversy. Researchers who favor a biological paradigm tend to favor genetic, brain-structure, and biochemical explanations. Other researchers focus primarily on the impact of psychological and social factors in the development of the disorder. We consider the strengths and weaknesses of the different approaches. At the end of the section on genetics, you should reach your own conclusion about what to tell the thirteen-year-old boy.

A Sure Sign of Genetic Influence   The Genain quadruplets, shown here at age sixty-three, all developed schizophrenia, which is unusual because the concordance rate for the disorder in identical twins is only 50 percent. Still, the sisters differed in terms of symptoms, level of recovery, and age of onset, all of which suggest that environmental influences were at work as well. Pictured from left to right are Edna, Wilma, Sarah, and Helen.

Heredity and Schizophrenia

"That genetic factors are involved in the etiology in schizophrenia is no longer a matter of controversy" is a conclusion that has been reached by many researchers (Cannon et al., 1998, p. 67; Wolkin & Rusinek, 2003). What remains controversial, however, is the degree and the nature of the contribution. Over forty years ago, one researcher posed the following challenge to his colleagues:

> You [are] required to write down a procedure for selecting an individual from the population who would be diagnosed as schizophrenic by a psychiatric staff; you have to wager $1,000 on being right. You may not include in your selection procedure any behavioral fact, such as a symptom or trait, manifested by the individual. (Meehl, 1962, p. 827)

According to Meehl, your best chance of winning this wager is to look for someone whose identical twin has already been diagnosed with schizophrenia. This solution reflects the belief that heredity is an important cause in the development of this disorder—a belief supported by research (Cannon et al., 1998; Erlenmeyer-Kimling et al., 1997; Heinrichs, 1993). However, what may be inherited "is not the disorder itself but a state of vulnerability manifested by neuropsychological impairment" (Byrne et al., 2003, p. 38).

Studies Involving Blood Relatives

Close blood relatives are genetically more similar than distant blood relatives. For example, first-degree relatives (parents, siblings, child) share 50 percent of their genes, whereas second-degree relatives (grandparents, uncles, aunts, nephews) share only 25

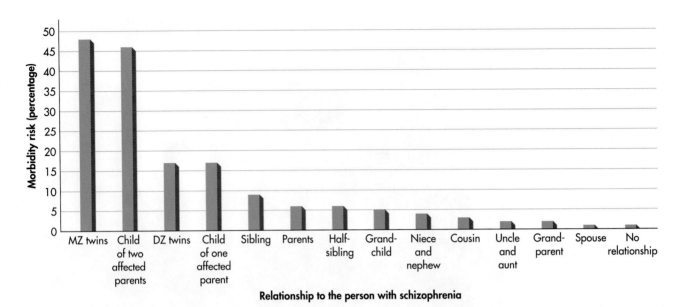

Figure 11.4 Morbidity Risk Among Blood Relatives of People with Schizophrenia
This figure reflects the estimate of the lifetime risk of developing schizophrenia—a risk that is strongly correlated with the degree of genetic influence. *Source:* Data from Gottesman (1978, 1991).

percent of their genes. If schizophrenia has a genetic basis, researchers should find the disorder more often among close relatives of people diagnosed with schizophrenia than among more distant relatives.

Figure 11.4 suggests that this situation is indeed the case. The data are summarized from several major studies on the prevalence of schizophrenia (Gottesman, 1978, 1991). They show that closer blood relatives of people diagnosed with schizophrenia run a greater risk of developing the disorder. Thus the boy described earlier has a 16 percent chance of being diagnosed with schizophrenia, but his mother's nieces or nephews have only a 4 percent chance. (It should be noted that the risk for the general population is 1 percent.)

Even if well-designed studies pointed to a relationship between degree of genetic relatedness and schizophrenia, however, they still do not clearly demonstrate the role of heredity. Why? Simply because closer blood relatives are more likely to share the same environmental factors or stressors, as well as the same genes. To confirm a genetic basis for schizophrenia, research must separate genetic influences from environmental influences.

Twin Studies

Earlier in this book we described the use of twin studies by researchers who seek to differentiate between the effects of heredity and those of environment. You may recall that identical, or monozygotic (MZ), twins are genetically identical, so differences between MZ twins are presumably caused by differences in their environments. If reared together, MZ twins share the same general environment, as well as the same hereditary makeup. But fraternal, or dizygotic (DZ), twins, though born at about the same time, are not genetically more similar than any other two siblings, and they may be of different sexes. If DZ twins are reared together, they share the same general environment, but their genetic makeup is, on the average, only 50 percent identical. In general, **concordance rates** (likelihood that both members of a twin pair will show the

concordance rate The likelihood that both members of a twin pair will show the same characteristic.

Separating the Effects of Heredity and Environment These monozygotic twin boys are genetically identical but also share the same environment. One of the problems with studying twins is the difficulty of separating heredity factors from environmental influences. Adoption studies are useful because heredity and environmental factors can be more clearly differentiated.

same characteristic) for schizophrenia among MZ twins are two to four times higher than among DZ twins. This seems to point to a strong genetic basis for the disorder.

Adoption Studies

Even with twin studies, it is difficult to separate the effects of heredity from the effects of environment because twins are usually raised together. Thus when the child of a parent with schizophrenia develops the disorder, three explanations are possible:

1. The mother or father with schizophrenia may have genetically transmitted schizophrenia to the child.

2. The parent, being disturbed, may have provided a stressful environment for the child.

3. The child's schizophrenia may have resulted from a combination of genetic factors and a stressful environment.

In what has become a classic effort to sort out the effects of heredity and environment, the incidence of schizophrenia and other disorders in a group of babies who were born to mothers with schizophrenia but who had no further contact with their mothers was determined (Heston, 1966; Heston & Denny, 1968). This condition eliminated the possibility that contact with the mother increased the chance of developing the disorder. The lives of these people were traced through the records of child-care institutions—all had been adopted by two-parent families. A control group, consisting of people who were born to mothers who did not have schizophrenia and who were adopted through the same child-care institutions, was selected and matched. Information regarding both the genetically at-risk and control groups was collected from many sources (including school records, court records, and interviews). The people themselves were interviewed and given psychological tests. Five individuals in the at-risk group (mothers with schizophrenia) were later diagnosed with schizophrenia, compared with none in the control group. These results are highly significant and support a genetic explanation for schizophrenia. Of special interest is the finding that nearly one-half of those in the at-risk group were "notably successful adults" who were more spontaneous when interviewed and had more colorful life histories than the control group (Heston, 1966, p. 825).

In another study designed to separate hereditary and environmental influences, investigators identified adults who were diagnosed with schizophrenia and who had been adopted in infancy. Then they located both the adoptive parents and the biological parents. If environmental factors play the major role in schizophrenia, the adoptive families should be more disturbed than the biological parents. Conversely, if heredity is more important, biological families should show more disturbance than adoptive families. Schizophrenia was found only among the biological relatives, thus supporting the importance of heredity (Kety et al., 1994).

Studies of High-Risk Populations

Perhaps the most comprehensive way to study the etiology of schizophrenia is to monitor a large group of children over time, noting the differences between those who eventually develop schizophrenia and those who do not. This sort of developmental study allows the investigator to see how the disorders develop. But because the prevalence of schizophrenia in the general population is only 1 percent, a prohibitively large group would have to be monitored if a random sample of children were chosen. Instead, investigators have chosen participants from "high-risk" populations; this procedure increases the probability that a smaller group of participants will include some who develop schizophrenia. In one study (Erlenmeyer-Kimling et al., 1997) children ages seven to twelve years of parents with schizophrenia (a high-risk group) and without schizophrenia were studied twenty-five years later. Those who developed schizophrenia (13.1 percent) were all in the high-risk group. This percentage is much higher than would have been predicted from the general population.

The best known developmental studies are those conducted by Mednick and colleagues (Mednick, 1970; Mednick et al., 1989) involving about 200 persons whose mothers had schizophrenia (the high-risk group) and about 100 persons whose mothers did not have schizophrenia (the low-risk control group). The researchers followed these people for more than thirty years. On the basis of existing data, they predicted the eventual outcome for both high-risk and low-risk persons. Their prediction was that approximately one-half of the high-risk group may eventually display some form of psychopathology, including but not limited to schizophrenia. At this time, fifteen of the high-risk individuals have developed schizophrenia; the researchers estimate that another fifteen will later receive this diagnosis. Because only a minority of the high-risk individuals will develop this disorder, environmental factors also play an etiological role.

▶ Physiological Factors in Schizophrenia

Two important areas of research into the causes of schizophrenia focus on brain chemistry and brain pathology. Logically, either could serve as a vehicle for the genetic transmission of schizophrenia, but no substantive evidence to that effect has yet been found. Currently, researchers have found no physiological sign or symptom that leads solely to an invariant diagnosis of schizophrenia. Nonetheless, research in these areas has implications for treatment, as well as etiology.

Table 11.2   Biological Findings in Schizophrenia and Some Problems Associated with Them

Biological Finding	Problem
Disturbed functioning in dopamine system	A large minority of people with schizophrenia are not responsive to antipsychotic medications affecting dopamine.
	Other effective medications (Clozapine) work primarily on the serotonin, rather than the dopamine, system.
	Neuroleptics block dopamine receptors quickly, but relief from symptoms is not seen for weeks.
Ventricular enlargement	Differences are relatively small compared with control groups.
	Reported in only 6 to 40 percent of patients with schizophrenia in a variety of studies.
	Also reported in some patients with mood disorders.
Diminished volume of frontal or temporal lobes	Differences are relatively small, compared with control groups.
	About 50 percent of patients with schizophrenia fall within range of control groups on this measure.
Low relative glucose metabolism in frontal areas	Participants are generally chronic patients on heavy neuroleptic medications.
	Some evidence indicates that neuroleptics influence cerebral blood flow even in patients who are currently medication free.
Cognitive dysfunctions (visual processing, attention problems, recall memory problems)	Some members of control groups also have such dysfunctions.
	May be a result of medication, hospitalization, or other such variables.
	Validity of measures is questionable.

Note: Although differences have been found in the functioning and structure of the brain in many people with schizophrenia, the findings are subject to different interpretations.
Source: Compiled from Chua & McKenna (1995); Faraone et al. (1995); Kane & Freeman (1994); Vita et al. (1995); Wiesel (1994).

Biochemistry: The Dopamine Hypothesis

Biochemical explanations of schizophrenia have a long history. A century ago, for example, Emil Kraepelin suggested that these disorders result from a chemical imbalance caused by abnormal sex gland secretion. Since then, a number of researchers have tried to show that biochemistry is involved in schizophrenia. Most have failed to do so. What generally happens is that a researcher finds a particular substance in the biochemical makeup of people with schizophrenia and does not find it in "normal" controls; however, other researchers cannot replicate those findings. In addition, patients with schizophrenia differ from normal persons in lifestyle and in food and medication intake, all of which affect body chemistry and tend to confound research results. Table 11.2 summarizes some of the problems associated with current biological research findings.

One promising line of biochemical research has focused on the neurotransmitter dopamine (Davis, Kahn, & Ko, 1991; Kapur, 2003). According to the **dopamine hypothesis** (discussed briefly in the chapter "Abnormal Behavior: Models and Treatments"), schizophrenia may result from excessive dopamine activity at certain synaptic sites. Support for the dopamine hypothesis has come from research with three types of drugs: phenothiazines, L-dopa, and the amphetamines.

dopamine hypothesis The suggestion that schizophrenia may result from excess dopamine activity at certain synaptic sites.

■ *Phenothiazines* are antipsychotic drugs that decrease the severity of thought disorders, alleviate withdrawal and hallucinations, and improve the mood of

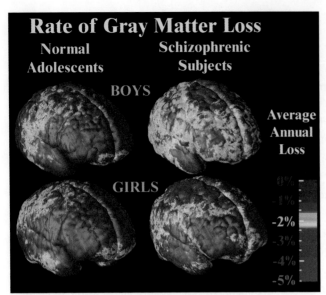

Rate of Gray Matter Loss

Normal Adolescents   Schizophrenic Subjects

BOYS

GIRLS

Average Annual Loss

0%
-1%
-2%
-3%
-4%
-5%

Rate of Gray Matter Loss in Teenagers with Schizophrenia   Male and female adolescents with schizophrenia show progressive loss of gray matter in the parietal, frontal, and temporal areas of the brain that is much greater than that found in "normal" adolescents. A similar pattern of gray matter loss in the different brain regions is found among both boys and girls with schizophrenia. How would you interpret this finding?

patients with schizophrenia. Evidence shows that the phenothiazines reduce dopamine activity in the brain by blocking dopamine receptor sites in postsynaptic neurons.

■ *L-dopa* is generally used to treat symptoms of Parkinson's disease, such as muscle and limb rigidity and tremors. The body converts L-dopa to dopamine, and the drug sometimes produces schizophrenic-like symptoms. By contrast, the phenothiazines, which reduce dopamine activity, can *produce* side effects that resemble Parkinson's disease.

■ Amphetamines are stimulants that increase the availability of dopamine and norepinephrine (another neurotransmitter) in the brain. When individuals not diagnosed with schizophrenia are given continual doses of amphetamines, they show symptoms very much like those of acute paranoid schizophrenia. And very small doses may increase the severity of symptoms in patients diagnosed with schizophrenia.

Thus a drug that is believed to block dopamine reception has the effect of reducing the severity of schizophrenic symptoms, whereas two drugs that increase dopamine availability either produce or worsen these symptoms. Such evidence obviously supports the idea that excess dopamine may cause schizophrenic symptoms.

The evidence is not all positive, however. For example, the dopamine hypothesis might lead us to expect that treating schizophrenia with phenothiazines would be effective in almost all cases. Yet about one-fourth of patients with schizophrenia responded very little or not at all to antipsychotic medication (Hoff & Kremen, 2003; Kane & Freeman, 1994).

Neurological Findings

Abnormal Neurological Findings   Do the symptoms of schizophrenia indicate neurological impairment? This is certainly a possibility. Anywhere from 20 to 75 percent of patients with schizophrenia show some signs of neurological abnormalities (Cannon & Marco, 1994; Coursey, Alford, & Safarjan, 1997; Crespo-Facorro et al., 2001; Pantelis et al., 2003). Sophisticated brain-imaging techniques have found that, compared with members of control groups, people with schizophrenia are more likely to show ventricular enlargement (enlarged spaces in areas of the brain), cerebral atrophy (Cahn et al., 2002; Keller et al., 2003), and a decrease in the size of the thalamus (Gaser et al., 2004; Staal et al., 2000; Wolkin et al., 1998). Ventricular enlargement may indicate only an increased susceptibility to schizophrenia, because healthy siblings of patients with schizophrenia also show ventricle enlargement (Staal et al., 2000).

In an interesting longitudinal study of brain changes among youths with and without schizophrenia, those with the disorder showed a striking loss of gray brain matter over a period of six years. The loss was so rapid that it was likened to a "forest fire" (Thompson et al., 2001.) The areas of brain loss were related to the symptoms associated with the disorder. It is not clear how generalizable the findings are because the sample involved adolescents with early-onset schizophrenia. Loss of cortical gray matter associated with schizophrenia has also been reported in other studies (Cahn et al., 2002).

Conclusions What can we conclude from studies of brain structure and functioning in schizophrenia? Neurological abnormalities tend to be reported more often in people with schizophrenia than in other individuals and more often in patients with negative symptoms of schizophrenia. At best, however, these differences are subtle. The observations are intriguing because they highlight the possibility that some subtypes of schizophrenia may be caused by structural brain pathology. Findings that abnormalities in the prefrontal cortex may be a factor are especially interesting because this area is involved with some of the intellectual symptoms associated with schizophrenia.

▷ CHECKPOINT REVIEW

concordance rate *(p. 288)*
dopamine hypothesis *(p. 291)*

Is there much chance of recovery from schizophrenia?
- ▪ The degree of recovery from schizophrenia is difficult to evaluate, in part because of changing definitions. Although most people assume that the prognosis for individuals with schizophrenia is not good, research is beginning to show that that may not be the case. Many of these individuals experience minimal or no lasting impairment and recover enough to lead relatively productive lives.

What causes schizophrenia?
- ▪ Much research and theorizing has focused on the etiology of schizophrenia, but methodological flaws and research design limitations restrict the kinds of conclusions that can be drawn. The best conclusion is that genetics, along with some type of environmental factors, combine to cause the disorder.

Is schizophrenia an inherited condition?
- ▪ Using research strategies such as twin studies and adoption studies, investigators have shown that heredity does influence this group of disorders. The degree of influence is open to question, however; when methodological problems are taken into account, it appears lower than previously reported. Heredity is a major factor but not sufficient to cause schizophrenia; environmental factors are also involved.

What supports the view that schizophrenia is a result of brain abnormalities?
- ▪ The process by which genetic influences are transmitted has not been explained. Brain structure and neurotransmitter differences have been found between individuals with and without schizophrenia. However, some of the findings report only small differences and are difficult to interpret.

▷ Environmental Factors in Schizophrenia

Obviously, genetic and biological research have not yet clarified the causes of the various schizophrenic disorders. Because the concordance rate is less than 50 percent in identical twins, nonshared environmental influences must also play a role. Most of these may be physical in nature, such as damage to a developing fetus from prenatal infections, obstetric complications, or early trauma (Jablensky & Kalaydjieva, 2003; Sanders & Gejman, 2001). Several studies have reported that individuals whose mothers were exposed to the influenza virus during the second trimester of pregnancy have higher-than-expected rates of schizophrenia (Machon, Mednick, & Huttunen, 1997). Although these findings may be coincidences, they illustrate the attempt to identify early environmental factors, such as infections during fetal or perinatal development, which could be related to schizophrenia.

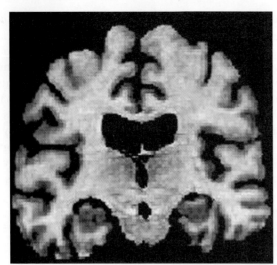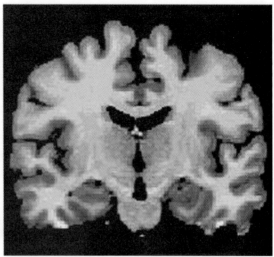

Coronal Sections of the Brain in a Patient with Schizophrenia   Structural brain abnormalities have been found in most individuals with schizophrenia. The degree and extent of the abnormalities appear to be related to outcome. Patients with poor outcome (represented by the left photo) show significantly greater loss of cerebral gray matter and greater enlargement of the ventricles than patients with a good outcome (represented by the photo on the right). *Source:* Staal et al. (2001).

As with the biological theories, environmental explanations are not sufficient to explain the etiology of schizophrenia. In this section we consider some of the more developed of these theories—those concerning the role of family dynamics, social class, and cultural differences.

Family Influences

It was once strongly believed that exposure to specific dysfunctional family patterns was enough to produce schizophrenia (Wahlberg et al., 1997). However, as Lehman and Steinwachs (1998) note, "Research has failed to substantiate hypothesized causal links between family dysfunction and the etiology of schizophrenia. . . . The presumption that family interaction causes schizophrenia . . . has led to serious disruptions in clinician/family trust" (p. 8). These researchers believe that unless a person has a genetic predisposition toward schizophrenia, environmental factors have little impact on the development of the disorder. Others strongly disagree. In this section, we consider theories that support psychological factors as either causes of or contributors to schizophrenia.

Theoretical Constructs   Studies of high-risk children have found that those who develop schizophrenia had a negative family environment (Marcus et al., 1987; Tienari et al., 1994). Several theories have attempted to pinpoint patterns of family interaction that could produce such a disorder. The first was proposed by psychodynamic theorists, who believed that certain behavioral patterns among parents could inhibit appropriate ego development in the child (Alanen, 1994). This, in turn, would make the child vulnerable to the severe regression characteristic of schizophrenia. Attention was focused mainly on the mother, who usually has a great deal of contact with the child. These theorists characterized the **schizophrenogenic** (or schizophrenia-producing) mother as being simultaneously or alternately cold and overprotecting, rejecting and dominating. This behavior pattern was believed to lead to the development of schizophrenia in the child.

The second theory involving family interaction asked another question: "Can some kind of communication pattern produce schizophrenia?" The **double-bind theory** (Bateson

schizophrenogenic Causing or producing schizophrenia; a term generally used to describe a parent who is simultaneously or alternately cold and overprotecting, rejecting and dominating.

double-bind theory The suggestion that schizophrenia develops as a result of repeated experiences that the preschizophrenic child has with one or more family members (usually the mother and father) in which the child receives contradictory messages.

et al., 1956) suggested that schizophrenia develops as a result of repeated experiences that a child has with one or more family members (usually the mother and father) in which the child receives contradictory messages. Because the child cannot discern the parent's meaning, it leads to difficulty in interpreting other people's communications and in accurately and appropriately conveying his or her own thoughts and feelings. To survive, children in such situations may resort to self-deception, falsely interpreting their own thoughts, as well as those communicated by others. They may develop a false concept of reality, an inability to communicate effectively, withdrawal, and other symptoms of schizophrenia.

Most studies conducted before the mid-1970s supported the view that communications were much more dysfunctional in families in which a member had schizophrenia than in other families. Methodological shortcomings, however, kept researchers from generalizing these results to a relationship between schizophrenia and family dynamics. Two flaws were most common: a family's interactions were studied only after one of its members had been diagnosed with schizophrenia, and studies generally lacked control groups. Thus even if negative family interaction was correlated with schizophrenia, researchers could not tell which was the cause and which the effect or whether the correlation was unique to schizophrenia.

Expressed Emotion   Current research is directed toward a specific behavior pattern called **expressed emotion (EE)**, a negative communication pattern that is found among some relatives of individuals with schizophrenia and that is associated with higher relapse rates. The EE index is determined by the number of critical comments made by a relative (criticism); the number of statements of dislike or resentment directed toward the patient by family members (hostility); and the number of statements reflecting emotional overinvolvement, overconcern, or overprotectiveness made about the patient. For example, high-EE relatives are likely to make a greater number of statements such as, "You are a lazy person" or "You've caused our family a lot of trouble" (Rosenfarb et al., 1995; Weisman et al., 2000). The EE construct strongly predicts the course of the disorder (Karno et al., 1987; Miklowitz, 1994; Mintz, Mintz, & Goldstein, 1987). A review of twenty-six studies (Kavanagh, 1992) indicated that the median relapse rate for patients living with high-EE relatives was 48 percent, compared with 21 percent for those living with low-EE relatives.

Although these studies are better designed than those discussed earlier, they are still correlational in nature and are therefore subject to different interpretations. Figure 11.5 indicates three possible interpretations.

1. A high-EE environment is stressful, and it may lead directly to relapse in the family member who has schizophrenia. Patients whose parents are rated high in EE are more likely to recount negative and stressful memories involving their parents than those whose parents are low on EE (Cutting & Docherty, 2000).

2. A more severely ill individual may be responsible for high-EE communication patterns in relatives. The severity of the illness also means that the chances of relapse are high. Schreiber, Breier, and Pickar (1995) found some support for this pattern. Expressed emotions may be a response of parents to the "chronic disabling aspect of this illness, and a belief by the parents that increased involvement would facilitate increased functioning of the child" (p. 649).

3. In the bidirectional model, the patient's odd behaviors or symptoms may cause family members to attempt to exert control and to react with frustration, which in turn produce more psychotic symptoms in the patient. An examination of communication patterns in families of patients with schizophrenia also shows some support for this view (Rosenfarb et al., 1995).

expressed emotion (EE) A type of negative communication pattern that is found in some families in which some members have schizophrenia and that is associated with higher relapse rates.

High-EE communication does not appear to be peculiar to schizophrenia. These patterns have also been found in the families of patients with depression, bipolar disorder, and eating disorders (Butzlaff & Hooley, 1998; Kavanagh, 1992). And although EE has been related to relapse, little evidence supports the idea that deviant family communication patterns are sufficient to produce schizophrenia.

Figure 11.5 Possible Relationships Between High Rates of Expressed Emotion and Relapse Rates in Patients with Schizophrenia Although some researchers believe that high expressed emotions among family members are related to relapse rates in schizophrenic patients, the precise relationship has not been determined. This figure shows several ways in which expressed emotions and relapse rates can be related.

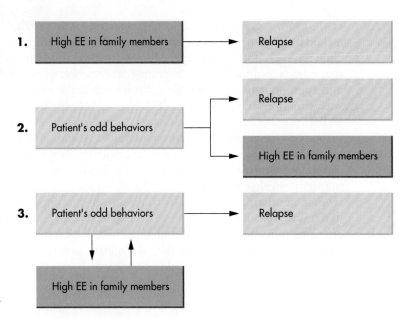

Effect of Social Class

One of the most consistent research findings is that the disorder is disproportionately concentrated among people in the poorest areas of large cities and in the occupations with the lowest status (Keith, Regier, & Rae, 1991; Olfson et al., 2002). This correlation between social class and schizophrenia has two possible explanations. First, low socioeconomic status is itself stressful. Physical and psychological stressors associated with poverty, a lack of education, menial employment, and the like may increase the chance that schizophrenia will develop *(breeder hypothesis)*. Second, people with schizophrenia may drift to the poorest urban areas and the lowest socioeconomic levels because they cannot function effectively elsewhere in society *(downward-drift theory)*.

One way to test downward-drift theory is to compare the occupations of individuals with this disorder with those of their fathers. If this comparison indicates a lower status for patients' jobs than for fathers' jobs, a downward-drift interpretation would be supported. In several studies, the patients with schizophrenia were found to have such lower status occupations (Gottesman, 1991). Overall, the evidence offers some support for both the breeder hypothesis and downward-drift theory. For some people, the stressors and limitations associated with membership in the lowest socioeconomic class facilitate the development of schizophrenia. But for others, low socioeconomic status is a result of the disorder.

Cross-Cultural Comparisons

As noted throughout this book, the study of cross-cultural perspectives on psychopathology is important because indigenous belief systems influence views of etiology and treatment. In India, the belief in the supernatural causation of schizophrenia is very widespread, which leads to consultation and treatment by indigenous healers (Banerjee & Roy, 1998). In a study of 281 individuals in Saudi Arabia and England, the researchers (Wahass & Kent, 1997) found that the Saudis were likely to believe that auditory hallucinations were due to Satanic or demonic powers or to a curse or magic. Only 18.7 percent believed these "voices" to be a symptom of schizophrenia. Most English respondents attributed auditory hallucinations to symptoms of schizophrenia or some form of brain damage. Figure 11.6 lists other comparisons from this study. Not surprisingly, beliefs influenced treatment choices. About two-thirds of the Saudi sample believed that

Some Neighborhoods May Nurture Schizophrenia   Schizophrenia is much more prevalent at lower socioeconomic levels. Some believe this is due to the increased stress of living in poverty (as illustrated by the homeless people sleeping in cardboard boxes), others believe that individuals with schizophrenia move into poor neighborhoods due to their inability to function fully. How would you determine which view is correct?

the most appropriate intervention would be religious assistance, whereas nearly two-thirds of the English sample believed that medication and psychological therapies would be treatments of choice. Cultural factors may also be present in the case of a thirteen-year-old child of a Tongan mother and a Caucasian father living in the United States:

> The girl appeared to have visual hallucinations, had become isolative, exhibited echolalia, had been observed conversing with herself, and reported hearing voices of a woman who sounded like her mother and a man who sounded like her dead grandfather. Although some improvement was observed with antipsychotic medication, the girl still reported being disturbed by ghosts and reported ideas of reference—that people were talking about her. The mother decided that her daughter suffered from "fakamahaki" (a culture-bound syndrome in which deceased relatives can inflict illness or possess the living when customs have been neglected) and took her daughter to Tonga to be treated. For five days, a traditional healer ("witch doctor") treated the girl with herbal potions. Vomiting was induced to remove toxins from the body. She also visited her grandfather's grave to allow proper mourning. The girl returned to the United States and was reevaluated. No symptoms of psychosis could be found. Follow-up contacts revealed that the girl was continuing to do well. This case is interesting because medication had only limited success, whereas traditional healing seemed to be effective. It might have been just that the disorder was time limited, but how can we account for the seemingly successful treatment of severe mental disorders through folk medicine? (Takeuchi, 2000)

Cultural differences are not confined solely to explanations of symptoms, however. Less developed countries seem to have a greater percentage of "hysterical psychoses," "possession syndromes," and other brief psychotic disorders. These psychoses tend to be rapid in onset and short in duration; they have a good prognosis.

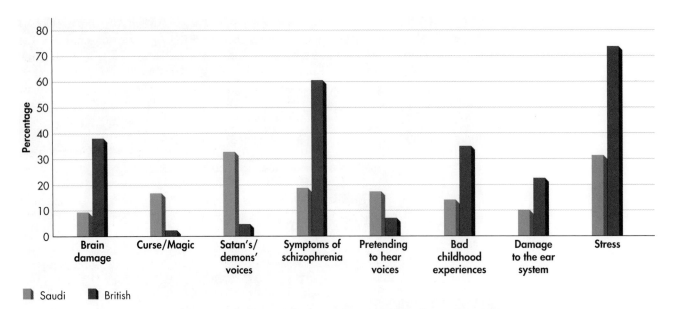

Figure 11.6 Members of Two Cultures Explain the Causes of Auditory Hallucinations
A study of 281 individuals in Saudi Arabia and England revealed that people from the different cultures had very different beliefs about the causes of auditory hallucinations. These differences in beliefs also influenced the respondents' recommendations for treatment. *Source:* Wahass & Kent (1997).

◀ The Treatment of Schizophrenia

Through the years, schizophrenia has been "treated" by a variety of means, including the "warehousing" of severely disturbed patients in overcrowded asylums and prefrontal lobotomy, a surgical procedure in which the frontal lobes are disconnected from the remainder of the patient's brain. Such radical procedures were generally abandoned in the 1950s, when the beneficial effects of antipsychotic drugs were discovered. Today schizophrenia is typically treated with antipsychotic medication, along with some type of psychosocial therapy. In recent years, the research and clinical perspective on people with schizophrenia has shifted from a focus on disease and deficit to one promoting health, competencies, independence, self-determination, and collaborative therapy with family members (Coursey et al., 1997; Fadden, 1998).

Antipsychotic Medication

> Peter was a twenty-nine-year-old man with chronic paranoid schizophrenia....even on medication, he heard voices talking about him and believed that his phone was bugged. When off medication, he had constant hallucinations, and his behavior became unpredictable....He was on 10 milligrams of haloperidol (Haldol) three times a day....Peter complained that he had been quite restless and did not want to take the medication. Over the next six months, Peter's psychiatrist gradually reduced Peter's medication to 4 milligrams per day....At this dose, Peter continued to have bothersome symptoms, but they remained moderate....He was no longer restless. (Liberman, Kopelowicz, & Young, 1994, p. 94)

The use of medication in Peter's case illustrates several points. First, antipsychotic drugs can reduce symptoms. Second, dosage levels should be carefully monitored, and third, side effects can occur as a result of medication.

Most mental health professionals consider the introduction of *Thorazine,* the first antipsychotic drug, the beginning of a new era in treating schizophrenia. For the first time, a medication was available that sufficiently relaxed even violent patients with schizophrenia and helped organize their thoughts to the point at which strait-jackets were no longer needed to contain the individuals. Three decades later, the phenothiazines, which are variations of Thorazine, are still viewed as the most effective drug treatment for schizophrenia. They are not, however, a "cure" for the condition.

The antipsychotic medications (also called **neuroleptics**) are, however, far from perfect and can produce a number of extremely unwelcome side effects that resemble neurological conditions. They quite effectively reduce the severity of the positive symptoms of schizophrenia, such as hallucinations, delusions, bizarre speech, and thought disorders. Most, however, offer little relief from the negative symptoms of social withdrawal, apathy, and impaired personal hygiene (Carpenter et al., 1995; Christison, Kirch, & Wyatt, 1991). Moreover, a "relatively large group" of people with schizophrenia do not benefit at all from antipsychotic medication (Wiesel, 1994; Silverman et al., 1987).

Some new antipsychotic drugs (including clozapine, risperidone, quetiapine, and olanzapine) were released for use in the United States in the 1990s. Over 50 percent of new prescriptions for treating schizophrenia are for the new atypical antipsychotics (Meltzer, 2000). These medications have fewer side effects than some older neuroleptics and are effective with up to 50 percent of patients who do not respond to traditional medications (Reid & Mason, 1998; Rivas-Vazquez et al., 2000).

Regulation and monitoring of antipsychotic drugs is especially important. However, a study of 719 patients diagnosed with schizophrenia revealed that the dosage levels of their antipsychotic medications were often outside the recommended treatment ranges (Lehman & Steinwachs, 1998). African American patients were also more likely to be on higher levels than white patients (American Psychiatric Association, 2004). Another study found that women were given higher doses of antipsychotic medication than their male counterparts and that women's medication was seldom reduced to a maintenance level after the acute stage passed (Zito et al., 1987). This may be problematic because women, especially those with late-onset schizophrenia, are more likely to develop tardive dyskinesia (neurological disturbances indicated by involuntary movements resulting from use of antipsychotic medications) (Lindamer et al., 2001).

Clinicians are also often unaware of negative effects of the drugs, such as tremors, motor restlessness, anxiety, agitation, extreme terror, and even the danger of impulsive suicide attempts (Drake & Ehrlich, 1985; Hirose, 2003; Lehman & Steinwachs, 1998). The inability to recognize these "side effects" in medicated patients is disturbing. The Mental Health and Society feature, "Should Patients Have the Right to Refuse Medication?" examines the issue of patients' rights in taking medication.

Psychosocial and Cognitive-Behavioral Therapy

Nearly three-fourths of patients with schizophrenia in one study reported that individual psychotherapy brought about positive changes in their lives (Coursey, Keller, & Farrell, 1995). Most patients felt that the best treatment was a combination of talking therapy with medication. The patients reported that the beneficial aspects of psychotherapy included giving them practical advice, helping them "get in touch with their feelings," understanding how they affect people, and determining the reasons for their actions and feelings. Along with psychotherapy, there have been attempts to address specific deficits shown by many individuals with schizophrenia, as illustrated in the following case:

neuroleptics Antipsychotic drugs that can help treat symptoms of schizophrenia but can produce undesirable side effects, such as symptoms that mimic neurological disorders.

mentaL HeaLth and society

Should Patients Have the Right to Refuse Medication?

Should individuals with schizophrenia have the right to refuse antipsychotic medications that may produce an increased risk of cardiac arrest (Herxheimer & Healy, 2002) or potentially hazardous side effects? Before you respond to this question, consider that there is no known effective treatment for some side effects, such as tardive dyskinesia. Tardive dyskinesia is characterized by involuntary and rhythmic movements of the protruding tongue; chewing, lip smacking, and other facial movements; and jerking movements of the limbs. At risk for this disorder are people who have been treated with antipsychotic medications—also known as neuroleptics—over a long period of time. The elderly appear to be especially vulnerable to neuroleptic side effects (Meltzer, 2000; Zayas & Grossberg, 1998). Women tend to have more severe tardive dyskinesia and a higher prevalence than men do (American Psychiatric Association, 2004; Yassa & Jeste, 1992). However, this syndrome is appearing increasingly more often in younger patients and nonpsychotic patients because neuroleptics are now being prescribed to treat anxiety, hyperactivity in children, aggression, and mood disorders. Legal and ethical issues are becoming involved, as the "cure may be worse than the illness."

In one large developmental study, nearly 20 percent of the sample developed tardive dyskinesia after being on the medication for four years. After eight years, 40 percent had tardive dyskinesia (Kane et al., 1986). As Kane and Freeman (1994) have observed, "In patients who are already socially disabled by negative and deficit symptoms, bizarre behavior, and impaired social skills, the addition of embarrassing and stigmatizing involuntary movements of [tardive dyskinesia] is certainly an added obstacle to optimal adjustment in the community" (p. 28). In most cases, the symptoms persist and cannot be eliminated (Glazer, Morgenstern, & Doucette, 1991).

The antipsychotic medications also have side effects that are reversible. Approximately 60 percent of patients on antipsychotic medications develop extrapyramidal side effects such as *Parkinsonism* (muscle tremors, shakiness, and immobility), *dystonia* (slow and continued contrasting movements of the limbs and tongue), *akathesis* (motor restlessness), and *neuroleptic malignant syndrome* (muscle rigidity and autonomic instability), the latter of which can be fatal if untreated (American Psychiatric Association, 1997). Other symptoms may involve the loss of facial expression, immobility, shuffling gait, tremors of the hand, rigidity of the body, and poor postural stability; these symptoms are usually reversible (Lehman & Steinwachs, 1998).

Patients have described a variety of reactions to the medication: "I feel restless; I cannot keep still; my nerves are jumpy; I feel like jumping out of my skin; my legs just want to keep moving; it's like having ants in my pants" (Sachdev & Loneragan, 1991, p. 383). Other side effects include drowsiness, skin rashes, blurred vision, dry mouth, nausea, and rapid heartbeat.

Groups that support the concept of patients' rights argue that forced administration of drugs violates a person's basic freedoms. Yet hospital staff members fear that violent patients may be dangerous to themselves, other patients, and staff if they are not medicated. As the funding of state mental institutions has decreased, the use of medication has increased.

Should patients who admit themselves voluntarily for treatment be able to refuse antipsychotic medications? What about those who are involuntarily committed? Should the state, institution, or psychiatrist be liable for the development of permanent side effects among patients? Can an individual who is currently undergoing a psychotic episode give "consent" to being treated with antipsychotic medications? States and the mental health profession are wrestling with these issues.

Philip's psychotic symptoms were reduced with medication. However, he was unable to obtain employment. The counselor suggested that his attire (sweatshirt, exercise pants, head band, and worn sneakers) might be inappropriate for a job interview. In addition, his skills for making a good first impression in interviews were lacking. Field trips allowed Philip to observe attire worn by individuals in different businesses. He was also trained in conversational topics and practiced job interviews with his counselor. Philip decided to apply for landscape work, wore a work shirt, blue jeans, and construction boots, and was hired by a landscaping contractor. (Heinssen & Cuthbert, 2001)

Many individuals with schizophrenia behave "strangely" and do not have positive conversational skills (Nisenson, Berenbaum, & Good, 2001). Only about 20 percent are employed (Mechanic, Bilder, & McAlpine, 2002). Heinssen and Cuthbert (2001) found that eccentricities in appearance, attire, communication patterns, and lack of discretion in discussing their illness impede employment or the establishment of social networks. These problems can be addressed through the use of psychotherapeutic interventions. With appropriate interventions, many more individuals with schizophrenia can acquire competitive employment. Major advances have been made in the use of cognitive and behavioral strategies in treating the symptoms of schizophrenia, especially among those who have not been fully helped through medications (Chadwick et al., 2000; Twamley, Jeste, & Bellack, 2003).

Interventions Focusing on Family Communication and Education

More than 50 percent of recovering patients now return to live with their families, and new psychological interventions address this fact. Family intervention programs have not only reduced relapse rates but have also lowered the cost of care (Fadden, 1998). They have been beneficial for families with and without communication patterns such as EE (Lehman & Steinwachs, 1998). Most programs include the following components (Marsh & Johnson, 1997; Mueser et al., 2001): (1) normalizing the family experience, (2) educating family members about schizophrenia, (3) identifying the strengths and competencies of the patient and family members, (4) developing skills in problem solving and managing stress, (5) learning to cope with the symptoms of mental illness and its repercussions on the family, (6) recognizing early signs of relapse (one study, by Stenberg, Jaaskelainen, and Royks, 1998, found that simply teaching family members to recognize early signs of relapse resulted in earlier treatment and shorter hospital stays), (7) creating a supportive family environment, and (8) understanding and meeting the needs of all family members.

The combination of medication and the new psychological interventions has provided hope for many patients with schizophrenia; continuing research points to an even more promising future.

▶ CHECKPOINT REVIEW

double-bind theory *(p. 294)*

expressed emotion (EE) *(p. 295)*

neuroleptics *(p. 299)*

schizophrenogenic *(p. 294)*

Can psychological factors "cause" schizophrenia?
- The search for an environmental basis for schizophrenia has met with no more success than has the search for genetic influences.
- Certain negative family patterns, involving parental characteristics or intrafamilial communication processes, have been hypothesized to result in schizophrenia.
- High expressed emotions (negative comments), or high EE, from family members may be related to relapse in people with schizophrenia.
- There is little evidence that psychological factors in and of themselves can cause the condition.

What is the best etiological model for schizophrenia?
- The research on the etiology of schizophrenia has suggested an interaction between genetic and environmental factors. When the vulnerable person is exposed to strong environmental stressors but does not have the resources to cope with them, a schizophrenic episode may result.

What kinds of treatments are currently available, and are they effective?
- Schizophrenia seems to involve both biological and environmental factors, and treatment programs that combine drugs with psychotherapy appear to hold the most promise.
- Drug therapy usually involves the phenothiazines, or antipsychotics.
- The accompanying psychosocial therapy consists of either supportive counseling or behavior therapy, with an emphasis on social-skills training and changing communication patterns among patients and family members.

FOCUS QUESTIONS

■ What are cognitive disorders?

■ What are the different types of cognitive disorders?

■ Why do people develop cognitive disorders?

■ What kinds of interventions can be used to treat people with cognitive disorders?

■ What is mental retardation?

12 *Cognitive Disorders*

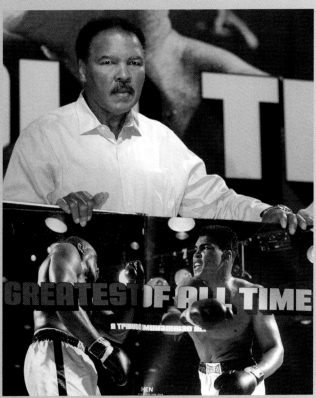

Still a Champion, but at What Cost? Muhammad Ali, one of the greatest heavyweight champion boxers ever, suffers from Parkinson-like symptoms, such as slurred speech, shuffling when walking, expressionless facial appearance, and occasional memory lapses. These symptoms are believed to be caused by the repeated blows to the head suffered by Ali during his boxing career. What cognitive symptoms are associated with this disease?

cognitive disorders Behavioral disturbances that result from transient or permanent damage to the brain.

In the ring, Muhammad Ali was able to "float like a butterfly, sting like a bee" as he won, lost, and twice regained the world heavyweight boxing championship. Outside the ring he was known for his ego, his wit and rapid-fire speech, and his never-ending rhyming. But it was a different Muhammad Ali who, at age fifty-four and retired from boxing, visited Cuba to donate medicine and supplies on behalf of two American relief organizations. His hands trembled and he could barely speak. He tended to shuffle when he walked; he often seemed remote and expressionless, constantly felt tired, and suffered occasional lapses of memory. Ali often spoke through hand signals that were translated by his wife.

Ali's symptoms resemble those of Parkinson's disease, a brain disorder, but his doctors ruled out that possibility. His disorder was diagnosed as Parkinson's syndrome, meaning that he has many symptoms of Parkinson's disease although he does not have the disorder. Ali's symptoms are probably due to some sort of brain trauma. Anti-Parkinson's medication has reduced the severity of some of the symptoms, but the prognosis is vague.

Like many other individuals, Ali suffers from a **cognitive disorder**—behavioral disturbances that result from transient or permanent damage to the brain. DSM-IV-TR (American Psychiatric Association, 2000a) characterizes them as disorders that affect thinking processes, memory, consciousness, perception, and so on and that are caused by brain dysfunction. Psychiatric conditions with associated cognitive symptoms (such as schizophrenia) are not considered in this category or in this chapter. We also discuss mental retardation. Although mental retardation is considered within the DSM-IV-TR category of disorders usually first diagnosed in infancy, childhood, or adolescence, we consider it in this chapter because it deals with cognitive and intellectual functioning. Strictly speaking, however, mental retardation is not considered a cognitive disorder.

DSM-IV-TR classifies cognitive disorders into four major categories: (1) dementia, (2) delirium, (3) amnestic disorders, and (4) cognitive disorders not otherwise specified (see Figure 12.1). DSM-IV-TR also attempts to specify the etiological agent for each disorder.

Possible causes of cognitive disorders include aging, trauma, infection, loss of blood supply, substance abuse, and various biochemical imbalances. These may result in cognitive, emotional, and behavioral symptoms that can resemble the symptoms of the mental disorders (Abeles & Victor, 2003).

The overall prevalence of cognitive disorders as found by the Epidemiologic Catchment Area (ECA) study (George et al., 1991), the largest epidemiological study

303

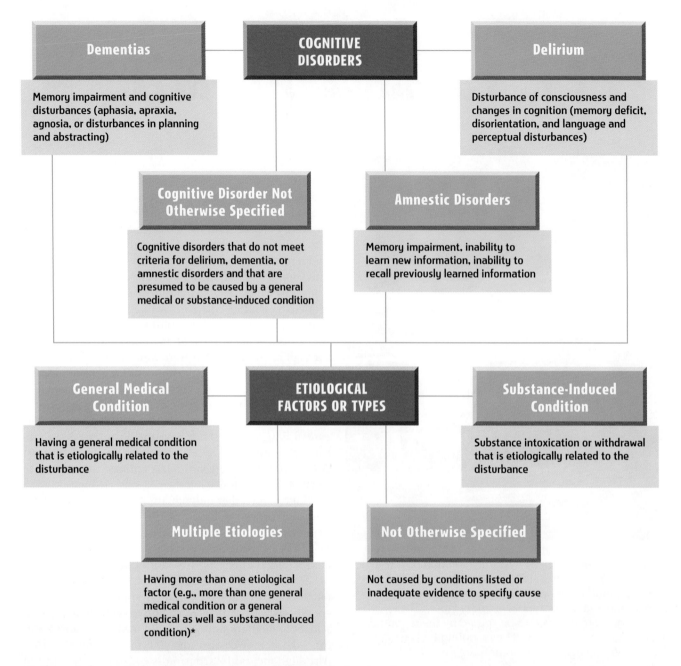

*In the case of amnestic disorders, the category of multiple etiologies is not used.

Figure 12.1 Disorders Chart: Cognitive Disorders   *Source:* Based on American Psychiatric Association (2000a).

conducted in the United States, is about 1 percent for severe disorders and 6 percent for mild disorders. The study also indicated that prevalence increases with age—for example, the severe cognitive impairment rate for persons age seventy-five and older is about twenty-two times higher than that for persons between the ages of eighteen and thirty-four. Gender differences were not meaningful, but one ethnic difference was— African Americans have a higher rate of severe cognitive disorders than is found among either white or Hispanic Americans.

COGNITIVE DISORDERS	Prevalence*	Gender Differences	Age of Onset	Course
Dementia	—	Usually none; depends on type of dementia	Depends on type; usually highest rates found among elderly	Depends on type; onset frequently gradual; may be temporary or progressively deteriorating
Delirium	—	Usually none; depends on type of delirium	Any age; but some variation, depending on type	Develops over hours to days; may persist for weeks; if underlying etiology is promptly corrected or is self-limiting, recovery is more likely to be complete
Amnestic Disorder	—	Usually none; depends on type of disorder	Variable	Variable; depends on type or etiology

*Prevalence for all cognitive disorders in the United States is about 6 percent.

Figure 12.1 **Disorders Chart: Cognitive Disorders (continued)**

Although behavioral disturbance stems from brain pathology, it is influenced by social and psychological factors, as well as by the specific pathology. People with similar types of brain damage may behave quite differently, depending on their premorbid personalities, their coping skills, and the availability of such resources as family support systems. Furthermore, people with cognitive impairments often are treated with insensitivity by other people, so they experience a lot of stress. This stress may add to or modify the symptoms that stem from the disorder.

Thus, physical, social, and psychological factors interact in complicated ways to produce the behaviors of people who have cognitive disorders (Binder, 1988). Treatment, too, often requires some combination of physical, medicinal, and psychological therapy; it may include behavior modification and skills training. For some patients who have severe and irreversible brain damage, the only available options may be rehabilitation, modified skills training, and the creation of a supportive environment.

We discussed the structure of the human brain in the chapter "Abnormal Behavior: Models and Treatments"; here we focus primarily on the types, major causes, and treatment of cognitive disorders.

▶ **CHECKPOINT REVIEW**

cognitive disorder *(p. 303)*

What are cognitive disorders?
- Cognitive disorders are behavioral disturbances that result from transient or permanent damage to the brain. The effects of brain damage vary greatly.
- The most common symptoms include impaired consciousness and memory, impaired judgment, orientation difficulties, and attentional deficits.
- The prevalence of cognitive disorders is about 1 percent for severe disorders and 6 percent for mild disorders.
- The prevalence is much higher among elderly persons than among younger persons.

Types of Cognitive Disorders

Pet Therapy in a Nursing Home   Caring for pets has been found to be beneficial, often reducing the levels of depression and boredom of individuals. Increasingly, in nursing homes and other settings people are allowed to play with and care for pets. Thus, pet therapy can be beneficial to both patients and pets. Why do you think that having pets can be therapeutic for elderly patients?

In each of the four major cognitive disorder categories listed in DSM-IV-TR—dementia, delirium, amnestic disorders, and cognitive disorders not otherwise specified—clinicians categorize the disorder according to its cause. In general, the causes are classified as due to a general medical condition, a substance-induced condition, multiple etiologies, or conditions not otherwise specified. For example, a client may be given the diagnosis of delirium. If the delirium is caused by the use of psychoactive substances, it is considered to be a case of substance-induced delirium. If the type of substance is identified, it is also specified (see Figure 12.1).

In some cases, individuals also have symptoms of other mental disorders (such as a mood, psychotic, or anxiety disorder) in which there is evidence that the disorder is due to a general medical condition. In this case, DSM-IV-TR lists the disorder within a category appropriate for the symptom pattern. For example, a mood disorder due to a general medical condition is classified under mood disorders, and an anxiety disorder due to a general medical condition is found under the category of anxiety disorders. Neither would be diagnosed as a cognitive disorder.

Dementia

Dementia is characterized by memory impairment and cognitive disturbances, such as *aphasia* (language disturbance), *apraxia* (inability to carry out motor activities despite intact comprehension and motor function), *agnosia* (failure to recognize or identify objects despite intact sensory function), or disturbances in planning and abstracting in thought processes. The multiple cognitive deficits are severe enough to hinder social and occupational activities and represent a significant decline from a previous level of functioning. People with dementia may forget to finish tasks, the names of significant others, and past events. (The Mental Health and Society feature, "Aphasia: At a Loss for Words," presents the case of an individual with aphasia.) Some people who exhibit dementia also display impulse control problems. They may, for example, disrobe in public or make sexual advances to strangers. Dementia is characterized by gradual onset and continuing cognitive decline. It should be noted that memory decline in normal aging is distinct from that found in dementia. In age-associated memory impairment, patients experience a gradual loss of memory in daily life activities (e.g., remembering names, misplacing objects, or forgetting phone numbers) but retain intact global intellectual functioning. This normal-aging memory loss does not represent early stages of Alzheimer's disease (Wise, Gray, & Seltzer, 1999).

Dementia can occur for numerous reasons. DSM-IV-TR lists the major etiological categories for dementia as (1) general medical conditions (such as Alzheimer's disease, cerebrovascular disease, Parkinson's disease, brain trauma); (2) substance-induced persisting dementia, in which the symptoms are associated with substance use; (3) multiple etiologies, in which more than one factor has caused the disorder (such as a general medical condition and substance use); and (4) dementia not otherwise specified, in which there is insufficient evidence to establish a specific etiology.

About 1.5 million Americans suffer from severe dementia, and an additional 1 million to 5 million have mild to moderate forms of the disorder (Read, 1991). Although

dementia A syndrome characterized by memory impairment and cognitive disturbances, such as aphasia, apraxia, agnosia, or disturbances in planning or abstraction in thought processes.

Mental Health and Society

Aphasia: At a Loss for Words

The loss of motor or sensory functions that are associated with language is known as aphasia. People who have aphasia and motor disturbances may have trouble expressing themselves via verbal language (speech aphasia), may be unable to recall the names of familiar objects (nominal aphasia), or may have problems in writing words (manual aphasia). Sensory aphasias include the inability to understand spoken words (auditory aphasia) and the inability to understand written words (visual aphasia or alexia). Aphasic problems may be extremely specific. For example, persons with visual aphasia lose the ability to understand written words, although they have no difficulty in reading the words aloud or in understanding spoken words. Thus impairment is manifested in listening, speaking, reading, and writing—although not necessarily to the same extent in each area (Chapey, 1994).

Two primary problems in aphasia are the loss of access to words and their meanings and the inability to retain words and their meanings (Schuell, 1974). Persons with aphasia may become quite emotional and frustrated over their deficits, and this, in turn, can impede efforts at rehabilitation.

The following dialogue illustrates some of the problems involved in aphasia. Albert Harris is a sixty-seven-year-old man who suffered a stroke. In addition to physical therapy

for his partially paralyzed right side, an effort was made to rehabilitate his speech. Mr. Harris was unable to communicate fully and expressed himself almost exclusively with the words "Mrs. Harris," his wife's name.

Psychologist: Hello, Mr. Harris.
Mr. Harris (responding to psychologist): Hello, Mrs. Harris. Hello, Mrs. Harris.
Psychologist: You look pretty cheerful today.
Mr. Harris: Yes, Mrs. Harris. Ah … Ah … Ah [apparently trying to elaborate on his response]. … Yes, Mrs. Harris. Ah … Ah (looking disappointed and frustrated).
Psychologist: I know it's hard to say what you want to say.
Mr. Harris: Yes, Mrs. Harris, yes. Things will get better, Mrs. Harris.
Psychologist: You've already shown improvement, don't you think?
Mr. Harris: Mrs. Harris a little bit better, yes. Slow but sure, Mrs. Harris.

Speech therapy and skills training are frequently used to treat aphasia. Although many patients recover from the problem, the reasons for recovery are not well understood. It is possible that other areas of the brain can be trained to compensate for the damaged areas.

dementia is most often encountered in older people, only a small proportion of them actually develop this syndrome. Among people over age sixty-five, about 5 to 7 percent have dementia (APA Working Group on the Older Adult, 1998), and 2 to 4 percent have dementia of the Alzheimer's type. (Alzheimer's disease is discussed in detail later in this chapter.) Other types of dementia are even less common. The prevalence of dementia increases with age, with a prevalence of over 20 percent or more in people over the age of eighty-five (American Psychiatric Association, 2000a).

Dementia can also occur with delusions, hallucinations, disturbances in perception and communication, and delirium. If these features are predominant, they are noted in the DSM-IV-TR classification.

Dementia is, in fact, associated with a range of disorders. C. E. Wells (1978) analyzed the records of 222 patients who displayed dementia as the primary sign, rather than a secondary sign, of a diagnosed disorder. The disorders associated with dementia included Alzheimer's disease, vascular disease, normal pressure hydrocephalus (the accumulation of an abnormal amount of cerebrospinal fluid in the cranium, which can damage brain tissues), dementia in alcoholics, intracranial masses, and Huntington's disease. These findings have important implications for diagnosis because such problems as depression, drug toxicity, normal pressure hydrocephalus, and benign intracranial masses can be corrected. Identifying noncorrectable causes of dementia is also important because specific therapeutic intervention may reduce or limit symptoms in some cases.

Delirium

Delirium is characterized by disturbance of consciousness and changes in cognition (memory deficit, disorientation, and language and perceptual disturbances). These impairments and changes are not attributable to dementia. The disorder develops rather rapidly over a course of hours or days. The patient often shows a reduced ability to focus, sustain, or shift attention and exhibits disorganized patterns of thinking, as manifested by rambling, irrelevant, or incoherent speech. At times patients show a reduced level of consciousness and disturbances in the cycle of sleep and waking. The following describes a case of a student who was treated for amphetamine-induced delirium:

> An eighteen-year-old high school senior was brought to the emergency room by police after being picked up wandering in traffic on the Triborough Bridge [in New York City]. He was angry, agitated, and aggressive and talked of various people who were deliberately trying to "confuse" him by giving him misleading directions. His story was rambling and disjointed, but he admitted to the police officer that he had been using "speed." In the emergency room he had difficulty focusing his attention and had to ask that questions be repeated. He was disoriented as to time and place and was unable to repeat the names of three objects after five minutes. The family gave a history of the patient's regular use of "pep pills" over the past two years, during which time he was frequently "high" and did very poorly in school. (Spitzer et al., 1994, p. 162)

Among individuals over age sixty-five who are hospitalized for a general medical condition, about 10 percent exhibit delirium on admission (American Psychiatric Association, 2000a). Certain groups of patients are at risk for developing delirium (Wise et al., 1999). They include: the elderly, individuals recovering from surgery, patients with preexisting brain dysfunction (e.g., stroke), patients in the withdrawal phase of drug dependency, patients with AIDS, and those with high illness burden (e.g., burn patients and elderly patients). Obviously, some patients have multiple risk factors, as found in those who are elderly, who have suffered a stroke, and who are recovering from surgery. When people grow older, they have less cerebral reserve and are more likely to develop delirium with medical illness, stress conditions, or surgical procedures (Wise, Hilty, & Cerda, 2001). As in the case of dementia, delirium is classified according to its cause: general medical condition, substance-induced condition, multiple etiologies, and not otherwise specified.

Amnestic Disorders

Amnestic disorders are characterized by memory impairment as manifested by an inability to learn new information and an inability to recall previously learned knowledge or past events. As a result, confusion and disorientation occur. The memory disturbance causes major problems in social or occupational functioning and does not occur exclusively during the course of dementia or delirium. As in the case of dementia and delirium, the etiology is specified. The memory impairment is not the result of a developmental process but rather the result of some insult to the central nervous system (Burke & Bohac, 2001). The most common causes of amnestic disorders include head trauma, stroke, and Wernicke's encephalopathy, which is an alcohol-induced organic mental disorder probably involving thiamine deficiency (Wise et al., 1999).

All three conditions—dementia, delirium, and amnestic disorders—have overlapping symptoms, especially those involving memory deficits. Some important differences distinguish the three, however. In dementia, the patients show not only memory impairment but also such conditions as aphasia, apraxia, or agnosia. In contrast, the memory dysfunctions that occur in delirium happen relatively quickly, unlike those of dementia, in which functioning gradually declines. Individuals with delirium also expe-

delirium A syndrome in which there is disturbance of consciousness and changes in cognition, such as memory deficit, disorientation, and language and perceptual disturbances.

amnestic disorders Disorders characterized by memory impairment as manifested by inability to learn new information and inability to recall previously learned knowledge or past events.

Figure 12.2 **Unique and Overlapping Symptoms in Dementia, Delirium, and Amnestic Disorders** Dementia, delirium, and amnestic disorders share some symptoms. The three overlapping circles show the unique and the overlapping areas. The symptoms that occur in all three include memory disturbance and impaired functioning. Where the circles do not overlap, symptoms are largely unique. For example, aphasia and apraxia are exhibited in dementia but not in delirium or amnestic disorders. Confusion and disorientation are more likely to occur in delirium and amnestic disorders than in dementia.

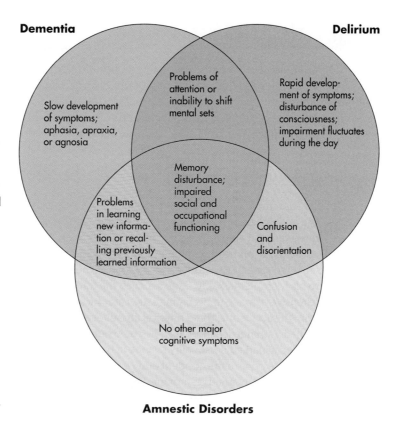

Dementia

Slow development of symptoms; aphasia, apraxia, or agnosia

Problems of attention or inability to shift mental sets

Delirium

Rapid development of symptoms; disturbance of consciousness; impairment fluctuates during the day

Problems in learning new information or recalling previously learned information

Memory disturbance; impaired social and occupational functioning

Confusion and disorientation

No other major cognitive symptoms

Amnestic Disorders

rience an impairment of consciousness. In amnestic disorders, the primary symptom involves memory. Figure 12.2 shows the unique characteristics, as well as the overlap in cognitive symptoms, of the three conditions.

Cognitive disorders that do not meet the criteria for dementia, delirium, or amnestic disorders would be classified as cognitive disorders not otherwise specified.

▶ CHECKPOINT REVIEW

amnestic disorders *(p. 308)*

delirium *(p. 308)*

dementia *(p. 306)*

What are the different types of cognitive disorders?

- DSM-IV-TR lists four major types of cognitive disorders: dementia, delirium, amnestic disorders, and other cognitive disorders.
- In dementia, memory is impaired and cognitive functioning declines, as revealed by aphasia (language disturbance), apraxia (inability to carry out motor activities despite intact comprehension and motor function), agnosia (failure to recognize or identify objects despite intact sensory function), or disturbances in planning, organizing, and abstracting in thought processes.
- Delirium is a condition in which there is an impairment in consciousness with reduced ability to focus, sustain, or shift attention. Changes in cognition (memory deficit, disorientation, and language or perceptual disturbance) are observed, and the disorder develops rather rapidly over a course of hours or days.
- Amnestic disorders are characterized by memory impairment, as manifested by the inability to learn new information and the inability to recall previously learned knowledge or past events.
- Cognitive impairments that do not meet the criteria for the other three are classified as other cognitive disorders.

Cognitive disorders can be caused by many different factors, and the same factor can result in dementia, delirium, or amnestic disorder. The sources of cognitive disorders discussed here are brain trauma; processes associated with aging, disease, and infection; tumors; epilepsy; and psychoactive substance-induced disorders. Toxic substances, malnutrition, and even brain surgery may also produce cognitive disorders.

Brain Trauma

> On September 13, 1848, at Cavendish, Vermont, Phineas Gage was working as foreman of a railroad excavation crew. A premature explosion of a blast sent a tamping iron—a three-foot rod about an inch in diameter—through the lower side of Gage's face and out of the top of his head. Exhibiting some convulsions and bleeding profusely, Gage soon regained speech. He was taken to his hotel, where he walked up a flight of stairs to get to his room. Remarkably, Gage survived the trauma, even though there must have been extensive damage to his brain tissue. Later, he appeared to have completely recovered from the accident with no physical aftereffects. However, Gage began to complain that he had a strange feeling, which he could not describe. Soon, his employers and others noticed a marked personality change in him. Although he had been a very capable employee prior to the accident and was known for his affable disposition, Gage now became moody, irritable, profane, impatient, and obstinate. So radically changed was Gage that his friends said that he was "no longer Gage." (Adapted from Harlow, 1868)

A **brain trauma** is a physical wound or injury to the brain, as in the case of Phineas Gage. Each year, an estimated 1.9 million Americans experience a traumatic injury to the brain (Schalock, 1998). The severity, duration, and symptoms may differ widely, depending on the person's premorbid personality and on the extent and location of the neural damage. Generally, the greater the tissue damage, the more impaired the functioning. In some cases, however, interactions among various parts of the brain, coupled with brain redundancy, in which different parts of the brain can control a specific function, may compensate for some loss of tissue.

Head injuries are usually classified as concussions, contusions, or lacerations. A *concussion* is a mild brain injury, typically caused by a blow to the head. Blood vessels in the brain are often ruptured, and circulatory and other brain functions may be disrupted temporarily. The person may become dazed or even lose consciousness and, on regaining consciousness, may experience postconcussion headaches, disorientation, confusion, and memory loss. The symptoms are usually temporary, lasting no longer than a few weeks. In some cases, symptoms may persist for months or years, for unknown reasons, without neurological signs of impairment (Binder, 1986).

In a *contusion*, the brain is forced to shift slightly and press against the side of the skull. The cortex of the brain may be bruised (that is, blood vessels may rupture) on impact with the skull. As in concussion, the person may lose consciousness for a few hours or even for days. Postcontusion symptoms often include headaches, nausea, an inability to concentrate, and irritability. Although the symptoms are similar to those of concussion, they are generally more severe and last longer.

> Thirteen-year-old Ron G. was a catcher for his school baseball team. During a game, a player on the other team lost his grip on the bat as he swung at a pitch, and the bat hit Ron on the forehead. Although his catcher's mask absorbed some of the force, the blow knocked Ron out. An hour elapsed before he regained consciousness at a nearby hospital, where he was diagnosed as having a cerebral contusion. Headaches, muscle weakness, and nausea continued for two weeks.

brain trauma A physical wound or injury to the brain.

Danger Just a Tumble Away   More than 8 million Americans suffer head injuries each year, such as concussions, contusions, and lacerations. In order to reduce the risk of head injuries, individuals are well advised to wear helmets while skateboarding, rollerblading, and bicycling. If you engage in these activities, do you wear a helmet?

Lacerations are brain traumas in which brain tissue is torn, pierced, or ruptured, usually by an object that has penetrated the skull. When an object also penetrates the brain, death may result. If the person survives and regains consciousness, a variety of temporary or permanent effects may be observed. Symptoms may be quite serious, depending on the extent of damage to the brain tissue and on the amount of hemorrhaging. Cognitive processes are frequently impaired, and the personality may change.

More than eight million Americans suffer head injuries each year, and about 20 percent of these result in serious brain trauma. The majority show deficits in attention and poor concentration, are easily fatigued, and tend to be irritable. Brain injuries are often sustained by abused women, and cognitive functioning is affected (Valera & Berenbaum, 2003). Personality characteristics may undergo change in the areas of motivation, subjective emotional experiences, or emotional expressions (Stuss, Gow, & Hetherington, 1992). One study examined twenty-three patients with severe traumatic brain injuries (seventeen closed-head injuries, three penetrating missile wounds, two cerebral contusions, and one brainstem contusion) who had spent an average of twenty days in coma. Every one displayed a distress syndrome characterized by depression, anxiety, tension, and nervousness—yet they all denied having these feelings (Sbordone & Jennison, 1983). It is, in fact, common for patients with severe traumatic injuries to deny emotional reactions and physical dysfunctions until they begin to recover from their injuries.

Closed-head injuries are the most common form of brain trauma and the most common reason that physicians refer patients younger than age forty to neurologists (Golden et al., 1983). They usually result from a blow that causes damage at the site of the impact and at the opposite side of the head. If the victim's head was in motion before the impact (as is generally the case in automobile accidents), the blow produces a forward-and-back movement of the brain, accompanied by tearing and hemorrhaging of brain tissue. Epilepsy develops in about 5 percent of closed-head injuries and in more than 30 percent of open-head injuries in which the brain tissue is penetrated. Damage to brain tissues in the left hemisphere often results in intellectual disorders, and affective problems more frequently result from damage to brain tissues in the right hemisphere.

Severe brain trauma has long-term negative consequences. Many young adults who are comatose for at least twenty-four hours later experience residual cognitive deficits that interfere with employment and psychosocial adjustment. Recovery from the trauma often does not ensure a return to the victim's premorbid level of functioning. Along with any physical or mental disabilities produced by the brain damage, motivational and emotional disturbances result from the frustration of coping with these physical or mental deficits. As a consequence, only one-third of patients with severe closed-head injuries can return to gainful employment after traditional rehabilitative therapy (Prigatano et al., 1984).

Aging and Disorders Associated with Aging

Before discussing the cognitive disorders often associated with aging, it seems appropriate to describe the nature of the older population. A growing proportion of the U.S. population, as well as that of the world, is sixty-five years of age or older (Powell & Whitla, 1994). This group, which numbered only 3.1 million in 1900, has increased more than tenfold, to 34.7 million, in the U.S. population (Takamura, 1998). By 2030, one of every five Americans will be sixty-five years or older (APA Working Group on the Older Adult, 1998). The increase is attributable both to longer life expectancy and to the relatively large numbers of people from the "baby-boom" generation who were born in the 1940s and who will be elderly by 2010.

The cognitive disorders most common among the elderly are strokes, Alzheimer's disease, and memory loss. These conditions are correlated with aging, but they also occur among younger people. Unfortunately, the elderly are less likely than younger individuals to seek help from mental health professionals (Clarkin & Levy, 2004). Because assessment of the cognitive functioning of the older adult has taken on increased importance, there have been calls to establish practical guidelines for this assessment (Baker, Lichtenberg, & Moye, 1998).

Cerebrovascular Accidents or Strokes   Although the brain represents only 2 percent of the body's weight, it requires 15 percent of the blood flow and 20 percent of the oxygen (Oliver et al., 1982). A *stroke* or **cerebrovascular accident** is a sudden stoppage of blood flow to a portion of the brain, leading to a loss of brain function. Stroke risk factors include hypertension, heart disease, cigarette smoking, diabetes mellitus, and excessive alcohol consumption. Vascular problems are the second leading cause of dementia, right behind Alzheimer's disease (Wise et al., 1999).

Strokes are the third major cause of death in the United States, afflicting more than 400,000 persons annually. Only about 50 to 60 percent of stroke victims survive, and they generally require long-term care while suffering from a variety of mental and sensory-motor disabilities (Oliver et al., 1982). Stroke victims are often frustrated and depressed by their handicaps, and they show greater depression and interpersonal sensitivity than other groups of patients. At least one-fourth of stroke victims appear to develop major depression (Conn, 1991), which in many cases tends to deepen with time (Magni & Schifano, 1984). Their depression, pessimism, and anxiety about their disabilities occasionally leads to further disability (Burruss, Travella, & Robinson, 2001).

The bursting of blood vessels (and the attendant intercranial hemorrhaging) causes 25 percent of all strokes and often occurs during exertion. Victims report feeling that something is wrong within the head, along with headaches and nausea. Confusion, paralysis, and loss of consciousness follow rapidly. Mortality rates for this type of stroke are extremely high.

cerebrovascular accident A sudden stoppage of blood flow to a portion of the brain, leading to a loss of brain function; also called *stroke*.

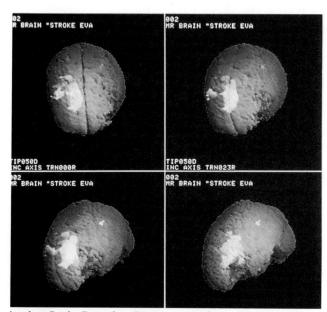

Losing Brain Function Due to a Stroke A stroke is a condition in which brain functioning is lost because blood flow to an area of the brain slows or stops. This stoppage is caused by burst or obstructed blood vessels. Shown are three-dimensional images of a brain stroke from four different angles.

Strokes may also be caused by the narrowing of blood vessels owing to a buildup of fatty material on interior walls *(atherosclerosis)* or by the blockage of blood vessels. In either case, the result is **cerebral infarction,** the death of brain tissue from a decrease in the supply of blood. These strokes often occur during sleep, and the person is paralyzed when he or she awakens. Approximately 20 percent die, 20 percent exhibit full to nearly full recovery, and 60 percent suffer residual disabilities (Lishman, 1978).

The residual loss of function after a stroke usually involves only one side of the body, most often the left. Interestingly, one residual symptom of stroke is a "lack of acknowledgment" of various stimuli on one side of the body. For example, a patient who is asked to copy a pattern may draw only half the pattern and may ignore the left side of his or her body (Golden et al., 1983).

Some functional reorganization of the brain may occur after a stroke to compensate for the loss of function. Three months after suffering a stroke owing to cerebral infarction, one patient showed significantly reduced cerebral blood flow in one area. An examination performed one year later showed no abnormalities. The pattern of blood flow, however, suggested increased activation in brain areas surrounding the affected area. It is possible that the patient's clinical improvement was due to brain reorganization, in which the function of the destroyed area was taken over by other areas.

A series of infarctions may lead to a syndrome known as **vascular dementia,** which is characterized by the uneven deterioration of intellectual abilities (although some mental functions may remain intact). The specific symptoms of this disruption depend on the area and extent of the brain damage. Both physical and intellectual functioning are usually impaired. The patient may show gradual improvement in intellectual functioning, but repeated episodes of infarction can occur, producing additional disability.

Memory Loss in Older People Memory loss occurs for a variety of reasons. It is one of the most obvious symptoms of Alzheimer's disease, which we discuss in depth in the next section. Memory loss may be part of a severe loss of intellectual functioning produced by brain cell deterioration as a result of aging, usually after age seventy-five. Research indicates, however, that age-related decreases in certain cognitive functions can be mitigated in cognitively active persons, such as professors, who maintain intellectual activities (Shimamura et al., 1995). Loss of memory may also be shown by elderly people suffering vascular dementia. And finally, occasional loss of memory, as well as an overall slowing of the speed of mental processing, is part of the normal aging process (Bashore, Ridderinkhof, & Van der Molen, 1997) and is not indicative of dementia (Wise et al., 1999).

Losing cognitive and mental capabilities is the symptom of aging most feared by elderly people. One eighty-two-year-old man commented, "It's not the physical decline I fear so much. It's becoming a mental vegetable inside of a healthy body. It is a shame that we can rehabilitate or treat so much of the physical ills, but when your mind goes, there's nothing you can do" (Gatz, Smyer, & Lawton, 1980, p. 12). It should be noted that, in general, reports of intellectual decline in aging have been exaggerated. Although tests of intellectual functioning indicate that performance abilities generally start to decline with advancing age, verbal fluency and cognitive skills are relatively

cerebral infarction The death of brain tissue resulting from a decrease in the supply of blood serving that tissue.

vascular dementia Dementia characterized by uneven deterioration of intellectual abilities and resulting from a number of cerebral infarctions.

Aging Well   The proportion of elderly individuals in the U.S. population is growing rapidly. Increasingly, older Americans are staying healthy and active longer than previous generations did. These women are receiving awards for their performances at the U.S. Senior Olympics in Baton Rouge, Louisiana. What skills are maintained or enhanced and what skills decline as a function of aging?

stable over time. Intellectual performance on knowledge acquired over the course of the socialization process is fairly stable, whereas fluid abilities (those abilities involving solutions to novel problems or requiring creativity) tend to decline with age (Poon & Siegler, 1991). Ivnik and colleagues (1995) have also found that stability depends on the particular cognitive ability being examined. About 75 percent of older people retain sharp mental functioning, and an additional 10 to 15 percent experience only mild to moderate memory loss (Butler, 1984). Although the structures and biochemistry of the brain are affected in that brain cells and cerebral blood flow are reduced, many researchers nevertheless now believe that the extent of brain atrophy has been overestimated (Duckett, 1991).

Alzheimer's Disease

The disorder perhaps most often associated with aging is **Alzheimer's disease,** in which brain tissue atrophies, leading to marked deterioration of intellectual and emotional functioning. It is one of the most prevalent forms of dementia, accounting for almost 80 percent of dementia in older persons (Teri & Wagner, 1992). The risk for the disease increases with age. The incidence (new cases) each year is 0.6 percent for ages sixty-five to sixty-nine, 1 percent for ages seventy to seventy-four, 2 percent for ages seventy-five to seventy-nine, 3.3 percent for ages eighty to eighty-four, and 8.4 percent for ages eighty-five and older (Wise et al., 1999). About 4 million Americans suffer from the disease (Nash, 1997). The disease affects about 8 to 15 percent of those above the age of sixty-five (DHHS, 1999). We have become increasingly aware of the disease because public figures such as former president Ronald Reagan have candidly discussed their condition.

Characteristics of Alzheimer's Disease   As noted, patients with Alzheimer's disease show marked deterioration of intellectual and emotional functioning. Early symptoms—memory dysfunction, irritability, and cognitive impairment—gradually worsen, and other symptoms, such as social withdrawal, depression, apathy, delusions, impulsive behaviors, and neglect of personal hygiene may eventually appear. At present, no curative or disease-reversing interventions exist for Alzheimer's disease (Rivas-Vazquez, 2001). Death usually occurs within five years of the onset of the disorder, which is the fourth leading cause of death in the United States (Francis & Bowen, 1994).

Alzheimer's disease A dementia in which brain tissue atrophies, leading to marked deterioration of intellectual and emotional functioning.

Elizabeth R., a forty-six-year-old woman diagnosed as suffering from Alzheimer's disease, is trying to cope with her increasing problems with memory. She writes notes to herself and tries to compensate for her difficulties by rehearsing conversations with herself, anticipating what might be said. However, she is gradually losing the battle and has had to retire from her job. She quickly forgets what she has just read, and she loses the

The Tragedy of Alzheimer's Disease   Jack Guren, an Alzheimer's patient living in a nursing home, is being visited by his son Peter. Alzheimer's disease is responsible for most cases of dementia among the elderly. Dementia is characterized by multiple and severe cognitive deficits, especially impairment of memory. Is Alzheimer's disease hereditary?

meaning of an article after reading only a few sentences. She sometimes has to ask where the bathroom is in her own house and is depressed by the realization that she is a burden to her family. (Clark et al., 1984, p. 60)

The deterioration of memory seems to be the most poignant and disturbing symptom for those who have Alzheimer's disease. They may at first forget appointments, phone numbers, and addresses. As the disorder progresses, they may lose track of the time of day, have trouble remembering recent and past events, and forget who they are (Reisberg, Ferris, & Crook, 1982). But even when memory is almost gone, contact with loved ones is still important.

> I believe the emotional memory of relationships is the last to go. You can see daughters or sons come to visit, for example, and the mother will respond. She doesn't know who they are, but you can tell by her expression that she knows they're persons to whom she is devoted. (Materka, 1984, p. 13)

Alzheimer's Disease and the Brain   Persons with this disease have an atrophy of cortical tissue within the brain. Autopsies performed on the brains of Alzheimer's victims reveal *neurofibrillary tangles* (abnormal fibers that appear to be tangles of brain tissue filaments) and *senile plaques* (patches of degenerated nerve endings). Both conditions are believed to disrupt the transmission of impulses among brain cells, thereby producing the symptoms of the disorder. Alzheimer's disease is generally considered a disease of the elderly, and its incidence does increase with increasing age. However, it also can attack people in their forties or fifties. It occurs more frequently in women.

Etiology of Alzheimer's Disease The etiology of Alzheimer's disease is unknown, although it is thought to be a product of hereditary and environmental factors (Hendrie, 2001). Many different explanations have been proposed. They include reduced levels of the neurotransmitter acetylcholine in the brain; repeated head injuries; infections and viruses; decreased blood flow in the brain; and the effect of plaques and tangles in disrupting cellular metabolism or in reducing glucose absorption from the bloodstream (Nash, 1997; Read, 1991). Some researchers believe that aluminum is the primary cause, because high concentrations of the substance have been found in the brains of Alzheimer's patients, because increased concentration of aluminum in drinking water is associated with higher incidence of the disease, and because aluminum has been experimentally found to pass through the blood-brain barrier, resulting in severe impairment of nerve cells (Yumoto et al., 1995). For a subgroup, heredity appears to be important. Approximately 50 percent of individuals with a family history of the disease, if followed into their eighties and nineties, develop the disease (DHHS, 1999). The gene that appears to be responsible for senile plaques and neurofibrillary tangles found in Alzheimer's disease is located on chromosome 21 (Clarke & Clarke, 1987). Furthermore, early-onset cases of Alzheimer's disease—those that occur before age sixty-five—may be caused by genetic anomalies (Mullan & Brown, 1994).

Although abnormalities are found in the brains of affected individuals, it is not clear whether the abnormalities are the cause, the effect, or an accompanying condition of Alzheimer's disease. Snowden and his colleagues (1997) studied two groups of individuals: those with and without neurofibrillary tangles and senile plaques. Presumably, those with the tangles and plaques met the neuropathological criteria for Alzheimer's disease. The investigators found that among individuals having Alzheimer's disease, those who also suffered brain infarcts exhibited poorer cognitive functioning and a higher prevalence of dementia than those without brain infarcts. However, individuals who suffered brain infarcts but did not have Alzheimer's disease exhibited better cognitive functioning than those suffering from both infarcts and Alzheimer's disease. The findings point to the possible interaction of other conditions with Alzheimer's disease in producing cognitive deficits.

Several protective factors have been identified that may delay the onset of Alzheimer's disease. These include genetic endowment with the ApoE-e2 allele, which decreases the risk for the disease; higher education; use of nonsteroidal anti-inflammatory drugs or estrogen replacement therapy; and taking vitamin E. The reasons why these factors may provide protection are unclear, but they may reduce the deleterious action of oxidative stress (via antioxidants such as vitamin E or estrogen) or the action of inflammatory mediators associated with plaque formation (DHHS, 1999).

Other Diseases and Conditions of the Brain

A wide variety of other diseases and conditions of the brain are considered cognitive disorders or have effects on cognitive functioning. They include:

1. Parkinson's disease—a progressively worsening disorder characterized by muscle tremors; a stiff, shuffling gait; a lack of facial expression; social withdrawal; and, in some cases, dementia and depression. In some persons, the disorder stems from causes such as infections of the brain, cerebrovascular disorders, brain trauma, and poisoning with carbon monoxide; in other persons, no specific origin can be determined.

2. AIDS (Acquired Immunodeficiency Syndrome)—the AIDS virus may reach the brain or a compromised immune system may allow infections that affect cognitive functioning.

3. Encephalitis—a brain inflammation caused by a viral infection.

On the Physical Trail of Alzheimer's The diseased brain tissue from an Alzheimer's patient shows senile plaques (patches of degenerated nerve endings) located in the gray matter. Some researchers believe that the plaques may interfere with transmission of nerve impulses in the brain, thereby causing the disease's symptoms.

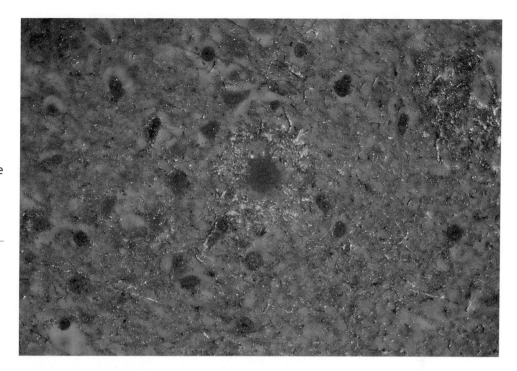

4. Epilepsy—a disorder characterized by intermittent and brief periods of altered consciousness often accompanied by seizures or excessive electrical discharge from brain cells.

Thus cognitive disorders can be caused by a number of different factors.

▶ CHECKPOINT REVIEW

Alzheimer's disease *(p. 314)*

brain trauma *(p. 310)*

cerebral infarction *(p. 313)*

cerebrovascular accident *(p. 312)*

vascular dementia *(p. 313)*

Why do people develop cognitive disorders?

■ Many different agents can cause cognitive disorders; among these are physical wounds or injuries to the brain, processes of aging, diseases that destroy brain tissue (such as Alzheimer's disease), and brain tumors.

■ Toxic substances, malnutrition, epilepsy, and even brain surgery may also produce cognitive disorders.

▶ Treatment Considerations

Because cognitive disorders can be caused by many different factors and are associated with different symptoms and dysfunctions, treatment approaches have varied widely. The major interventions have been surgical, medical, psychological, and environmental. Most treatment programs are comprehensive in nature, providing patients with medication, rehabilitation, therapy, and environmental modifications (see Cohen & Weiner, 1994). Neuropsychologists are often asked to provide assessment of the cognitive problems and determine longitudinal progress of patients (Nelson & Adams, 1997). Surgical procedures may be used to remove cerebral tumors, relieve the pressure caused by tumors, or restore ruptured blood vessels. Psychotherapy may help patients deal with the emotional aspects of these disorders. And some patients who have lost motor skills can be retrained to compensate for their deficiencies or can be retaught these skills. Sometimes, patients with cognitive disorders need complete hospital care. We examine the use of medication and cognitive and behavioral approaches in more detail.

Medication

Drugs can prevent, control, or reduce the symptoms of brain disorders, as L-dopa does in Parkinson's disease. Medication is of the most benefit in controlling some symptoms of cognitive disorders. For example, more than 50 percent of the people with epilepsy can control their seizures with medication such as Dilantin; another 30 percent can reduce the frequency of seizures. However, side effects can occur, such as a decrease in the speed of motor responding, tremors, weight gain, and swollen gums (Dodrill & Matthews, 1992; Hauser, 1994). Only 20 percent of patients with epilepsy fail to improve on the medications (Epilepsy Foundation of America, 1983).

Sometimes medication is used to control emotional problems that may accompany cognitive impairment. Antidepressant drugs, for example, can alleviate the depression found in many patients with Alzheimer's disease (Teri & Wagner, 1992). Alzheimer's disease has also been treated using acetylcholinesterase inhibitors that increase the availability of acetylcholine in the synaptic clefts of the brain (DHHS, 1999). Interestingly, the regular use of some anti-inflammatory medications such as ibuprofen may cut the risk of developing the disease by as much as one-half (Nash, 1997). The goals of current treatment approaches have been to delay the onset of symptoms, slow the progression of the disease, improve symptoms and reduce disease morbidity, modify risk factors, and prevent the disease (Masterman & Cummings, 2001).

Cognitive and Behavioral Approaches

The cognitive therapeutic approaches also appear to be particularly promising. Memory-improvement techniques and other strategies have been used (Schalock, 1998). Researchers have hypothesized, for example, that the impaired attention and concentration shown by head-injured people result from the disruption of private speech, which regulates behavior and thought processes (Luria, 1982). One therapeutic program uses self-instructional training to enhance the self-regulation of speech and behavior (Webster & Scott, 1983). The program was used to treat a twenty-four-year-old construction worker who had been in a coma for four days as a result of a car accident. Tests showed him to have poor recall, poor concentration, and attentional difficulties; he couldn't concentrate on any task for a long period of time. He also complained that intrusive nonsexual thoughts kept him from maintaining an erection during intercourse. The patient was told to repeat the following self-instructions aloud before doing anything:

1. "To really concentrate, I must look at the person speaking to me."
2. "I also must focus on what is being said, not on other thoughts which want to intrude."
3. "I must concentrate on what I am hearing at any moment by repeating each word in my head as the person speaks."
4. "Although it is not horrible if I lose track of conversation, I must tell the person to repeat the information if I have not attended to it." (Webster & Scott, 1983, p. 71)

After he had learned to use these vocalized instructions, rephrased in his own words, he was taught to repeat them subvocally before each task. His concentration and attention soon improved greatly, and he returned to his former job. He also successfully blocked intrusive thoughts during sexual intercourse by focusing on his partner.

Help For People Who Experience Memory Problems
Memory loss can be extremely frustrating. Affected individuals may require constant attention and aid from others in locating items. With labels, those with memory problems are able to function more independently. What other strategies can be used to assist those with memory difficulties?

Such self-vocalizations often increase a person's effectiveness at the task at hand (Kohlenberg & Tsai, 1991).

A similar program was developed to eliminate the anger response that brain-injured people sometimes display, either as a result of the brain damage or in reaction to their deficits. One twenty-two-year-old patient had suffered a severe head trauma in a motorcycle accident at age sixteen. After two months of intensive medical treatment, he had returned home to live with his parents. There he showed outbursts of anger toward people and objects, a low frustration level, and impulsiveness. These behaviors led to many failures in a vocational rehabilitation program. Medication did not help control his outbursts.

A stress inoculation program was developed for this patient. Twelve 30-minute sessions, spread over three weeks, focused on the following areas:

1. *Cognitive preparation* The function and appropriateness of anger were explained, as were alternatives to being destructive. The situations that produced anger were identified, and appropriate responses were demonstrated.

2. *Skills acquisition* The patient was taught to stop himself from becoming angry, to reevaluate anger-evoking situations, and to use self-verbalizations that were incompatible with the expression of anger.

3. *Application training* A hierarchy of situations evoking anger was developed. The patient role-played and practiced the use of cognitive and behavioral skills to cope with progressively greater anger-evoking stimuli. He also used these techniques in the hospital setting and received feedback about his performance.

Before treatment, the patient had averaged about three outbursts each week. No outbursts at all were recorded immediately after treatment, and a follow-up five months later indicated that the gain had been maintained. He found a part-time job as a clerk and was living independently.

In an early seizure-prevention program using classical conditioning (Efron, 1956, 1957), one woman who suffered from tonic-clonic seizures learned to prevent the occurrence of the tonic (body extended and stiff) and clonic (rapid alternation of muscle contraction and relaxation) phases by sniffing an unpleasant odor during the initial stage of an attack. Researchers first presented the odor to the woman while she stared at a bracelet, then paired the smell with the bracelet over a period of several days. At that point, the bracelet alone was enough to elicit thoughts of the unpleasant odor, and the patient could stop a seizure by staring at it when she felt an attack starting. Eventually she could cut an attack short by just thinking about the bracelet. Other behavior modification and biofeedback techniques have also been helpful in reducing seizure activity (Devinsky, 1994).

Environmental Interventions and Caregiver Support

The effects of many cognitive disorders are largely irreversible. This raises the issue of how family and friends can assist those with cognitive disorders. There are a variety of means by which people with these disorders may be helped to live comfortably and with dignity while making use of those abilities that remain. The following interventions have been proposed by Butler (1984):

1. To preserve the patient's sense of independence and control over his or her life, the environment must be modified to make it safer. Rails can be installed to allow the patient to move freely in the house. A chair that is easy to get into and out of, a remote-control device for the television set, and guard rails for the bathtub will help the patient do things for himself or herself. The patient should be encouraged to make as many personal decisions as possible—to choose which clothing to wear and which activities to take part in—even if the choices are not always perfect.

2. Continued social contacts are important, but visits by friends and relatives should be kept short so that the patient does not feel pressured to continue the social interaction. Visits should not involve large groups of individuals, which could overwhelm the patient.

3. Diversions, such as going out for a walk, are important. It is better to stroll through a calm and peaceful area than to visit a crowded shopping mall, where the environment tends to be unpredictable.

4. Tasks should be assigned to the patient to increase his or her sense of self-worth. These tasks may not be completed to perfection, but they will provide a very important sense of having contributed. In addition, older people can be taught to use memory aids and other strategies to facilitate remembering.

The family and friends who provide care may, themselves, need support. They often feel overwhelmed, helpless, frustrated, anxious, or even angry at having to take care of someone with a cognitive impairment. They may worry about how to take proper care of a loved one who has a cognitive disorder or feel guilty if the loved one is injured or deteriorates under their care. Role relationships may change, as the child becomes the primary caregiver for a parent with a disability (Feldman, Mosbach, et al., 1994). In all of these circumstances, caregivers should learn as much as possible about the disorder and the means of taking care of loved ones, realize that the role of a caregiver is stressful, and seek out personal support (such as through self-help groups composed of other caregivers).

▷ CHECKPOINT REVIEW

What kinds of interventions can be used to treat people with cognitive disorders?
- Treatment strategies include corrective surgery and cognitive and behavioral training. Medication is often used, either alone or with other therapies, to decrease or control the symptoms of the various cognitive disorders.
- Caregivers can learn to provide assistance to loved ones with cognitive disorders.

◁ Mental Retardation

A teenager with **mental retardation** told his fellow students, during a high school assembly, how he felt about his handicap:

> My name is Tim Frederick.... I would like to tell you what it is like to be retarded.... I am doing this so that you might be able to understand people like me. I do chores at home. I have to take care of all the animals—twelve chickens, three cats, a dog, three goldfish, and a horse. That's a lot of mouths to feed.... After I graduate from school, I hope to live in an apartment.... The hardest thing is when people make fun of me. I went to a dance a few weeks ago, and no girl would dance with me. Can you guys imagine how you would feel if that happened to you? Well, I feel the same way. (Smith, 1988, pp. 118–119)

mental retardation Significant subaverage general intellectual functioning accompanied by deficiencies in adaptive behavior, with onset before age eighteen.

Table 12.1   Mental Retardation: Prevalence, Onset, and Course

Disorder	Prevalence	Gender Differences	Age of Onset	Course
Mental retardation	1 to 3%	1.5 to 1 (male to female)	Before age eighteen; precise age of onset depends on etiology and severity	Depends on severity; with appropriate training, many individuals learn good adaptive skills

Source: Based on American Psychiatric Association (2000a).

The perception of mental retardation, formerly considered a hopeless condition that required institutionalization, is undergoing a fundamental change. Tim Frederick's mother was told that her son's development would be delayed and that he might never be able to walk or talk. We now know that the effects of mental retardation are variable and that with training, even people with severe retardation can make intellectual and social gains (see Table 12.1).

The Association for Retarded Citizens, an advocacy organization, has estimated that 75 percent of children with mental retardation can become completely self-supporting adults if given appropriate education and training. Another 10 to 15 percent have the potential to be self-supporting. The challenge is to develop appropriate programs to ensure the greatest success. The movement away from institutionalization will continue to increase contact between people with mental retardation and the general population. In 1967, more than 200,000 people with mental retardation lived in public institutions. By 1984, this number had decreased to 110,000 (Landesman & Butterfield, 1987). It is now widely accepted that these people should have the opportunity to live, work, learn, and develop relationships with the general population in integrated settings. People are beginning to question assumptions about what individuals with mental retardation can do. A dance troupe called "Images in Motion," composed of individuals with IQ scores between 30 and 60, has won rave reviews (Walker, 1991). The next frontier will be fuller integration of people into the social fabric (Wolfensberger, 1988).

Diagnosing Mental Retardation

About 7 million or more persons in the United States have IQ scores of about 70 or less (Madle, 1990). Prevalence figures for the United States are 1–3 percent, depending primarily on the definition of adaptive functioning (Popper & West, 1999). As mentioned earlier, mental retardation is categorized by DSM-IV-TR as one of the disorders usually first diagnosed in infancy, childhood, or adolescence. It is not considered a cognitive disorder, although we have included it in this chapter simply because mental retardation affects cognitive functioning. The definition of mental retardation in DSM-IV-TR includes the following criteria:

1. *Significant subaverage general intellectual functioning* (ordinarily interpreted as an IQ score of 70 or less on an individually administered IQ test).

2. *Concurrent deficiencies in adaptive behavior* (social and daily living skills, degree of independence lower than would be expected by age or cultural group).

3. *Onset before age eighteen* (subaverage intellectual functioning arising after age eighteen is typically categorized as dementia).

Table 12.2 Alternative Explanations for Lower Performance by African Americans on IQ Tests

Disadvantage/Oppression Explanations

Legacy of slavery

Teacher racism/prejudice

Inadequate schools
- Lack of funds, resources
- Lack of parental involvement

Inadequate home environment
- Poverty
- Lack of opportunities to learn
- Deficient mother-child interactions
- Lack of parental support
- Lack of academic role models

Cultural Difference Explanations

Cultural bias in tests
- Lack of African Americans in standardization samples
- Preference for "dynamic" vs. "static" testing
- Item loading on white middle-class culture
- Different race of the examiner from test taker
- Lack of "test-wiseness"

Afrocentric home/Eurocentric school mismatch
- Active opposition to "white" cultural values
- Lack of cultural competence in teachers
- Lack of multicultural curricula
- Preference for cooperative vs. competitive learning
- Preference for African American English vs. standard English
- African American behavioral/learning style

Psychological Maladjustment Explanations

Expectancy of failure due to low teacher expectations

Low self-esteem (negative self-concept)
- Caused by segregation from whites
- Caused by integration with whites

Lack of motivation to achieve

Test/performance anxiety

Learned helplessness

Negative peer pressure (burden of acting white)

Source: Adapted from Frisby (1995).

Common characteristics that accompany mental retardation are dependency, passivity, low self-esteem, low tolerance of frustration, depression, and self-injurious behavior (American Psychiatric Association, 2000a). Relative to the general population, persons with mental retardation are much more likely to suffer from psychiatric problems (Dykens & Hodapp, 1997). The more severe levels of mental retardation are associated with speech difficulties, neurological disorders, cerebral palsy, and vision and hearing problems (McQueen et al., 1987). Individuals with autism may also exhibit cognitive deficits, but mental retardation has been distinguished from autism on various mental and perceptual tasks (Shulman, Yirmiya, & Greenbaum, 1995).

Issues Involved in Diagnosing Mental Retardation Arguments have been raised against the use of IQ scores to determine mental retardation, especially among members of ethnic minority groups. The validity of IQ scores is questionable, especially when they are used to test members of minority groups. This controversy resurfaced with the publication of *The Bell Curve* (Herrnstein & Murray, 1994), which attributes African Americans' poorer performance on IQ tests to genetic factors. Frisby (1995), however, points out that alternative explanations for IQ performance can be made (see Table 12.2). IQ tests also may measure familiarity with mainstream middle-class culture, not intelligence. Jane Mercer (1988) argued that the IQ test has been inappropriately used and that it is unfair to attempt to "measure" intelligence by using items drawn from one culture to test individuals from a different cultural group. In addition,

Table 12.3   Estimated Number of Mentally Retarded People by Level of Retardation

Level	Range of Wechsler IQ	Percentage of All Mentally Retarded	Number
Mild	50–70	85	7,926,000
Moderate	35–49	10	933,000
Severe	20–34	3–4	326,700
Profound	0–19	1–2	140,000

Note: Estimates based on percentages from the American Psychiatric Association (2000a) and applied to the normal probability distribution of intelligence based on a U.S. population of 274 million.

IQ tests do not acknowledge the positive coping characteristics of persons from various ethnic minority groups.

In a 1979 ruling in the *Larry P. v. Riles* case, Judge Robert Peckham of the Federal District Court for the Northern District of California held that IQ tests were culturally biased and were not to be used in decisions regarding the placement of African Americans in classes for children with mental retardation. He broadened his decision in 1986 by saying that IQ tests could not be used—even with parental consent—to determine the educational needs of African American children as part of a comprehensive educational program. His decision was challenged by the mother of an African American child who requested IQ testing. She argued that this was a case of reverse discrimination, as IQ tests can be administered for special education services to European Americans, Hispanic Americans, Asian Americans, and American Indians. On September 1, 1992, Judge Peckham reversed his 1986 ruling. IQ tests can again be used with African American children as part of a special education assessment. However, the 1979 ruling still holds. They cannot be used to place African American children in classes for those with mental retardation.

Levels of Retardation DSM-IV-TR specifies four different levels of mental retardation, which are based only on IQ score ranges, as measured on the revised Wechsler scales (WISC-R and WAIS-R): (1) mild (IQ score 50–55 to 70), (2) moderate (IQ score 35–40 to 50–55), (3) severe (IQ score 20–25 to 35–40), and (4) profound (IQ score below 20 or 25). Social and vocational skills and degree of adaptability may vary greatly within each category. Table 12.3 contains estimates of the number of people within each level in the United States.

It should be noted that the American Association on Mental Retardation (AAMR), unlike the American Psychiatric Association with DSM-IV-TR, does not use a classification of mental retardation based on levels of intellectual functioning as revealed in IQ scores. Instead, AAMR considers limitations in both the intellectual and adaptive skills of the individual. Adaptive skills include those required in communication, self-care, social interactions, health and safety, work, and leisure. Furthermore, the skills are placed in the context of one's culture and community. Mental retardation is diagnosed only if low intelligence is accompanied by impaired adaptive functioning. Low intelligence alone, or deficits in adaptive behaviors alone, do not result in a diagnosis of mental retardation according to AAMR (Popper & West, 1999). Although DSM-IV-TR and AAMR use intellectual and adaptive functioning as criteria in the diagnosis of mental retardation, AAMR focuses more on adaptive functioning and

Table 12.4   Predisposing Factors Associated with Mental Retardation

Factor	Percentage of Cases	Examples
Heredity	5	Errors of metabolism (Tay-Sachs), single gene abnormalities (tuberous sclerosis), chromosome aberrations (translocation Down syndrome, fragile X syndrome)
Alteration of embryonic development	30	Chromosomal changes (Down syndrome, trisomy 21), prenatal damage due to toxins (fetal alcohol syndrome), infections
Pregnancy and perinatal complications	10	Malnutrition, prematurity, hypoxia, traumas, infections
Infancy or childhood medical conditions	5	Traumas, infections, lead ingestion
Environmental influences and other mental conditions	15–20	Social, linguistic, and nurturance deprivation. Severe mental disorders (autistic disorder)
Etiology unknown	30–40	Etiological factors cannot be identified

Source: Based on DSM-IV-TR (American Psychiatric Association, 2000a).

specifies the type and nature of psychosocial supports needed in adaptive functioning (Harris, 2001).

Etiology of Mental Retardation

Mental retardation is thought to be produced by environmental factors (such as poor living conditions), biological factors, or some combination of the two (see Table 12.4). The etiology is dependent to some extent on the level of mental retardation. Mild retardation is generally idiopathic (having no known cause) and familial, whereas severe retardation is typically related to genetic factors or to brain damage (Popper & West, 1999).

Environmental Factors   Certain features of the environment may contribute to retardation. Among these are the absence of stimulating factors or situations, a lack of attention and reinforcement from parents or significant others, and chronic stress and frustration. In addition, poverty, lack of adequate health care, poor nutrition, and inadequate education place children at a disadvantage. A lower socioeconomic status generally implies a lower mean group IQ score (Ardizzone & Scholl, 1985).

Genetic Factors   Genetic factors in mental retardation include genetic variations and genetic abnormalities (Thapar et al., 1994). Mental retardation caused by normal genetic variation simply reflects the fact that in a normal distribution of traits, some individuals will fall in the upper range and some in the lower. Researchers have suggested that the normal range of intelligence lies between the IQ scores of 50 and 150, and that some individuals simply lie on the lower end of this normal range (Zigler, 1967). No organic or physiological anomaly associated with mental retardation is usually found in this type of retardation. Most people classified with mild retardation have normal health, appearance, and physical abilities.

The most common inherited form of mental retardation that is caused by genetic anomalies is called the fragile X syndrome because an abnormal gene is present on the bottom end of the X chromosome (Hagerman, 1996). Although impairment in functioning varies among those with inherited forms of mental retardation, many affected persons have severe deficits. Those with profound retardation (about 1 to 2 percent of those with the disorder) may be so intellectually deficient that they require constant and total care and supervision. Many also have significant sensorimotor impairment (Irwin & Gross, 1990) and are confined to a bed or wheelchair by the congenital defects that produced the retardation. Even with teaching, there is minimal, if any, acquisition of self-help skills among these individuals. Their mortality rate during childhood is extremely high, with more than one-half dying before age twenty (Ramer & Miller, 1992). Associated physical problems such as neuromuscular disorders, impairment of vision or hearing, and seizures may coexist (Irwin & Gross, 1990).

Down syndrome is a condition produced by the presence of an extra chromosome (trisomy 21, an autosomal, or nonsex, chromosome) and resulting in mental retardation and distinctive physical characteristics. It may occur as often as once in every thousand live births (Thapar et al., 1994). About 10 percent of children with severe or moderate retardation show this genetic anomaly. The prevalence rate increases dramatically with the age at which the mother gives birth (U.S. Department of Health and Human Services, 1995a).

The well-known physical characteristics of Down syndrome are short incurving fingers, short broad hands, slanted eyes, furrowed protruding tongue, flat and broad face, harsh voice, and incomplete or delayed sexual development. Some Down syndrome children receive cosmetic surgery (consisting mostly of modifying tongue size) to make their physical appearance more nearly normal and to allow them to speak more clearly and to eat more normally. The procedure is intended to enable people with Down syndrome to fit in as much as possible with their peers to enhance their social interactions and communication abilities (May & Turnbull, 1992).

People with Down syndrome who live past age forty are at high risk for developing Alzheimer's disease, discussed earlier in this chapter. The gene responsible for the amyloid plaques and neurofibrillary tangles found in Alzheimer's disease is located on chromosome 21, indicating a possible relationship between Down syndrome and Alzheimer's disease (Clarke & Clarke, 1987). People who have Down syndrome show a greater intellectual decline after the age of thirty-five than do other individuals with mental retardation (Young & Kramer, 1991). Congenital heart abnormalities are also common in people with Down syndrome, causing a high mortality rate. Surgical procedures have improved the probability of surviving these heart defects and have resulted in both a longer life expectancy and a healthier life (Carr, 1994).

Prenatal detection of Down syndrome is possible through **amniocentesis,** a screening procedure in which a hollow needle is inserted through the pregnant woman's abdominal wall and the amniotic fluid is withdrawn from the fetal sac. This procedure is performed during the fourteenth or fifteenth week of pregnancy. The fetal cells from the fluid are cultivated and, within three weeks, can be tested to determine whether Down syndrome is present. This procedure involves some risk for both mother and fetus, so it is employed only when the chance of finding Down syndrome is high—as, for example, with women older than age thirty-five. Remember, however, that the greater percentage of babies with Down syndrome are born to younger mothers, and yet testing for Down syndrome through amniocentesis occurs primarily among older women.

A procedure that allows earlier detection of Down syndrome is *chorionic villus sampling*. Tests are made of cells on the hairlike projections (villi) on the sac that surrounds the fetus and can be performed after the ninth week of pregnancy (Pueschel, 1991).

Down syndrome A condition produced by the presence of an extra chromosome (trisomy 21) and resulting in mental retardation and distinctive physical characteristics.

amniocentesis A screening procedure in which a hollow needle is inserted through the pregnant woman's abdominal wall and amniotic fluid is withdrawn from the fetal sac; used during the fourteenth or fifteenth week of pregnancy to determine the presence of Down syndrome and other fetal abnormalities.

A Blind Adoptive Parent with Son Who Has Brain Damage from Fetal Alcohol Syndrome   Our society is becoming increasingly aware of the importance and necessity of helping each other. There is also growing recognition of the roles that people can play in helping others regardless of physical challenges or disabilities.

Other, less common genetic anomalies—such as Turner's syndrome, Klinefelter's syndrome, phenylketonuria (PKU), Tay-Sachs disease, and cretinism—can also produce mental retardation.

Nongenetic Biological Factors   Mental retardation may be caused by a variety of environmental mishaps during the prenatal (from conception to birth), perinatal (during the birth process), or postnatal (after birth) periods.

During the prenatal period, the developing organism is susceptible to viruses and infections (such as German measles), drugs, radiation, poor nutrition, and other nongenetic influences.

Increasing attention is being focused on the problem of mental deficits related to alcohol consumption during pregnancy. Some children born to alcoholic mothers have **fetal alcohol syndrome (FAS)**, a group of congenital physical and mental defects including small body size and *microcephaly*, an anomaly whose most distinguishing feature is an unusually small brain. Such children are generally mildly retarded, but many are either moderately retarded or of average intelligence. Those with normal intelligence seem to have significant academic and attentional difficulties, however, as well as a history of hyperactivity and behavioral deficits (Streissguth, 1994). Smoking and poor nutrition may increase the likelihood that an alcoholic mother will have FAS offspring. Available information suggests that one case of FAS occurs in each 750 live births, which places alcohol among the most common causes of retardation for which an etiology can be determined (Streissguth et al., 1980). Among the different ethnic groups in the United States, the rate of FAS is especially high among American Indians (U.S. Department of Health and Human Services, 1995b).

During the perinatal period, mental retardation can result from birth trauma, prematurity, or asphyxiation. After birth or during the postnatal period, head injuries, infections, tumors, malnutrition, and ingestion of toxic substances such as lead can cause brain damage and consequent mental retardation. Compared with prenatal factors, however, these hazards account for only a small proportion of organically caused mental retardation.

The most common birth condition associated with mental retardation is prematurity and low birth weight. Although most premature infants develop normally, approximately 20 percent show signs of neurological problems reflected in learning disabilities and mental retardation (Pound, 1987). In a study of more than 53,000 U.S. women and their children, researchers found that low birth weight was generally associated with low IQ scores. The average IQ score of children who had birth weights between 26 ounces and 52.5 ounces was 86, whereas those with birth weights between 122 ounces and 140 ounces had an average IQ score of 105 (Broman, Nichols, & Kennedy, 1975).

Although most types of mental retardation now have decreasing incidence rates, mental retardation owing to postnatal causes is on the increase. For example, direct trauma to the head produces hemorrhaging and tearing of the brain tissue, often as the result of an injury sustained in an automobile accident or from child abuse. Depending

fetal alcohol syndrome (FAS) A group of congenital physical and mental defects found in some children born to alcoholic mothers; symptoms include small body size and microcephaly, in which the brain is unusually small and mild retardation may occur.

on the definition of *child abuse,* estimates of the number of cases of child abuse per year range from 35,000 to 1.9 million. Of this group, a large percentage are subjected to violent abuse that could cause serious injury (Gelard & Sanford, 1987). Other postnatal causes include brain infections, neurological disease, toxic exposure, and even extreme malnutrition (Popper & West, 1999).

Programs for People with Mental Retardation

Early Intervention Programs such as Head Start have not produced dramatic increases in intellectual ability among at-risk children (those from low-income families). But long-term follow-up studies have found that they do produce positive results (Royce, Lazar, & Darlington, 1983; Zigler & Bergman, 1983). Children who participated in early intervention programs were found to perform better in school than nonparticipants, and the difference between the two groups continued to widen until the twelfth grade. In addition, a greater proportion of the participants in early intervention finished high school, which no doubt helped them obtain and hold better jobs. The families of participants were also positively influenced by the programs. They rated the programs as personally helpful, spent more time working with their children on school tasks, and perceived their children as becoming happier and healthier.

Employment Programs People with mental retardation can achieve more than was previously thought. The parents of one teenage boy, for example, were told that he would always be childlike and that the only job he would ever be fit for was stringing beads. Another person with moderate retardation, who spent most of his time staring at his hands and rubbing his face, also appeared to have a dismal future. Both of these men now have paying jobs, one as a janitor and the other as a dishwasher. Programs designed to help people with mental retardation learn occupational skills are largely responsible for the improved outcome of these men and others like them (McLeod, 1985). Gains made in social and vocational skills appear to be maintained or increased in follow-up studies (Foxx & Faw, 1992).

Living Arrangements Institutionalization of people with mental retardation is declining, as more individuals are placed in group homes or in situations in which they can live independently or semi-independently within the community. The idea is to provide the "least restrictive environment" that is consistent with their condition and that will give them the opportunity to develop more fully. Although the implication seems to be that institutions are bad places, they do not have uniformly negative effects. Nor do group homes always provide positive experiences. What seems to be most important are program goals; programs that promote social interaction and the development of competence have positive effects on the residents of either institutions or group homes (Tjosvold & Tjosvold, 1983).

Nontraditional group arrangements, in which a small number of people live together in a home, sharing meals and chores, provide increased opportunity for social interactions. These "normalized" living arrangements were found to produce benefits such as increased adaptive functioning, improved language development, and socialization (Kleinberg & Galligan, 1983; MacEachron, 1983). Many of these positive behaviors, however, were already part of the residents' repertoires; what they need are systematic programs that will teach them additional living skills (Kleinberg & Galligan, 1983). Merely moving people with mental retardation from one environment to another does not by itself guarantee that they will be taught the skills they need. Nonetheless, properly planned and supported deinstitutionalization does provide these individuals an opportunity to experience a more "normal" life.

Early Intervention and Training Can Make a Difference   Many mentally retarded individuals can lead productive and satisfying lives, especially if they have access to programs designed to help them learn occupational skills. Here, a woman with Down syndrome is working successfully at McDonald's. Do you feel people often stereotype individuals with mental retardation? What kinds of stereotypes exist?

Finally, it should be noted that living arrangements, environmental supports, and interventions should be tailored to the type of retardation and severity of limitations found among the individuals (Dykens & Hodapp, 1997). Research has found that customized or consumer-directed services are more effective than traditional agency-directed services (President's New Freedom Commission on Mental Health, 2003).

As mentioned earlier, parents and family members often serve as caregivers for a significant period of time. When this occurs, the family members may need education and training in dealing with someone who has mental retardation. Overcoming myths about the disorder, finding out how to deal with the affected family member, identifying supports and resources, and handling emotional problems (e.g., anxiety, guilt, and anger) within the family are important tasks for caregivers (Harris, 2001).

▷ **CHECKPOINT REVIEW**

amniocentesis *(p. 325)*

Down syndrome *(p. 325)*

fetal alcohol syndrome (FAS) *(p. 326)*

mental retardation *(p. 320)*

What is mental retardation?

- DSM-IV-TR identifies four different levels of mental retardation, which are based only on IQ scores: mild (IQ score 50 to 70), moderate (IQ score 35 to 49), severe (IQ score 20 to 34), and profound (IQ score below 20).
- Causes of retardation include environmental factors, normal genetic processes, genetic anomalies, and other biological abnormalities such as physiological or anatomical defects.
- Most mental retardation does not have an identifiable organic cause and is associated with only mild intellectual impairment.

- The vast majority of those with mental retardation can become completely self-supporting with appropriate education and training.
- Public schools provide special programs for children and adolescents; even people with severe retardation are given instruction and training in practical self-help skills.
- Various approaches—behavioral therapy in particular—are used successfully to help people with mental retardation acquire needed "living" skills.

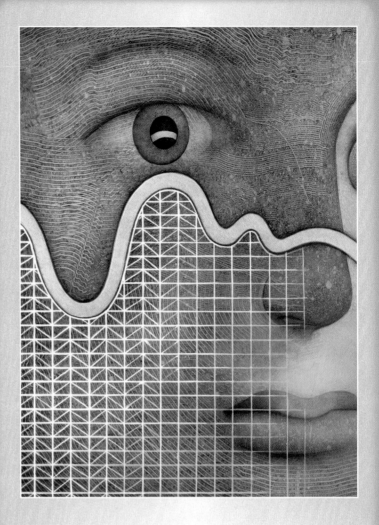

FOCUS QUESTIONS

- What are pervasive developmental disorders?
- Who is most likely to suffer from autism, and how debilitating is it?
- What are the causes of autism?
- What are some of the characteristics of attention deficit/hyperactivity disorder, and what are the subtypes of this disorder?
- What is the difference between conduct disorder and oppositional defiant disorder?
- What is the general prognosis for children with anxiety disorders?
- Which adult mood disorders are also seen in children and adolescents?
- What are tic disorders?
- What are elimination disorders, and what is their prognosis?

13 Disorders of Childhood and Adolescence

Much of the public continues to cling to the popular notion that childhood is a period relatively free of stress and that it represents a carefree and happy existence. Because children are less able to express unhappiness or fears verbally, their problems often go unnoticed unless they become glaringly extreme, as in the following cases:

The five-and-one-half-year-old preschooler sat apart from the other children. In his hand, Ahmed held a toy truck, and he was spinning its wheels and humming aloud as if to mimic the sound. He then stood and placed the truck in the corner of the room before moving to the window. Peering out, he ran his right forefinger along the sill exactly five times. He then returned to the corner, picked up the truck, and repeated the entire sequence again, as he had been doing all morning. If by chance one of the other children accidentally moved or handled the truck, Ahmed seemed panic stricken and filled with rage. Caretakers' attempts to comfort him were unsuccessful. He showed no response when they talked to him, and he seldom looked in their eyes. Ahmed seemed to live in a world of his own, and he treated people as if they were inanimate objects that stood in his way. *Diagnosis:* autistic disorder

The mother sat in the psychiatrist's office, watching apprehensively as her ten-year-old son fidgeted in his seat and played with the ornaments hanging from the nearby Christmas tree. The mother explained to the psychiatrist that Adam had been expelled from school twice for disruptive classroom behavior. He had difficulty concentrating in class, and he was failing. The school psychologist had said Adam was "hyperactive" and recommended that they seek professional help. Throughout the interview, the mother admonished the child, saying, "Sit still," "Don't play with those," and "Pay attention." Each time, the child appeared remorseful, and his behavior abated briefly. But remaining still seemed impossible for Adam, and he was soon fidgeting again. By the end of the session, he had been in and out of his seat some half dozen times and had accidentally broken two ornaments. *Diagnosis:* attention deficit/hyperactivity disorder

The father had never struck Kim before, but he was on the verge of doing so now. He was enraged and incensed at his fourteen-year-old son's defiance and argumentative nature. Standing before his father with a scowl on his face and both hands clenched in fists, Kim refused to come out of his room to meet friends and relatives attending his mother's surprise birthday party. Just hours before, he and his father had had a heated encounter over picking up his room and helping with chores around the house. Kim had steadfastly refused. Even when he was threatened with being "grounded," Kim only stated, "You can't make me do anything." *Diagnosis:* oppositional defiant disorder

At eight years of age, Nina was suffering from multiple anxieties. During the day, she could not tolerate having her mother out of sight, and at night she was tormented by unrealistic fears and nightmares. Leaving her at school was becoming increasingly difficult because Nina would cling to her mother and often refused to leave the car. Even when her mother walked her to the classroom, Nina fussed and cried in front of the other children. The child's problem seemed to be worsening: she was complaining of stomachaches and headaches in school, and she had exaggerated fears that the school would burn down. Nina was now frequently sent to the school nurse for her physical symptoms. *Diagnosis:* separation anxiety disorder

Although it is easy for us to dismiss such childhood disorders as rare and unusual, it is estimated that almost 21 percent of the children in the United States between the ages of nine and seventeen have a diagnosable mental or addictive disorder associated with at least a minimal level of impairment, with 11 percent having significant impairment and 5 percent having an extreme degree of impairment (Schaffer et al., 1996). Children and adolescents are subject not only to childhood disorders but also to many of the "adult" disorders discussed in previous chapters. Unless effective intervention takes place early in the child's life, an untreated disorder may develop into a lifelong pattern that creates problems in future years.

The disorders of childhood and adolescence encompass a wide variety of behavioral problems, ranging from severe disturbances that affect many aspects of behavior to those that are less severe. One of the most disturbing is a cluster of impairments called *pervasive developmental disorders*. Autistic disorder (as in the first case study) is a particularly baffling and debilitating condition that all too often dooms a child to constant dependent care. Also disturbing are disorders that involve attention deficits and/or hyperactivity that become especially pronounced during the school years (as in the second case study). Attention deficit/hyperactivity disorder (ADHD) has become a controversial diagnosis because of the criticisms leveled at the frequent use of Ritalin to control the problem. The third case study is a typical example of the class of problems called disruptive behavior disorders. In this case, the son can be described as suffering from an oppositional defiant disorder. Children can also suffer from excessive anxieties, as in the fourth case study, or from other forms of emotional or mood problems.

Pervasive Developmental Disorders

The **pervasive developmental disorders** are childhood disorders involving severe impairment in areas such as social interaction and communication skills and the display of stereotyped interests and behaviors. The pervasive developmental disorders differ distinctly from the psychotic conditions observed in adolescents and adults; they do not include symptoms such as hallucinations, delusions, loosening of associations, or incoherence. A child showing these symptoms probably would be diagnosed with schizophrenia. The impairments shown in the pervasive developmental disorders are not simply delays in development but are distortions that would not be normal at any developmental stage (Kabot, Masi, & Segal, 2003).

DSM-IV-TR identifies several categories of pervasive developmental disorders. Asperger's disorder, for example, involves children who have significant impairment in social interaction skills, limited and repetitive interests and activities, and lack of emotional reciprocity. They show no significant delay in cognitive development, and difficulties with communication skills tend to be subtle. Asperger's disorder is diagnosed five times more frequently in males than females (American Psychiatric Association, 2000a). But by far the most disabling and baffling of the childhood disorders is autism.

Autistic Disorder

pervasive developmental disorders Severe childhood disorders in which qualitative impairment in verbal and nonverbal communication and social interaction are the primary symptoms; include autistic disorder, Asperger's disorder, and pervasive developmental disorders not otherwise specified.

Jim, currently twenty-nine years old, received a diagnosis of autism during his preschool years. His parents reported that Jim was not "cuddly." He would stiffen when touched and preferred being alone. Jim found touching aversive because it produced soundlike sensations, as well as tactile ones. This was confusing to him. In talking about his reactions, Jim found it difficult to discuss sensations because he believed that his sensory and perceptual sensations were different from those of others. On responding to external stimuli, he replied, "Sometimes the channels get confused, as when sounds come through as color. Sometimes I know that something is coming in somewhere, but I can't

> tell right away what sense it's coming through" (Cesaroni & Garber, 1991, p. 305). Jim engaged in stereotyped movements involving rocking and twirling. He can now consciously control these behaviors, but they still occur when he is tired and not consciously aware. Any environmental change was very distressing to him. He strongly responded to the sale of the family car as the "loss of a family member." Jim feels different from others and is unable to understand social signals. He describes himself as "communication impaired." He is most comfortable when communication is concrete but not when different subjects or informal conversation occurs. Relationships are enormously difficult to form because of the communication problems.

In 1943 Leo Kanner, a child psychiatrist, identified a triad of behaviors that have come to define the essential features of autism: an extreme isolation and inability to relate to people; a psychological need for sameness; and significant difficulties with communication. The puzzling symptoms displayed by the children Kanner described (see the first case study in this chapter) fit the diagnostic criteria for **autistic disorder** in DSM-IV-TR—qualitative impairment in social interaction and/or communication; restricted, stereotyped interest and activities; and delays or abnormal functioning in a major area before the age of three.

Autistic disorder is quite rare—about two to twenty cases in every 10,000 children. The prevalence of autism has not been found to vary across socioeconomic classes, nor are there any significant racial or ethnic variations (Bristol et al., 1996). Autistic disorder occurs four to five times more frequently in boys than in girls (American Psychiatric Association, 2000a). Unfortunately, only one-third of children with autism are able to lead even partially independent lives as adults (American Psychiatric Association, 2000a).

Impairments Impairments found with this disorder occur in three major areas: social interactions, verbal and nonverbal communication, and activities and interests (American Psychiatric Association, 2000a; Gillberg, 1992; Klin, Volkmar, & Sparrow, 1992).

- *Social Interactions* Unusual lack of interest in others is a primary aspect of this disorder. Individuals with autism interact as though other people were unimportant objects, and they show little interest in establishing friendships, imitating behaviors, or playing games (Stone & Lemanek, 1990). As a result, children with autistic disorder often fail to develop peer relationships. Disturbances may be displayed in body postures, gestures, facial expressions, and eye contact.

  Autistic children appear to be unaware of other people's identity and emotions. They appear not to need physical contact with or emotional response from their caretakers. For example, although children with autistic disorder are as likely as other children to smile when they successfully complete a task, they are much less likely to look at an adult to convey this feeling (Kasari et al., 1993). Mothers often describe infants with autism as content to be left alone and as showing no anticipatory response to being picked up.

- *Verbal and Nonverbal Communication* About 50 percent of autistic children do not develop meaningful speech. Those who do generally show oddities such as echolalia (echoing what has previously been said). One child constantly repeated the words "How do you spell relief?" without any apparent reason. In addition, the child may reverse pronouns. For example, *you* might be used for *I*, and *I* for *me*. Even when they can speak, such children may be unable or unwilling to initiate conversations. Children with this disorder also use more nonsensical and idiosyncratic language than that of matched controls (Volden & Lord, 1991).

- *Activities and Interests* Children with autistic disorder engage in few activities. They often have unusual repetitive habits such as spinning objects, whirling themselves, or fluttering or flapping their arms. They may show intense interest

autistic disorder A severe childhood disorder characterized by qualitative impairment in social interaction and/or communication; restricted, stereotyped interest and activities; and delays or abnormal functioning in a major area before the age of three.

in self-induced sounds or in staring at their hands and fingers. They may stare into space and be totally self-absorbed. Minor changes in the environment may produce rages and tantrums. Children with this disorder also show a lack of imaginary activities.

As many as three-fourths of children with autistic disorder have IQ scores lower than 70. High-functioning individuals, such as Jim in the preceding case study or the person played by Dustin Hoffman in the movie *Rain Man,* account for only a minority of people with this disorder—about 20 percent—who have average to above-average intelligence (Freeman, 1993; Gillberg, 1988). In the past, some theorists believed that children with autism were unusually bright. They based their beliefs on two phenomena. First, some of them display *splinter skills*—that is, they often do well on one or more isolated tasks such as drawings, puzzle construction, and rote memory but perform poorly on verbal tasks and tasks requiring language skills and symbolic thinking. Second, they sometimes display unusual abilities and are referred to as "autistic savants." One Chinese boy with autism could identify the day of the week on which different dates fell and could convert the Gregorian calendar to the Chinese calendar. He also knew the lottery numbers and their drawing dates for the previous three months, the titles of songs in the popular charts for the previous ten years and their dates of release, and the numbers and routes of buses throughout the city (Ho, Tsang, & Ho, 1991). It is difficult to know whether autistic savants have particular cognitive strengths or whether the unusual skills are due to their perseverative attention to selected tasks (Miller, 1999).

As mentioned earlier, some theorists (Baron-Cohen, Leslie, & Frith, 1985; Tager-Flushberg & Sullivan, 1994; Frith, 1991) believe that individuals with autism lack a "theory of mind," that they are unable to attribute mental states to others or to understand that others think and have feelings. As Cowley (1995) described it, "Their worlds are peopled not by fellow beings with thoughts, feelings and agendas but by skin-covered bags that approach and withdraw unpredictably" (p. 67). Their inability to apply mental states to others results in a corresponding inability to lie, deceive, or understand jokes. Parents have said that their child "[is] embarrassingly honest," "wouldn't know what a white lie was," "tells jokes but they don't make any sense," and "knows you laugh at the end of [a joke]" (Leekam & Prior, 1994).

Individuals with autistic disorder seem unable to understand that others think and have beliefs. This inability to appreciate other people's mental states appears to be long lasting. Children who showed this deficit displayed unchanged performance seven years later, even though their experience had increased (Holroyd & Baron-Cohen, 1993). Even when children with autism "pass" tests in identifying thoughts in others, they do not demonstrate the ability to apply this skill in real-life situations (Leekham & Prior, 1994).

Autistic Girl Wearing a Helmet Besides having problems with social interactions and communication, autistic children can show a variety of symptoms, such as impulsivity, temper tantrums, and self-injurious behavior. Here a child is wearing a helmet to prevent damage from head banging. How do self-injurious behaviors arise?

Etiology There are four major etiological groupings in autism (Gillberg, 1992): (1) familial autism, (2) autism related to a medical condition, (3) autism associated with nonspecific brain dysfunction, and (4) autism without a family history or associated brain dysfunction. One very puzzling aspect of this disorder is that different factors are associated with different cases (Folstein & Rutter, 1988; Gillberg, 1992; Volkmar et al., 1988). How the syndrome of autism can develop from so many different conditions is not known. One important implication of the four sets of conditions is that no single cause for autism is likely to be found. Because of the early lack of normal development and distinct social and cognitive deficits, researchers increasingly believe that autism results from biological rather than psychosocial factors. However, the early explanations for autism, evolving from psychodynamic theory, involved parent-child relationships.

Psychodynamic Theories Early psychodynamic theories of autism stressed the importance of deviant parent-child interactions in producing this condition. Kanner (1943), who named the syndrome, concluded that cold and unresponsive parenting is responsible for the development of autism. He described the parents as "successfully autistic," "cold, humorless perfectionists who preferred reading, writing, playing music, or thinking" (p. 663). These individuals "happened to defrost long enough to produce a child" (Steffenburg & Gillberg, 1989). Kanner has since changed his position and now believes the disorder is "innate."

Psychological factors are implicated in many disorders, but they do not seem to be involved in autism. Unfortunately, many mental health professionals continue to inflict guilt on parents who already bear the burden of raising a child with this disorder. Parents of children with autism show much stress and are particularly concerned about the well-being of their children after they can no longer take care of them (Koegel et al., 1992). In light of current research, no justification exists for allowing parents to think they caused their child's autism.

Family and Genetic Studies Current research is continuing to focus on genetics and the understanding of brain abnormalities that underlie autistic disorder (National Institute of Neurological Disorders and Stroke, 2001a). About 2 to 9 percent of siblings of children with autism also have this disorder; this rate is 100 to 200 times greater than that of the general population (American Psychiatric Association, 2000a; Bolton et al., 1994; Ritvo et al., 1989; Smalley & Asarnow, 1990). These findings are supportive of genetic influences. E. H. Cook (1998) reported much greater concordance in identical than in fraternal twins. A well-controlled twin study was performed by Folstein and Rutter (1977). They recruited fraternal and identical twins, some of whom were discordant and some concordant. (That is, in some pairs both twins had autism; in others only one twin had the disorder.) Identification as identical or fraternal was determined through blood analysis, and diagnoses were made without knowing who the twins' siblings were or whether the twins were fraternal or identical. The concordance rate for twenty-one pairs of twins was 36 percent for identical twins and 0 percent for fraternal twins. An interesting finding of the Folstein and Rutter study is that seven of the discordant identical twins showed some language impairment—one characteristic of autism. Folstein and Rutter (1977) also believe that the diathesis-stress model could account for some of their findings. In twelve of the seventeen discordant twin pairs, the twin with autism had suffered some birth complication. So a predisposition interacting with an environmental stressor may result in the disorder.

Central Nervous System Impairment Autistic disorder appears to be a neurodevelopmental disorder involving some form of inherited brain dysfunction (Rutter, 1994). However, what is confusing is that autistic disorder seems to be associated with many organic conditions (Bolton et al., 1989; Ghaziuddin et al., 1992), none of which are specific only to autism. Conditions such as the fragile X syndrome (malformation of the X chromosome), tuberous sclerosis (a congenital hereditary disease associated with brain tumors), neurofibromatosis (tumors of the peripheral nerves), phenylketonuria (PKU), and intrauterine rubella (measles) have been reported among children with autistic disorder. These diseases affect the central nervous system, but most people undergo them without developing autism. It is estimated that between one-fourth to one-third of those diagnosed with a pervasive developmental disorder eventually demonstrate seizures (American Psychiatric Association, 2000a; National Institute of Neurological Disorders and Stroke, 2001b).

The fact that so many organic conditions are associated with autism has caused some researchers to search for central nervous system impairment—possibly in the left hemisphere, which is associated with cognition and language. Results have been mixed. Researchers have reported some differences in brain structure between autistic and nonautistic individuals (Courchesne, 1995; Courchesne et al., 1988). For example, Hashimoto and his colleagues (1995) found that certain parts of the brainstem and cerebellum are significantly smaller in individuals with autism than in members of control groups. However, other researchers found no difference in similar comparisons (Garber & Ritvo, 1992).

No consistent pattern of impairment has yet been found, which is perhaps to be expected, given the different subgroups of autism. Rutter, MacDonald, and colleagues (1990) believe that some of the confusion is due to including samples of "atypical" autism and other pervasive developmental disorders in studies of autism. Each of these may have etiological components that differ from those of "true" autism. The etiological picture may become clearer once the distinctions among the different pervasive developmental disorders are accepted.

Biochemical Studies Researchers are also interested in the role that neurotransmitters may play in autistic disorder. But the studies are difficult to interpret because they often use different intellectual and behavioral measures and because they may study different subgroups of people with autism (DuVerglas, Banks, & Guyer, 1988). Nevertheless, some children with this disorder do have elevated serotonin and dopamine levels. Ritvo and colleagues (1984) reported elevated blood serotonin levels in a minority of such patients. The significance of this elevation is still not clear, but it suggests a promising line of research. Nelson et al. (2001) report that, based on a study involving the archiving and later study of blood samples taken at birth, children who later developed mental retardation or autistic disorder showed elevated levels of neural growth factors, a protein important in the prenatal formation of the central nervous system.

Prognosis

The prognosis for children with pervasive developmental disorders is mixed. Approximately 25 percent are able to function in a supported environment, and another 25 percent will be able to live independently although social impairment continues (Ratey, Grandin, & Miller, 1992). The prognosis is somewhat better for those who are considered high functioning with good verbal skills. For example, Temple Grandin overcame the symptoms of autistic disorder to earn a doctorate in animal science and is now a recognized leader in the field of livestock handling (Ratey et al., 1992). The prognosis for those with Asperger's disorder tends to be the most promising. Many individuals with the disorder are self-sufficient and successfully employed. There are reports of significant intellectual success for some with Asperger's disorder; in fact, it is reported that compelling evidence exists that Albert Einstein exhibited symptoms consistent with Asperger's disorder or high-functioning autism (Perner, 2001).

Treatment

Because patients with these disorders have communication or social impairments, pervasive developmental disorders are very difficult to treat. Therapy with the parents, family therapy, drug therapy, and behavior modification techniques are all currently being used, with limited success. Intensive behavior modification programs seem the most promising treatment. Interventions for those with Asperger's disorder can include verbally mediated therapies, such as structured problem-solving therapy, due to the higher level of language development demonstrated by this group compared with those with other pervasive developmental disorders (Volkmar et al., 2000).

Drug Therapy The antipsychotic medication haloperidol can produce modest reductions in withdrawal, stereotypical movements, and fidgetiness. However, long-term use produces movement problems and other side effects in many children (Gadow, 1991). Overall, treatment with psychotropic medication has not produced particularly promising results.

There has been significant interest in ongoing research on the use of secretin, a hormone that controls digestion, which is routinely administered during diagnostic gastrointestinal procedures. Interest in this hormone began when Victoria Beck made the connection between her son's infusion with secretin during a GI endoscopy procedure and the subsequent reduction of his autistic symptoms (Autism Society of Wisconsin, 2001; Paulson, 1999). Similar improvement in symptoms following secretin use has been reported in other children (Hovarth et al., 1998). Studies are now in progress using secretin as a treatment for autistic symptoms, and the results suggest that a subset of autistic individuals seem particularly responsive to the therapy. Issues concerning who the best candidates for this treatment are, what the best dosage and optimal administration schedules are, and the close monitoring of side effects, including reports of secretin-induced seizures, will be closely addressed by those involved in research (Rimland, 2000).

Behavior Modification Behavior modification procedures have been used effectively to eliminate echolalia, self-mutilation, and self-stimulation. They also have effectively increased attending behaviors, verbalizations, and social play through social interaction training (Harris, 1995; Oke & Schreibman, 1990; Plienis et al., 1987). Shiver, Allen, and Mathews (1999) indicate that applied behavior analysis has by far the strongest empirical support in the treatment of autistic disorder.

Comprehensive early childhood treatment programs have shown positive results, particularly with respect to measured IQ. Effective programs involve a curriculum focused extensively on social and communication skills, a structured teaching environment, a predictable routine, and use of choices to prevent problem behaviors. Family involvement and a carefully planned transition into the elementary school environment are also important factors. Research is still needed regarding the optimal intensity of intervention (Gresham, Beebe-Frankenberger, & MacMillan, 1999).

Even with intervention, certain symptoms of social impairment generally remain (Seigel, 2003). Even high-functioning adults with autistic disorder display problem behaviors involving inappropriate communication and poor interpersonal skills. One group of high-functioning autistic adults had problems obtaining employment because of behaviors such as rudely terminating or interrupting conversations, walking sideways, or waving arms in a robotlike fashion. Through behavioral interventions, these adults were able to become competitively employed, although some oddities of behavior remained (Burt, Fuller, & Lewis, 1991; Estrada & Pinsof, 1995).

CHECKPOINT REVIEW

autistic disorder *(p. 333)*
pervasive developmental disorders *(p. 332)*

What are pervasive developmental disorders?
- This class of disorders is characterized by severe impairments in social interaction and communications skills and a display of stereotyped interest and behaviors. The most dramatic illustration is autism.

Who is most likely to suffer from autism, and how debilitating is it?
- Although autism is quite rare, we know it occurs more frequently in boys, that it generally produces IQ scores less than 70, and that only one-third of autistic individuals are able to lead semi-independent lives.

What are the causes of autism?
- Although many psychological theories abound in explaining the disorder, there is general consensus that genetics, central nervous system impairment, or brain abnormalities underlie autism.

Other Developmental Disorders

How do we know whether a child has a childhood disorder? Such decisions are often based on vague and arbitrary interpretations of the extent to which a given child deviates from some "acceptable" norm. And, as some critics have observed, the decision frequently depends on the tolerance of the referring agent. Cultural factors also play a role in the types of problems identified. In Thailand, where aggression is discouraged and values such as peacefulness, politeness, and deference are encouraged, clinic referrals are primarily for overcontrolled behaviors (fearfulness, sleep problems, somatization). In the United States, where independence and competitiveness are emphasized, problems generally involve undercontrolled behaviors (disobedience, fighting, arguing; Tharp, 1991).

The less severe childhood and adolescent disturbances cover a wide range of problems. In this section we discuss some of the more common disorders: attention deficit/hyperactivity disorders, disruptive disorders, separation-anxiety disorders, tic disorders, and elimination disorders.

Attention Deficit/Hyperactivity Disorders and Disruptive Behavior Disorders

These disorders involve symptoms that are often socially disruptive and distressing to others (see Figure 13.1). They include attention deficit/hyperactivity disorders (ADHD), conduct disorder, and oppositional defiant disorder. These disorders often occur together and have overlapping symptoms. Without intervention, these disorders tend to persist (Farmer, 1995; Fergusson, Horwood, & Lynskey, 1995; Root & Resnick, 2003). In a longitudinal study of "hard to manage" preschoolers followed from age three until school entry and then to age nine, 67 percent showed clinically significant problems at age six and met the criteria for one of the disorders in this category (Campbell & Ewing, 1990). The children displayed problem behaviors such as inattention, overactivity, and aggression, and they required supervision. Early identification and intervention are necessary to interrupt the negative course of these disorders.

Raising a child with a disruptive behavior disorder is difficult. Parents report more negative feelings about parenting, higher stress levels, and a more negative impact on their social lives than do parents of normally developing children (Donenberg & Baker, 1993).

Attention Deficit/Hyperactivity Disorders

> Ron, an only child, was always on the go as a toddler and preschooler. He had many accidents because of his continual climbing and risk taking. Temper outbursts were frequent. In kindergarten Ron had much difficulty staying seated for group work and in completing projects. The quality of his work was poor. In the first grade, Ron was referred to the school psychologist for evaluation. Although his high activity level and lack of concentration were not so pronounced in this one-on-one situation, his impulsive approach to tasks and short attention span were evident throughout the interview. Ron was referred to a local pediatrician who specializes in attention deficit disorders. The pediatrician prescribed Ritalin, which helped reduce Ron's activity level.

attention deficit/hyperactivity disorders (ADHD) Disorders of childhood and adolescence characterized by socially disruptive behaviors—either attentional problems or hyperactivity—that are present before age seven and persist for at least six months.

Attention deficit/hyperactivity disorder (ADHD) is characterized by socially disruptive behaviors—either attentional problems or hyperactivity—that are present before age seven and persist for at least six months. *Hyperactivity* is a confusing term because it refers to both a diagnostic category and behavioral characteristics. Children who are "overactive" or who have "short attention spans" are often referred to as "hyperactive," even though they may not meet the diagnostic criteria for this disorder. Whether a child is merely overactive or has ADHD is often difficult to determine.

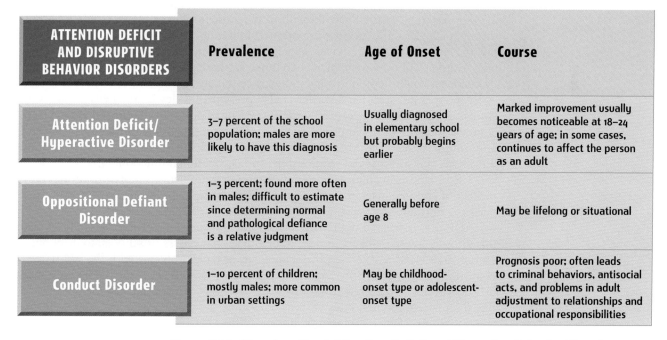

Figure 13.1 Disorders Chart: Attention Deficit and Disruptive Behavior Disorders
Sources: Data from DSM-IV-TR; Gaub & Carlson (1997); Lewinsohn et al. (1993).

Attention Deficit/Hyperactive Disorder

Symptoms are present before age seven

Disruptive behavior in either one or both of the following:
• Attentional problems (distractible, inattentive, not completing tasks)
• Hyperactivity (impulsive, heightened motor activity, interrupts)

Symptoms are present in two or more settings

Clear evidence of interference with social or academic functioning

ATTENTION DEFICIT AND DISRUPTIVE BEHAVIOR DISORDERS

These disorders involve socially disruptive behaviors that distress others. Disruptive behavior pattern must be present for at least six months.

Oppositional Defiant Disorder

Pattern of negativistic, hostile, and defiant behavior

Often loses temper, argues with adults, and defies or refuses adult requests

Does not take responsibility for actions

Angry and resentful

Often blames others

Often spiteful and vindictive

Conduct Disorder

Often bullies or threatens others

Lying and cheating common

Deliberately destroys property

Steals

Often truant from school

May be physically cruel to people and animals

Often initiates physical fights

Serious violations of rules

ATTENTION DEFICIT AND DISRUPTIVE BEHAVIOR DISORDERS	Prevalence	Age of Onset	Course
Attention Deficit/Hyperactive Disorder	3–7 percent of the school population; males are more likely to have this diagnosis	Usually diagnosed in elementary school but probably begins earlier	Marked improvement usually becomes noticeable at 18–24 years of age; in some cases, continues to affect the person as an adult
Oppositional Defiant Disorder	1–3 percent; found more often in males; difficult to estimate since determining normal and pathological defiance is a relative judgment	Generally before age 8	May be lifelong or situational
Conduct Disorder	1–10 percent of children; mostly males; more common in urban settings	May be childhood-onset type or adolescent-onset type	Prognosis poor; often leads to criminal behaviors, antisocial acts, and problems in adult adjustment to relationships and occupational responsibilities

Three types of attention deficit/hyperactivity disorders are recognized:

- *ADHD, predominantly hyperactive-impulsive type,* is characterized by behaviors such as heightened motoric activity (fidgeting and squirming), short attention span, distractibility, impulsiveness, and lack of self-control. Children with this type of ADHD tend to have a pattern of being rejected by peers and sustaining more accidental injuries (American Psychiatric Association, 2000a).

- *ADHD, predominantly inattentive type,* is characterized by problems such as distractibility, difficulty with sustained attention, inattention to detail, and difficulty completing tasks. Children with attentional deficits tend to have less severe conduct problems and impulsivity than children with the hyperactive form of ADHD. Instead, they are more likely to be described as sluggish, daydreamers, anxious, and shy; they respond to lower doses of stimulants than do children with hyperactivity (Frick & Lahey, 1991). This type of ADHD affects approximately the same number of boys and girls and tends to have the greatest impact on academic performance (American Psychiatric Association, 2000a).

- *ADHD, combined type,* is probably the most common form of the disorder. In this case, the criteria for both the hyperactive and inattentive types are met.

A confusing aspect of attention deficit/hyperactivity disorder is the apparent inconsistency. Attentional deficit and excessive motor activity are not necessarily observed in all settings. Boys with ADHD, for example, may show greater motor activity during academic tasks but may not differ from normally functioning children during lunch, recess, and physical education activities. Thus a child might be identified as hyperactive in one situation but not in others. To receive a diagnosis of ADHD, the individual must display these characteristics in two or more situations (DSM-IV-TR).

ADHD is relatively common. Estimates of its prevalence range from 3 to 7 percent of school-age children, with boys much more likely to receive this diagnosis than girls, especially the hyperactive-impulsive subtype (American Psychiatric Association, 2000a). ADHD is particularly difficult to diagnose in preschool-age children because there is such variability in their attentional skills and activity levels, in addition to the fact that preschoolers face fewer demands for sustained attention. ADHD is a persistent disorder. Children with ADHD continue to show problems with impulsivity, family conflicts, and attention during adolescence (Gaub & Carlson, 1997). This is especially likely if a disruptive disorder is also present (Barkley et al., 1991). Follow-up studies suggest that between 30 and 50 percent of children diagnosed with ADHD continue to experience symptoms such as inattention, fidgeting, difficulty sitting still, and impulsive actions throughout adulthood (Jackson & Farrugia, 1997). These difficulties may affect social relationships and occupational functioning.

The prognosis in children with only attentional problems is more promising. Forty percent of children display attentional problems at some point in their lives, but they persist in only about 5 percent of cases (Palfrey et al., 1985).

ADHD is associated with many behavioral and academic problems. Children with this disorder are more likely to need to attend special classes or schools, to drop out of school, and to misbehave, become delinquent, or have problems with the law (Greene et al., 1996; Lambert, 1988; Mariani & Barkley, 1997). Boys with ADHD have more difficulty in less structured situations or in activities demanding sustained attention. Based on parent reports, boys with ADHD show more sadness, anger, and guilt than those without ADHD (Braaten & Rosen, 2000). It is crucial to understand ADHD within the psychosocial context of the individual child (Johnston et al., 2000).

Etiology Many researchers believe that the symptoms of overactivity, short attention span, and impulsiveness suggest central nervous system involvement. In fact, many conditions thought to cause neurological impairment—such as lead poisoning, chromosomal abnormalities, neurotransmitter deficits, oxygen deprivation during birth, and fetal

Boys Eating Candy Many parents and professionals believe that the ingestions of sugar or certain food additives can lead to hyperactivity in children and adults. Why does this belief remain even though most well-designed studies do not find this link?

alcohol syndrome—have been associated with ADHD (DHHS, 1999; Hynd et al., 1991). The affected areas of the brain are thought to be the reticular activating system (attention), frontal lobes (voluntary control of attention and inhibition of inappropriate emotional or behavioral responses), and the temporal-parietal regions (involuntary attention). Because ADHD seems to respond to stimulant medications, which increase the availability of dopamine (a neurotransmitter that affects alertness, purposeful movement, and motivation), it has been suggested that ADHD may be caused by inadequate dopamine in the central nervous system; this possibility has led to genetic research involving the dopamine-receptor genes on chromosomes 5 and 11 (DHHS, 1999). Researchers are continuing to examine the neuroanatomy of the brain and the relationship of differences or dysfunction to the symptoms seen in the various subtypes of ADHD (Castellanos et al., 2001; Erk, 2000). The recent use of ionizing radiation using a SPECT (single-photon emission computed tomography) scan has led to many questions about how to interpret the findings due to the lack of comparative data from nonsymptomatic controls. It has been recommended (Giedd, 2001) that before using any kind of imaging procedure it is important to answer the question, Will the outcome of this procedure influence the course of treatment for this child? Neuroimaging studies are providing insight into the psychophysiology of disorders; however, given the lack of control data and the wide range of normal findings, they have limited use as a diagnostic tool other than ruling out obvious problems such as brain tumors (Giedd, 2001).

Some researchers believe that certain foods or food additives produce physiological changes in the brain or other parts of the body, resulting in hyperactive behaviors. This view was promoted by Feingold (1977), who developed a diet excluding these substances. Sugar has also been suspected as a causal factor in ADHD (Chollar, 1988). Approximately 45 percent of physicians have recommended low-sugar diets for children with ADHD (Bennett & Sherman, 1983). Many parents have tried the recommended diets for their children, and many claim that their children's behavior improved. But parental expectations or treating the children differently (e.g., going shopping with them to buy only certain foods) might result in behavioral changes. In one study (Hoover & Millich, 1994), mothers were told that their "sugar-sensitive" sons had just received a drink that contained sugar or a sugar substitute (placebo). All children received only the sugar substitute. The mothers were asked to rate the behavior of their sons as viewed during a videotaped play session. The mothers who believed their sons ingested sugar rated the sons as significantly more hyperactive, even though the videotapes recorded no increases in motor activity in the sons. Clearly, expectations can also result in misperceptions.

To determine whether certain chemicals or sugars are implicated in hyperactivity, carefully controlled double-blind studies have also been conducted. Some of these studies involved a "biological challenge test." In this design, the diets of the children were alternated so that some of the time they ate food with the additive and other times without. The parents were not aware of the type of food they were giving their children. Reviews of such studies showed that eliminating food additives or certain chemicals from the diets of hyperactive children had little effect on their behavior (Consensus Development Panel, 1982; Milich & Pelham, 1986; Wolraich, Wilson, & White, 1995).

Family variables also seem related to ADHD, although it is not clear whether genetic or environmental factors or some combination of the two is involved. Evidence supporting the hypothesis of genetic transmission includes higher prevalence rates for the disorder in the first- and second-degree relatives of children with ADHD and higher concordance rates for this disorder among identical twins (Gillis et al., 1992; Knopf, 1984). Recent twin and sibling pair studies in Australia also support the idea that ADHD symptoms are highly heritable in both boys and girls (Rhee et al., 1999).

Treatment Many children with ADHD have been treated with drug therapy. Approximately 75–90 percent of children with ADHD respond positively to stimulant medication (DHHS, 1999). The drugs seem to treat the symptoms of ADHD (particularly hyperactivity, impulsivity, and inattention) rather than its causes, so drug therapy alone does not produce any long-term benefits. Direct effects on the school achievement of ADHD children are seldom seen (Cantwell, 1996).

Satterfield, Hoppe, and Schell (1982) believe that using medication alone may be harmful because drug therapy fails to address such problems as antisocial behavior, poor peer relationships, and learning difficulties. In fact, some studies that compared medication and behavior therapy in treating ADHD report that combining the two treatments produces the most positive results (Carlson et al., 1992; DuPaul & Barkley, 1993). Other clinicians have suggested that both physicians and therapists should pay more attention to family dynamics and child management problems rather than relying solely on pharmacological intervention. The Mental Health and Society feature, "Are We Overmedicating Children?" focuses on some issues surrounding drug therapy. Self-instructional procedures, modeling, role playing, classroom contingency management programs, and parent training programs have been useful in dealing with the problems of children with ADHD (Abramowitz & O'Leary, 1991; Whalen & Henker, 1991). It has been strongly suggested that mental health professionals working with children with suspected ADHD use systematic observation and data gathering to look for environmental factors that may be overtly or inadvertently encouraging problem behaviors (Northup & Gulley, 2001). Interventions based on functional behavior assessment have resulted in almost complete elimination of aggressive behavior in children with high activity levels (Boyajian et al., 2001). The National Institute of Mental Health instituted the NIMH Multimodal Study of ADHD with the goal of obtaining information regarding best practices in the use of medication with ADHD; it was concluded that, even when used without other interventions, carefully managed and monitored use of simulant medication is effective in reducing ADHD symptoms and that behavioral treatment seems to have the greatest benefit for non-ADHD symptoms (Greenhill et al., 1998).

Oppositional Defiant Disorder

Oppositional defiant disorder (ODD) is characterized by a negativistic, argumentative, and hostile behavior pattern. Children with this disorder often lose their tempers, argue with adults, and defy or refuse adult requests. They may refuse to do chores and to take responsibility for their actions. The defiant behavior is directed primarily toward parents, teachers, and other people in authority. Anger, resentment, blaming others, and spiteful and vindictive behaviors are common. Although confrontation often occurs, it does not involve the more serious violations of the rights of others that are involved in conduct disorders. Before puberty more males than females meet the criterion for this disorder, with closer to equal numbers after puberty (American Psychiatric Association, 2000a).

Oppositional defiant disorder is a relatively new category and is certainly one of the more controversial childhood disorders. It is often difficult to separate this disorder from milder forms of conduct disorder and from normal developmental difficulties in children and adolescents (Paternite, Loney, & Roberts, 1995). Most children and adolescents go through a period or several periods of defiant behaviors. In DSM-IV-TR, a criterion indicating that the problem causes "significant impairment in social or academic functioning" was added to try to discriminate between "normal" and "pathological" defiance. ODD tends to be associated with parent-child conflict, the espousing of unreasonable beliefs, and negative family interactions (Barkley et al., 1992). Because DSM-IV

oppositional defiant disorder (ODD) A childhood disorder characterized by a pattern of negativistic, argumentative, and hostile behavior in which the child often loses his or her temper, argues with adults, and defies or refuses adult requests; refusal to take responsibility for actions, anger, resentment, blaming others, and spiteful and vindictive behavior are common, but serious violations of other's rights are not.

mental Health and society

Are We Overmedicating Children?

A large number of medications are being prescribed to treat childhood disorders. They include tranquilizers, stimulants, and antipsychotic medications. As with adults, the use of medications with children and adolescents has been increasing dramatically. Drug companies are now advertising directly to the public via television and magazines. Ritalin production increased ninefold from 1985 to 1995 (Guttman, 1995). Controversy continues over the "quick fix" nature of medication, the large number of children for whom medications are prescribed, and the need to carefully determine whether medication, therapy, or intervention that focuses on other factors affecting the child (such as bullying at school or domestic violence within the home) is the best course of action for children experiencing difficulties (Marsa, 2000).

Concerns about the overprescription of psychoactive drugs for children, especially stimulant medication, have resulted in recent legislative efforts to prohibit schools from recommending, requiring, or, in some cases, even discussing the idea of a child being evaluated for possible ADHD. Others suggest that the increased use of stimulant medication is related to better diagnosis and public awareness of the disorder and increased participation in ADHD treatment by females and adolescents, previously underdiagnosed groups (DHHS, 1999). Additionally, ADHD is now diagnosed at earlier ages and, subsequently, medication therapy begins earlier, resulting in more prescriptions being given (Zito et al., 2000). In fact, recent reports have shown that only 2–3 percent of school-age children receive medication for ADHD, suggesting that reports that ADHD is overdiagnosed or that stimulant medications are overprescribed may not be accurate (Goldman et al., 1998; Jensen et al., 1999).

Unfortunately, apart from the more extensively researched stimulant medications used for ADHD, concerns remain regarding the "off-label" use of medication and the paucity of controlled studies on the safety and efficiency of specific medications being prescribed. It is particularly important for physicians to receive information on the effects of specific drug concentrations, frequency of dose, and the use of medication combined with other therapies (Schaffer et al., 1996).

Several questions are raised. Are the medications that are being used with children safe and effective in treating the specific disorders? Are medications being prescribed too freely? Is there adequate assessment or evaluation to determine whether medication is appropriate? Is there adequate monitoring of the effects of the drug and identification of possible side effects? Is there adequate information on the use of the specific medication with children? For example, clinicians recommend that Ritalin be prescribed only after a comprehensive diagnostic and evaluation procedure. The particular symptom or symptoms to be treated should be identified and the dosage modified if necessary. Prescribing any medication also necessitates the communication of possible side effects and contraindications to the patient and parent. Unfortunately, a large percentage of physicians and psychiatrists do not follow these guidelines (DuPaul & Barkley, 1993), and there is very limited research on some medications used with children, particularly mood stabilizers and newer antipsychotic medications (DHHS, 1999).

attempted to raise the threshold for the diagnosis of ODD, it is not clear how this will affect conclusions of studies that use a lower threshold.

Conduct Disorders

Charles was well known to school officials for his many fights with peers. After a stabbing incident at school, he was put on probation and then transferred to another junior high school. Two months later, at age fourteen, Charles was charged with armed robbery and placed in a juvenile detention facility. He had few positive peer contacts at the juvenile facility and seemed unwilling or unable to form close relationships. Some progress was achieved with a behavioral contract program that involved positive reinforcement from adults and praise for refraining from aggression in handling conflicts. He was transferred to a maximum-security juvenile facility when he seriously injured two of his peers, whose teasing had angered him. Charles completed a vocational training program in this second facility, but he couldn't hold a regular job. He was sent to prison following a conviction for armed robbery.

"DON'T YOU REALIZE, JASON, THAT WHEN YOU THROW FURNITURE OUT THE WINDOW AND TIE YOUR SISTER TO A TREE, YOU MAKE MOMMY AND DADDY VERY SAD?"

The Origins of Conduct Disorder   Many parents of adolescents with conduct disorder report a pattern of development—including bullying, lying, cheating, and aggressive behavior—that begins long before the teenage years.

Conduct disorders are characterized by a persistent pattern of antisocial behaviors that violate the rights of others. Many children and adolescents display isolated instances of antisocial behavior, but this diagnosis is given only when the behavior is repetitive and persistent. Conduct disorders may include behaviors such as bullying, lying, cheating, fighting, destruction of property, stealing, setting fires, cruelty to people and animals, assaults, rape, and truant behavior. The pattern of misconduct must last for at least twelve months to warrant this diagnosis (DSM-IV-TR).

The diagnosis of conduct disorder applies only when the behaviors reflect dysfunction in the individual rather than a reaction to the individual's social and economic environment. Males with this disorder tend to display confrontational aggressiveness such as fighting, stealing, and vandalism, whereas females are more likely to display truancy, running away, substance abuse, prostitution, or chronic lying. Estimates of prevalence range from 1 to 10 percent of the population. It is more common in males and in urban settings (American Psychiatric Association, 2000a).

Conduct disorders in adolescence represent a serious societal problem. In the United States, approximately 83,000 juveniles are housed in correctional institutions for antisocial behaviors, and 1.75 million were arrested in 1990 (Zigler, Taussig, & Black, 1992). Parents often report the following pattern in the development of the disorder: early arguments, stubbornness and tantrums, oppositional behaviors leading to fire setting and stealing and then truancy, vandalism, and substance abuse (Robins, 1991). Children and adolescents with conduct disorders have a greater tendency to seek novel situations and are less concerned about avoiding risk or harm (Schmeck & Poustka,

conduct disorders Disorders of childhood and adolescence characterized by a persistent pattern of antisocial behaviors that violate the rights of others; repetitive and persistent behaviors include bullying, lying, cheating, fighting, temper tantrums, destruction of property, stealing, setting fires, cruelty to people and animals, assaults, rape, and truant behavior.

2001). Although oppositional defiant disorder frequently precedes childhood-onset conduct disorder, it is important to note that many children with oppositional defiant disorder do not later exhibit a conduct disorder. Although many childhood disorders remit over time, children are less likely to outgrow conduct disorders. Lambert and colleagues (2001) emphasize the global nature of the difficulties experienced by children with conduct disorder. Children with this disorder not only show the externalizing aggressive behaviors that define the disorder but also may display internalizing symptoms, such as withdrawal and major depression, perhaps due to the social alienation created by their behaviors. It is interesting to note that childhood depression has been found to be a strong predictor of personality disorder in adulthood, including antisocial personality, although it is not clear whether the relationship is related to genetics or to the psychological outcomes of depressed mood (Harrington, 2001). Barry et al. (2000) found that subgroups of children with severe conduct disorder who also show callous, unemotional personality traits do not show much distress about their behavioral difficulties, a pattern consistent with that of adults who have antisocial personality traits. It may be that the group of children who show conduct-disordered behavioral symptoms but who do not have callous, unemotional personalities are, in fact, distressed by the lack of social connectedness that results from their behavior. As noted, prognosis for conduct disorders is poor; they often lead to criminal behavior, antisocial personality, and problems in marital and occupational adjustment during adulthood (Kazdin, Siegel, & Bass, 1992).

Many people with these disorders show early involvement with alcohol and illegal drugs (Lynskey & Fergusson, 1995). Many delinquent adolescents later become adult criminals. Nearly all adult offenders have a history of repeated antisocial behavior as children, and about 25 percent develop an antisocial personality disorder (Robins, 1991). The key factor associated with negative outcome is aggression. Highly aggressive children tend to remain aggressive over time, whereas other childhood adjustment problems show much less stability (Lerner et al., 1988). A particularly negative sign is sexually aggressive behavior. Individuals who engage in sexual assaults are more likely to show subsequent violence (both sexual and nonsexual) than are individuals who commit nonsexual violence (Rubinstein et al., 1993). Prognosis is better for males who have higher IQ scores and whose parents do not have antisocial personalities (Lahey et al., 1995). Females also have a better prognosis. (See the Mental Health and Society feature, "School Violence: A Sign of the Times?")

Treatment Although conduct disorders have resisted traditional forms of psychotherapy, training in social and cognitive skills appears promising (Chamberlain & Rosicky, 1995; Estrada & Pinsof, 1995). One program (Kolko, Loar, & Sturnick, 1990), for example, focused on helping aggressive boys develop the verbal skills to enter groups, play cooperatively, and provide reinforcement for peers. The cognitive element included using problem-solving skills to identify behavior problems, generate solutions to them, and select alternative behaviors. In addition, the children learned positive social skills through viewing videotapes and role-playing with therapists and peers. Dishion, McCord, and Poulin (1999) caution that group interventions involving the aggregation of young high-risk adolescents need to be considered carefully for use with delinquent youth because of possible "deviancy training effects" that may occur, resulting in increases in substance abuse and in antisocial and violent behavior. They propose mobilizing adult mentors (Chamberlain & Reid, 1998) or interventions targeting the parents of delinquent youths as powerful alternatives.

Parent management training has also been successful (Patterson, 1986; Webster-Stratton, 1991). These programs, which have evolved over a period of more than twenty years of work with problem children, teach specific skills so that parents learn how to establish appropriate rules for the child, implement consequences, and reward positive behaviors. The parents first practice their newly learned skills on simple problems and gradually work on more difficult problems, as they become more proficient in management techniques. A combination of building children's cognitive and social

mental health and society

School Violence: A Sign of the Times?

What accounts for the increase in dramatic episodes of violence in schools? What can we do to keep students safe and prevent such tragedies? There is increased national focus on these issues, particularly following violent events such as those that have occurred in schools in Colorado, Kentucky, Arkansas, Georgia, Oregon, and California.

Goldstein (1999) has focused on the link between low-level aggression and higher levels of aggression, concluding that it is critical to "catch it low to prevent it high" (i.e., not tolerating behaviors such as bullying, harassment, intimidation, vandalism, insults, or threats) and to provide comprehensive intervention for students who display these behaviors. The importance of working with gang-involved youth and adolescents and of understanding the characteristics of gang development (including initiation and recruitment practices) and the signs and symbols used by regional gangs has also been emphasized in efforts to prevent school and community violence (Goldstein & Kodluboy, 1998).

In addition, researchers continue to emphasize the complex effects that exposure to violence in the community has on children and adolescents, including internalized symptoms such as anxiety, depression, lack of concentration, and suicidal thinking and the externalized symptoms of aggressive, antisocial, and violent behaviors (Mazza & Overstreet, 2000). It is also important to recognize that, although school violence generates extensive media attention, it is only a subset of the overall pattern of violent crime committed by juveniles in the United States (Evans & Rey, 2001).

Given the reality that episodes of violence span the geographic and socioeconomic spectrum, researchers now recognize that violence is possible at any school. In response to public concern, the United States Department of Education has funded the Safe and Comprehensive Schools Project, an effort to examine actions that can be taken both to prevent violence and to recognize and intervene when there may be the potential of violence. Schools involved in the project have focused on three levels of intervention: (1) comprehensive planning to create a positive climate within the school—students are taught social skills and ways of peacefully solving conflict; (2) developing procedures for early identification and intervention for students who may be undergoing emotional difficulties or who appear to have violent tendencies or preoccupation with violent themes; and (3) developing effective responses to violence, with a philosophy not only of zero tolerance for any level of harassment or aggression but

skills and training parents in management techniques appears to produce the most marked and durable changes in children with conduct disorders (Kazdin et al., 1992). A curricular intervention for aggressive behavior on the playground showed clear reductions in aggressive actions, especially for those children who were initially the most aggressive (Stoolmiller, Eddy, & Reid, 2000). It has been suggested that early intervention targeting young children with high aggression, in addition to other risk factors such as low levels of parent education and early childbearing, is particularly important (Nagin & Tremblay, 2000).

Anxiety Disorders

Children and adolescents suffer from a variety of problems involving chronic anxiety—fears, nightmares, school phobia, shyness, timidity, and lack of self-confidence. Children with these disturbances display exaggerated autonomic responses and are apprehensive in new situations, preferring to stay at home or in other familiar environments. They report more negative thoughts about events and are overly self-critical (Bell-Dolan & Wessler, 1994). In contrast to the disruptive behavior disorders, which are socially disruptive and undercontrolled, the anxiety disorders are considered to be internalizing or overcontrolled. Higher distress scores are obtained from those with internalizing disorders than from those with externalizing disorders (McGee & Stanton, 1992).

The prognosis or course of internalizing disorders, even without treatment, is very promising (Esser, Schmidt, & Woerner, 1990). Some researchers believe that specific

also of creating procedures for responding to these behaviors and providing support to students about whom chronic or acute concerns exist.

Another challenge for schools is encouraging students to report to school officials when they become aware that a student has made comments or threats suggesting that they may harm others. Although it is recognized that potential reasons for not reporting might include a belief that the person is "only joking," concerns about retaliation or getting a friend in trouble, or concern about being labeled a "narc" or a "squealer," there is a need for systematic research to explore why students are not reporting threats of violence and to understand the characteristics of schools in which students do report potential problems (Lazarus, 2001). Understanding how to create a school environment in which students are willing to report potential danger is particularly important in view of reports that in over 75 percent of the cases of school violence studied by the Secret Service, the attacker had talked to at least one person about the plan prior to the attack. In addition, in about 70 percent of the attacks, the violent actions were actually encouraged by peers who knew about the plan (Vossekuil et al., 2000).

Some signs of the times: students as young as kindergarten age practice lockdown procedures and are trained in safety procedures in the event of violence in the schools in the same manner that earthquake and fire drills have been practiced for years.

MTV has developed a partnership with the American Psychological Association to provide a public outreach campaign to help end school violence.

Homicide is the second leading cause of death among children and adolescents. African American males between the ages of fourteen and nineteen are especially at risk; they are ten times more likely to die of homicide than are white males of the same age (Hammond & Yung, 1993).

Researchers continue to share concerns about the link between aggressive behavior and exposure to violent media (Bushman & Anderson, 2001).

In summary, recent efforts in the prevention of school violence have shifted from a focus on harsh consequences to a focus on prevention, encouraging students to report harassment and threats of violence, and schoolwide awareness of characteristics of students at risk for violent behavior or in need of mental health services. Comprehensive individualized intervention with a student who displays behaviors of significant concern is an essential component of these efforts. In addition, school systems are developing local and regional crisis response teams and plans for responding to catastrophic events, including procedures for "locking down" the entire school to ensure student safety.

personality patterns may predispose a child toward developing anxiety and other childhood disorders. Researchers (Weems, Silverman, & La Greca, 2000) examined the worries of children referred for treatment of anxiety disorders and found that their worries (health, school, disasters, and personal harm) were very similar to reports of worries of children in a community sample.

Children who suffer from a **separation anxiety disorder (SAD)** show excessive anxiety when separated from parents or home. They constantly seek their parents' company and may worry too much about losing them. Separation may produce physical symptoms, such as vomiting, diarrhea, and headaches. During separation, the child often expresses negative emotions, such as crying (Shouldice & Stevenson-Hinde, 1992). To receive a diagnosis of separation anxiety disorder, a child must display at least three of the following symptoms:

1. Excessive anxiety about separation from the attachment figure.
2. Unrealistic fear that the attachment figure will be harmed.
3. Reluctance to attend school.
4. Persistent refusal to go to sleep unless the attachment figure is nearby.
5. Persistent avoidance of being alone.
6. Nightmares involving themes of separation.
7. Repeated physical complaints when separated.
8. Excessive distress when separation is anticipated.

separation anxiety disorder (SAD)
A childhood disorder characterized by excessive anxiety over separation from parents and home.

The Anxiety of Separating   It is normal for very young children to feel distress when separating from their primary caretakers. Only when the distress is severe and prolonged is a diagnosis of separation anxiety disorder made.

This pattern must last at least four weeks and must occur before the age of eighteen (DSM-IV-TR). Children with this disorder tend to come from caring and close-knit families. There is a decrease in separation anxiety disorder from childhood to adolescence. Separation anxiety disorder may be a risk factor in developing a panic disorder (Battaglia et al., 1995). However, recent outcome data suggest that most children with separation anxiety disorder do not have continued anxiety disorders as adults (American Psychiatric Association, 2000a).

One type of separation anxiety disorder that has been studied extensively is *school phobia*, such as that exhibited by Nina in the case study at the beginning of this chapter. The physical symptoms may occur merely in response to the prospect of having to go to school. In a sample of high school students, about 6 percent of females and 2.5 percent of males indicated having had this disorder sometime in their lives (Lewinsohn et al., 1993). School refusal is common among children referred for treatment. It occurs more frequently in European American children than in African American children and is more common in children from lower socioeconomic backgrounds (Last & Perrin, 1993).

Psychodynamic explanations of school phobia stress the child's overdependence on the mother. The reluctance to attend school is not seen as a fear of school but as anxiety over separation from the mother. If separation anxiety is the primary etiological factor in this disorder, however, it should occur in the early school history of the child. But many cases of school phobia do not develop until the third or fourth grade. Also, these children often do not display "separation anxiety" in other situations that require separation from their mothers.

School phobia has also been explained in terms of learning principles. Parents are important sources of reinforcement during a child's preschool period. Going to school requires a child to develop new skills and to encounter uncertain and anxiety-arousing situations. If a parent reinforces the child's fears (for example, by continually warning the child not to get lost), the child may seek refuge away from school, where the kind of reinforcement he or she received earlier in life is available.

Cognitive-behavioral treatment of anxiety disorders in children has been found to be effective for children with anxiety alone or those with co-occurring psychiatric disorders (Kendall, Brady, & Verduin, 2001). Medication is sometimes used to treat childhood anxiety disorders. Luvox, which increases levels of the brain chemical serotonin and has been approved for the treatment of obsessive-compulsive disorder in children, has also been found effective in reducing symptoms of social phobia, separation anxiety, and generalized anxiety disorder in children (Vedantam, 2001).

Mood Disorders

Since infancy, David had had a history of depressive reactions to unpleasant events, which had become increasingly severe. Two events seemed to have produced affective pain and to have triggered the depressive acting out which led to his referral: one was a cerebral stroke suffered by his maternal grandmother with whom he was very close, and the second was learning of his mother's fourth pregnancy. . . . His parents described him as fearful and socially isolated and as making self-deprecating statements. His behavior at the time of referral was passive, quiet, and motorically slow, punctuated with occasional hostile outbursts. Suicidal ideation surfaced for several months—twice during the course of therapy. (O'Connor, 1987, p. 106)

The five-year-old boy just described displays many symptoms of depression. Although DSM-IV-TR does not list childhood depression under childhood disorders, children and adolescents may suffer from either major depressive disorder or the more chronic form of depression, dysthymic disorder, which often has its onset in childhood or adolescence and can persist for years (Kovacs et al., 1997). Recent attention has been given to bipolar disorder in children and adolescents. In adults who have bipolar disorder, depressive episodes alternate with episodes of mania (extreme energy, overconfidence, racing thoughts and/or speech, reduced need for sleep, reckless behavior). Children with bipolar disorder tend to have much more rapid cycling of moods, often with many mood changes occurring within the period of a day. A combination of hyperactivity, irritability, and shifting moods, particularly in a child with a first-degree relative with a mood disorder, suggests that an evaluation for bipolar disorder may be warranted (Papolos & Papolos, 1999). The most common form of depression in children, however, is reactive depression—depression lasting a limited period of time in response to a specific stressful situation. This depressive response is seen as a normal adjustment reaction and does not typically last longer than a few weeks, after which time the child or adolescent returns to normal functioning.

Estimates of depression range from 2 to 7 percent among children and adolescents (Kazdin, 1994; Petersen et al., 1993). Major depressive episodes can begin very early in life, even in infancy. During a five-year longitudinal study of third-grade children, the percentage of children who scored at a "serious" level of depression ranged from 4.9 percent to 11.3 percent (Nolen-Hoeksema et al., 1992). Children who were depressed during the first year of the study tended to also be depressed throughout the five-year period. Correlated with depressive scores were stressful life events, high levels of helplessness in social and academic situations, and a more pessimistic explanatory style. Depressive symptoms can co-occur with other disorders. Psychotic features are usually not seen in depressed children; however, the incidence of anxiety disorders and somatic complaints is greater than that seen in samples of depressed adults. In a sample of children and adolescents with dysthymic disorder, 33 percent of the children also showed separation anxiety, and 67 percent of the adolescents had a generalized anxiety disorder; however, only 14 percent of the sample displayed externalizing behaviors (Masi et al., 2001).

Depressed mood is more prevalent during adolescence and is more likely to be reported in adolescent girls than in boys (Weiss et al., 1992). Moderate to intense depressive symptoms were reported in 10 percent of adolescent boys and 40 percent of adolescent girls. Clinical depression is found in about 42 percent of psychiatric samples of adolescents and about 7 percent of nonclinical samples (Petersen et al., 1993). Mood disorders are of particular concern during middle adolescence because the risk of attempted suicide is greatest at this age (Centers for Disease Control and Prevention, 1999).

Clearly, depression does occur in childhood and adolescence. Children are especially vulnerable to environmental factors because they lack the maturity and skills to deal with various stresses. Conditions such as poor or inconsistent parenting, parental illness, loss of an attachment figure, and neglect or abuse often produce lowered self-esteem and increased vulnerability to depression. The connection between depression and abuse is notable, as about one of every ten children is the victim of physical abuse each year (McClain, 1995; see the Mental Health and Society feature, "Child Abuse").

Depressed children show many of the same characteristics exhibited by depressed adults. They have more negative self-concepts and are more likely to engage in self-blame

MENTAL HEALTH and SOCIETY

Child Abuse

Because the three-and-one-half-year-old boy had defecated in his pants once too often, the mother forced him to sit for two whole days on the toilet. She told her son that he would not be allowed to get up or eat unless he evacuated his stools. When the son became constipated and did not respond appropriately, the mother pulled him from the toilet seat and lashed his buttocks. She did this every hour on the hour, until they were raw and bleeding. Despite the son's pleading, the mother became so enraged that she gave him an enema with scalding water. The youngster lost consciousness and had to be hospitalized.

"Children are our most precious resource." "The future of society depends upon the youths of today." "Caring and nurturance of children are important responsibilities of a civilized society." These statements are repeated often by parents, teachers, social scientists, and politicians. Yet the maltreatment of children remains a significant national problem (Dogden, 2000). The following statistics present a shameful and dismal picture of how we value and care for our children:

- The U.S. Advisory Board on Child Abuse and Neglect (1995) conservatively estimates that nearly 2,000 infants and young children die from abuse and neglect

by parents or caretakers each year; that's an average of 5 children each day.

- Abuse and neglect kills 5.4 children out of every 100,000 who are age four and under (McClain, 1995).
- Approximately 1 child in 10 is the victim of severe physical abuse each year; 1 in 5 lives below the poverty line (McClain, 1995).
- An estimated 1 million or more youngsters run away from home (at an average age of fifteen); many do so to escape an intolerable home situation of physical or sexual abuse (Famularo et al., 1990; Feitel et al., 1992).
- Abuse of children results in tens of thousands of victims who are overwhelmed with lifelong psychological trauma and who continue to bear physical and psychological scars as adults; 18,000 children a year are left permanently disabled (Baladerian, 1991).

The Abused

Since the 1960s, when child abuse was recognized as a major social problem, reports of abuse have increased. Whether that increase reflects better reporting or an actual rise in abusive practices by parents is unclear. We do know, however, that children who are abused are more prone to

---

and self-criticism. Programs involving social skills training, cognitive behavioral therapy, family therapy (Beardslee et al., 1996; Winnett et al., 1987), and supportive therapy (Kazdin, 1994; O'Connor, 1987) have been effective in treating childhood depression. Medication is now more commonly used with depression in children and adolescents, especially when there has not been any response to therapeutic intervention. Prescriptions of antidepressants for this age group have increased from three to five times between 1980 and 1994 (Zito et al., 2000). As with adult mood disorders, appropriate diagnosis, particularly differentiating bipolar disorder from major depressive disorder, is critical in guiding the choice of medication (Papolos & Papolos, 1999).

Tic Disorders

tics Involuntary, repetitive, and nonrhythmic movements or vocalizations.

transient tic disorder Childhood onset disorder that lasts longer than four weeks but less than one year and that is characterized by involuntary, repetitive, and nonrhythmic movements or vocalizations.

chronic tic disorders Childhood-onset disorders that last longer than one year and are characterized by involuntary, repetitive, and nonrhythmic movements or vocalizations.

Tics are involuntary, repetitive, and nonrhythmic movements or vocalizations. Transient and chronic tic disorders and Tourette's disorder compose this group of disorders. Most individuals with tic disorders report bodily sensations or urges that precede the tic (Leckman, Walker, & Cohen, 1993). Most tics in children are *transient* and disappear without treatment. If a tic lasts longer than four weeks but less than one year, it is diagnosed as a **transient tic disorder.** A diagnosis of **chronic tic disorder** is given when the tic or tics last more than a year. Chronic tic disorders may persist into and through adulthood.

exhibit significant direct and indirect physical and psychological problems. The physical consequences of abuse range from mild bruises and lacerations to quite severe long-term damage, including brain damage, mental retardation, and cerebral palsy. Orthopedic injuries such as broken bones are not uncommon. X-rays of children who have been abused frequently reveal evidence of multiple old fractures and breaks that have healed.

Psychological effects of abuse include impaired memory, depression, self-destructive behavior, low self-esteem, and aggressive impulsivity (Alessandri, 1991; Sternberg et al., 1992; Toth, Manly, & Cicchetti, 1992). Abused children may show excessive anxiety, which can lead to bedwetting, nightmares, eating and sleeping disorders, and—in the teenage years—conduct disorders. Although physical and mental abuse can by itself be devastating, the impact of abuse is even more complex when it involves sexual molestation, incest, or rape (Kendall-Tackett, Williams, & Finkelhor, 1993). There is no one symptom or cohesive syndrome that characterizes children who have been abused (Saywitz et al., 2000), nor does DSM-IV-TR include child abuse as a disorder under the category of disorders usually first diagnosed in infancy, childhood, or adolescence. However, children who have experienced the trauma of sexual or physical abuse may show symptoms, either in childhood or later in life, of posttraumatic stress disorder (see the chapter titled "Anxiety Disorders") with experiences such as flashbacks, nightmares, feelings of alienation, or high levels of anxiety. Men who were sexually abused as children make up 2 to 5 percent of the general population. These individuals are themselves more prone to substance abuse and to lifelong sexual problems, such as exhibitionism, homophobic behavior, and sexual dysfunctions, than is the general population. Women who were abused as children tend to have poorer social and sexual relationships than do other women (Watkins & Bentovim, 1992; Jackson et al., 1990).

The Abuser

Why would parents abuse their own children? This is a very difficult question to answer. We know, for example, that most people who abuse were themselves abused as children. Most are under the age of thirty, are more likely to come from lower socioeconomic levels, are rarely psychotic, may show personality disorders, and often abuse alcohol and drugs (Petersen & Brown, 1994; Whipple & Webster-Stratton, 1991). Some studies indicate that abusive parents experience greater stressors (marital discord, unemployment, and poverty), tend to have low levels of tolerance for frustration, are more aggressive and selfish, and exhibit lower impulse control than their nonabusing counterparts (Hillson & Kuiper, 1994). It is clear that many factors contribute to abuse. Some, like poverty, are situational; others, such as immaturity and lack of parenting skills, are more related to individual temperament.

The most common tics are eye blinking and jerking movements of the face and head, although sometimes the extremities and larger muscle groups may be involved. In tic disorders, the movements, which are normally under voluntary control, occur automatically and involuntarily. Examples of tics reported in the literature include eye blinking, facial grimacing, head jerking, foot tapping, flaring of the nostrils, flexing of the elbows and fingers, and contractions of the shoulders or abdominal muscles. Vocal tics can range from coughing, grunting, throat clearing, and sniffing to repeating words. A tic disorder that has become very visible in our society because of its unusual nature is illustrated by the following example:

> Saul Lubaroff, a disc jockey in Iowa City, is able to deliver smooth news reports on the weather, news, and sports. However, whenever he turns off his microphone, an explosive, involuntary stream of obscenities follows. In high school, his classmates would mock and threaten him. Even today, his outbursts are highly embarrassing to him. He has shouted "HEY" and "I MASTURBATE" in a fancy restaurant. However, Saul does have control while he is on the air. He indicates that "I have no problem announcing. I can turn off my 'noises' for 20 to 25 seconds, sometimes up to two minutes." (Dutton, 1986, p. c1)

Tourette's disorder A childhood disorder characterized by multiple motor and one or more verbal tics that may develop into coprolalia (compulsion to shout obscenities).

Saul Lubaroff has a severe form of Tourette's disorder. According to DSM-IV-TR, a diagnosis of **Tourette's disorder** requires that the individual has demonstrated multiple motor tics and one or more vocal tics; tics must begin before age eighteen and have been apparent for at least one year (American Psychiatric Association, 2000a). Although there have been reports of Tourette's disorder in children as young as age two, the median age of onset is age seven, with a single tic (often eye-blinking) presenting as the first symptom. Vocal tics may include grunting and barking sounds or, on rare occasions, may involve explosive *coprolalia*, the compulsion to shout obscenities. Stress increases the severity of tic symptoms (Silva et al., 1995). Tourette's disorder is relatively rare, with a prevalence of 5 to 30 cases per 10,000 children; it occurs three to five times more frequently in males than in females in clinic samples and twice as often in community samples.

Elimination Disorders

Eight-year-old Billy did not want to go to school anymore. He was embarrassed about his inability to control his bladder, he frequently wet his pants while in class, and he had to put up with merciless teasing by classmates. Billy had been continent by age five, but he started wetting the bed again around the age of seven. His father was especially irate about his son's problem. He constantly berated Billy for being "a baby" and said he "should wear diapers again." The problem had become so severe that it disrupted the family's travel plans. On long outings by automobile, Billy—fearful that he would wet his pants—requested restroom stops every thirty minutes. For the first time, the family canceled their annual visit to their families on the East Coast. The trip would require traveling by plane, and both parents felt that the number of times Billy would visit the restroom on the plane and his tendency to wet his pants at the most inopportune times would ruin their pleasure in the vacation.

Most psychologists would agree with Freud that toilet training represents a major source of potential conflict for the child. It is one of the first times that demands for control of normal biological urges (urinating and defecating) are placed on the child. Most children handle this developmental milestone well, with no resulting problems. A small percentage of children like Billy experience elimination disorders—problems of bladder or bowel control.

Enuresis is the habitual voiding of urine during the day or night into one's clothes, bed, or floor. The behavior is generally involuntary, but in rare situations it may be intentional. Enuresis is most likely to occur during sleep, but it is not uncommon during the daytime. To be diagnosed with enuresis, the child must be at least five years old and must void inappropriately at least twice per week for at least three months. Enuresis is also associated with clinically significant distress and with impairment in social, academic, or other areas of functioning. It is a fairly common disorder, experienced by 5 to 10 percent of five-year-olds and 3 to 5 percent of ten-year-olds. Most children have outgrown the disorder by adolescence, although 1 percent of individuals with enuresis continue to have symptoms in adulthood (American Psychiatric Association, 2000a).

Both psychological and biological explanations have been associated with enuresis. Psychological stressors—unrealistic toilet training demands placed on the child, delayed or lax toilet training, a stressful life situation (such as death of a parent or birth of a new sibling), disturbed family patterns, or the presence of other emotional problems—can all be predisposing factors (Haug Schnabel, 1992; Olmos de Paz, 1990). Biological determinants may include delayed maturation of the urinary tract, delays in the development of normal rhythms of urine production, or a hypersensitive or small bladder.

Interventions often involve using medications that decrease the depth of sleep (allowing the child to recognize the bladder urges) or that decrease urine volume

enuresis An elimination disorder in which a child who is at least five years old voids urine during the day or night into his or her clothes or bed or on the floor, at least twice weekly for at least three months.

encopresis An elimination disorder in which a child who is at least four years old defecates in his or her clothes, on the floor, or other inappropriate places, at least once a month for at least three months.

(thereby decreasing enuretic events; Dahl, 1992). The most successful psychological procedures involve behavioral methods, such as parents giving constant reinforcement to the child, awakening the child to use the toilet, and giving the child responsibility for making up his or her own bed should an accident occur. A bedtime urine alarm treatment is particularly effective (Schulman et al., 2000).

Although less common than enuresis, **encopresis** may be more disturbing because it involves repeated defecating onto one's clothes, the floor, or other inappropriate places. To be diagnosed with this disorder, the child must be at least four years old and must have defecated inappropriately at least once a month for at least three months. The incidents must not be due to the use of laxatives. Estimates of the prevalence of encopresis vary, but it appears to occur in 1 percent of children in the grade school years, with boys far outnumbering girls. Intermittent episodes of encopresis can persist for years.

The most common means of treatment include proper medical evaluation (especially when constipation is present) and the use of behavioral and family forms of therapy. Parent and child education about toileting regimens and a well-organized bowel management program can produce dramatic results (Loening-Baucke, 2000).

▶ CHECKPOINT REVIEW

attention deficit/ hyperactivity disorders (ADHD) *(p. 338)*

chronic tic disorder *(p. 350)*

conduct disorders *(p. 344)*

encopresis *(p. 353)*

enuresis *(p. 352)*

oppositional defiant disorder (ODD) *(p. 342)*

separation anxiety disorder (SAD) *(p. 347)*

tics *(p. 350)*

Tourette's disorder *(p. 351)*

transient tic disorder *(p. 350)*

What are some of the characteristics of attention deficit/hyperactivity disorder, and what are the subtypes of this disorder?
- Attention deficit/hyperactivity disorder, or ADHD, is characterized by overactivity, restlessness, distractibility, short attention span, and impulsiveness.
- ADHD is relatively common, more likely to be present in boys than girls, and is often associated with behavioral and academic problems.
- It is believed that central nervous system involvement may be the culprit, as many conditions such as lead poisoning, chromosomal abnormalities, oxygen deprivation at birth, and fetal alcohol syndrome are associated with ADHD.
- Three types of ADHD are recognized: predominantly hyperactive-impulsive, predominantly inattentive, and combined.
- Medication is widely used to treat ADHD.

What is the difference between conduct disorder and oppositional defiant disorder?
- Oppositional defiant disorder (ODD) is characterized by a pattern of hostile, defiant behavior toward authority figures. Children with ODD do not display the more serious violations of others' rights that are symptomatic of conduct disorders. Conduct disorders, especially those that have an early onset, show a clear continuity with adult problems.

What is the general prognosis for children with anxiety disorders?
- Children's anxiety reactions are usually transitory and disappear with age.

Which adult mood disorders are also seen in children and adolescents?
- Depression, dysthmic disorder, and bipolar disorder can occur in childhood; these disorders become even more prevalent during adolescence.

What are tic disorders?
- Tics and other stereotyped movements often occur in children and adolescents. In most cases, tics are transient and disappear with or without treatment. Tics that last longer than a year are diagnosed as chronic tic disorders.
- A more complex problem is Tourette's disorder, which involves both vocal and motor tics.

What are elimination disorders, and what is their prognosis?
- Enuresis and encopresis are elimination disorders that are diagnosed when children pass an age at which bladder or bowel control should normally exist.
- Enuresis is the usually involuntary voiding of urine into one's own clothes or bed.
- Encopresis is the usually involuntary expulsion of feces into one's own clothes or bed.
- Although they cause considerable distress to the child, both elimination disorders usually abate with increasing age.

FOCUS QUESTIONS

- How can people with anorexia nervosa not realize that they are starving themselves to death?
- How does bulimia nervosa differ from anorexia?
- When do food binges turn into binge-eating disorder?
- What other kinds of eating disorders are there?
- Why has there been such an increase in disordered eating?
- How can we treat eating disorders?

14 Eating Disorders

Types of Eating Disorders

> Three years ago, doctors diagnosed Tara as having anorexia nervosa—an eating disorder characterized by self-starvation and severe weight loss. But Tara, at 5 feet 5 inches and 94 pounds, thinks she looks beautiful, but she wants to be even thinner. She admires her sharp collarbones and her pointy hipbones in the mirror. She likes how nice and small she feels in her boyfriend's arms. ("Anorexia's Web," 2001, p. 1)

> I would eat crazy amounts of food.... I'd eat ten pieces of bread and butter, a box of crackers, two bowls of cereal, and anything else that was sitting around in the kitchen. It was like I was in an alcoholic trance and I couldn't stop myself. In the morning I'd wake up thinking, I am so stupid. How can I be so stupid? (Jacobson & Alex, 2001, p. 1)

Eating disorders are becoming more prevalent in the United States, especially among young people. At some colleges, "vomit" signs are posted around women's bathrooms in the vicinity of dining halls urging women to clean up after themselves after vomiting. Cleaning equipment such as buckets, gloves, cleaning solutions, and sponges are often supplied (Palmer, 2001). The concern over body shape and weight is reflected in national surveys indicating that nearly 50 percent of adolescent females and 20 percent of adolescent males report dieting to control their weight. Weight concerns are so great that a reported 13.4 percent of girls and 7.1 percent of boys have engaged in disordered eating patterns (see Table 14.1). Factors associated with disordered eating patterns included being overweight, low self-esteem, depression, substance use, and suicidal ideation (Neumark-Sztainer, Hannan, & Stat, 2000). Paradoxically, the increasing emphasis on thinness, especially for women, is occurring as the population of the United States is becoming heavier (James, 2001). Size 14 is now the average clothing size for women and 41 for the jacket size for men (Zernike, 2004).

Adolescent boys and college males also show weight dissatisfaction, but their goals are to be heavier and more muscular. This more positive response to greater weight in males was reflected in their ratings. Men who were overweight rated themselves as more attractive and healthier than overweight women rated themselves, whereas underweight women felt more attractive and healthier than underweight men did (McCreary & Sadava, 2001). Similar findings about weight were reported with college men in Germany, France, and the United States. In the study (Pope et al., 2000), images of men with different degrees of fatness and muscularity were shown to a group of research participants. The males were asked to choose images that represented their own bodies, the bodies they would like to have, the body of an average man their age, and the male body they thought women preferred. In all three countries, the men picked an ideal body that was about 28 pounds more muscular than they themselves were and estimated that women preferred a male body 30 pounds more muscular than they were. In actuality, women indicated a preference for an ordinary male body without added muscle. Thus it would appear that both men and women suffer from body dissatisfaction.

Table 14.1   Prevalence of Weight Concerns of Youth in Grades 5–12

Concern	Females (%)	Males (%)
Very important not to be overweight	68.5	54.3
Ever been on a diet	45.4	20.2
Diet recommended by parent	14.5	13.6
Diet to "look better"	88.5	62.2
Engage in binge/purge behaviors	13.4	7.1
Binge/purge at least once a day	8.9	4.1

Source: Data from national survey of 6,728 adolescents (Neumark-Sztainer, Hannan, & Stat, 2000).

Weight and body shape concerns exist not only among young white females but also among older women and minorities (Andersen, 2001). With the exception of binge-eating disorder, males are much less likely than females to be diagnosed with an eating disorder. However, in certain areas, such as the sport of wrestling, males have been found to have high rates of eating disorders; in addition, the sociocultural emphasis on bodybuilding may underlie the fact that some men are also exhibiting an extreme fear of becoming fat (Holbrook & Weltzin, 1998).

Mass media may also be responsible for the increase in the percentage of men who are dissatisfied with their bodies: "no abs, thin chest, small muscles" (Morgan, 2002). Women's magazines have shown a dramatic increase in the number of ads displaying the male body. During the 1970s photos exhibited men in bathing suits on beaches; ads today, however, show undressed male bodies with electronics, telephones, furniture, and beverage products in which the display of the male body has no direct relevance (Pope et al., 2001). Perhaps the emphasis on the male body is responsible for the finding that between 6 and 7 percent of boys between the ages of fifteen and eighteen have taken anabolic steroids to gain more muscle mass (Kanayama, Pope, & Hudson, 2001).

Minority group members are not immune to society's emphasis on physical appearance. Rates of eating disorders are high among Hispanic Americans and American Indians and are increasing among Asian females (Kim, 2003; Sherwood, Harnack, & Story, 2000; Wax, 2000). Although African American women are less likely than white women to have eating disorders, there is some indication that prevalence rates are increasing.

Disordered eating patterns because of preoccupation with weight and body dimensions sometimes become so extreme that they may develop into one of the eating disorders—anorexia nervosa, bulimia nervosa, or binge-eating disorder (see Figure 14.1). More than 7 million women and 1 million men in the United States suffer from an eating disorder (National Association of Anorexia Nervosa and Associated Disorders, 2003).

Unfortunately, disordered eating attitudes and behaviors are becoming more common and are occurring even in children (Jones et al., 2001). In this chapter we attempt to determine the reason for the increase in eating disorders. In doing so, we consider the characteristics, associated features, etiology, and treatment of anorexia nervosa and bulimia nervosa, as well as binge-eating disorder, which was proposed as a category for inclusion in DSM-IV-TR (American Psychiatric Association, 2000a; see Table 14.2).

Anorexia Nervosa

Types: restricting; binge eating/purging

Refusal to maintain a body weight above the minimum normal weight for one's age and height (is more than 15 percent below expected weight)

Intense fear of becoming obese, which does not diminish even with weight loss

Body image distortion (not recognizing one's thinness)

In females, absence of at least three consecutive menstrual cycles otherwise expected to occur

EATING DISORDERS

Characterized by physically and/or psychologically harmful eating patterns

Bulimia Nervosa

Types: purging/nonpurging

Recurrent episodes of binge eating

Loses control of eating behavior when bingeing

Uses vomiting, exercise, laxatives, or dieting to control weight

Two or more eating binges a week, occurring for three or more months

Overconcern with body weight and shape

Binge-Eating Disorder

Proposed category

Recurrent episodes of binge eating

Loses control of eating when bingeing

No regular use of inappropriate compensatory activities to control weight

Binge eating occurs two or more times a week for six months

Concern about the effect of bingeing on body shape and weight

Marked distress over binge eating

EATING DISORDERS	Lifetime Prevalence and Sex Ratio	Age of Onset	Course
Anorexia Nervosa	Over 90 percent are white females; 0.5 percent prevalence	Usually after puberty or late adolescence	Highly variable; some recover completely; majority continue to be of low weight; 10 percent continue to meet diagnostic criteria 10 years after treatment
Bulimia Nervosa	Over 90 percent are white females; 1–3 percent prevalence rate	Late adolescence or early adulthood	Frequently begins after dieting; usually persists for at least several years; may be chronic or intermittent
Binge-Eating Disorder	0.7–4 percent; 1.5 times more prevalent in females than males; about 30 percent in weight control clinics have this disorder	Late adolescence or early 20s	Unknown; may be chronic among individuals seeking treatment

Figure 14.1 Disorders Chart: Eating Disorders *Sources:* Data from DSM-IV-TR; Hoffman (1998); Sullivan et al. (1998); Walsh & Devlin (1998).

Table 14.2   Do You Have an Eating Disorder?

Questions for Possible Anorexia Nervosa

1. Are you considered to be underweight by others? (What is your weight?)
   (Screening question. If yes, continue to next questions)
2. Are you intensely fearful of gaining weight or becoming fat even though you are underweight?
3. Do you feel that your body or a part of your body is too fat?
4. If you had periods previously, have they stopped?

Questions for Possible Bulimia Nervosa

1. Do you have binges in which you eat a lot of food?
   (Screening question, If yes, continue to next questions)
2. When you binge, do you feel a lack of control over eating?
3. Do you make yourself vomit, take laxatives, or exercise excessively because of overeating?
4. Are you very dissatisfied with your body shape or weight?

Questions for Possible Binge Eating Disorder

1. Do you have binges in which you eat a lot of food?
2. When you binge, do you feel a lack of control over eating?
3. When you binge, do three or more of the following apply?
   a. You eat more rapidly than usual
   b. You eat until uncomfortably full
   c. You eat large amounts even when not hungry
   d. You eat alone because of embarrassment from overeating
   e. You feel disgusted, depressed, or guilty about binge eating
4. Do you feel great distress regarding your binge eating?

Note: These questions are derived from the diagnostic criteria for DSM-IV-TR (American Psychiatric Association,, 2000a). For anorexia nervosa, the individual's weight must be 85 percent less than normal for age and height; for bulimia nervosa the binges must occur, on average, about twice a week for three months; and for binge eating the binges must occur, on average, at least two days a week for six months. If the full criteria for these disorders are not met and disturbed eating patterns exist, they may represent subclinical forms of the eating disorders or be diagnosed as eating disorder not otherwise specified.

Anorexia Nervosa

> Marya Hornbacher is an award-winning writer who fights a continuing battle with anorexia nervosa. At the age of eighteen, she weighed only fifty-two pounds and was so thin that she got bruises from lying in bed. As a fourth grader, Marya had become concerned about being "chubby," and she experimented with vomiting to control her weight. She ate highly colored foods so that she could identify them after throwing up. At twenty-three, Marya now weighs ninety pounds—healthier but still underweight—and she continues to struggle with eating. Her anorexia has left her with a variety of physical ailments: her heart muscle has been weakened, her stomach and esophagus are lacerated, her bones are brittle, and her immune system has been weakened. The disease has probably shortened her lifespan. Although fighting anorexia is difficult, Marya still believes that "it's your choice.…We are not just victims of external disease—we have choices." (Marshall, 1998, p. D2)

Although anorexia nervosa has been known for more than 100 years, it is receiving increased attention owing to greater public knowledge of the disorder and the apparent increase in its incidence. The disorder occurs primarily in adolescent girls and young women and only rarely in males. Estimates of its prevalence range from 0.5 to 1 percent of the female population. The rate peaks among fifteen- to nineteen-year-olds (American Psychiatric Association, 2000a; Walsh & Devlin, 1998). One disturbing finding is an increase in early-onset anorexia in girls between the ages of eight and thirteen (Lask & Bryant-Waugh, 1992). The causes of this condition are similar to those in women and include the pursuit of thinness, preoccupation with body weight and shape, disparagement of body shape, low self-esteem, and perfectionism. Although some men also develop this eating disorder, they are more likely to display "reverse anorexia"—they believe they are "too small." A small group of bodybuilders displayed disturbed patterns of eating and exercising, but their goal was to gain weight or muscle mass. In this study, the bodybuilders displayed body dissatisfaction, felt too fat, and were more preoccupied with food than a control group of college men (Mangweth et al., 2001). Among men who develop anorexia nervosa, clinical symptoms are similar to those of women with the disorder (Woodside et al., 2001). A major concern with anorexia nervosa is that it is associated with serious medical complications. The mortality rate is the highest of any major psychiatric disorder, with many deaths occurring suddenly, usually from ventricular arrhythmias (Panagiotopoulos et al., 2000).

Anorexia nervosa is characterized by a refusal to maintain a body weight above the minimum normal weight for one's age and height; an intense fear of becoming obese, which does not diminish with weight loss; body image distortion; and, in girls, the absence of at least three consecutive menstrual cycles otherwise expected to occur. A person with this puzzling disorder literally engages in self-starvation.

A very frightening characteristic of anorexia nervosa is that, even when they are clearly emaciated, most people with this disorder continue to insist that they are overweight. Others will acknowledge that they are thin but claim that some parts of their bodies are "too fat." They may measure or estimate their body size frequently and believe that weight loss is a sign of achievement but that gaining weight is a failure of self-control (American Psychiatric Association, 2000a). One eighteen-year-old woman with anorexia nervosa vomited up to ten times daily, took laxatives, and exercised four hours each day. Yet when her friends said, "You look sick," or "You need to eat," she viewed their comments as a sign of jealousy (Tarkan, 1998). Other times, peers will inadvertently provide reinforcement by expressing admiration for thinness. One woman, Rachel, hid her thin starving body under layers of bulky clothing. Some of her friends commented positively on her figure, which increased her determination to starve (Holahan, 2001a). In most cases, the body image disturbance is profound. As one researcher noted more than twenty years ago, people with this disorder "vigorously defend their often gruesome emaciation as not being too thin. . . . They identify with the skeleton-like appearance, actively maintain it, and deny its abnormality" (Bruch, 1978, p. 209).

Subtypes of Anorexia Nervosa There are two subgroups of patients with anorexia nervosa. Those with the restricting type accomplish weight loss through dieting or exercising. Those with the binge-eating/purging type lose weight through the use of self-induced vomiting, laxatives, or diuretics. Most, but not all, of this group binge eat. In one study of 105 patients hospitalized with this disorder, 53 percent had lost weight through constant fasting (restricting type); the remainder had periodically resorted to binge eating followed by purging or vomiting (binge-eating/purging type). Although both groups vigorously pursued thinness, they differed in some aspects. Those with restricting anorexia were more introverted and tended to deny that they suffered hunger and psychological distress. Those with the binge-eating/purging type were more extroverted. They reported more anxiety, depression, and guilt, admitted more frequently to having a strong appetite, and tended to be older.

Physical Complications Self-starvation produces a variety of physical complications along with weight loss. Patients with anorexia often exhibit cardiac arrhythmias because

anorexia nervosa An eating disorder characterized by a refusal to maintain a body weight above the minimum normal weight for the person's age and height; an intense fear of becoming obese that does not diminish with weight loss; body image distortion; and, in females, the absence of at least three consecutive menstrual cycles otherwise expected to occur.

Anorexia Claims a Victim Karen Carpenter, of the award-winning musical duo The Carpenters, is shown at a healthy weight in 1974 (left). In 1981, Karen showed visible signs of her illness (right). She died two years later of heart failure due to an anorexia-related complication. How can such individuals not realize they are starving themselves?

of electrolyte imbalance; most have low blood pressure and slow heart rates. They may be lethargic, have dry skin, brittle hair, and swollen parotid glands (from purging) that result in a chipmunk-like face, and exhibit hypothermia. For example, one woman had to wear heavy clothing even when the temperature was over 90 degrees (Bryant, 2001). Irreversible osteoporosis, vertebra contraction, and stress fractures are also significant complications of the disorder. Males with the bulimic type of anorexia are also prone to osteoporosis and are more likely than women to have comorbid substance use disorder and antisocial personality (American Psychiatric Association, 2000a). In addition, the heart muscle is often damaged and weakened because the body may use it as a source of protein during starvation. One result of such complications is a mortality rate of up to 20 percent, according to long-term follow-up studies (American Psychiatric Association, 2000b; Hoffman, 1998). Unfortunately, even with the severe health and emotional damage associated with the disorder, support groups advocating anorexia as a lifestyle choice have appeared on the Internet (see the Mental Health and Society feature, "Anorexia's Web," for the controversy over these Web sites).

Associated Characteristics A number of associated characteristics or mental disorders are comorbid (coexist) with anorexia nervosa. Obsessive-compulsive behaviors and thoughts that may or may not involve food or exercise are often reported (Milos et al., 2003; Rogers & Petrie, 2001). The manner in which these symptoms are related

mental health and society

Anorexia's Web

One individual writes, "I love the feeling I get when I can feel my bones stick out. I love feeling empty. I love knowing I went the whole day without eating. I love losing weight. I love people telling me 'you're too skinny!'" Another wrote, "I only had three olives, two cookies and some chicken curry today and puked it up so I'm starting to get back into the swing of things" (Hellmich, 2001, p. 2). Some of the names used in online discussion groups include "thinspiration," "puking pals," "disappearing acts," "anorexiangel," and "chunkee monkeee." Mottos such as "It's better to be thin and dead than fat and living" indicate the repugnance displayed to fat on these Web sites (Atkins, 2002).

Although anorexia nervosa has been associated with negative medical consequences and unhappiness for its victims, as many as 400 pro-eating-disorder Web sites have recently appeared. The Web sites include pictures of ultra-thin models, tips for dieting, and ways to conceal the thinness from family members and friends. The Anorexic Nation Web site features support groups to get or remain sick. Participants talk about how it is important to have friends that are like them and argue that anorexia is a lifestyle choice and not an illness. A woman on one site writes, "I am very much for anorexia and this webpage is a reflection of that. If you are recovered or recovering from an eating disorder, please, please, PLEASE do not visit my site. I can almost guarantee it will trigger you! But if you are like me and your eating disorder is your best friend and you aren't ready to give it up, please continue" (Hellmich, 2001, p. 3). These Web sites are visited by thousands of people each day, and medical experts are deeply concerned

that the sites will produce a surge in eating-disorder cases, especially among susceptible individuals. Judy Sargent, who is recovering from the disorder, says, "These sites don't tell you that you're going to die if you don't get treatment" ("Anorexia's web," 2001, p. 2). Eating-disorder organizations have been alarmed with these sites and have petitioned Yahoo! and other hosts to remove the forums. Initially the response they received was "no," because the issue involved freedom of speech. In August 2001, Yahoo! did agree to remove the pro-eating-disorder Web site; however, many sites have switched to other servers, and there has been a flood of e-mail, some expressing suicidal feelings for being denied access to their "community" (Holahan, 2001b). However, Anorexic Nation responds on its Web site by writing, "We are not going anywhere. We will not let anybody chase us off the Internet so easily. The pro-ana witch hunts must end. Society must deal with us now, and on our own terms."

Helpful resources for individuals with body dissatisfaction do exist online, such as www.mirror-mirror.org/college.htm, the American Anorexia/Bulimia Association, Eating Disorders Awareness and Prevention, Anorexia Nervosa and Related Eating Disorders, and the Eating Disorder Referral and Information Center. In addition, Web sites also exist that focus on helping people feel comfortable with their bodies. Bodypositive.com is an online magazine that offers different perspectives on larger body sizes. About-face.com addresses positive body esteem in women and delves into the impact of mass media on women's physical, mental, and emotional well-being (Maltais, 2001).

to anorexia nervosa is unclear because of the possibility that malnutrition or starvation may cause or exacerbate obsessive symptoms. Some investigators also believe that a characteristic of anorexia nervosa involves control. One individual noted that "It's a misguided way of coping with stress, a way of imposing control" (Erdely, 2004, p. 116). Personality disorders and other characteristics have also been linked to anorexia nervosa, although the restricting and binge-eating/purging types may differ in the characteristics with which they are linked. The restricting type is more likely to be linked to traits of introversion, conformity, perfectionism, and rigidity, whereas the bingeing/purging type is more likely to be associated with extroverted, histrionic, and emotionally volatile personalities, impulse control problems, and substance abuse.

Course and Outcome Anorexia nervosa tends to develop during adolescence, and the course is highly variable. Individuals with the binge-eating/purging type tend to have a better outcome and fit the profile of being high-functioning but chronically self-critical and perfectionistic. People with anorexia may form a heterogeneous group, with some developing the disorder because they fear their impulses and want to attempt to prove they can regulate them; others as an act of competitiveness or out of a sense of achievement; others as a form of self-punishment or a means of demonstrating control over one aspect of their lives. Greater severity of the disorder is associated with the constricted/overcontrolled profile that is manifested in the restriction of pleasure, needs, emotions, self-knowledge, sexuality, and relationships (Westen & Harnden-Fischer, 2001). A difficulty in attempting to determine outcome by anorexia nervosa type is that many patients who have the restricting type later develop the binge-eating/purging subtype.

Approximately 44 percent of individuals treated for anorexia recover completely and remain within 15 percent of their recommended weight, another 28 percent show some weight gain but remain underweight, and the outcome for 24 percent is poor. About two-thirds continue to have weight and body image preoccupations, and up to 40 percent have bulimic symptoms. Depending on the length of the follow-up period, mortality—primarily from cardiac arrest or suicide—ranged from 5 percent to 20 percent (American Psychiatric Association, 2000b). Death from suicide is especially high among individuals with anorexia who abuse alcohol (Keel et al., 2003). In a recent five-year follow-up study of ninety-five women patients age fifteen years and older with anorexia, 59 percent of the patients had initially had the restricting type and 41 percent had had the binge-eating/purging type. At follow-up, over 50 percent no longer had a diagnosable eating disorder, but three had died within the five-year period. Most still showed disturbed eating patterns, poor body image, and psychosocial difficulties (Ben-Tovim et al. 2001).

Bulimia Nervosa

> At first, after eating too much, I would just go to the toilet and make myself sick. I hadn't heard of bulimia.... I started eating based on how I was feeling about myself. If my hair looked bad, I'd stuff down loads of candy. After a while, I started exercising excessively because I felt so guilty about eating. I'd run for miles and miles and go to the gym for three hours. (Dirmann, 2003, p. 60)

Ex-Spice Girl and actress Geri Halliwell struggled with bulimia nervosa for almost ten years. The anguish over losing control of her eating caused her to research the disorder on the Internet and to seek treatment.

Bulimia nervosa is an eating disorder characterized by recurrent episodes of binge eating (the rapid consumption of large quantities of food) at least twice a week for three months, during which the person loses control over eating. Two subtypes exist: the purging type, in which the individual regularly vomits or uses laxatives, diuretics, or enemas; and the nonpurging type, in which excessive exercise or fasting are used in an attempt to compensate for binges. A persistent overconcern with body image and weight also characterizes this disorder. Eating episodes may be stopped when abdominal pain develops or when vomiting is induced.

Individuals with bulimia nervosa evaluate themselves critically in terms of body shape and weight. They overestimate their body size. Compared with women at similar weight levels but without the disorder, women with bulimia exhibited more psychopathology, a greater external locus of control, lower self-esteem, and a lower sense of personal effectiveness (Shisslak, Pazda, & Crago, 1990; Williams, Taylor, & Ricciardelli, 2000). They also have a negative self-image, feelings of inadequacy, dissatisfaction with their bodies, and a tendency to perceive events as more stressful than most people would (Vanderlinden, Norre, & Vandereycken, 1992). These characteristics of patients diagnosed with bulimia may be a result of their loss of control over eating patterns, however, rather than the cause of the disorder.

People with bulimia realize that their eating patterns are not normal, and they are frustrated by that knowledge. They become disgusted and ashamed of their eating and hide it from others. The binges characterized by rapid consumption of foods typically

bulimia nervosa An eating disorder characterized by recurrent episodes of binge eating (the rapid consumption of large quantities of food) at least twice a week for three months, during which the person loses control over eating and uses vomiting, laxatives, and excess exercise to control weight.

occur in private. Some eat nothing during the day but lose control and binge in late after-noon or evening. The loss of self-control over eating is characteristic of this disorder, and the individual feels difficulty stopping once a binge has begun. Consequences of binge eating are controlled through vomiting or the use of laxatives, which produce feelings of relief from physical discomfort and the fear of gaining weight. Those with the nonpurg-ing type of bulimia often follow overeating episodes with a commitment to a severely restrictive diet, fasting, or engaging in excessive exercising or physical activity.

Bulimia is much more prevalent than anorexia. Up to 3 percent of women may suffer from bulimia nervosa (Gordon, 2001; Walsh & Devlin, 1998). An additional 10 percent of women report some symptoms but do not meet all the criteria for the diag-nosis. The incidence of bulimia appears to be increasing in women and is especially prevalent in urban areas. Few males exhibit the disorder, presumably because there is less cultural pressure for them to remain thin, although it is estimated that about 10 percent of those affected by this disorder are males.

A person's weight seems to have little to do with whether or not the individual devel-ops bulimia. Most are within the normal weight range (Gordon, 2001). Of a sample of forty women with the disorder, twenty-five were of normal weight, two were overweight, one was obese, and twelve were underweight. These women averaged about twelve binges per week, and the estimated calories consumed in a binge could be as high as 11,500. Typical binge foods were ice cream, candy, bread or toast, and donuts.

Physical Complications   People with this disorder use a variety of measures—fasting, self-induced vomiting, diet pills, laxatives, and exercise—to control the weight gain that accompanies binge eating. More than 75 percent of patients with this disorder practice self-induced vomiting (McGilley & Prior, 1998). Side effects and complica-tions may result from this practice or from the excessive use of laxatives. The effects of vomiting include erosion of tooth enamel from vomited stomach acid; dehydration; swollen parotid glands, which produces a puffy facial appearance; and lowered potas-sium, which can weaken the heart and cause arrhythmia and cardiac arrest (American Dietetic Association, 2001; Hoffman, 1998). In rare cases, binge eating can cause the stomach to rupture. Other possible gastrointestinal disturbances include esophagitis and gastric and rectal irritation.

Associated Features   Some evidence has shown that individuals with bulimia eat not only out of hunger but also as an emotionally soothing response to distressing thoughts or external stressors. As noted earlier, women with this disorder tend to perceive events as more stressful than most people would. Such difficulties may lead them to consume food for gratification. In one study, eating and emotional states were monitored over a six-day period using handheld computers as recorders. Among the women, binges were preceded by poor mood, feelings of poor eating control, and the craving for sweets. Interestingly, a control sample of women without the disorder also reported frequent binges due to emotional states. Weight preoccupation is also related to the type of coping response an individual shows to life stressors. Mood disorders are common, and rates of seasonal affective disorder, a syndrome characterized by depression during the dark win-ter months followed by remission during the spring and summer months, are higher among those with bulimia nervosa than in the general population (Lam et al., 2001).

Course and Outcome   Bulimia nervosa has a somewhat later onset than anorexia ner-vosa, beginning in late adolescence or early adult life. Outcome studies have shown a mixed course, although the prognosis is more positive than for anorexia nervosa. In a five-year community study of 102 participants with bulimia nervosa, only a minority still met the criteria for the disorder at the end of the study period. However, each year about one-third would improve, and another one-third would relapse. Most continued to show disturbed eating patterns and low self-esteem, and 40 percent met the criteria for a major depressive disorder (Fairburn et al., 2000). Another five-year study of individuals with bulimia nervosa reported a more positive outcome. Almost three-fourths had no diagnosable eating disorder at the end of the study (Ben-Tovim et al., 2001). A history of substance use and a longer duration before treatment are associated with a poorer outcome (Keel et al., 1999).

Binge-Eating Disorder

> Ms. A was a thirty-eight-year-old African American woman who was single, lived alone, and was employed as a personnel manager ... she weighed 292 lb. ... Her chief reason for coming to the clinic was that she felt her eating was out of control and, as a result, she had gained approximately 80 lb over the previous year. ... A typical binge episode consisted of the ingestion of two pieces of chicken, one small bowl of salad, two servings of mashed potatoes, one hamburger, one large serving of french fries, one large chocolate shake, one large bag of potato chips, and 15 to 20 small cookies—all within a 2-hour period ... she was embarrassed by how much she was eating, and felt disgusted with herself and very guilty after eating. (Goldfein, Devlin, & Spitzer, 2000, p. 1052)

Binge-eating disorder (BED) is a diagnostic category that has been "provided for further study" in DSM-IV-TR (American Psychiatric Association, 2000a). Further research will be conducted to determine whether BED should be adopted as a distinct diagnostic category in DSM-V. Studies do seem to indicate that it may be an appropriate subgroup to be included as an eating disorder (Pull, 2004). The disorder is similar to bulimia nervosa in that they both involve the consumption of large amounts of food over a short period of time, an accompanying feeling of loss of control, and "marked distress" over eating during the episodes. However, in BED, the episodes are not generally followed by "the regular use of compensatory behaviors" such as vomiting, excessive exercise, or fasting. As in the case of bulimia nervosa, the individual with this disordered eating pattern eats large amounts of food, is secretive about this activity, and may eat large amounts even when not hungry. To be diagnosed with BED, an individual must have a history of binge-eating episodes at least two days a week for six months.

Females are one and one-half times more likely to have this disorder than males, and a prevalence range from 0.7 percent to 4 percent in the general community has been reported (American Psychiatric Association, 2000a; Stice, Telch, & Rizvi, 2000). White women make up the vast majority of clinic cases, whereas in community samples, the percentages of African American and white women with BEDs are roughly equal (Wilfley et al., 2001). However, African American women are more likely to be obese, but they show lower levels of eating, shape, and weight concerns and psychiatric distress (Pike et al., 2001; see Figure 14.2). American Indian women also appear to be at higher risk for BED, with a 10 percent prevalence rate reported in one study (Sherwood, Harnack, & Story, 2000).

Associated Characteristics In contrast to those with bulimia nervosa, individuals suffering from binge-eating disorder are likely to be overweight. Most have a history of weight fluctuation. It is estimated that from 20 to 40 percent of individuals in weight-control programs have BED. In the general population, its prevalence ranges from 2 to 5 percent (Telch & Stice, 1998). The risk factors associated with this disorder include adverse childhood experiences, parental depression, vulnerability to obesity, and repeated exposure to negative comments from family members about body shape, weight, or eating (Fairburn et al., 1998). The binges are often preceded by poor mood, low alertness, feelings of poor eating control, and cravings for sweets (Greeno, Wing, & Shiffman, 2000). The complications from this disorder are due to medical conditions associated with obesity, such as high blood pressure, high cholesterol, and diabetes. People with BED are also likely to suffer from depression (Hoffman, 1998).

As with the other eating disorders, comorbid features and mental disorders are associated with BED. In one study that compared 162 individuals with BED with psy-

binge-eating disorder (BED) A diagnostic category that is provided for further study in DSM-IV-TR and that involves a large consumption of food over a short period of time at least twice weekly for six months; unlike bulimia, it does not involve extreme behavioral attempts to vomit or excessive exercise as compensation.

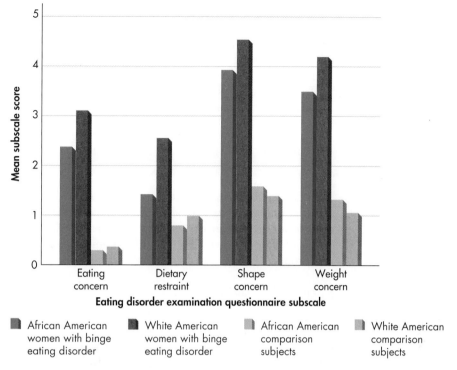

Figure 14.2 Binge-Eating Disorder   *Source:* Pike et al. (2001).

chiatric samples, the lifetime rate for major depressive disorder was higher among those with BED. Obsessive-compulsive personality disorder and avoidant personality disorder were also higher among the individuals with BED (Wilfley et al., 2000).

Course and Outcome   The onset of binge-eating disorder is similar to that of bulimia nervosa, typically beginning in late adolescence or early adulthood. The natural course of BED in young women appears to be relatively positive in comparison with the other eating disorders. Over a five-year period, most individuals with BED made a full recovery even without treatment. They showed improved self-esteem and higher social functioning. Only 18 percent had an eating disorder of clinical severity versus 51 percent of the bulimia nervosa cohort. However, their weight remained high, and 39 percent eventually met the criteria for obesity (Fairburn et al., 2000).

CHECKPOINT REVIEW

anorexia nervosa *(p. 359)*

binge-eating disorder (BED) *(p. 364)*

bulimia nervosa *(p. 362)*

How can people with anorexia nervosa not realize that they are starving themselves to death?

■ Individuals with anorexia nervosa suffer from body image distortion. They feel fat no matter how thin they get. They weigh less than 85 percent of their expected weight and suffer from effects of starvation but are still deathly afraid of getting fat.

How does bulimia nervosa differ from anorexia?

■ An individual with bulimia nervosa is generally of normal weight, engages in binge eating, feels a loss of control over eating during these periods, and uses vomiting, exercise, or laxatives to attempt to control weight. Some people with anorexia nervosa also engage in binge eating/purging but weigh less than 85 percent of their expected weight.

When do food binges turn into binge-eating disorder?

■ Although many people have engaged in binge eating, the diagnosis for the disorder is given only when the individual has regularly recurrent episodes in which she or he feels a loss of control over eating and shows marked distress about the activity. Most of these individuals are overweight.

What other kinds of eating disorders are there?

- Atypical patterns of severely disordered eating that do not fully meet the criteria for anorexia nervosa, bulimia nervosa, or binge-eating disorder would be given the diagnosis of Eating Disorder Not Otherwise Specified. Currently, binge-eating disorders are subsumed under this category.

◀ Etiology of Eating Disorders

The etiology of eating disorders is believed to be determined by social, gender, psychological, familial, biological, and cultural factors (Tripp & Petrie, 2001). See Table 14.3 for some of the risk factors in eating disorders. In this section we present some of the etiological factors involved. Usually it is a combination of variables rather than one factor that produces eating disorders, and this combination may differ for specific individuals.

Societal Influences

In the United States physical appearance is a very important attribute, especially for females. The average American woman is 5 feet 3 inches tall and weighs 152 pounds, but teenage girls describe their ideal body as 5 feet 7 inches, weighing 110 pounds, and fitting into a size 5 dress. Although this ideal is far from the actual statistics for body size, it is consistent with the image portrayed in mass media. It is estimated that only about 5 percent of American women can achieve the size required for fashion models (Irving, 2001). See the height and weight table, Table 14.4. Women are socialized to be conscious of their body shape and weight. As a result, many researchers believe that eating disorders result from the sociocultural demand for thinness in females, which produces a preoccupation with body image ("Risk Factors," 2003; Stice, Shaw, & Nemeroff, 1998). Society's increasing emphasis on thinness over the past twenty years has been accompanied by an increasing incidence of eating disorders. By fifth grade, over 31 percent of girls are already dieting, and 11.3 percent are engaging in disordered eating (Neumark-Sztainer et al., 2000).

The mass media are one route by which these messages can be delivered. Unrealistic body images of women are shown on movies, television, magazines, computer games, and even in toys. The thinness of many celebrities and models is unattainable for the vast majority of American women. A number of studies have indicated that in mass media, body slimness is associated with social rewards, whereas a fat body is socially stigmatized (Harrison & Cantor, 1997; Spitzer, Henderson, & Zivian, 1999).

Adolescent girls gave the following reasons for dieting and concern over their bodies: mass media (magazines, television, advertising, fashions), peer influences (wanting to fit in), and criticisms by family members about their weight (Wertheim et al., 1997). The beginning of dating and mixed-gender social activities is also related to dieting and disordered eating, especially for young women who have recently experienced menarche (Cauffman &

Table 14.3	Overview of Major Risk Factors for Eating Disorders

Biological
- Dieting
- Obesity/overweight/pubertal weight gain

Psychological
- Body image/dissatisfaction/distortions
- Low self-esteem
- Premorbid OCD
- Childhood sexual abuse

Family
- Parental attitudes and behaviors
- Parental comments regarding appearance
- Eating-disordered mothers
- Misinformation about ideal weight

Sociocultural
- Peer pressure regarding weight/eating
- Media: TV, magazines
- Distorted images: Toys
- Elite athletes as at-risk groups

Source: White (2000).

Idealized Image?   The Barbie doll illustrates some of the unrealistic physical standards that girls are exposed to. If the proportions of Barbie were applied to the woman on the left, she would have to be a foot taller, increase her breast size by four inches, and reduce her waist by five inches. Does exposure to the Barbie doll affect the body image of young girls?

Steinberg, 1996). Unfortunately, high school and college females may not be aware of the psychologically harmful effect of the super-slim standard for women. When asked to examine forty magazine ads featuring potentially harmful female stereotypes, they picked out ones that portray women as helpless or dumb, as sex objects, or as using alcohol or cigarettes. They appeared to overlook the ultra-thin models, possibly because they were accustomed to seeing this or have accepted it as a social-cultural norm (Gustafson, Popovich, & Thomsen, 2001).

Body dissatisfaction among male and female college students was studied by Forbes and colleagues (2001). Participants were asked to choose, from drawings of different figures, (1) the one that was closest to their own, (2) the one that they would most like to have, (3) the one that their gender would like, and (4) the one that the opposite sex would like best (see Figure 14.3). For males, the figure they chose as "matching their own" was smaller than the one that they believed most men or most women would prefer. In contrast, female participants chose a figure "matching their own" as much larger than the one they would like to have and that they believed most women or men would prefer. Although society's emphasis on body

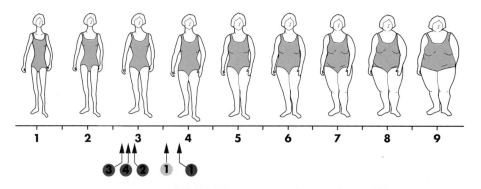

For Female Participants	Mean Rating
❶ Which body type closely matches your own?	3.85
❷ Which body type would you most like to have?	2.99
❸ Which body type would most women like to have?	2.69
❹ Which body type do you believe men like best?	2.85

For Male Participants	Mean Rating
❶ Which body type do you find most attractive?	3.52

Figure 14.3 Preferences for Female Body Types by Female and Male College Students
Source: Forbes et al. (2001).

Table 14.4   Height and Weight Table for Women

Height Feet Inches	Small Frame	Medium Frame	Large Frame
4' 10"	102–111	109–121	118–131
4' 11"	103–113	111–123	120–134
5' 0"	104–115	113–126	122–137
5' 1"	106–118	115–129	125–140
5' 2"	108–121	118–132	128–143
5' 3"	111–124	121–135	131–147
5' 4"	114–127	124–138	134–151
5' 5"	117–130	127–141	137–155
5' 6"	120–133	130–144	140–159
5' 7"	123–136	133–147	143–163
5' 8"	126–139	136–150	146–167
5' 9"	129–142	139–153	149–170
5' 10"	132–145	142–156	152–173
5' 11"	135–148	145–159	155–176
6' 0"	138–151	148–162	158–179

Note: Weights at ages 25–59 based on lowest mortality. Weight in pounds according to frame (in indoor clothing weighing 3 lbs.; shoes with 1" heels.)

Source: MetLife®. Copyright 1996, 1999 Metropolitan Life Insurance Company, One Madison Avenue, New York, NY 10010. All Rights Reserved. Reprinted with the permission of MetLife. This information is not intended to be a substitute for professional medical advice and should not be regarded as an endorsement or approval of any product or service.

types for males and especially for females may lead to general body dissatisfaction, it is important to identify individuals who are most influenced by the standard. The researchers found that among both males and females, those of either gender with low self-esteem displayed the greatest degree of body dissatisfaction.

Women in their twenties have a much higher standard of thinness than girls do. This might indicate that a need to be increasingly thin begins to develop in adolescence and becomes deeply ingrained when the young woman reaches full adulthood. Especially intriguing is the finding that 27 percent of adolescent girls who rate themselves as being at the "right weight" are still trying to lose weight (Walsh & Devlin, 1998). In fact, one study of 288 girls between the ages of ten and fifteen found that girls wanted thinner bodies than they thought boys found attractive (Cohn et al., 1987). Variables other than a desire to be attractive to men must be involved. An independent standard of thinness might be one factor. Some support for this view was found by Silverstein and Perdue (1988). They found that women equated thinness with attractiveness and with professional success and intelligence.

Can Ballerinas Be of Normal Weight?   We expect ballerinas to be thin and tall. What is your reaction to these students in a ballet class? If they plan to be successful ballerinas, will they be exposed to pressure to become unusually thin?

Height Feet Inches	Small Frame	Medium Frame	Large Frame
5' 2"	128–134	131–141	138–150
5' 3"	130–136	133–143	140–153
5' 4"	132–138	135–145	142–156
5' 5"	134–140	137–148	144–160
5' 6"	136–142	139–151	146–164
5' 7"	138–145	142–154	149–168
5' 8"	140–148	145–157	152–172
5' 9"	142–151	148–160	155–176
5' 10"	144–154	151–163	158–180
5' 11"	146–157	154–166	161–184
6' 0"	149–160	157–170	164–188
6' 1"	152–164	160–174	168–192
6' 2"	155–168	164–178	172–197
6' 3"	158–172	167–182	176–202
6' 4"	162–176	171–187	181–207

Table 14.4 continued   Height and Weight Table for Men

Note: Weights at ages 25–59 based on lowest mortality. Weight in pounds according to frame (in indoor clothing weighing 5 lbs.; shoes with 1" heels.)

Mass media portrayals of lean, muscular male bodies are also increasing. There appears to be a gradual shift away from traditional measures of masculinity that include wealth and power toward physical appearance. If this is true, we may see dramatic increases in eating disorders among men in the near future (Pope et al., 2001). The gay male subculture places a great deal of value on physical attractiveness, resulting in more concern over body size and appearance and disturbed eating patterns (Strong et al., 2000). Some studies indicate that gay males constitute 30 percent of males with eating disorders (Carlat, Camargo, & Herzog, 1997; Heffernan, 1994). Subcultural influences on attractiveness are also apparent in the fact that lesbians appear to be less concerned about physical appearance and report that they are less influenced by the media (Pope et al., 2001).

What kind of predisposition or characteristic leads some people to interpret images of thinness in the media as evidence of their own inadequacy? Are people who develop eating disorders chronically self-conscious to begin with, or do they develop eating disorders because agents in their social environment make them chronically self-conscious? How does exposure to mass media portrayals of thinness influence the values and norms of young people? Harrison (2001) believes that the development of disordered eating and preoccupation with body image may involve multiple processes (see Figure 14.4): First, exposure to ultra-thin media models can lead to thin-body-image internalization, which could lead to patterns of eating intended to bring about this ideal. Second, exposure to a thin ideal could increase negative feelings about oneself, which then triggers dieting. Third, exposure to the thin ideal can promote social comparison, which can lead to disordered eating to meet external standards of beauty. Although societal emphasis on thinness is related to an increase in disordered eating, it is not a sufficient explanation. Only a relatively small percentage of individuals in our media-conscious society develop eating disorders.

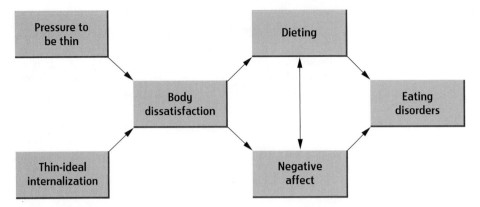

Figure 14.4   **Route to Eating Disorders**   *Source:* Adapted from Stice (2001).

Family and Peer Influences

Interpersonal interaction patterns with parents and peers have also been put forth as explanations of eating disorders. The early psychodynamic formulation, which was based primarily on anorexia nervosa, hypothesized the following family characteristics. The girl with the disorder has problems with maturation. She is afraid of having to grow up, which would lead to having to separate from her family and develop her own identity. By staying thin and not menstruating, she fulfills the unconscious desire to remain a child (Bruch, 1978; Halmi et al., 2000). Other family characteristics are believed by some to be important in eating disorders. In their book, *Psychosomatic Families: Anorexia in Context,* Minuchin, Rosman, and Baker (1978) describe communication patterns between family members as problematic and characterized by parental control, emotional enmeshment, and unexpressed conflicts and tensions. This pattern of family relationships is believed to result in anorexia. Other unhealthy family patterns

Ideal Male Bodies?   Most males prefer to be heavier and more muscular. Will the exposure in the media of physically powerful men produce body image distortion and dissatisfaction among men?

that are thought to be important etiological factors are maternal overprotectiveness, parental rejection, and less paternal affection (Leung, Thomas, & Waller, 2000). Unfortunately, the reported findings are difficult to interpret. Most are based on case studies or family systems theory or depend on the perception of family members of their relationships. Also, family patterns may change as a result of dealing with an eating disorder. Parents may become more "controlling" in an attempt to force the person with the eating disorder to gain weight or to establish a healthier eating pattern. At this point we don't know if the described "family characteristics should be considered cause, consequence, or means of coping with an eating disorder" (Herzog et al., 2000, p. 360).

Stice and Bearman (2001) believe that socialization agents such as peers or family members can produce pressure to be thin by engaging in criticism of weight, encouragement to diet, and the praise of ultra-slim models.

Healthy or Overweight?   In high school, Jamie-Lynn DiScala, who plays Meadow on "The Sopranos," would get up at 4 a.m. to exercise for two hours. Her dinner consisted merely of fat-free yogurt. She was so thin that size 0 clothing was too large for her. Now recovered, she has received criticisms from some fans that she is overweight and fat!

Perceived pressure from family, friends, dating partners, or the media to have a slender figure was associated with the thin-ideal internalization and feelings of depression. Part of the depressive reaction arises from the view that "one should be able to diet or exercise to lose weight"—in other words, that obtaining a slim figure is under voluntary control. Later, eating "too much," unsuccessful dieting, and guilt from purging or loss of control contributes to depressive feelings. One woman with an eating disorder remembers being teased about her weight by her family. Her nickname was "Checker." It was not until she was a teenager that her mother told her the name came from Chubby Checker (Goldfein et al., 2000). This revelation increased the young woman's sensitivity about her weight. Teasing and criticism about body weight or shape by family members has been found to predict ideal-body internalization, body dissatisfaction, dieting, and eating problems (Vincent & McCabe, 2000).

Problems in relationships can also increase susceptibility to developing problem eating patterns. Jamie-Lynn DiScala, who plays Tony Soprano's daughter Meadow on "The Sopranos," focused on dieting and exercising after breaking up with her boyfriend during high school. She lost so much weight that she could not fit into size 0 clothing and resorted to wearing children's sizes. She is now at a healthy weight and educates people about the disorder. Ironically, some fans believe she has gained too much and have posted emails to her website calling her "fat" (DiPasquale & Karnopp, 2004, p. 28).

Other family and peer relationships are associated with eating disorders. Peer relationships can either serve as a buffer to eating disorders or produce pressure to lose weight. Girls exist in a subculture in which thinness is emphasized and weight issues are frequently discussed. Nearly 50 percent of adolescent girls in one study reported being encouraged to lose weight by their mothers, friends, or sisters (Mukai, 1996). Mothers who dieted also indirectly transmitted the message of the importance of slimness and the thin ideal and had a significant influence on their daughters' weight-loss behaviors. For boys, peer and father encouragement to lose weight was related to more severe disordered eating patterns (Vincent & McCabe, 2000).

mental health and society

Is Our Society Creating Eating Disorders?

There appears to have been a dramatic increase in eating disorders over the past twenty years, which is correlated with our society's emphasis on thinness and attractiveness. Even fourth-grade girls are beginning to diet, and 31 percent of nine-year-old girls are worried about being fat. About 80 percent of American girls report having dieted by the age of thirteen (Gardner, 1998). Liposuction is the leading cosmetic surgical procedure; nearly 150,000 individuals had this procedure in 1997, more than triple the rate for 1992 ("Liposuction vs. American fat," 1998). Equating thinness with success and attractiveness has taken a toll, especially among women. As many as 64 percent of women exhibit symptoms of eating disorders, and even more are dissatisfied with their body shapes (American Anorexia/Bulimia Association, 1998).

What role has society played in eating disorders, and why do they appear primarily in Western societies? Eating disorders are rare in China, Singapore, Malaysia, and Hong Kong (Lee, Hsu, & Wing, 1992; Tsai & Gray, 2000) and in other non-Western cultures (Bhadrinath, 1990). Root (1990) believes that thinness represents success and control in Western societies. Other societies do not place such emphasis on thinness. Is it possible that eating disorders are culture-bound syndromes and are attempts by women to resolve identity issues?

As psychologists, we are interested in the etiology or causes of problems. What do you think about the opinion that the "pursuit of thinness" is a culture-bound phenomenon? Do contemporary women gain status or identity through their physical appearance? Why have Western cultures been so susceptible to eating disorders? Do you think eating disorders will increase in the future in other societies? If society continues to equate desirable characteristics with thinness, how can we change its message? How have African Americans been able to insulate themselves from this standard?

The women's movement stressed the importance of ability over appearance. Why, given the greater freedom and power that women have gained, is there an increase in the importance of appearance?

We are also beginning to see more physically attractive men in the mass media. (In one study of twenty-five college men with an eating disorder, they expressed dissatisfaction with their body images and used vomiting, laxatives, and exercise to control their weight; Olivardia et al., 1995.) Are such attitudes an early warning sign for a dramatic increase in eating disorders in men?

Cultural Factors

Some observers believe that eating disorders are a culture-bound syndrome found only in Western cultures (see the Mental Health and Society feature, "Is Our Society Creating Eating Disorders?"). Few reports of eating disorders are found in Latin America, South America, and Asia, whereas they appear to be high or increasing in European countries, Israel, and Australia (Miller & Pumariega, 2001). Countries or groups that have been exposed to Western values show an increasing concern over eating (Srinivasan, Suresh, & Jayaram, 1998). Although the standard of beauty among African American women in South Africa is based on fuller figures, black teenage girls are being drawn to Western standards of thinness, resulting in a dramatic increase in eating disorders among this group (Simmons, 2002). Asian female adolescents born in Britain also have concerns over body shape and eating (Hill & Bhatti, 1995). Among Pakistani adolescent girls, those who were the most exposed to Western culture had the highest rates of abnormal eating attitudes (Mumford, Whitehouse, & Choudry, 1992). In a shocking discovery, Becker (1995) found that Fijian girls displayed dieting and disordered eating during a three-year exposure to Western media. Prior to this period, these behaviors were virtually unknown. The girls reported that television influenced their beliefs regarding the thin body ideal. What is more astounding is that in Fiji the norm for an attractive woman is larger size with a good appetite (Irving, 2001).

Interestingly, African Americans appear to be somewhat insulated from the thinness standard. Even though they tend to be heavier, African American girls and women are more satisfied with their body size, weight, and appearance than are white females. They

Table 14.5   Differences in Body Image and Weight Concerns Among African American and White Females

Concern	African American Females	White American Females
Satisfied with current weight or body shape	70 percent	11 percent
Body image	Perceive selves to be thinner than they actually are.	Perceive selves to be heavier than they actually are.
Attitude toward dieting	Better to be a little overweight than underweight (65 percent of respondents in a survey).	Need to diet to produce a slender body. Fear of being overweight.
Definition of beauty	Well groomed, "style," and overall attractiveness. Beauty is the right "attitude and personality."	Slim; 5'7"; 100 to 110 pounds. Perfect body can lead to success and the good life.
Being overweight	Of those who were overweight, 40 percent considered their figures attractive or very attractive.	Those who considered selves as not having a weight problem were 6 to 14 pounds under the lower limit of the "ideal" weight range.
Age and beauty	Believed they would get more beautiful with age (65 percent chose this response).	Beauty is fleeting and decreases with age.

Sources: From Desmond et al. (1989); Kumanyika, Wilson, & Guilford-Davenport (1993); Lovejoy (2001); Parker et al. (1995); Rand & Kuldau (1990).

also have a lower level of negative attitudes toward body size and weight and less motivation for thinness (Lovejoy, 2001). Findings from a national survey of adolescents on dieting and disordered eating appear to support this view (Newmark-Sztainer et al., 2000). Ethnic comparisons revealed that dieting was lowest among African American girls (37.6 percent) and highest among white girls (51.3 percent). Disordered eating patterns (bingeing and purging) were highest among Hispanic American girls (19.1 percent) and lowest among African American girls (11.4 percent). Although the results may indicate that African American girls appear to experience lower levels of body dissatisfaction than girls from other ethnic groups, a substantial percentage of them also diet and binge or purge. The impact of ethnicity and dieting or disordered eating was more difficult to interpret in the case of boys. No relationship was found between ethnicity and dieting, but 13.9 percent of African American and 13.1 percent of Hispanic American boys engaged in disordered eating as compared with only 4.4 percent of white boys. Why nonwhite boys in the study were more likely to report bingeing and purging is unclear (Story et al., 1998).

Although fewer African American women appear to have either anorexia nervosa or bulimia nervosa, they are as likely as other groups of women to have binge-eating disorder (Dolan, 1991; Lovejoy, 2001). African Americans appear to be able to ignore the white media messages that equate thinness with beauty. Table 14.5 compares some differences in body image and weight concerns among African American and white women. It is possible that African American girls and women are protected by several cultural factors. First, because they do not identify with white women, media messages of thinness have less impact. Second, their definition of attractiveness is broad, encompassing style of dress, personality, and confidence and does not focus just on external characteristics such as body shape and weight. Third, African American women tend to be assertive and egalitarian in relationships, which allows them to have important roles in the community. In this way, they may be less influenced by gender-restrictive messages than white women.

However, not all African American women are protected from majority-culture messages. Many engage in binge eating and attempt to diet. As with white American women, self-esteem and body dissatisfaction among African American women is related to bulimic symptoms. This relationship is greatest among those who have internalized U.S. societal values concerning attractiveness (Lester & Petrie, 1998). In a study of African American and white women with or without binge-eating disorder, certain differences were found (Pike et al., 2001). African American women had higher body weight than white women and had fewer weight and shape concerns, regardless of whether or not they had the disorder. Among those with binge-eating disorder, African Americans had significantly lower scores on eating concerns, dietary restraint, and shape and weight concern (see Table 14.5). Thus African American women with binge-eating disorder differed in certain eating disorder characteristics from their white counterparts. The drive for thinness may be less an etiological factor for African Americans than for white Americans. Among Hispanic American female college students, weight and adherence to mainstream values were positively related to bulimic symptoms (Lester & Petrie, 1995). Thus it appears that ethnic minorities are becoming increasingly vulnerable to societal messages regarding attractiveness and may be at especially high risk for developing eating disorders, as a greater percentage of ethnic minority children and adults, especially females, are overweight ("Update: Prevalence of Overweight," 1997).

Other Suggested Etiological Factors in Eating Disorders

Additional research has focused on personality characteristics, negative emotional moods, and sexual abuse as causal factors in eating disorders. Individuals with eating disorders often display low self-esteem and feelings of helplessness, resulting in the use of food or weight control as a means of handling stress or anxieties (Walsh & Devlin, 1998). Individuals with anorexia have been described as perfectionistic, obedient, good students, excellent athletes, and model children. It is hypothesized that the emphasis on weight allows them to have control over an aspect of their lives. Dieting and weight loss are individual activities over which one has nearly total control (Hoffman, 1998). Perfectionism has also been found to be a predictor of bulimic symptoms among women who perceived themselves as being overweight (Joiner et al., 1997). For both men and women, higher scores on characteristics such as passivity, low self-esteem, dependence, and nonassertiveness are associated with higher scores on disordered eating. Dieting may be used to demonstrate self-control and improve self-esteem and body image (Lakkis, Ricciardelli, & Williams, 1999). Depression often accompanies eating disorders. One interesting finding is that binge eating, purging, and mood varied seasonally among patients with bulimia nervosa (Blouin et al., 1992). The researchers hypothesize that for some people, a relationship between bulimia and seasonal affective disorder may exist. The cycle of bingeing and purging may be associated with availability of light.

Although it is widely believed that sexual abuse is a causal factor in eating disorders, several studies have failed to find such a connection (Conners & Morse, 1993; Pope & Hudson, 1992; Pope et al., 1994). Sexual abuse may be indirectly related to eating disorders in that it produces body disparagement or bodily shame, which affects body image (Tripp & Petrie, 2001).

Genetic Influences

Genetic influences may also contribute to eating disorders, which appear to run in families, especially among female relatives (Hoffman, 1998). Strober et al. (2000) examined the lifetime rates of full or partial anorexia nervosa and bulimia nervosa among first-degree relatives of patients with these eating disorders. The rate was compared with that of relatives of matched, never-ill comparison participants. Support was found for a genetic contribution to the disorders. Whereas anorexia nervosa and bulimia nervosa were relatively rare among the relatives of the never-ill group, these disorders occurred at significantly high levels among the first-degree relatives of those with eating disorders (see Table 14.6). Interestingly, in this study, the relatives of those with anorexia nervosa were as likely to develop bulimia as anorexia. The reverse was also true. There may be a shared

Table 14.6   Lifetime Rates of Illness in Female First-Degree Relatives of Probands with Anorexia Nervosa, or No Psychiatric Illness

Proband Diagnosis	Number of Female Relatives	Female Relatives with Diagnosis									
		Anorexia Nervosa		Partial Anorexia Nervosa		Bulimia Nervosa		Partial Bulimia Nervosa		Total and Partial Illness	
		n	%	*n*	%	*n*	%	*n*	%	*n*	%
Anorexia nervosa	290	10	3.4	10	3.4	11	3.8	10	3.4	41	14.4
Bulimia nervosa	297	11	3.7	10	3.4	12	4.0	11	3.7	44	14.8
Never ill	318	1	0.3	2	0.6	3	0.9	4	1.3	10	3.1

Source: Strober et al. (2000).

familial factor between the two eating disorders. However, the studies have not been able to consider the impact of shared environmental influences (Fairburn & Harrison, 2003).

Treatment of Eating Disorders

Prevention programs have been developed in schools to reduce the incidence of eating disorders and disordered eating patterns. A school-based group intervention program was developed for adolescent girls who were showing some problems with eating, body image, and self-esteem (Daigneault, 2000). The goals for the girls involved: (1) learning to develop a more positive attitude toward their bodies; (2) becoming aware of societal messages of "what it means to be female"; (3) developing healthier eating and exercise habits; (4) increasing their comfort in expressing their feelings to peers, family members, and significant others; (5) developing healthy strategies to deal with stress and pressures; and (6) increasing assertiveness skills. These points were addressed through group discussions and the use of videos, magazines, and examples from mass media. The program focuses on teaching girls and women to reexamine the consequences of gender messages, and some of these elements have been included in the treatment of anorexia nervosa, bulimia nervosa, and binge-eating disorder. Because people with eating disorders are often ambivalent about changing their eating patterns, a collaborative treatment approach is more likely to be accepted and adhered to (Geller et al., 2003).

Anorexia Nervosa

A female undergoing treatment for anorexia nervosa who was 5 feet, 3 inches tall and weighed 81 pounds and still felt fat reported, "I did gain 25 pounds, the target weight of my therapist and nutritionist. But everyday was really difficult. I would go and cry. A big part of anorexia is fear. Fear of fat, fear of eating. But (my therapist) taught me about societal pressures to be ultrathin comes from the media, TV, advertising.... She talked me through what I was thinking and how I had completely dissociated my mind from my body.... I'm slowly reintroducing foods one thing at a time. I'd like to think I am completely better, but I'm not. I'm still extremely self-conscious about my appearance. But I now know I have a problem and my family and I are finding ways to cope with it." (Bryant, 2001, p. B4)

As you have seen, eating disorders, especially anorexia nervosa, can be life threatening. Treatment for anorexia nervosa can be delivered on either an outpatient or an inpatient basis, depending on the weight and health of the individual. Because it is a complex disorder, there is a need for teamwork between physicians and mental health professionals.

Because the individual is starving, the initial goal is to restore weight. Restoration of weight should not be attempted without psychological support. Typically, the individual with anorexia nervosa will become terrified of gaining weight and need the opportunity to discuss her or his reactions. During the weight restoration period, new foods have to be introduced, because the individual's choices are not sufficiently high in calories. The physical condition of the person has to be carefully monitored because sudden and severe physiological reactions can occur during refeeding. Psychological interventions are used to help the patient (1) understand and cooperate with nutritional and physical rehabilitation, (2) identify and understand the dysfunctional attitudes related to the eating disorder, (3) improve interpersonal and social functioning, and (4) address comorbid psychopathology and psychological conflicts that reinforce eating-disorder behavior (American Dietetic Association, 2001; American Psychiatric Association, 2000b; Walsh & Devlin, 1998). Once the patient has gained sufficient weight to become an outpatient, family therapy sessions may be implemented. Experience has shown that this approach helps maintain the treatment gains achieved in the hospital.

Bulimia Nervosa

During the initial assessment of patients with bulimia nervosa, conditions that might contribute to vomiting, such as esophageal reflux disease, should be identified. Physical conditions resulting from purging include muscle weakness, cardiac arrhythmias, dehydration, and electrolyte imbalance. Gastrointestinal problems involving the stomach or esophagus should also be carefully assessed. In many patients, dental erosion can also be quite serious. As with anorexia nervosa, bulimia nervosa should involve an interdisciplinary team that includes a physician and psychotherapist. One important goal in treatment is to normalize the eating pattern and to eliminate the binge-purge cycle. A routine of eating three meals a day with one to three snacks a day is used to break up the disordered eating pattern. Cognitive-behavioral therapy and the use of antidepressant medication have been helpful in treating this condition (American Dietetic Association, 2001; American Psychiatric Association, 2000b; Hoffman, 1998).

Cognitive-behavioral approaches have also been effective in helping individuals with bulimia and binge-eating disorder develop a sense of self-control (Parrott, 1998). These individuals learn to replace urges to binge with exercise, relaxation, or other alternative behaviors (Fairburn et al., 1991, 1995; Garner et al., 1993; Thiels et al., 1998). Common components of cognitive-behavioral treatment plans are encouraging the consumption of three or more balanced meals a day, reducing rigid food rules and body image concerns, and developing cognitive and behavioral strategies. This approach was as successful as antidepressant medication in treating bulimia nervosa, although combined treatment was the most effective (Agras et al., 1992). Even with these approaches, only about 50 percent of those with the disorder fully recover (Fairburn et al., 2003).

Binge-Eating Disorder

Treatments for binge-eating disorder are similar to those for bulimia nervosa, although BED presents fewer physical complications because of a lack of purging. Individuals with BED do differ in some ways from those with bulimia nervosa. Most are overweight. Most overeat without regular compensatory behaviors that involve vomiting, laxatives, fasting, or excessive exercising, and most have to deal with stereotypes of overweight individuals. Because of the health consequences of weight problems, some therapy programs also attempt to help the individual lose weight.

In general, treatment follows three phases (Ricca et al., 2000). First, cognitive factors underlying the eating disorder are determined. The clients also are taught to use strategies that reduce eating binges. One patient, Mrs. A., had very rigid rules concerning eating that, when violated, would result in her "going the whole nine yards." She thought that exceeding her caloric intake would mean that she was a "bad" person. Two types of triggers were identified for her binges: emotional distress, involving anger, anxiety, sadness, or frustration, and work stressors (long hours, deadlines). Interventions were applied to help her develop more flexible rules regarding eating and to deal with her stressors. In many of these programs, body weight is recorded weekly, and a healthy pattern of three meals and two snacks a day is implemented. Food diaries may be utilized to determine type and amount of the food consumed and the psychological states preceding eating. Information about obesity, proper nutrition, and physical exercise is provided.

Second, cognitive strategies are employed regarding distorted beliefs about eating. The thoughts are identified and eliminated by changing the individual's thought patterns. The client is asked to prepare a list of "forbidden" foods and to rank them in order of "dangerousness." Gradually, the foods are introduced into normal eating, with those perceived as being less dangerous first. Having clients observe their own bodies in a mirror helps them reduce or eliminate cognitive distortions associated with their bodies. The prejudices of society about body size are discussed, and realistic expectations about the amount of change are addressed. The clients may also be asked to observe attractive individuals with larger body sizes to help them consider positive qualities other than focusing on the body. After performing this "homework," Mrs. A. discovered that overweight women can look attractive, and she bought more fashionable clothes for herself. She was astonished at the positive reactions and comments from friends and coworkers. Although she had lost twelve pounds, she attributed the attention to her confidence and improved body image (Goldfein et al., 2000). Another aspect of treatment involves the patient's acceptance of her or his current body.

Third, relapse prevention strategies are utilized to identify potential obstacles and setbacks, and the patient practices methods of dealing with them. Because weight loss is very difficult, most therapists believe that treatment is successful if binges are eliminated, healthier eating patterns established, and greater acceptance of one's body has occurred. Cognitive-behavioral therapy produced significant reductions in binge eating but was less successful in reducing weight (Carter & Fairburn, 1998; Ricca et al., 2000).

▶ CHECKPOINT REVIEW

Why has there been such an increase in disordered eating?
- It is believed that the societal emphasis on thinness as being attractive may contribute to the increasing incidence of eating disorder. This is believed to lead to an internalized thin ideal that girls and women aspire to achieve.
- Most women suffer from some body image distortion in that they believe they weigh more than they actually do.
- Males also appear to be influenced by mass media presentation of muscular male bodies. Most prefer to be more heavily muscled.
- Countries that are influenced by Western standards are also reporting an increased incidence of eating disorders in women.

How can we treat eating disorders?
- Many of the therapies attempt to teach the clients to identify the impact of societal messages regarding thinness and encourage them to develop healthier goals and values.
- For individuals with anorexia nervosa, medical, as well as psychological, treatment is necessary because the body is in a starvation mode. The goal is to help them gain weight, normalize their eating patterns, understand and alter their thoughts related to body image, and develop more healthy methods of dealing with stress.
- With bulimia nervosa, medical assistance may also be required because of the physiological changes associated with purging.
- Because many people with binge-eating disorder are overweight or obese, weight reduction strategies are also included in treatment.
- With both bulimia nervosa and binge-eating disorder, the therapy involves normalizing eating patterns, developing a more positive body image, and dealing with stress in a healthier fashion.

FOCUS QUESTIONS

- Does insanity mean the same thing as being mentally disturbed?
- What legal means are available for hospitalizing or committing someone to a mental institution?
- Is everything confidential in a therapy session? What are the exceptions?
- What impact have the changing racial-cultural demographics had on the mental health profession?

15 Legal and Ethical Issues in Abnormal Psychology

Public interest in the workings of the legal system has never been more pronounced than it has been since the impeachment hearings of President Clinton, and the O. J. Simpson, Martha Stewart, and Kobe Bryant trials. Sitting as a mass-media jury, Americans speculated not only about the guilt or innocence of these individuals but also about their states of mind. What would make President Clinton act so recklessly? Was he addicted to sex? If Simpson did kill his ex-wife, Nicole Brown Simpson, and her friend, Ronald Goldman, what could have motivated him to do so? With all her wealth, why would Martha Stewart engage in insider trading that would save her only a fraction of her vast fortune? Kobe Bryant is married to an attractive woman, is considered handsome, and possesses fame and fortune. Why would he engage in an alleged rape when it could negatively affect his marriage and career? Were these acts premeditated or impulsive, born of extreme and uncontrollable rage?

Increasingly, psychologists and other mental health professionals are being asked to answer such questions. They are playing an important role in determining the state of mind of defendants and are participating in decisions and actions of the legal system that affect human relationships, such as custody issues and jury selection (Stromberg, Lindberg, & Schneider, 1995). In the past, psychologists dealt primarily with evaluation of competency and issues related to criminal cases. Now, however, their expanded roles include giving expert opinions on child custody, organic brain functioning, traumatic injury, suicide, and even deprogramming activities (see Table 15.1). And just as psychologists have influenced decisions in the legal system, they have also been influenced by mental health laws passed at local, state, and federal levels. The following two case examples illustrate the complex relationship between mental health issues and the law.

On July 24, 1998, Russell Weston, Jr., carried a concealed gun into the nation's Capitol building as literally hundreds of tourists crowded through the security machines. Setting off an alarm as he passed through, Weston was confronted by Capitol guards and exchanged volleys of gunfire with them. Tourists ran panic stricken throughout the hallways as Weston killed two police officers and wounded a tourist.

Weston was subsequently captured, arrested, and charged with murder. Prosecutors offered no motive for the killings, but court papers revealed that the early investigation focused on Weston's alleged belief that federal agents had placed land mines on his Montana property. Family members testified that Weston had a twenty-year history of mental illness, suffered from paranoid schizophrenia, and believed government agents were out to get him. A government psychiatrist concluded that Weston "suffers from a mental disease or defect rendering him mentally incapable of assisting in his defense" and that he should be hospitalized indefinitely, until he is capable of understanding the proceedings. In order to improve his condition and render him competent, psychiatrists attempted to administer antipsychotic drugs. When consent forms for the medication were presented to Weston, he refused to sign.

On August 20, 1989, two brothers, Erik and Lyle Menendez, killed their parents, José Menendez and Mary Louise (Kitty) Menendez. The brothers, then eighteen and twenty-one, admitted emptying their two pump-action Mossberg shotguns into their parents. Prosecutors claimed that the brothers killed their millionaire parents to inherit the family's

379

fortune; indeed, just days after the slayings, the brothers went on a shopping spree, charging purchases on their credit cards. As support for their case, the prosecution played tapes of the Menendez brothers' therapy sessions in which they confessed to the killings.

The defense, however, argued that the killings were due to (1) an irrational fear that their lives were in danger, (2) years of sexual molestation by the father, (3) constant physical abuse and intimidation, and (4) threats that they would be killed if the "family secret" was ever exposed. The defense portrayed the brothers as "the victims" who endured years of sexual, psychological, and physical abuse and who, as a result, killed out of "mind-numbing, adrenaline-pumping fear." The prosecution argued for a first-degree murder conviction and sought the death penalty. The brothers were tried separately, and in each case the jury was deadlocked, unable to reach a verdict. The brothers were retried and a second jury convicted them of first-degree murder in March 1996. They were sentenced to life in prison without possibility of parole.

Both of the preceding examples make it clear that clinical or mental health issues are often intertwined with legal and ethical ones as well. This is evident in the Capitol Hill shooting of two police officers, for which the court psychiatrist ruled that Russell Weston, Jr., was not competent to stand trial. Yet how do we determine whether a person is competent to stand trial or whether he or she is insane or sane? What criteria do we use? If we call on experts, we find that professionals often disagree with one another. Might defendants in criminal trials attempt to fake mental disturbances to escape guilty verdicts?

Or consider the issues raised by the case of the Menendez brothers. If their claim that they suffered from years of excessive abuse is true, do such reasons excuse them from the moral or legal obligations of a wrongful act? Increasingly, lawyers are using clients' claims of child abuse, domestic violence, and other psychological traumas to explain the criminal actions of their clients. In 1994, for example, a jury found Lorena Bobbitt not guilty of charges related to cutting off her husband's penis because she had suffered physical and sexual abuse throughout her married life. Should people like the Menendez brothers and Lorena Bobbitt be held responsible for their actions?

Should This Man Be Committed?   Should this homeless man be considered mentally disturbed and committed to an institution? Is he a danger to himself or to others? Residents in the neighborhood where Larry Hogue lives claim that he has been frightening people for years. He has been arrested numerous times for threatening people and damaging property, but he has never been permanently confined.

An Abuse and Mental Illness Claim that Almost Worked Erik (right) and Lyle Menendez killed their parents in August 1989. The defense argued that the brothers killed out of fear of their father and trauma suffered from years of sexual and physical abuse from him. The brothers were tried separately, and both cases resulted in hung juries. After a second trial, the brothers were found guilty.

Table 15.1   The Intersection of Psychology and the Law

Increasingly, psychologists are finding that their expertise is either being sought in the legal system or being influenced by the law. Only a few of these roles and activities are described here:

Assessing dangerousness   This is a primary function that undergirds many of the other activities. The psychologist engaged in assessing dangerousness—suicide and homicide potential, child endangerment, civil commitment, and so on—must be knowledgeable about the clinical and research findings affecting such determinations.

Child custody evaluations in divorce proceedings
Psychologists often use their expertise to help courts and social service agencies to determine the "best interests of the child" in custody cases involving parenting arrangements, termination of parental rights, and issues of neglect and abuse.

Psychological evaluations in child protection matters
When a child is at risk for harm, courts may ask a psychologist to become involved. While being mindful of the parents' civil and constitutional rights, the psychologist will attempt to determine whether abuse or neglect has occurred, whether the child is at risk for harm, and what, if any, corrective action should be recommended.

Repressed/recovered or false memory determinations   One of the most controversial situations a psychologist faces is determining the accuracy and validity of repressed memories—claims by adults that they have recovered repressed memories of childhood abuse. Although psychologists are usually called as expert witnesses by the lawyers defending or prosecuting the alleged abuser, they sometimes play another role: suits have also been filed against mental health professionals for promoting the recall of false memories.

Civil commitment determination   Psychologists are asked to become involved in the civil commitment of an individual or the discharge of a person who has been so confined. They must determine whether the person is at risk of harm to self or others, is too mentally disturbed to take care of himself or herself, or lacks the appropriate resources for care if left alone.

Determination of sanity or insanity   Mental health professionals are often asked by the court, prosecution, or defense to determine the sanity or insanity of someone accused of a crime. The results are usually presented via a private hearing in the judge's chamber or expert testimony in front of a jury.

Determination of competency to stand trial
Psychologists may be asked to determine whether an individual is competent to stand trial. Is the accused sufficiently rational to aid in his or her own defense? Note that competence does not refer to the state of mind during the alleged crime.

Jury selection   A new breed of psychologists called jury specialists help attorneys determine whether prospective jurors might favor one side or the other. Jury specialists use clinical knowledge in an attempt to screen out individuals who might be biased against their clients.

Profiling of serial killers, mass murderers, or specific criminals   In the field of forensic psychology, law enforcement officers now work hand in hand with psychologists and psychiatrists in developing profiles of criminals. The Unabomber Theodore Kaczynski, for example, was profiled with amazing accuracy.

Testifying in malpractice suits   A psychologist may be called in a civil suit to give expert testimony on whether another practicing clinician failed to follow the "standards of the profession" and is thus guilty of negligence or malpractice and/or on whether the client bringing the suit suffered psychological harm or damage as a result of the clinician's actions.

Protection of patient rights   Psychologists may become involved in seeing that patients are not grievously wronged by the loss of their civil liberties on the grounds of mental health treatment. Some of these valued liberties are the right to receive treatment, to refuse treatment, and to live in the least restrictive environment.

▶ Criminal Commitment

criminal commitment Incarceration of an individual for having committed a crime.

A basic premise of criminal law is that all of us are responsible beings who exercise free will and are capable of choices. If we do something wrong, we are responsible for our actions and should suffer the consequences. **Criminal commitment** is the incarceration of an individual for having committed a crime. Abnormal psychology accepts different perspectives on free will; criminal law does not. Yet criminal law does recognize that some people lack the ability to discern the ramifications of their actions because

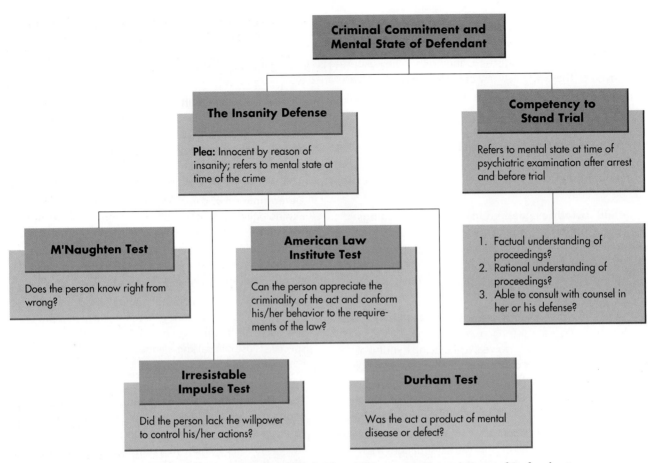

Figure 15.1 Legal Standards That Address the Mental State of Defendants

they are mentally disturbed. Although they may be technically guilty of a crime, their mental state at the time of the offense exempts them from legal responsibility. Let us explore the landmark cases that have influenced this concept's evolution and application. Standards arising from these cases and some other important guidelines are summarized in Figure 15.1.

The Insanity Defense

For five months between 1977 and 1978, Los Angeles was terrorized by a series of murders of young women whose bodies were left on hillsides. All the women had been raped and strangled; some had been brutally tortured. The public and press dubbed the culprit the Hillside Strangler, and a massive hunt for the killer ensued. A major break occurred one year after the Los Angeles murders, when twenty-seven-year-old Kenneth Bianchi was arrested for two unrelated murders of college students in Bellingham, Washington. His fingerprints matched those found at the scene of the Hillside murders.

Bianchi was an unlikely murder suspect because many who knew him described him as dependable and conscientious—"the boy next door." Furthermore, despite the strong evidence against Bianchi, he insisted he was innocent. Police noticed that he was unable to remember much of his past life. During interviews in which hypnosis was used, a startling development occurred: Bianchi exhibited another personality (Steve). Steve freely admitted to killing the women, calling Ken a "turkey," and laughing at Ken's ignorance of his existence.

Faking Mental Illness to Use the Insanity Plea
Confessed Hillside Strangler Kenneth Bianchi is shown giving testimony against his cousin Angelo Buono. From 1977 to 1978, both men raped, tortured, and murdered a number of young Los Angeles women. Wanting to use the insanity plea in order to get a reduced sentence, Bianchi tried to convince psychiatrists that he suffered from multiple personality. His scheme was exposed as a fake by psychologist and hypnosis expert Martin Orne, and Bianchi was found guilty of murder and sentenced to life in prison without parole.

insanity defense The legal argument used by defendants who admit they have committed a crime but plead not guilty because they were mentally disturbed at the time the crime was committed.

M'Naghten Rule A cognitive test of legal insanity that inquires whether the accused knew right from wrong when he or she committed the crime.

The concept of "innocent by reason of insanity" has provoked much controversy among legal scholars, mental health practitioners, and the general public. The **insanity defense** is a legal argument used by defendants who admit they have committed a crime but plead not guilty because they were mentally disturbed at the time the crime was committed. The insanity plea recognizes that under specific circumstances people may not be held accountable for their behavior. The fear that such a plea might be used by a guilty individual to escape criminal responsibility was portrayed in a popular film, *Primal Fear,* in which actor Richard Gere, playing a high-powered attorney, was duped into believing that his client suffered from a dissociative identity disorder (formerly known as multiple personality disorder). The client was found not guilty by reason of insanity at the trial, only to have Gere's character discover the ghastly truth. We need not go to the movies, however, to see the danger of misuse of the insanity plea. The Kenneth Bianchi case is a prime real-life example.

The question confronting the state prosecutors, defense attorney, and mental health experts in the Bianchi case was whether the defendant was a shrewd, calculating, cold-blooded murderer or a person with true dissociative identity disorder. It is important to note, however, that any number of psychiatric conditions may be used in an insanity plea.

Psychologist Martin Orne, an internationally recognized expert on hypnosis, was asked by the prosecution to examine Bianchi. Orne knew that Bianchi was either suffering from a dissociative personality disorder or was just a clever liar. He reasoned that if Bianchi was pretending, he would be highly motivated to convince others of his disorder. Orne thought that if he told Bianchi that multiple personalities rarely show just two distinct personalities, Bianchi might show still another personality to convince Orne that his was a true case. After hinting to Bianchi in the waking state that two personalities are rare, Orne placed Bianchi under hypnosis. Bianchi took the bait. Another personality—Billy—emerged. (Other experts were unable to draw out more than two personalities.) Orne also noticed that Bianchi's behaviors were unusual for someone under hypnosis and that many symptoms he feigned were inconsistent with dissociative identity disorder. Orne's work, coupled with other evidence, forced a change in Bianchi's plea from "not guilty by reason of insanity" to "guilty." Unfortunately, the rare but highly publicized cases—such as those of the Hillside Strangler, John Hinckley (the person who attempted to assassinate President Ronald Reagan), and the Menendez brothers—seem to have the greatest impact and to provoke public outrage and suspicion (Rogers, 1987).

Legal Precedents In this country, a number of different standards are used as legal tests of insanity. One of the earliest is the *M'Naghten Rule*. In 1843, Daniel M'Naghten, a grossly disturbed woodcutter from Glasgow, Scotland, claimed that he was commanded by God to kill the English prime minister, Sir Robert Peel. He killed a lesser minister by mistake and was placed on trial, at which it became obvious that M'Naghten was quite delusional. Out of this incident emerged the **M'Naghten Rule,**

popularly known as the "right-wrong" test, which holds that people can be acquitted of a crime if it can be shown that, at the time of the act, they (1) had such defective reasoning that they did not know what they were doing or (2) were unable to comprehend that the act was wrong. The M'Naghten Rule has come under tremendous criticism from some who regard it as being exclusively a cognitive test (knowledge of right or wrong) that does not consider volition, emotion, and other mental activity. Further, it is often difficult to evaluate a defendant's awareness or comprehension.

The second major precedent that strengthened the insanity defense was the **irresistible impulse test**. In essence, the doctrine says that a defendant is not criminally responsible if he or she lacked the will power to control his or her behavior. In other words, a verdict of not guilty by reason of insanity could be obtained if it was shown that the defendant was irresistibly impelled to commit the act. Criticisms of the irresistible impulse defense revolve around what constitutes an irresistible impulse. Shapiro (1984, p. 30) asked the question, "What is the difference between an *irresistible* impulse (*unable* to exert control) and an *unresisted* impulse (*choosing* not to exert control)?" For example, is a person with a history of antisocial behavior unable to resist his or her impulses, or is he or she choosing not to exert control? Neither the mental health profession nor the legal profession has answered this question satisfactorily.

In the case of *Durham v. United States* (1954), the U.S. Court of Appeals broadened the M'Naghten Rule with the so-called products test. An accused person was not considered criminally responsible if his or her unlawful act was the *product* of mental disease or defect. The *Durham* standard also has its drawbacks. The term *product* is vague and difficult to define because almost anything can cause anything. Further, relying on psychiatric testimony only serves to confuse the issues because both the prosecution and defense bring in psychiatric experts, who often present conflicting testimony (Otto, 1989).

In 1962, the **American Law Institute (ALI)**, in its **Model Penal Code**, produced guidelines to help jurors determine the validity of the insanity defense on a case-by-case basis. The guidelines combined features from the previous standards.

1. A person is not responsible for criminal conduct if at the time of such conduct as a result of mental disease or defect he lacks substantial capacity either to appreciate the criminality of his conduct or to conform his conduct to the requirements of the law.

2. As used in the Article, the terms "mental disease or defect" do not include an abnormality manifested by repeated criminal or otherwise antisocial conduct (Sec. 401, p. 66).

The second point was intended to eliminate the insanity defense for people diagnosed as antisocial personalities. With the attempt to be more specific and precise, the ALI guidelines moved the burden of determining criminal responsibility to jurors. Previous standards, particularly the *Durham* standard, gave great weight to expert testimony, and many feared that it would usurp the jury's responsibilities. By using phrases such as "substantial capacity," "appreciate the criminality of his conduct," and "conform his conduct to the requirements of the law," the ALI standard was intended to allow the jurors the greatest possible flexibility in ascribing criminal responsibility.

Guilty, but Mentally Ill

Perhaps no other trial has more greatly challenged the use of the insanity plea than the case of John W. Hinckley, Jr. Hinckley's attempt to assassinate President Ronald Reagan and Hinckley's subsequent acquittal by reason of insanity outraged the public, as well as legal and mental health professionals. As a result, Congress passed the Insanity Reform Act of 1984, which based the definition of insanity totally on the individual's ability to understand what he or she did.

Some states have also adopted alternative pleas, such as "culpable and mentally disabled," "mentally disabled, but neither culpable nor innocent," and "guilty, but mentally

irresistible impulse test One test of insanity, which states that a defendant is not criminally responsible if he or she lacked the will power to control his or her behavior.

***Durham* standard** A test of legal insanity known as the products test—an accused person is not responsible if the unlawful act was the product of mental disease or defect.

American Law Institute (ALI) Model Penal Code A test of legal insanity that combines both cognitive criteria (diminished capacity) and motivational criteria (specific intent). Its purpose is to give jurors increased latitude in determining the sanity of the accused.

Not Guilty by Reason of Insanity   John Hinckley, Jr., was charged with the attempted murder of President Ronald Reagan. His acquittal by reason of insanity created a furor among the American public over use of the insanity defense. The outrage forced Congress to pass the Insanity Reform Act.

ill." These pleas are attempts to separate mental illness from insanity and to hold people responsible for their acts (Slovenko, 1995; Steadman et al., 1993). Such pleas allow jurors to reach a decision that not only convicts individuals for their crimes and holds them responsible but also ensures that they will be given treatment for their mental illnesses.

Just such a decision was handed down in the case of John E. Du Pont, the fifty-seven-year-old heir to the Du Pont family fortune. Du Pont killed an Olympic wrestling champion on his 800-acre estate in 1997, but it was obvious to many that he was mentally disturbed. His attempt to use the insanity plea failed, and the jury found him guilty of third-degree murder but mentally ill. Despite attempts at reform, however, states and municipalities continue to use different tests of insanity with varying outcomes, and the use of the insanity plea remains controversial.

Competency to Stand Trial

The term **competency to stand trial** refers to a defendant's mental state at the time of psychiatric examination after arrest and before trial. It has nothing to do with the issue of criminal responsibility, which refers to an individual's mental state or behavior at the time of the offense. If you recall from the case of Russell Weston, Jr., who killed the two Capitol police officers, the court-appointed psychiatrist declared Weston not competent to stand trial. In such cases, our system of law states that an accused person cannot be tried unless three criteria are satisfied (Shapiro, 1984):

1. Does the defendant have a factual understanding of the proceedings?
2. Does the defendant have a rational understanding of the proceedings?
3. Can the defendant rationally consult with counsel in presenting his or her own defense?

competency to stand trial A judgment that a defendant has a factual and rational understanding of the proceedings and can rationally consult with counsel in presenting his or her own defense; refers to the defendant's mental state at the time of psychiatric examination.

Given this third criterion, a defendant who is suffering from paranoid delusions could not stand trial because a serious impairment exists.

Determination of competency to stand trial is meant to ensure that a person understands the nature of the proceedings and is able to help in his or her own defense. This effort is an attempt to protect mentally disturbed people and to guarantee preservation of criminal and civil rights. But being judged incompetent to stand trial may have unfair negative consequences as well. A person may be committed for a long period of time, denied the chance to post bail, and isolated from friends and family, all without having been found guilty of a crime.

Such a miscarriage of justice was the focus of a U.S. Supreme Court ruling in 1972 in the case of *Jackson v. Indiana*. In that case, a severely retarded, brain-damaged person who could neither hear nor speak was charged with robbery but was determined incompetent to stand trial. He was committed indefinitely, which in his case probably meant for life, because it was apparent by the severity of his disorders that he would never be competent. His lawyers filed a petition to have him released on the basis of deprivation of **due process**—the legal checks and balances that are guaranteed to everyone, such as the right to a fair trial, the right to face accusers, the right to present evidence, the right to counsel, and so on. The U.S. Supreme Court ruled that a defendant cannot be confined indefinitely solely on the grounds of incompetency. After a reasonable time, a determination must be made as to whether the person is likely or unlikely to regain competency in the foreseeable future. If, in the hospital's opinion, the person is unlikely to do so, the hospital must either release the individual or initiate civil commitment procedures.

▶ Civil Commitment

> She was a well-known "bag lady" in the downtown Oakland, California, area. By night, she slept on any number of park benches and in store fronts. By day she could be seen pushing her Safeway shopping cart full of boxes, extra clothing, and garbage, which she collected from numerous trash containers. According to her only surviving sister, the woman had lived this way for nearly ten years and had been tolerated by local merchants. Over the past six months, however, the woman's behavior had become progressively intolerable. She had always talked to herself, but recently she had begun shouting and screaming at anyone who approached her. Her use of profanity was graphic, and she often urinated and defecated in front of local stores. She was occasionally arrested and detained for short periods of time by local law-enforcement officials, but she always returned to her familiar haunts. Finally, her sister and several merchants requested that the city take action to commit her to a mental institution.

Sometimes action seems necessary when people are severely disturbed and exhibit bizarre behaviors that can pose a threat to themselves or others. Government has a long-standing precedent of *parens patriae* ("father of the country" or "power of the state"), in which it has authority to commit disturbed individuals for their own best interest. **Civil commitment** is the involuntary confinement of a person judged to be a danger to himself, herself, or others, even though the person has not committed a crime. Factors relevant to civil commitment are displayed in Figure 15.2. The commitment of a person in acute distress may be viewed as a form of protective confinement (Bednar et al., 1991) and concern for the psychological and physical well-being of that person or others. Hospitalization is considered in the case of potential suicide or assault, bizarre behavior, destruction of property, and severe anxiety leading to loss of impulse control.

Involuntary hospitalization should, however, be avoided if at all possible because it has many potentially negative consequences. It may result in the lifelong social stigma associated with psychiatric hospitalization, major interruption in the person's life, losing

due process Legal checks and balances that are guaranteed to everyone (the right to a fair trial, the right to face accusers, the right to present evidence, the right to counsel, and so on).

civil commitment The involuntary confinement of a person judged to be a danger to himself or herself or to others, even though the person has not committed a crime.

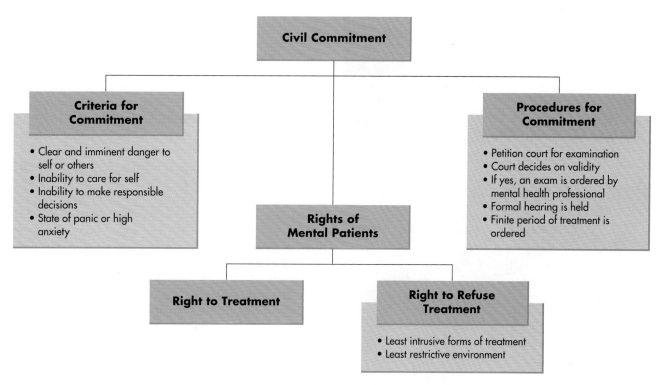

Figure 15.2 **Factors in the Civil Commitment of a Nonconsenting Person**

control of his or her life and being dependent on others, and loss of self-esteem and self-concept. To this we would add a possible loss or restriction of civil liberties—a point that becomes even more glaring when we consider that the person has actually committed no crime other than being a nuisance or assailing people's sensibilities. The "bag lady" described earlier had certainly committed no crime, although she had violated many social norms. But at what point do we confine people simply because they fail to conform to our standards of "decency" or "socially appropriate" behavior?

Criteria for Commitment

States vary in the criteria used to commit a person, but there do appear to be certain general standards. It is not enough that a person be mentally ill: additional conditions need to exist before hospitalization is considered (Turkheimer & Parry, 1992).

1. *The person presents a clear and imminent danger to self or others.* An example is someone who is displaying suicidal behavior or threatening to harm someone.

2. *The person is unable to care for himself or herself or does not have the social network to provide for such care.* Most civil commitments are based primarily on this criterion. The details vary, but states generally specify an inability to provide sufficient shelter, clothing, or food to sustain a minimal level of life.

3. *The person is unable to make responsible decisions about appropriate treatment and hospitalization.* As a result, there is a strong chance of deterioration.

4. *The person is in an unmanageable state of fright or panic.* Such people may believe and feel that they are on the brink of losing control.

Certainly the example of the homeless lady would seem to fulfill the second criterion and possibly the third. In the past, commitments could be obtained solely on the

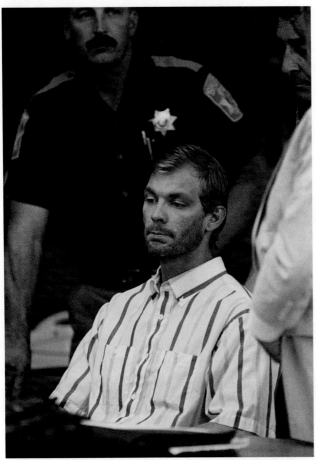

A Tragic Case of Failing to Predict Dangerousness
Convicted serial killer Jeffrey Dahmer killed at least seventeen men and young boys over a period of many years. Besides torturing many of his victims, Dahmer admitted to dismembering them and devouring their bodies in a celebration of cannibalism. Although Dahmer had been imprisoned in 1988 for sexual molestation, it would have been difficult to predict his degree of dangerousness. Despite an attempt to use the insanity plea, Dahmer was found guilty in 1994, imprisoned, and subsequently killed by another inmate.

basis of mental illness and a person's need for treatment, which was often determined arbitrarily. Increasingly, the courts have tightened up civil commitment procedures and have begun to rely more on a determination of whether the person presents a danger to self or others. How do we determine this possibility? Many people would not consider the homeless woman a danger to herself or others. Some, however, might believe that she could be assaultive to others and injurious to herself.

Most studies have indicated that mental health professionals have difficulty predicting whether their clients will commit dangerous acts and that they often overpredict violence (Buchanan, 1997; McNiel & Binder, 1991; Monahan & Walker, 1990). The fact that civil commitments are often based on a determination of **dangerousness**—the person's potential for doing harm to himself or herself or to others—makes this conclusion even more disturbing. The difficulty in predicting this potential seems linked to four factors.

1. *The rarer something is, the more difficult it is to predict.* A frequent misconception shared by both the public and the courts is that mental illnesses are in and of themselves dangerous. Studies have indicated that approximately 90 percent of people suffering from mental disorders are neither violent nor dangerous (Swanson et al., 1990), and few psychotic patients are assaultive: estimates range from 10 percent of hospitalized patients to about 3 percent in outpatient clinics (Tardiff, 1984; Tardiff & Koenigsburg, 1985; Tardiff & Sweillam, 1982). Homicide is even rarer: a psychiatric patient is no more likely to commit a homicide than is someone in the population at large (Monahan, 1981).

2. *Violence seems as much a function of the context in which it occurs as a function of the person's characteristics.* Although it is theoretically possible for a psychologist to accurately assess an individual's personality, we can have little idea about the situations in which people will find themselves.

3. *The best predictor of dangerousness is probably past criminal conduct or a history of violence or aggression.* Such a record, however, is frequently ruled irrelevant or inadmissible by mental health commissions and the courts.

4. *The definition of dangerousness is itself unclear.* Most of us would agree that murder, rape, torture, and physical assaults are dangerous. But are we confining our definition to physical harm only? What about psychological abuse or even destruction of property?

Rights of Mental Patients

dangerousness A person's potential for doing harm to himself or herself or to others.

Many people in the United States are concerned about the balance of power among the state, our mental institutions, and our citizens. The U.S. Constitution guarantees certain "inalienable rights" such as trial by jury, legal representation, and protection against self-incrimination. In recent decades, some courts have ruled that commitment for any purpose constitutes a major deprivation of liberty that requires due process protection.

Because of this concern, several major cases (*Lessard v. Schmidt,* 1972, Wisconsin Federal Court; and *Dixon v. Weinberger,* 1975) have introduced the **least restrictive environment concept.** This means that people have a right to the least restrictive alternative to freedom that is appropriate to their condition. Only patients who cannot adequately care for themselves are confined to hospitals. Those who can function acceptably should be given alternative choices, such as boarding homes and other shelter.

Right to Treatment One of the primary justifications for commitment is that treatment will improve a person's mental condition and increase the likelihood that he or she will be able to return to the community. If we confine a person involuntarily and do not provide the means for release (therapy), isn't this deprivation of due process? Several cases have raised this problem as a constitutional issue. Together, they have determined that mental patients who have been involuntarily committed have a **right to treatment**—a right to receive therapy that would improve their emotional state.

In 1966, in a lawsuit brought against St. Elizabeth's Hospital in Washington, D.C. *(Rouse v. Cameron),* the court held that (1) right to treatment is a constitutional right and (2) failure to provide treatment cannot be justified by lack of resources. In other words, a mental institution or the state could not use lack of funding facilities or labor power as reasons for not providing treatment. Court rulings have also specified standards of adequate treatment, such as staff-patient ratios, therapeutic environmental conditions, and professional consensus about appropriate treatment. Further, mental patients cannot be forced to work (scrub floors, cook, serve food, wash laundry, and so on) or to engage in work-related activities aimed at maintaining the institution in which they live. This practice, widely used in institutions, was declared unconstitutional. Moreover, patients who volunteered to perform tasks had to be paid at least the minimum wage to do them instead of merely being given token allowances or special privileges.

One major dilemma facing the courts in all cases of court-ordered treatment is what constitutes treatment. As discussed in earlier chapters, treatment can range from rest and relaxation to psychosurgery, medication, and aversion therapy. Mental health professionals believe that they are in the best position to evaluate the type and efficacy of treatment, a position supported by the case of *Youngberg v. Romeo* (1982). The court ruled that Nicholas Romeo, a boy with mental retardation, had a constitutional right to "reasonable care and safety," and it deferred judgment to the mental health professional as to what constitutes therapy.

Right to Refuse Treatment Russell Weston, the man suffering from paranoid schizophrenia who killed two U.S. Capitol police officers in 1998, has refused antipsychotic drugs (see the chapter-opening case study). As you recall, he was declared mentally incompetent to stand trial, and he refused to take medication to make him competent. Court-appointed psychiatrists have testified that his mental condition has worsened and that without treatment he could be dangerous. His attorneys, however, have supported his right to refuse treatment and have fought government officials on this point. Many believe that the refusal is based on a Supreme Court ruling *(Ford vs. Wainwright)* that the government cannot execute an incompetent convict. Unresolved, so far, is the issue of whether the government has a right to medicate a convict against his will to restore competence for his own execution.

Although it may be easy for us to surmise the reason for Weston's attorneys to refuse treatment to make him better, does it make sense for others? Patients frequently refuse medical treatment on religious grounds or because the treatment would only prolong a terminal illness. In many cases, physicians are inclined to honor such

least restrictive environment concept A person's right to the least restrictive alternative to freedom that is appropriate to his or her condition.

right to treatment The concept that mental patients who have been involuntarily committed have a right to receive therapy that would improve their emotional state.

refusals, especially if they seem to be based on reasonable grounds. But should mental patients have a right to refuse treatment? At first glance, it may appear illogical. After all, why commit patients for treatment and then allow them to refuse it? Furthermore, isn't it possible that mental patients may be incapable of deciding what is best for themselves? For example, a man with a paranoid delusion may refuse treatment because he believes the hospital staff is plotting against him. If he is allowed to refuse medication or other forms of therapy, his condition may deteriorate more. The result is that the client may become even more dangerous or incapable of caring for himself outside of hospital confinement.

Proponents of the right to refuse treatment argue, however, that many forms of treatment, such as medication or electroconvulsive therapy (ECT), may have long-term side effects, as discussed in earlier chapters. They also point out that involuntary treatment is generally much less effective than treatment accepted voluntarily (Shapiro, 1984). People forced into treatment seem to resist it, thereby nullifying the potentially beneficial effects.

The case of *Rennie v. Klein* (1978) involved several state hospitals in New Jersey that were forcibly medicating patients in nonemergency situations. The court ruled that people have a constitutional right to refuse treatment (psychotropic medication) and to be given due process. In another related case, *Rogers v. Okin* (1979), a Massachusetts court supported these guidelines. Both cases made the point that psychotropic medication was often used only to control behavior or as a substitute for treatment. Further, the decisions noted that drugs might actually inhibit recovery.

In these cases, the courts supported the right to refuse treatment under certain conditions and extended the least restrictive alternative principle to include *least intrusive forms of treatment*. Generally, psychotherapy is considered less intrusive than somatic or physical therapies (ECT and medication). Although this compromise may appear reasonable, other problems present themselves. First, how do we define *intrusive treatment*? Are insight therapies as intrusive as behavioral techniques (punishment and aversion procedures)? Second, if patients are allowed to refuse certain forms of treatment and if the hospital does not have alternatives for them, can clients sue the institution? These questions remain unanswered.

▶ CHECKPOINT REVIEW

American Law Institute (ALI)
    Model Penal Code *(p. 384)*

civil commitment *(p. 386)*

competency to stand trial *(p. 385)*

criminal commitment *(p. 381)*

dangerousness *(p. 388)*

due process *(p. 386)*

Durham standard *(p. 384)*

insanity defense *(p. 383)*

irresistible impulse test *(p. 384)*

least restrictive environment
    concept *(p. 389)*

M'Naghten Rule *(p. 383)*

right to treatment *(p. 389)*

Does insanity mean the same thing as being mentally disturbed?

■ Insanity is a legal concept. Several standards have been used.

■ The M'Naghten Rule holds that people can be acquitted of a crime if it can be shown that their reasoning was so defective that they were unaware of or could not comprehend the wrongness of their actions.

■ The irresistible impulse test holds that people are innocent if they are unable to control their behavior.

■ The *Durham* decision acquits people if their criminal actions were products of mental disease or defects.

■ The American Law Institute guidelines state that people are not responsible for a crime if they lack substantial capacity to appreciate the criminality of their conduct or to conform their conduct to the requirements of the law.

■ Weaknesses in the standards and public outrage with the acquittal of some highly publicized people have led to the "guilty, but mentally ill" plea, an attempt to separate mental illness from insanity and to hold people responsible for their actions.

■ The phrase "competency to stand trial" refers to defendants' mental state at the time they are being examined. It is a separate issue from criminal responsibility, which refers to past behavior at the time of the offense. Although competency to stand trial is important in ensuring fair trials, being judged incompetent can have negative consequences, such as unfair and prolonged denial of civil liberties.

What legal means are available for hospitalizing or committing someone to a mental institution?

- Concern with denial of civil liberties is also present in civil commitment cases. People who have committed no crime can be confined against their will if it can be shown that (1) they present a clear and imminent danger to themselves or others, (2) they are unable to care for themselves, (3) they are unable to make responsible decisions about appropriate treatment and hospitalization, and (4) they are in an unmanageable state of fright or panic.
- Courts have tightened criteria and rely more than ever on the concept of dangerousness. Mental health professionals have great difficulty in predicting dangerousness because dangerous acts depend as much on social situations as on personal attributes and because the definition is unclear.
- Concern with patients' rights has become an issue because many practices and procedures seem to violate constitutional guarantees. As a result, court rulings have established several important precedents.

The Therapist-Client Relationship

The therapist-client relationship involves a number of legal, moral, and ethical issues. Three primary concerns are issues of confidentiality and privileged communication; the therapist's duty to warn others of a risk posed by a dangerous client; and the therapist's obligation to avoid sexual intimacies with clients.

Confidentiality and Privileged Communication

Basic to the therapist-patient relationship is the premise that therapy involves a deeply personal association in which clients have a right to expect that whatever they say will be kept private. Therapists believe that genuine therapy cannot occur unless clients trust their therapists and believe that they will not divulge confidential communications. Without this guarantee, clients may not be completely open with their thoughts and may thereby lose the benefits of therapy. This assumption raises several questions. First, what professional ethics and legal statutes govern the therapist-client relationship? Under what conditions can a therapist breach the confidentiality of the relationship? Second, what if, in a conflict between clinical issues (need for trust) and legal ones (need to disclose), the therapist chooses trust? What are the consequences? Third, if a therapist decides to disclose information to a third party, what effects can the disclosure have on the therapist-client relationship? Last, how can a therapist discuss the limits of confidentiality in a way that would be least likely to disrupt the therapeutic relationship?

Confidentiality is an ethical standard that protects clients from disclosure of information without their consent. The belief in the importance of confidentiality is also shared by the public. In one study it was found that 74 percent of respondents thought everything told to a therapist should be confidential; indeed, 69 percent believed that whatever they discussed was never disclosed (Miller & Thelen, 1986). Confidentiality, however, is an ethical, not a legal, obligation. **Privileged communication,** a narrower legal concept, protects privacy and prevents the disclosure of confidential communications without a client's permission (Corey, Corey, & Callanan, 1998; Herlicky & Sheeley, 1988). An important part of this concept is that the "holder of the privilege" is the client, not the therapist. In other words, if a client waives this privilege, the therapist has no grounds for withholding information. Shapiro (1984) pointed out that our society recognizes how important certain confidential relationships are and protects them by law. These relationships are the husband-wife, attorney-client, pastor-congregant, and therapist-client relationships. Psychiatric practices are regulated in all fifty states

confidentiality An ethical standard that protects clients from disclosure of information without their consent; an ethical obligation of the therapist.

privileged communication A therapist's legal obligation to protect a client's privacy and to prevent the disclosure of confidential communications without a client's permission.

and the District of Columbia, and forty-two states have privileged communication statutes (Herlicky & Sheeley, 1988).

Exemptions from Privileged Communication   Although states vary considerably, all states recognize certain situations in which communications can be divulged. Corey and associates (1998) summarized these conditions:

1. In situations that deal with civil or criminal commitment or competency to stand trial, the client's right to privilege can be waived. For example, a court-appointed therapist who determines that the client needs hospitalization for a psychological disorder may disclose the results of the examination to an appropriate third party (judge, mental health professionals, or those intimately involved in the decision-making process).

2. Disclosure can also be made when a client sees a therapist and introduces his or her mental condition as a claim or defense in a civil action. For example, a woman who sues an employer for harassment and uses "mental distress" to justify her claim may force the therapist to disclose information relevant to her claim.

3. When the client is younger than sixteen years of age or is a dependent elderly person and information leads the therapist to believe that the individual has been a victim of crime (incest, rape, or child and elder abuse), the therapist must provide that information to the appropriate protective services agency.

4. When the therapist has reason to believe that a client presents a danger to himself or herself (possible injury or suicide) or may potentially harm someone else, the therapist must act to ward off the danger.

Privilege in communication is not absolute. Rather, it strikes a delicate balance between the individual's right to privacy and the public's need to know certain information (Leslie, 1991). Problems arise when we try to determine what the balance should be and how important various events and facts are in individual cases.

The Duty-to-Warn Principle

In a much discussed case (*Tarasoff v. Board of Regents of the University of California,* 1976), Prosenjit Poddar, a male graduate student, killed Tatiana Tarasoff, another student, after notifying his therapist that he intended to take her life. Before the homicide and during the counseling sessions, the therapist had concluded that Poddar was dangerous and likely to carry out his threat, and he had notified the director of the Cowell Psychiatric Clinic that the client was dangerous. He also informed the campus police, hoping that they would detain the student.

Although the therapist believed he had done everything possible, the California Supreme Court ruled that he had not. In the *Tarasoff* **ruling**, the court stated that when a therapist determines, according to the standards of the mental health profession, that a patient presents a serious danger to another, the therapist is obligated to warn the *intended victim*. The court went on to say that protective privilege ends where public peril begins. In general, courts have ruled that therapists have a responsibility to protect the public from dangerous acts of violent clients and have held therapists accountable for (1) failing to diagnose or predict dangerousness, (2) failing to warn potential victims, (3) failing to commit dangerous individuals, and (4) prematurely discharging dangerous clients from a hospital.

Criticism of the Duty-to-Warn Principle   The *Tarasoff* ruling seems to place the therapist in the unenviable role of being a double agent (Bednar et al., 1991). Therapists have an ethical and legal obligation to their clients, but they also have legal obligations to society. Not only can these dual obligations conflict with one another, but they can also be quite ambiguous. Many situations exist in which state courts must

Tarasoff ruling   Commonly referred to as the "duty-to-warn" principle; obligates mental health professionals to break confidentiality when their clients pose clear and imminent danger to another person.

rule to clarify the implications and uncertainties of the "duty-to-warn" rule (Fulero, 1988; see the Mental Health and Society feature, "Does the Duty-to-Warn Principle Apply to AIDS?").

Siegel (1979) loudly criticized the *Tarasoff* ruling, stating that it was a "day in court for the law and not for the mental health professions." He reasoned that if confidentiality had been an absolute policy, Poddar might have been kept in treatment, thus ultimately saving Tarasoff's life. Other mental health professionals have echoed this theme in one form or another. Hostile clients with pent-up feelings and emotions may be less likely to act out or become violent when allowed to vent their thoughts. The irony, according to critics, is that the duty-to-warn principle may actually be counterproductive to its intent to protect the potential victim.

Another controversial issue surrounding the duty-to-warn principle relates not just to determining danger but to when that determination should be made. Stimulated mainly by the *Tarasoff* ruling, mental health professionals and government and private institutions are developing guidelines for dealing with dangerous clients. These guidelines have several common elements. One is the recognition that the therapist's principal duty is to the client and that confidentiality is a crucial aspect of the therapeutic relationship.

Another is that therapy necessarily encourages people to engage in open dialogue with the therapist and to share their innermost thoughts and feelings. It is not unusual for clients to voice thoughts about ending their own lives or harming others. Relatively few of these threats are actually carried out, and therapists are not expected to routinely report all of them.

A third common element in the guidelines for dealing with dangerous clients is that the duty-to-warn principle can be invoked only in the most extraordinary circumstances. During the therapy session, however, the therapist should continue to treat the client and, if therapeutically appropriate, should attempt to dissuade the client from the threatened violence.

A final point is that somewhere in the therapy process, the therapist must discuss the limits of confidentiality and inform the client about the possible actions he or she must take to protect a third party. In other words, professionals are obligated to inform their clients that they have a duty to warn others about the threatened actions of their clients. Although some therapists fear that such actions might prevent the client from being open and honest, studies suggest that informing clients about the limits of confidentiality has little impact in inhibiting clients' disclosures and does not necessarily have negative consequences (Applebaum, 1994; Muehleman, Pickens, & Robinson, 1985).

Sexual Relationships with Clients

Therapeutic practice can also be legally regulated by civil lawsuits brought by clients against their therapists for professional malpractice. To be successful, however, these lawsuits must satisfy four conditions: (1) the plaintiff must have been involved in a professional therapeutic relationship with the therapist, (2) there must have been negligence in the care of the client, (3) demonstrable harm must have occurred, and (4) there must be a cause-effect relationship between the negligence and harm. If these four conditions are demonstrated, a jury may find the therapist guilty and award the plaintiff monetary damages. Although malpractice claims can be brought in any number of situations, by far the most common type involves sexual intimacies with a current or former client (Corey et al., 1998; Olarte, 1997).

Traditionally, mental health practitioners have emphasized the importance of separating their personal and professional lives. They reasoned that therapists need to be objective and removed from their clients because becoming emotionally involved with them was nontherapeutic. A therapist in a personal relationship with a client may be less confrontive, may fulfill his or her own needs at the expense of the client, and may

MenTaL HeaLTh and socieTy

Does the Duty-to-Warn Principle Apply to AIDS?

George, a twenty-four-year-old graduate student, had known for some time that he was HIV-infected. He entered counseling at the university psychiatric services center because of extreme feelings of guilt associated with his dishonesty in not disclosing his infection to a woman student with whom he had recently become intimate. He had hidden his medical condition from family, friends, and past lovers because of the social stigma involved and the fear that others would find out that he had often engaged in bisexual relationships. On numerous occasions, George had unprotected sex with his partners, but he had started to use condoms with his current woman friend. However, she did not like condoms and had encouraged George to avoid their use in lovemaking. Several times, George had complied with her request.

Before reading further, take a few minutes to contemplate your answers to these questions: If you were George's therapist, what would you do? What ethical or legal obligations do you have toward George and toward the larger society? Should you maintain the confidentiality of the therapeutic relationship or inform others about George's HIV condition? If you choose to disclose this information, whom would you notify? From your reading in the section on the *Tarasoff* decision, are there any guidelines that could help you decide?

Proponents of maintaining confidentiality believe that any violation of the therapeutic trust would decrease the likelihood that clients will discuss their health status with a counselor. Under the Family Education Rights and Privacy Act (McGowan, 1991), student records are confidential, and strong prohibitions warn against releasing information. HIV- and AIDS-positive students are guaranteed confidentiality because of their right to privacy. In addition, a public diagnosis of HIV or AIDS may stigmatize the student and subject him or her to social ostracism and discrimination. Those who hold this position believe it would be more beneficial in the long run if the counselor explored with students their motives for concealing their condition and encouraged them to discuss it with their sexual partners.

Others, however, have less faith in the counselor's ability to persuade infected students to be honest with their partners (Hoffman, 1991). Studies indicate that dishonesty about one's sexual history and infectious state is quite common (Kegeles, Catania, & Coates, 1988): among gay or bisexual men who were diagnosed as HIV-positive, 12 percent said they did not plan to tell their primary sexual partners; 27 percent said they would not tell their nonprimary partners. In another study of heterosexual men, 20 percent

unintentionally exploit the client because of his or her position (Corey, Corey, & Callahan, 1993, 1998). Although some people question the belief that a social or personal relationship is necessarily antitherapeutic, matters of personal relations with clients, especially those dealing with erotic and sexual intimacies, are receiving increasing attention.

Sexual misconduct of therapists is considered to be one of the most serious of all ethical violations. Indeed, virtually all professional organizations condemn sexual intimacies in the therapist-client relationship. The American Psychological Association (1995) states explicitly, "Psychologists do not engage in sexual intimacies with current patients or clients" (p. 474).

But how do practitioners view sexual intimacies with clients? How often do such intimacies really occur? Who does what to whom? Some studies indicate that being sexually attracted to a client or engaging in sexual fantasy about one is not uncommon among therapists (Pope, Tabachnick, & Keith-Spiegel, 1987; Pope & Tabachnick, 1993). Furthermore, complaints to state licensing boards about sexual misconduct by therapists have increased significantly (Zamichow, 1993). Although these are indisputable facts, the vast majority of psychologists are able to control their sexual feelings and to behave in a professional manner.

In an early nationwide study, Holroyd and Brodsky (1977) reported that 5.5 percent of male therapists and 0.6 percent of female therapists have had sexual intercourse with clients. Sexual intimacy is almost always between male therapists and

said they would lie about being HIV-positive, and 35 percent said they had lied to female partners about their past sexual behavior (Elias, 1988). Some counselors would argue that breaking confidentiality is a small price to pay when a client's unknowing partner may be receiving the equivalent of a death sentence.

So far there have been no legal tests of the *Tarasoff* decision and its relationship to HIV infection (Corey et al., 1998). Furthermore, state laws are often confusing and conflict with one another. Pennsylvania law does not allow therapists to break confidentiality, but they are expected to persuade clients to change their behaviors voluntarily (Corey et al., 1998). Some states forbid disclosure to any third party. Others allow some disclosure to at-risk third parties by medical personnel but not by mental health professionals. Indeed, some state laws consider any such action malpractice. Most state statutes, however, are silent on this question.

The *Tarasoff* decision, however, does have important ramifications for a therapist's decision to breach confidentiality. Three criteria have been identified as important in that decision (Hoffman, 1991):

1. *A (fiduciary) special relationship of trust must exist between the counselor and client.* A therapeutic relationship fulfills this criterion.

2. *There must be an identifiable potential victim.* Remember, the duty to warn extends only to identifiable victims rather than to all persons whom the client could conceivably infect. Anonymous partners or casual partners who are unknown to the counselor would not fall within the duty-to-warn principle. Partners who live with the person under a monogamous or exclusive relationship would probably meet this criterion.

3. *The assessment of dangerousness must be made.* Three factors need to be clarified under this criterion: (1) the certainty of the client's HIV, (2) the extent to which the client engages in behaviors that carry a high risk of HIV transmission, and (3) the use or nonuse of safer-sex techniques.

Given these criteria, how would you apply them to the case of George? Perhaps it would be helpful to form small groups to discuss these issues and come to a decision. Remember, even with these criteria, many gray areas exist. For example, not all sexual practices are high risk with regard to transmission. Thus not all sexual practices would create a legal obligation to report. As mentioned, there have been no legal tests of the *Tarasoff* criteria with HIV-infected persons, and the American Psychological Association guidelines (1995) are silent on this matter.

female clients. Of those who had sexual intercourse with clients, 80 percent were likely to repeat the practice. Of those responding, 88 percent of female and 70 percent of male therapists believed that erotic contact is never beneficial to clients. However, 4 percent of the respondents thought that erotic contact with clients was beneficial. Although in the minority, these therapists took the position that sexual intimacy may be beneficial to clients because it validates the clients as sexual beings, frees them from inhibitions and guilt, and allows them to enjoy their sexuality.

Critics of these arguments find them weak and self-serving (American Psychological Association, 1995; Olarte, 1997). First, sexual intimacy represents an abuse of the therapist's power. Clients who discuss the most intimate aspects of their lives (sexual desires and struggles) are very vulnerable, and it is extremely easy for therapists to take advantage of their clients' trust and to exploit it. Second, sexual intimacy fosters dependency in clients, who look toward the therapist as an "ideal" and as someone who has "the answers." An individual's personal therapeutic goals become subordinate to a desire to please the therapist or to live up to his or her standards. Third, objectivity may also be lost. When therapists become sex partners, they cease to be therapists. Fourth, clients often feel exploited, used, embittered, and angry. Their self-esteem is also harmed.

Statistics on the harmful effects of sexual intimacy on clients have supported these conclusions. In one survey of patients who became sexually involved with their therapists, 90 percent were deemed adversely affected (Bouhoutsos et al., 1983). The harm included mistrust of opposite-gender relationships, hospitalizations, deterioration of their relationships with primary partners, and suicide. Many victims of therapist-client sexual contact showed responses that seemed similar to those of the rape syndrome and the battered-spouse syndrome, as well as to symptoms displayed by victims of child abuse (Olarte, 1997; Pope, 1988; Pope & Vetter, 1991; Sherman, 1993). The Committee on Women in Psychology of the American Psychological Association (1989) took the position that sexual relationships between therapists and clients are never the fault of the client and that the therapist can never be excused for sexual misconduct.

Most professional organizations and states have procedures for filing and processing ethical complaints related to sexual intimacies between therapist and client. In the state of California, the Board of Medical Quality Assurance—the parent organization of the Psychology Examining Committee—has power to suspend or revoke the license of a therapist who engages in sexual misconduct with clients. And, as noted earlier, clients always have legal recourse to sue their therapists for malpractice. Therapists who engage in sex with clients have few arguments they can use in court because the courts have generally rejected claims of consent (Austin, Moline, & Williams, 1990). Many cases of misconduct, however, probably go unreported because of the clients' shame and guilt over their "complicity." In any case, the consensus is that sexual intimacy with clients is unethical, antitherapeutic, and detrimental.

◄► Cultural Competence and the Mental Health Profession

Many mental health professionals assert that the prevailing concepts of mental health and mental disorders are culture bound and that contemporary theories of therapy are based on values specific to a middle-class, white, highly individualistic, and ethnocentric population (American Psychological Association, 1993, 2003; Samuda, 1998; Sue & Sue, 2003). As a result, misdiagnosis and inappropriate treatments often victimize ethnic-minority clients.

Sue and Sue (2003) have made it clear that working with culturally different clients is unethical unless the mental health professional has adequate training and expertise in multicultural psychology. Such a position has resulted in the development of "Guidelines for Providers of Psychological Services to Ethnic, Linguistic, and Culturally Diverse Populations" (American Psychological Association, 1993) and "Guidelines for Psychotherapy with Lesbian, Gay, and Bisexual Clients" (American Psychological Association, 2000). Inherent in both documents is their call for "cultural competence" and the conclusion that psychotherapy may represent biased, discriminatory, and unethical treatment if the racial/cultural backgrounds of clients are ignored and if the therapist does not possess adequate training in working with a culturally diverse population.

From this perspective, mental health professionals have a moral and professional responsibility to become culturally competent if they work with people who differ from them in terms of race, culture, ethnicity, gender, sexual orientation, and so forth. To become culturally competent requires mental health professionals to strive toward attaining three goals (Sue & Sue, 2003): (1) to become aware of and deal with the biases, stereotypes, and assumptions that affect their practice; (2) to become aware of the culturally different client's values and worldview; and (3) to develop appropriate intervention strategies that take into account the social, cultural, historical, and environmental influences on culturally different clients. As we have seen, the increased awareness of multicultural influences in our understanding of abnormal psychology is reflected in the most recent version of the *Diagnostic and Statistical Manual of the American Psychiatric Association* (DSM-IV-TR; APA, 2000a). For the first time since its publication in 1952, DSM is acknowledging the importance of culture in the diagnosis and treatment of mental disorders.

In further recognition of the importance of cultural differences in psychotherapy, a joint collaboration of three divisions of the American Psychological Association—Division 17: Society of Counseling Psychology; Division 44: Society for the Psychological Study of Gay, Lesbian and Bisexual Issues; and Division 45: The Society for the Psychological Study of Ethnic Minority Issues—submitted a document, "Guidelines on Multicultural Education, Training, Research, Practice, and Organizational Change for Psychologists" (APA, 2003), to the American Psychological Association that was recently approved and has become formal policy. One of the most comprehensive guidelines on racial/ethnic minorities to be proposed, the document makes it clear that service providers need to become aware of how their own culture, life experiences, attitudes, values, and biases have influenced them. It also emphasizes the importance of cultural and environmental factors in diagnosis and treatment, and it insists that therapists respect and consider using traditional healing approaches intrinsic to a client's culture. Finally, it suggests that therapists learn more about cultural issues and seek consultation when confronted with cultural-specific problems.

▶ CHECKPOINT REVIEW

confidentiality *(p. 391)*

privileged communication *(p. 391)*

Tarasoff ruling *(p. 392)*

Is everything confidential in a therapy session? What are the exceptions?

- Most mental health professionals believe that confidentiality is crucial to the therapist-client relationship.

- Exceptions to this privilege include situations that involve (1) civil or criminal commitment and competency to stand trial, (2) a client's initiation of a lawsuit for malpractice or a civil action in which the client's mental condition is introduced, (3) the belief that child or elder abuse has occurred, (4) a criminal action, or (5) the danger a client poses to himself or herself or to others.

- Although psychologists have always known that privileged communication is not an absolute right, the *Tarasoff* decision makes therapists responsible for warning a potential victim to avoid liability.

- Mental health professionals are beginning to recognize that ethical and moral values permeate the therapeutic process. The most controversial issues involve erotic and sexual intimacy. Sexual intimacy with clients is almost universally condemned by therapists as immoral, unethical, and antitherapeutic.

What impact have the changing racial-cultural demographics had on the mental health profession?

- Major demographic changes are forcing mental health professionals to consider culture, ethnicity, gender, and socioeconomic status as powerful variables in (1) the manifestation of mental disorders and (2) the need to provide culturally appropriate intervention strategies for minority groups.

- Increasingly, mental health organizations are taking the position that it is unethical to treat members of minority groups without adequate training and expertise in cross-cultural psychology.

Glossary

abnormal behavior Behavior that departs from some norm and that harms the affected individual or others.

abnormal psychology The scientific study whose objectives are to describe, explain, predict, and treat behaviors that are considered strange or unusual.

acute stress disorder (ASD) Exposure to a traumatic stressor that results in dissociation, reliving the experience, and attempts to avoid reminders of the events and that lasts for more than two and less than thirty days.

agoraphobia An intense fear of being in public places where escape or help may not be readily available; in extreme cases, a fear of leaving one's home.

alcoholic Person who abuses alcohol and is dependent on it.

alcoholism Substance-related disorder characterized by abuse of, or dependency on, alcohol, which is a depressant.

Alzheimer's disease A dementia in which brain tissue atrophies, leading to marked deterioration of intellectual and emotional functioning.

American Law Institute (ALI) Model Penal Code A test of legal insanity that combines both cognitive criteria (diminished capacity) and motivational criteria (specific intent). Its purpose is to give jurors increased latitude in determining the sanity of the accused.

amnestic disorders Disorders characterized by memory impairment as manifested by inability to learn new information and inability to recall previously learned knowledge or past events.

amniocentesis A screening procedure in which a hollow needle is inserted through the pregnant woman's abdominal wall and amniotic fluid is withdrawn from the fetal sac; used during the fourteenth or fifteenth week of pregnancy to determine the presence of Down syndrome and other fetal abnormalities.

amphetamines Drugs that speed up central nervous system activity and produce increased alertness, energy, and, sometimes, feelings of euphoria and confidence; also called "uppers."

analogue study An investigation that attempts to replicate or simulate, under controlled conditions, a situation that occurs in real life.

anorexia nervosa An eating disorder characterized by a refusal to maintain a body weight above the minimum normal weight for the person's age and height; an intense fear of becoming obese that does not diminish with weight loss; body image distortion; and, in females, the absence of at least three consecutive menstrual cycles otherwise expected to occur.

antisocial personality disorder A personality disorder characterized by a failure to conform to social and legal codes, by a lack of anxiety and guilt, and by irresponsible behaviors.

anxiety Feelings of fear and apprehension.

anxiety disorders A group of disorders that are primarily characterized by extreme, unrealistic, or debilitating anxiety. The anxiety itself is the major disturbance, and it may nearly always be present or manifested only in particular situations.

assessment With regard to psychopathology, the process of gathering information and drawing conclusions about the traits, skills, abilities, emotional functioning, and psychological problems of an individual.

asthma A chronic inflammatory disease of the airways in the lungs, in which the airways become constricted, making it difficult to empty the lungs and therefore reducing the amount of air that can be inhaled.

attention deficit/hyperactivity disorders (ADHD) Disorders of childhood and adolescence characterized by socially disruptive behaviors—either attentional problems or hyperactivity—that are present before age seven and persist for at least six months.

autistic disorder A severe childhood disorder characterized by qualitative impairment in social interaction and/or communication; restricted, stereotyped interest and activities; and delays or abnormal functioning in a major area before the age of three.

aversion therapy Conditioning procedure in which the response to a stimulus is decreased by pairing the stimulus with an aversive stimulus.

aversive conditioning A classical conditioning technique in which an undesirable behavior is paired with an unpleasant stimulus to suppress the undesirable behavior.

avoidant personality disorder A personality disorder characterized by a fear of rejection and humiliation and a reluctance to enter into social relationships.

axon A long, thin extension at the end of neuron that sends signals to other neurons.

barbiturates Substances that are a powerful depressant of the central nervous system; commonly used to induce relaxation and sleep; and capable of inducing psychological and physical dependency.

behavioral medicine A number of disciplines that study social, psychological, and lifestyle influences on health.

behavioral models Theories of psychopathology that are concerned with the role of learning in abnormal behavior.

binge-eating disorder (BED) A diagnostic category that is provided for further study in DSM-IV-TR and that involves a large consumption of food over a short period of time at least twice weekly for six months; unlike bulimia, it does not involve extreme behavioral attempts to vomit or excessive exercise as compensation.

biofeedback training A therapeutic technique in which the person is taught to voluntarily control a particular physiological function, such as heart rate or blood pressure.

biological markers Biological indicators of a disorder that may or may not be causal.

biological view The belief that mental disorders have a physical or physiological basis.

biopsychosocial approach The belief that biological, psychological, and social factors must all be considered in explaining and treating mental disorders.

bipolar disorder A category of mood disorders characterized by one or more manic or hypomanic episodes and, usually, by one or more depressive episodes.

body dysmorphic disorder (BDD) A somatoform disorder that involves preoccupation with an imagined physical defect in a normal-appearing person, or an excessive concern with a slight physical defect.

borderline personality disorder A personality disorder characterized by intense fluctuations in mood, self-image, and interpersonal relationships.

brain pathology Dysfunction or disease of the brain.

brain trauma A physical wound or injury to the brain.

brief psychotic disorder Psychotic disorder that lasts no longer than one month.

bulimia nervosa An eating disorder characterized by recurrent episodes of binge eating (the rapid consumption of large quantities of food) at least twice a week for three months, during which the person loses control over eating and uses vomiting, laxatives, and excess exercise to control weight.

case study Intensive study of one individual that relies on observation, psychological tests, and historical and biographical data.

catatonic schizophrenia Rare schizophrenic disorder characterized by marked disturbance in motor activity—either extreme excitement or motoric immobility; symptoms may include motoric immobility or stupor; excessive purposeless motor activity; extreme negativism or physical resistance; peculiar voluntary movements; or echolalia or echopraxia.

cathartic method The therapeutic use of verbal expression to release pent-up unconscious conflicts.

cerebral infarction The death of brain tissue resulting from a decrease in the supply of blood serving that tissue.

cerebrovascular accident A sudden stoppage of blood flow to a portion of the brain, leading to a loss of brain function; also called *stroke*.

chronic tic disorders Childhood-onset disorders that last longer than one year and are characterized by involuntary, repetitive, and nonrhythmic movements or vocalizations.

civil commitment The involuntary confinement of a person judged to be a danger to himself or herself or to others, even though the person has not committed a crime.

classical conditioning A principle of learning in which involuntary responses to stimuli are learned through association.

classification system With regard to psychopathology, a system of distinct categories, indicators, and nomenclature for different patterns of behavior, thought processes, and emotional disturbances.

cluster headache Excruciating headache that produces stabbing or burning sensations in an eye or cheek.

cocaine Substance extracted from the coca plant; induces feelings of euphoria and self-confidence in users.

cognitive disorders Behavioral disturbances that result from transient or permanent damage to the brain.

cognitive model A principle of learning that holds that conscious thought mediates, or modifies, an individual's emotional state and/or behavior in response to a stimulus.

comorbidity The co-occurrence of different disorders.

competency to stand trial A judgment that a defendant has a factual and rational understanding of the proceedings and can rationally consult with counsel in presenting his or her own defense; refers to the defendant's mental state at the time of psychiatric examination.

compulsion The need to perform acts or to dwell on thoughts to reduce anxiety.

concordance rate The likelihood that both members of a twin pair will show the same characteristic.

conditioned response (CR) In classical conditioning, the learned response made to a previously neutral stimulus that has acquired some of the properties of another stimulus with which it has been paired.

conditioned stimulus (CS) In classical conditioning, a previously neutral stimulus that has acquired some of the properties of another stimulus with which it has been paired.

conduct disorders Disorders of childhood and adolescence characterized by a persistent pattern of antisocial behaviors that violate the rights of others; repetitive and persistent behaviors include bullying, lying, cheating, fighting, temper tantrums, destruction of property, stealing, setting fires, cruelty to people and animals, assaults, rape, and truant behavior.

confidentiality An ethical standard that protects clients from disclosure of information without their consent; an ethical obligation of the therapist.

continuous amnesia An inability to recall any events that have occurred between a specific time in the past and the present time; the least common form of psychogenic amnesia.

conversion disorder A somatoform disorder in which patients complain of physical problems or impairments of sensory or motor functions controlled by the voluntary nervous system, all suggesting a neurological disorder, but for which no underlying physical cause can be found.

coronary heart disease (CHD) A narrowing of the arteries in or near the heart, resulting in the restriction or partial blockage of the flow of blood and oxygen to the heart.

correlation The extent to which variations in one variable are accompanied by increases or decreases in a second variable.

covert sensitization Aversive conditioning technique in which the individual imagines a noxious stimulus occurring in the presence of a behavior.

criminal commitment Incarceration of an individual for having committed a crime.

cultural relativism The belief that what is judged to be normal or abnormal may vary from one culture to another.

cultural universality The belief that the origin, process, and manifestation of disorders are equally applicable across cultures.

cyclothymic disorder A chronic and relatively continual mood disorder characterized by hypomanic episodes and depressed moods that do not meet the criteria for major depressive episode.

dangerousness A person's potential for doing harm to himself or herself or to others.

defense mechanisms In psychoanalytic theory, ego-protection strategies that shelter the individual from anxiety, that operate unconsciously, and that distort reality.

delirium A syndrome in which there is disturbance of consciousness and changes in cognition, such as memory deficit, disorientation, and language and perceptual disturbances.

delusion A false belief that is firmly and consistently held despite disconfirming evidence or logic.

delusional disorder A disorder characterized by persistent, nonbizarre delusions that are not accompanied by other unusual or odd behavior.

dementia A syndrome characterized by memory impairment and cognitive disturbances, such as aphasia, apraxia, agnosia, or disturbances in planning or abstraction in thought processes.

dendrites Rootlike structures that are attached to the body of the neuron and that receive signals from other neurons.

dependent personality disorder A personality disorder characterized by reliance on others and an unwillingness to assume responsibility.

dependent variable A variable that is expected to change when an independent variable is manipulated in a psychological experiment.

depersonalization disorder A dissociative disorder in which feelings of unreality concerning the self or the environment cause major impairment in social or occupational functioning.

depressant Substance that causes generalized depression of the central nervous system and a slowing down of responses; a sedative.

depression An emotional state characterized by intense sadness, feelings of futility and worthlessness, and withdrawal from others.

depressive disorders DSM-IV-TR category including major depressive disorders, dysthymic disorder, and depressive disorders not otherwise specified; also known as unipolar disorders because no mania is exhibited.

detoxification Alcohol or drug treatment phase characterized by removal of the abusive substance; after that removal, the user is immediately or eventually prevented from consuming the substance.

diathesis-stress theory The theory that a predisposition to develop a mental illness—not the mental illness itself—is inherited and that this predisposition may or may not be activated by environmental forces.

disorganized schizophrenia A schizophrenic disorder characterized by grossly disorganized behaviors manifested by disorganized speech and behavior and flat or grossly inappropriate affect.

dissociative amnesia A dissociative disorder characterized by the partial or total loss of important personal information, sometimes occurring suddenly after a stressful or traumatic event.

dissociative disorders Mental disorders in which a person's identity, memory, or consciousness is altered or disrupted; include dissociative amnesia, dissociative fugue, dissociative identity disorder (multiple-personality disorder), and depersonalization disorder.

dissociative fugue Confusion over personal identity accompanied by unexpected travel away from home; also called *fugue state*.

dissociative identity disorder (DID) A dissociative disorder in which two or more relatively independent personalities appear to exist in one person; formerly known as multiple-personality disorder.

dopamine hypothesis The suggestion that schizophrenia may result from excess dopamine activity at certain synaptic sites.

double-bind theory The suggestion that schizophrenia develops as a result of repeated experiences that the preschizophrenic child has with one or more family members (usually the mother and father) in which the child receives contradictory messages.

Down syndrome A condition produced by the presence of an extra chromosome (trisomy 21) and resulting in mental retardation and distinctive physical characteristics.

due process Legal checks and balances that are guaranteed to everyone (the right to a fair trial, the right to face accusers, the right to present evidence, the right to counsel, and so on).

Durham standard A test of legal insanity known as the products test—an accused person is not responsible if the unlawful act was the product of mental disease or defect.

dyspareunia Recurrent or persistent pain in the genitals before, during, or after sexual intercourse.

dysthymic disorder A disorder characterized by chronic and relatively continual depressed mood that does not meet the criteria for major depression.

electroconvulsive therapy (ECT) The application of electric voltage to the brain to induce convulsions; used to reduce depression; also called electroshock therapy.

encopresis An elimination disorder in which a child who is at least four years old defecates in his or her clothes, on the floor, or other inappropriate places, at least once a month for at least three months.

enuresis An elimination disorder in which a child who is at least five years old voids urine during the day or night into his or her clothes or bed or on the floor, at least twice weekly for at least three months.

essential hypertension Chronic high blood pressure, usually with no known biological cause; the most common disease in the United States.

etiology The causes or origins of a disorder.

exhibitionism Disorder characterized by urges, acts, or fantasies about the exposure of one's genitals to strangers.

existential approach A set of attitudes that has many commonalities with humanism but is less optimistic, focusing on (1) human alienation in an increasingly technological and impersonal world, (2) the individual in the context of the human condition, and (3) responsibility to others, as well as to oneself.

exorcism Ritual in which prayer, noise, emetics, and extreme measures such as flogging and starvation were used to cast evil spirits out of an afflicted person's body.

experiment A technique of scientific inquiry in which a prediction—an experimental hypothesis—is made about two variables; the independent variable is then manipulated in a controlled situation, and changes in the dependent variable are measured.

experimental hypothesis A prediction concerning how an independent variable affects a dependent variable in an experiment.

exposure therapy A therapy technique in which the patient is introduced to encounters (can be gradual or rapid) with the feared situation.

expressed emotion (EE) A type of negative communication pattern that is found in some families in which some members have schizophrenia and that is associated with higher relapse rates.

factitious disorders Disorders in which symptoms of physical or mental illnesses are deliberately induced or simulated with no apparent incentive.

family systems model A model of psychopathology that emphasizes the family's influence on individual behavior.

female orgasmic disorder A sexual dysfunction in which the woman experiences persistent delay or inability to achieve an orgasm with stimulation that is adequate in focus, intensity, and duration after entering the excitement phase; also known as inhibited orgasm.

female sexual arousal disorder The inability to attain or maintain physiological response and/or psychological arousal during sexual activity.

fetal alcohol syndrome (FAS) A group of congenital physical and mental defects found in some children born to alcoholic mothers; symptoms include small body size and microcephaly, in which the brain is unusually small and mild retardation may occur.

fetishism Sexual attraction and fantasies involving inanimate objects, such as female undergarments.

flat affect Little or no emotion in situations in which strong reactions are expected.

flooding A behavioral treatment that attempts to extinguish fear by placing the client in continued *in vivo* (actual) or imagined anxiety-provoking situations; a form of exposure therapy.

free association A psychoanalytic method that involves the patient saying whatever comes to mind, regardless of how illogical or embarrassing it may seem, for the purpose of revealing the contents of the patient's unconscious.

frotteurism Disorder characterized by recurrent and intense sexual urges, acts, or fantasies of touching or rubbing against a nonconsenting person.

gender identity disorder Disorder characterized by conflict between a person's anatomical sex and his or her gender identity, or self-identification as male or female.

general adaptation syndrome (GAS) A three-stage model for understanding the body's physical and psychological reactions to biological stressors.

generalized amnesia An inability to remember anything about one's past life.

generalized anxiety disorder (GAD) Disorder characterized by persistent high levels of anxiety and excessive worry over many life circumstances.

genetic linkage studies Studies that attempt to determine whether a disorder follows a genetic pattern.

genotype A person's genetic makeup.

hallucinations Sensory perceptions that are not directly attributable to environmental stimuli.

hallucinogen Substance that produces hallucinations, vivid sensory awareness, heightened alertness, or increased insight.

hardiness A concept developed by Kobasa and Maddi that refers to a person's ability to deal well with stress.

histrionic personality disorder A personality disorder characterized by self-dramatization, the exaggerated expression of emotions, and attention-seeking behaviors.

humanism Philosophical movement that emphasizes human welfare and the worth and uniqueness of the individual.

humanistic perspective The optimistic viewpoint that people are born with the ability to fulfill their potential and that abnormal behavior results from disharmony between the person's potential and his or her self-concept.

hypochondriasis A somatoform disorder characterized by persistent preoccupation with one's health and physical condition, even in the face of physical evaluations that reveal no organic problems.

hypothesis A conjectural statement, usually describing a relationship between two variables.

implosion A behavioral treatment that attempts to extinguish a fear by having the client imagine the anxiety-provoking situation at full intensity.

incest Sexual relations between people too closely related to marry legally.

incidence Onset or occurrence of a given disorder over some period of time.

independent variable A variable or condition that an experimenter manipulates to determine its effect on a dependent variable.

insanity defense The legal argument used by defendants who admit they have committed a crime but plead not guilty because they were mentally disturbed at the time the crime was committed.

intoxication Condition in which a substance affecting the central nervous system has been ingested and certain maladaptive behaviors or psychological changes, such as belligerence and impaired functioning, are evident.

irresistible impulse test One test of insanity, which states that a defendant is not criminally responsible if he or she lacked the will power to control his or her behavior.

learned helplessness Acquiring the belief that one is helpless and unable to affect the outcomes in one's life.

least restrictive environment concept A person's right to the least restrictive alternative to freedom that is appropriate to his or her condition.

lethality The probability that a person will choose to end his or her life.

life-change model An explanation of stress that assumes that all changes in a person's life—large or small, desirable or undesirable—can act as stressors and that the accumulation of small changes can be as powerful as one major stressor.

lifetime prevalence The total proportion of people in a population who have ever had a disorder in their lives.

localized amnesia The most common type of amnesia; an inability to recall all the events that happened during a specific period, often centered on some highly painful or disturbing event.

loosening of associations Continual shifting from topic to topic without any apparent logical or meaningful connection between thoughts.

M'Naghten Rule A cognitive test of legal insanity that inquires whether the accused knew right from wrong when he or she committed the crime.

major depression A disorder in which a group of symptoms, such as depressed mood, loss of interest, sleep disturbances, feelings of worthlessness, and an inability to concentrate, are present for at least two weeks.

male erectile disorder An inability to attain or maintain an erection sufficient for sexual intercourse.

male orgasmic disorder Persistent delay or inability to achieve an orgasm after the excitement phase has been reached and sexual activity has been adequate in focus, intensity, and duration; usually restricted to an inability to ejaculate within the vagina (also known as inhibited male orgasm).

malingering Faking a disorder to achieve some goal, such as an insurance settlement.

mania An emotional state characterized by elevated mood, expansiveness, or irritability, often resulting in hyperactivity.

marijuana The mildest and most commonly used hallucinogen; also known as "pot" or "grass."

masochism A paraphilia in which sexual urges, fantasies, or acts are associated with being humiliated, bound, or made to suffer.

mass madness Group hysteria, in which large numbers of people exhibit similar symptoms that have no apparent cause.

mental retardation Significant subaverage general intellectual functioning accompanied by deficiencies in adaptive behavior, with onset before age eighteen.

migraine headache Severe headache characterized by constriction of cranial arteries, followed by dilation of the cerebral blood vessels, resulting in moderate to severe pain.

model An analogy used by scientists, usually to describe or explain a phenomenon or process that they cannot directly observe.

modeling The process of learning by observing models and later imitating them; also known as *vicarious conditioning*.

modeling therapy A therapeutic approach to phobias in which the person with the phobia observes a model in the act of coping with, or responding appropriately in, the fear-producing situation.

mood disorders Disturbances in emotions that cause subjective discomfort, hinder a person's ability to function, or both; depression and mania are central to these disorders.

moral treatment movement A shift to more humane treatment of the mentally disturbed; its initiation is generally attributed to Philippe Pinel.

multicultural psychology A field of psychology that stresses the importance of culture, race, ethnicity, gender, age, socioeconomic class, and other similar factors in its efforts to understand and treat abnormal behavior.

narcissistic personality disorder A personality disorder characterized by an exaggerated sense of self-importance, an exploitative attitude, and a lack of empathy.

narcotics Drugs such as opium and its derivatives—morphine, heroin, and codeine—which depress the central nervous system; act as sedatives to provide relief from pain, anxiety, and tension; and are addictive.

negative symptoms In schizophrenia, symptoms that are associated with inferior premorbid social functioning and carry a poorer prognosis than positive symptoms; they include flat affect, poverty of speech, anhedonia, apathy, and avolition.

neuroleptics Antipsychotic drugs that can help treat symptoms of schizophrenia but can produce undesirable side effects, such as symptoms that mimic neurological disorders.

neurons Nerve cells that transmit messages throughout the body.

neurotransmitters Chemical substances that are released by axons of sending neurons and that are involved in the transmission of neural impulses to the dendrites of receiving neurons.

observational learning theory A theory of learning that holds that an individual can acquire behaviors simply by watching other people perform them.

obsession An intrusive and repetitive thought or image that produces anxiety.

obsessive-compulsive disorder (OCD) Disorder characterized by intrusive and repetitive thoughts or images, or by the need to perform acts or dwell on thoughts to reduce anxiety.

obsessive-compulsive personality disorder A personality disorder characterized by perfectionism, a tendency to be interpersonally controlling, devotion to details, and rigidity.

operant behavior A voluntary and controllable behavior that "operates" on an individual's environment.

operant conditioning A theory of learning that applies primarily to voluntary behaviors and that holds that these behaviors are controlled by the consequences that follow them.

operational definitions Definitions of the variables under study.

oppositional defiant disorder (ODD) A childhood disorder characterized by a pattern of negativistic, argumentative, and hostile behavior in which the child often loses his or her temper, argues with adults, and defies or refuses adult requests; refusal to take responsibility for actions, anger, resentment, blaming others, and spiteful and vindictive behavior are common, but serious violations of other's rights are not.

organicity Damage or deterioration in the central nervous system.

pain disorder A somatoform disorder characterized by reports of severe pain that has no physiological or neurological basis, is greatly in excess of that expected with an existing condition, or lingers long after a physical injury has healed.

panic disorder Anxiety disorder characterized by severe and frightening episodes of apprehension and feelings of impending doom.

paranoid personality disorder A personality disorder characterized by unwarranted suspiciousness, hypersensitivity, and a reluctance to confide in others.

paranoid schizophrenia A schizophrenic disorder characterized by one or more systematized delusions or auditory hallucinations and the absence of such symptoms as disorganized speech and behavior or flat affect.

paraphilias Sexual disorders of at least six months' duration in which the person has either acted on, or is severely distressed by, recurrent urges or fantasies involving nonhuman objects, nonconsenting persons, or suffering or humiliation.

pedophilia A disorder in which an adult obtains erotic gratification through urges, acts, or fantasies involving sexual contact with a prepubescent child.

personality disorder A disorder characterized by inflexible and maladaptive personality traits that cause significant functional impairment or subjective distress for the individual.

person-centered therapy A humanistic therapy that emphasizes the therapist's attitudes in the therapeutic relationship rather than the precise techniques to be used in therapy.

pervasive developmental disorders Severe childhood disorders in which qualitative impairment in verbal and nonverbal communication and social interaction are the primary symptoms; include autistic disorder, Asperger's disorder, and pervasive developmental disorders not otherwise specified.

phenotype The observable results of the interaction of a person's genotype and the environment.

phobia A strong, persistent, and unwarranted fear of some specific object or situation.

pleasure principle Usually associated with the id in Freudian theory; the impulsive, pleasure-seeking aspect of our being that seeks immediate gratification of instinctual needs regardless of moral or realistic concerns.

polysubstance dependence Substance dependence in which dependency is not based on the use of any single substance but on the repeated use of at least three groups of substances (not including caffeine and nicotine) for a period of twelve months.

positive symptoms Symptoms that are present during the active phase of schizophrenia and that tend to disappear with treatment; they may include hallucinations and delusions, as well as disorganized speech and behavior, inappropriate affect, and formal thought disorders.

posttraumatic stress disorder (PTSD) An anxiety disorder that lasts for more than thirty days; develops in response to a specific extreme stressor; characterized by intrusive memories of the traumatic event, emotional withdrawal, and heightened autonomic arousal.

premature ejaculation Ejaculation with minimal sexual stimulation before, during, or shortly after penetration.

prevalence The percentage of people in a population who have a disorder at a given point in time.

privileged communication A therapist's legal obligation to protect a client's privacy and to prevent the disclosure of confidential communications without a client's permission.

prognosis A prediction of the future course of a particular disorder.

projective personality test A personality assessment technique in which the test taker is presented with ambiguous stimuli and is asked to respond to them in some way.

psychoanalysis Therapy based on the Freudian view that unconscious conflicts must be aired and understood by the patient if abnormal behavior is to be eliminated.

psychodiagnosis An attempt to describe, assess, and systematically draw inferences about an individual's psychological disorder.

psychodynamic models Models based on the view that adult disorders arise from traumas or anxieties originally experienced in childhood but later repressed because they are too threatening for the adult to face.

psychological autopsy The systematic examination of existing information for the purpose of understanding and explaining a person's behavior before his or her death.

psychological tests and inventories A variety of standardized test instruments used to assess personality, maladaptive behavior, development of social skills, intellectual abilities, vocational interests, and cognitive impairment.

psychological view The belief or theory that mental disorders are caused by psychological and emotional factors, rather than organic or biological factors.

psychopathology Clinical term meaning abnormal behavior.

psychopharmacology The study of the effects of drugs on the mind and on behavior; also known as *medication* and *drug therapy*.

psychophysiological disorder Any physical disorder that has a strong psychological basis or component.

psychosexual stages In psychoanalytic theory, the sequence of stages—oral, anal, phallic, latency, and genital—through which human personality develops.

psychosurgery Brain surgery performed for the purpose of correcting a severe mental disorder.

reality principle Usually associated with the ego in Freudian theory; an awareness of the demands of the environment and of the need to adjust behavior to meet these demands.

reinforcing abstinence Giving behavioral reinforcements for abstinence from substance use.

relaxation training A therapeutic technique in which the person acquires the ability to relax the muscles of the body in almost any circumstances.

reliability The degree to which a procedure or test will yield the same results repeatedly, under the same circumstances.

residual schizophrenia A category of schizophrenic disorder reserved for people who have had at least one previous schizophrenic episode but are now showing an absence of prominent psychotic features and continuing evidence of two or more symptoms, such as marked social isolation, peculiar behaviors, blunted affect, odd beliefs, or unusual perceptual experiences.

resistance During psychoanalysis, the process in which the patient unconsciously attempts to impede the analysis by preventing the exposure of repressed material; tactics include silence, late arrival, failure to keep appointments, and others.

right to treatment The concept that mental patients who have been involuntarily committed have a right to receive therapy that would improve their emotional state.

sadism Form of paraphilia in which sexually arousing urges, fantasies, or acts are associated with inflicting physical or psychological suffering on others.

schizoid personality disorder A personality disorder characterized by social isolation, emotional coldness, and indifference to others.

schizophrenia A group of disorders characterized by severely impaired cognitive processes, personality disintegration, affective disturbances, and social withdrawal.

schizophreniform disorder Psychotic disorder that last more than one month but less than six months.

schizophrenogenic Causing or producing schizophrenia; a term generally used to describe a parent who is simultaneously or alternately cold and overprotecting, rejecting and dominating.

schizotypal personality disorder A personality disorder characterized by peculiar thoughts and behaviors and by poor interpersonal relationships.

scientific method A method of inquiry that provides for the systematic collection of data through controlled observation and for the testing of hypotheses.

selective amnesia An inability to remember certain details of an incident.

self-actualization An inherent tendency to strive toward the realization of one's full potential.

self-concept An individual's assessment of his or her own value and worth.

self-report inventories An assessment tool that requires test takers to answer specific written questions or to select specific responses from a list of alternatives.

separation anxiety disorder (SAD) A childhood disorder characterized by excessive anxiety over separation from parents and home.

sexual arousal disorders Problems occurring during the excitement (arousal) phase and relating to difficulties with feelings of sexual pleasure or with the physiological changes associated with sexual excitement.

sexual desire disorders Sexual dysfunctions that are related to the appetitive phase and are characterized by a lack of sexual desire.

sexual dysfunction A disruption of any part of the normal sexual response cycle.

single-participant experiment An experiment performed on a single individual in which some aspect of the person's own behavior is used as a control or baseline for comparison with future behaviors.

skills training Teaching skills for resisting peer pressures or temptations, resolving emotional conflicts or problems, or for more effective communication.

social phobia An intense, excessive fear of being scrutinized in one or more social situations.

somatization disorder A somatoform disorder in which the person chronically complains of a number of bodily symptoms that have no physiological basis; complaints include at least four symptoms in different sites, two gastrointestinal symptoms, one sexual symptom, and one pseudoneurological symptom.

somatoform disorders Mental disorders that involve physical symptoms or complaints that have no physiological basis; include somatization disorder, conversion disorder, pain disorder, hypochondriasis, and body dysmorphic disorder.

specific phobia An extreme fear of a specific object or situation; a phobia that is not classified as either agoraphobia or a social phobia.

stimulant Substance that is a central nervous system energizer, inducing elation, grandiosity, hyperactivity, agitation, and appetite suppression.

stress An internal response to a stressor.

stressor An external event or situation that places a physical or psychological demand on a person.

substance abuse Maladaptive pattern of recurrent use that extends over a period of twelve months; leads to notable impairment or distress; and continues despite social, occupational, psychological, physical, or safety problems.

substance dependence Maladaptive pattern of use extending over a twelve-month period and characterized by unsuccessful efforts to control use, despite knowledge of harmful effects; taking more of substance than intended; tolerance; or withdrawal.

substance-related disorders Disorders resulting from the use of psychoactive substances that affect the central nervous system, causing significant social, occupational, psychological, or physical problems, and that sometimes result in abuse or dependence.

sudden death syndrome Unexpected abrupt death that seems to have no specific physical basis.

suicide The intentional, direct, and conscious taking of one's own life.

synapse A minute gap between the axon of the sending neuron and the dendrites of the receiving neuron.

syndrome A cluster of symptoms that tend to occur together and that are believed to represent a particular disorder with its own unique cause, course, and outcome.

systematic desensitization (1) A form of counterconditioning aimed at reducing anxiety by overcoming it with an antagonistic response. (2) A behavioral therapy technique in which relaxation is used to eliminate the anxiety associated with phobias and other fear-evoking situations.

systematized amnesia The loss of memory for only selected types of information, such as all members of one's family.

***Tarasoff* ruling** Commonly referred to as the "duty-to-warn" principle; obligates mental health professionals to break confidentiality when their clients pose clear and imminent danger to another person.

tension headache A headache thought to be produced by prolonged contraction of the scalp and neck muscles, resulting in vascular constriction.

theory A group of principles and hypotheses that together explain some aspect of a particular area of inquiry.

therapy A program of systematic intervention whose purpose is to modify a client's behavioral, affective (emotional), or cognitive state.

tics Involuntary, repetitive, and nonrhythmic movements or vocalizations.

token economy A treatment program, based on principles of operant conditioning, that rewards patients for appropriate behaviors with tokens, which can then be exchanged for hospital privileges, food, or weekend passes.

tolerance Condition in which increasing doses of a substance are necessary to achieve the desired effect.

Tourette's disorder A childhood disorder characterized by multiple motor and one or more verbal tics that may develop into coprolalia (compulsion to shout obscenities).

transaction model of stress Explanation of stress that states that stress resides neither in the person alone nor in the situation alone, but rather in a transaction between the two.

transference During psychotherapy, a process in which the patient reenacts early conflicts by carrying over and applying to the therapist feelings and attitudes that the patient had toward significant others (primarily parents) in the past.

transient tic disorder Childhood onset disorder that lasts longer than four weeks but less than one year and that is characterized by involuntary, repetitive, and nonrhythmic movements or vocalizations.

transsexualism A strong and persistent cross-gender identification and persistent discomfort with one's anatomical sex, which cause significant impairment in social, occupational, or other areas of functioning.

transvestic fetishism Intense sexual arousal obtained through cross-dressing (wearing clothes appropriate to the opposite gender); not to be confused with transsexualism.

trephining An ancient surgical technique in which part of the skull was chipped away to provide an opening through which evil spirits could escape.

unconditioned response (UCR) In classical conditioning, the unlearned response made to an unconditioned stimulus.

unconditioned stimulus (UCS) In classical conditioning, the stimulus that elicits an unconditioned response.

undifferentiated schizophrenia A schizophrenic disorder in which the person's behavior shows prominent psychotic symptoms that do not meet the criteria for paranoid, disorganized, or catatonic schizophrenia.

undifferentiated somatoform disorder At least one physical complaint with no physical basis that has lasted for six months or more.

vaginismus Involuntary spasm of the outer third of the vaginal wall, preventing or interfering with sexual intercourse.

validity The extent to which a test or procedure actually performs the function it was designed to perform.

vascular dementia Dementia characterized by uneven deterioration of intellectual abilities and resulting from a number of cerebral infarctions.

voyeurism Urges, acts, or fantasies involving observation of an unsuspecting person disrobing or engaging in sexual activity.

withdrawal Condition characterized by distress or impairment in social, occupational, or other areas of functioning or by physical or emotional symptoms such as shaking, irritability, and inability to concentrate after reducing or ceasing intake of a substance.

References

Abebimpe, V. R., Chu, C. C., Klein, H. E., & Lange, M. H. (1982). Racial and geographic differences in the psychopathology of schizophrenia. *American Journal of Psychiatry, 139,* 888–891.

Abel, G. G., & Osborn, C. (1992). The paraphilias: The extent and nature of sexually deviant and criminal behavior. *Psychiatric Clinics of North America, 15,* 675–687.

Abeles, N., & Victor, T. (2003). Unique opportunities for psychology in mental health care for older adults. *Clinical Psychology: Science and Practice, 10,* 120–124.

Abramowitz, A. J., & O'Leary, S. G. (1991). Behavioral interventions for the classroom: Implications for students with ADHD. *School Psychology Review, 20,* 220–234.

Abramowitz, J. S., Foa, E. B., & Franklin, M. E. (2003). Exposure and ritual prevention for obsessive-compulsive disorder: Effects of intensive versus twice-weekly sessions. *Journal of Consulting and Clinical Psychology, 71,* 394–398.

Abramson, J., Berger, A., Krubholz, H. M., & Vaccarino, V. (2001). Depression and risk of heart failure among older persons with isolated systolic hypertension. *Archives of Internal Medicine, 161,* 1725–1730.

Abramson, L. Y., Metalsky, G. I., & Alloy, L. B. (1989). Hopelessness in depression: A theory-based subtype of depression. *Psychological Review, 96*(2), 358–372.

Abramson, L. Y., Seligman, M. E. P., & Teasdale, J. D. (1978). Learned helplessness in humans: Critique and reformulation. *Journal of Abnormal Psychology, 87,* 49–74.

Adler, J., & Rogers, A. (1999, January 11). The new war against migraines. *Newsweek,* pp. 46–52.

Adler, R. H., Zamboni, P., Hofer, T., Hemmler, W., Hurny, C., Minder, C., Radvila, A., & Zlot, S. I. (1997). How not to miss a somatic needle in the haystack of chronic pain. *Journal of Psychosomatic Research, 42,* 499–506.

Agras, W. S., Rossiter, E. M., Arnow, B., Schneider, J. A., Telch, C. F., Raeburn, S. D., Bruce, B., Perl, M. & Koran, L. M. (1992). Pharmacologic and cognitive-behavioral treatment for bulimia nervosa: A controlled comparison. *American Journal of Psychiatry, 149,* 82–87.

Ahles, T. A., Cassens, H. L., & Stalling, R. B. (1987). Private body consciousness, anxiety and the perception of pain. *Journal of Behavior Therapy and Experimental Psychiatry, 18,* 215–222.

Alanen, Y. O. (1994). An attempt to integrate the individual-psychological and interactional concepts of the origins of schizophrenia. *British Journal of Psychiatry, 164,* 56–61.

Aldridge-Morris, R. (1989). *Multiple personality. An exercise in deception.* Hove, United Kingdom: Erlbaum.

Alessandri, S. (1991). Play and social behavior in maltreated preschoolers. *Development and Psychopathology, 3,* 191–205.

Alexander, F. (1950). *Psychosomatic medicine.* New York: Norton.

Alexander, F. G., & Selesnick, S. T. (1966). *The history of psychiatry.* New York: Harper & Row.

Alford, G. S. (1980). Alcoholics Anonymous: An empirical outcome study. *Addictive Behaviors, 5,* 359–370.

Allen, L. A., Gara, M. A., Escobar, J. I., Waitzkin, H., & Silver, R. C. (2001). Somatization: A debilitating syndrome in primary care. *Psychosomatics, 42,* 63–67.

Allgeier, E. R., & Allgeier, A. R. (1998). *Sexual interactions.* Boston: Houghton Mifflin.

Althof, S. E., Turner, L. A., Levine, S. B., Risen, C., Kursch, E. D., Bodner, D., & Resnick, M. (1987). Intracavernosal injection in the treatment of impotence: A prospective study of sexual, psychological, and marital functioning. *Journal of Sex and Marital Therapy, 13,* 155–167.

Amador, X. F., Falum, M., Andreasen, N. C., Strauss, D. H., Yale, S. A., Clark, S. C., & Gorman, J. M. (1994). Awareness of illness in schizophrenia and schizoaffective and mood disorders. *Archives of General Psychiatry, 51,* 826–836.

American Association of Retired Persons. (1999, September-October). Sex and sexuality [Special issue]. *Modern Maturity.*

American Anorexia/Bulimia Association. (1998). General information on eating disorders (Online). http://members.aol.com/amabu/index.html.

American Dietetic Association. (2001). Position of the American Dietetic Association: Nutrition intervention in the treatment of anorexia nervosa, bulimia nervosa, and eating disorders not otherwise specified (EDNOS). *Journal of the American Dietetic Association, 101,* 810–819.

American Heart Association. (1998). *Biostatistical fact sheets.* Author.

American Psychiatric Association. (1952). *Diagnostic and statistical manual of mental disorders* (1st ed.) [DSM-I]. Washington, DC: Author.

American Psychiatric Association. (1968). *Diagnostic and statistical manual of mental disorders* (2nd ed.) [DSM-II]. Washington, DC: Author.

American Psychiatric Association. (1980). *Diagnostic and statistical manual of mental disorders* (3rd ed.). [DSM-III]. Washington, DC: Author.

American Psychiatric Association. (1987). *Diagnostic and statistical manual of mental disorders* (3rd ed.). [DSM-III-R]. Washington, DC: Author.

American Psychiatric Association. (1994). *Diagnostic and statistical manual of mental disorders* (4th ed.). [DSM-IV]. Washington, DC: Author.

American Psychiatric Association. (1997). Practice guidelines for the treatment of patients with schizophrenia. *American Journal of Psychiatry, 154,* 1–40.

American Psychiatric Association. (1998). Practice guidelines for the treatment of patients with panic disorder. *American Journal of Psychiatry, 155,* 1–34.

American Psychiatric Association. (2000a). *Diagnostic and statistical manual of mental disorders* (4th ed., Text revision). Washington, DC: Author.

American Psychiatric Association. (2000b). Practice guideline for the treatment of patients with eating disorders (revision). *American Journal of Psychiatry, 157,* 1–39.

American Psychological Association. (1992). Ethical principles of psychologists and code of conduct. *American Psychologist, 47,* 1597–1611.

American Psychological Association. (1993). Guidelines for providers of psychological services to ethnic, linguistic, and culturally diverse populations. *American Psychologist, 48,* 45–48.

American Psychological Association. (1995). *Ethical principles of psychologists and code of conduct.* Washington, DC: Author.

American Psychological Association. (2000). Guidelines for psychotherapy with lesbian, gay, and bisexual clients. *American Psychologist, 55*(12), 1440–1451.

American Psychological Association. (2003). Guidelines on multicultural education, training, research, practice, and organizational change for psychologists. *American Psychologist, 58*(5), 377–402.

APA Working Group on the Older Adult. (1998). What practitioners should know about working with older adults. *Professional Psychology: Research and Practice, 29,* 413–427.

Anastasi, A. (1982). *Psychological testing.* New York: Macmillan.

Andersen, A. E. (2001). Progress in eating disorders research. *American Journal of Psychiatry, 158,* 515–517.

Andersen, B. L., & Cyranowski, J. M. (1995). Women's sexuality: Behaviors, responses, and individual differences. *Journal of Consulting and Clinical Psychology, 63,* 891–906.

Anderson, T., & Strupp, H. H. (1996). The ecology of psychotherapy research. *Journal of Consulting and Clinical Psychology, 64,* 776–782.

Andreasen, N. C. (1984). *The broken brain.* New York: Harper & Row.

Andreasen, N. C. (1989). Nuclear magnetic resonance imaging. In N. C. Andreasen (Ed.), *Brain imaging: Applications in psychiatry* (pp. 67–121). Washington, DC: American Psychiatric Press.

Andreasen, N. C., Arndt, S., Alliger, R., Miller, D., & Flaum, M. (1995). Symptoms of schizophrenia: Methods, meanings, and mechanisms. *Archives of General Psychiatry, 52,* 341–351.

Anorexia's web. (2001, September 7). *Current Events, 101,* 1–3.

Anthony, J. C., & Helzer, J. E. (1991). Syndromes of drug abuse and dependence. In L. N. Robins & D. A. Regier (Eds.), *Psychiatric disorders in America: The Epidemiologic Catchment Area study* (pp. 116–154). New York: Free Press.

Antony, M. M., Brown, T. A., & Barlow, D. H. (1997). Heterogeneity among specific phobia types in *DSM-IV. Behaviour Research and Therapy, 35,* 1089–1100.

Applebaum, P. S. (1994). *Almost a revolution: Mental health law and the limits of change.* New York: Oxford University Press.

Ardizzone, J., & Scholl, G. T. (1985). Mental retardation. In G. T. Scholl (Ed.), *The school psychologist and the exceptional child.* Reston, VA: Council for Exceptional Children.

Arndt, S., Andreasen, N. C., Flaum, M., Miller, D., & Nopoulous, P. (1995). A longitudinal study of symptom dimensions in schizophrenia. *Archives of General Psychiatry, 52,* 352–360.

Arndt, W. B., Jr. (1991). *Gender disorders and the paraphilias.* Madison, CT: International Universities Press.

Asmundson, G. J. G., & Norton, G. R. (1993). Anxiety sensitivity and its relationship to spontaneous and cued panic attacks in college students. *Behaviour Research and Therapy, 31,* 199–201.

Assalian, P. (1988). Clomipramine in the treatment of premature ejaculation. *Journal of Sex Research, 24,* 213–215.

Associated Press. (1994, January 30). Long-term HIV survivors intrigue scientists. *Bellingham Herald,* p. A10.

Associated Press. (1998, August 14). Psychiatrist is sued over multiple bad personalities. *Seattle Post Intelligencer,* p. A12.

Atkins, L. (2002, July 23). Health: "It's better to be thin and dead than fat and living." *Guardian, 2,* 10.

Atkinson, D. R., Morten, G., & Sue, D. W. (1998). *Counseling American Minorities: A cross-cultural perspective.* New York: McGraw-Hill.

Austin, K. M., Moline, M. M., & Williams, G. T. (1990). *Confronting malpractice: Legal and ethical dilemmas in psychotherapy.* Newbury Park, CA: Sage.

Ausubel, D. P. (1961). Causes and types of narcotic addiction: A psychosocial view. *Psychiatric Quarterly, 35,* 523–531.

Autism Society of Wisconsin. (2001). *Secretin and links.* Retrieved from http://www.gsw4autism.org/secretin.htm.

Ayanian, J. Z., Udvarhelyi, I. S., Pashos, C. L., & Epstein, A. M. (1993). Racial differences in the use of revascularization procedures after coronary angiography. *Journal of the American Medical Association, 269,* 2642–2646.

Bacon, N. M. K., Bacon, S. F., Atkinson, J. H., Slater, M. A. (1994). Somatization symptoms in chronic low back pain patients. *Psychosomatic Medicine, 56,* 118–127.

Bagby, R. M., Rogers, R., Nicholson, R. A., Buis, T., Seeman, M. V., & Rector, N. A. (1997). The effectiveness of the MMPI-2 validity indicators in the detection of defensive responding in clinical and nonclinical samples. *Psychology Assessment, 9,* 406–413.

Bahnson, C. B. (1981). Stress and cancer: The state of the art. *Psychosomatics, 22,* 207–209.

Bak, M., Myin-Germeys, I., Hanssen, M., Bijl, R., et al. (2003). When does experience of psychosis result in a need for care? A prospective general population study. *Schizophrenia Bulletin, 29,* 349–356.

Baker, L. A., & Clark, R. (1990). Introduction to special feature on genetic origins of behavior: Implications for counselors. *Journal of Counseling and Development, 68,* 597–605.

Baker, R. R., Lichtenberg, P. A., & Moye, J. (1998). A practice guideline for assessment of competency and capacity of the older adult. *Professional Psychology: Research and Practice, 29,* 149–154.

Bakker, A., Spinhoven, P., Van Balkom, A. J. L. M., & Van Dyck, R. (2002). Relevance of assessment of cognitions during panic attacks in the treatment of panic disorder. *Psychotherapy and Psychosomatics, 71,* 158–162.

Baladerian, N. J. (1991). Abuse causes disabilities. *In Disability and the family.* Culver City, CA: Spectrum Institute.

Ballenger, J. C., Davidson, J. R. T., Lecrubier, Y., Nutt, D. J., et al. (2000). Consensus statement on generalized anxiety disorder from the International Consensus Group on depression and anxiety. *Journal of Clinical Psychiatry, 62,* 53–58.

Bancroft, J. (1989). *Human sexuality and its problems.* New York: Churchill-Livingstone.

Bandura, A. (1969). *Principles of behavior modification.* New York: Holt, Rinehart & Winston.

Bandura, A., & Walters, R. H. (1963). *Social learning and personality development.* New York: Holt, Rinehart & Winston.

Banerjee, G., & Roy, S. (1998). Determinants of help-seeking behaviour of families of schizophrenic patients attending a teaching hospital in India: An indigenous explanatory model. *International Journal of Social Psychiatry, 44,* 199–214.

Barber, J. P., & Luborsky, L. (1991). A psychodynamic view of simple phobias and prescriptive matching: A commentary. *Psychotherapy, 28,* 469–472.

Barber, J. P., Morse, J. Q., Krakauer, I. D., Chittams, J., & Crits-Cristoph, K. (1997). Change in obsessive-compulsive and avoidant personality disorders following time-limited supportive-expressive therapy. *Journal of Psychotherapy, 34,* 133–143.

Barkley, R. A., Anastopoulous, A. D., Guevremont, D. C., & Fletcher, K. E. (1992). Adolescents with attention deficit hyperactivity disorder: Mother-child-adolescent interactions, family beliefs and conflicts, and psychopathology. *Journal of Abnormal Child Psychology, 20,* 263–288.

Barkley, R. A., Fischer, M., Edelbrock, C., & Smallish, L. (1991). The adolescent outcome of hyperactive children diagnosed by research criteria–III. Mother-child interactions, family conflicts and maternal psychopathology. *Journal of Child Psychology and Psychiatry, 32,* 233–255.

Barlow, D. H., Abel, G., & Blanchard, E. (1979). Gender identity change in transsexuals. *Archives of General Psychiatry, 36,* 1001–1007.

Barlow, D. H., Gorman, J. M., Shear, M. K., & Woods, S. W. (2000). Cognitive-behavioral therapy, imipramine, or their combination for panic disorder: A randomized controlled trial. *Journal of the American Medical Association, 283,* 2529–2536.

Baron, M. (1991). Genetics of manic depressive illness: Current status and evolving concepts. In P. R. McHugh & V. A. McKusick (Eds.), *Genes, brain, and behavior* (pp. 153–164). New York: Raven Press.

Baron-Cohen, L., Leslie, A. M., & Frith, U. (1985). Does the autistic child have a "theory of mind"? *Cognition, 21*, 37–46.

Barry, C. T., Frick, P. J., DeShazo, T. M., McCoy, M. G., Ellis, M., & Loney, B. R. (2000). The importance of callous-unemotional traits for extending the concept of psychopathology to children. *Journal of Abnormal Psychology, 109*, 335–340.

Barsky, A. J., Cleary, P. D., Sarnie, M. K., & Klerman, G. L. (1993). The course of transient hypochondriasis. *American Journal of Psychiatry, 150*, 484–488.

Barsky, A. J., Wool, C., Barnett, M. C., & Cleary, P. D. (1995). Histories of childhood trauma in adult hypochondriacal patients. *American Journal of Psychiatry, 151*, 397–401.

Barsky, A. J., & Wyshak, G. (1990). Hypochondriasis and somatosensory amplification. *British Journal of Psychiatry, 157*, 404–409.

Barsky, A. J., Wyshak, G., & Klerman, G. L. (1992). Psychiatric comorbidity in DSM-III-R hypochondriasis. *Archives of General Psychiatry, 49*, 101–108.

Bashore, T. R., Ridderinkhof, K. R., & Van der Molen, M. W. (1997). The decline of cognitive processing speed in old age. *Current Directions in Psychological Science, 6*, 163–169.

Basoglu, M. L., Livanou, M. L., & Salcioglu, E. (2003). A single session with an earthquake simulator for traumatic stress in earthquake survivors. *American Journal of Psychiatry, 160*, 788–790.

Bateson, G., Jackson, D., Haley, J., & Weakland, J. (1956). Toward a theory of schizophrenia. *Behavioral Science, 1*, 251–264.

Battaglia, M., Bertella, S., Politi, E., Bernardeschi, L., Perna, G., Gabriele, A., & Bellodi, L. (1995). Age at onset of panic disorder: Influence of familial liability to the disease and of childhood separation anxiety. *American Journal of Psychiatry, 152*, 1362–1364.

Baum, A., & Posluszny, D. M. (1999). Health psychology: Mapping biobehavioral contributions to health and illness. *Annual Review of Psychology, 50*, 137–163.

Baumeister, R. F. (1988). Masochism as escape from self. *Journal of Sex Research, 25*, 28–59.

Beardslee, W. R., Wright, E., Rothberg, P. C., Salt, P., & Versage, E. (1996). Response of families to two preventative intervention strategies: Long-term differences in behavior and attitude change. *Journal of American Child and Adolescent Psychiatry, 35*, 774–782.

Beck, A. T. (1974). The development of depression: A cognitive model. In R. J. Friedman & M. M. Katz (Eds.), *The psychology of depression: Contemporary theory and research*. New York: Wiley.

Beck, A. T. (1976). *Cognitive therapy and emotional disorders*. New York: International Universities Press.

Beck, A. T., Freeman, A., & Associates. (1990). *Cognitive therapy of personality disorders*. New York: Guilford Press.

Beck, A. T., & Rector, N. A. (2000). Cognitive therapy of schizophrenia: A new therapy for the new millennium. *American Journal of Psychotherapy, 54*, 291–300.

Beck, A. T., Ward, C. H., Mendelson, M., Mock, J. E., & Erbaugh, J. (1961). An inventory for measuring depression. *Archives of General Psychiatry, 4*, 561–571.

Beck, A. T., & Weishaar, M. E. (1989). Cognitive therapy. In R. J. Corsini & D. Wedding (Eds.), *Current psychotherapies* (pp. 285–320). Itasca, IL: Peacock.

Becker, A. E. (1995). *Body, self, and society: The view from Fiji*. Philadelphia: University of Pennsylvania Press.

Bednar, R. L., Bednar, S. C., Lambert, M. J., & Waite, D. R. (1991). *Psychotherapy with high-risk clients: Legal and professional standards*. Pacific Grove, CA: Brooks/Cole.

Beers, M. H., & Berkow, R. (Eds.) (1999). *The Merck manual of diagnosis and therapy* (17th ed.). Whitehouse Station, NJ: Merck Publications.

Bell, A. P., & Weinberg, M. S. (1978). *Homosexualities: A study of diversity among men and women*. New York: Simon & Schuster.

Bell, A. P., Weinberg, M. S., & Hammersmith, S. K. (1981). *Sexual preference: Its development in men and women*. Bloomington: Indiana University Press.

Bell-Dolan, D., & Wessler, A. E. (1994). Attribution style of anxious children: Extensions from cognitive theory and research on adult anxiety. *Journal of Anxiety Disorders, 8*, 79–94.

Bellodi, L., Cavallini, M. C., Bertelli, S., Chiapparino, D., et al. (2001). Morbidity risk for obsessive-compulsive spectrum disorders in first-degree relatives of patients with eating disorders. *American Journal of Psychiatry, 158*, 563–569.

Bender, L. (1938). A visual motor gestalt test and its clinical use. *Research Monograph of the American Orthopsychiatric Association, 3*(11), 176.

Benedict, J. G., & Donaldson, D. W. (1996). Recovered memories threaten all. *Professional Psychology: Research and Practice, 27*, 427–428.

Benjamin, L. S., & Karpiak, C. P. (2002). Personality disorders. In J. C. Norcross (Ed.), *Psychotherapy relationships that work* (pp. 423–440). New York: Oxford University Press.

Benjamin, L. S., & Wonderlich, S. A. (1994). Social perceptions and borderline personality disorder: The relation to mood disorders. *Journal of Abnormal Psychology, 103*, 610–624.

Bennett, L. F. C., & Sherman, R. (1983). Management of childhood "hyperactivity" by primary care physicians. *Journal of Developmental and Behavioral Pediatrics, 4*, 88–93.

Ben-Tovim, D. I., Walker, K., Gilchrist, P., Freeman, R., et al. (2001). Outcome in patients with eating disorders: A five-year study. *Lancet, 357*, 1254–1257.

Beratis, S., Gabriel, J., & Hoidas, S., (1994). Age at onset in subtypes of schizophrenic disorders. *Schizophrenic Bulletin, 20*, 287–296.

Berkowitz, A., & Perkins, H. W. (1988). Personality characteristics of children of alcoholics. *Journal of Consulting and Clinical Psychology, 56*, 206–209.

Bernstein, S. M., Steiner, B. W., Glaisler, J. T. D., & Muir, C. F. (1981). Changes in patients with gender identity problems after parental death. *American Journal of Psychiatry, 138*, 41–45.

Bersoff, D. N. (1981). Testing and the law. *American Psychologist, 36*, 1047–1057.

Bhadrinath, B. R. (1990). Anorexia nervosa in adolescents of Asian extraction. *British Journal of Psychiatry, 156*, 565–568.

Bickel, W. K., Amass, L., Higgins, S. T., Badger, G. J., & Esch, R. A. (1997). Effects of adding behavioral treatment to opiod detoxification with buprenorphine. *Journal of Consulting and Clinical Psychology, 65*, 803–810.

Binder, L. M. (1986). Persisting symptoms after mild head injury: A review of the postconcussive syndrome. *Journal of Clinical and Experimental Neuropsychology, 8*, 323–346.

Binder, R. L. (1988). Organic mental disorders. In H. H. Goldman (Ed.), *Review of general psychiatry* (pp. 252–265). Norwalk, CT: Appleton & Lange.

Biondi, M., Picardi, A., Bakker, A., Spinhoven, P., et al. (2003). Attribution of improvement to medication and increased risk of relapse of panic disorder with agoraphobia [Reply]. *Psychotherapy and Psychosomatics, 72*, 110–111.

Black, D. W., Noyes, R., Goldstein, R. B., & Blum, N. (1992). A family study of obsessive-compulsive disorder. *Archives of General Psychiatry, 49*, 362–368.

Black, S. T. (1993). Comparing genuine and simulated suicide notes: A new perspective. *Journal of Consulting and Clinical Psychology, 67*, 699–702.

Blakeslee, S. (1993, June 2). New therapies are helping men to overcome impotence. *New York Times*, p. C12.

Blanchard, J. J., Gangestad, S. W., Brown, S. A., & Horan, W. P. (2000). Hedonic capacity and schizotypy revisited: A taxometric analysis of social anhedonia. *Journal of Abnormal Psychology, 109*, 87–95.

Blanchard, J. J., Horan, W. P., & Brown, S. A. (2001). Diagnostic differences in social anhedonia: A longitudinal study of schizophrenia and major depressive disorder. *Journal of Abnormal Psychology, 110*, 363–371.

Blanchard, R. (1988). Nonhomosexual gender dysphoria. *Journal of Sex Research, 24*, 188–193.

Blanchard, R., Racansky, I. G., & Steiner, B. W. (1986). Phallometric detection of fetishistic arousal. *Journal of Sex Research, 22*, 452–462.

Bleuler, E. (1950). *Dementia praecox or the group of schizophrenias* (J. Zinkin, Trans.). New York: International Universities Press. (Original work published 1911)

Blier, P., Szabo, S. T., Haddjeri, N., & Dong, J. (2000). Orbitofrontal cortex-basal ganglia system in OCD. *International Journal of Neuropsychopharmacology, 3*, 1–14.

Bliss, E. L. (1984). Hysteria and hypnosis. *Journal of Nervous and Mental Disease, 172*, 203–208.

Bloomberg, D. (2000, January/February). Bennett Braun case settled: Two-year loss of license, five years probation. *Skeptical Inquirer*, 7–8.

Blouin, A., Blouin, J., Aubin, P., Carter, J., Goldstein, C., Boyer, H., & Perez, E. (1992). Seasonal patterns of bulimia nervosa. *American Journal of Psychiatry, 149*, 73–81.

Boll, T. J. (1983). Neuropsychological assessment. In I. B. Weiner (Ed.), *Clinical methods in psychology*. New York: Wiley.

Bolton, P., Macdonald, H., Pickles, A., Rios, P., Goode, S., Crowson, M., Bailey, A., & Rutter, M. (1994). A case-control family history of autism. *Journal of Child Psychology and Psychiatry, 35*, 877–900.

Bolton, P., Rutter, M., Butler, L., & Summers, D. (1989). Females with autism and the fragile X. *Journal of Autism and Developmental Disorders, 19*, 473–476.

Bongar, B. (1992). Effective risk management and the suicidal patient. *Register Report, 18*, 1–3, 21–27.

Boon, S., & Draijer, N. (1993). Multiple personality disorder in the Netherlands: A clinical investigation of 71 patients. *American Journal of Psychiatry, 150*, 489–494.

Borch-Jacobsen, M. (1997). Sybil—The making of a disease: An interview with Dr. Herbert Spiegel. *New York Review of Books, 44*, 60–64.

Borkovec, T. D., & Ruscio, A. M. (2001). Psychotherapy for generalized anxiety disorder. *Journal of Clinical Psychiatry, 62*, 37–42.

Bornstein, R. F. (1997). Dependent personality disorder in the DSM-IV and beyond. *Clinical Psychology, 4*, 175–187.

Bouhoutsos, J., Holroyd, J., Lerman, H., Forer, B. R., & Greenberg, M. (1983). Sexual intimacy between psychotherapists and patients. *Professional Psychology: Research and Practice, 14*, 185–196.

Boyajian, A. E., DuPaul, G. J., Handler, M. W., Eckert, T. L., & McGoey, K. E. (2001). The use of classroom based brief functional analysis with preschoolers at risk for ADHD. *School Psychology Review, 30*, 278–293.

Bozzuto, J. C. (1975). Cinematic neurosis following *The Exorcist*. *Journal of Nervous and Mental Disease, 161*, 43–48.

Brandsma, J. (1979). *Outpatient treatment of alcoholism*. Baltimore: University Park Press.

Brawman-Mintzer, O., Lydiard, R. B., Rickels, K., & Small, G. W. (1997). Biological basis of generalized anxiety disorder: Discussion. *Journal of Clinical Psychology, 58*, 16–23.

Breier, A., Albus, M., Pickar, D., Zahn, T. P., Wolkowitz, O. M., & Paul, S. M. (1987). Controllable and uncontrollable stress in humans: Alterations in mood and neuroendocrine and psychophysiological function. *American Journal of Psychiatry, 144*, 1419–1425.

Breuer, J., & Freud, S. (1957). *Studies in hysteria*. New York: Basic Books. (Original work published 1895)

Brewin, C. R., Andrews, B., & Rose, S. (2003). Diagnostic overlap between acute stress disorder and PTSD in victims of violent crime. *American Journal of Psychiatry, 160*, 783–785.

Brewslow, N., Evans, L., & Langley, J. (1986). Comparisons among heterosexual, bisexual, and homosexual male sadomasochists. *Journal of Homosexuality, 13*, 83–107.

Brislin, R. (1993). *Understanding culture's influence on behavior*. New York: Harcourt Brace Jovanovich.

Bristol, M. M., Cohen, D. J., Costello, E. J., Deckla, M. B., Eckberg, T. J., Kallen, R., Kraemer, H. C., Lord, C., Maurer, R., McIlvane, W. J., Minchew, N., Sigman, M., & Spence, M. A. (1996). State of the science in autism: Report to the National Institute of Health. *Journal of Autism and Developmental Disorders, 26*, 121–154.

Broman, S. H., Nichols, P. L., & Kennedy, W. A. (1975). *Preschool IQ: Prenatal and early developmental correlates*. Hillsdale, NJ: Erlbaum.

Brown, T. A., & Cash, T. F. (1990). The phenomenon of nonclinical panic: Parameters of panic fear, and avoidance. *Journal of Anxiety Disorders, 4*, 15–29.

Brown, T. A., Di Nardo, P. A., Lehman, C. L., & Campbell, L. A. (2001). Reliability of DSM-IV anxiety and mood disorders: Implications for the classification of emotional disorders. *Journal of Abnormal Psychology, 110*, 49–58.

Bruch, H. (1978). Obesity and anorexia nervosa. *Psychosomatics, 19*, 208–221.

Bruch, M. A., Fallon, M., & Heimberg, R. G. (2003). Social phobia and difficulties in occupational adjustment. *Journal of Counseling Psychology, 50*, 109–117.

Bruch, M. A., & Heimberg, R. G. (1994). Differences in perceptions of parental and personal characteristics between generalized and nongeneralized social phobics. *Journal of Anxiety Disorders, 8*, 155–168.

Bryant, K. (2001, February 20). Eating disorders: In their own words. *Atlanta Constitution*, p. B4.

Buchanan, A. (1997). The investigation of acting on delusions as a tool for risk assessment in the mentally disordered. *British Journal of Psychiatry, 170*, 12–14.

Bunney, W. E., Pert, A., Rosenblatt, J., Pert, C. B., & Gallaper, D. (1979). Mode of action of lithium: Some biological considerations. *Archives of General Psychiatry, 36*, 898–901.

Burchard, E. G., Avila, P. C., Nazario, S., Casal, J., et al. (2004). Lower bronchodilator responsiveness in Puerto Rican than in Mexican subjects with asthma. *American Journal of Respiratory and Critical Care Medicine, 169*, 386–392.

Burgess, A. W., Hartman, C. R., McCausland, M. P., Powers, P. (1984). Response pattern in children and adolescents exploited through sex rings and pornography. *American Journal of Psychiatry, 141*, 656–662.

Burgess, A. W., & Holmstrom, L. L. (1979). Rape: Sex disruption and recovery. *American Journal of Orthopsychiatry, 49*, 648–657.

Burgy, M. (2001). The narcissistic function in obsessive-compulsive neurosis. *American Journal of Psychotherapy, 55*, 65–73.

Burke, W. J., & Bohac, D. L. (2001). Amnestic disorder due to a general medical condition and amnestic disorder not otherwise specified. In G. O. Gabbard (Ed.), *Treatment of psychiatric disorders* (pp. 609–624). Washington, DC: American Psychiatric Press.

Burruss, J. W., Travella, J. I., & Robinson, R. G. (2001). Vascular dementia. In G. O. Gabbard (Ed.), *Treatment of psychiatric disorders* (pp. 515–534). Washington, DC: American Psychiatric Press.

Burt, D. B., Fuller, S. P., & Lewis, K. R. (1991). Brief report: Competitive employment of adults with autism. *Journal of Autism and Developmental Disorders, 21,* 237–242.

Burt, V. L., Whelton, P., Roccella, E. J., Higgins, M., Horan, M. J., & Labarthe, D. (1995). Prevalence of hypertension in the U.S. adult population: Results from the Third National Health and Nutrition Examination Survey, 1988–1991. *Hypertension, 25,* 305–313.

Bushman, B. J., & Anderson, C. A. (2001). Media violence and the American public: Scientific facts versus media misinformation. *American Psychologist, 56,* 477–489.

Butcher, J. N. (1990). *The MMPI-2 in psychological treatment.* New York: Oxford University Press.

Butler, L. D., Duran, R. E. F., Jasiukaitis, P., Koopman, C., & Spiegel, D. (1996). Hypnotizability and traumatic experience. *American Journal of Psychiatry, 153,* 42–59.

Butler, R. N. (1984). Senile dementia: Reversible and irreversible. *Counseling Psychologist, 12,* 75–79.

Butzlaff, R. L., & Hooley, J. M. (1998). Expressed emotion and psychiatric relapse: A meta-analysis. *Archives of General Psychiatry, 55,* 547–553.

Byrne, M., Clafferty, B. A., Cosway, R., Grant, E., Hodges, A., Whalley, H. C., et al. (2003). Neuropsychology, genetic liability, and psychotic symptoms in those at high risk of schizophrenia. *Journal of Abnormal Psychology, 112,* 38–48.

Cadoret, R. J., & Cain, C. (1981). Environmental and genetic factors in predicting adolescent antisocial behavior in adoptees. *Psychiatric Journal of the University of Ottawa, 6,* 220–225.

Cadoret, R. J., & Wesner, R. B. (1990). Use of the adoption paradigm to elucidate the role of genes and environment and their interaction in the genesis of alcoholism. In C. R. Cloninger & H. Begleiter (Eds.), *Genetics and biology of alcoholism* (pp. 31–42). Cold Spring Harbor, NY: Cold Spring Harbor Laboratory Press.

Cahn, W., Pol, H. E. H., Lems, E. B. T. E., & van Haren, N. E. M. (2002). Brain volume changes in first-episode schizophrenia: A 1-year follow-up study. *Archives of General Psychiatry, 59,* 1002–1011.

Camara, W. J., Nathan, J. S., & Puente, A. E. (2000). Psychological test usage: Implications in professional psychology. *Professional Psychology: Research and Practice, 31,* 141–154.

Campbell, R. J. (1981). *Psychiatric dictionary* (5th ed.). New York: Oxford University Press.

Campbell, S. B., & Ewing, L. J. (1990). Follow-up of hard-to-manage preschoolers: Adjustment at age 9 and predictors of continuing symptoms. *Journal of Child Psychology and Psychiatry, 31,* 871–889.

Campo, J. A., Frederikx, M., Nijman, H. & Merckelback, H. (1998). Schizophrenia and changes in physical appearance. *Journal of Clinical Psychiatry, 59,* 197–198.

Cannon, T. D., Kaprio, J., Lonnqvist, J., Huttunen, M., & Koskenvuo, M. (1998). The genetic epidemiology of schizophrenia in a Finnish twin cohort. *Archives of General Psychiatry, 55,* 67–74.

Cannon, T. D., & Marco, E. (1994). Structural brain abnormalities as indicators of vulnerability to schizophrenia. *Schizophrenia Bulletin, 20,* 89–100.

Cantor, P. (1991). Developmental perspective on prevention and treatment of suicidal youth. In A. A. Leenaars (Ed.), *Life span perspectives of suicide: Time-lines in the suicide process.* New York: Plenum.

Cantwell, D. P. (1996). Attention deficit disorder: A review of the past 10 years. *Journal of the American Academy of Child and Adolescent Psychiatry, 35,* 978–987.

Caplan, P. J. (1995). *They say you're crazy.* Reading, MA: Addison-Wesley.

Cardemil, E., & Barber, J. P. (2001). Building a model for prevention practice: Depression as an example. *Professional Psychology: Research and Practice, 32,* 392–401.

Carels, R. A., Cacciapaglia, H., Perez-Benitez, C. I., Douglass, O., Christie, S., & O'Brien, W. H. (2003). The association between emotional upset and cardiac arrhythmia during daily life. *Journal of Consulting and Clinical Psychology, 71,* 613–618.

Carey G., & DiLalla, D. L. (1994). Personality and psychopathology: Genetic perspectives. *Journal of Abnormal Psychology, 103,* 32–43.

Carlat, D. J., Camargo, C. A., & Herzog, D. B. (1997). Eating disorders in males: A report on 135 patients. *American Journal of Psychiatry, 154,* 1127–1132.

Carlin, A. S., Hoffman, H. G., & Weghorst, S. (1997). Virtual reality and tactile argumentation in the treatment of spider phobia: A case report. *Behaviour Research and Therapy, 35,* 153–158.

Carlson, C. L., Pelham, W. E. Jr., Milich, R., & Dixon, J. (1992). Single and combined effects of methylphenidate and behavior therapy on the classroom performance of children with attention-deficit hyperactivity disorder. *Journal of Abnormal Child Psychology, 20,* 213–232.

Carpenter, W. T., Conley, R. R., Buchanan, R. W., Breier, A., & Tamminga, C. A. (1995). Patient response and resource management: Another view of clozapine treatment of schizophrenia. *American Journal of Psychiatry, 152,* 827–832.

Carr, J. (1994). Annotation: Long-term outcome for people with Down syndrome. *Journal of Child Psychology and Psychiatry, 35,* 425–439.

Carter, J. C., & Fairburn, C. G. (1998). Cognitive-behavioral self-help for binge eating disorder: A controlled effectiveness study. *Journal of Consulting and Clinical Psychology, 66,* 616–623.

Cartwright, S. (1967). "A report on the diseases and peculiarities of the Negro race" (1851). *DeBow's Review, Southern and Western States, 11* (New Orleans). Reprint New York: AMS Press.

Cash, R. (1998). Losing it? *Essence, 28,* pp. 34–37.

Castellanos, F. X., Giedd, J. N., Berquin, P. C., & Walter, J. M. (2001). Quantitative brain magnetic resonance imaging in girls with attention-deficit/hyperactive disorder. *Archives of General Psychiatry, 58,* 289–295.

Castle, D. J., & Murray, R. M. (1993). The epidemiology of late-onset schizophrenia. *Schizophrenia Bulletin, 22,* 691–699.

Catz, S. L., Kelly, J. A., Bogart, L. M., Benotsch, E. G., & McAuliffe, T. L. (2000). Patterns, correlates, and barriers to medication adherence among persons prescribed new treatments for HIV disease. *Healthy Psychology, 19,* 124–133.

Cauffman, E., & Steinberg, L. (1996). Interactive effects of menarcheal status and dating on dieting and disordered eating among adolescent girls. *Developmental Psychology, 32,* 631–635.

Cautela, J. R. (1966). Treatment of compulsive behavior by covert sensitization. *Psychological Record, 16,* 33–41.

Centers for Disease Control and Prevention. (1999). *Suicide deaths and rates per 100,000.* Retrieved from http://www.cdc.gov/ncipc/data/us9794/suic.htm.

Centers for Disease Control and Prevention. (2002). Self-reported increase in asthma severity after September 11 attacks on the World Trade Center—Manhattan, New York, 2001. *Mortality and Morbidity Weekly Report, 51,* 781–784.

Cesaroni, L., & Garber, M. (1991). Exploring the experience of autism through firsthand accounts. *Journal of Autism and Developmental Disorders, 21,* 303–313.

Chadwick, P., & Birchwood, M. (1994). The omnipotence of voices: A cognitive approach to auditory hallucinations. *British Journal of Psychiatry, 164,* 190–201.

Chadwick, P., Sambrooke, S., Rasch, S., & Davies, E. (2000). Challenging the omnipotence of voices: Group cognitive behavior therapy for voices. *Behaviour Research and Therapy, 38,* 993–1003.

Chamberlain, P., & Reid, J. B. (1998). Comparison of two community alternatives to incarceration for chronic juvenile offenders. *Journal of Consulting and Clinical Psychology, 6*, 624–633.

Chamberlain, P., & Rosicky, J. G. (1995). The effectiveness of family therapy in the treatment of adolescents with conduct disorders and delinquency. *Journal of Marital and Family Therapy, 21*, 441–459.

Chapey, R. (1994). Assessment of language disorders in adults. In R. Chapey (Ed.), *Language intervention strategies in adult aphasia* (pp. 80–120). Baltimore: Williams & Wilkins.

Chen, E., Bloomberg, G. R., Fisher, E. B., & Strunk, R. C. (2003). Predictors of repeated hospitalizations in children with asthma: The role of psychosocial and socioenvironmental factors. *Health Psychology, 22*, 12–18.

Chodoff, P. (1987). Letter to the editor. *American Journal of Psychiatry, 144*, 124.

Choi, P. Y. L., Pope, H. G, Jr., Olivardia, R., & Cash, T. F. (2002). Muscle dysphoria: A new syndrome in weightlifters. *British Journal of Sports Medicine, 36*, 375–377.

Chollar, S. (1988). Food for thought. *Psychology Today, 22*, 30–34.

Christensen, L., & Duncan, K. (1995). Distinguishing depressed from nondepressed individuals using energy and psychosocial variables. *Journal of Consulting and Clinical Psychology, 63*, 495–498.

Christensen, S. C., Martin, S. B., Schleicher, N. C., Koziol, J. A., & Zuraw, B. L. (1996). Current prevalence of asthma-related symptoms in San Diego's predominantly Hispanic inner-city children. *Journal of Asthma, 33*, 17–26.

Christison, G. W., Kirch, D. G. & Wyatt, R. J. (1991). When symptoms persist: Choosing among alternative somatic treatments for schizophrenia. *Schizophrenic Bulletin, 17*, 217–245.

Chua, S. E., & McKenna, P. J. (1995). Schizophrenia: A brain disease? A critical review of structural and functional cerebral abnormality in the disorder. *British Journal of Psychiatry, 166*, 563–582.

Chun, K. M., Eastman, K. L., Wang, G. C. S. & Sue, S. (1998). In N. W. S. Zane & L. C. Lee (Eds.), *Handbook of Asian American Psychology* (pp. 457–483), Thousand Oaks, CA: Sage.

Chung, R., & Okazaki, S. (1991). Counseling Americans of Southeast Asian descent: The impact of the refugee experience. In C. C. Lee & B. L. Richardson (Eds.), *Multicultural issues in counseling: New approaches to diversity* (pp. 107–126). Alexandria, VA: American Association for Counseling and Development.

Cinciripini, P. M., Lapitsky, L., Seay, S., Wallfisch, A., Kitchens, K., & Van Vunakis, H. (1995). The effects of smoking schedules on cessation outcome: Can we improve on common methods of gradual and abrupt nicotine withdrawal? *Journal of Consulting and Clinical Psychology, 63*, 388–400.

Clark, D. M. (1996). Panic disorder: From theory to therapy. In P. M. Salkovskis (Ed.), *Frontiers of cognitive therapy* (pp. 318–344). New York: Guilford Press.

Clark, M., Gosnell, M., Witherspoon, J., Huck, J., Hager, M., Junkin, D., King, P., Wallace, A., & Robinson, T. (1984, December 3). A slow death of the mind. *Newsweek*, pp. 56–62.

Clarke, A. D. B., & Clarke, A. M. (1987). Research on mental handicap, 1957–1958: A selective review. *Journal of Mental Deficiency Research, 31*, 317–328.

Clarkin, J. F., Hurt, S. W., & Mattis, S. (1999). Psychological and neurological assessment. In R. E. Hales, S. C. Yudofsky & J. A. Talbott (Eds.), *Textbook of psychiatry* (pp. 253–280). Washington, DC: American Psychiatric Press.

Clarkin, J. F., & Levy, K. N. (2004). The influence of client variables on psychotherapy. In M. J. Lambert (Ed.), *Bergin and Garfield's handbook of psychotherapy and behavior change* (5th ed., pp. 194–226). New York: Wiley.

Clarkin, J. F., Marziali, E., & Munroe-Blum, H. (1991). Group and family treatments for borderline personality disorder. *Hospital and Community Psychiatry, 42*, 1038–1043.

Classen, C., Koopman, C., Hales, R., & Spiegel, D. (1998). Acute stress disorder as a predictor of posttraumatic stress symptoms. *American Journal of Psychiatry, 155*, 620–624.

Clay, R. A. (2001). Marijuana youth treatment study produces promising results. *SAMHSA News, 9*(1), 17–19.

Cleckley, J. (1976). *The mask of sanity* (5th ed.). St. Louis, MO: Mosby.

Clemmensen, L. H. (1990). The "real-life test" for surgical candidates. In R. Blanchard & B. W. Steiner (Eds.), *Clinical management of gender identity disorders in children and adults* (pp. 119–136). Washington, DC: American Psychiatric Press.

Clomipramine Collaborative Study Group. (1991). Clomipramine in the treatment of patients with obsessive-compulsive disorder. *Archives of General Psychiatry, 48*, 730–738.

Cloninger, C. R., Reich, T., Sigvardsson, S., Von Knorring, A. L., & Bohman, M. (1986). The effects of changes in alcohol use between generations or the inheritance of alcohol abuse. In American Psychological Association (Ed.), *Alcoholism: A medical disorder: Proceedings of the 76th Annual Meeting of the American Psychological Association.*

Cochran, S. D., Sullivan, J. G., & Mays, V. M. (2003). Prevalence of mental disorders, psychological distress, and mental health services use among lesbian, gay, and bisexual adults in the United States. *Journal of Consulting and Clinical Psychology, 71*, 53–61.

Coffman, J. A. (1989). Computed tomography in psychiatry. In N. C. Andreasen (Ed.), *Brain imaging: Applications in psychiatry* (pp. 1–65). Washington, DC: American Psychiatric Press.

Cohen, A. M., & Weiner, W. J. (Eds.) (1994). *The comprehensive management of Parkinson's disease.* New York: Demos Publications.

Cohen, S., Frank, E., Doyle, W. J., Skoner, D. P., Rabin, B. S., & Gwaltney, J. M. (1998). Types of stressors that increase susceptibility in the common cold in healthy adults. *Health Psychology, 17*, 214–223.

Cohen, S., & Herbert, T. B. (1996). Health psychology: Psychological factors and physical disease from the perspective of human psychoneuroimmunology. *Annual Review of Psychology, 47*, 113–123.

Cohen, S., & Rodriguez, M. S. (1995). Pathways linking affective disturbances and physical disorders. *Health Psychology, 14*, 374–380.

Cohn, L. D., Adler, N. E., Irwin, C. E., Jr., Millstein, S. G., Kegeles, S. M., & Stone, G. (1987). Body-figure preferences in male and female adolescents. *Journal of Abnormal Psychology, 96*, 276–279.

Colon, E. A., Callies, A. L., Popkin, M. K., & McGlave, P. B. (1991). Depressed mood and other variables related to bone marrow transplantation survival in acute leukemia. *Psychosomatics, 32*, 420–425.

Colt, G. H., & Hollister, A. (1998, April). Were you born that way? *Life*, pp. 39–48.

Comings, D. E., & Comings, B. G. (1987). Hereditary agoraphobia and obsessive-compulsive behaviour in relatives of patients with Gilles de la Tourette's syndrome. *British Journal of Psychiatry, 151*, 195–199.

Committee on Women in Psychology, American Psychological Association. (1989). If sex enters into the psychotherapy relationship. *Professional Psychology: Research and Practice, 20*, 112–115.

Compas, B. E., Haaga, D. A. F., Keefe, F. J., Leitenberg, H., & Williams, D. A. (1998). Sampling of empirically supported psychological treatments from health psychology: Smoking, chronic pain, cancers, and bulimia nervosa. *Journal of Consulting and Clinical Psychology, 66,* 89–112.

Conn, D. K. (1991). Delirium and other organic mental disorders. In J. Sadavoy, L. W. Lazarus, & L. F. Jarvik (Eds.), *Comprehensive review of geriatric psychiatry* (pp. 11–336). Washington, DC: American Psychiatric Press.

Conners, M. E., & Morse, W. (1993). Sexual abuse and eating disorders: A review. *International Journal of Eating Disorders, 13,* 1–11.

Consensus Development Panel. (1982). Defined diets and childhood hyperactivity. *Clinical Pediatrics, 21,* 627–630.

Cook, E. H., Jr. (1998). Genetics of autism. *Mental Retardation and Developmental Disabilities Research Reviews, 4,* 113–120.

Cook, E. W., III, Hodes, R. L., & Lang, P. J. (1986). Preparedness and phobia: Effects of stimulus content on human visceral conditioning. *Journal of Abnormal Psychology, 95,* 195–207.

Cooney, N. L., Litt, M. D., Morse, P. A., Bauer, L. O., & Gaupp, L. (1997). Alcohol cue reactivity, negative-mood reactivity, and relapse in treated alcoholic men. *Journal of Abnormal Psychology, 106,* 243–250.

Coons, P. M. (1994). Confirmation of childhood abuse in child and adolescent cases of multiple personality disorder and dissociative disorder not otherwise specified. *Journal of Nervous and Mental Disease, 182,* 461–464.

Cooper, A., & McCormack, W. A. (1992). Short-term group treatment for adult children of alcoholics. *Journal of Counseling Psychology, 39,* 350–355.

Cooper, A. J. (1969). A clinical study of coital anxiety in male potency disorders. *Journal of Psychosomatic Research, 13,* 143–147.

Cooper, J. E., Kendell, R. E., Gurland, B. J., Sharp, L., Copeland, J. R. M., & Simon, R. (1972). *Psychiatric diagnosis in New York and London.* Maudsley Monograph Series No. 20. London: Oxford University Press.

Cooper, M. L., Russell, M., & George, W. H. (1988). Coping, expectancies, and alcohol abuse: A test of social learning formulations. *Journal of Abnormal Psychology, 97,* 218–230.

Corbitt, E. M., & Widiger, T. A. (1995). Sex differences among the personality disorders: An exploration of the data. *Clinical Psychology: Science and Practice, 2,* 225–238.

Corey, G. (2001). *Theory and practice of counseling and psychotherapy* (6th ed.). Belmont, CA: Brooks/Cole.

Corey, G., Corey, M. S., & Callanan, P. (1993). *Issues and ethics in the helping professions* (3rd ed.). Pacific Grove, CA: Brooks/Cole.

Corey, G., Corey, M. S., & Callanan, P. (1998). *Issues and ethics in the helping professions.* Pacific Grove, CA: Brooks/Cole.

Corin, E. (1998). The thickness of being: Intentional worlds, strategies of identity, and experience among schizophrenics. *Psychiatry, 61,* 133–146.

Cormier, J. F., & Thelen, M. H. (1998). Professional skepticism of multiple personality disorder. *Professional Psychology: Research and Practice, 29,* 163–167.

Cornelius, J. R., Salloum, I. M., Mezzich, J., Cornelius, M. D., Fabrega, H., Ehler, J. G., Ulrich, R. F., Thase, M. E., & Mann, J. J. (1995). Disproportionate suicidality in patients with comorbid major depression and alcoholism. *American Journal of Psychiatry, 152,* 358–364.

Cottone, R. R. (1992). *Theories and paradigms of counseling and psychotherapy.* Boston: Allyn & Bacon.

Courchesne, E. (1995). New evidence of cerebellar and brainstem hypoplasia in autistic infants, children, and adolescents: The MR imaging study by Hashimoto and colleagues. *Journal of Autism and Developmental Disorders, 25,* 19–22.

Courchesne, I., Yeung-Courchesne, R., Press, G. A., Hesselink, J. R., & Jernigan, T. L. (1988). Hypoplasia of cerebellar vermal lobules VI and VII in autism. *New England Journal of Medicine, 318,* 1349–1354.

Coursey, R. D., Alford, J., & Safarjan, B. (1997). Significant advances in understanding and treating serious mental illness. *Professional Psychology: Research and Practice, 28,* 205–216.

Coursey, R. D., Keller, A. B., & Farrell, E. W. (1995). Individual psychotherapy and persons with serious mental illness: The clients' perspective. *Schizophrenia Bulletin, 21,* 283–299.

Cousins, N. (1979). *Anatomy of an illness.* New York: Norton.

Cowley, G. (1995). Blind to other minds. *Newsweek,* August 14, p. 67

Cowley, G., & Underwood, A. (1997, May 26). Why Ebonie can't breathe. *Newsweek,* 58–63.

Cox, B. J., Fergus, K. D., & Swinson, R. P. (1994). Patient satisfaction with behavioral treatments for panic disorder with agoraphobia. *Journal of Anxiety Disorders, 8,* 193–206.

Cox, D. J., & McMahon, B. (1978). Incidence of male exhibitionism in the United States as reported by victimized college students. *International Journal of Law and Psychiatry, 1,* 453–457.

Crandall, C. S., Preisler, J. J., & Aussprung, J. (1992). Measuring life event stress in the lives of college students: The Undergraduate Stress Questionnaire (USQ). *Journal of Behavioral Medicine, 15,* 627–662.

Crespo-Facorro, B., Paradiso, S., Andreasen, N. C., O'Leary, D. S., et al. (2001). Neural mechanisms of anhedonia in schizophrenia: A PET study of response to unpleasant and pleasant odors. *Journal of the American Medical Association, 286,* 427–435.

Crimlisk, H. L., Bhatia, K., Cope, H., & David, A. (1998). Slater revisited: Six-year follow-up study of patients with medically unexplained motor symptoms. *British Medical Journal, 316,* 582–586.

Cruess, D. G., Antoni, M. H., Schneiderman, N., Ironson, G., McCabe, P., Fernandez, J. B., Cruess S. E., Klimas, N., & Kumar, M. (2000). Cognitive-behavioral stress management increases free testosterone and decreases psychological distress in HIV-seropositive men. *Health Psychology, 19,* 12–20.

Cummings, N. A. (1995). Behavioral health after managed care: The next golden opportunity for professional psychology. *Register Report, 20,* 1, 30–33.

Curran, P. J., Stice, E., & Chassin, L. (1997). The relation between adolescent alcohol use and peer alcohol use: A longitudinal random coefficients model. *Journal of Consulting and Clinical Psychology, 65,* 130–140.

Cutting, L. P., & Docherty, N. M. (2000). Schizophrenia outpatients' perceptions of their parents: Is expressed emotion a factor? *Journal of Abnormal Psychology, 109,* 266–272.

Dahl, R. E. (1992). The pharmacologic treatment of sleep disorders. *Psychiatric Clinical America, 15,* 161–178.

Dahlstrom, W. G., & Welsh, G. S. (1965). *An MMPI handbook.* Minneapolis: University of Minnesota Press.

Daigneault, S. D. (2000). Body talk: A school-based group intervention for working with disordered eating behaviors. *Journal for Specialists in Group Work, 25,* 191–213.

Daley, S. E., Burge, D., & Hammen, C. (2000). Borderline personality disorder symptoms as predictors of four-year romantic relationship dysfunction in young women: Addressing issues of specificity. *Journal of Abnormal Psychology, 109,* 451–460.

Dana, R. H. (1998). *Understanding cultural identity in intervention and assessment.* Thousand Oaks, CA: Sage.

Dana, R. H. (2000). Psychological assessment in the diagnosis and treatment of ethnic group members. In J. F. Aponte & J. Wohl (Eds.), *Psychological interventions and cultural diversity* (2nd ed., pp. 59–74). Boston: Allyn & Bacon.

Dar, R., Rish, S., Hermesh, H., Taub, M., & Fux, M. (2000). Realism of confidence in obsessive-compulsive checkers. *Journal of Abnormal Psychology, 109,* 673–678.

Dardick, H. (2004, February 13). Psychiatric patient tells of ordeal in treatment. *Chicago Tribune*, 1.

Davey, G. C. L., McDonald, A. S., Hirisave, U., Prabhu, G. G., Iwawaki, S. Jim, C. I., Merckelbach, H., deJong, P. J., Leung, P. W. L., & Reimann, B. C. (1998). A cross-cultural study of animal fears. *Behaviour Research and Therapy, 36*, 735–750.

Davidson, J. R. T. (2000). Pharmacotherapy of posttraumatic stress disorder: Treatment options, long-term follow-up and predictors of outcome. *Journal of Clinical Psychiatry, 61*, 52–56.

Davidson, J. R. T., Rothbaum, B. O., Van der Kolk, B. A., Sikes, C. R., & Farfel, G. M. (2001). Multicenter, double-blind comparison of sertraline and placebo in the treatment of post-traumatic stress disorder. *Archives of General Psychiatry, 58*, 485–492.

Davidson, K., Hall, P., & MacGregor, M. (1997). Gender differences in the relation between interview-derived hostility scores and resting blood pressure. *Journal of Behavioral Medicine, 19*, 185–201.

Davis, K. L., Kahn, R. S., & Ko, G. (1991). Dopamine in schizophrenia: A review and reconceptualization, *American Journal of Psychiatry, 148*, 1474–1486.

Davis, P. J., & Gibson, M. G. (2000). Recognition of posed and genuine facial expressions of emotion in paranoid and nonparanoid schizophrenia. *Journal of Abnormal Psychology, 109*, 445–450.

deJong, G. M., Timmerman, I. G. H., & Emmelkamp, P. M. G. (1996). The survey of recent life experience: A psychometric evaluation. *Journal of Behavioral Medicine, 19*, 529–542.

deJong, P. J., Vorage, I., & van den Hout, M. A. (2000). Counterconditioning in the treatment of spider phobia: Effects on disgust, fear and valence. *Behaviour Research and Therapy, 38*, 1055–1069.

Dekker, J. (1993). Inhibited male orgasm. In W. O'Donohue & J. H. Geer (Eds.), *Handbook of sexual dysfunctions: Assessment and treatment* (pp. 279–301). Boston: Allyn & Bacon.

Delgado, P. L., & Gelenberg, A. J. (2001). Antidepressant and antimanic medications. In G. O. Gabbard (Ed.), *Treatment of psychiatric disorders* (pp. 1137–1179). Washington, DC: American Psychiatric Press.

Dent, C. W., Sussman, S., Stacy, A. W., Craig, S., Burton, D., & Flay, B. R. (1995). Two-year behavior outcomes of Project Towards No Tobacco Use. *Journal of Consulting and Clinical Psychology, 63*, 676–677.

Department of Health and Human Services. (1999). *Mental health: A report of the Surgeon General*. Rockville, MD: Author.

DeSilva, P. (1988). Phobias and preparedness: Replication and extension. *Behaviour Research and Therapy, 26*, 97–98.

Desmond, S., Price, J., Hallinan, C., & Smith, D. (1989). Black and White adolescents' perceptions of their weight. *Journal of School Health, 59*, 353–358.

Deutsch, A. (1949). *The mentally ill in America* (2nd ed.). New York: Columbia University Press.

DeVellis, B. M., & Blalock, S. J. (1992). Illness attributions and hopelessness depression: The role of hopelessness expectancy. *Journal of Abnormal Psychology, 101*, 257–264.

Devinsky, O. (1994). *A guide to understanding and living with epilepsy*. Philadelphia: F. A. Davis.

Diekstra, R. F., Kienhorst, C. W. M., & de Wilde, E. J. (1995). Suicide and suicidal behaviour among adolescents. In M. Rutter & D. J. Smith (Eds.), *Psychological disorders in young people*. Chichester, England: Wiley.

DiPasquale, C., & Karnopp, K. (2004, March 2). DiScala's mission: "Sopranos" star helps others with eating disorders. *Chicago Tribune*, p. 28.

Dirmann, T. (2003, September 8). Ex-Spice girl Geri Halliwell: How I beat my eating disorder. *Us Weekly*, p. 60.

Dishion, T. J., McCord, J., & Poulin, F. (1999). When interventions harm: Peer groups and problem behavior. *American Psychologist, 54*, 755–764.

Dodrill, C. B., & Matthews, C. G. (1992). The role of neuropsychology in the assessment and treatment of persons with epilepsy. *American Psychologist, 47*, 1139–1142.

Dogden, D. (2000). Science policy and the protection of children. *American Psychologist, 55*, 1034–1035.

Dolan, B. (1991). Cross-cultural aspects of anorexia nervosa and bulimia: A review. *International Journal of Eating Disorders, 10*, 67–69.

Domb, Y., & Beaman, K. (1991). Mr. X—A case of amnesia. *British Journal of Psychiatry, 158*, 423–425.

Donenberg, G., & Baker, B. L. (1993). The impact of young children with externalizing behaviors on their families. *Journal of Abnormal Child Psychology, 21*, 179–198.

Dong, Q., Yang, B., & Ollendick, T. H. (1994). Fears in Chinese children and adolescents and their relations to anxiety and depression. *Journal of Child Psychology and Psychiatry, 35*, 351–363.

Drake, R. E., & Ehrlich, J. (1985). Suicide attempts associated with akathisia. *American Journal of Psychiatry, 142*, 499–501.

Drossman, D. A. (1998). Presidential address: Gastrointestinal illness and the biopsychosocial model. *Psychosomatic Medicine, 60*, 258–267.

Duberstein, P. R., & Conwell, Y. (1997). Personality disorders and completed suicide: A methodological and conceptual review. *Clinical Psychology 4*, 502–504.

Dubovsky, S. L., & Buzan, R. (1999). Mood disorders. In R. E. Hales, S. C. Yudofsky & J. A. Talbott (Eds.), *Textbook of psychiatry* (pp. 479–565). Washington, DC: American Psychiatric Press.

Duckett, S. (1991). The normal aging human brain. In S. Duckett (Ed.), *The pathology of the aging human nervous system* (pp. 1–19). Philadelphia: Lea & Febiger.

Dugas, M. J., & Ladouceur, R. (2000). Treatment of GAD: Targeting intolerance of uncertainty in two types of worry. *Behavior Modification, 24*, 635–657.

DuPaul, G. J., & Barkley, R. A. (1993). Behavioral contributions to psychopharmacology: The utility of behavioral methodology in medication treatment of children with attention deficit hyperactivity disorder. *Behavior Therapy, 24*, 47–65.

Durkheim, E. (1951). *Suicide*. New York: Free Press. (Original work published 1897)

Dutton, J. (1986, September 30). Doctors seek reason for bizarre syndrome. *Bellingham Herald*, p. C1.

Du Verglas, G., Banks, S. R., & Guyer, K. E. (1988). Clinical effects of fenfluramine on children with autism: A review of the research. *Journal of Autism and Developmental Disorders, 18*, 297–308.

Dworkin, S., VonKorff, M., & LeResche, L. (1990). Multiple pains and psychiatric disturbance. *Archives of General Psychiatry, 47*, 239–244.

Dykens, E. M., & Hodapp, R. M. (1997). Treatment issues in genetic mental retardation syndromes. *Professional Psychology: Research and Practice, 28*, 263–270.

Eaton, W. W., Holzer, C. E., III, Von Korff, M., Anthony, J. C., Helzer, J. E., George, L., Brunam, A., Boyd, J. H., Kessler, L. G., & Locker, B. Z. (1984). The design of the Epidemiologic Catchment Area surveys. *Archives of General Psychiatry, 41*, 942–948.

Edwards, S., & Dickerson, M. (1987). On the similarity of positive and negative intrusions. *Behaviour Research and Therapy, 25*, 207–211.

Efron, R. (1956). The effect of olfactory stimuli in arresting uncinate fits. *Brain, 79*, 267–281.

Efron, R. (1957). The conditioned inhibitions of uncinate fits. *Brain, 80,* 251–262.

Ehlers, A. (1993). Introception and panic disorder. *Advances in Behavioural Research and Therapy, 15,* 3–21.

Eisen, A. R., & Silverman, W. K. (1998). Prescriptive treatment for generalized anxiety disorder in children. *Behaviour Therapy, 29,* 105–121.

Elias, M. (1988, August 15). Many lie about AIDS risk. *USA Today,* p. D–1.

Ellason, J. W., & Ross, C. A. (1997). Two-year follow-up of inpatients with dissociative identity disorder. *American Journal of Psychiatry, 154,* 832–839.

Ellickson, P. L., Hays, R. D., & Bell, R. M. (1992). Stepping through the drug use sequence: Longitudinal scalogram analysis of initiation and regular use. *Journal of Abnormal Psychology, 101,* 441–451.

Ellis, A. (1962). *Reason and emotion in psychotherapy.* New York: Stuart.

Ellis, A. (1989). Rational-emotive therapy. In R. J. Corsini & D. Wedding (Eds.), *Current psychotherapies* (pp. 197–238). Itasca, IL: Peacock.

Ellis, A. (1997). The evolution of Albert Ellis and rational emotive behavior therapy. In J. K. Zeig (Ed.), *The evolution of psychotherapy: The third conference.* New York: Brunner/Mazel.

Emmelkamp, P. M. (2004). Behavior therapy with adults. In M. J. Lambert (Ed.), *Bergin and Garfield's handbook of psychotherapy and behavior change* (5th ed., pp. 393–446). New York: Wiley.

Emslie, G. J., & Rosenfeld, A. (1983). Incest reported by children and adolescents hospitalized for severe psychiatric problems. *American Journal of Psychiatry, 140,* 108–111.

Endler, N. (1982). *Holiday of darkness.* New York: Wiley.

Endler, N. (1990). *Holiday of darkness: A psychologist's journey out of his depression* (rev. ed.). Toronto: Wall & Thompson.

Epilepsy Foundation of America. (1983). *Questions and answers about epilepsy.* Landover, MD: Author.

Erdely, S. R. (2004, March). What women sacrifice to be slim. *Redbook,* 114–120.

Erickson, W. D., Luxenberg, M. G., Walbek, N. H., & Seely, R. K. (1987). Frequency of MMPI two-point code types among sex offenders. *Journal of Consulting and Clinical Psychology, 55,* 566–570.

Erickson, W. D., Walbek, N. H., & Seely, R. K. (1988). Behavior patterns of child molesters. *Archives of Sexual Behavior, 17,* 77–86.

Erk, R. R. (2000). The framework for increasing understanding and effective treatment of attention-deficit/hyperactive disorder: Predominantly inattentive type. *Journal of Counseling and Development, 78,* 389–399.

Erlenmeyer-Kimling, L., Adamo, U. H., Rock, D., Roberts, S. A., Bassett, A. S., Squires-Wheeler, E., Cornblatt, B. A., Endicott, J., Pape, S., & Gottesman, I. (1997). The New York High-Risk Project. *Archives of General Psychiatry, 54,* 1096–1102.

Esser, G., Schmidt, M. H., & Woerner, W. (1990). Epidemiology and course of psychiatric disorders in school-age children: Results of a longitudinal study. *Journal of Child Psychology and Psychiatry, 31,* 243–263.

Estrada, A. U., & Pinsof, W. M. (1995). The effectiveness of family therapies for selected behavioral disorders of childhood. *Journal of Marital and Family Therapy, 21,* 403–440.

Evans, G., & Rey, J. (2001). In the echoes of gunfire: Practicing psychologists' response to school violence. *Professional Psychology: Research and Practice, 32,* 157–164.

Evans, S. J. (1997, April 11). How regular is your heartbeat? *Newsweek,* pp. 28–34.

Everson, S. A., Lynch, J. W., Kaplan, G. A., Lakka, T. A., Sivenius, J., & Salonen, J. T. (1999). Stress-induced blood pressure reactivity and incident stroke in middle-aged men. *Psychosomatic Medicine, 61,* 125–126.

Exner, J. E. (1990). *A Rorschach workbook for the Comprehensive System* (2nd ed.). Asheville, NC: Rorschach Workshops.

Fadden, G. (1998). Family intervention on psychosis. *Journal of Mental Health, 7,* 115–122.

Fagan, J., & McMahon, P. P. (1984). Incipient multiple personality in children: Four cases. *Journal of Nervous and Mental Disease, 172,* 26–36.

Fairburn, C. G., Cooper, Z., Doll, H. A., Norman, P., & O'Connor, M. (2000). The natural course of bulimia nervosa and binge eating disorder in young women. *Archives of General Psychiatry, 57,* 659–665.

Fairburn, C. G., Doll, H. A., Welch, S. L., Hay, P. J., et al. (1998). Risk factors for binge eating disorder: A community-based, case-control study. *Archives of General Psychiatry, 55,* 425–429.

Fairburn, C. G., & Harrison, P. J. (2003). Eating disorders. *Lancet, 361,* 407–416.

Fairburn, C. G., Jones, R., Peveler, R. C., Carr, S. J., Solomon, R. A., O'Connor, M. E., Burton, J., & Hope, R. A. (1991). Three psychological treatments for bulimia nervosa: A comparative trial. *Archives of General Psychiatry, 48,* 463–469.

Fairburn, C. G., Norman, P. A., Welch, S. L., O'Connor, M. E., Doll, H. A., & Peveler, R. C. (1995). A prospective study of bulimia nervosa and the long-term effects of three psychological treatments. *Archives of General Psychiatry, 52,* 304–312.

Fairburn, C. G., Stice, E., Cooper, Z., Doll, H. A., Norman, P. A., & O'Connor, M. E. (2003). Understanding persistence in bulimia nervosa: A 5-year naturalistic study. *Journal of Consulting and Clinical Psychology, 71,* 103–109.

Famularo, R., Kinscherff, R., Fenton, T., & Bolduc, S. M. (1990). Child maltreatment histories among runaways and delinquent children. *Clinical Pediatrics, 29,* 713–718.

Fang, C. Y., & Myers, H. F. (2001). The effects of racial stressors and hostility on cardiovascular reactivity in African American and Caucasian men. *Health Psychology, 20,* 64–70.

Faraone, S. V., Kremen, W. S., Lyons, M. J., Pepple, J. R., Seidman, L. J., & Tsuang, M. T. (1995). Diagnostic accuracy and linkage analysis: How useful are schizophrenia spectrum phenotypes? *American Journal of Psychiatry, 152,* 1286–1290.

Farley, F. (1986). World of the type T personality. *Psychology Today, 20,* 45–52.

Farmer, E. M. Z. (1995). Extremity of externalizing behavior and young adult outcomes. *Journal of Child Psychology and Psychiatry, 36,* 617–632.

Farrell, A. D., & White, K. S. (1998). Peer influences and drug use among urban adolescents: Family structure and parent-adolescent relationship as protective factors. *Journal of Consulting and Clinical Psychology, 66,* 248–252.

Fava, G. A., Zielezny, M., Savron, G., & Grandi, S. (1995). The long-term behavioral treatment for panic disorder with agoraphobia. *British Journal of Psychiatry, 166,* 87–92.

Feingold, B. F. (1977). Behavioral disturbances linked to the ingestion of food additives. *Delaware Medical Journal, 49,* 89–94.

Feitel, B., Margetson, N., Chamas, J., & Lipman, C. (1992). Psychosocial background and behavioral and emotional disorders of homeless and runaway youth. *Hospital Community Psychiatry, 43,* 155–159.

Feldman, H. A., Goldstein, I., Hatzichristou, D. G., Krane, R. J., & McKinlay, J. B. (1994). Impotence and its medical and psychosocial correlates: Results of the Massachusetts Male Aging Study. *Journal of Urology, 151,* 54–61.

Feldman, R. G., Mosbach, P., Thomas, C., & Perry, L. M. (1994). Psychosocial factors in the treatment of Parkinson's disease: A contextual approach. In A. M. Cohen & W. J. Weiner (Eds.), *The comprehensive management of Parkinson's disease* (pp. 193–208). New York: Demos Publications.

Fenichel, O. (1945). *The psychoanalytic theory of neuroses.* New York: Norton.

Fergusson, D. M., Horwood, L. J., & Lynskey, M. T. (1995). The stability of disruptive childhood behaviors. *Journal of Abnormal Child Psychology, 23,* 379–396.

Fine, C. G. (1999). The tactical-integration model for the treatment of dissociative identity disorder and allied dissociative disorders. *American Journal of Psychotherapy, 53,* 361–376.

Finkelhor, D. (1980). Sex among siblings: A survey on prevalence, variety, and effects. *Archives of Sexual Behavior, 9,* 171–194.

Flaherty, M. L., Infante, M., Tinsley, J. A., & Black, J. L., III (2001). Factitious hypertension by pseudoephedrine. *Psychosomatics, 42,* 150–153.

Flavin, D. K., Franklin, J. E., & Frances, R. J. (1990). Substance abuse and suicidal behavior. In S. J. Blumenthal & D. J. Kupfer (Eds.), *Suicide over the life cycle: Risk factors, assessment, and treatment of suicidal patients.* Washington, DC: American Psychiatric Press.

Fleer, J., & Pasework, R. A. (1982). Prior public health agency contacts of individuals committing suicide. *Psychological Reports, 50,* 1319–1324.

Foa, E. B. (2000). Psychosocial treatment of posttraumatic stress disorder. *Journal of Clinical Psychiatry, 61,* 43–53.

Foa, E. B., Dancu, C. V., Hembree, E. A., Jaycox, L. H., Meadows, E. A., & Street, G. P. (1999). A comparison of exposure therapy, stress inoculation training, and their combination in reducing posttraumatic stress disorder in female assault victims. *Journal of Consulting and Clinical Psychology, 67,* 194–200.

Foa, E. B., & Kozak, M. J. (1986). Emotional processing of fear: Exposure to corrective information. *Psychological Bulletin, 99,* 20–35.

Foa, E. B., & Kozak, M. J. (1995). DSM-IV field trial: Obsessive-compulsive disorder. *American Journal of Psychiatry, 152,* 90–96.

Follette, W. C., & Houts, A. C. (1996). Models of scientific progress and the role of theory in taxonomy development: A case study of the *DSM. Journal of Consulting and Clinical Psychology, 64,* 1120–1132.

Folstein, S., & Rutter, M. (1977). Infantile autism: A genetic study of 21 twin pairs. *Journal of Child Psychology, 18,* 297–321.

Folstein, S., & Rutter, M. (1988). Autism: Familial aggregation and genetic implications. *Journal of Autism and Developmental Disorders, 18,* 3–30.

Forbes, G. B., Adams-Curtis, L. E., Rade, B., & Jaberg, P. (2001). Body dissatisfaction in women and men: The role of gender-typing and self-esteem. *Sex Roles, 44,* 461–484.

Fordyce, W. E. (1982). A behavioral perspective on chronic pain. *British Journal of Clinical Psychiatry, 21,* 313–320.

Fordyce, W. E. (1988). Pain and suffering: A reappraisal. *American Psychologist, 43,* 276–283.

Forgac, G. E., Cassel, C. A., & Michaels, E. J. (1984). Chronicity of criminal behavior and psychopathology in male exhibitionists. *Journal of Clinical Psychology, 40,* 827–832.

Forgac, G. E., & Michaels, E. J. (1982). Personality characteristics of two types of male exhibitionism. *Journal of Abnormal Psychology, 91,* 287–293.

Foxx, R., & Brown, R. (1979). Nicotine fading and self-monitoring for cigarette abstinence or controlled smoking. *Journal of Applied Behavior Analysis, 12,* 111–125.

Foxx, R. M., & Faw, G. D. (1992). An eight-year follow-up of three social skills training studies. *Mental Retardation, 30,* 63–66.

Francis, P. T., & Bowen, D. M. (1994). Neuronal pathology in relation to molecular biology and treatment of Alzheimer's disease. In F. Owen & R. Itzhaki (Eds.), *Molecular and cell biology of neuropsychiatric diseases* (pp. 24–54). New York: Chapman and Hall.

Franklin, J. E., & Frances, R. J. (1999). Alcohol and other psychoactive substance use disorders. In R. E. Hales, S. C. Yudofsky, & J. A. Talbott (Eds.), *Textbook of psychiatry* (pp. 363–423). Washington, DC: American Psychiatric Press.

Franklin, M. E., Abramowitz, J. S., Kozak, M. J., Levitt, J. T., & Foa, E. B. (2000). Effectiveness of exposure and ritual prevention for obsessive-compulsive disorder: Randomized compared with nonrandomized samples. *Journal of Consulting and Clinical Psychology, 68,* 594–602.

Freedman, D. X. (1984). Psychiatric epidemiology counts. *Archives of General Psychiatry, 41,* 931–933.

Freeman, B. J. (1993). The syndrome of autism: Update and guidelines for diagnosis. *Infants and Young Children, 6,* 1–11.

Freeston, M. H., & Ladouceur, R. (1993). Appraisal of cognitive intrusions and response style: Replication and extension. *Behaviour Research and Therapy, 31,* 185–191.

Freeston, M. H., & Ladouceur, R. (1997). What do patients do with their obsessive thoughts? *Behaviour Research and Therapy, 35,* 335–347.

Fremouw, W. J., Perczel, W. J., & Ellis, T. E. (1990). *Suicide risk: Assessment and response guidelines.* Elmsford, New York: Pergamon.

Freud, S. (1959). *Beyond the pleasure principle.* New York: Bantam. (Original work published 1909)

Freud, S. (1917). *Mourning and melancholia.* Standard ed., Vol. 14 (1955, pp. 737–858). London: Hogarth Press.

Freud, S. (1938). The psychopathology of everyday life. In A. B. Brill (Ed.), *The basic writings of Sigmund Freud.* New York: Modern Library.

Freud, S. (1949). *An outline of psychoanalysis.* New York: Norton.

Frick, P. J., & Lahey, B. B. (1991). Nature and characteristics of attention-deficit hyperactivity disorder. *School Psychology Review, 20,* 163–173.

Friedman, M., & Rosenman, R. H. (1974). *Type A behavior.* New York: Knopf.

Frisby, C. L. (1995). When facts and orthodoxy collide: The bell curve and the robustness criterion. *School Psychology Review, 24,* 12–19.

Frith, U. (1991). *Autism and Asperger syndrome.* Cambridge: Cambridge University Press.

Fulero, S. M. (1988). Tarasoff: 10 years later. *Professional Psychology: Research and Practice, 19,* 184–190.

Furman, T., Tillfors, M., Marteinsdottir, I., Fischer, H., et al. (2002). Common changes in cerebral blood flow in patients with social phobia treated with citalopram or cognitive-behavioral therapy. *Archives of General Psychiatry, 59,* 425–432.

Furr, S. R., Westfeld, J. S., McConnell, G. N., & Jenkins, J. M. (2001). Suicide and depression among college students: A decade later. *Professional Psychology: Research and Practice, 32,* 97–100.

Gabbard, G. O. (2001). Psychodynamic psychotherapies. In G. O. Gabbard (Ed.), *Treatment of psychiatric disorders* (pp. 1227–1245). Washington, DC: American Psychiatric Press.

Gadow, K. D. (1991). Clinical issues in child and adolescent psychopharmacology. *Journal of Consulting and Clinical Psychology, 59,* 842–852.

Gallant, D. (2001). Alcoholism. In G. O. Gabbard (Ed.), *Treatment of psychiatric disorders* (pp. 665–678). Washington, DC: American Psychiatric Press.

Gangadhar, B., Kapur, R., & Kalyanasundaram, S. (1982). Comparison of electroconvulsive therapy with imipramine in endogenous depression: A double blind study. *British Journal of Psychiatry, 141,* 367–371.

Garber, H. J., & Ritvo, E. R. (1992). Magnetic resonance imaging of the posterior fossa in autistic adults. *American Journal of Psychiatry, 149,* 245–247.

Garcia, J. (1981). The logic and limits of mental aptitude testing. *American Psychologist, 36,* 1172–1180.

Gardner, M. (1998, December 16). Children and body images: Getting beyond Barbie. *Christian Science Monitor,* pp. 17–18.

Garner, D. M., Rockert, W., Davis, R., Garner, M. V., Olmsted, M. P., & Eagle, M. (1993). Comparison of cognitive-behavioral and supportive-expressive therapy for bulimia nervosa. *American Journal of Psychiatry, 150,* 37–46.

Garrett, M., & Silva, R. (2003). Auditory hallucinations, source monitoring, and the belief that "voices" are real. *Schizophrenia Bulletin, 29,* 445–458.

Gartner, A. F., & Gartner, J. (1988). Borderline pathology in postincest female adolescents. *Bulletin of the Menninger Clinic, 52,* 101–113.

Gaser, C., Nenadic, I., Buchsbaum, B. R., Hazlett, E. A., & Buchsbaum, M. S. (2004). Ventricular enlargement in schizophrenia related to volume reduction of the thalamus, striatum, and superior temporal cortex. *American Journal of Psychiatry, 161,* 154–159.

Gass, C. S. (2002). Personality assessment of neurologically impaired patients. In J. N. Butcher (Ed.), *Clinical personality assessment: Practical approaches* (pp. 208–224). New York: Oxford University Press.

Gatz, M. (1990). Interpreting behavioral genetic results: Suggestions for counselors and clients. *Journal of Counseling and Development, 68,* 601–605.

Gatz, M., Smyer, M. A., & Lawton, M. P. (1980). The mental health system and the older adult. In L. W. Poon (Ed.), *Aging in the 1980s.* Washington, DC: American Psychological Association.

Gaub, M., & Carlson, C. L. (1997). Behavioral characteristics of *DSM-IV* ADHD subtypes in a school-based population. *Journal of Abnormal Child Psychology, 25,* 103–111.

Gawin, F. H. (1991). Cocaine addiction: Psychology and neurophysiology. *Science, 251,* 1580–1586.

Gelard, M. S., & Sanford, E. E. (1987). Child abuse and neglect: A review of the literature. *School Psychology Review, 16,* 137–155.

Geller, J., Brown, K. E., Zaitsoff, S. L., Goodrich, S., & Hastings, F. (2003). Collaborative versus directive interventions in the treatment of eating disorders: Implications for care providers. *Professional Psychology: Research and Practice, 34,* 406–413.

George, L. K., Landerman, R., Blazer, D. G., Anthony, J. C. (1991). Cognitive impairment. In L. N. Robins & D. A. Regier (Eds.), *Psychiatric disorders in America: The Epidemiologic Catchment Area study* (pp. 291–327). New York: Free Press.

George, M. S., Trimble, M. R., Ring, H. A., Sallee, F. R., & Robertson, M. M. (1993). Obsessions in obsessive-compulsive disorder with and without Gilles de la Tourette's syndrome. *American Journal of Psychiatry, 150,* 93–97.

Gerhardt, P. (1998, August 2). Hearing my sister's voice. *Washington Post,* C01.

Ghaziuddin, M., Tsai, L., Eilers, L., & Ghaziuddin, N. (1992). Brief report: Autism and herpes simplex encephalitis. *Journal of Autism and Developmental Disorders, 22,* 107–113.

Giancola, P. R., & Zeichner, A. (1997). The biphasic effects of alcohol on human physical aggression. *Journal of Abnormal Psychology, 106,* 598–607.

Giedd, J. N. (2001). Neuroimaging of pediatric neuropsychiatric disorders: Is a picture really worth a thousand words? *Archives of General Psychiatry, 58,* 443–445.

Gillberg, C. (1988). The neurobiology of infantile autism. *Journal of Child Psychology and Psychiatry, 29,* 257–266.

Gillberg, C. (1992). Autism and autistic-like conditions: Subclasses among disorders of empathy. *Journal of Child Psychology and Psychiatry, 33,* 813–842.

Gillis, J. J., Gilger, J. W., Pennington, B. F., & DeFries, J. C. (1992). Attention deficit in reading-disabled twins: Evidence for a genetic etiology. *Journal of Abnormal Child Psychology, 20,* 303–315.

Gillum, R. F. (1997). Sudden cardiac death in Hispanic American and African Americans. *American Journal of Public Health, 87,* 1461–1464.

Girard, S. S., Toth, S. A., Davis, R. H., Donnelly, R. E., Muma, R. D., & Taft, J. M. (1998). Guidelines for the diagnosis and management of asthma. *Journal of American Academy of Physician Assistants, 11,* 45–48.

Glasgow, R. E., & Lichtenstein, E. (1987). Long-term effects of behavioral smoking cessation intervention. *Behavior Therapy, 18,* 297–324.

Glassman, J. N. S., Magulac, M., & Darko, D. F. (1987). Folie a famille: Shared paranoid disorder in a Vietnam veteran and his family. *American Journal of Psychiatry, 144,* 658–660.

Glazer, W. M., Morgenstern, H., & Doucette, J. T. (1991). The prediction of chronic persistent versus intermittent tardive dyskinesia. *British Journal of Psychiatry, 158,* 822–828.

Goff, D. C. (1993). Reply to Dr. Armstrong. *Journal of Nervous and Mental Disease, 181,* 604–605.

Goff, D. C., & Simms, C. A. (1993). Has multiple personality disorder remained consistent over time? *Journal of Nervous and Mental Disease, 181,* 595–600.

Goisman, R. M., Warshaw, M. G., Steketee, G. S., & Fierman, E. J. (1995). DSM-IV and the disappearance of agoraphobia without a history of panic disorder: New data on a controversial diagnosis. *American Journal of Psychiatry, 152,* 1438–1442.

Goldberg, D. (1996). Psychological disorders in general medical settings. *Social Psychiatry, 31,* 1–2.

Golden, C. J. (1989). The Nebraska Neuropsychological Children's Battery. In C. R. Reynolds & E. Fletcher-Janzen (Eds.), *Handbook of clinical child neuropsychology* (pp. 193–204). New York: Plenum Press.

Golden, C. J., Graber, B., Blose, I., Berg, R., Coffman, J., & Bloch, S. (1981). Differences in brain densities between chronic alcoholic and normal control patients. *Science, 211,* 508–510.

Golden, C. J., Moses, J. A., Coffman, J. A., Miller, W. R., & Strider, F. D. (1983). *Clinical neuropsychology.* New York: Grune & Stratton.

Goldenberg, H., & Goldenberg, I. (1995). Family therapy. In R. J. Corsini & D. Wedding (Eds.), *Current psychotherapies* (5th ed.). Itasca, IL: Peacock.

Goldenhar, L. M., Swanson, N. G., Hurrell, J. J., Jr., Ruder, A., & Deddens, J. (1998). Stressors and adverse outcomes for female construction workers. *Journal of Occupational Health Psychology, 3,* 19–32.

Goldfein, J. A., Devlin, M. J., & Spitzer, R. L. (2000). Cognitive behavioral therapy for the treatment of binge eating disorder: What constitutes success? *American Journal of Psychiatry, 157,* 1051–1056.

Goldman, H. H. (1988). Psychiatric epidemiology and mental health services research. In H. H. Goldman (Ed.), *Review of general psychiatry* (pp. 143–156). Norwalk, CT: Appleton & Lange.

Goldman, L. S., Genel, M., Bezman, R. J., & Slanetz, P. J. (1998). Diagnosis and treatment of attention-deficit/hyperactivity disorder in children and adolescents. *Journal of the American Medical Association, 279,* 1100–1107.

Goldstein, A. (1999). *Low level aggression: First steps on the ladder to violence.* Champaign, IL: Research Press.

Goldstein, A. P., & Kodluboy, D. W. (1998). *Gangs in school: Signs, symbols and solutions.* Champaign, IL: Research Press.

Goma, M., Perez, J., & Torrubia, R. (1988). Personality variables in antisocial and prosocial disinhibitory behavior. In T. E. Moffitt & S. A. Mednick (Eds.), *Biological contributions to crime causation* (pp. 211–222). Boston: Martinus Nijhoff Publishers.

Gonsiorek, J. C. (1982). The use of diagnostic concepts in working with gay and lesbian populations. In J. C. Gonsiorek (Ed.), *Homosexuality and psychotherapy.* New York: Hayworth Press.

Goodwin, D. W. (1979). Alcoholism and heredity. *Archives of General Psychiatry, 36,* 57–61.

Goodwin, D. W. (1985). Alcoholism and alcoholic psychoses. In H. I. Kaplan & B. J. Sadock (Eds.), *Comprehensive textbook of psychiatry* (Vol. 4, pp. 1016–1025). Baltimore: Williams & Wilkins.

Goodwin, D. W., & Guze, S. B. (1984). *Psychiatric diagnosis* (3rd ed.). New York: Oxford University Press.

Gordon, A. (2001). Eating disorders: 2. Bulimia nervosa. *Hospital Practice, 36,* 71–73.

Gorman, J. M. (2001). Generalized anxiety disorder. *Clinical Cornerstone, 3,* 37–46.

Gorman, J. M., Kent, J. M., Sullivan, G. M., & Coplan, J. D. (2000). Neuroanatomical hypothesis of panic disorder, revised. *American Journal of Psychiatry, 157,* 493–505.

Gotham, H. J., Sher, K. J., & Wood, P. K. (1997). Predicting stability and change in frequency of intoxication for the college years to beyond: Individual-difference and role transition variables. *Journal of Abnormal Psychology, 106,* 619–629.

Gottesman, I. I. (1978). Schizophrenia and genetics: Where are we? Are you sure? In L. C. Wynne, R. L. Cromwell, & S. Matthysse (Eds.), *The nature of schizophrenia: New approaches to research and treatment* (pp. 59–69). New York: Wiley.

Gottesman, I. I. (1991). *Schizophrenia genesis.* New York: W. H. Freeman & Co.

Graham, J. R. (1990). MMPI-2: *Assessing personality and psychopathology.* New York: Oxford University Press.

Gramling, S. E., Clawson, E. P., & McDonald, M. K. (1996). Perceptual and cognitive abnormality of hypochondriasis: Amplification and physiological reactivity in women. *Psychosomatic Medicine, 58,* 423–431.

Grant, J. E., Kim, S. W., & Crow, S. J. (2001). Prevalence and clinical features of body dysmorphic disorder in adolescent and adult psychiatric inpatients. *Journal of Clinical Psychiatry, 62,* 517–522.

Green, B. (2003). Post-traumatic stress disorder: Symptom profiles in men and women. *Current Medical Research Opinion, 19,* 200–204.

Green, R. (1987). *The "sissy boy syndrome" and the development of homosexuality.* New Haven: Yale University Press.

Green, R., & Blanchard, R. (1995). Gender-identity disorders. In H. I. Kaplan & B. J. Sadock (Eds.), *Comprehensive textbook of psychiatry* (Vol. 6, pp. 1345–1360). Baltimore: Williams & Wilkins.

Green, R., Mandel, J. B., Hotvedt, M. E., Gray, J., & Smith, L. (1986). Lesbian mothers and their children: A comparison with solo parent heterosexual mothers and their children. *Archives of Sexual Behavior, 15,* 167–184.

Greene, R. L. (1991). *The MMPI-2/MMPI: An interpretive manual.* Boston: Allyn & Bacon.

Greene, R. W., Biederman, J., Faraone, S. V., & Oullette, C. (1996). Toward a new psychometric definition of social disability in children with attention-deficit hyperactivity disorder. *Journal of the American Academy of Child and Adolescent Psychiatry, 35,* 571–578.

Greenhill, L., Abikoff, H., Arnold, L., Cantwell, D., Conners, C., Cooper, T., Crowley, K., Elliot, G., Davies, M., Halperin, J., Hectman, L., Hinshaw, S., Jensen, P., Klein, R., Lerner, M., March, J., MacBurnett, K., Pelham, W., Severe, J., Sharma, V., Swanson, J., Vallaro, G., Vitello, B., Wingal, T., & Zametkin, A. (1998). *Psychopharmacological treatment manual: NIMH multimodal treatment study of children with attention deficit hyperactivity disorder (MTA study).* New York: Psychopharmacology Subcommittee of the MTA Steering Committee.

Greeno, C. G., Wing, R. R., & Shiffman, S. (2000). Binge antecedents in obese women with and without binge eating disorder. *Journal of Consulting and Clinical Psychology, 68,* 95–102.

Greer, S. (1991). Psychological response to cancer and survival. *Psychological Medicine, 21,* 43–49.

Gresham, F. M., Beebe-Frankenberger, M. E., & MacMillan, D. L. (1999). A selective review of treatment of children with autism: Description and methodological considerations. *School Psychology Review, 28,* 559–575.

Griffith, E. E., Gonzalez, C. A., & Blue, H. C. (1999). The basics of cultural psychiatry. In R. E. Hales, S. C. Yudofsky & J. A. Talbott (Eds.), *Textbook of psychiatry* (pp. 1463–1492). Washington, DC: American Psychiatric Press.

Grinker, R. R., & Robbins, F. P. (1954). *Psychosomatic case book.* New York: Blakiston.

Groopman, L. C., & Cooper, A. M. (2001). Narcissistic personality disorder. In G. O. Gabbard (Ed.), *Treatment of psychiatric disorders* (pp. 2309–2326). Washington, DC: American Psychiatric Press.

Gross, P. R., & Eifert, G. H. (1990). Components of generalized anxiety: The role of intrusive thoughts vs. worry. *Behaviour Research and Therapy, 28,* 421–428.

Grove, M. W., Lebow, B. S., Clementz, B. A., Cerri, A., Medus, C., & Iacono, W. G. (1991). Familial prevalence and coaggregation of schizotypy indicators: A multitrait family study. *Journal of Abnormal Psychology, 100,* 115–121.

Guadagnoli, E., Ayanian, J. Z., Gibbons, G., McNeil, B. J., & LoGerfo, F. W. (1995). The influence of race on the use of surgical procedures for treatment of peripheral vascular disease of the lower extremities. *Archives of Surgery, 130,* 381–386.

Guerin, P. J., Jr., & Chabot, D. R. (1992). Development of family systems theory. In D. K. Freedheim (Ed.), *History of psychotherapy* (pp. 225–260). Washington, DC: American Psychological Association.

Gunderson, J. G., & Links, P. S. (2001). Borderline personality disorder. In G. O. Gabbard (Ed.), *Treatment of psychiatric disorders* (pp. 2273–2291). Washington, DC: American Psychiatric Press.

Gureje, O., Simon, G. E., Ustun, T. B., & Goldberg, D. P. (1997). Somatization in cross-cultural perspective: A World Health Organization study in primary care. *American Journal of Psychiatry, 154,* 989–995.

Gustafson, R., Popovich, M., & Thomsen, S. (2001). Subtle ad images threaten girls more. *Marketing News, 35,* 12–13.

Guttman, M. (1995, October 27–29). The Ritalin generation. *USA Weekend,* pp. 4–6.

Haas, K., & Haas, A. (1993). *Understanding human sexuality.* St. Louis, MO: Mosby.

Haenen, M. A., deJong, P. J., Schmidt, A. J. M., Stevens, S., & Visser, L. (2000). Hypochondriacs' estimation of negative outcomes: Domain-specificity and responsiveness to reassuring and alarming information. *Behaviour Research and Therapy, 38,* 819–833.

Hafner, H. an der Heiden, W., Behrens, S., Gattaz, W. F., Hambrecht, M., Loffler, W., Maurer, K., Munk-Jorgensen, P., Mowotny, B., Riecher-Rossler, A., & Stein, A. (1998). Causes and consequences of gender difference in age at onset of schizophrenia. *Schizophrenia Bulletin, 24,* 99–113.

Hagerman, R. J. (1996). Biomedical advances in development psychology: The case of fragile X syndrome. *Developmental Psychology, 32,* 416–424.

Hall, R. G., Sachs, D. P. L., Hall, S. M., & Benowitz, N. L. (1984). Two-year efficacy and safety of rapid smoking therapy in patients with cardiac and pulmonary disease. *Journal of Consulting and Clinical Psychology, 52,* 574–581.

Hallak, J. E. C., Crippa, J. A. S., & Zuardi, A. W. (2000). Treatment of koro with citalopram. *Journal of Clinical Psychology, 61,* 951–952.

Halmi, K. A., Sunday, S. R., Strober, M., Kaplan, A., et al. (2000). Perfectionism in anorexia nervosa: Variation by clinical subtype, obsessionality, and pathological eating disorder. *American Journal of Psychiatry, 157,* 1799–1805.

Hammen, C. L. (1985). Predicting depression: A cognitive-behavioral perspective. In P. Kendall (Ed.), *Advances in cognitive-behavioral research and therapy* (Vol. 4). New York: Academic Press.

Hammond, W. R., & Yung, B. (1993). Psychology's role in the public health–response to assaultive violence among young African-American men. *American Psychologist, 48,* 142–154.

Harenstam, A., Theorell, T., & Kaijser, L. (2000). Coping with anger-provoking situations, psychosocial working conditions, and the ECG-detected signs of coronary heart disease. *Journal of Occupational Health Psychology, 5,* 191–203.

Hare, R. D. (1968). Psychopathy, autonomic functioning and the orienting responses. *Journal of Abnormal Psychology, 73,* 1–24.

Harlow, J. M. (1868). Recovery from the passage of an iron bar through the head. *Publication of the Massachusetts Medical Society, 2,* 327.

Harrington, R. C. (2001). Childhood depression and conduct disorder: Different routes to the same outcome? *Archives of General Psychiatry, 58,* 237–240.

Harris, J. C. (2001). Psychiatric disorders in mentally retarded persons. In G. O. Gabbard (Ed.), *Treatment of psychiatric disorders* (pp. 75–107). Washington, DC: American Psychiatric Press.

Harris, S. L. (1995). Autism. In M. Hersen & R. T. Ammerman (Eds.), Advanced abnormal psychology. Hillsdale, NJ: Lawrence Erlbaum.

Harrison, K. (2001). Ourselves, our bodies: Thin-ideal media, self-discrepancies, and eating disorder symptomatology in adolescents. *Journal of Social and Clinical Psychology, 20,* 289–299.

Harrison, K., & Cantor, J. (1997). The relationship between media exposure and eating disorders. *Journal of Communication, 47,* 40–67.

Harvey, A. G., & Bryant, R. A. (2002). Acute stress disorder: A synthesis and critique. *Psychological Bulletin, 128,* 886–902.

Harvey, A. G., Bryant, R. A., & Dang, S. T. (1998). Autobiographical memory in acute stress disorder. *Journal of Consulting Clinical Psychology, 66,* 500–506.

Harvey, A. G., Clark, D. M., Ehlers, A., & Rapee, R. M. (2000). Social anxiety and self-impression. *Behaviour Research and Therapy, 38,* 1183–1192.

Hashimoto, T., Tayama, M., Murakawa, K., Yoshimoto, T., Miyazaki, M., Harada, M., & Kuroda, Y. (1995). Development of brainstem and cerebellum in autistic patients. *Journal of Autism and Developmental Disorders, 25,* 1–18.

Hathaway, S. R., & McKinley, J. C. (1943). *Manual for the Minnesota Multiphasic Personality Inventory.* New York: Psychological Corporation.

Haug Schnabel, G. (1992). Daytime and nighttime enuresis: A functional disorder and its ethological decoding. *Behavior, 120,* 232–262.

Hauser, W. A. (1994). The distribution of mild and severe forms of epilepsy. In M. R. Trimble & W. E. Dodson (Eds.), *Epilepsy and quality of life* (pp. 249–257). New York: Raven Press.

Hawton, K., Catalan, J., Martin, P., & Fagg, J. (1986). Long-term outcome of sex therapy. *Behaviour Research and Therapy, 24,* 665–675.

Hayes, S. C., Wilson, K. G., Gifford, E. V., Follette, V. M., & Strosahl, K. (1996). Experimental avoidance and behavioral disorders: A functional dimensional approach to diagnosis and treatment. *Journal of Consulting and Clinical Psychology, 64,* 1152–1168.

Haynes, S. N. (2001). Clinical applications of analogue behavioral observation: Dimensions of psychometric evaluation. *Psychological Assessment, 13,* 73–85.

Heckman, T. G., Anderson, E. S., Sikkema, K. J., Kochman, A., Kalichman, S. C., & Anderson, T. (2004). Emotional distress in nonmetropolitan persons living with HIV disease enrolled in a telephone-delivered, coping improvement group intervention. *Health Psychology, 23,* 94–100.

Heffernan, K. (1994). Sexual orientation as a factor in risk for binge eating and bulimia nervosa: A review. *International Journal of Eating Disorders, 16,* 335–347.

Heinrichs, R. W. (1993). Schizophrenia and the brain. *American Psychologist, 48,* 221–233.

Heinssen, R. K., & Cuthbert, B. N. (2001). Barriers to relationship formation in schizophrenia: Implications for treatment, social recovery, and translational research. *Psychiatry, 64,* 126–132.

Helgeson, V. S., Snyder, P., & Seltman, H. (2004). Psychological and physical adjustment to breast cancer over 4 years: Identifying trajectories of change. *Health Psychology, 23,* 3–15.

Hellmich, N. (2001, July 25). Super-thin, super-troubling. *USA Today,* p. D7.

Hellstrom, K., Fellenius, J., & Öst, L-G. (1996). One versus five sessions of applied tension in the treatment of blood phobia. *Behaviour Research and Therapy, 34,* 101–112.

Hendrie, H. C. (2001). Exploration of environmental and genetic risk factors for Alzheimer's disease: The value of cross-cultural studies. *Current Directions in Psychological Science, 10,* 98–101.

Herbener, E. S., & Harrow, M. (2002). The course of anhedonia during 10 years of schizophrenic illness. *Journal of Abnormal Psychology, 111,* 237–248.

Herlicky, B., & Sheeley, V. L. (1988). Privileged communication in selected helping professions: A comparison among statutes. *Journal of Counseling & Development, 65,* 479–483.

Herman, J., & Hirschman, L. (1981). Families at risk for father-daughter incest. *American Journal of Psychiatry, 38,* 967–970.

Herrnstein, R. J., & Murray, C. (1994). *The bell curve: Intelligence and class structure in American life.* New York: Free Press.

Herschkowitz, S., & Dickes, R. (1978). Suicide attempts in a female-to-male transsexual. *American Journal of Psychiatry, 135,* 368–369.

Herxheimer, A., & Healy, D. (2002). Arrhythmias and sudden death in patients taking antipsychotic drugs. *British Medical Journal, 325,* 1253–1254.

Herzog, W., Kronmuller, K.-T., Hartmann, M., Bergmann, G., & Kroger, F. (2000). Family perception of interpersonal behavior as a predictor in eating disorders: A prospective, six-year follow-up study. *Family Process, 39,* 359–374.

Heston, L. L. (1966). Psychiatric disorders in foster-home-reared children of schizophrenic mothers. *British Journal of Psychiatry, 122,* 819–825.

Heston, L. L., & Denny, D. (1968). Interactions between early life experience and biological factors in schizophrenia. In D. Rosenthal & S. Kety (Eds.), *The transmission of schizophrenia.* New York: Pergamon Press.

Hettema, J. M., Annas, P., Neale, M. C., Kendler, K. S., & Fredrickson, M. (2003). A twin study of the genetics of fear conditioning. *Archives of General Psychiatry, 60,* 702–709.

Hidalgo, R. B., & Davidson, J. R. T. (2000). Posttraumatic stress disorder: Epidemiology and health-related considerations. *Journal of Clinical Psychiatry, 61,* 5–13.

Hill, A. J., & Bhatti, R. (1995). Body shape perception and dieting in preadolescent British Asian girls: Links with eating disorders. *International Journal of Eating Disorders, 17,* 175–183.

Hill, C. E., & Lambert, M. J. (2004). Methodological issues in studying psychotherapy processes and outcomes. In M. J. Lambert (Ed.), *Bergin and Garfield's handbook of psychotherapy and behavior change* (5th ed., pp. 84–135). New York: Wiley.

Hill, D., & Watterson, D. (1942). Electroencephalographic studies of the psychopathic personality. *Journal of Neurology and Psychiatry, 5,* 47–64.

Hill, S. K., Ragland, J. D., Gur, R. C., & Gur, R. E. (2001). Neuropsychological differences among empirically derived clinical subtypes of schizophrenia. *Neuropsychology, 15,* 492–501.

Hillson, J. M., & Kuiper, N. A. (1994). Stress and coping model of child treatment. *Clinical Psychological Review, 14,* 261–285.

Hilsenroth, M. J., Fowler, J. C., Padawer, J. R., & Handler, L. (1997). Narcissism in the Rorschach revisited: Some reflections on empirical data. *Psychological Assessment, 9,* 113–121.

Hirose, S. (2003). The causes of underdiagnosing akathisia. *Schizophrenia Bulletin, 29,* 547–553.

Hirschfield, R. M., & Davidson, L. (1989). Clinical risk factors for suicide. *Psychiatric Annals, 18,* 628–635.

Hirschfield, R. M., & Shea, T. (1985). Affective disorders: Psychosocial treatment. In H. I. Kaplan & B. J. Sadock (Eds.), *Comprehensive textbook of psychiatry* (4th ed., pp. 786–810). Baltimore: Williams & Wilkins.

Ho, D. D., Neumann, A. U., Perelson, A. S., Chen, W., Leonard, J. M., & Markowitz, M. (1995). Rapid turnover of plasma virions and CD4 lymphocytes in HIV-1 infection. *Nature, 373,* 123–126.

Ho, E. D. F., Tsang, A. K. T., & Ho, D. Y. F. (1991). An investigation of the calendar calculation ability of a Chinese calendar savant. *Journal of Autism and Developmental Disorders, 21,* 315–327.

Hodgins, D. C., El-Guebaly, N., & Armstrong, S. (1995). Prospective and retrospective reports of mood states before relapse to substance use. *Journal of Consulting and Clinical Psychology, 63,* 400–407.

Hoehn-Saric, R., Pearlson, G. D., Harris, G. J., Machlin, S. R., & Camargo, E. E. (1991). Effects of fluoxetine on regional cerebral blood flow in obsessive-compulsive patients. *American Journal of Psychiatry, 148,* 1243–1245.

Hoff, A. L., & Kremen, W. S. (2003). Neuropsychology in schizophrenia: An update. *Current Opinion in Psychiatry, 16,* 149–155.

Hoff, A. L., Kremen, W. S., Weineke, M. H., Lauriello, J., et al. (2001). Association of estrogen levels with neuropsychological performance in women with schizophrenia. *American Journal of Psychiatry, 158,* 1134–1139.

Hoffman, L. (1998). *Eating disorders.* Rockville, MD: National Institutes of Health.

Hoffman, M. A. (1991). Counseling the HIV-infected client: A psychosocial model for assessment and intervention. *Counseling Psychologist, 19,* 467–542.

Hofman, S. G. (2000). Self-focused attention before and after treatment of social phobia. *Behaviour Research and Therapy, 38,* 717–725.

Hofmann, S. G., Lehman, C. L., & Barlow, D. H. (1997). How specific are specific phobias? *Journal of Behavior Therapy and Experimental Psychiatry, 28,* 233–240.

Holahan, C. (2001a, August 28). Hidden eating disorders concealment is growing, specialists say. *Boston Globe,* p. C4.

Holahan, C. (2001b, August 4). Yahoo removes pro-eating-disorder Internet sites. *Boston Globe,* p. A2.

Holbrook, T., & Weltzin, T. E. (1998). Eating disorders in males. *Treatment Today, 10,* 52–53.

Holcomb, H. H., Links, J., Smith, C., & Wong, D. (1989). Positron emission tomography: Measuring the metabolic and neurochemical characteristics of the living human nervous system. In N. C. Andreasen (Ed.), *Brain imaging: Applications in psychiatry* (pp. 235–370). Washington, DC: American Psychiatric Press.

Holden, N. L. (1987). Late paraphrenia or the paraphrenias? A descriptive study with a 10-year follow-up. *British Journal of Psychiatry, 150,* 635–639.

Hollon, S. D., & Fawcett, J. (2001). Combined medication and psychotherapy. In G. O. Gabbard (Ed.), *Treatment of psychiatric disorders* (pp. 1247–1266). Washington, DC: American Psychiatric Press.

Holmes, T. S., & Holmes, T. H. (1970). Short-term intrusion into the life style routine. *Journal of Psychosomatic Research, 14,* 121–132.

Holroyd, J., & Brodsky, A. (1977). Psychologists' attitudes and practices regarding erotic and nonerotic physical contact with patients. *American Psychologist, 32,* 839–843.

Holroyd, S., & Baron-Cohen, S. (1993). Brief report: How far can people with autism go in developing a theory of mind? *Journal of Autism and Developmental Disorders, 23,* 379–385.

Hong, G. K., & Domokos-Cheng Ham, M. (2001). *Psychotherapy and counseling with Asian American clients.* Thousand Oaks, CA: Sage.

Hooper, J. (1998, August). Science in the sack: Beyond Viagra. *Health and Fitness,* pp. 108–113.

Hoover, D. W., & Millich, R. (1994). Effects of sugar ingestion expectancies on mother-child interactions. *Journal of Abnormal Child Psychology, 22,* 501–515.

Houston case may sink Texas sodomy law. (1998, November 7). *San Francisco Chronicle,* p. A7.

Hovarth, K., Stefanatos, G., Sokolski, K. N., Wachtel, R., Nabors, L., & Tildon, J. J. (1998). Improved social and language skills after secretin administration in patients with autistic spectrum disorders. *Journal for the Association for Academic Minority Physician, 9,* 9–15.

Howard, R. (1992). Folie a deux involving a dog. *American Journal of Psychiatry, 149,* 414.

Howard, R., Rabins, P. V., Seeman, M. V., & Jeste, D. V. (2000). International late onset schizophrenia group: Late-onset schizophrenia and very-late-onset schizophrenia-like psychosis—An international consensus. *American Journal of Psychiatry, 157,* 172–178.

Hu, S., Pattatucci, A. M. L., & Patterson, C. L. L. (1995, November). Linkage between sexual orientation and chromosome Xq28 in males but not in females. *Nature Genetics, 11,* 248–256.

Hudson, J. I., Manoach, D. S., Sabo, A. N., & Sternbach, S. E. (1991). Recurrent nightmares in posttraumatic stress disorder: Association with sleep paralysis, hypnopompic hallucinations, and REM sleep. *Journal of Nervous and Mental Disease, 179,* 572–573.

Hull, J. C., & Bond, C. F. (1986). Social and behavioral consequences of alcohol consumption and expectancy: A meta-analysis. *Psychological Bulletin, 99,* 347–360.

Hunfeld, J. A. M., Perquin, C. W., Hazelbroek-Kampschreur, A. A. J. M., & Passchier, J., et al. (2002). Physically unexplained chronic pain and its impact on children and their families: The mother's perception. *Psychology and Psychotherapy, 75,* 251–257.

Hunter, R., & Macalpine, I. (1963). *Three hundred years of psychiatry, 1535–1860.* London: Oxford University Press.

Hurley, R. A., Saxena, S., Rauch, S. L., Hoehn-Saric, R., & Taber, K. H. (2002). Predicting treatment response in obsessive-compulsive disorder. *Journal of Neuropsychiatry and Clinical Neurosciences, 14,* 249–255.

Hurtig, A. L., & Rosenthal, I. M. (1987). Psychological findings in early treated cases of female pseudohermaphroditism caused by virilizing congenital adrenal hyperplasia. *Archives of Sexual Behavior, 16,* 209–223.

Hutchings, B., & Mednick, S. A. (1977). Criminality in adoptees and their adoptive and biological parents: A pilot study. In S. A. Mednick & K. L. Christianson (Eds.), *Biosocial bases of criminal behavior*. New York: Garden Press.

Hynd, G. W., Hern, K. L., Voeller, K. K., & Marshall, R. M. (1991). Neurobiological basis of attention-deficit hyperactivity disorder. *School Psychology Review, 20,* 174–186.

Irving, L. M. (2001). Media exposure and disordered eating: Introduction to the special section. *Journal of Social and Clinical Psychology, 20,* 259–263.

Irwin, A., & Gross, A. M. (1990). Mental retardation in childhood. In M. Hersen & C. G. Last (Eds.), *Handbook of child and adult psychopathology* (pp. 325–336). New York: Pergamon Press.

Irwin, H. J. (1998). Attitudinal predictors of dissociation: Hostility and powerlessness. *Journal of Psychology, 132,* 389–404.

Isenberg, S. A., Lehrer, P. M., & Hochron, S. (1992). The effects of suggestion and emotional arousal on pulmonary function in asthma: A review and a hypothesis regarding vagal medication. *Psychosomatic Medicine, 54,* 192–216.

Ivnik, R. J., Smith, G. E., Malec, J. F., Petersen, R. C., & Tangalos, E. G. (1995). Long-term stability and intercorrelations of cognitive abilities in older persons. *Psychological Assessment, 7,* 155–161.

Iwamasa, G. Y., Larrabee, A. L., & Merritt, R. D. (2000). Are personality disorder criteria ethnically biased? A card-sort analysis. *Cultural Diversity and Ethnic Minority Psychology, 6,* 284–296.

Jablensky, A. V., & Kalaydjieva, L. V. (2003). Genetic epidemiology of schizophrenia: Phenotypes, risk factors, and reproductive behavior. *American Journal of Psychiatry, 160,* 425–429.

Jackson, B., & Farrugia, D. (1997). Diagnosis and treatment of adults with attention deficit hyperactive disorder. *Journal of Counseling and Development, 75,* 312–319.

Jackson, J. L., Calhoun, K., Amick, A. E., Maddever, H. M., & Habif, V. (1990). Young adult women who experienced childhood intrafamilial sexual abuse: Subsequent adjustment. *Archives of Sexual Behavior, 19,* 211–221.

Jackson, K. M., Sher, K. J., Gotham, H. J., & Wood, P. K. (2001). Transitioning into and out of large-effect drinking in young adulthood. *Journal of Abnormal Psychology, 110,* 378–391.

Jacobs, D., & Klein, M. E. (1993). The expanding role of psychological autopsies. In A. A. Leenaars (Ed.), *Suicidology.* Northvale: Jason Aronson.

Jacobson, S., & Alex, P. (2001, February 19). Waist management: Men aren't immune to eating disorders, but they do their best to disguise them. *Record,* p. 1.

James, D. C. (2001). Eating disorders, fertility, and pregnancy: Relationships and complications. *Journal of Perinatal and Neonatal Nursing, 15,* 36–48.

Jamison, K. R. (1996). Manic-depressive illness, genes, and creativity. In L. L. Hall (Ed.), *Genetics and mental illness: Evolving issues for research and society* (pp. 111–132). New York: Plenum Press.

Janssen, K. (1983). Treatment of sinus tachycardia with heart-rate feedback. *Psychiatry and Human Development, 17,* 166–176.

Janus, S. S., & Janus, C. L. (1993). *The Janus report on sexual behavior.* New York: Wiley.

Jason, L. A. (1998). Tobacco, drug and HIV prevention media interventions. *American Journal of Community Psychology, 26,* 151–187.

Jawed, S. Y. (1991). A survey of psychiatrically ill Asian children. *British Journal of Psychiatry, 158,* 268–270.

Jellinek, E. M. (1971). Phases of alcohol addiction. In G. Shean (Ed.), *Studies in abnormal behavior.* Chicago: Rand McNally.

Jenike, M. A. (2001). A forty-five-year-old woman with obsessive-compulsive disorder. *Journal of the American Medical Association, 285,* 2121–2128.

Jensen, P. S., Bhatara, V. S., Vitiello, B., Hoagwood, K., Feil, M., & Burke, L. B. (1999). Proactive medication prescribing practices for U.S. children: Gaps between research and clinical practice. *Journal of the American Academy of Child and Adolescent Psychiatry, 38,* 557–565.

Jilek, W. G. (2001). Cultural factors in psychiatric disorders. Paper presented at the Twenty-sixth Congress of the World Federation for Mental Health, July.

Johnson, W. G. (1990). Multifactorial diseases and other disorders with non-Mendelian inheritance. In H. E. Hendrie, L. G. Mendelsohn, & C. Readhead (Eds.), *Brain aging: Molecular biology, the aging process and neurodegenerative disease* (pp. 5–19). Bern, Germany: Hans Huber.

Johnston, C., Fine, S., Weiss, M., & Weiss, J. (2000). Effects of stimulant medication treatment on mothers and children's attribution for the behavior of children with ADHD. *Journal of Abnormal Child Psychology, 28,* 371–382.

Joiner, T. E., Heatherton, T. F., Rudd, M. D., & Schmidt, N. B. (1997). Perfectionism, perceived weight status, and bulimic symptoms: Two studies testing a diathesis-stress model. *Journal of Abnormal Psychology, 106,* 145–153.

Jones, D. R., Harrell, J. P., Morris-Prather, C. E., Thomas, J., & Omowale, N. (1996). Affective and physiological responses to racism. The role of Afrocentrism and mode of presentation. *Ethnicity and Disease, 6,* 109–122.

Jones, J. M. (1995). Headache: Benign or catastrophic? *Physician Assistant, 19,* 25–44.

Jones, J. M. (1996). Treating acute pain in a desperate headache. *Journal of the American Academy of Physician Assistants, 9,* 26–50.

Jones, J. M., Bennett, S., Olmsted, M. P., Lawson, M. L., & Rodin, G. (2001). Disordered eating attitudes and behaviours in teenaged girls: A school-based study. *Canadian Medical Association Journal, 165,* 547–551.

Jones, K. L., Shainberg, L. W., & Byer, C. O. (1977). *Sex and people.* New York: Harper & Row.

Joseph, E. (1991). Psychodynamic personality theory. In K. Davis, H. Klar, & J. J. Coyle (Eds.), *Foundations of psychiatry.* Philadelphia: Saunders.

Joseph, J. (2001). Separated twins and the genetics of personality differences: A critique. *American Journal of Psychology, 114,* 1–30.

Julkunen, J., Idanpaan-Heikkila, U., & Saarinen, T. (1993). Components of type A behavior and the first-year prognosis of a myocardial infarction. *Journal of Psychosomatic Research, 37,* 11–18.

Kabot, S., Masi, W., & Segal, M. (2003). Advances in the diagnosis and treatment of autism spectrum disorders. *Professional Psychology: Research and Practice, 34*(1), 26–33.

Kaivanto, K. K., Estlander, A. M., Moneta, G. B., & Vanharanta, H. (1995). Isokinetic performance in low back pain patients: The predictive power of the self-efficacy scale. *Journal of Occupational Rehabilitation, 5,* 87–99.

Kamphaus, R. W., Petoskey, M. D., & Rowe, E. W. (2000). Current trends in psychological testing of children. *Professional Psychology: Research and Practice, 31,* 155–164.

Kanas, N. (1988). Psychoactive substance use disorders: Alcohol. In H. H. Goldman (Ed.), *Review of general psychiatry* (pp. 286–298). Norwalk, CT: Appleton & Lange.

Kanayama, G., Pope, H. G., Jr., & Hudson, J. I. (2001). "Body image" drugs: A growing psychosomatic problem. *Psychotherapy and Psychosomatics, 70,* 61–64.

Kane, J. M., & Freeman, H. L. (1994). Towards more effective antipsychotic treatment. *British Journal of Psychiatry, 165,* 22–31.

Kane, J. M., Woerner, M., Borenstein, M., Wegner, J., & Lieberman, J. (1986). Investigating the incidence and prevalence of tardive dyskinesia. *Psychopharmacology Bulletin, 22,* 254–258.

Kang, S. H., Chen, A. M., Lew, R., Min, K., Moskowithz, J. M., Wismer, B. A., & Tager, I. B. (1997). Behavioral risk factor survey of Korean Americans: Alameda County, California, 1994. *MMWR, 46,* 774–777.

Kanner, L., & Lesser, L. I. (1958). Early infantile autism. *Pediatrics Clinic of North America, 5,* 711–730.

Kaplan, H. S. (1974). No nonsense therapy for six sexual malfunctions. *Psychology Today, 8,* 76–80, 83, 86.

Kapur, S. (2003). Psychosis as a state of aberrant salience: A framework linking biology, phenomenology, and pharmacology in schizophrenia. *American Journal of Psychiatry, 160,* 13–23.

Karno, M., Hough, R. L., Burnam, A., Escobar, J. I., Timbers, D. M., Santana, F., & Boyd, J. H. (1987). Lifetime prevalence of specific psychiatric disorders among Mexican Americans and non-Hispanic whites in Los Angeles. *Archives of General Psychiatry, 44,* 695–701.

Kasari, C., Sigman, M. D., Baumgartner, P., & Stipek, D. J. (1993). Pride and mastery in children with autism. *Journal of Child Psychology and Psychiatry, 34,* 353–362.

Kaszniak, A. W., Nussbaum, P. D., Berren, M. R., & Santiago, J. (1988). Amnesia as a consequence of male rape: A case report. *Journal of Abnormal Psychology, 97,* 100–104.

Kaufman, A. S., Kamphaus, R. W., & Kaufman, N. L. (1985). The Kaufman Assessment Battery for Children (K-ABC). In C. S. Newmark (Ed.), *Major psychological assessment instruments* (pp. 249–276). Boston: Allyn & Bacon.

Kavanagh, D. J. (1992). Recent developments in expressed emotions and schizophrenia. *British Journal of Psychiatry, 160,* 601–620.

Kawachi, I., Sparrow, D., Vonkonas, P. S., & Weiss, S. T. (1994). Symptoms of anxiety and risk of coronary heart disease: The Normative Aging Study. *Circulation, 90,* 2225–2229.

Kazdin, A. E. (1987). Treatment of antisocial behavior in children: Current status and future directions. *Psychological Bulletin, 102,* 187–203.

Kazdin, A. E. (1994). Psychotherapy for children and adolescents. In A. E. Bergin & S. L. Garfield (Eds.), *Handbook of psychotherapy and behavior change* (pp. 543–594). New York: Wiley.

Kazdin, A. E., Siegel, T. C., & Bass, D. (1992). Cognitive problem-solving skills training and parent management training in the treatment of antisocial behavior in children. *Journal of Consulting and Clinical Psychology, 60,* 733–747.

Keel, P. K., Dorer, D. J., Eddy, K. T., Franko, D., et al. (2003). Predictors of mortality in eating disorders. *Archives of General Psychiatry, 60,* 179–185.

Keel, P. K., Mitchell, J. E., Miller, K. B., Davis, T. L., & Crow, S. J. (1999). Long-term outcome of bulimia nervosa. *Archives of General Psychiatry, 56,* 63–69.

Kegeles, T., Catania, J., & Coates, T. (1988). Intentions to communicate positive HIV status to sex partners (letters to the editor). *Journal of the American Medical Association, 259,* 216–217.

Keith, S. J., Regier, D. A., & Rae, D. S. (1991). Schizophrenic disorders. In L. N. Robins & D. A. Regier (Eds.), *Psychiatric disorders in America* (pp. 33–52). New York: Free Press.

Keller, A., Castellanos, F. X., Vaituzis, A. C., Jeffries, N. O., et al. (2003). Progressive loss of cerebellar volume in childhood-onset schizophrenia. *American Journal of Psychiatry, 160,* 128–133.

Kellner, R. (1985). Functional somatic symptoms and hypochondriasis. *Archives of General Psychiatry, 42,* 821–833.

Kellner, R., Hernandez, J., & Pathak, D. (1992). Hypochondriacal fears and beliefs, anxiety, and somatization. *British Journal of Psychiatry, 160,* 525–532.

Kendall, P. C., Brady, E. U., & Verduin, T. L. (2001). Comorbidity in childhood anxiety disorders and treatment outcomes. *Journal of the American Academy of Child and Adolescent Psychology, 40,* 787–794.

Kendall, P. C., Holmbeck, G., & Verduin, T. (2004). Methodology, design, and evaluation in psychotherapy research. In M. J. Lambert (Ed.), *Bergin and Garfield's handbook of psychotherapy and behavior change* (5th ed., pp. 16–43). New York: Wiley.

Kendall-Tackett, K. A., Williams, L. M., & Finkelhor, D. (1993). Impact of sexual abuse on children: A review and synthesis of recent empirical studies. *Psychological Bulletin, 113,* 164–180.

Kendler, K. S. (1988). Familial aggregation of schizophrenia and schizophrenic spectrum disorders. *Archives of General Psychiatry, 45,* 377–383.

Kendler, K. S., Myers, J., & Prescott, C. A. (2002). The etiology of phobias: An evaluation of stress-diathesis model. *Archives of General Psychiatry, 59,* 242–249.

Kendler, K. S., Myers, J., Prescott, C. A., & Neale, M. C. (2001). The genetic epidemiology of irrational fears and phobias in men. *Archives of General Psychiatry, 58,* 257–265.

Kendler, K. S., Neale, M. C., Kessler, R. C., Heath, A. C., & Eaves, L. J. (1992). Generalized anxiety disorder in women. *Archives of General Psychiatry, 49,* 267–271.

Kernberg, O. F. (1975). *Borderline conditions and pathological narcissism.* New York: Jason Aronson.

Kernberg, O. (1976). Technical considerations in the treatment of borderline personality organization. *Journal of the American Psychoanalytic Association, 24,* 795–829.

Kessler, R. C., McGonagle, K. A., Zhao, S., Nelson, C. B., Hughes, M., Eshleman, S., Wittchen, H.-U., & Kendler, K. S. (1994). Lifetime and twelve-month prevalence of DSM-III-R psychiatric disorders in the United States. *Archives of General Psychiatry, 51,* 8–19.

Kessler, R. C., Sonnega, A., Bromet, E., Hughes, M., & Nelson, B. (1995). Posttraumatic stress disorder in the National Comorbidity Survey. *Archives of General Psychiatry, 52,* 1048–1068.

Kety, S. S., Wender, P. H., Jacobsen, B., Ingraham, L. J., Jansson, L., Faber, B., & Kinney, D. K. (1994). Mental illness in the biological and adoptive relatives of schizophrenic adoptees. *Archives of General Psychiatry, 51,* 442–455.

Khanna, S., Desai, N. G., & Channabasavanna, S. M. (1987). A treatment package for transsexualism. *Behavior Therapy, 2,* 193–199.

Kiecolt-Glaser, J. K., Dura, J. R., Speicher, C. E., Trask, O. J., et al. (1991). Spousal caregivers of dementia victims: Longitudinal changes in immunity and health. *Psychosomatic Medicine, 53,* 345–362.

Kiecolt-Glaser, J. K., & Glaser, R. (1993). Mind and immunity. In D. Goleman & J. Gurin (Eds.), *Mind/body medicine* (pp. 39–64). New York: Consumer Reports Books.

Kiecolt-Glaser, J. K., Glaser, R., Cacioppo, J. T., MacCallum, R. C., Snydersmith, M., Kim, C., & Malarky, W. B. (1997). Marital conflict in older adults: Endocrinological and immunological correlates. *Psychosomatic Medicine, 59,* 339–349.

Kiecolt-Glaser, J. K., Glaser, R., Dyer, C., Shuttleworth, E. C., Ogrocki, P., & Speicher, C. E. (1987). Chronic stress and immune function in family care-givers of Alzheimer's disease victims. *Psychosomatic Medicine, 49,* 523–535.

Killen, J. D., Robinson, T. N., Haydel, K. F., Hayward, C., Wilson, D. M., Hammer, L. D., Litt, I. F., & Taylor, C. B. (1997). Prospective study of risk factors for the initiation of cigarette smoking. *Journal of Consulting and Clinical Psychology, 65,* 1011–1016.

Kilmann, P. R., & Auerbach, R. (1979). Treatments of premature ejaculation and psychogenic impotence: A critical review of the literature. *Archives of Sexual Behavior, 8,* 81–100.

Kim, E. A. (2003, Jan 28). Asian Americans and eating disorders: A silent struggle. *Seattle Post–Intelligencer*, E1.

Kim, U., & Berry, J. W. (1993). *Indigenous psychologies*. Thousand Oaks, CA: Sage.

Kinderman, P., & Bentall, R. P. (1996). Self-discrepancies and persecutory delusions: Evidence for a model of paranoid ideation. *Journal of Abnormal Psychology, 105*, 106–113.

Kinderman, P., & Bentall, R. P. (1997). Casual attributions in paranoia and depression: Internal, personal, and situational attributions for negative events. *Journal of Abnormal Psychology, 106*, 341–345.

King, N. J., Clowes-Hollins, V., & Ollendick, T. H. (1997). The etiology of dog phobia. *Behaviour Research and Therapy, 35*, 77.

King, N. J., Eleonora, G., & Ollendick, T. H. (1998). Etiology of childhood phobias: Current status of Rachman's three pathways theory. *Behavior Research and Therapy, 36*, 297–309.

King, N. J., Gullione, E., Tonge, B. J., & Ollendick, T. H. (1993). Self-reports of panic attacks and manifest anxiety in adolescents. *Behaviour Research and Therapy, 31*, 11–116.

Kinsey, A. C., Pomeroy, W. B., & Martin, C. E. (1948). *Sexual behavior in the human male*. Philadelphia: W. B. Saunders.

Kinsey, A. C., Pomeroy, W. B., Martin, C. E., & Gebhard, P. H. (1953). *Sexual behavior in the human female*. Philadelphia: Saunders.

Klein, D. N., Norden, K. A., Ferro, T., Leader, J. B., Kasch, K. L., Klein, L. M., Schwartz, J. E., & Aronson, T. A. (1998). Thirty-month naturalistic follow-up study of early-onset dysthymic disorder: Course, diagnostic stability, and prediction of outcome. *Journal of Abnormal Psychology, 107*, 338–348.

Kleinberg, J., & Galligan, B. (1983). Effects of deinstitutionalization on adaptive behavior of mentally retarded adults. *American Journal of Mental Deficiency, 88*, 21–27.

Kleinman, A. (1991, April). *Culture and DSM-IV: Recommendations for the introduction and for the overall structure*. Paper presented at the Conference on Culture and DSM-IV, Pittsburgh.

Klerman, G. L., Weissman, M. M., Markowitz, J., Glick, I., Wilner, P. J., Mason, B., & Shear, M. K. (1994). Medication and psychotherapy. In A. E. Bergin & S. L. Garfield (Eds.), *Handbook of psychotherapy and behavior change* (pp. 734–782). New York: Wiley.

Klesges, R. C., Winders, S. E., Meyers, A. W., Eck, L. H., Ward, K. D., Hultquist, C. M., Ray, J. W., & Shadish W. R. (1997). How much weight gain occurs following smoking cessation? A comparison of weight gain using both continuous and point prevalence abstinence. *Journal of Consulting and Clinical Psychology, 65*, 286–291.

Klin, A., Volkmar, F. R., & Sparrow, S. S. (1992). Autistic social dysfunction: Some limitations of the theory of mind hypothesis. *Journal of Child Psychology and Psychiatry, 33*, 861–876.

Klopfer, B., & Davidson, H. (1962). *The Rorschach technique*. New York: Harcourt, Brace & World.

Kluft, R. P. (1987). Dr. Kluft replies. *American Journal of Psychiatry, 144*, 125.

Kluft, R. P. (1996). Treating the traumatic memories of patients with dissociative identity disorder. *American Journal of Psychiatry, 153*, 103–108.

Knapp, S., & VandeCreek, L. (1996). Risk management for psychologists: Treating patients who recover lost memories of childhood abuse. *Professional Psychology, Research and Practice, 27*, 452–459.

Kneisel, P. J., & Richards, G. P. (1988). Crisis intervention after the suicide of a teacher. *Professional Psychology: Research and Practice, 19*, 165–169.

Knopf, I. J. (1984). *Childhood psychopathology* (2nd ed.). Englewood Cliffs, NJ: Prentice-Hall.

Knott, J., Platt, E., Ashley, M., & Gottlieb, J. (1953). A familial evaluation of the electroencephalogram of patients with primary behavior disorder and psychopathic personality. *EEG and Clinical Neurophysiology, 5*, 363–370.

Kobasa, S. C., Hilker, R. J., & Maddi, S. R. (1979). Psychological hardiness. *Journal of Occupational Medicine, 21*, 595–598.

Kockott, G., & Fahrner, E.-M. (1987). Transsexuals who have not undergone surgery: A follow-up study. *Archives of Sexual Behavior, 16*, 511–522.

Koegel, R. L., Screibman, L., Loos, L. M., Dirlich-Wilhelm, H., Dunlap, G., Robbins, F. R., & Plienis, A. J. (1992). Consistent stress profiles in mothers of children with autism. *Journal of Autism and Developmental Disorders, 22*, 205–216.

Koh, K. B. (1998). Emotion and immunity. *Journal of Psychosomatic Research, 45*, 107–115.

Kohlenberg, R. J., & Tsai, M. (1991). *Functional analytic psychotherapy*. New York: Plenum.

Kohon, G. (1987). Fetishism revisited. *International Journal of Psychoanalysis, 68*, 213–228.

Kolko, D. J., Loar, L. L., & Sturnick, D. (1990). Inpatient social-cognitive skills training groups with conduct disordered and attention deficit disordered children. *Journal of Child Psychology and Psychiatry, 31*, 734–748.

Kovacs, M., Devlin, B., Pollock, M., Richards, C., & Mukerji, P. (1997). A controlled family history study of childhood-onset depressive disorder. *Archives of General Psychiatry, 54*, 613–623.

Kraepelin, E. (1923). *Textbook of psychiatry* (8th ed.). New York: Macmillan. (Original work published 1883)

Krahn, L. E., Li, H., & O'Connor, M. K. (2003). Patients who strive to be ill: Factitious disorder with physical symptoms. *American Journal of Psychiatry, 160*, 1163–1169.

Kremer, L. (1999, January 2). Whatever happened to . . . Jody Roberts drops plan for book and television movie about her life. *News Tribune*, p. B1.

Kresin, D. (1993). Medical aspects of inhibited sexual desire disorder. In W. O'Donahue, & J. Geer (Eds.), *Handbook of sexual dysfunctions*. Boston: Allyn & Bacon.

Krieger, N., & Sidney, S. (1996). Racial discrimination and blood pressure: The CARDIA study of young black and white adults. *American Journal of Public Health, 86*, 1370–1380.

Krueger, R. F., Caspi, A., Moffitt, T. E., & Silva, P. A. (1998). The structure and stability of common mental disorders (DSM-III-R): A longitudinal-epidemiological study. *Journal of Abnormal Psychology, 107*, 216–227.

Kubany, E. S., Hill, E. E., Owens, J. A., Iannce-Spencer, C., et al. (2004). Cognitive trauma therapy for battered women with PTSD (CTT-BW). *Journal of Consulting and Clinical Psychology, 72*, 3–18.

Kubiszyn, T. W., Meyer, G. J., Finn, S. E., Eyde, L. D., Kay, G. G., Moreland, K. L., Dies, R. R., & Eisman, E. J. (2000). Empirical support for psychological assessment in clinical health care settings. *Professional Psychology: Research and Practice, 31*, 119–130.

Kuipers, E. L. Garety, P., Fowler, D., & Dunn, G. (1997). London-East Anglia randomized controlled trial of cognitive-behavioural therapy for psychosis: I. Effects of treatment phase. *British Journal of Psychiatry, 171*, 319–325.

Kumanyika, S., Wilson, J., & Guilford-Davenport, M. (1993). Weight-related attitudes and behaviors of Black women. *Journal of the American Dietetic Association, 93*, 416–422.

Kusek, K. (2001). Could a fear wreak havoc on your life? *Cosmopolitan, 230*, 182–184.

Kushner, H. I. (1995). Women and suicidal behavior: Epidemiology, gender, and lethality in historical perspective. In S. S. Canetto & D. Lester (Eds.), *Women and suicidal behavior*. New York: Springer.

Kushner, M. (1965). The reduction of a long-standing fetish by means of aversive conditioning. In L. P. Ullmann & L. Krasner (Eds.), *Case studies in behavior modification*. New York: Holt, Rinehart & Winston.

Lackner, J. M., Carosella, A. M., & Feuerstein, M. (1996). Pain expectancies, pain, and functional self-efficacy expectancies as determinants of disability in patients with chronic low back disorders. *Journal of Consulting and Clinical Psychology, 64,* 212–220.

Lader, M., & Bond, A. J. (1998). Interaction of pharmacological and psychological treatments of anxiety. *British Journal of Psychiatry, 173,* 41–48.

Ladouceur, R., Dugas, M. J., Freeston, M. H., Leger, E., Gagnon, F., & Thibodeau, N. (2000). Efficacy of a cognitive-behavioral treatment for generalized anxiety disorder. *Journal of Consulting and Clinical Psychology, 68,* 957–964.

Ladouceur, R., Freeston, M. H., Fournier, S., Rheaume, J., Dugas, M. J., Gagnon, F., & Thibodeau, N. (2000). Strategies used with intrusive thoughts: A comparison of OCD patients with anxious and community controls. *Journal of Abnormal Psychology, 109,* 179–187.

LaGreca, A. M., Silverman, W. K., Vernberg, E. M., & Prinstein, M. J. (1996). Symptoms of posttraumatic stress in children after Hurricane Andrew: A prospective study. *Journal of Consulting and Clinical Psychology, 64,* 712–723.

Lahey, B. B., Loeber, R., Hart, E. L., Frick, P. J., Applegate, B., Zhang, Q., Green, S. M., & Russo, M. R. (1995). Four-year longitudinal study of conduct disorders in boys: Patterns and predictors of persistence. *Journal of Abnormal Psychology, 104,* 89–93.

Lai, J. Y., & Linden, W. (1992). Gender anger expression style, and opportunity for anger release determine cardiovascular reaction to and recovery from anger provocation. *Psychosomatic Medicine, 54,* 297–310.

Laird, J., & Green, R. J. (1996). *Lesbians and gays in couples and families.* San Francisco: Jossey-Bass.

Lakkis, J., Ricciardelli, L. A., & Williams, R. J. (1999). Role of sexual orientation and gender-related traits in disordered eating. *Sex Roles, 41,* 1–16.

Lam, R. W., Lee, S. K., Tam, E. M., Grewal, A., & Yatham, L. N. (2001). An open trial of light therapy for women with seasonal affective disorder and comorbid bulimia nervosa. *Journal of Clinical Psychiatry, 62,* 164–168.

Lambert, E. W., Wahler, R. G., Andrade, A. R., & Bickman, L. (2001). Looking for the disorder in conduct disorder. *Journal of Abnormal Psychology, 110,* 110–123.

Lambert, M. J., & Ogles, B. M. (2004). The efficacy and effectiveness of psychotherapy. In M. J. Lambert (Ed.), *Bergin and Garfield's handbook of psychotherapy and behavior change* (5th ed., pp. 139–193). New York: Wiley.

Lambert, N. M. (1988). Adolescent outcomes for hyperactive children. *American Psychologist, 43,* 786–799.

Lambley, P. (1974). Treatment of transvestism and subsequent coital problems. *Journal of Behavior Therapy and Experimental Psychiatry, 5,* 101–102.

Landesman, S., & Butterfield, E. C. (1987). Normalization and deinstitutionalization of mentally retarded individuals. *American Psychologist, 42,* 809–816.

Langevin, R., Paitich, D., Ramsay, G., Anderson, C., Kamrad, J., Pope, S., Geller, G., Pearl, L., & Newman, S. (1979). Experimental studies of exhibitionism. *Archives of Sexual Behavior, 8,* 307–331.

Larkin, K. T., & Zayfert, C. (1996). Anger management training with mild essential hypertensive patients. *Journal of Behavioral Medicine, 19,* 415–433.

Larson, C. A., & Carey, K. B. (1998). Caffeine: Brewing trouble in mental health settings? *Professional Psychology, Research and Practice, 29,* 373–376.

Lask, B., & Bryant-Waugh, R. (1992). Early-onset anorexia nervosa and related eating disorders. *Journal of Child Psychology and Psychiatry, 33,* 281–300.

Last, C. G., & Perrin, S. (1993). Anxiety disorders in African-American and white children. *Journal of Abnormal Child Psychology, 21,* 153–162.

Laudenslager, M. L., Ryan, S. M., Drugan, R. C., Hyson, R. L., & Maier, S. F. (1983). Coping and immunosuppression: Inescapable but not escapable shock suppresses lymphocyte proliferation. *Science, 220,* 568–570.

Laumann, E. O., Gagnon, J. H., Michael, R. T., & Michaels, S. (1994). *The social organization of sexuality.* Chicago: University of Chicago Press.

Lazarus, P. (2001, May). Breaking the code of silence: What schools can do about it. *NASP Communique,* 28–29.

Lazarus, R. S. (1966). *Psychological stress and the coping process.* New York: McGraw-Hill.

Leary, W. E. (1992, December 10). Medical panel says most sexual impotence in men can be treated without surgery. *New York Times,* p. D20.

Leckman, J. F., Walker, D. E., & Cohen, D. J. (1993). Premonitory urges in Tourette's syndrome. *American Journal of Psychiatry, 150,* 98–102.

Lee, S., Hsu, L. K., & Wing, Y. K. (1992). Bulimia nervosa in Hong Kong Chinese patients. *British Journal of Psychiatry, 161,* 545–551.

Lee, T. M. C., Chen, E. Y. H., Chan, C. C. H., Paterson, J. G., Janzen, H. L., & Blashko, C. A. (1998). Seasonal affective disorder. *Clinical Psychology: Science and Practice, 5,* 275–290.

Leekam, S. R., & Prior, M. (1994). Can autistic children distinguish lies from jokes? A second look at second-order belief attribution. *Journal of Child Psychology and Psychiatry, 35,* 901–915.

Leenaars, A. A. (1992). Suicide notes, communication, and ideation. In R. W. Maris, A. L. Berman, J. T. Maltsberger, & R. I. Yufit (Eds.), *Assessment and prediction of suicide.* New York: Guilford.

Leferink, K. (1998). Private and public in the lives of chronic schizophrenic patients. *Psychiatry, 61,* 147–162.

Legato, M. J. (1996). What we know about coronary artery disease in women. *Physician Assistant, 20,* 93–100.

Lehman, A. F., & Steinwachs, D. M. (1998). At issue: Translating research into practice: The schizophrenia patient outcome research team (PORT) treatment recommendations. *Schizophrenia Bulletin, 24,* 1–10.

Leibbrand, R., Hiller, W., & Fichter, M. M. (2000). Hypochondriasis and somatization: Two distinct aspects of somatoform disorders. *Journal of Clinical Psychology, 56,* 63–72.

Leiblum, S. R., & Rosen, R. C. (1991). Couples therapy for erectile disorders: Conceptual and clinical considerations. Special issue: The treatment of male erectile disorders. *Journal of Sex and Marital Therapy, 17,* 147–159.

Lenzenweger, M. F. (2001). Reaction time slowing during high-load, sustained-attention task performance in relation to psychometrically identified schizotypy. *Journal of Abnormal Psychology, 110,* 290–296.

Lenzenweger, M. F., Cornblatt, B. A., and Putnick, M. (1991). Schizotypy and sustained attention. *Journal of Abnormal Psychology, 100,* 84–89.

Leppard, W., Ogletree, S. M., & Wallen, E. (1993). Stereotyping in medical advertising: Much ado about something? *Sex Roles, 29,* 829–838.

Lerner, J. V., Hertzog, C., Hooker, K. A., Hassibi, M., & Thomas, A. (1988). A longitudinal study of negative emotional states.

Lester, D. (1994). Are there unique features of suicide in adults of different ages and developmental stages? *Omega Journal of Death and Dying, 29,* 337–348.

Lester, R., & Petrie, T. A. (1998). Physical, psychological, and societal correlates of bulimic symptomatology among African American college women. *Journal of Counseling Psychology, 45,* 315–321.

Leung, N., Thomas, G., & Waller, G. (2000). The relationship between parental bonding and core beliefs in anorexic and bulimic women. *British Journal of Clinical Psychology, 39,* 205–210.

Levenstein, C., Prantera, C., Varvo, V., Scribano, M. L., Berto, E., Luzi, C., & Andreoli, A. (1993). Development of the Perceived Stress Questionnaire: A new tool for psychosomatic research. *Journal of Psychosomatic Research, 37,* 19–32.

Levin, M. (2002). The many causes of headache: Migraine, vascular, drug-induced, and more. *Postgraduate Medicine, 112,* 67–78.

Levis, D. J. (1985). Implosive therapy: A comprehensive extension of conditioning theory of fear/anxiety to psychology. In S. Reiss & R. R. Bootzin (Eds.), *Theoretical issues in behavior therapy.* New York: Academic Press.

Lewinsohn, P. M. (1974). A behavioral approach to depression. In R. J. Friedman & M. M. Katz (Eds.), *The psychology of depression: Contemporary theory and research.* New York: Wiley.

Lewinsohn, P. M., Hoberman, H. M., Teri, L., & Hautzinger, M. (1985). An integrative theory of depression. In S. Reiss & R. R. Bootzin (Eds.), *Theoretical issues in behavioral therapy* (pp. 331–359). Orlando, FL: Academic Press.

Lewinsohn, P. M., Hopps, H., Roberts, R. E., Seeley, J. R., & Andrews, J. A. (1993). Adolescent psychopathology: I. Prevalence and incidence of depression and other DSM-III-R disorders in high school students. *Journal of Abnormal Psychology, 102,* 133–144.

Lezon, D. (2002, May 25). Everybody a stranger. *Houston Chronicle,* A–33.

Liberini, P., Faglia, L., Salvi, F., & Grant, R. P. J. (1993). Cognitive impairment related to conversion disorder: A two-year follow-up study. *Journal of Nervous and Mental Disease, 181,* 325–327.

Liberman, R. P., Kopelowicz, A., & Young, A. S. (1994). Biobehavioral treatment and rehabilitation of schizophrenia. *Behavior Therapy, 25,* 89–107.

Lichtenstein, E., & Danaher, B. (1976). Modification of smoking behavior: A critical analysis of theory, research, and practice. In M. Hersen, R. Eisler, & P. Miller (Eds.), *Progress in behavior modification: 3.* New York: Academic Press.

Lichtenstein, E., & Glasgow, R. E. (1977). Rapid smoking: Side effects and safeguards. *Journal of Consulting and Clinical Psychology, 45,* 815–821.

Lichtenstein, E., & Rodrigues, M. (1977). Long-term effects of rapid smoking treatment for dependent cigarette smokers. *Addictive Behaviors, 2,* 109–112.

Lickey, M. E., & Gordon, B. (1991). *Medicine and mental illness.* New York: W. H. Freeman.

Lieberman, J. A. (1995). Signs and symptoms. *Archives of General Psychiatry, 52,* 361–363.

Lilienfeld, S. O., Lynn, S. J., Kirsch, I., Chaves, J. F., Sarbin, T. R., Ganaway, G. K., et al. (1999). Dissociative identity disorder and the sociocognitive model: Recalling the lessons of the past. *Psychological Bulletin, 125,* 507–523.

Lilienfeld, S. O., Wood, J. M., & Garb, H. N. (2000). The scientific status of projective techniques. *Psychological Science in the Public Interest, 1,* 17–66.

Lindamer, L. A., Lohr, J. B., Caligiuri, M. P., & Jeste, D. V. (2001). Relationship of gender and age of onset of schizophrenia to severity of dyskinesia. *Journal of Neuropsychiatry and Clinical Neurosciences, 13,* 399–401.

Linehan, M. M. (1987). Dialectical behavior therapy for borderline personality disorder. Theory and method. *Bulletin of the Menninger Clinic, 51,* 261–276.

Linehan, M. M. (1993). *Cognitive-behavioral treatment of borderline personality disorder.* New York: Guilford Press.

Liposuction vs. American fat. (1998). *USA Today, 127,* pp. 8–9.

Li-Repac, D. (1980). Cultural influences on clinical perceptions: A comparison between Caucasian and Chinese-American therapists. *Journal of Cross-Cultural Psychology, 11,* 327–342.

Lishman, W. A. (1978). *The psychological consequences of cerebral disorder.* Oxford, England: Blackwell.

Loeber, R. (1990). Development and risk factors of juvenile antisocial behavior and delinquency. *Clinical Psychology Review, 10,* 1–42.

Loening-Baucke, V. (2000). Clinical approach to fecal soiling in children. *Clinical Pediatrics, 39,* 603–607.

Loewenstein, R. (1994). Diagnosis, epidemiology, clinical course, treatment, and cost effectiveness of treatment for dissociative disorders and MPD: Report submitted to the Clinton administration task force on health care reform. *Dissociation, 7,* 3–11.

Loftus, E. F., Garry, M., & Feldman, J. (1994). Forgetting sexual trauma: What does it mean when 38 percent forget? *Journal of Consulting and Clinical Psychology, 62,* 1177–1181.

Looper, K. J., & Kirmayer, L. J. (2002). Behavioral medicine approaches to somatoform disorders. *Journal of Consulting and Clinical Psychology, 70,* 810–827.

Lopez, S. R. (1989). Patient variable biases in clinical judgment: Conceptual overview and methodological considerations. *Psychological Bulletin, 106,* 1–20.

LoPiccolo, J. (1995). Sexual disorders and gender identity disorders. In R. J. Comer, *Abnormal Psychology.* New York: W. H. Freeman.

LoPiccolo, J. (1997). Sex therapy: A postmodern model. In S. J. Lynn & J. P. Garske (Eds.), *Contemporary psychotherapies: Models and methods.* New York: Guilford.

LoPiccolo, J., & Freidman, J. R. (1988). Broad spectrum treatment of low sexual desire: Integration of cognitive, behavioral, and systemic treatment. In S. Leiblum & R. Rosen (Eds.), *Sexual desire disorders.* New York: Guilford.

LoPiccolo, J., & Stock, W. E. (1986). Treatment of sexual dysfunction. *Journal of Consulting and Clinical Psychology, 54,* 158–167.

Lovaas, O. I. (1977). *The autistic child: Language development through behavior modification.* New York: Halsted Press.

Lovaas, O. I., Schaeffer, B., & Simmons, J. Q. (1965). Building social behavior in autistic children by use of electric shock. *Journal of Experimental Research in Personality, 1,* 99–109.

Lovejoy, M. (2001). Disturbances in the social body: Differences in body image and eating problems among African American and white women. *Gender and Society, 15,* 239–261.

Lowe, C. F., & Chadwick, P. D. J. (1990). Verbal control of delusions. *Behavior Therapy, 21,* 461–479.

Luecken, L. J., Suarez, E. C., Kuhn, C. M., Barefoot, J. C., Blumenthal, J. A., Siegler, I. C., & Williams, R. B. (1997). Stress in employed women: Impact of marital status and children at home on neurohormone output and home strain. *Psychosomatic Medicine, 59,* 352–359.

Luria, A. R. (1982). *Language and cognition.* New York: Oxford University Press.

Lydiard, R. B. (1996). Recent developments in the psychopharmacology of anxiety disorders. *Journal of Consulting and Clinical Psychology, 64,* 660–668.

Lykken, D. T. (1982). Fearlessness: Its carefree charm and deadly risks. *Psychology Today, 16,* 20–28.

Lynskey, M. T., & Fergusson, D. M. (1995). Childhood conduct problems, and adolescent alcohol, tobacco, and illicit drug use. *Journal of Abnormal Child Psychology, 23,* 281–302.

Mace, C. J., & Trimble, M. R. (1996). Ten-year prognosis of conversion disorder. *British Journal of Psychiatry, 169,* 282–288.

MacEachron, A. E. (1983). Institutional reform and adaptive functioning of mentally retarded persons: A field experiment. *American Journal of Mental Deficiency, 88,* 2–12.

Machon, R. A., Mednick, S. A., & Huttunen, M. O. (1997). Adult major affective disorder after prenatal exposure to an influenza epidemic. *Archives of General Psychiatry, 54*, 322–328.

Machover, K. (1949). *Personality projection in the drawing of the human figure: A method of personality investigation.* Springfield, IL: Thomas.

Maddi, S. R. (1972). *Personality theories.* Homewood, IL: Dorsey.

Madle, R. A. (1990). Mental retardation in adulthood. In M. Hersen & C. G. Last (Eds.), *Handbook of child and adult psychopathology* (pp. 337–352). New York: Pergamon Press.

Magic Johnson. (2002). *Jet, 101,* 54–58.

Magni, G., & Schifano, F. (1984). Psychological distress after stroke. *Journal of Neurology, Neurosurgery and Psychiatry, 47,* 567–568.

Mallik, I. (2001). Hypertension. *Heart, 86,* 251.

Maltais, M. (2001, May 31). E-briefing: Body of knowledge: The Web offers a wealth of information about self-image and resources for the size and shape conscious. *Los Angeles Times,* p. T3.

Maltby, N., Kirsch, I., Mayers, M., & Allen, G. J. (2002). Virtual reality exposure therapy for the treatment of fear of flying: A controlled investigation. *Journal of Consulting and Clinical Psychology, 70,* 1112–1118.

Maltsberger, J. T. (1991). The prevention of suicide in adults. In A. A. Leenaars (Ed.), *Life span perspectives of suicide: Timelines in the suicide process.* New York: Plenum.

Manderscheid, R. W., & Sonnenschein, M. A. (1992). *Mental health, United States, 1992.* Rockville, MD: U.S. Department of Health and Human Services.

Mangweth, B., Pope, H. G., Jr., Kemmler, G., Ebenbichler, C., et al. (2001). Body image and psychopathology in male body builders. *Psychotherapy and Psychosomatics, 70,* 38–42.

Manjiviona, J., & Prior, M. (1995). Comparison of Asperger syndrome and high-functioning autistic children on a test of motor impairment. *Journal of Autism and Developmental Disorders, 25,* 23–39.

Mann, S. J., & James, G. D. (1998). Defensiveness and essential hypertension. *Journal of Psychosomatic Research, 45,* 139–148.

Marantz, S., & Coates, S. (1991). Mothers of boys with gender identity disorder: A comparison of matched controls. *Journal of the American Academy of Child and Adolescent Psychiatry, 30,* 310–315.

Marcus, J., Hans, S. L., Nagler, S., Auerbach, J. G., Mirsky, A. F., & Aubrey, A. (1987). Review of the NIMH Israeli kibbutz-city study and the Jerusalem Infant Developmental study. *Schizophrenia Bulletin, 13,* 425–437.

Mariani, M. A., & Barkley, R. A. (1997). Neuropsychological and academic functioning in preschool boys with attention deficit hyperactivity disorder. *Developmental Neuropsychology, 13,* 111–129.

Marlatt, G. A. (1978). Craving for alcohol, loss of control and relapse: A cognitive-behavioral analysis. In P. E. Nathan & G. A. Marlatt (Eds.), *Experimental and behavioral approaches to alcoholism.* New York: Plenum.

Marlatt, G. A. (1983). The controlled-drinking controversy: A commentary. *American Psychologist, 38,* 1097–1110.

Marlatt, G. A., Baer, J. S., Kivlahan, D. R., Dimeff, L. A., Larimer, M. E., Quigley, L. A., Somers, J. M., & Williams, E. (1998). Screening and brief intervention for high-risk college student drinkers: Results from a two-year follow-up assessment. *Journal of Consulting and Clinical Psychology, 66,* 604–615.

Marlatt, G. A., Demming, B., & Reid, J. (1973). Loss-of-control drinking in alcoholics: An experimental analogue. *Journal of Abnormal Psychology, 81,* 233–241.

Marmar, C. R. (1988). Personality disorders. In H. H. Goldman (Ed.), *Review of general psychiatry* (pp. 401–424). Norwalk, CT: Appleton & Lange.

Marmot, M. G., & Syme, S. L. (1976). Acculturation and coronary heart disease in Japanese-Americans. *American Journal of Epidemiology, 104,* 225–247.

Marquadt, W. H. (2000). Update on migraine management. *Journal of the American Academy of Physician Assistants, 13,* 60–72.

Marrugat, J., Sala, J., Masia, R., Pavesi, M., Sanz, G., Valle, V., Molina, L. Seres, L., & Elosua, R. (1998). Mortality differences between men and women following first myocardial infarction. *Journal of the American Medical Association, 280,* 1405–1409.

Marsa, L. (2000, April 3). Children's health issue—The drug dilemma: The increased use of powerful psychiatric medicines in children under six has raised concerns about overmedication and long-term effects. *Los Angeles Times,* p. S1.

Marsella, A. J. (1988). Ethnocultural issues in the assessment of psychopathology. In S. Wetzler (Ed.), *Measuring mental illness.* (pp. 7–21). Washington, DC: American Psychiatric Press.

Marsh, D. T., & Johnson, D. L. (1997). The family experience of mental illness: Implications for intervention. *Professional Psychology: Research and Practice, 28,* 229–237.

Marshall, J. (1998, February 23). Memoir of anorexia and bulimia is a harrowing story. *Seattle Post-Intelligencer,* pp. D1–D2.

Martin, P. R. (1993). *Psychological management of chronic headaches.* New York: Guilford Press.

Martin, P. R., & Seneviratne, H. M. (1997). Effects of food deprivation and a stressor on head pain. *Health Psychology, 16,* 310–318.

Martin, R. A. (2001). Humor, laughter, and physical health: Methodological issues and research findings. *Psychological Bulletin, 127,* 504–519.

Masi, G., Favilla, L., Mucci, M., Poli, P., & Romano, R. (2001). Depressive symptoms in children and adolescents with dysthymic disorder. *Psychopathology, 34,* 29–35.

Maslow, A. H. (1954). *Motivation and personality.* New York: Harper & Row.

Masserman, J., Yum, K., Nicholson, J., & Lee, S. (1944). Neurosis and alcohol: An experimental study. *American Journal of Psychiatry, 101,* 389–395.

Masterman, D. L., & Cummings, J. L. (2001). Alzheimer's disease. In G. O. Gabbard (Ed.), *Treatment of psychiatric disorders* (pp. 481–514). Washington, DC: American Psychiatric Press.

Masters, W. H., & Johnson, V. E. (1966). *Human sexual response.* Boston: Little, Brown.

Masters, W. H., & Johnson, V. E. (1970). *Human sexual inadequacy.* London: Churchill.

Masters, W. H., & Johnson, V. E. (1979). *Homosexuality in perspective.* Boston: Little, Brown.

Masters, J. H., Johnson, V. E., & Kolodny, R. C. (1992). *Human sexuality.* New York: HarperCollins.

Masterson, J. F. (1981). *The narcissistic and borderline disorders: An integrated developmental approach.* New York: Brunner/Mazel.

Matarazzo, J. D. (1992). Psychological testing and assessment in the twenty-first century. *American Psychologist, 47,* 1007–1018.

Materka, P. R. (1984). Families caring, coping with Alzheimer's disease. *Michigan Today, 16,* 13–14.

May, D. C., & Turnbull, N. (1992). Plastic surgeons' opinions of facial surgery for individuals with Down syndrome. *Mental Retardation, 30,* 29–33.

Mazza, J., & Overstreet, S. (2000). Children and adolescents exposed to community violence: A mental health perspective for school psychologists. *School Psychology Review, 29,* 86–101.

McCarthy, K. (2002). Family dynamics affect asthma in at-risk kids. *Psychology Today, 35,* 30–31.

McCauley, E., & Ehrhardt, A. A. (1984). Follow-up of females with gender identity disorders. *Journal of Nervous and Mental Disease, 172,* 353–358.

McClain, P. (1995). Centers for Disease Control and Prevention, Atlanta, GA.

McCord, W., & McCord, J. (1964). *The psychopath: An essay on the criminal mind.* Princeton, NJ: Van Nostrand.

McCracken, L. M., & Larkin, K. T. (1991). Treatment of paruresis with in vivo desensitization: A case report. *Journal of Behavior Therapy and Experimental Psychiatry, 22,* 57–62.

McCrady, B. S. (1994). Alcoholics Anonymous and behavior therapy: Can habits be treated as diseases? Can diseases be treated as habits? *Journal of Consulting and Clinical Psychology, 62,* 1159–1166.

McCreary, D. R., & Sadava, S. W. (2001). Gender differences in relationships among perceived attractiveness, life satisfaction, and health in adults as a function of body mass index and perceived weight. *Psychology of Men and Masculinity, 2,* 108–116.

McCullough, P. K., & Maltsberger, J. T. (2001). Obsessive-compulsive personality disorder. In G. O. Gabbard (Ed.), *Treatment of psychiatric disorders* (pp. 2341–2351). Washington, DC: American Psychiatric Press.

McDaniel, S. H., & Speice, J. (2001). What family psychology has to offer women's health: The examples of conversion, somatization, infertility treatment, and genetic testing. *Professional Psychology: Research & Practice, 32,* 44–51.

McDermut, W., Miller, I. W., & Brown, R. A. (2001). The efficacy of group psychotherapy for depression: A meta-analysis and review of the empirical research. *Clinical Psychology: Science and Practice, 8,* 98–116.

McDowell, D. M. (2001). Club drugs. In G. O. Gabbard (Ed.), *Treatment of psychiatric disorders* (pp. 749–758). Washington, DC: American Psychiatric Press.

McGee, R., & Stanton, W. R. (1992). Sources of distress among New England adolescents. *Journal of Child Psychology and Psychiatry, 33,* 999–1010.

McGilley, B. M., & Pryor, T. L. (1998). Assessment and treatment of bulimia nervosa. *American Family Physician, 57,* 2743–2750.

McGowan, S. (1991, November). Confidentiality and the ethical dilemma. *Guidepost, 34,* 1, 6, 10.

McGue, M., & Christensen, K. (1997). Genetic and environmental contributions to depression symptomology: Evidence from Danish twins 75 years of age and older. *Journal of Abnormal Psychology, 106,* 439–448.

McGuire, P. A. (1999). More psychologists are finding that discrete uses of humor promote healing in their patients. *APA Monitor Online, 30,* 1–5.

McKenzie, N., Marks, I., & Liness, S. (2001). Family and past history of mental illness as predisposing factors in posttraumatic stress disorder. *Psychotherapy and Psychosomatics, 70,* 163–167.

McLellan, A. T., Alterman, A. I., Metzger, D. S., Grissom, G. R., Woody, G. E., Luborsky, L., & O'Brien, C. P. (1994). Similarity of outcome predictors across opiate, cocaine, and alcohol treatments: Role of treatment services. *Journal of Consulting and Clinical Psychology, 62,* 1141–1158.

McLeod, B. (1985). Real work for real pay. *Psychology Today, 19,* 42–50.

McNamee, H. B., Mello, N. K., & Mendelson, J. H. (1968). Experimental analysis of drinking patterns of alcoholics: Concurrent psychiatric observations. *American Journal of Psychiatry, 124,* 1063–1069.

McNiel, D. E., & Binder, R. L. (1991). Clinical assessment of the risk of violence among psychiatric inpatients. *American Journal of Psychiatry, 148,* 1317–1321.

McQueen, P. C., Spence, M. W., Garner, J. B., Pereira, L. H., & Winson, E. J. T. (1987). Prevalence of major mental retardation and associated disabilities in the Canadian Maritime Provinces. *American Journal of Mental Deficiency, 91,* 460–466.

Mechanic, D., Bilder, S., & McAlpine, D. D. (2002). Employing persons with serious mental illness. *Health Affairs, 21,* 242–253.

Mednick, S. A. (1970). Breakdown in individuals at high risk for schizophrenia: Possible predispositional perinatal factors. *Mental Hygiene, 54,* 50–63.

Mednick, S. A., Cannon, T., Parnas, J., & Schulsinger, F. (1989). Twenty-seven-year follow-up of the Copenhagen high-risk for schizophrenia project: Why did some of the high-risk offspring become schizophrenic? *Schizophrenia Research, 2,* 14.

Mednick, S. A., & Christiansen, K. O. (Eds.). (1977). *Biosocial bases of criminal behavior.* New York: Gardner Press.

Mednick, S. A., & Kandel, E. (1988). Genetic and perinatal factors in violence. In T. E. Moffitt & S. A. Mednick (Eds.), *Biological contributions to crime causation* (pp. 40–54). Boston: Martinus Nijhoff.

Meehl, P. E. (1962). Schizotaxia, schizotypia, schizophrenia. *American Psychologist, 17,* 827–838.

Meichenbaum, D. H. (1993). The personal journey of a psychotherapist and his mother: In G. Brannigan & M. R. Merrens (Eds.), *The undaunted psychologist: Adventures in research.* New York: McGraw-Hill.

Meissner, W. W. (2001). Paranoid personality disorder. In G. O. Gabbard (Ed.), *Treatment of psychiatric disorders* (pp. 2227–2236). Washington, DC: American Psychiatric Press.

Meloy, J. R. (2001). Antisocial personality disorder. In G. O. Gabbard (Ed.), *Treatment of psychiatric disorders* (pp. 2251–2271). Washington, DC: American Psychiatric Press.

Meltzer, H. Y. (2000). Side effects of antipsychotic medications: Physician's choice of medication and patient compliance. *Journal of Clinical Psychiatry, 61,* 3–4.

Mendlein, J. M., Freedman, D. S., Peter, D. G., Allen, B., Percy, C. A., Ballew, C., Mokdad, A. H., & Whie, L. L. (1997). Risk factors for coronary heart disease among Navajo Indians: Findings from the Navajo Health and Nutrition Survey. *Journal of Nutrition, 127,* 2099–2105.

Mendlowicz, M. V., Rapaport, M. H., Fontenelle, L., Jean-Louis, G., et al. (2002). Amnesia and neonaticide. *American Journal of Psychiatry, 159,* 498.

Menzies, R. P. D., Fedoroff, J. P., Green, C. M., & Isaacson, K. (1995). Prediction of dangerous behavior in male erotomania. *British Journal of Psychiatry, 166,* 529–536.

Mercer, J. R. (1988). Death of the IQ paradigm: Where do we go from here? In W. J. Lonner & V. O. Tyler (Eds.), *Cultural and ethnic factors in learning and motivation: Implications for education.* Bellingham, WA: Western Washington University.

Merryman, K. (1997, July 17). Medical experts say Roberts may well have amnesia: Parts of her life match profile of person who might lose memory. *News Tribune,* pp. A8–A9.

Merskey, H. (1995). Multiple personality disorder and false memory syndrome. *British Journal of Psychiatry, 166,* 281–283.

Merz, C. N. B. (1997, April 11). Heart Disease: The stress connection. *Newsweek,* pp. 9–16.

Meyer, G. J., Finn, S. E., Eyde, L. D., Kay, G. G., Moreland, K. L., Dies, R. R., Eisman, E. J., Kubiszyn, T. W., & Reed, G. M. (2001). Psychological testing and psychological assessment: A review of evidence and issues. *American Psychologist, 56,* 128–165.

Meyer, G. J., Finn, S. E., Eyde, L. D., Kay, G. G., Moreland, K. L., Dies, R. R., et al. (2003). Psychological testing and psychological assessment: A review of the evidence and issues. In A. E. Kazdin (Ed.), *Methodological issues and strategies in clinical research* (pp. 265–345). Washington, DC: American Psychological Association.

Meyer, J., & Peter, D. (1979). Sex reassignment: Follow-up. *Archives of General Psychiatry, 36,* 1010–1015.

Meyer, R. G., & Osborne, Y. V. H. (1982). *Case studies in abnormal behavior.* Boston: Allyn & Bacon.

Meyer, W. S., & Keith, C. R. (1991). Homosexual and preoedipal issues in the psychoanalytic psychotherapy of a female-to-male transsexual. In C. W. Socarides & V. D. Volkan (Eds.), *The homosexualities and the therapeutic process* (pp. 75–96). Adison, CT: International Universities Press.

Meyers, W. A. (1991). A case history of a man who made obscene telephone calls and practiced frotteurism. In G. I. Fogel & W. A. Myers (Eds.), *Perversions and near-perversions in clinical practice* (pp. 109–126). New Haven, CT: Yale University Press.

Miklowitz, D. J. (1994). Family risk indicators in schizophrenia. *Schizophrenia Bulletin, 20,* 137–148.

Mileno, M. D., Barnowski, C., Fiore, T., Gormley, J., Rich, J. D., Emgushov, R.-T., & Carpenter, C. C. J. (2001). Factitious HIV syndrome in young women. *AIDS Reader, 11,* 263–268.

Milich, R., & Pelham, W. E. (1986). Effects of sugar ingestion on the classroom and playground behavior of attention deficit disordered boys. *Journal of Consulting and Clinical Psychology, 54,* 714–718.

Miller, D. J., & Thelen, M. H. (1986). Knowledge and beliefs about confidentiality in psychotherapy. *Professional Psychology, 17,* 15–19.

Miller, M., & Kantrowitz, B. (1999, January 25). Unmasking Sybil. *Newsweek,* pp. 66–68.

Miller, M. N., & Pumariega, A. J. (2001). Culture and eating disorders: A historical and cross-cultural review. *Psychiatry, 64,* 93–110.

Miller, S. B., Friese, M., Dolgoy, L., Sita, A., Lavoie, K., & Campbell, T. (1998). Hostility, sodium consumption, and cardiovascular response to interpersonal stress. *Psychosomatic Medicine, 60,* 71–77.

Millon, T. (1981). *Disorders of personality: DSM-III-R, Axis II.* New York: Wiley-Interscience.

Millon, T., & Everly, G. S. (1985). *Personality and its disorders.* New York: Wiley.

Milos, G. F., Spindler, A. M., Buddeberg, C., & Crameri, A. (2003). Axis I and II comorbidity and treatment experiences in eating disorder subjects. *Psychosomatics, 72,* 276–284.

Milstein, V. (1988). EEG topography in patients with aggressive violent behavior. In T. E. Moffitt & S. A. Mednick (Eds.), *Biological contributions to crime causation* (pp. 121–134). Boston: Martinus Nijhoff.

Milstone, C. (1997). Sybil minds. *Saturday Night, 112,* 35–42.

Mintz, J., Mintz, L., & Goldstein, M. (1987). Expressed emotion and relapse in first episodes of schizophrenia. *British Journal of Psychiatry, 151,* 314–320.

Minuchin, S., Rosman, B., & Baker, L. (1978). *Psychosomatic families: Anorexia nervosa in context.* Cambridge, MA: Harvard University Press.

Mitchell, A. (1998, June 17). Controversy over Lott's view of homosexuality. *New York Times,* p. 24.

Mohr, D. C., & Beutler, L. E. (1990). Erectile dysfunction: A review of diagnostic and treatment procedures. *Clinical Psychology Review, 10,* 123–150.

Monahan, J. (1981). *The clinical prediction of violent behavior.* Rockville, MD: National Institute of Mental Health.

Monahan, J., & Walker, L. (Eds.). (1990). *Social science in law: Cases and materials* (2nd ed.). Westbury, NJ: Foundation Press.

Money, J. (1987). Masochism: On the childhood origin of paraphilia, opponent-process theory, and antiandrogen therapy. *Journal of Sex Research, 23,* 273–275.

Monroe, M., & Simons, A. D. (1991). Diathesis-stress theories in the context of life stress research: Implications for the depressive disorders. *Psychological Bulletin, 110,* 406–425.

Morenz, B. & Becker, J. V. (1995). The treatment of youthful sex offenders. *Applied and Preventive Psychology, 4,* 247–256.

Morey, L. C., & Zanarini, M. C. (2000). Borderline personality: Traits and disorder. *Journal of Abnormal Psychology, 109,* 733–737.

Morgan, R. (2002). More male students report body-image and eating problems. *Chronicle of Higher Education, 48,* A53–A54.

Morgenstern, J., Labouvie, E., McCrady, B. S., Kahler, C. W., & Frey, R. M. (1997). Affiliation with Alcoholics Anonymous after treatment: A study of its therapeutic effects and mechanisms of action. *Journal of Consulting and Clinical Psychology, 65,* 768–777.

Morihisa, J. M., Rosse, R. B., Cross, C. D., Balkoski, V., & Ingraham, C. A. (1999). Laboratory and other diagnostic tests in psychiatry. In R. E. Hales, S. C. Yudofsky & J. A. Talbott (Eds.), *Textbook of psychiatry* (pp. 281–316). Washington, DC: American Psychiatric Press.

Morrison, A. P., & Baker, C. A. (2000). Intrusive thoughts and auditory hallucinations: A comparative study of intrusions in psychosis. *Behaviour Research and Therapy, 38,* 1097–1106.

Moser, C., & Levitt, E. E. (1987). An exploratory-descriptive study of a sadomasochistically oriented sample. *Journal of Sex Research, 23,* 322–337.

Moser, G., Wenzel-Abatzi, T-A., Stelzeneder, M., & Wenzel, T. (1998). Globus sensation: Pharngyoesophageal function, psychometric and psychiatric findings, and follow-up in eighty-eight patients. *Archives of Internal Medicine, 158,* 1365–1372.

Mrazek, D. A. (1993). Asthma: Stress, allergies, and the genes. In D. Goleman & J. Gurin (Eds.), *Mind/body medicine* (pp. 193–205). New York: Consumer Reports Books.

Muehleman, T., Pickens, B. K., & Robinson, F. (1985). Informing clients about the limits to confidentiality, risks, and their rights: Is self-disclosure inhibited? *Professional Psychology: Research and Practice, 16,* 385–397.

Mueser, K. T., Sengupta, A., Schooler, N. R., Bellack, A. S., Xie, H., Glick, I. D., & Keith, S. J. (2001). Family treatment and medication dosage reduction in schizophrenia: Effects on patient social functioning, family attitudes, and burden. *Journal of Consulting and Clinical Psychology, 69,* 3–12.

Mukai, T. (1996). Mothers, peers, and perceived pressure to diet among Japanese adolescent girls. *Journal of Research on Adolescence, 6,* 309–324.

Mulder, R. T., Beautrais, A. L., Joyce, P. R., & Fergusson, D. M. (1998). Relationship between dissociation, childhood sexual abuse, childhood physical abuse, and mental illness in a general population sample. *American Journal of Psychiatry, 155,* 806–811.

Mulkens, S. A. N., de Jong, P. J., & Merckelbach, H. (1996). Disgust and spider phobia. *Journal of Abnormal Psychology, 105,* 464–468.

Mullan, M., & Brown, F. (1994). The clinical features of Alzheimer's disease and the search for clinico-aetiologic correlates. In D. Nicholson (Ed.), *Anti-dementia agents: Research and prospects for therapy* (pp. 1–12). San Diego: Academic Press.

Mumford, D. B., Whitehouse, A. M., & Choudry, I. Y. (1992). Survey of eating disorders in English-medium schools in Lehore, Pakistan. *International Journal of Eating Disorders, 11,* 173–184.

Mungadze, J. (1997). Treating dissociative identity disorder: An update. *Treatment Centers Magazine, 9,* 2.

Muris, P., & Merckelbach, H. (2000). How serious are common childhood fears? II. The parent's point of view. *Behaviour Research and Therapy, 38,* 813–818.

Muris, P., Merckelbach, H., & Clavan, M. (1997). Abnormal and normal compulsions. *Behaviour Research and Therapy, 35,* 249–252.

Muris, P., Merckelbach, H. & Collaris, R. (1997). Common childhood fears and their origins. *Behaviour Research and Therapy, 35,* 929–936.

Muris, P., Merckelbach, H., Ollendick, T. H., King, N. J., & Bogie, N. (2001). Children's nighttime fears: Parent-child ratings of frequency, content, origins, coping behaviors and severity. *Behaviour Research and Therapy, 39,* 13–28.

Murphree, O. D., & Dykman, R. A. (1965). Litter patterns in the offspring of nervous and stable dogs: I. Behavioral tests. *Journal of Nervous and Mental Disorders, 141,* 321–332.

Murphy, J. K., Stoney, C. M., Alpert, B. S., & Walker, S. S. (1995). Gender and ethnicity in children's cardiovascular reactivity: Seven years of study. *Health Psychology, 14,* 48–55.

Murray, H. A., & Morgan, H. (1938). *Explorations in personality.* New York: Oxford University Press.

Myers, J. K., Weissman, M. M., Tischler, G. L., Holzer, C. E., Leaf, P. J., Orvaschel, H., Anthony, J. C., Boyd, J. H., Burke, J. D., Kramer, M., & Stoltzman, R. (1984). Six-month prevalence of psychiatric disorders in three communities. *Archives of General Psychiatry, 41,* 959–967.

Mystkowski, J. L. L., Mineka, S., Vernon, L. L., & Zinbarg, R. E. (2003). Changes in caffeine states enhance return of fear in spider phobia. *Journal of Consulting and Clinical Psychology, 71,* 243–250.

Nagin, D. S., & Tremblay, R. E. (2001). Parental and early childhood predictors of persistent physical aggression in boys from kindergarten to high school. *Archives of General Psychiatry, 58,* 389–397.

Nash, J. M. (1997, March 24). Gift of love. *Time,* pp. 81–82.

Nathan, P. E. (1976). Alcoholism. In H. Leitenberg (Ed.), *Handbook of behavior modification and behavior therapy.* Englewood Cliffs, NJ: Prentice-Hall.

Nathan, P. E. (1988). The addictive personality is the behavior of the addict. *Journal of Consulting and Clinical Psychology, 56,* 183–188.

National Association of Anorexia and Associated Disorders. (2003). Facts about eating disorders. Retrieved from http://www.anad.org/site/anadweb

National Center for Health Statistics (1988). *Advance report of final mortality statistics, 1986. NCHS Monthly Vital Statistics Report, 37*(6). Hyattsville, MD: U.S. Public Health Service.

National Center for Health Statistics (1994). Advance report of final mortality statistics, 1991, *Monthly Vital Statistics Report, 42.*

National Center for Health Statistics. (2001a). *Asthma.* Hyattsville, MD: U.S. Department of Health and Human Services.

National Center for Health Statistics. (2001b). *Hypertension.* Hyattsville, MD: U.S. Department of Health and Human Services.

National Council on the Aging. (1998, September, 29). *San Francisco Chronicle,* A4.

National Institute of Mental Health. (1985). *Mental Health: United States, 1985.* Washington, DC: U.S. Government Printing Office.

National Institute of Mental Health. (1995). *Mental illness in America: The National Institute of Mental Health agenda.* Rockville, MD: Author.

National Institute of Mental Health. (1999). *Facts about panic disorder.* Washington, DC: National Institute of Mental Health.

National Institute of Mental Health. (2000). *Anxiety disorders.* Bethesda, MD: U.S. Department of Health and Human Services.

National Institute of Mental Health. (2001). *When someone has schizophrenia.* Washington, DC: U.S. Government Printing Office.

National Institute of Neurological Disorders and Stroke. (2001a). *Autism fact sheet.* Bethesda, MD: National Institutes of Health.

National Institute of Neurological Disorders and Stroke. (2001b). *NINDS headache information fact sheet.* Bethesda, MD: National Institutes of Health.

National Institute on Drug Abuse. (1991). *National household survey on drug abuse: Main findings 1990.* Washington, DC: U.S. Government Printing Office.

National Institutes of Health. (1989). *Report on the expert panel on detection, evaluation, and treatment of high blood cholesterol in adults.* Rockville, MD: Author.

Nelson, C. B., Heath, A. C., & Kessler, R. C. (1998). Temporal progression of alcohol dependence symptoms in the U. S. household population: Results from the National Comorbidity Survey. *Journal of Consulting and Clinical Psychology, 66,* 474–483.

Nelson, K. B., Grether, J. K., Croen, L. A., Dambrosia, J. M., Dickens, B. F., Jelliffe, L. L., Hansen, R. L., & Philips, T. M. (2001). Neuropeptides and neurotrophins in neonatal blood of children with autism or mental retardation. *Annals of Neurology, 49,* 597–606.

Nelson, L. D., & Adams, K. M. (1997). Challenges for neuropsychology in the treatment and rehabilitation of brain-injured patients. *Psychological Assessment, 9,* 368–373.

Nelson-Gray, R. O. (1991). DSM-IV: Empirical guidelines from psychometrics. *Journal of Abnormal Psychology, 100,* 308–315.

Nemeroff, C. B. (1998). Psychopharmacology of affective disorders in the twenty-first century. *Biological Psychiatry, 44,* 517–525.

Neugebauer, R. (1979). Medieval and early modern theories of mental illness. *Archives of General Psychiatry, 36,* 477–483.

Neumark-Sztainer, D., Hannan, P. J., & Stat, M. (2000). Weight-related behaviors among adolescent girls and boys. *Archives of Pediatric Adolescent Medicine, 154,* 569–577.

Nevid, J. S., Fichner-Rathus, L., & Rathus, S. A. (1995). *Human sexuality.* Boston: Allyn & Bacon.

Neziroglu, F., & Yaryura-Tobias, J. A. (1997). A review of cognitive behavioral and pharmacological treatment of body dysmorphic disorder. *Behavior Modification, 21,* 324–340.

Niaura, R. S., Rohsenow, D. J., Binkoff, J. A., Monti, P. M., Pedraza, M., & Abrams, D. B. (1988). Relevance of cue reactivity to understanding alcohol and smoking relapse. *Journal of Abnormal Psychology, 97,* 133–152.

Nicotine: Powerful grip on the brain. (1995, September 22). *Los Angeles Times,* pp. A1, A37.

Nigg, J. T., Lohr, N. E., Westen, D., Gold, L. J., & Silk, K. R. (1992). Malevolent object representations in borderline personality disorder and major depression. *Journal of Abnormal Psychology, 101,* 61–67.

Nisenson, L. G., Berenbaum, H., & Good, T. L. (2001). The development of interpersonal relationships in individuals with schizophrenia. *Psychiatry, 64,* 111–125.

Noble, J., & McConkey, K. M. (1995). Hypnotic sex change: Creating and challenging a delusion in the laboratory. *Journal of Abnormal Psychology, 104,* 69–74.

Nolen-Hoeksema, S. (1987). Sex differences in unipolar depression: Evidence and theory. *Psychological Bulletin, 101,* 259–282.

Nolen-Hoeksema, S., Girgus, J. S., & Seligman, M. E. (1992). Predictors and consequences of childhood depressive symptoms: A 5-year longitudinal study. *Journal of Abnormal Psychology, 101,* 405–422.

Norcross, J. C., & Freedheim, D. K. (1992). Into the future: Retrospect and prospect in psychotherapy. In D. K. Freedheim (Ed.), *History of psychotherapy: A century of change* (pp. 881–900). Washington, DC: American Psychological Association.

Northup, J., & Gulley, V. (2001). Some contributions of functional analysis to the assessment of behaviors associated with ADHD and the effects of stimulant medication. *School Psychology Review, 30,* 227–238.

Norton, P. J., & Hope, D. A. (2001). Analogue observational methods in the assessment of social functioning in adults. *Psychological Assessment, 13,* 59–72.

Noyes, R., Jr., Langbehn, D. R., Happel, R. L., Stout, L. R., et al. (2001). Personality dysfunction among somatizing patients. *Psychosomatics, 42,* 320–329.

Nussbaum, N. L., & Bigler, E. D. (1989). Halstead-Reitan neuropsychological test batteries for children. In C. R. Reynolds & E. Fletcher-Janzen (Eds.), *Handbook of clinical child neuropsychology* (pp. 181–191). New York: Plenum Press.

Nutt, D. J. (2001). Neurobiological mechanisms in generalized anxiety disorder. *Journal of Clinical Psychiatry, 62,* 22–27.

O'Connor, K. (1987). The interaction of hostile and depressive behaviors: A case study of a depressed boy. *Journal of Child and Adolescent Psychotherapy, 3,* 105–108.

O'Connor, T. G., McGuire, S., Reiss, D., Hetherington, E. M., & Plomin, R. (1998). Co-occurrence of depressive symptoms and antisocial behavior in adolescence: A common genetic liability. *Journal of Abnormal Psychology, 107,* 27–37.

Office of National Drug Control Policy. (1998). *1997 national household survey on drug abuse: Selected findings.* Washington, DC: Author.

Ofshe, R. J. (1992). Inadvertent hypnosis during interrogation: False confession due to dissociative state; misidentified multiple personality and the satanic cult hypothesis. *International Journal of Clinical and Experimental Hypnosis, 40,* 125–156.

Ohaeri, J. U., & Odejide, O. A. (1994). Somatization symptoms among patients using primary health care facilities in a rural community in Nigeria. *American Journal of Psychiatry, 151,* 728–731.

Ohayon, M. M. (2004). Prevalence and risk factors on morning headache in the general population. *Archives of Internal Medicine, 164,* 97–103.

Okazaki, S., & Sue, S. (1995). Cultural considerations in psychological assessment of Asian Americans. In J. N. Butcher (Ed.), *Clinical personality assessment: Practical approaches* (pp. 107–119). New York: Oxford University Press.

Oke, N. J., & Schreibman, L. (1990). Training social imitations to a high-functioning autistic child: Assessment of collateral behavior change and generalization in a case study. *Journal of Autism and Developmental Disorders, 20,* 479–497.

Olarte, S. W. (1997). Sexual boundary violations. In *The Hatherleigh guide to ethics in therapy* (pp. 195–209). New York: Hatherleigh Press.

Olfson, M., Lewis-Fernandez, R., Weissman, M. M., Feder, A., et al. (2002). Psychotic symptoms in a urban general medicine practice. *American Journal of Psychiatry, 159,* 1412–1419.

Olivardia, R., Pope, H. G., Mangweth, B., & Hudson, J. I. (1995). Eating disorders in college men. *American Journal of Psychiatry, 152,* 1279–1285.

Oliver, J., Shaller, C. A., Majovski, L. V., & Jacques, S. (1982). Stroke mechanisms: Neuropsychological implications. *Clinical Neuropsychology, 4,* 81–84.

Ollendick, T. H., & King, N. J. (1998). Empirically supported treatments for children with phobic and anxiety disorders: Current status. *Journal of Clinical Child Psychology, 27,* 156–167.

Olmos de Paz, T. (1990). Working-through and insight in child psychoanalysis. *Melanie Kelin and Object Relations, 8,* 99–112.

Oren, D. A., & Rosenthal, N. E. (2001). Light therapy. In G. O. Gabbard (Ed.), *Treatment of psychiatric disorders* (pp. 1295–1306). Washington, DC: American Psychiatric Press.

Orr, S. P., Lasko, N. B., Shalev, A. Y., & Pitman, R. K. (1995). Physiologic responses to loud tones in Vietnam veterans with posttraumatic stress disorder. *Journal of Abnormal Psychology, 104,* 75–82.

Osbourne, L. (2001, May 6). Regional disturbances. *New York Times Magazine,* pp. 6–14.

Öst, L.-G. (1987). Age of onset in different phobias. *Journal of Abnormal Psychology, 96,* 223–229.

Öst, L.-G. (1992). Blood and injection phobia: Background and cognitive, physiological, and behavioral variables. *Journal of Abnormal Psychology, 101,* 68–74.

Öst, L.-G., & Hugdahl, K. (1981). Acquisition of phobias and anxiety response patterns in clinical patients. *Behaviour Research and Therapy, 19,* 439–447.

Öst, L.-G., & Westling, B. E. (1995). Applied relaxation vs. cognitive behavior therapy in the treatment of panic disorder. *Behaviour Research and Therapy, 33,* 145–158.

O'Sullivan, G. A., & Tiggermann, M. (1997). Body dissatisfaction and body image distortion in men who train with weights. *Journal of Gender, Culture, and Health, 2,* 321–329.

Othmer, E., & Othmer, S. C. (1994). *The clinical interview using DSM-IV. Volume 1: Fundamentals.* Washington, DC: American Psychiatric Press.

Otto, M. W., Pollack, M. H., & Sabatino, S. A. (1996). Maintenance of remission following cognitive behavior therapy for panic disorder: Possible deleterious effects of concurrent medication treatment. *Behavior Therapy, 27,* 473–482.

Otto, M. W., Wilhelm, S., Cohen, L. S., & Harlow, B. L. (2001). Prevalence of body dysmorphic disorder in a community sample of women. *American Journal of Psychiatry, 158,* 2061–2063.

Otto, R. K. (1989). Bias and expert testimony of mental health professionals in adversarial proceedings: A preliminary investigation. *Behavioral Science and Law, 7,* 267–273.

Overholser, J. C., & Beck, S. (1986). Multimethod assessment of rapists, child molesters, and three control groups in behavioral and psychological measures. *Journal of Consulting and Clinical Psychology, 54,* 682–687.

Ozer, E. J., Best, S. R., Lipsey, T. L., & Weiss, D. S. (2003). Predictors of posttraumatic stress disorder and symptoms in adults: A meta-analysis. *Psychological Bulletin, 129,* 52–73.

Paley, A.-M. (1988). Growing up in chaos: The dissociative response. *American Journal of Psychoanalysis, 48,* 72–83.

Palfrey, J. S., Levine, M. D., Walker, D. K., & Sullivan, M. (1985). The emergence of attention deficits in early childhood: A prospective study. *Developmental and Behavioral Pediatrics, 6,* 339–348.

Palmer, K. S. (2001, May 10). Colleges start to realize men need body-image help too. *USA Today,* p. A15.

Panagiotopoulos, C., McCrindle, B. W., Hick, K., & Katzman, D. K. (2000). Electrocardiographic findings in adolescents with eating disorders. *Pediatrics, 105,* 1100–1105.

Pantelis, C., Velakoulis, D., McGorry, P. D., Wood, S. J., et al. (2003). Neuroanatomical abnormalities before and after onset of psychosis: A cross-sectional and longitudinal MRI comparison. *Lancet, 361,* 281–291.

Papolos, D., & Papolos, J. (1999). *The bipolar child: The definitive and reassuring guide to childhood's most misunderstood disorder.* New York: Broadway Books.

Parker, S., Nichter, M., Vuckovic, N., Sims, C., & Ritenbaugh, C. (1995). Body image and weight concerns among African-American and White adolescent females: Differences that make a difference. *Human Organization, 54,* 103–114.

Parrott, C. (1998). Treating binge eating disorder. *Counseling Psychology Quarterly, 11,* 265–281.

Paternite, C. E., Loney, J., & Roberts, M. A. (1995). External validation of oppositional disorder and attention deficit disorder with hyperactivity. *Journal of Abnormal Child Psychology, 23,* 453–469.

Patterson, G. R. (1986). Performance models for antisocial boys. *American Psychologist, 41,* 432–444.

Paulson, T. (1999, May 11). UW team joins study of autism treatment: Story of hormone secretin is like "Lorenzo's Oil." *Seattle Post Intelligencer,* p. C1, 3, 5.

Payne, R. L. (1992). First person account: My schizophrenia. *Schizophrenia Bulletin, 18,* 725–728.

Penava, S. J., Otto, M. W., Maki, K. M., & Pollack, M. H. (1998). Rate of improvement during cognitive-behavioral group treatment for panic disorder. *Behaviour Research and Therapy, 36,* 665–673.

Pendery, M. L., Maltzman, I. M., & West, L. J. (1982). Controlled drinking by alcoholics? New findings and a reevaluation of a major affirmative study. *Science, 217,* 169–175.

Penninx, B. W. J. H., Beekman, A. T. F., Honig, A., Deeg, D. J. H., et al. (2001). Depression and cardiac mortality: Results from a community-based longitudinal study. *Archives of General Psychiatry, 58,* 221–227.

Perner, L. E. (2001, August). Literal detours: Propositions on abstraction in high functioning autistic individuals. Paper presented at the meeting of the American Psychological Association, San Francisco.

Perris, C. (1966). A study of bipolar (manic-depressive) and unipolar recurrent depressive psychosis. *Acta Psychiatrica Scandinavica* (Suppl. 194).

Perry, J. C. (2001). Dependent personality disorder. In G. O. Gabbard (Ed.), *Treatment of psychiatric disorders* (pp. 2353–2368). Washington, DC: American Psychiatric Press.

Persons, J. B. (1986). The advantages of studying psychological phenomena rather than psychiatric diagnosis. *American Psychologist, 41,* 1252–1260.

Petersen, A. C., Compas, B. E., Brooks-Gunn, J., Stemmler, M., Ey, S., & Grant, K. E. (1993). Depression in adolescence. *American Psychologist, 48,* 155–168.

Petersen, L., & Brown, D. (1994). Integrating child injury and abuse-neglect research: Common histories, etiologies, and solutions. *Psychological Bulletin, 116,* 293–315.

Petry, N. M., Martin, B., Cooney, J. L., & Kranzler, H. R. (2000). Give them prizes, and they will come: Contingency management for treatment of alcohol dependence. *Journal of Consulting and Clinical Psychology, 68,* 250–257.

Peveler, R. (1998). Understanding medically unexplained physical symptoms: Faster progress in the next century than in this? *Journal of Psychosomatic Research, 45,* 93–97.

Pfuhlmann, B., & Stober, G. (1997). The importance of differentiated psychopathology of catatonia. *Acta Psychiatrica Scandinavia, 95,* 357–359.

Phillips, D. P., Todd, E. R., & Wagner, L. M. (1993). Psychology and survival. *Lancet, 342,* 1142–1145.

Phillips, K. A., & Gunderson, J. G. (1999). Personality disorders. In R. E. Hales, S. C. Yudofsky & J. A. Talbott (Eds.), *Textbook of psychiatry* (pp. 795–823). Washington, DC: American Psychiatric Press.

Phillips, K. A., McElroy, S. L., Dwight, M. M., Eisen, J. L., & Rasmussen, S. A. (2001). Delusionality and response to open-label fluvoxamine in body dysmorphic disorder. *Journal of Clinical Psychiatry, 62,* 87–91.

Phillips, K. A., McElroy, S. L., Keck, P. E., Pope, H. G., Jr., & Hudson, J. I. (1993). Body dysmorphic disorder: Thirty cases of imagined ugliness. *American Journal of Psychiatry, 150,* 302–308.

Piacentini, J., Gitow, A., Jaffer, M., Graael, F., & Whitaker, A. (1994). Outpatient behavioral treatment of child and adolescent obsessive-compulsive disorder. *Journal of Anxiety Disorders, 8,* 277–289.

Pigott, T. A. (1996). OCD: Where the serotonin selectivity story begins. *Journal of Clinical Psychiatry, 57,* 11–20.

Pike, J. L., Smith, T. L., Hauger, R. L., Nicassio, P. M., Patterson, T. L., McClintick, J., Costlow, C., & Irwin, M. R. (1997). Chronic life stress alters sympathetic, neuroendocrine, and immune responsivity to an acute psychological stressor in humans. *Psychosomatic Medicine, 59,* 447–457.

Pike, K. M., Dohn, F.-A., Streigel-Moore, R., Wilfley, D. E., & Fairburn, C. G. (2001). A comparison of black and white women with binge eating disorder. *American Journal of Psychiatry, 158,* 1455–1461.

Pilisuk, M. (1975). The legacy of the Vietnam veteran. *Journal of Social Issues, 31*(4), 3–12.

Plienis, A. J., Hansen, D. J., Ford, F., Smith, S., Jr., Stark, L. J., & Kelly, J. A. (1987). Behavioral small group training to improve the social skills of emotionally-disordered adolescents. *Behavior Therapy, 18,* 17–32.

Plomin, R., Owen, M. J., & McGuffin, P. (1994). The genetic basis of complex human behaviors. *Science, 264,* 1733–1739.

Polivy, J., Schueneman, A. L., & Carlson, K. (1976). Alcohol and tension reduction: Cognitive and physiological effects. *Journal of Abnormal Psychology, 85,* 595–600.

Ponterotto, J. G., & Casas, J. M. (1991). *Handbook of racial/ethnic minority counseling research.* Springfield, IL: Thomas.

Poon, L. W., & Siegler, I. C. (1991). Psychological aspects of normal aging. In J. Sadavoy, L. W. Lazarus, & L. F. Jarvik (Eds.), *Comprehensive review of geriatric psychiatry* (pp. 117–145). Washington, DC: American Psychiatric Press.

Pope, H. G., Jr., Gruber, A. J., Mangweth, B., Bureau, B., et al. (2000). Body image perception among men in three countries. *American Journal of Psychiatry, 157,* 1297–1301.

Pope, H. G., Jr., & Hudson, J. I. (1992). Is childhood sexual abuse a risk factor for bulimia nervosa? *American Journal of Psychiatry, 149,* 455–463.

Pope, H. G., Jr., Mangweth, B., Negrao, A. B., Hudson, J. I., & Cordas, T. A. (1994). Childhood sexual abuse and bulimia nervosa: A comparison of American, Austrian, and Brazilian women. *American Journal of Psychiatry, 151,* 732–737.

Pope, H. G., Jr., Oliva, P. S., Hudson, J. I., Bodkin, J. A., & Gruber, A. J. (1999). Attitudes toward DSM-IV dissociative disorders diagnoses among board-certified American psychiatrists. *American Journal of Psychiatry, 156,* 321–323.

Pope, H. G., Jr., Olivardia, R., Borowiecki, J. J., III, & Cohane, G. H. (2001). The growing commercial value of the male body: A longitudinal survey of advertising in women's magazines. *Psychotherapy and Psychosomatics, 70,* 189–193.

Pope, K. S. (1988). How clients are harmed by sexual contact with mental health professionals: The syndrome and its prevalence. *Journal of Counseling and Development, 67,* 222–226.

Pope, K. S., & Tabachnick, B. G. (1993). Therapists' anger, hate, fear, and sexual feelings: National survey of therapist responses, client characteristics, critical events, formal complaints, and training. *Professional Psychology: Research and Practice, 24,* 142–152.

Pope, K. S., Tabachnick, B. G., & Keith-Spiegel, P. (1987). Ethics of practice: The beliefs and behaviors of psychologists as therapists. *American Psychologist, 42,* 993–1166.

Pope, K. S., & Vetter, V. A. (1991). Prior therapist-patient sexual involvement among patients seen by psychologists. *Psychotherapy, 28,* 429–438.

Popper, C., & West, S. A. (1999). Disorders usually first diagnosed in infancy, childhood, or adolescence. In R. E. Hales, S. C. Yudofsky & J. A. Talbott (Eds.), *Textbook of psychiatry* (pp. 825–954). Washington, DC: American Psychiatric Press.

Poulton, R., Trainor, P., Stanton, W., McGee, R., Davies, S., & Silva, P. (1997). The (in)stability of adolescent fears. *Behaviour Research and Therapy, 35,* 159–163.

Poulton, R., Waldie, K. E., Craske, M. G., Menzies, R. G., & McGee, R. (2000). Dishabituation processes in height fear and dental fear: An indirect test of the non-associative model of fear acquisition. *Behaviour Research and Therapy, 38,* 909–919.

Poulton, R., Waldie, K. E., Menzies, R. G., Craske, M. G., & Silva, P. A. (2001). Failure to overcome "innate" fear: A developmental test of the non-associative model of fear acquisition. *Behaviour Research and Therapy, 39,* 375–387.

Pound, E. J. (1987). Children and prematurity. In A. Thomas & J. Grimes (Eds.), *Children's needs: Psychological perspectives* (pp. 441–450). Washington, DC: National Association of School Psychologists.

Powell, D. H., & Whitla, D. K. (1994). Normal cognitive aging: Toward empirical perspectives. *Current Directions in Psychological Science, 3,* 27–31.

Powell, J. (1998). First-person account: Paranoid schizophrenia—a daughter's story. *Schizophrenia Bulletin, 24,* 175–177.

President's New Freedom Commission on Mental Health. (2003). *Achieving the promise: Transforming mental health care in America* (Report of the President's New Freedom Commission on Mental Health). Retrieved April 28, 2004, from http://www.mentalhealthcommission.gov/reports/FinalReport/toc.html

Prichard, J. C. (1837). *Treatise on insanity and other disorders affecting the mind.* Philadelphia: Haswell, Barrington & Haswell.

Prigatano, G. P., Fordyce, D. J., Zeiner, H. K., Roueche, J. R., Pepping, M., & Wood, B. C. (1984). Neuropsychological rehabilitation after closed head injury in young adults. *Journal of Neurology and Neuropsychology, 47,* 505–513.

Pueschel, S. M. (1991). Ethical considerations relating to prenatal diagnosis of fetuses with Down syndrome. *Mental Retardation, 29,* 185–190.

Pull, C. B. (2004). Binge eating disorder. *Current Opinion in Psychiatry, 17,* 43–48.

Quay, H. C. (1965). Psychopathic personality as pathological stimulation seeking. *American Journal of Psychiatry, 122,* 180–183.

Rabatin, J., & Keltz, L. B. (2002). Generalized anxiety and panic disorder. *Western Journal of Medicine, 176,* 164–169.

Rachman, S., & DeSilva, P. (1987). Abnormal and normal obsessions. *Behaviour Research and Therapy, 16,* 233–248.

Radloff, L. S., & Rae, D. S. (1981). The components of the sex difference in depression. In R. G. Simmons (Ed.), *Research in community and mental health* (Vol. 2). Greenwood, CT: JAI Press.

Rahe, R. H. (1994). The more things change . . . *Psychosomatic Medicine, 56,* 306–307.

Ramer, J. C., & Miller, G. (1992). Overview of mental retardation. In G. Miller & J. C. Ramer (Eds.), *Static encephalopathies of infancy and childhood* (pp. 1–10). New York: Raven Press.

Ranchor, A. V., Sanderman, R., Bouma, J., Buunk, B. P., & van den Heuvel, W. J. (1997). An exploration of the relation between hostility and disease. *Journal of Behavioral Medicine, 20,* 223–240.

Rand, C., & Kuldau, J. (1990). The epidemiology of obesity and self-defined weight problem in the general population: Gender, race, age, and social class. *International Journal of Eating Disorders, 9,* 329–343.

Rapee, R. M. (1995). Psychological factors influencing the affective response to biological challenge procedures in panic disorder. *Journal of Anxiety Disorders, 9,* 59–74.

Rassin, E., Muris, P., Schmidt, H., & Merckelbach, H. (2000). Relationships between thought-action fusion, thought suppression and obsessive-compulsive symptoms: A structural equation modeling approach. *Behaviour Research and Therapy, 38,* 889–897.

Ratey, J. J., Grandin, T., & Miller, A. (1992). Defense behavior and coping in an autistic savant: The story of Temple Grandin, PhD. *Psychiatry, 55,* 382–391.

Read, J. P., Kahler, C. W., & Stevenson, J. F. (2001). Bridging the gap between alcoholism treatment research and practice: Identifying what works and why. *Professional Psychology: Research and Practice, 32,* 227–238.

Read, S. (1991). The dementias. In J. Sadavoy, L. W. Lazarus, & L. F. Jarvik (Eds.), *Comprehensive review of geriatric psychiatry* (pp. 287–309). Washington, DC: American Psychiatric Press.

Rechlin, T., Loew, T. H., & Joraschky, P. (1997). Pseudoseizure "status." *Journal of Psychosomatic Research, 42,* 495–498.

Reed, G. M., Levant, R. F., Stout, C. E., Murphy, M. J., & Phelps, R. (2001). Psychology in the current mental health marketplace. *Professional Psychology: Research and Practice, 32*(1), 65–70.

Regier, D. A., Boyd, J. H., Burke, J. D., Rae, D. S., Myers, J. K., Kramer, M., Robins, L. N., George, L. K., Karno, M., & Locke, B. Z. (1988). One-month prevalence of mental disorders in the U.S.: Based on five Epidemiologic Catchment Area (ECA) sites. *Archives of General Psychiatry, 45,* 977–986.

Regier, D. A., Narrow, W. E., Rae, D. S., Manderscheid, R. W., Locke, B. Z., & Goodwin, F. K. (1993). The de facto U.S. Mental and Addictive Disorders Service System: Epidemiologic Catchment Area prospective one-year prevalence rates of disorders in services. *Archives of General Psychiatry, 50,* 85–94.

Reich, J. (1987). Sex distribution of DSM-III personality disorders in psychiatric outpatients. *American Journal of Psychiatry, 144,* 485–488.

Reid, W. H. (1981). The antisocial personality and related symptoms. In J. R. Lion (Ed.), *Personality disorders: Diagnosis and management.* Baltimore: Williams & Wilkins.

Reid, W. H., & Mason, M. (1998). Psychiatric hospital utilization in patients treated with clozapine for up to 4.5 years in a state mental health care system. *Journal of Clinical Psychiatry, 59,* 189–194.

Reisberg, B., Ferris, S. H., Crook, T. (1982). Signs, symptoms, and course of age-associated cognitive decline. In S. Corkin, K. L. Davis, J. H. Growdon, E. Usdin, & R. J. Wurtman (Eds.), *Alzheimer's disease: A report of progress.* New York: Raven Press.

Reiser, D. E. (1988). The psychiatric interview. In H. H. Goldman (Ed.), *Review of general psychiatry* (pp. 184–192). Norwalk, CT: Appleton & Lange.

Repressed memory claims expected to soar. (1995, May). *National Psychologist, 4,* 3.

Reus, V. I. (1988). Affective disorders. In H. H. Goldman (Ed.), *Review of general psychiatry* (pp. 332–348). Norwalk, CT: Appleton & Lange.

Rhee, S. H., Waldman, I. D., Hay, D. A., & Levy, F. (1999). Sex differences in genetic and environmental influences in DSM-III-R ADHD. *Journal of Abnormal Psychology, 108,* 24–41.

Ricca, V., Mannucci, E., Zucchi, T., Rotella, C. M., & Faravelli, C. (2000). Cognitive-behavioral therapy for bulimia nervosa and binge eating disorder: A review. *Psychotherapy and Psychosomatics, 69,* 287–295.

Richards, J. C., Alvarenga, M., & Hoff, A. (2000). Serum lipids and their relationships with hostility and angry affect and behaviors in men. *Health Psychology, 19,* 393–398.

Richardson, L. F. (1998). Psychogenic dissociation in childhood: The role of the counseling psychologist. *Counseling Psychologist, 26,* 69-100.

Rickels, K., & Schweizer, E. (1997). The clinical presentation of generalized anxiety in primary-care settings: Practical concepts of classification and management. *Journal of Clinical Psychology, 58,* 4–9.

Ridley, C. R. (1995). *Overcoming unintentional racism in counseling and therapy: A practitioner's guide to intentional intervention.* Thousand Oaks, CA: Sage.

Rietveld, S., Everaerd, W., & van Beest, I. (2000). Excessive breathlessness through emotional imagery in asthma. *Behaviour Research and Therapy, 38,* 1005–1014.

Rietveld, S., van Beest, I., & Everaerd, W. (2000). Psychological confounds in medical research: The example of excessive cough in asthma. *Behaviour Research and Therapy, 38,* 791–800.

Rimland, B. (2000, October). Secretin: New studies reveal GI effects; which autistic children benefit? *Autism Research Review International.* Retrieved from http://www.autism.com/ari/secretin.htm.

Risk factors for the onset of eating disorders in adolescent girls: Results of the McKnight longitudinal risk factor study. (2003). *American Journal of Psychiatry, 160,* 248–254.

Riskind, J. H., Moore, R., & Bowley, L. (1995). The looming of spiders: The fearful perceptual distortion of movement and menace. *Behaviour Research and Therapy, 33,* 171–178.

Ritvo, E. R., Freeman, B. J., Yuwiler, A., Geller, E., Yokota, A., Schroth, P., & Novak, P. (1984). Study of fenfluramine in outpatients with the syndrome of autism. *Journal of Pediatrics, 105,* 823–828.

Ritvo, E. R., Jorde, L. B., Mason-Brothers, A., Freeman, B. J., Pingree, C., Jones, M. B., McMahon, W. M., Petersen, B., Jenson, W. R., & Mo, A. (1989). The UCLA–University of Utah epidemiologic survey of autism: Recurrent risk estimates and genetic counseling. *American Journal of Psychiatry, 146,* 1032–1036.

Rivas-Vazquez, R. A. (2001). Cholinesterase inhibitors: Current pharmacological treatments for Alzheimer's disease. *Professional Psychology: Research and Practice, 32,* 433–436.

Rivas-Vazquez, R. A., & Blais, M. A. (1997). Selective serotonin reuptake inhibitors and atypical antidepressants: A review and update for psychologists. *Professional Psychology: Research and Practice, 28,* 526–536.

Rivas-Vazquez, R. A., Blais, M. A., Rey, G. J., & Rivas-Vazquez, A. A. (2000). Atypical antipsychotic medications: Pharmacological profiles and psychological implications. *Professional Psychology: Research and Practice, 31,* 628–640.

Roberto, L. (1983). Issues in diagnosis and treatment of transsexualism. *Archives of Sexual Behavior, 12,* 445–473.

Roberts, W. (1995). Postvention and psychological autopsy in the suicide of a 14-year-old public school student. *School Counselor, 42,* 322–330.

Robins, L. N. (1991). Conduct disorder. *Journal of Child Psychology and Psychiatry, 32,* 193–212.

Robins, L. N., Helzer, J. E., Weisinann, M. M., Orvaschel, H., Gruenberg, E., Burke, J. D., & Regier, D. A. (1984). Lifetime prevalence of specific psychiatric disorders in three sites. *Archives of General Psychiatry, 41,* 949–958.

Robins, L. N., Locke, B. Z., & Regier, D. A. (1991). An overview of psychiatric disorders in America. In L. N. Robins & D. A. Regier (Eds.), *Psychiatric disorders in America: The Epidemiologic Catchment Area study* (pp. 328–366). New York: Free Press.

Robins, L. N., & Regier, D. A. (Eds.) (1991). *Psychiatric disorders in America: The Epidemiologic Catchment Area study.* New York: Free Press.

Robins, L. N., Tipp, J., & Przybeck, T. (1991). Antisocial personality. In L. N. Robins & D. A. Regier (Eds.), *Psychiatric disorders in America: The Epidemiologic Catchment Area study* (pp. 258–290). New York: Free Press.

Robinson, J. P., Shaver, P. R., & Wrightsman, L. S. (Eds.). (1991). *Measures of personality and social psychological attitudes.* San Diego, CA: Academic Press.

Rogers, C. R. (1951). *Client-centered therapy.* Boston: Houghton Mifflin.

Rogers, C. R. (1959). A theory of therapy, personality, and interpersonal relationships, as developed in client-centered framework. In S. Koch (Ed.), *Psychology: A study of science* (Vol. 3). New York: McGraw-Hill.

Rogers, C. R. (1961). *On becoming a person.* Boston: Houghton Mifflin.

Rogers, C. R. (1987). The underlying theory: Drawn from experiences with individuals and groups. *Counseling and Values, 32,* 38–45.

Rogers, J. R. (1992). Suicide and alcohol: Conceptualizing the relationship from a cognitive-social paradigm. *Journal of Counseling and Development, 70,* 540–543.

Rogers, R. L., & Petrie, T. A. (2001). Psychological correlates of anorexic and bulimic symptomatology. *Journal of Counseling and Development, 79,* 178–187.

Rohsenow, D. J., Monti, P. M., Hutchinson, K. E., Swift, R. M., Colby, S. M., & Kaplan, G. B. (2000). Naltrexone's effects on reactivity to alcohol cues among alcoholic men. *Journal of Abnormal Psychology, 109,* 738–742.

Rollason, D. H., Jr. (1995). Clinical asthma: Fundamental concepts of diagnosis and treatment. *Physician Assistant,* Supplement, 3–15.

Root, M. P. (1990). Disordered eating in women of color. *Sex Roles, 22,* 525–536.

Root, M. P. (1996). *The multiracial experience.* Thousand Oaks, CA: Sage.

Root, R. W., II, & Resnick, R. J. (2003). An update on the diagnosis and treatment of attention-deficit/hyperactivity disorder. *Professional Psychology: Research and Practice, 34*(1), 34–41.

Rosen, J. C., Reiter, J., & Orosan, P. (1995). Assessment of body image in eating disorders with the body dysmorphic disorder examination. *Behaviour Research and Therapy, 33,* 77–84.

Rosen, R. C., & Leiblum, S. R. (1987). Current approaches to the evaluation of sexual desire disorders. *Journal of Sex Research, 23,* 141–162.

Rosen, R. C., & Leiblum, S. R. (1995). Hypoactive sexual desire. *Psychiatric Clinics of North America, 13,* 107–121.

Rosenfarb, I. S., Goldstein, M. J., Mintz, J., & Nuechterlein, K. H. (1995). Expressed emotion and subclinical psychopathology observable within the transactions between schizophrenic patients and their family members. *Journal of Abnormal Psychology, 104,* 259–267.

Rosenfield, A. H. (1985). Discovering and dealing with deviant sex. *Psychology Today, 19,* 8–10.

Rosenstreich, D. L., Eggleston, P., & Kattan, M. (1997). The role of cockroach allergy and exposure to cockroach allergen in causing morbidity among inner-city children with asthma. *New England Journal of Medicine, 336,* 1356–1363.

Rosenthal, D. (1970). *Genetic theory and abnormal behavior.* New York: McGraw-Hill.

Rosenthal, D. (1971). *Genetics of psychopathology.* New York: McGraw-Hill.

Roth, R. M., Flashman, L. A., Saykin, A. J., McAllister, T. W., & Vidaver, R. (2004). Apathy in schizophrenia: Reduced frontal lobe volume and neuropsychological deficits. *American Journal of Psychiatry, 161,* 157–161.

Royce, J. M., Lazar, I., & Darlington, R. B. (1983). Minority families, early education, and later life changes. *American Journal of Orthopsychiatry, 53,* 706–720.

Rubinstein, M., Yaeger, C. A., Goodstein, C., & Lewis, D. O. (1993). Sexually assaultive male juveniles: A follow-up. *American Journal of Psychiatry, 150,* 262–265.

Ruscio, J., & Ruscio, A. M. (2000). Informing the continuity controversy: A taxometric analysis of depression. *Journal of Abnormal Psychology, 109,* 473–487.

Rutter, M. (1994). Debate and argument: There are connections between brain and mind and it is important that Rett syndrome be classified somewhere. *Journal of Child Psychology and Psychiatry, 35,* 379–381.

Rutter, M., MacDonald, H., LeCouteur, A., Harrington, R., Bolton, P., & Bailey, A. (1990). Genetic factors in child psychiatric disorders–II. Empirical findings. *Journal of Child Psychology and Psychiatry, 31,* 39–83.

Rutter, M. L. (1997). Nature-nurture integration: The example of antisocial behavior. *Journal of the American Psychological Association, 52,* 390–398.

Sable, P. (1997). Attachment, detachment, and borderline personality disorder. *Journal of Psychotherapy, 34,* 171–181.

Sachdev, P., & Loneragan, C. (1991). The present status of akathisia. *Journal of Nervous and Mental Disease, 179,* 381–391.

Sadovsky, R. (1998). Evaluation of patients with transient global amnesia. *American Family Physician, 57,* 2237–2238.

Saklofske, D. H., Hildebrand, D. K., & Gorsuch, R. L. (2000). Replication of the factor structure of the Wechsler Adult Intelligence Scale—Third Edition with a Canadian sample. *Psychological Assessment, 12,* 436–439.

Salaberria, K., & Echeburua, E. (1998). Long-term outcome of cognitive therapy's contributions to self-exposure in vivo to the treatment of generalized social phobia. *Behavior Modification, 22,* 262–284.

Salovey, P., Rothman, A. J., Detweiler, J. B., & Steward, W. T. (2000). Emotional state and physical health. *American Psychologist, 55,* 110–121.

Salyer, S. J. (1997, February 25). Virtual reality therapy shrinks fear of spiders away. *Bellingham Herald,* pp. C1–C2.

Samuda, R. (1998). *Psychological testing of American minorities.* Thousand Oaks, CA: Sage.

Sanders, A. R., & Gejman, P. V. (2001). Influential ideas and experimental progress in schizophrenia genetics research. *Journal of the American Medical Association, 285,* 2831–2833.

Sarbin, T. R. (1997). On the futility of psychiatric diagnostic manuals (DSMs) and the return of personal agency. *Journal of Applied and Preventative Psychology, 6,* 233–244.

Satterfield, J. H., Hoppe, C. M., & Schell, A. M. (1982). A prospective study of delinquency in 110 adolescent boys with attention deficit disorder and 88 normal adolescent boys. *American Journal of Psychiatry, 139,* 795–798.

Sawchuk, C. N., Lohr, J. M., Tolin, D. F., Lee, T. C., & Kleinknecht, R. A. (2000). Disgust sensitivity and contamination fears in spider and blood-injection-injury phobias. *Behaviour Research and Therapy, 38,* 753–762.

Saxena, S., Winograd, A., Dunkin, J. J., Maidment, K., et al. (2001). A retrospective review of clinical characteristics and treatment response in body dysmorphic versus obsessive-compulsive disorder. *Journal of Clinical Psychiatry, 62,* 67–72.

Saywitz, K. J., Mannarino, A. P., Berliner, L., & Cohen, J. A. (2000). Treatment for sexually abused children and adolescents. *American Psychologist, 55,* 1040–1049.

Sbordone, R. J., & Jennison, J. H. (1983). A comparison of the OBD-168 and MMPI to assess the emotional adjustment of traumatic brain-injured inpatients to their cognitive deficits. *Clinical Neuropsychology, 5,* 87–88.

Schacht, T. E. (1985). DSM-III and the politics of truth. *American Psychologist, 40,* 513–521.

Schacht, T. E., & Nathan, P. E. (1977). But is it good for the psychologists? Appraisal and status of DSM-III. *American Psychologist, 32,* 1017–1025.

Schachter, S., & Latane, B. (1964). Crime, cognition, and the autonomic nervous system. *Nebraska Symposium on Motivation, 12,* 221–274.

Schafer, J., & Brown, S. A. (1991). Marijuana and cocaine effect expectancies and drug use patterns. *Journal of Consulting and Clinical Psychology, 59,* 558–565.

Schaffer, D., Fisher, P., Dulcan, M. K., Davies, M., Piacentini, J., Schwab-Stone, M. E., Lahey, B. B., Bourdon, K., Jensen, P. S., Bird, H. R., Canino, G., & Regier, D. (1996). The NIMH Diagnostic Interview for Children Version 2.3: Description, acceptability, prevalence rates and performance in the MECA study methods for the epidemiology of child and adolescent mental health disorders study. *Journal of the American Academy of Child and Adolescent Psychiatry, 35,* 865–877.

Schalock, R. L. (1998). Traumatic brain injury: Implications for practice. *Applied and Preventative Psychology, 7,* 247–253.

Schiavi, R. C. (1990). Sexuality and aging in men. *Annual Review of Sex Research, 1,* 227–249.

Schiavi, R. C. & Segraves, R. T. (1995). The biology of sexual dysfunction. *Psychiatric Clinics of North America, 18,* 7–23.

Schmauk, F. J. (1970). Punishment, arousal, and avoidance learning. *Journal of Abnormal Psychology, 76,* 325–335.

Schmeck, K., & Poustka, F. (2001). Temperament and disruptive behavior disorder. *Psychopathology, 34,* 159–164.

Schmidt, N. B., & Harrington, P. (1995). Cognitive-behavioral treatment of body dysmorphic disorder: A case report. *Journal of Behavior Therapy and Experimental Psychiatry, 26,* 161–167.

Schmidt, N. B., Lerew, D. R., & Trakowski, J. H. (1997). Body vigilance in panic disorder: Evaluating attention to bodily perturbations. *Journal of Consulting and Clinical Psychology, 65,* 214–220.

Schover, L. R., Friedman, J. M., Weiler, S. J., Heiman, J. R., & Lo-Piccolo, J. (1982). Multiaxial problem-oriented system for sexual dysfunctions. *Archives of General Psychiatry, 39,* 614–619.

Schreiber, F. R. (1973). *Sybil.* Chicago: Regnery.

Schreiber, J. L., Breier, A., & Pickar, D. (1995). Expressed emotion: Trait or state? *British Journal of Psychiatry, 166,* 647–649.

Schuckit, M. A. (1994). A clinical model of genetic influences in alcohol dependence. *Journal of Studies on Alcohol, 55,* 5–17.

Schuell, H. (1974). *Aphasia theory and therapy: Selected lectures and papers of Hildred Schuell.* Baltimore: University Park Press.

Schulman, S. L., Collish, Y., von Zuben, F. C., & Kodman-Jones, C. (2000). Effectiveness of treatments for nocturnal enuresis in a heterogeneous population. *Clinical Pediatrics, 39,* 359–364.

Schulsinger, F. (1972). Psychopathy: Heredity and environment. *International Journal of Mental Health, 1,* 190–206.

Schulz, R., Bookwala, J., Knapp, J. E., Scheier, M., & Williamson, G. M. (1996). Pessimism, age, and cancer mortality. *Psychology and Aging, 11,* 304–309.

Schwartz, B. S., Stewart, W. F., Simon, D., & Lipton, R. B. (1998). Epidemiology of tension-type headache. *Journal of the American Medical Association, 279,* 381–383.

Schwartz, L., Slater, M. A., & Birchler, G. R. (1994). Interpersonal stress and pain behaviors in patients with chronic pain. *Journal of Consulting and Clinical Psychology, 62,* 861–864.

Scroppo, J. C., Drob, S. L., Weinberger, J. L., & Eagle, P. (1998). Identifying dissociative identity disorder: A self-report and projective study. *Journal of Abnormal Psychology, 107,* 272–284.

Segraves, R. T., Schoenberg, H. W., & Ivanoff, J. (1983). Serum testosterone and prolactin levels in erectile dysfunction. *Journal of Sex and Marital Therapy, 9,* 19–26.

Seligman, M. E. P. (1971). Phobias and preparedness. *Behavior Therapy, 2,* 307–320.

Seligman, M. E. P. (1975). *Helplessness.* San Francisco: Freeman.

Seligman, M. E. P. (1987). Stop blaming yourself. *Psychology Today, 21,* 30–32, 34, 36–39.

Selvin, I. P. (1993). The incidence and prevalence of sexual dysfunctions. *Archives of Sexual Behavior, 19,* 389–408.

Selye, H. (1956). *The stress of life.* New York: McGraw-Hill.

Selye, H. (1982). Stress: Eustress, distress, and human perspectives. In S. B. Day (Ed.), *Life stress* (pp. 3–13). New York: Van Nostrand Reinhold.

Semans, J. H. (1956). Premature ejaculation: A new approach. *Southern Medical Journal, 49,* 353–357.

Sexton, T. L., Alexander, J. F., & Mease, A. L. (2004). Levels of evidence for the models and mechanisms of therapeutic change in family and couple therapy. In M.J. Lambert (Ed.), *Bergin and Garfield's handbook of psychotherapy and behavior change* (5th ed., pp. 590–646). New York: Wiley.

Shafran, R., Booth, R., & Rachman, S. (1993). The reduction of claustrophobia—II: Cognitive analysis. *Behaviour Research and Therapy, 31,* 75–85.

Shaibani, A., & Sabbagh, M. N. (1998). Pseudoneurologic syndromes: Recognition and diagnosis. *American Family Physician, 57,* 2485–2494.

Shalev, A. Y., Freedman, S., Peri, T. & Brandes, D. (1998). Prospective study of posttraumatic stress disorder and depression following trauma. *American Journal of Psychiatry, 155,* 630–637.

Shapiro, D. L. (1984). *Psychological evaluation and expert testimony.* New York: Van Nostrand Reinhold.

Shapiro, J. P. (1991). Interviewing children about psychological issues associated with sexual abuse. *Psychotherapy, 28,* 55–65.

Shapiro, M. K. (1991). Bandaging a "broken heart:" Hypnoplay therapy in the treatment of multiple personality disorder. *American Journal of Clinical Hypnosis, 34,* 1–9.

Sharma, V., Murthy, S., Kumar, K., Agarwal, M., & Wilkinson, G. (1998). Comparison of people with schizophrenia from Liverpool, England and Sakalwara-Bangalore, India. *International Journal of Social Psychiatry, 44,* 225–230.

Sher, K. J., & Trull, T. J. (1994). Personality and disinhibitory psychopathology: Alcoholism and antisocial personality disorder. *Journal of Abnormal Psychology, 103,* 92–102.

Sherman, C. (1993). Behind closed doors: Therapist-client sex. *Psychology Today, 26*(3), 64–72.

Sherwood, N. E., Harnack, L., & Story, M. (2000). Weight-loss practices, nutrition beliefs, and weight-loss program preferences of urban American Indian women. *Journal of the American Dietetic Association, 100,* 442–446.

Shimamura, A. P., Berry, J. M., Mangels, J. A., Rusting, C. L., & Jurica, P. J. (1995). Memory and cognitive abilities in university professors: Evidence for successful aging. *Psychological Science, 6,* 271–277.

Shisslak, C. M., Pazda, S. L., & Crago, M. (1990). Body weight and bulimia as discriminators of psychological characteristics among anorexic, bulimic, and obese women. *Journal of Abnormal Psychology, 99,* 380–384.

Shiver, M. D., Allen, K. D., & Mathews, R. (1999). Introduction to the mini-series: Assessment and treatment of children with autism in the schools. *School Psychology Review, 28,* 535–537.

Shnek, Z. M., Irvine, J., Stewart, D., & Abbey, S. (2001). Psychological factors and depressive symptoms in ischemic heart disease. *Health Psychology, 20,* 141–145.

Shouldice, A., & Stevenson-Hinde, J. (1992). Coping with security distress: The Separation Anxiety Test and attachment classification at 4.5 years. *Journal of Child Psychology and Psychiatry, 33,* 331–348.

Shulman, C., Yirmiya, N., & Greenbaum, C. W. (1995). From categorization to classification: A comparison among individuals with autism, mental retardation, and normal development. *Journal of Abnormal Psychology, 104,* 601–609.

Shusta, S. R. (1999). Successful treatment of refractory obsessive-compulsive disorder. *American Journal of Psychotherapy, 53,* 377–391.

Siegel, B. (2003). *Helping children with autism learn.* New York: Oxford University Press.

Siegel, M. (1979). Privacy, ethics, and confidentiality. *Professional Psychology, 10,* 249–258.

Siegel, R. A. (1978). Probability of punishment and suppression of behavior in psychopathic and nonpsychopathic offenders. *Journal of Abnormal Psychology, 87,* 514–522.

Siever, L. J. (1981). Schizoid and schizotypal personality disorders. In J. R. Lion (Ed.), *Personality disorders: Diagnosis and management.* Baltimore: Williams & Wilkins.

Silberstein, S. D. (1998). *Migraine and other headaches: A patient's guide to treatment.* Chicago: American Medical Association.

Silva, R. R., Munoz, D. M., Barickman, J., & Friedhoff, A. J. (1995). Environmental factors and related fluctuation of symptoms in children and adolescents with Tourette's disorder. *Journal of Child Psychology and Psychiatry, 36,* 305–312.

Silverman, J. M., Mohs, R. C., Davidson, M., Losonczy, M. F., Keefe, R. S. E., Breitner, J. C. S., Sorokin, J. E., & Davis, K. L. (1987). Familial schizophrenia and treatment response. *American Journal of Psychiatry, 144,* 1271–1276.

Silverstein, B., & Perdue, L. (1988). The relationship between role concerns, preference of slimness, and symptoms of eating problems among college women. *Sex Roles, 18,* 101–160.

Simeon, D., Gross, S., Guralnik, O., Stein, D. J., et al. (1997). Feeling unreal: Thirty cases of DSM-III-R depersonalization disorder. *American Journal of Psychiatry, 154,* 1107–1113.

Simeon, D., Guralnik, O., Hazlett, E. A., Spiegel-Cohen, J., et al. (2000). Feeling unreal: A PET study of depersonalization disorder. *American Journal of Psychiatry, 157,* 1782–1788.

Simeon, D., Guralnik, O., Schmeidler, J., Sirof, B., & Knutelska, M. (2001). The role of childhood interpersonal trauma in depersonalization disorder. *American Journal of Psychiatry, 158,* 1027–1033.

Simmons, A. M. (2002, January 13). Eating disorders on rise for South African Blacks. *Los Angeles Times,* A3.

Simon, G. E., & Vonkorff, M. (1991). Somatization and psychiatric disorder in the NIMH Epidemiologic Catchment Area study. *American Journal of Psychiatry, 148,* 1494–1500.

Simon, L. M. J. (1998). Does criminal offender treatment work? *Journal of Applied and Preventative Psychology, 7,* 137–159.

Simons, J., Correia, C. J., Carey, K. B., & Borsari, B. E. (1998). Validating a five-factor marijuana motives measure: Relations with use, problems, and alcohol motives. *Journal of Counseling Psychology, 45,* 265–273.

Simonton, O. C., Mathews-Simonton, S., & Creighton, J. (1978). *Getting well again: A step-by-step, self-help guide to overcoming cancer for patients and their families.* Los Angeles: Tarcher.

Singh, S. P., & Lee, A. S. (1997). Conversion disorders in Nottingham: Alive but not kicking. *Journal of Psychosomatic Research, 43,* 425–430.

Slovenko, R. (1995). *Psychiatry and criminal culpability.* New York: Wiley.

Slutske, W. S., Heath, A. C., Dinwiddie, S. H., Madden, P. A. F., Bucholz, K. K., Dunne, M. P., Statham, D. J., & Martin, N. G. (1997). Modeling genetic and environmental influences in the etiology of conduct disorder: A study of 2,682 adult twin pairs. *Journal of Abnormal Psychology, 106,* 266–279.

Slutske, W. S., Heath, A. C., Dinwiddie, S. H., Madden, P. A. F., Bucholz, K. K., Dunne, M. P., Statham, D. J., & Martin, N. G. (1998). Common genetic risk factors for conduct disorders and alcohol dependence. *Journal of Abnormal Psychology, 107,* 363–374.

Smalley, S. L., & Asarnow, R. F. (1990). Brief report: Cognitive subclinical markers in autism. *Journal of Autism and Developmental Disorders, 20,* 271–278.

Smith, D., & Kraft, W. A. (1983). DSM-III: Do psychologists really want an alternative? *American Psychologist, 38,* 777–785.

Smith, D. E., & Landry, M. J. (1988). Psychoactive substance use disorders: Drugs and alcohol. In H. H. Goldman (Ed.), *Review of general psychiatry* (pp. 266–285). Norwalk, CT: Appleton & Lange.

Smith, G. C., Clarke, D. M., Handrinos, D., Dunsis, A., & McKenzie, D. P. (2000). Consultation-liaison psychiatrists' management of somatoform disorders. *Psychosomatics, 41,* 481–489.

Smith, G. T., Goldman, M. S., Greenbaum, P. E., & Christiansen, B. A. (1995). Expectancy for social facilitation from drinking: The divergent paths of high-expectancy and low-expectancy adolescents. *Journal of Abnormal Psychology, 104,* 32–40.

Smith, J. E., Meyers, R. J., & Delaney, H. D. (1998). The community reinforcement approach with homeless alcohol-dependent individuals. *Journal of Consulting and Clinical Psychology, 66,* 541–548.

Smith, K. (1988, May). Loving him was easy. *Reader's Digest,* pp. 115–119.

Smith, T. W., Ruiz, J. M., & Uchino, B. N. (2000). Vigilance, active coping, and cardiovascular reactivity during social interaction in young men. *Health Psychology, 19,* 382–393.

Snowden, D. A., Greiner, L. H., Mortimer, J. A., Riley, K. P., Greiner, P. A., & Markesbery, W. R. (1997). Brain infarction and the clinical expression of Alzheimer's Disease. *Journal of the American Medical Association, 277,* 813–817.

Spanos, N. P. (1978). Witchcraft in histories of psychiatry: A critical analysis and an alternative conceptualization. *Psychological Bulletin, 85,* 417–439.

Spanos, N. P. (1994). Multiple identity enactments and multiple personality disorder: A sociocognitive perspective. *Psychological Bulletin, 116,* 143–165.

Spark, R. F. (1991). *Male sexual health: A couple's guide.* Mount Vernon, NY: Consumer Reports Books.

Spector, I. P., & Carey, M. P. (1990). Incidence and prevalence of sexual dysfunctions: A critical review of the empirical literature. *Archives of Sexual Behavior, 19,* 389–408.

Spencer, S. L., & Zeiss, A. M. (1987). Sex roles and sexual dysfunction in college students. *Journal of Sex Research, 23,* 338–347.

Spiro, A. III, Aldwin, C. M., Ward, K. D., & Mroczek, D. K. (1995). *Health Psychology, 14,* 563–569.

Spitzer, B. L., Henderson, K. A., & Zivian, M. T. (1999). Gender differences in population versus media body sizes: A comparison over four decades. *Sex Roles, 40,* 545–565.

Spitzer, R. L., Gibbon, M., Skodol, A. E., Williams, J. B., & First, M. B. (Eds.). (1994). *DSM-IV: Casebook.* Washington, DC: American Psychiatric Press.

Spitzer, R. L., Skodol, A. E., Gibbon, M., & Williams, J. B. W. (1981). *DSM-III casebook.* Washington, DC: American Psychiatric Association.

Srinivasan, T. N., Suresh, T. R., & Jayaram, V. (1998). Emergence of eating disorders in India: Study of eating distress syndrome and development of a screening questionnaire. *International Journal of Social Psychiatry, 44,* 189–198.

Srole, L., Langer, T. S., Michael, S. T., Opler, M. K., & Rennie, T. A. (1962). *Mental health in the metropolis: The midtown Manhattan study.* New York: McGraw-Hill.

Staal, W. G., Pol, H. E. H., Schnack, H. G., van Haren, N. E. M., et al. (2001). Structural abnormalities in chronic schizophrenia at the extremes of the outcome spectrum. *American Journal of Psychiatry, 158,* 1140–1142.

Stader, S. R., & Hokanson, J. E. (1998). Psychosocial antecedents of depressive symptoms: An evaluation using daily experiences methodology. *Journal of Abnormal Psychology, 107,* 17–26.

Stampfl, T., & Levis, D. (1967). Essentials of implosive therapy: A learning-theory-based psychodynamic behavioral therapy. *Journal of Abnormal Psychology, 72,* 496–503.

Stanley, M. A., Beck, J. G., Novy, D. M., Averill, P. M., Swann, A. C., Diefenbach, G. J., & Hopko, D. R. (2003). Cognitive-behavioral treatment of late-life generalized anxiety disorder. *Journal of Consulting and Clinical Psychology, 71,* 309–319.

Stanley, M. A., & Turner, S. M. (1995). Current status of pharmacological and behavioral treatment of obsessive-compulsive disorder. *Behavior Therapy, 26,* 163–186.

Stark, E. (1984). The unspeakable family secret. *Psychology Today, 18,* 38–46.

Stark, M. J. (1992). Dropping out of substance abuse treatment: A clinically oriented review. *Clinical Psychology Review, 12,* 93–116.

Steadman, H. J., Monahan, J., Robbins, P. C., Appelbaum, P., Grisso, T., Klassen, D., Mulvey, E. P., & Roth, L. (1993). From dangerousness to risk assessment: Implications for appropriate research strategies. In S. Hodgins (Ed.), *Mental disorder and crime.* New York: Sage Publications.

Steege, J. F., Stout, A. L., & Carson, C. C. (1986). Patient satisfaction in Scott and small-Carrion penile implant recipients: A study of 52 patients. *Archives of Sexual Behavior, 15,* 171–177.

Steele, C. M., & Josephs, R. A. (1988). Drinking your troubles away II: An attention-allocation model of alcohol's effect on psychological stress. *Journal of Abnormal Psychology, 97,* 196–205.

Steele, C. M., & Josephs, R. A. (1990). Alcohol myopia: Its prized and dangerous effects. *American Psychologist, 45,* 921–933.

Steele, M. S., & McGarvey, S. T. (1997). Anger expression, age, and blood pressure in modernizing Samoan adults. *Psychosomatic Medicine, 59,* 632–637.

Steffen, J. J., Nathan, P. E., & Taylor, H. A. (1974). Tension-reducing effects of alcohol: Further evidence and methodological considerations. *Journal of Abnormal Psychology, 83,* 542–547.

Steffenburg, S., & Gillberg, C. (1989). The etiology of autism. In C. Gillberg (Ed.), *Diagnosis and treatment of autism* (pp. 63–82). New York: Plenum Press.

Stein, D. J. (2001). Comorbidity in generalized anxiety disorder: Impact and implications. *Journal of Clinical Psychiatry, 62,* 29–34.

Stein, D. J. (2002). Obsessive-compulsive disorder. *Lancet, 360,* 397–405.

Stenberg, J-H., Jaaskelainen, I. P., & Royks, R. (1998). The effect of symptom self-management training on rehospitalization for chronic schizophrenia in Finland. *International Review of Psychiatry, 10,* 58–61.

Stern, J., Murphy, M., & Bass, C. (1993). Personality disorders in patients with somatisation disorder: A controlled study. *British Journal of Psychiatry, 163,* 785–789.

Sternberg, K. J., Lamb, M. B., Greenbaum, C., & Cicchetti, D. (1992). Effects of domestic violence on children's behavior problems and depression. *Developmental Psychology, 29,* 44–52.

Stevens, J. (1987). Brief psychoses: Do they contribute to the good prognosis and equal prevalence of schizophrenia in developing countries? *British Journal of Psychiatry, 151,* 393–396.

Stewart, W. F., Lipton, R. B., Celentano, D. D., & Reed, M. L. (1992). Prevalence of migraine headache in the United States. *Journal of the American Medical Association, 267,* 64–69.

Stice, E. (2001). A prospective test of the dual-pathway model of bulimic pathology: Mediating effects of dieting and negative affect. *Journal of Abnormal Psychology, 110,* 124–135.

Stice, E., & Bearman, S. K. (2001). Body-image and eating disturbances prospectively predict increases in depressive symptoms in adolescent girls: A growth curve analysis. *Developmental Psychology, 37,* 597–607.

Stice, E., Shaw, H., & Nemeroff, C. (1998). Dual pathway model of bulimia nervosa: Longitudinal support for dietary restraint and affect-regulation mechanisms. *Journal of Social and Clinical Psychology, 17,* 129–149.

Stice, E., Telch, C. F., & Rizvi, S. L. (2000). Development of validation of the Eating Disorder Diagnostic Scale: A brief self-report measure of anorexia, bulimia, and binge-eating disorder. *Psychological Assessment, 12,* 123–131.

Stone, A. A., Smyth, J. M., Kaell, A., & Hurewitz, A. (2000). Structured writing about stressful events: Exploring potential psychological mediators of positive health effects. *Health Psychology, 19,* 619–624.

Stone, M. H. (2001). Schizoid and schizotypal personality disorders. In G. O. Gabbard (Ed.), *Treatment of psychiatric disorders* (pp. 2237–2250). Washington, DC: American Psychiatric Press.

Stone, W. L., & Lemanek, K. L. (1990). Parental report of social behaviors in autistic preschoolers. *Journal of Autism and Developmental Disorders, 20,* 513–522.

Stoolmiller, M., Eddy, J. M., & Reid, J. B. (2000). Detecting and describing preventative intervention effects in a universal school-based randomizing trial: Targeting delinquent and violent behavior. *Journal of Consulting and Clinical Psychology, 68*, 296–306.

Story, M., Neumark-Sztainer, D., Sherwood, N., Stang, J., & Murray, D. (1998). Dieting status and its relationship to eating and physical activity behaviors in a representative sample of U. S. adolescents. *Journal of the American Dietetic Association, 98*, 1127–1135.

Stout, C., Kotses, H., & Creer, T. L. (1997). Improving perception of air flow obstruction in asthma patients. *Psychosomatic Medicine, 59*, 201–206.

Streissguth, A. P. (1994). A long-term perspective of FAS. *Alcohol Health and Research World, 18*, 74–81.

Streissguth, A. P., Landesman-Dwyer, S., Martin, J. C., & Smith, D. W. (1980). Teratogenic effects of alcohol in humans and laboratory animals. *Science, 209*, 353–361.

Strickland, B. R. (1992). Women and depression. *Current Directions in Psychological Science, 1*(4), 132–135.

Stripling, S. (1986, August 3). Crossing over. *Seattle Post Intelligencer*, pp. K1–K2.

Strober, M., Freeman, R., Diamond, C. L. J., & Kaye, W. (2000). Controlled family study of anorexia nervosa and bulimia nervosa: Evidence of shared liability and transmission of partial syndromes. *American Journal of Psychiatry, 157*, 393–401.

Strohman, R. (2001, April). Beyond genetic determinism. *California Monthly, 111*(5), 24–27.

Stromberg, C., Lindberg, D., & Schneider, J. (1995, January). A legal update on forensic psychology. *The Psychologists' Legal Update, No. 6*. Washington, DC: National Register of Health Service Providers in Psychology.

Strong, B., & DeVault, C. (1994). *Human sexuality*. Mountain View, CA: Mayfield.

Strong, S. M., Williamson, D. A., Netemeyer, R. G., & Geer, J. H. (2000). Eating disorder symptoms and concerns about body differ as a function of gender and sexual orientation. *Journal of Social and Clinical Psychology, 19*, 240–255.

Stuart, F. M., Hammond, D. C., & Pett, M. A. (1987). Inhibited sexual desire in women. *Archives of Sexual Behavior, 16*, 91–106.

Stuss, D. T., Gow, C. A., & Hetherington, C. R. (1992). "No longer Gage": Frontal lobe dysfunction and emotional changes. *Journal of Consulting and Clinical Psychology, 60*, 349–359.

Sue, D. (1979). Erotic fantasies of college students during coitus. *Journal of Sex Research, 15*, 299–305.

Sue, D. W. (1995). Toward a theory of multicultural counseling and psychotherapy. In J. A. Banks & C. A. Banks, *Handbook of research on multicultural education*. New York: Macmillan.

Sue, D. W. (2001). Multidimensional facets of cultural competence. *The Counseling Psychologist, 29*, 790–821.

Sue, D. W. (2003). *Overcoming our racism: The journey to liberation*. San Francisco: Jossey-Bass.

Sue, D. W., Carter, R. T., Casas, J. M., Fouad, N. A., Ivey, A. E., Jensen, M., LaFromboise, T., Manese, J. E., Ponterotto, J. G., & Vasquez-Nuttall, E. (1998). *Multicultural counseling competencies: Individual and organizational development*. Thousand Oaks, CA: Sage.

Sue, D. W., & Sue, D. (1999). *Counseling the culturally different* (3rd ed.). New York: Wiley.

Sue, D. W., & Sue, D. (2003). *Counseling the culturally diverse: Theory and practice*. New York: Wiley.

Sue, S., & Abe, J. (1988). *Predictors of academic achievement among Asian American and white students*. New York: College Board.

Sue, S., & Morishima, J. K. (1982). *The mental health of Asian Americans*. San Francisco: Jossey-Bass.

Sue, S., & Nakamura, C. Y. (1984). An integrative model of physiological and social/psychological factors in alcohol consumption among Chinese and Japanese Americans. *Journal of Drug Issues, 14*, 349–364.

Sugiura, T., Sakamoto, S., Tanaka, E., Tomada, A., & Kitamura, T. (2001). Labeling effects of Seishin-Bunretsu-Byou, the Japanese translation for schizophrenia: An argument for relabeling. *International Journal of Social Psychiatry, 47*, 43–51.

Sullivan, P. F., Bulik, C. M., Fear, J. L., & Pickering, A. (1998). Outcome of anorexia nervosa. *American Journal of Psychiatry, 155*, 939–946.

Sulser, F. (1979). Pharmacology: New cellular mechanisms of antidepressant drugs. In S. Fielding & R. C. Effland (Eds.), *New frontiers in psychotropic drug research*. Mount Kisco, NY: Futura.

Sundel, M., & Sundel, S. S. (1998). Psychopharmacological treatment of panic disorder. *Research of Social Work Practice, 8*, 426–451.

Suokas, J., & Lonnqvist, J. (1995). Suicide attempts in which alcohol is involved: A special group in general hospital emergency rooms. *Acta Psychiatrica Scandinavia, 91*, 36–40.

Sutherland, S. M. (2001). Avoidant personality disorder. In G. O. Gabbard (Ed.), *Treatment of psychiatric disorders* (pp. 2327–2340). Washington, DC: American Psychiatric Press.

Suzuki, K., Takei, N., Kawai, M., Minabe, Y., & Mori, N. (2003). Is Taijin Kyofusho a culture-bound syndrome? *American Journal of Psychiatry, 160*, 1358.

Swanson, J., Holzer, C., Ganju, V., & Jono, R. (1990). Violence and psychiatric disorder in the community: Evidence from the Epidemiological Catchment Area Surveys. *Hospital Community Psychiatry, 41*, 761–770.

Swartz, M., Landerman, R., George, L. K., Blazer, D. G., & Escobar, J. (1991). Somatization disorder. In L. N. Robins and D. A. Regier (Eds.). *Psychiatric disorders in America* (pp. 220–255). New York: Free Press.

Swedo, S. E., Rapoport, J. L., Leonard, H., Lenane, M., & Cheslow, D. (1989). Obsessive-compulsive disorder in children and adolescents. *Archives of General Psychiatry, 46*, 335–341.

Szasz, T. S. (1987). Justifying coercion through theology and therapy. In J. K. Zeig (Ed.), *The evolution of psychotherapy*. New York: Brunner/Mazel.

Tager-Flushberg, H., & Sullivan, K. (1994). Predicting and explaining behavior: A comparison of autistic, mentally retarded, and normal children. *Journal of Child Psychology and Psychiatry, 35*, 1059–1075.

Takamura, J. C. (1998). An aging agenda for the twenty-first century: The opportunities and challenges of population longevity. *Professional Psychology: Research and Practice, 29*, 411–412.

Takeuchi, J. (2000). Treatment of a biracial child with schizophreniform disorder: Cultural formulation. *Cultural Diversity and Ethnic Minority Psychology, 6*, 93–101.

Tarasoff vs. The Board of Regents of the University of California, 17 Cal. 3d 435, 551 P.2d, 334, 131 Cal. Rptr. 14, 83 Ad. L. 3d 1166 (1976).

Tardiff, K. (1984). Characteristics of assaultive patients in private psychiatric hospitals. *American Journal of Psychiatry, 141*, 1232–1235.

Tardiff, K., & Koenigsberg, H. W. (1985). Assaultive behavior among psychiatric outpatients. *American Journal of Psychiatry, 142*, 960–963.

Tardiff, K., & Sweillam, A. (1982). Assaultive behavior among chronic inpatients. *American Journal of Psychiatry, 139*, 212–215.

Tarkan, C. L. (1998). Diary of an eating disorder. *Joe Weider's Shape, 18*, 116–119.

Tarter, R. E., & Vanyukov, M. (1994). Alcoholism: A developmental disorder. *Journal of Consulting and Clinical Psychology, 62*, 1096–1107.

Taylor, E. H. (1990). The assessment of social intelligence. *Psychotherapy, 27,* 445–457.

Taylor, S., Thordarson, D. S., Maxfield, L., Fedoroff, I. C., Lovell, K., & Ogrodniczuk, J. (2003). Comparative efficacy, speed, and adverse effects of three PTSD treatments: Exposure therapy, EMDR, and relaxation training. *Journal of Consulting and Clinical Psychology, 71,* 330–338.

Taylor, S., Woody, S., Koch, W. J., McLean, P. D., & Anderson, K. W. (1996). Suffocation fear alarms and efficacy of cognitive behavioral therapy for panic disorder. *Behavior Therapy, 27,* 115–126.

Teachman, B. A., & Woody, S. R. (2003). Automatic processing in spider phobia: Implicit fear associations over the course of treatment. *Journal of Abnormal Psychology, 112,* 100–109.

Telch, C. F., & Stice, E. (1998). Psychiatric comorbidity in women with binge eating disorder: Prevalence rates from a non-treatment-seeking example. *Journal of Consulting and Clinical Psychology, 66,* 768–776.

Temoshok, L., & Dreher, H. (1992). *The type C connection: The mind-body link to cancer and your health.* New York: Penguin.

Teri, L., & Wagner, A. (1992). Alzheimer's disease and depression. *Journal of Consulting and Clinical Psychology, 60*(3), 379–391.

Terman, L. M., & Merrill, M. A. (1960). *Stanford-Binet intelligence scale.* Boston: Houghton Mifflin.

Thacker, A. J. (1994). Formal communication disorder: Sign language in deaf people with schizophrenia. *British Journal of Psychiatry, 165,* 818–823.

Thapar, A., Gottesman, I. I., Owen, M. J., O'Donovan, M. C., & McGuffin, P. (1994). The genetics of mental retardation. *British Journal of Psychiatry, 164,* 747–758.

Tharp, R. G. (1991). Cultural diversity and treatment of children. *Journal of Consulting and Clinical Psychology, 59,* 799–812.

Thiels, C., Schmidt, U., Treasure, J., Garthe, R., & Troop, N. (1998). Guided self-change for bulimia nervosa incorporating use of a self-care manual. *American Journal of Psychiatry, 155,* 947–953.

Thigpen, C. H., & Cleckley, H. M. (1984). On the incidence of multiple personality disorder: A brief communication. *International Journal of Clinical and Experimental Hypnosis, 32,* 63–66.

Thomas, P. (1995). Thought disorder or communication disorder: Linguistic science provides a new approach. *British Journal of Psychiatry, 166,* 287–290.

Thompson, P. M., Vidal, C., Giedd, J. N., Gochman, P., Blumenthal, J., Nicolson, R., Toga, A. W., & Rapoport, J. L. (2001). Mapping adolescent brain change reveals dynamic wave of accelerated gray matter loss in very early-onset schizophrenia. *Proceedings of the National Academy of Science, 98,* 11650–11655.

Thorndike, R. L., Hagen, E. P., & Sattler, J. M. (1986). *The Stanford-Binet intelligence scale: Guide for administration and scoring* (3rd ed.). Chicago: Riverside.

Thorpe, S.J., & Salkovskis, P. M. (1998). Studies on the role of disgust in the acquisition and maintenance of specific phobias. *Behaviour Research and Therapy, 36,* 877–893.

Tienari, P., Wynne, L. C., Moring, J., Lahti, I., Naarala, M., Sorri, A., Wahlberg, K.-E., Saarento, O., Seitamaa, M., Kaleva, M., & Laksy, K. (1994). The Finnish adoptive family study of schizophrenia: Implications for family research. *British Journal of Psychiatry, 164,* 20–26.

Tierney, J. (1988, July 3). Research finds lower-level workers bear brunt of workplace stress. *Seattle Post Intelligencer,* pp. K1–K3.

Titone, D., Levy, D. L., & Holzman, P. S. (2000). Contextual insensitivity in schizophrenic language processing: Evidence from lexical ambiguity. *Journal of Abnormal Psychology, 109,* 761–767.

Tjosvold, D., & Tjosvold, M. M. (1983). Social psychological analysis of residences for mentally retarded persons. *American Journal of Mental Deficiency, 88,* 28–40.

Tobin, J. J., & Friedman, J. (1983). Spirits, shamans, and nightmare death: Survivor stress in a Hmong refugee. *American Journal of Orthopsychiatry, 53,* 439–448.

Tolan, P. H., Gorman-Smith, D., Huesmann, L. R., & Zelli, A. (1997). Assessment of family relationship characteristics: A measure to explain risk for antisocial behavior and depression among urban youth. *Psychological Assessment, 9,* 212–223.

Tollefson, G. D., Rampey, A. H., Potvin, J. H., Jenike, M. A., Rush, A. J., Dominguez, R. A., Koran, L. M., Shear, M. K., Goodman, W., & Genduso, L. A. (1994). A multicenter investigation of fixed-dose fluoxetine in the treatment of obsessive-compulsive disorder. *Archives of General Psychiatry, 51,* 559–567.

Torgalsboen, A-K., & Rund, B. R. (1998). "Full recovery" from schizophrenia in the long term: A ten-year follow-up of eight former schizophrenic patients. *Psychiatry, 61,* 20–34.

Torpy, J. M. (2002). Heart disease and women. *Journal of the American Medical Association, 288,* 3230–3232.

Toth, S. L., Manly, J. T., & Cicchetti, D. (1992). Child maltreatment and vulnerability to depression. *Developmental Psychopathology, 4,* 97–112.

Trierweiler, S. J., Neighbors, H. W., Munday, C., Thompson, E. E., Binion, V. J., & Gomez, J. P. (2000). Clinician attributions associated with the diagnosis of schizophrenia in African American and non–African American patients. *Journal of Consulting and Clinical Psychology, 68,* 171–175.

Tripp, M. M., & Petrie, T. A. (2001). Sexual abuse and eating disorders: A test of a conceptual model. *Sex Roles, 44,* 17–32.

Troxel, W. M., Matthews, K. A., Bromberger, J. T., & Tyrrell, K. S. (2003). Chronic stress burden, discrimination, and subclinical carotid artery disease in African American and Caucasian women. *Health Psychology, 22,* 300–309.

Trull, T. J. (1995). Borderline personality disorder features in nonclinical young adults: 1. Identification and validation. *Psychological Assessment, 7,* 33–41.

Trull, T. J., Useda, J. D., Conforti, K., & Doan, B.-T. (1997). Borderline personality disorder features in nonclinical young adults, Part 2: Two-year outcome. *Journal of Abnormal Psychology, 106,* 307–314.

Tsai, G., & Gray, J. (2000). The Eating Disorders Inventory among Asian American college women. *Journal of Social Psychology, 140,* 527–529.

Tsoi, W. F. (1993). Male and female transsexuals: A comparison. *Singapore Medical Journal, 33,* 182–185.

Tuomisto, M. T. (1997). Intra-arterial blood pressure and heart rate reactivity to behavioral stress in normotensive, borderline, and mild hypertensive men. *Health Psychology, 16,* 554–565.

Turkheimer, E., & Parry, C. D. H. (1992). Why the gap? *American Psychologist, 47,* 646–655.

Turner, W. J. (1995). Homosexuality, Type 1: An Xq28 phenomenon. *Archives of Sexual Behavior, 24,* 109–134.

Tutkun, H., Sar, V., Yargic, L. I., & Ozpulat, T. (1998). Frequency of dissociative disorders among psychiatric inpatients in a Turkish university clinic. *American Journal of Psychiatry, 155,* 800–805.

Twamley, E. W., Jeste, D. V., & Bellack, A. S. (2003). A review of cognitive training in schizophrenia. *Schizophrenia Bulletin, 29,* 359–372.

Tyrer, P., Lee, I., & Alexander, J. (1980). Awareness of cardiac function in anxious, phobic, and hypochondriacal patients. *Psychological Medicine, 10,* 171–174.

U.S. Advisory Board on Child Abuse and Neglect. (1995). *A national shame: Fatal child abuse and neglect in the United States* (5th report). Washington, DC: Government Printing Office.

U.S. Bureau of the Census. (1992). *We, the American . . .* Washington, DC: U.S. Government Printing Office.

U.S. Department of Health and Human Services. (1995a). Down syndrome prevalence at birth–United States, 1983–1990. *Morbidity and Mortality Weekly Report, 43,* 617–623.

U.S. Department of Health and Human Services. (1995b). Update: Trends in fetal alcohol syndrome. *Morbidity and Mortality Weekly Report, 44,* 249–251.

U.S. Surgeon General. (1999). *Mental health: A report of the Surgeon General.* Washington, DC: U.S. Government Printing Office.

Uba, L. (1994). *Asian Americans: Personality patterns, identity, and mental health.* New York: Guilford.

Uchino, B. N., & Garvey, T. S. (1997). The availability of social support reduces cardiovascular reactivity to acute psychological stress. *Journal of Behavioral Medicine, 20,* 15–27.

Ullmann, L. P., & Krasner, L. (1975). *A psychological approach to abnormal behavior* (2nd ed.). Englewood Cliffs, NJ: Prentice-Hall.

United States Public Health Service. (1999). *The Surgeon General's call to action to prevent suicide.* Washington, DC: U.S. Public Health Services.

Update: Prevalence of overweight among children, adolescents, and adults—United States, 1988–1994. (1997). *MMWR—Morbidity and Mortality Weekly Report, 46,* 199–202.

Ursano, R. J. (1997). Disaster: Stress, immunologic function, and health behavior. *Psychosomatic Medicine, 59,* 142–143.

Vaillant, G. E. (1975). Sociopathy as a human process: A viewpoint. *Archives of General Psychiatry, 32,* 178–183.

Vaillant, G. E. (1994). Ego mechanisms of defense and personality psychopathology. *Journal of Abnormal Psychology, 103,* 44–50.

Vaillant, G. E., & Perry, J. C. (1985). Personality disorders. In H. I. Kaplan & B. J. Sadock (Eds.), *Comprehensive textbook of psychiatry* (4th ed., pp. 958–986). Baltimore: Williams & Wilkins.

Valenstein, E. S. (1986). *Great and desperate cures: The rise and decline of psychosurgery and other radical treatments for mental illness.* New York: Basic Books.

Valera, E. M., & Berenbaum, H. (2003). Brain injury in battered women. *Journal of Consulting and Clinical Psychology, 71,* 794–804.

Van Evra, J. P. (1983). *Psychological disorders of children and adolescents.* Boston: Little, Brown.

Vanderlinden, J., Norre, J., & Vandereycken, W. (1992). *A practical guide to the treatment of bulimia nervosa.* New York: Brunner/Mazel.

Vedantam, S. (2001). Drug found to curb kid's debilitating social anxiety. *Washington Post,* p. A1.

Vedhara, K., & Nott, K. (1996). The assessment of the emotional and immunological consequences of examination stress. *Journal of Behavioral Medicine, 19,* 467–478.

Vega, W., & Rumbaut, R.G. (1991). Ethnic minorities and mental health. *Annual Review of Sociology, 17,* 351–383.

Velting, O. N., Setzer, N. J., & Albano, A. M. (2004). Update and advances in assessment and cognitive-behavioral treatment of anxiety disorders in children and adolescents. *Professional Psychology: Research and Practice, 35,* 42–54.

Vincent, M. A., & McCabe, M. P. (2000). Gender differences among adolescents in family, and peer influences on body dissatisfaction, weight loss, and binge eating disorders. *Journal of Youth and Adolescence, 29,* 205–221.

Visintainer, M. A., Volpicelli, J. R., & Seligman, M. E. P. (1982). Tumor rejection in rats after inescapable or escapable shock. *Science, 216,* 437–439.

Vita, A., Bressi, S., Perani, D., Invernizzi, G., Giobbio, G. M., Dieci, M., Garbarini, M., Del Sole, A., & Fazio, F. (1995). High-resolution SPECT study of regional cerebral blood flow in drug-free and drug-naive schizophrenic patients. *American Journal of Psychiatry, 152,* 876–882.

Volden, J., & Lord, C. (1991). Neologisms and idiosyncratic language in autistic speakers. *Journal of Autism and Developmental Disorders, 21,* 109–130.

Volkmar, F. R., Cicchetti, D. V., Dykens, E., Sparrow, S. S., Leckman, J. F., & Cohen, D. J. (1988). An evaluation of the Autism Behavior checklist. *Journal of Autism and Developmental Disorders, 18,* 81–97.

Volkmar, F. R., Klin, A., Schultz, R. T., Rubin, E., & Bronen, R. (2000). Asperger's disorder. *American Journal of Psychiatry, 157,* 262–267.

Vontress, C. E., & Epps, L. R. (1997). Historical hostility in the African American client: Implications for counseling. *Journal of Multicultural Counseling and Development, 25,* 170–185.

Vossekuil, G., Reddy, M., Fein, R., Borum, R., & Modzeleski, W. (2000). *U.S. Secret Service Schools Initiative: An interim report on the prevention of targeted violence in schools.* Washington, DC: U.S. Secret Service, National Threat Assessment Center.

Wahass, S., & Kent, G. (1997). A cross-cultural study of the attitudes of mental health professionals toward auditory hallucinations. *International Journal of Social Psychiatry, 43,* 184–192.

Wahlberg, K.-E., Wynne, L. C., Oja, H., & Keskitalo, P. (1997). Gene-environment interaction in vulnerability to schizophrenia: Findings from the Finnish adoptive family study of schizophrenia. *American Journal of Psychiatry, 154,* 355–362.

Waldrop, D., Lightsey, O. R., Ethington, C. A., Woemmel, C. A., & Coke, A. L. (2001). Self-efficacy, optimism, health competence, and recovery from orthopedic surgery. *Journal of Counseling Psychology, 48,* 233–238.

Walker, L. E. (1991). Posttraumatic stress disorder in women: Diagnosis and treatment of battered woman syndrome. *Psychotherapy, 28,* 21–29.

Walkup, J. (1995). A clinically based rule of thumb for classifying delusions. *Schizophrenia Bulletin, 21,* 323–331.

Walsh, B. T., & Devlin, M. J. (1998). Eating disorders: Progress and problems. *Science, 280,* 1387–1390.

Walter, H. J. (2001). Substance abuse and substance use disorders. In G. O. Gabbard (Ed.), *Treatment of psychiatric disorders* (pp. 325–338). Washington, DC: American Psychiatric Press.

Warner, R. (1986). Hard times and schizophrenia. *Psychology Today, 20,* 51–52.

Wartik, N. (1994, February). Fatal attention. *Redbook,* pp. 62–69.

Warwick, H. M. C., & Marks, I. M. (1988). Behavioural treatment for illness phobia and hypochondriasis. *British Journal of Psychiatry, 152,* 239–241.

Wassertheil-Smoller, S., Shumaker, S., Ockene, J., Talavera, G. A., et al. (2004). Depression and cardiovascular sequelae in postmenopausal women: The women's health initiative (WHI). *Archives of Internal Medicine, 164,* 289–299.

Watkins, B., & Bentovim, A. (1992). The sexual abuse of male children and adolescents: A review of current research. *Journal of Child Psychology and Psychiatry, 33,* 197–248.

Watson, J. B., & Rayner, R. (1920). Conditioned emotional responses. *Journal of Experimental Psychology, 3,* 1–14.

Watson, J. B., & Rayner, R. (2000). Conditioned emotional reactions. *American Psychologist, 55,* 313–317.

Wax, E. (2000, March 6). Immigrant girls are starving to be American, studies find. *Washington Post,* p. B1.

Webster, J. S., & Scott, R. P. (1983). The effects of self-instruction training in attention deficit following head injury. *Clinical Neuropsychology, 5,* 69–74.

Webster-Stratton, C. (1991). Annotation: Strategies for helping families with conduct disordered children. *Journal of Child Psychology and Psychiatry, 32,* 1047–1062.

Wechsler, D. (1981). *Wechsler Adult Intelligence Scale.* New York: Harcourt, Brace, Jovanovich.

Weddington, W. W. (1979). Single case study: Conversion reaction in an 82-year-old man. *Journal of Nervous and Mental Diseases, 167,* 368–369.

Weems, C. F., Hayward, C., Killen, J., & Taylor, C. B. (2002). A longitudinal investigation of anxiety sensitivity in adolescence. *Journal of Abnormal Psychology, 111,* 471–477.

Weems, C., Silverman, W. K., & LaGreca, A. M. (2000). What do youth referred for anxiety problems worry about? *Journal of Abnormal Child Psychology, 28,* 63–72.

Weiller, J., Bisserbe, C., Maier, W., & Lecrubier, Y. (1998). Prevalence and recognition of anxiety syndromes in five European primary care settings. *British Journal of Psychiatry, 173,* 18–23.

Weinberg, T. S. (1987). Sadomasochism in the United States: A review of recent sociological literature. *Journal of Sex Research, 23,* 50–69.

Weiner, I. B. (1995). How to anticipate ethical and legal challenges in personality assessments. In J. N. Butcher (Ed.), *Clinical personality assessment: Practical approaches* (pp. 95–106). New York: Oxford University Press.

Weiner, I. B. (2003). Prediction and postdiction in clinical decision making. *Clinical Psychology: Science and Practice, 10,* 335–338.

Weinman, J., & Petrie, K. J. (1997). Illness perceptions: A new paradigm for psychosomatics. *Journal of Psychosomatic Research, 42,* 113–116.

Weintraub, W. (1981). Compulsive and paranoid personalities. In J. R. Lion (Ed.), *Personality disorders: Diagnosis and management.* Baltimore: Williams & Wilkins.

Weiser, B. (2000, December 16). Judge rules defendant's amnesia is feigned in terror case. *New York Times,* p. B2.

Weisman, A. G., Nuechterlein, K. H., Goldstein, M. J., & Snyder, K. S. (2000). Controllability perceptions and reactions to symptoms of schizophrenia: A within-family comparison of relatives with high and low expressed emotions. *Journal of Abnormal Psychology, 109,* 167–171.

Weiss, B., Weisz, J. R., Politano, M., Carey, M., Nelson, W. M., & Finch, A. J. (1992). Relations among self-reported depressive symptoms in clinic referred children versus adolescents. *Journal of Abnormal Psychology, 101,* 391–397.

Weiss, D. S. (1988). Personality assessment. In H. H. Goldman (Ed.), *Review of general psychiatry* (pp. 221–232). Norwalk, CT: Appleton & Lange.

Weissberg, M. (1993). Multiple personality disorder and iatrogenesis: The cautionary tale of Anna O. *International Journal of Clinical and Experimental Hypnosis, 41,* 15–34.

Weissman, M. M. (1993). The epidemiology of personality disorders: A 1990 update. *Journal of Personality Disorders, Supplement 1,* 44–62.

Weissman, M. M., Bland, R. C., Canino, G. J., Faravelli, C., Greenwald, S., Hwu, H-G., Joyce, P. R., Karam, E. G., Lee, C-K., Lellouch, J., Lepine, J-P., Newman, S. C., Oakley-Browne, M. A., Rubio-Stipec, M., Wells, J. E., Wickramaratne, P. J., Wittchen, H-U., & Yeh, E-K. (1997). The cross-national epidemiology of panic disorder. *Archives of General Psychiatry, 54,* 305–309.

Weissman, M. M., Bruce, M. L., Leaf, P. J., Florio, L. P., & Holzer, C. (1991). Affective disorders. In L. N. Robins & D. A. Regier (Eds.), *Psychiatric disorders in America: The Epidemiologic Catchment Area study* (pp. 53–80). New York: Free Press.

Wells, A., & Papageorgiou, C. (1999). The observer perspective: Biased imagery in social phobia, agoraphobia, and blood/injury phobia. *Behaviour Research & Therapy, 37,* 653–658.

Wells, C. E. (1978). Role of stroke in dementia. *Stroke, 9,* 1–3.

Wells, K. B., Sturm, R., Sherbourne, C. D., & Meredith, L. S. (1996). *Caring for depression.* Cambridge, MA: Harvard University Press.

Wen, P. (2001, April 10). Thinking the unspeakable, the "silent epidemic" of obsessive dark thoughts. *Boston Globe,* p. B6.

Wender, P. H., & Klein, D. F. (1981, February). The promise of biological psychiatry. *Psychology Today, 15,* 25–41.

Wenger, N. K. (1997). Coronary heart disease: An older woman's health risk. *British Medical Journal, 315,* 1085–1089.

Wertheim, E. H., Paxton, S. J., Schutz, H. K., & Muir, S. L. (1997). Why do adolescent girls watch their weight? An interview study examining sociocultural pressures to be thin. *Journal of Psychosomatic Research, 42,* 345–355.

Westen, D. (1991). Cognitive-behavioral interventions in the psychoanalytic psychotherapy of borderline personality disorders. *Clinical Psychology Review, 11,* 211–230.

Westen, D., & Harnden-Fischer, J. (2001). Personality profiles in eating disorders: Rethinking the distinction between axis I and axis II. *American Journal of Psychiatry, 158,* 547–562.

Whalen, C. K., & Henker, B. (1991). Therapies for hyperactive children: Comparisons, combinations, and compromises. *Journal of Consulting and Clinical Psychology, 59,* 126–137.

Whipple, E., & Webster-Stratton, C. (1991). The role of parental stress in physically abusive families. *Child Abuse and Neglect, 15,* 279–291.

White, G. M. (1982). The role of cultural explanations in "somatization" and "psychologization." *Social Science Medicine, 16,* 1519–1530.

White, J. II. (2000). The prevention of eating disorders: A review of the research on risk factors with implications for practice. *Journal of Child and Adolescent Psychiatric Nursing, 13,* 76–88.

White, J. L., & Parham, T. A. (1990). *The psychology of Blacks.* Englewood Cliffs, NJ: Prentice-Hall.

White, P. D., & Moorey, S. (1997). Psychosomatic illnesses are not "all in the mind." *Journal of Psychosomatic Research, 42,* 329–333.

Whittal, M. L., & Goetsch, V. L. (1995). Physiological, subjective, and behavioral responses to hyperventilation in clinical and infrequent panic. *Behaviour Research and Therapy, 33,* 415–422.

Whittal, M. L., Suchday, S., & Goetsch, V. L. (1994). The panic attack questionnaire: Factor analysis of symptom profiles and characteristics of undergraduates who panic. *Journal of Anxiety Disorders, 8,* 237–245.

Widiger, T. A., & Coker, L. A. (2002). Assessing personality disorders. In J. N. Butcher (Ed.), *Clinical personality assessment: Practical approaches* (pp. 407–434). New York: Oxford University Press.

Widiger, T. A., & Spitzer, R. L. (1991). Sex bias in the diagnosis of personality disorders: Conceptual and methodological issues. *Clinical Psychology Review, 11,* 1–22.

Widom, C. S. (1976). Interpersonal and personal construct systems in psychopaths. *Journal of Consulting and Clinical Psychology, 44,* 614–623.

Wiens, A. N. (1983). The assessment interview. In I. B. Weiner (Ed.), *Clinical methods in psychology.* New York: Wiley.

Wiersma, D., Nienhuis, F. J., Sloof, C. J., & Giel, R. (1998). Natural course of schizophrenic disorders: A fifteen-year follow-up of a Dutch incidence cohort. *Schizophrenia Bulletin, 24,* 75–85.

Wiesel, F.-A. (1994). II. The treatment of schizophrenia. *British Journal of Psychiatry, 164,* 65–70.

Wilfley, D. E., Dounchis, J. Z., Stein, R. I., Welch, R. R., Friedman, M. A., & Ball, S. A. (2000). Comorbid psychopathology in binge eating disorder: Relationship to eating disorder severity at baseline and following treatment. *Journal of Consulting and Clinical Psychology, 68,* 641–649.

Wilfley, D. E., Pike, K. M., Dohm, F.-A., Striegel-Moore, R. H., & Fairburn, C. G. (2001). Bias in binge eating disorder: How representative are recruited clinic samples? *Journal of Consulting and Clinical Psychology, 69,* 383–388.

Williams, J. B. (1999). Psychiatric classification. In R. E. Hales, S. C. Yudofsky & J. A. Talbott (Eds.), *Textbook of psychiatry* (pp. 227–252). Washington, DC: American Psychiatric Press.

Williams, K. E., Chambless, D. L., & Steketee, G. (1998). Behavioral treatment of obsessive-compulsive disorder in African Americans: Clinical issues. *Journal of Behavior Therapy and Experimental Psychiatry, 29,* 163–170.

Williams, L. M., & Finkelhor, D. (1990). The characteristics of incestuous fathers: A review of recent studies. In W. L. Marshall, D. R. Laws, & H. E. Barbaree (Eds.), *Handbook of sexual assault: Issues, theories, and treatment of the offender* (pp. 231–256). New York: Plenum Press.

Williams, R. (1974). The problem of match and mismatch. In L. Miller (Ed.), *The testing of black children.* Englewood Cliffs, NJ: Prentice-Hall.

Williams, R. J., & Chang, S. Y. (2000). A comprehensive and comparative review of adolescent substance abuse treatment outcome. *Clinical Psychology: Science and Practice, 7,* 138–166.

Williams, R. J., Taylor, J., & Ricciardelli, L. A. (2000). Brief report: Sex-role traits and self-monitoring as dimensions in control: Women with bulimia nervosa versus controls. *British Journal of Clinical Psychology, 39,* 317–320.

Williamson, D., Robinson, M. E., & Melamed, B. (1997). Patient behavior, spouse responsiveness, and marital satisfaction in patients with rheumatoid arthritis. *Behavior Modification, 21,* 97–106.

Wilson, G. T. (1984). Clinical issues and strategies in the clinical practice of behavior therapy. In C. M. Franks, G. T. Wilson, K. D. Brownell, & P. Kendall (Eds.), *Annual review of behavior therapy: Theory and practice* (p. 8). New York: Guilford Press.

Wincze, J. P., Hoon, E. F., & Hoon, P. W. (1978). Multiple measure analysis of women experiencing low sexual arousal. *Behaviour Research and Therapy, 16,* 43–49.

Windle, M., & Windle, R. C. (2001). Depressive symptoms and cigarette smoking among middle adolescents: Prospective associations and intrapersonal and interpersonal influences. *Journal of Consulting and Clinical Psychology, 69,* 215–226.

Winnett, R. L., Bornstein, P. H., Cogsuell, K. A., & Paris, A. E. (1987). Cognitive-behavioral therapy for childhood depression: A levels-of-treatment approach. *Journal of Child and Adolescent Psychotherapy, 4,* 283–286.

Winokur, G., Clayton, P. J., & Reich, T. (1969). *Manic depressive illness.* St. Louis: Mosby.

Wise, M. G., Gray, K. F., & Seltzer, B. (1999). Delirium, dementia, and amnestic disorders. In R. E. Hales, S. C. Yudofsky & J. A. Talbott (Eds.), *Textbook of psychiatry* (pp. 317–362). Washington, DC: American Psychiatric Press.

Wise, M. G., Hilty, D. M., & Cerda, G. M. (2001). Delirium due to a general medical condition, delirium due to multiple etiologies, and delirium not otherwise specified. In G. O. Gabbard (Ed.), *Treatment of psychiatric disorders* (pp. 387–412). Washington, DC: American Psychiatric Press.

Wise, R. A. (1988). The neurobiology of craving: Implications for understanding and treatment of addiction. *Journal of Abnormal Psychology, 97,* 118–132.

Wise, T. N., Fagan, P. J., Schmidt, C. W., & Ponticas, Y. (1991). Personality and sexual functioning of transvestitic fetishists and other paraphilics. *Journal of Nervous and Mental Disorders, 179,* 694–698.

Woike, B. A., & McAdams, D. P. (2001). TAT-based personality measures have considerable validity. *APS Observer, 14,* 10.

Wolfensberger, W. (1988). Common assets of mentally retarded people that are commonly not acknowledged. *Mental Retardation, 26,* 63–70.

Woliver, R. (2000, March 26). 44 personalities, but artist shines. *New York Times,* pp. 6–9.

Wolkin, A., & Rusinek, H. (2003). A neuropathology of psychosis? *Lancet, 361,* 270–271.

Wolkin, A., Rusinek, H., Vaid, G., & Arena, L. (1998). Structural magnetic resonance image averaging in schizophrenia. *American Journal of Psychiatry, 155,* 1064–1073.

Wolpe, J. (1958). *Psychotherapy by reciprocal inhibition.* Stanford, CA: Stanford University Press.

Wolpe, J. (1973). *The practice of behavior therapy.* New York: Pergamon.

Wolraich, M. L., Wilson, D. B., & White, J. W., (1995). The effect of sugar on behavior or cognition in children. *Journal of the American Medical Association, 274,* 1617–1621.

Woodruff, P. G., & Fahy, J. V. (2001). Asthma: Prevalence, pathogenesis, and prospects for novel therapies. *Journal of the American Medical Association, 286,* 1–10.

Woodside, D. B., Garfinkel, P. E., Lin, E., Goering, P., et al. (2001). Comparisons of men with full or partial eating disorders, men without eating disorders, and women with eating disorders in the community. *American Journal of Psychiatry, 158,* 570–574.

Woody, G. E., & Cacciola, J. (1994). Review of remission criteria. In T. A. Widiger, A. J. Frances, H. A. Pincus, M. B. First, R. Ross, & W. Davis (Eds.), *DSM-IV Sourcebook* (Vol. 1, pp. 67–80). Washington, DC: American Psychiatric Association.

Woody, S. R., Chambless, D. L., & Glass, C. R. (1997). Self-focused attention in the treatment of social phobia. *Behavior Research and Therapy, 35,* 117–129.

World Health Organization. (1973). Report on the international pilot study of schizophrenia (Vol. 1). Geneva: World Health Organization.

World Health Organization. (2002). *World report on violence and health.* Geneva: World Health Organization.

Wren, C. (2002). Sudden death in children and adolescents. *Heart, 88,* 426–434.

Yassa, R., & Jeste, D. V. (1992). Gender differences in tardive dyskinesia: A critical review of the literature. *Schizophrenia Bulletin, 18,* 701–715.

Yasumatsu, K. (1993). One's own body odor and eye-to-eye phobias in high school students: A cross-sectional questionnaire study. *Japanese Journal of Child and Adolescent Psychiatry, 34,* 261–267.

Yehuda, R. (2000). Biology of posttraumatic stress disorder. *Journal of Clinical Psychiatry, 61,* 14–21.

Yehuda, R., & McFarlane, A. C. (1995). Conflict between current knowledge about posttraumatic stress disorder and its original conceptual basis. *American Journal of Psychiatry, 152,* 1705–1713.

Yen, S., Shea, M. T., Sanislow, C. A., Grilo, C. M., McGlashan, T. H., Skodol, A. E., et al. (2003). Axis I and Axis II disorders as predictors of prospective suicide attempts: Findings from the Collaborative Longitudinal Personality Disorders Study. *Journal of Abnormal Psychology, 112,* 375–381.

Yeung, A., & Deguang, H. (2002). Somatoform disorders. *Western Journal of Medicine, 176,* 253–256.

Yonkers, K. A., Zlotnick, C., Allsworth, J., & Warshaw, M. (1998). Is the course of panic disorder the same in women and men? *American Journal of Psychiatry, 155,* 596–602.

Young, E. C., & Kramer, B. M. (1991). Characteristics of age-related language decline in adults with Down syndrome. *Mental Retardation, 29,* 75–79.

Young, M. (1980). Attitudes and behavior of college students relative to oral-genital sexuality. *Archives of Sexual Behavior, 9,* 61–67.

Yumoto, S., Kakimi, S., Ogawa, Y., Nagai, H., Imamura, M., & Kobayashi, K. (1995). Aluminum neurotoxicity and Alzheimer's disease. In I. Hanin, M. Yoshida, & A. Fisher (Eds.), *Alzheimer's and Parkinson's diseases: Recent developments* (pp. 223–229). New York: Plenum Press.

Zamichow, N. (1993, February 15). The dark corner of psychology. *Los Angeles Times,* p. A1.

Zayas, E. M., & Grossberg, G. T. (1998). The treatment of psychosis in later life. *Journal of Clinical Psychiatry, 59,* 5–9.

Zernike, K. (2004, March 1). National survey confirms that we're getting bigger. *Seattle Post-Intelligencer,* A2.

Zhang, A. Y., & Snowden, L. R. (1999). Ethnic characteristics of mental disorders in five U.S. communities. *Cultural Diversity and Ethnic Minority Psychology, 5,* 134–146.

Zigler, E. (1967). Familial mental retardation: A continuing dilemma. *Science, 155,* 292–298.

Zigler, E., & Bergman, W. (1983). Discerning the future of early childhood intervention. *American Psychologist, 38,* 893–905.

Zigler, E., Taussig, C., & Black, K. (1992). Early childhood intervention: A promising preventative for juvenile delinquency. *American Psychologist, 47,* 997–1006.

Zilbergeld, B. (1983). *The shrinking of America.* Boston: Little, Brown.

Zilboorg, G., & Henry, G. W. (1941). *A history of medical psychology.* New York: Norton.

Zito, J. M., Craig, T. J., Wanderling, J., & Siegel, C. (1987). Pharmaco-epidemiology in 136 hospitalized schizophrenic patients. *American Journal of Psychiatry, 144,* 778–782.

Zito, J. M., Safer, D. J., dos Reis, S., Gardner, J. F., Boles, M., & Lynch, F. (2000). Trends in the prescribing of psychotropic medications to preschoolers. *Journal of the American Medical Association, 283,* 1025–1030.

Zucker, K. J. (1990). Gender identity disorders in children: Clinical descriptions and natural history. In R. Blanchard & B. W. Steiner (Eds.), *Clinical management of gender identity disorders in children and adults* (pp. 1–24). Washington, DC: American Psychiatric Press.

Zuckerman, M. (1996). Sensation seeking. In C. G. Costello (Ed.), *Personality characteristics of the personality disordered* (pp. 317–330). New York: Wiley.

Zverina, J., Lachman, M., Pondelickova, J., & Vanek, J. (1987). The occurrence of atypical sexual experience among various female patient groups. *Archives of Sexual Behavior, 16,* 321–326.

Credits

Text Credits

Chapter 3: p. 74 *Figure 3.2:* From *The Bender Visual Motor Gestalt Test.* Copyright © 1938 by *The American Journal of Orthopsychiatry.* Reprinted with permission. **Chapter 4: p. 92** *Figure 4.3: American Journal of Psychiatry,* Vol. 157, 493–505 (2000). Copyright (2000), the American Psychiatric Association; http://AJP.psychiatryonline.org. Reprinted by permission. **Chapter 6: p. 153** *Figure 6.2: Archives of General Psychiatry,* Vol. 58, 221–226 (2001). Copyright (2001), the American Medical Association. Reprinted by permission. All rights reserved. **p. 159** *Figure 6.4: Newsweek*—Cowley and Underwood, p. 61. © 1997 Newsweek, Inc. All rights reserved. Reprinted by permission. **Chapter 11: p. 279** *Figure 11.1: Archives of General Psychiatry,* October 1994, Vol. 51, p. 830. Copyright © 1994. American Medical Association. All rights reserved. **Chapter 12: p. 322** *Table 12.2:* From, "Alternative Explanations for Black Scholastic Underachievement Relative to Whites" from *School Psychology Review* quarterly journal, Vol. 24, No. 1, Table 1. Copyright 1995 by the National Association of School Psychologists, Bethesda, MD. Adapted with permission of the publisher. **Chapter 14: p. 365** *Figure 14.2: American Journal of Psychiatry,* Vol. 158, 493–505 (2001). Copyright (2001), the American Psychiatric Association; http://AJP.psychiatryonline.org. Reprinted by permission. **p. 367** *Figure 14.3:* G. B. Forbes, L. E. Adams-Curtis, B. Rade, & P. Jaberg, "Body dissatisfaction in women and men: The role of gender-typing and self-esteem," *Sex Roles,* 44, (2001): 461–484. From Danish adoption register for the study of obesity and thinness, in S. Kety, L. P. Rowland, R. L. Sidman, & S. W. Matthysse (Eds.), *The Genetics of Neurological and Psychiatric Disorders* (pp. 115–120) (Raven Press). Reprinted by permission of Lippincott, Williams, & Wilkins. **pp. 368–369** *Table 14.4:* Reprinted with the permission of MetLife. This information is not intended to be a substitute for professional medical advice and should not be regarded as an endorsement or approval of any product or service. **p. 375** *Table 14.6: American Journal of Psychiatry,* Vol. 157, 393–401 (2000). Copyright (2000), the American Psychiatric Association; http://AJP.psychiatryonline.org. Reprinted by permission.

Photo Credits

Chapter 1: p. 2 James Endicott/The Stock Illustration Source. **p. 6** Jeffrey Dunn Studios. **p. 8 (top)** Jerry Irwin/Getty Images. **(bottom)** Ilene Perlman/Stock Boston. **p. 11** Joseph Sohm/ChromoSohm Inc./Corbis. **p. 13** Neg. #312263 photo by Julius Krishner, 1928/Courtesy Dept. of Library Services, American Museum of Natural History. **p. 14** Corbis/Bettmann. **p. 16** Archives of American Psychology. **p. 22** Dan McCoy/Rainbow. **p. 23** Leo Abbett Cartoons.

Chapter 2: p. 30 James Endicott/The Stock Illustration Source. **p. 40** Library of Congress/WoodfinCamp & Associates. **p. 41 (left)** Rob Crandall/The Image Works. **(right)** Laura Dwight/Peter Arnold, Inc. **p. 46** AP/Wide World Photos. **p. 47** Spencer Grant/PhotoEdit. **p. 53** Corbis. **p. 58 (left)** Bill Pierce/Rainbow. **(right)** Monkmeyer/Dollarhide. **Chapter 3: p. 64** James Endicott/The Stock Illustration Source. **p. 67 (left)** Richard T. Nowitz/Photo Researchers, Inc. **(right)** Dan McCoy/Rainbow. **p. 70** Rorschach H: Diagnostics. **p. 71** © 1971 By the President and Fellows of Harvard College. **p. 76 (left, right, bottom)** Dan McCoy/Rainbow. **p. 77** Dan McCoy/Rainbow. **p. 83** Leo Abbett Cartoons. **Chapter 4: p. 84** James Endicott/The Stock Illustration Source. **p. 89** Scala/Art Resource. **p. 91** CATHY ©2002 Cathy Guisewite. Reprinted with permission of Universal Press Syndicate. All rights reserved. **p. 96** David Ulmer/Stock Boston. **p. 98** ©The New Yorker Collection 2000 Robert Mankoff from cartoonbank.com. All Rights Reserved. **p. 101** J. Cancolusil/Stock Boston. **p. 104** Thomas R. Fletcher/Stock Boston. **p. 108** David Butow/Corbis Saba. **p. 109** Bob Daemmrich/The Image Works. **p. 110** Marianne Armshaw/Wide World Photos. **Chapter 5: p. 112** James Endicott/The Stock Illustration Source. **p. 117 (top)** Getty Images. **(bottom)** George Tooker, The Subway, 1950. Egg tempera $18\frac{1}{8}$ x $26\frac{1}{8}$ in. Whitney Museum of American Art, New York. Purchased with funds from the Juliana Force Purchase Award 50.23. **p. 119** Gordon M. Grant. **p. 120** Jacques Jangoux/Photo Researchers, Inc. **p. 124** Tom Minehart/AP/Wide World Photos. **p. 131** Steve Smith/Outline. **p. 133** The Image Bank. **p. 138** John Gress/AP/Wide World. **Chapter 6: p. 140** James Endicott/The Stock Illustration Source. **p. 143** Fred Prouser/Reuters/Corbis. **p. 144** Gary A. Conner/PhotoEdit. **p. 145** Michael Newman/PhotoEdit. **p. 148 (top)** John S. Abbott. **(bottom)** NIBSC/Science Photo Library/Photo Researchers, Inc. **p. 149** Mark Richards/PhotoEdit. **p. 150** Newport Daily News Press. **p. 153** Dan McCoy/Rainbow. **p. 155** Spencer Platt/Getty Images. **p. 157** Michael Newman/PhotoEdit. **p. 162** Michael Newman/PhotoEdit. **p. 164** Owen Franken/Corbis. **Chapter 7: p. 166** James Endicott/The Stock Illustration Source. **p. 168** Spencer Platt/Getty Images. **p. 173** Cindy Charles/PhotoEdit, Inc. **p. 174** Shooting Star. **p. 175** Shooting Star. **p. 182** Corbis. **p. 183** Bob Daemmrich/The Image Works. **p. 187** Craig Prentis/Allsport/Getty Images. **Chapter 8: p. 190** James Endicott/The Stock Illustration Source. **p. 197** David Frazier/The Image Works. **p. 198** Daniel Hulshizer/AP/Wide World Photos. **p. 202** David Yong-Wolff/PhotoEdit. **p. 205** Tom Prettyman/PhotoEdit. **p. 206** Rufus F. Folkks/Corbis. **p. 212** Billy E. Barnes/Stock Boston. **p. 214** Cartoonists and Writers Syndicate. **Chapter 9: p. 218** James Endicott/The Stock Illustration Source. **p. 220 (left)** Jeff Greenberg/PhotoEdit.

(**right**) © Esbin-Anderson/The Image Works. **p. 221** Ira Wyman/Corbis-Sygma. **p. 225** Cleo/Picture Cube/Index Stock. **p. 229** Leo Abbett Cartoons. **p. 237** (**left**) AP/Wide World Photos. (**right**) Corbis/Bettmann. **p. 241** © Abaca/Burton/Corbis Kipa. **p. 243** CustomMedical StockPhotos. **Chapter 10: p. 246** James Endicott/The Stock Illustration Source. **p. 250** Sidney Harris Cartoons. **p. 251** Pool photo/Getty Images. **p. 253** Robert F. Bukaty/Wide World Photos. **p. 255** AP/Wide World Photos. **p. 256** Mary Kate Denny/PhotoEdit. **p. 257** M. Grecco/Stock Boston. **p. 262** The New Yorker Collection ©1993 Tom Cheney from Cartoonbank.com. **p. 264** (**left**) John Duricka/AP/Wide World Photos. (**right**) Seth Rossman/AP/Wide World Photos. **p. 266** (**left**) Ken Hayman/Black Star. (**right**) Jay Blakesberg/Corbis Sygma. **Chapter 11: p. 272** James Endicott/The Stock Illustration Source. **p. 274** Corbis Bettmann. **p. 275** Rex Arbogast/AP/Wide World Photos. **p. 276** Cartoonists and Writers Syndicate. **p. 278** Prinzhorn Sammlung/Foto Klinger. **p. 283** (**left**) Mary Ellen Mark. (**right**) Monkmeyer/Grannitus. **p. 287** Edna Murlock. **p. 289** Jose Luis Pelaez, Inc./Corbis. **p. 292** Dr. Paul Thompson PhD, Dept. of Neurology, UCLA School of Medicine. **p. 294** (**left, right**) Dr. Wouter G. Staal, PhD, Dept. of Psychiatry, University Hospital Utrecht, The Netherlands. **p. 297** Mark Peterson/Corbis. **Chapter 12: p. 302** James Endicott/The Stock Illustration Source. **p. 303** AP/Wide World Photos. **p. 306** Frank Siteman/Stock Boston. **p. 311** John Boykin/PhotoEdit. **p. 313** Cemax, Inc./Phototake. **p. 314** Bob Daemmrich/Stock Boston. **p. 315** James Schnepf/Getty Images. **p. 317** Science Source/Photo Researchers, Inc. **p. 319** David Young-Wolff/PhotoEdit. **p. 326** Andy Levin/Photo Researchers, Inc. **p. 328** James Shaffer/PhotoEdit. **Chapter 13: p. 330** James Endicott/The Stock Illustration Source. **p. 334** Tony Freeman/PhotoEdit. **p. 341** Jeff Isaac Greenberg/Photo Researchers, Inc. **p. 344** Sidney Harris Cartoons. **p. 348** Ken Cavanaugh/Photo Researchers, Inc. **Chapter 14: p. 354** James Endicott/The Stock Illustration Source. **p. 360** (**left**) Tom Graham/Getty Images. (**right**) AP/Wide World Photos. **p. 367** Jill Greenberg ©1998 the Walt Disney Company/Discover Magazine. **p. 368** Paul Conklin/PhotoEdit. **p. 370** AP/Wide World Photos. **p. 371** Bryan Bedder/Getty Images. **Chapter 15: p. 378** James Endicott/The Stock Illustration Source. **p. 380** (**left**) AP/Wide World Photos. (**right**) Reuters/Corbis Bettmann. **p. 383** AP/Wide World Photos. **p. 385** Corbis/UPI/Bettmann. **p. 388** Saba.

Name Index

Hippocrates, 13, 14
Hirose, S., 299
Hirschfield, R. M., 264, 269
Hirschman, L., 243
Hitler, A., 9, 265
Ho, D. D., 144
Ho, D. Y. F., 334
Ho, E. D., 334
Hochron, S., 160–161
Hodapp, R. M., 322, 328
Hodes, R. L., 47
Hodgins, D. D., 209
Hoehn-Saric, R., 105
Hof, A., 154, 155
Hoff, A. L., 273
Hoffman, D., 334
Hoffman, H. G., 100
Hoffman, L., 357, 360, 363, 364, 374, 376
Hoffman, M. A., 394, 395
Hofman, S. G., 101
Hofmann, S. G., 93
Hogue, L., 380
Hoidas, S., 280
Hokanson, J. E., 258
Holahan, C., 359, 361
Holbrook, T., 356
Holcomb, H. H., 75
Holden, N. L., 282
Hollister, A., 35
Hollon, S. D., 265
Holmbeck, G., 66
Holmes, T. H., 144
Holmes, T. S., 144
Holmstrom, L. L., 233
Holroyd, J., 394
Holroyd, S., 334
Holzman, P. S., 278
Hong, G. K., 8
Hooley, J. M., 295
Hoon, E. F., 232
Hoon, P. W., 232
Hooper, J., 226, 229, 232
Hoover, D. W., 341
Hope, D. A., 66
Hoppe, C. M., 342
Horan, W. P., 278
Horwood, L. J., 338
Hovarth, K., 9, 337
Howard, R., 8, 273, 276
Hsu, L. K., 372
Hu, S., 224
Hudson, J. I., 107, 356, 374
Hugdahl, K., 98
Hull, J. C., 198
Hunfeld, J. A. M., 132
Hunter, M., 123
Hunter, R., 12–13
Hurley, R. A., 106
Hurt, S. W., 69
Hurtig, A. L., 236
Hutchings, B., 185
Hutchinson, K. E., 212
Huttunen, M. O., 293
Hynd, G. W., 341

Idanpaan-Heikkila, U., 154
Irving, L. M., 366, 372
Irwin, A., 325
Irwin, H. J., 121
Isenberg, S. A., 160–161
Ivanoff, J., 229

Ivnik, R. J., 314
Iwamasa, G. Y., 20

Jaaskelainen, I. P., 301
Jablensky, A. V., 293
Jackson, B., 340
Jackson, J. L., 351
Jackson, K. M., 197
Jacobs, D., 266
Jacobson, S., 355
James, G. D., 154, 161
James, W., 16
Jamison, K. R., 251
Janssen, K., 163
Janus, C. L., 220, 224, 225, 228
Janus, S. S., 220, 224, 225, 228
Janus Report, 228
Jason, L. A., 216
Jawed, S. Y., 127
Jayaram, V., 372
Jellinek, E. M., 198
Jenike, M. A., 102, 103, 106
Jennison, J. H., 311
Jensen, P. S., 343
Jeste, D. V., 300, 301
Jilek, W. G., 279
Johnson, D. L., 301
Johnson, V., 220, 221
Johnson, V. E., 224, 225, 229, 231, 233, 234, 243
Johnson, W. G., 56
Johnston, C., 340
Joiner, T. E., 374
Jones, J., 265, 356
Jones, J. M., 157, 158, 159
Jones, K. L., 240
Joplin, J., 205
Joraschky, P., 131
Joseph, E., 43
Josephs, R. A., 209
Julkunen, J., 154

Kabot, S., 332
Kaczynski, T., 381
Kahler, C., 216
Kahn, R. S., 291
Kaijser, L., 153
Kaivanto, K. K., 150
Kalaydjieva, L. V., 293
Kalyanasundaram, S., 263
Kamphaus, R. W., 74
Kanas, N., 206, 211
Kanayama, G., 356
Kane, J. M., 291, 300
Kang, S. H., 157
Kanner, L., 333, 335
Kantrowitz, B., 125
Kaplan, H. S., 233, 234
Kapur, R., 263
Kapur, S., 291
Karnopp, K., 371
Karpiak, C. P., 168, 177
Kasari, C., 5, 333
Kaszniak, A. W., 121
Kattan, M., 160
Kaufman, A. S., 74
Kaufman, N. L., 74
Kavanagh, D. J., 295
Kawachi, I., 153, 154
Kazdin, A. E., 189, 345, 346, 349, 350
Keel, P. K., 362, 364

Kegeles, T., 394
Keith, C. R., 236
Keith, S. J., 296
Keith-Spiegel, P., 394
Keller, A., 292
Keller, A. B., 299
Kellner, A., 132
Kellner, R., 133, 135
Keltz, L. B., 91
Kendall, P. C., 66, 348
Kendall-Tackett, K. A., 351
Kendler, K. S., 91, 92, 98, 172
Kennedy, W. A., 326
Kent, G., 296, 298
Kernberg, O. F., 43, 174, 176
Kessler, R. C., 12, 80, 88, 108, 196
Kety, S. S., 290
Khanna, S., 237
Kiecolt-Glaser, J. K., 148
Kienhorst, C. W. M., 267
Killen, J., 90
Killen, J. D., 207
Kilmann, P. R., 231, 233
Kim, E. A., 356
Kim, S. W., 133
Kim, U., 8, 56
Kinderman, P., 281
King, N. J., 88, 97, 98, 101
Kinsey, A. C., 220, 222, 228
Kirch, D. G., 299
Kirmayer, L. J., 137, 138
Klein, D. F., 39
Klein, D. N., 250
Klein, M., 43
Klein, M. E., 266
Kleinberg, J., 327
Kleinman, A., 258
Klerman, G. L., 37, 39, 132
Klesges, R. C., 214
Klin, A., 333
Klopfer, B., 69
Kluft, R. P., 121, 125
Knapp, S., 123
Kneisel, P. J., 270
Knopf, I. J., 342
Knott, J., 185
Ko, G., 291
Kobasa, S. C., 149
Kockott, G., 238
Kodluboy, D. W., 346
Koegel, R. L., 335
Koenigsburg, H. W., 388
Koh, K. B., 148
Kohlenberg, R. J., 319
Kohut, H., 43
Kolko, D. J., 345
Kolodny, R. C., 243
Kopelowicz, A., 298
Koresh, D., 265
Kotses, H., 160
Kozak, M. J., 47, 103
Kraepelin, E., 17, 79, 274, 285
Kraft, K. A., 81
Krahn, L. E., 129
Kramer, B. M., 325
Krasner, L., 184
Kremer, L., 116
Kresin, D., 231
Krieger, N., 157
Krueger, R. F., 80, 81

Kubany, E. S., 107
Kubiszyn, T. W., 75
Kuiper, N. A., 351
Kuipers, E. L., 277
Kuldau, J., 373
Kumanyika, S., 373
Kusek, K., 88
Kushner, M., 245, 268
Kyofusho, T., 95

Lackner, J. M., 150
Lader, M., 100
Ladouceur, R., 89, 90, 91, 92, 102, 103
LaGreca, A. M., 108, 347
Lahey, B. B., 340, 345
Lai, J. Y., 156
Laird, J., 223
Lakkis, J., 374
Lam, R. W., 363
Lambert, E. W., 116, 340, 345
Lambert, M. J., 68, 265
Lambley, P., 241
Landesman, S., 321
Landry, M. J., 199
Lang, P. J., 47
Langevin, R., 241
Langley, J., 244
Larkin, K. T., 101, 164
Larrabee, A. L., 20
Larson, C. A., 201
Lask, B., 359
Last, C. G., 348
Latane, B., 187
Laudenslager, M. L., 149
Laumann, E. O., 222, 230, 234
Lawton, M. P., 36, 313
Lazar, I., 327
Lazarus, A. A., 145
Lazarus, J., 347
Lazarus, R., 145
Leary, W. E., 229
Leckman, J. F., 350
Lee, A. S., 130, 131
Lee, I., 137
Lee, S., 372
Lee, T. M. C., 254
Leekam, S. R., 334
Leenaars, A. A., 267
Leferink, K., 275
Legato, M. J., 152
Lehman, A. F., 294, 299, 300, 301
Lehman, C. L., 93
Lehrer, P. M., 160–161
Leibbrand, R., 132
Leiblum, S. R., 228, 230, 233
Lemanek, K. L., 333
Lenzenweger, M. F., 172
Leppard, W., 154
LeResche, L., 135
Lerew, D. R., 90
Lerner, J. V., 345
Leslie, A. M., 334
Leslie, R., 392
Lester, D., 267
Lester, R., 374
Leung, N., 371
Levenstein, C., 145
Levin, M., 158
Levis, D. J., 47

Levitt, E. E., 244
Levy, D. L., 278
Levy, K. N., 79, 83, 167, 168, 312
Lewinsky, M., 222
Lewinsohn, P. M., 255, 339, 348
Lewis, K. R., 337
Lezon, D., 113
Li, H., 129
Liberini, P., 130
Liberman, R. P., 298
Lichtenberg, P. A., 312
Lichtenstein, E., 47, 213
Lickey, M. E., 18, 19, 35, 39
Lieberman, J. A., 278
Lightner, C., 198
Lilienfeld, S., 122
Lilienfeld, S. O., 71
Lindamer, L. A., 299
Lindberg, D., 379
Linden, W., 156
Linehan, M. M., 176, 177
Liness, S., 108
Links, P. S., 177
Li-Repac, D., 77
Lishman, W. A., 313
Livanou, M. L., 109
Loar, L. L., 345
Locke, B. Z., 10, 80
Loeber, R., 184
Loening-Baucke, V., 353
Loew, T. H., 131
Loftus, E. F., 122
Lonergan, C., 300
Loney, J., 342
Lonnqvist, J., 269
Looper, K. J., 137, 138
Lopez, M. and R., 148
Lopez, S. R., 20
LoPiccolo, J., 222, 226, 228, 229, 230, 231, 232, 233, 234
Lord, C., 333
Lott, T., 222
Lovaas, O. I., 48
Lovejoy, M., 373
Lowe, C. F., 276
Luborsky, L., 97
Luecken, L. J., 148
Luria, A. R., 318
Lydiard, R. B., 106
Lykken, D. I., 186
Lynskey, M. I., 338, 345

Macalpine, I., 12–13
MacDonald, H., 336
Mace, C. J., 131
MacEachron, A. E., 327
MacGregor, M., 155
Machon, R. A., 293
Machover, K., 70
MacMillan, D. L., 337
Maddi, S. R., 52, 149
Madle, R. A., 321
Magic, J., 141
Magni, G., 312
Magulac, M., 281
Mahler, M., 43
Mallik, I., 156
Maltais, M., 361
Maltby, N., 100
Maltsberger, J. T., 179, 269

Maltzman, I. M., 215
Manderscheid, R. W., 19
Mangweth, B., 359
Manly, J. T., 351
Mann, S. J., 154, 161
Marantz, S., 236
Marco, E., 292
Marcus, J., 294
Mariani, M. A., 340
Marks, I., 108
Marks, I. M., 137
Marlatt, G. A., 208, 209, 214, 215–216
Marmar, C. R., 170, 174, 178, 179
Marmot, M. G., 162
Marquardt, W. H., 158
Marquis de Sade, 243
Marrugat, J., 154
Marsa, L., 343
Marsella, A. J., 7
Marsh, D. T., 301
Marshall, J., 358
Martin, C. E., 220
Martin, P. R., 158, 161
Martin, R. A., 151
Marziali, E., 177
Masi, G., 349
Masi, W., 332
Maslow, A. H., 52
Mason, M., 299
Masserman, J., 208
Masterman, D. L., 318
Masters, J. H., 224, 225, 229, 231, 233, 234, 243
Masters, W., 220, 221
Masterson, J. F., 176
Matarazzo, J. D., 76
Materka, P. R., 315
Mathews, R., 337
Mathews-Simonton, S., 150
Matthews, C. G., 318
Mattis, S., 69
May, D. C., 325
Mays, V. M., 88
Mazza, J., 346
McAdams, D. P., 70
McAlpine, D. D., 301
McCabe, M. P., 371
McCarthy, K., 160
McCauley, E., 238
McClain, P., 350
McConkey, K. M., 25
McCord, J., 184, 345
McCord, W., 184
McCormack, W. A., 197
McCracken, L. M., 101
McCrady, B. S., 211
McCreary, D. R., 355
McCullough, P. K., 179
McDaniel, S. H., 130
McDermut, W., 264
McDonald, M. K., 135, 137
McDowell, D. M., 203
McElroy, S. L., 126, 134
McFarlane, A. C., 109
McGarvey, S. T., 161
McGee, R., 346
McGilley, B. M., 363
McGowan, S., 394
McGue, M., 259
McGuffin, P., 35, 36

McGuire, P. A., 151, 276
McKenna, P. J., 291
McKenzie, N., 108
McKinley, J. C., 71
McLellan, A. T., 216
McLeod, B., 327
McMahon, B., 241
McMahon, P. P., 121
McNamee, H. B., 209
McNiel, D. E., 388
McQueen, P. C., 322
Mease, A. L., 211
Mechanic, D., 301
Mednick, S. A., 184, 185, 290, 293
Meehl, P. E., 39, 287
Meichenbaum, D. H., 49
Meissner, W. W., 169
Melamed, B., 136
Mello, N. K., 209
Meloy, J. R., 188
Meltzer, H. Y., 299, 300
Mendelson, J. H., 209
Mendlein, J. M., 157
Mendlowicz, M. V., 115
Menendez family, 379, 380
Menzies, R. P. D., 282
Mercer, J., 322
Merckelbach, H., 95, 98, 104
Merrill, J., 73
Merritt, R. D., 20
Merryman, K., 115, 116
Merskey, H., 120, 122
Merz, C. N. B., 141
Metalsky, G. I., 257
Meyer, G. J., 69, 77
Meyer, J., 238
Meyer, R. G., 188
Meyer, W. S., 236
Meyers, R. J., 213
Meyers, W. A., 236
Michaels, E. J., 241
Michelangelo, 251
Miklowitz, D. J., 295
Mileno, M. D., 129
Milich, R., 341
Miller, D. J., 391
Miller, G., 324
Miller, I. W., 264
Miller, M., 125, 334
Miller, M. N., 372
Miller, S. B., 154, 155
Millich, R., 341
Millon, T., 175, 176, 177, 184
Milos, G. F., 360
Milstein, V., 185
Milstone, C., 119
Mintz, J., 295
Mintz, L., 295
Minuchin, S., 370
Mitchell, A., 222
Mohr, D. C., 232
Moline, M. M., 396
Monahan, J., 388
Money, J., 244
Monroe, M., 258, 265
Monti, P. M., 212
Moore, R., 98
Moorey, S., 143, 146
Morenz, B., 242
Morey, L. C., 177
Morgan, H., 69

Morgan, R., 356
Morgenstern, H., 300
Morgenstern, J., 211
Morihisa, J. M., 76
Morishima, J. K., 279
Morrison, A. P., 276
Morrison, J., 205
Morse, W., 374
Morten, G., 57
Moser, G., 127, 244
Moye, J., 312
Mrazek, D. A., 160, 161
Muehleman, T., 393
Mueser, K. T., 301
Mukai, T., 371
Mulder, R. T., 118
Mulkens, S. A. N., 98, 99
Mullan, M., 316
Mumford, D. B., 372
Munch, E., 89
Mungadze, J., 125
Munroe-Blum, H., 177
Muris, P., 95, 98, 104
Murphree, O. D., 36
Murphy, J. K., 157
Murphy, M., 130
Murray, C. 3, 322
Murray, H. A., 69
Murray, R. M., 273
Myers, H. F., 157
Myers, J., 98
Myers, J. K., 10, 250
Mystkowski, J. L. L., 100

Nagin, D. S., 346
Nakamura, C. Y., 207
Narcotics Anonymous, 211
Nash, J., 275
Nash, J. M., 314, 316, 318
Nathan, J. S., 75
Nathan, P. E., 81, 207, 208, 209
National Association of Anorexia Nervosa and Associated Disorders, 356
National Center for Health Statistics (NCHS), 156, 160, 267
National Council on the Aging, 225
National Institute of Neurological Disorders and Stroke, 335
National Institute on Drug Abuse, 196
National Institute on Drug Abuse, 208
National Institutes of Mental Health (NIMH), 4, 10, 19, 85, 86, 88, 89, 94, 95, 107, 154, 342
NCHS (National Center for Health Statistics), 156, 160, 268
Nelson, C. B., 196, 197
Nelson, L. D., 317
Nelson-Gray, R. O., 81
Nelsoni, K. B., 336
Nemeroff, C., 366
Nemeroff, C. B., 18
Neugebauer, R., 13

Neumark-Sztainer, D., 355, 356, 366, 373
Nevid, J. S., 223, 244
Neziroglu, F., 135, 138
Niaura, R. S., 214
Nichols, P. L., 326
Nigg, J. T., 175
NIMH (National Institute of Mental Health), 4, 10, 19, 85, 86, 88, 89, 94, 95, 107, 154, 342
Nisenson, L. G., 300
Noble, J., 25
Nolen-Hoeksema, S., 256, 258, 349
Norcross, J. C., 47
Norre, J., 362
Northup, J., 342
Norton, G. R., 88
Norton, P. J., 66
Nott, K., 148
Noyes, R., 126
Nussbaum, N. L., 75
Nutt, D. J., 91

O'Connor, K., 349, 350
O'Connor, M. K., 129
O'Connor, T. G., 185
Odejide, O. A., 128
Office of National Drug Control Policy, 191, 196, 197, 202, 203
Ofshe, R. J., 122
Ogles, B. M., 265
Ogletree, S. M., 154
Ohaeri, J. U., 128
Ohayon, M. M., 158
Okazaki, S., 77, 257
Oke, N. J., 337
Olarte, S. W., 394, 396
O'Leary, S. G., 342
Olendick, T. H., 97
Olfson, M., 296
Olivardia, R., 372
Oliver, J., 312
Ollendick, T. H., 95, 98, 101
Oren, D. A., 254
Orne, M., 383
Orosan, P., 138
Orr, S. P., 107, 109
Osborn, C., 240
Osborne, Y. V. H., 188
Osbourne, L., 118
Ost, L. G., 92, 95, 98
O'Sullivan, G. A., 134
Othmer, E., 68
Othmer, S. C., 68
Otto, M. W., 92, 134
Otto, R. K., 384
Overholser, J. C., 242
Overstreet, S., 346
Owen, M. J., 35, 36
Ozer, E. J., 108

Paley, A. M., 121
Palfrey, J. S., 340
Palmer, K. S., 355
Panagiotopoulos, C., 359
Pantelis, C., 292
Papageorgiou, C., 94
Papolos, D., 349, 350
Papolos, J., 349, 350

Parham, T. A., 56
Parker, S., 373
Parrish, G., 142
Parrott, C., 376
Parry, C. D. H., 387
Pasewark, R. A., 266
Paternite, C. E., 342
Pathak, D., 132
Pattatucci, A. M. L., 224
Patterson, C. L. L., 224
Patterson, G. R., 345
Paulson, T., 337
Pavlov, I., 43–44
Payne, R. L., 276
Pazda, S. L., 362
Peel, R., 383
Pelham, W. E., 341
Penava, S. J., 92
Pendery, M. L., 215
Penninx, B. W. J. H., 152, 153
Perczel, W. J., 267
Perdue, L., 368
Perez, J., 186
Perkins, H. W., 197
Perner, L. E., 336
Perrin, S., 348
Perris, C., 259
Perry, J. C., 179, 184
Persons, J. B., 83
Peter, D., 238
Petersen, A. C., 349
Petersen, L., 351
Petoskey, M. D., 74
Petrie, K., 143
Petrie, T. A., 360, 366, 374
Petry, N. M., 215
Pett, M. A., 228
Peveler, R., 126
Pfuhlmann, B., 280
Phillips, D. P., 150
Phillips, K. A., 126, 133, 138, 167, 168, 173, 177, 178, 180, 184
Phoenix, R., 205
Piacentini, J., 85
Pickaro, D., 295
Pickens, B. K., 393
Pigott, T. A., 106
Pike, J. L., 148
Pike, K. M., 364, 369, 374
Pilisuk, M., 210
Pinel, P., 15, 16
Pinsof, W. M., 337, 345
Plato, 13, 14
Plienis, A. J., 337
Plomin, R., 35, 36
Poddar, P., 392, 393
Polivy, J., 209
Pollack, M. H., 92
Pomeroy, W. B., 220
Ponterotto, J. G., 56, 59
Poon, L. W., 314
Pope, H. G., 120, 355, 356, 374
Pope, K. S., 394, 396
Popovich, M., 367
Popper, C., 321, 323, 324, 327
Posluszny, D. M., 150
Poulin, F., 345
Poulton, R., 95, 98
Poustka, F., 334, 335
Powell, D. H., 312
Powell, J., 273

Preisler, J. J., 145
Prescott, C. A., 98
President's New Freedom Commission on Mental Health, 11, 247, 264, 328
Prichard, J. C., 181–182
Prigatano, G. P., 313
Prinze, F., 265
Prior, M., 334
Prior, T. L., 363
Przybeck, T., 182
Puente, A. E., 75
Pueschel, S. M., 325
Pull, C. B., 364
Pumariega, A. J., 372
Putnick, M., 172

Quay, H. C., 186

Rabatin, J., 91
Rachman, S., 98, 103
Radloff, L. S., 258
Rae, D. S., 258, 296
Rahe, R. H., 144
Ramer, J. C., 324
Ranchor, A. V., 155, 161
Rand, C., 373
Rapee, R. M., 90
Raskin, R., 237
Rassin, E., 105
Rathus, S. A., 244
Rayner, R., 45, 98
Read, J. P., 216
Read, S., 306, 316
Rechlin, T., 131
Rector, N. A., 277
Reed, G. M., 12
Regier, D. A., 10, 12, 80, 208, 296
Reich, J., 167
Reich, T., 259
Reid, J., 208
Reid, J. B., 345, 346
Reid, W. H., 188, 299
Reisberg, B., 315
Reiser, D. E., 67
Reitan, R. M., 75
Reiter, J., 138
Resnick, R. J., 338
Reus, V. I., 250
Rey, J., 346
Rhee, S. H., 342
Ricca, V., 376, 377
Ricciardelli, L. A., 362, 374
Richards, G. P., 270
Richards, J. C., 154, 155
Richards, R., 237
Richardson, L. F., 119, 121
Rickels, K., 89
Ridderinkhof, K. R., 313
Ridley, C. R., 20, 59
Rietveld, S., 160, 161
Rimland, B., 337
Riskind, J. H., 98
Ritvo, E. R., 335, 336
Rivas-Vazquez, R. A., 261, 299, 314
Rizvi, S. L., 364
Robbins, F. P., 136
Robert, P., 323
Roberto, L., 237

Roberts, J., 116
Roberts, M. A., 342
Roberts, W., 266
Robertson, P., 222
Robins, L. N., 10, 12, 80, 182, 208, 247, 344, 345
Robinson, F., 393
Robinson, J. P., 65
Robinson, M. E., 136
Robinson, R. G., 312
Rodman, D., 241
Rodrigues, M., 213
Rodriguez, M. S., 146, 147
Rogers, A., 157
Rogers, C. R., 52, 53, 268, 383
Rogers, R. L., 360
Rohsenow, D. J., 212
Rollason, D. H., 160
Romeo, N., 389
Ronald, R., 384
Root, M. P., 57, 372
Root, R. W., 338
Rorschach, H., 69–70
Rose, S., 107
Rosen, J. C., 138
Rosen, L. A., 340
Rosen, R. C., 228, 230, 233
Rosenfarb, I. S., 295
Rosenfeld, A., 243
Rosenfield, A. H., 240
Rosenman, R. H., 154
Rosenstreich, D. L., 160
Rosenthal, D., 39, 206
Rosenthal, I. M., 236
Rosenthal, N. E., 254
Rosicky, J. G., 345
Rosman, B., 370
Ross, C. A., 125
Roth, R. M., 275
Rowe, E. W., 74
Roy, S., 296
Royce, J. M., 327
Royks, R., 301
Rubinstein, M., 345
Ruiz, J. M., 156
Rumbaut, R. G., 257
Rund, B. R., 285
Ruscio, A. M., 82, 91
Ruscio, J., 82
Rush, B., 16
Rusinek, H., 287
Russell, M., 214
Rutter, M., 334, 335, 336
Rutter, M. L., 185

Saarinen, J., 154
Sabatino, S. A., 92
Sabbagh, M. N., 126
Sable, P., 176
Sachdev, P., 300
Sadava, S. W., 355
Sadovsky, R., 116
Safarjan, B., 292
Saklofske, D. H., 73
Salcioglu, E., 109
Salkovskis, P. M., 99
Salovey, P., 151
Salyer, S. J., 100
Samson, 265
Samuda, R., 56, 396
Sanders, A. R., 293
Sanford, E. E., 327

Santorum, R., 221
Sarbin, T. R., 81
Sargent, J., 361
Sartorius, 286
Satterfield, J. H., 342
Sattler, J. M., 73
Sawchuk, C. N., 99
Saxena, S., 135
Saywitz, K. J., 351
Sbordone, R. J., 311
Schacht, T. E., 81
Schachter, S., 187
Schaeffer, B., 48
Schafer, J., 210
Schaffer, D., 343
Schalock, R. L., 310, 318
Schaudinn, F., 35
Schell, A. M., 342
Schiavi, R. C., 231, 232
Schifano, F., 312
Schmauk, F. J., 188
Schmeck, K., 334, 335
Schmidt, M. H., 346
Schmidt, N. B., 90, 133, 134
Schneider, J., 379
Schoenberg, H. W., 229
Scholl, G. T., 324
Schover, L. R., 228
Schreiber, J. L., 295
Schreibman, L., 337
Schuckit, M. A., 269
Schueneman, A. L., 209
Schulman, S. L., 353
Schulsinger, F., 185
Schulz, R., 161
Schwartz, B. S., 158
Schwartz, L., 136
Schweizer, E., 89
Scott, R. P., 318
Scroppo, J. C., 119
Seely, R. K., 242
Segal, M., 332
Segraves, R. T., 229, 231, 232
Selesnick, S. T., 12, 15
Seligman, M. E. P., 98, 149, 256, 257
Seltman, H., 150
Seltzer, B., 306
Selvin, I. P., 236
Selye, H., 143–144
Semans, J. H., 234
Seneviratne, H. M., 161
Setzer, N. J., 100
Sexton, T. L., 211
Shafran, R., 98
Shaibani, A., 126
Shainberg, L. W., 240
Shalev, A. Y., 108
Shapiro, D. L., 390, 391
Shapiro, M. K., 113, 119
Sharma, V., 286
Shaver, P. R., 65
Shaw, H., 366
Shea, T., 264
Sheeley, B. L., 391, 392
Sher, K. J., 207
Sherman, C., 396
Sherman, R., 341
Sherwood, N. E., 356, 364
Shiffman, S., 364
Shimamura, A. P., 313
Shisslak, C. M., 362

Shiver, M. D., 337
Shnek, Z. M., 146
Shouldice, A., 347
Shulman, C., 322
Shusta, S. R., 125
Sidney, S., 157
Siegel, B., 337
Siegel, M., 393
Siegel, R. A., 188
Siegel, T. C., 345, 346
Siegler, I. C., 314
Siever, L. J., 170, 172
Silberstein, S. D., 158, 159, 161
Silva, R., 276
Silva, R. R., 352
Silverman, J. M., 299
Silverman, W. K., 89, 92, 347
Silverstein, B., 368
Simeon, D., 117
Simmons, A. M., 372
Simmons, J. Q., 48
Simms, C. A., 119, 122
Simon, G. E., 136
Simon, L. M. J., 188
Simons, A. D., 258
Simons, J., 203
Simonton, O. C., 150
Simpson, N. B., 379
Simpson, O. J., 379
Singh, S. P., 130, 131
Sizemore, C., 124
Skinner, B. F., 46
Slater, M. A., 136
Slovenko, R., 385
Slutske, W. S., 185, 206
Smalley, S. L., 335
Smith, D., 81
Smith, D. E., 199, 320
Smith, G. C., 126, 136, 138
Smith, G. T., 208
Smith, J. E., 213
Smith, T. W., 156
Smyer, M. A., 36, 313
Snowden, D. A., 316
Snowden, L. R., 103
Sonnenschein, M. A., 19
Spanos, N. P., 13, 15, 122
Spark, R. F., 231
Sparrow, S. S., 333
Spector, I. P., 226, 228, 230, 231, 238
Speice, J., 130
Spencer, S. L., 233
Spiegel, H., 122
Spiro, A., 161
Spitzer, B. L., 366
Spitzer, R. L., 167, 170, 176, 308, 364, 371, 377
Srinivasan, T. N., 372
Srole, L., 10
Staal, W. G., 292, 294
Stader, S. R., 258
Stalling, R. B., 137
Stampfl, T., 47
Stanley, M. A., 106
Stanton, W. R., 346
Stark, E., 243
Stark, M. J., 216
Starr, K., 222
Stat, M., 355, 356, 366
Steadman, H. J., 385
Steege, J. F., 232

Steele, C. M., 209
Steele, M. S., 161
Steffen, J. J., 209
Steffenburg, S., 335
Stein, D. J., 86, 89, 105
Steinberg, L., 366–367
Steinwachs, D. M., 294, 299, 300, 301
Steketee, G., 105
Stenberg, J. H., 301
Stern, J., 130
Sternberg, K. J., 351
Stevens, J., 286
Stevenson, J. F., 216
Stevenson-Hinde, J., 347
Stewart, M., 379
Stewart, W. F., 158
Stice, E., 207–208, 364, 366, 370, 371
Stober, G., 280
Stock, W. E., 229, 231, 232, 233, 234
Stone, A. A., 143, 147, 164
Stone, M. H., 170, 172
Stone, W. L., 333
Stoolmiller, M., 346
Story, M., 356, 364, 373
Stout, A. L., 232
Stout, C., 160
Streissguth, A. P., 326
Strickland, B. R., 258
Strober, M., 374, 375
Strohman, R., 33
Stromberg, C., 379
Strong, B., 224, 226–227
Strong, S. M., 369
Strupp, H. H., 22
Stuart, F. M., 228, 233
Sturnick, D., 345
Stuss, D. T., 311
Suchday, S., 88
Sue, D. W., 7, 19, 20, 56, 57, 58, 127, 244, 396
Sue, S., 77, 78, 207, 279
Sugiura, T., 279
Sullivan, J. G., 88
Sullivan, K., 334
Sullivan, P. F., 357
Sulser, F., 261
Sultanoff, S., 151
Sundel, M., 100
Sundel, S. S., 100
Suokas, J., 269
Suresh, T. R., 372
Sutherland, S. M., 178
Suzuki, K., 95
Swanson, J., 388
Swartz, M., 126, 130
Swedo, S. E., 103
Sweillam, A., 388
Swinson, R. P., 92
"Sybil," 119, 120, 122, 125
Syme, S. L., 162
Synder, P., 150
Szasz, T., 9

Tabachnick, B. G., 394
Tager-Flushberg, H., 334
Takamura, J. C., 312
Takeuchi, J., 297
Tardiff, K., 388
Tarkan, C. L., 359

Tarter, R. E., 207
Taussig, C., 344
Taylor, C. B., 90
Taylor, E. H., 73
Taylor, H. A., 209
Taylor, J., 362
Taylor, S., 92, 109
Tchaikovsky, L., 251
Teachman, B. A., 98
Teasdale, J. D., 257
Telch, C. F., 364
Temoshok, L., 150
Teri, L., 314
Terman, L. M., 73
Thacker, A. J., 277
Thapar, A., 324, 325
Tharp, R. G., 331
Thelen, M. H., 120, 391
Theorell, T., 153
Thiels, C., 376
Thigpen, C. H., 120
Thomas, G., 371
Thomas, P., 277
Thompson, P. M., 292
Thomsen, S., 367
Thorndike, R. L., 73
Thorpe, S. J., 99
Tienari, P., 294
Tierney, J., 155
Tiggermann, M., 134
Timmerman, I. G. H., 144
Tipp, J., 182
Titone, D., 278
Tjosvold, D., 327
Tjosvold, M. M., 327
Tobin, J. J., 142
Todd, E. R., 150
Tolan, P. H., 184
Tollefson, G. D., 106
Tooker, G., 117
Torgalsboen, A. K., 285
Torpy, J. M., 152
Torrubia, R., 186
Toth, S. L., 351
Trakowski, J. H., 90
Travella, J. I., 312
Tremblay, R. E., 346
Trierweiler, S. J., 20
Trimble, M. R., 131
Tripp, M. M., 366, 374
Troxel, W. M., 157
Trull, T. J., 175, 176, 207
Tsai, G., 372
Tsai, M., 319
Tsang, A. K. T., 334
Tsoi, W. F., 235, 238
Tuke, W., 16
Tuomisto, M. T., 156
Turkheimer, E., 387
Turnbull, N., 325
Turner, S. M., 106
Turner, W. J., 224
Tutkun, H., 120
Twamley, E. W., 301
Tyrer, P., 137

Uba, L., 20
Uchino, B. N., 156
Ullmann, L. P., 184
Underwood, A., 159
Ursano, R. J., 148
U.S. Census, 19, 57

Subject Index

Duty-to-warn principle, 392–393, 394–395
Dysaethesia Aethiopica, 20
Dysfunction, 5, 7
Dyspareunia, 226, 229–230, 231
Dysthymic disorder, 250, 252–253
Dystonia, 300

Eating disorders, 355–377
　anorexia nervosa, 358–362, 375–376
　binge-eating disorder (BED), 364–365, 376–377
　bulimia nervosa, 362–364, 376
　etiology, 366–375
　mental health and society, 361, 372
　treatment, 375–377
Eccentric behaviors and personality disorders, 168–172
Ecstasy or MDMA (methylenedioxymethamphetamine), 203
ECT (electroconvulsive therapy), 36, 37, 262, 263
Education:
　incidence and prevalence of mental disorders, 12
　schizophrenia treatment, 301
　school phobia, 348
　school psychology, 4
　school violence, 346
　sex therapy, 233–234, 236
EE (expressed emotion), schizophrenia, 295–296
EEG (electroencephalograph), 75, 185
Ego, 40
Ego ideal, and superego, 40
Eighteenth-century views to abnormal behavior, 15–16
Einstein, Albert, 336
Elderly persons, See Aging and aging-related disorders
Electroconvulsive therapy (ECT), 36, 37, 262, 263
Electroencephalograph (EEG), 75, 185
Electroshock therapy, 36
Elimination disorders, 352–353
Ellis' cognitive theories, 49–51
Emetics, 213
Emotions and emotional arousal:
　asthma, 160
　cultural repression of, 161–162
　histrionic personality disorder, 170–171, 173–174
　moods, 149–151, 175
　personality disorders, 173–177
　psychological states, 146, 147
　treatment of problems, 318
Employment programs and mental retardation, 327
Encephalitis, 316
Endorphins, 37
Enlargement of the ventricles, 294

Enuresis, 352
Environmental influences:
　cognitive disorders treatment, 319–320
　dependent personality disorder, 178–179
　depression, 261
　humanistic view, 52
　mental retardation, 324
　schizophrenia, 293–298
　stressors, 39
Epidemiologic Catchment Area (ECA) study, 194, 303–304
Epidemiology of mental disorders, 10–12, 19–21
Epilepsy, 311–312, 317
Erectile dysfunction, 229–230
Erratic behaviors and personality disorders, 173–177
Errors, 69
Essential hypertension, 156
Estrogen, 231, 273
Ethical issues, See Legal and ethical issues
Etiology:
　acute stress disorders (ASD), 108–110
　ADHD, 340–341
　Alzheimer's Disease, 316
　antisocial personality disorder, 181–188
　anxiety disorders, 89–91, 96–99, 104–105, 108–110
　autistic disorder, 334–335
　childhood and adolescent disorders, 334–335, 340–342
　cognitive disorders, 304, 310–317
　defined, 79
　depression, 254–261
　dissociative disorders, 120–123
　eating disorders, 366–375
　gender identity disorders, 236
　generalized anxiety disorder (GAD), 89–91
　mental retardation, 324–329
　mood disorders, 254–261
　obsessive-compulsive disorder (OCD), 104–105
　panic disorder, 89–91
　paraphilias, 244–245
　perspectives on, 160–162
　phobias, 96–99
　psychophysiological disorder, 160–162
　schizophrenia, 285–287
　sexual dysfunction, 231–234
　somatoform disorders, 135–137
　substance-related disorders, 204–210
Eurasian, as label, 57
European Americans, as label, 57
See also White Americans
Evaluation, 82
Exaggeration, Beck's, 50
Excited catatonia, disorganized schizophrenia, 283
Exercising, anorexia nervosa, 359

Exhaustion stage, general adaptation model of stress, 144
Exhibitionism, 238, 239, 241–242
Existential models of psychopathology, 51–53, 54, 61, 63
Exorcism, 13
Expectancy, alcohol use and abuse, 209, 210
Experiment, defined, 22
Experimental group, 23
Experimental hypothesis, 22
Experimental research methods, 22–24
Expert witnesses, 381
Exposure therapy, phobias, 100
Expressed emotion (EE), schizophrenia, 295–296
External stressors, panic and anxiety disorders, 89–90

Factitious disorders, 127, 129
False memory, 381
Familial alcoholism, 206
Families: Anorexia in Context (Minuchin, Rosman, and Baker), 370
Family and peer influences:
　alcohol use and abuse, 206, 207–208
　autism, 335
　borderline personality disorders, 177
　depression, 258–259
　eating disorders, 366, 370–371, 374–375
　schizophrenia, 286, 287–288, 294–296, 301
Family Education Rights and Privacy Act, 294
Family systems model of psychopathology, 32, 54–55, 61, 62, 184
FAS (fetal alcohol syndrome), 199, 326
Fasting, anorexia nervosa, 359
Fat, See Eating disorders
Fatal Attraction (film), 175
Fathers, incestuous, 242–243
Faulty thinking, Beck's six types of, 50
Fearful behaviors and personality disorders, 177–181
Fearlessness, antisocial personality disorder, 186
Feedback loop, panic attacks, 90
Feeling, See Humanistic models of psychopathology
Feeling (humanistic-existential), 63
Female orgasmic disorder, 226, 230, 231, 234
Females, See Gender differences
Female sexual arousal disorder, 226, 230
Fetal alcohol syndrome (FAS), 199, 326
Fetishism, 239, 240–241
"Fighting spirit" and cancer survival, 150, 151
Flat affect, 275, 278

Flooding, 47, 106
fMRI (functional magnetic resonance imaging), 76
Foods or food additives, ADHD, 341
Ford v. Wainwright, 389
Forebrain, 34
Formal standardized interview, 68
Fragile X syndrome, 324–325, 335
Free association, psychoanalysis, 42
Free-floating anxiety, 86, 88
Frequency of suicide, 268
Freud, Sigmund, 18, 40
Frontal lobotomy, 298
Frotteurism, 239, 240, 242
Fugue state, 116
Functional magnetic resonance imaging (fMRI), 76

GABA (gamma amino-butyric acid), 37
GAD, *See* Generalized anxiety disorder (GAD)
Gage, Phineas, 310
Gamma amino-butyric acid (GABA), 37
Gamma hydroxybutyrate (GHB), 203
GAS (general adaptation syndrome), 144
Genain quadruplets, 287
Gender bias, 154, 167, 171
Gender differences:
　aging and sexual activity, 224–225
　alcohol use and abuse, 197
　antisocial personality disorder, 175, 182
　anxiety disorders, 86
　asthma, 160
　benzodiazepine use, 200
　bipolar disorders, 253
　body image and satisfaction, 355, 367–368, 373–374
　cognitive disorders, 305
　coronary heart disease (CHD), 152–153
　depression, 253, 258, 259
　dissociative disorders, 118
　dyspareunia, 229–230
　eating disorders, 356, 357, 359, 364, 371, 373–374
　gender identity disorders, 236
　headaches, 158, 159
　hostility and coronary heart disease (AHA), 155
　hypertension, 156–157
　hypoactive sexual desire disorder, 228
　incidence and prevalence of mental disorders, 11, 12
　marriage, 12, 148, 268
　marriage and psychophysiological disorders, 148
　mental retardation, 321
　mood disorders, 253
　obsessive-compulsive disorder, 103
　orgasmic disorders, 230–231

Phenotype, 36
Phenylketonuria (PKU), 335
Phobias, 93–102
    agoraphobia, 94
    behavioral treatment of, 47–48
    classical conditioning, 45
    defined, 93
    disorder chart, 86–87
    etiology, 96–99
    incidence, 10, 11
    social phobias, 94–95
    specific phobias, 96
    treatment, 99–101
Phobophobia, 93, 94
Phone sex, 222
Physiological view:
    acute stress disorders (ASD), 108
    asthma, 159–160
    coronary heart disease (CHD), 152–155
    depression, 248, 249
    eating disorders, 359–360, 363
    generalized anxiety disorder (GAD), 88–89
    headaches, 157–159
    mania, 249, 250
    panic attacks, 90
    posttraumatic stress disorder (PTSD), 108
    schizophrenia, 290–293
    stress and hypertension, 155–157
    See also Biological view and treatment; Somatoform disorders
PKU (phenylketonuria), 335
Placebo control groups, 23
Plague, 15
Pleasure principle, and id, 40
Polarized thinking, Beck's, 50
Politics, and mental disorders concerns, 9
Polysubstance-use, 200, 205
Positive correlation, 24–25
Positive symptoms of schizophrenia, 274–278
Positron emission tomography (PET) scan, 75, 105
"Possession" and schizophrenia, 296–298
Post-Freudian views, psychodynamic model, 43
Postpartum depression, 251, 254
Posttraumatic stress disorder (PTSD), 106–110
"Pot" (marijuana), 192–193, 195, 203, 210
Predictive validity, 65
Predisposing factors, sexual disorders, 233
Prehistoric beliefs, and abnormal behavior, 13
Premature ejaculation, 226, 231, 234
Prematurity, and mental retardation, 326–327
Preparedness theory, phobias, 99
Prevalence of disorder:
    antisocial personality disorder, 182, 189

anxiety disorders, 87, 88, 89, 103, 107, 108
autistic disorders, 333
avoidant personality disorder, 177
bipolar disorders, 253
childhood and adolescent disorders, 332, 339
cognitive disorders, 303–304, 305
defined, 9
dependent personality disorder, 179
depression, 247, 253
dissociative disorders, 115
eating disorders, 357
mental retardation, 321
mood disorders, 247, 253
panic disorder, 88, 89
personality disorders, 167, 169, 171, 173, 174, 175
rates described, 82
schizophrenia, 273, 281
sexual dysfunction, 227
somatoform disorders, 127
substance-related disorders, 191, 193, 194, 199, 201
youth weight concerns, 356
Prevention:
    substance-related disorders, 215–216
    suicide, 269–271
Primal Fear (film), 383
Primary erectile dysfunction, 229
Primary gain, somatoform disorder, 136
Primary inhibited female orgasm, 230
Primary orgasmic dysfunction, 230
Primary symptoms, schizophrenia, 278
Privileged communication, therapist-client, 391–392
Process emphasis, and cognitive therapy, 49–50
Prodromal phase, schizophrenia, 284
Products test (Durham standard), 384
Profiling, criminal, 381
Prognosis, 80, 284–286, 321, 336
Programs, mental retardation, 327–328
Projection, as defense mechanism, 42
Projective personality tests, 69–71
Protection of patient rights, 381
Prozac (fluoxetine hydrochloride), 262
Psychiatric epidemiology, 9–12
Psychiatric social work, 4
Psychiatry, 4
Psychoanalysis, 4, 18, 40
    See also Psychodynamic view and treatment (psychoanalysis)
Psychodiagnosis, 3

Psychodynamic models of psychopathology, 39–44
    criticism of, 43–44
    defense mechanisms, 41–42
    integrative, 59
    personality structure, 40
    post-Freudian views, 43
    psychodynamic therapy, 42–43
    psychosexual stages, 40–41
    as psychosocial model, 32, 60
Psychodynamic Perspective, 160, 161
Psychodynamic view and treatment (psychoanalysis):
    alcohol use and abuse, 206–207
    antisocial personality disorder, 184
    autism, 335
    borderline personality disorders, 176
    depression, 254–255
    dissociative disorders, 120–121
    generalized anxiety disorder (GAD), 89–90
    obsessive-compulsive disorder (OCD), 104
    panic disorder, 89–90
    paraphilias, 244–245
    phobias, 97
    psychophysiological disorders, 160–161
    sexuality, 220
    somatoform disorder, 135–136, 137
    as therapy, 42–43
Psychological autopsy, 266
Psychological Stress and the Coping Process (Lazarus), 145
Psychological tests and inventories, 68–75
    assessment of abnormal behavior, 68–75
    cognitive impairment tests, 74–75
    cultural issues, 77–78
    defined, 68–69
    intelligence tests, 73
    Kaufman Assessment Battery for Children (K-ABC), 74
    Luria-Nebraska Neuropsychological Battery, 75
    Minnesota Multiphasic Personality Inventory (MMPI-2), 71–73
    neuropsychological, 75
    projective personality test, 69–71
    reliability and validity, 70–71
    Rorschach technique, 69–70, 71
    self-report inventories, 71–73
    test-retest reliability, 65
    Thematic Apperception Test (TAT), 69–70
Psychological view and treatment:
    abnormal psychology, 3–4, 18–21
    child protection evaluations, 381

clinical psychology, 4, 5
depression, 254–258
eating disorders, 375–377
factors affecting medical conditions, 141–165
indigenous psychologies, 56
intersection of psychology and the law, 381
involvement in specific physical disorders, 152–162
multicultural psychology, 18, 19–21, 53–59, 61, 62
psychological autopsy, 266
sexual dysfunctions, 231–232
stress and coping, 145
See also Psychological tests and inventories
Psychology, See Psychological view and treatment
Psychomotor retardation, 248
Psychopathic inferiority/personality, See Antisocial personality disorder
Psychopathology, 31, 59–60
See also Models of psychopathology; specific topics
Psychopaths, 187–188
Psychopharmacology, 38
Psychophysiological disorders, 140–165
    asthma, 159–160
    as behavioral medicine, 162–163
    biofeedback, 163
    characteristics of, 142–143
    cognitive-behavioral interventions, 164
    coronary heart disease (CHD), 152–155
    defined, 141
    etiology, 160–162
    headaches, 157–159
    hypertension and stress, 155–157
    immune system and stress, 146–151
    mental health and society, 151, 154
    models for understanding stress, 143–146
    relaxation techniques, 163
    sexual dysfunctions, 231–232
    specific physical disorders, 152–162
    stress, 143–151, 155–157
    treatment of, 162–165
Psychosexual stages, Freudian, 40–41
Psychosocial models of psychopathology:
    behavioral models, 44–48
    cognitive models, 48–51
    family systems model, 54–55
    humanistic models, 51–53
    multicultural models, 19–21, 32, 53–59, 62
    psychodynamic models, 39–44
    schizophrenia treatment, 298–300

Treatment *(cont.)*
  cognitive disorders, 317–320
  conduct disorders, 345–346
  depressive disorders, 261–264
  dissociative disorders, 123–125
  eating disorders, 375–377
  gender bias in medical, 154
  gender identity disorders, 236–238
  generalized anxiety disorder (GAD), 91–93
  mood disorders, 261–265
  obsessive-compulsive disorder (OCD), 105–106
  panic disorder, 91–93
  paraphilias, 244–245
  phobias, 99–101
  psychophysiological disorders, 162–165
  refusal of, 389–390
  rights of mental patients, 389–390
  sexual dysfunction, 231–234
  somatoform disorders, 137–138
  substance-related disorders, 210–217
Trephining, 13
Trial, competency to participate in, 381, 382, 385–386
Tricyclic antidepressants (TCAs), 260, 262
Trisomy 21 (Down syndrome), 325
Tuberous sclerosis, 335
Tuke, William, 16
Twin studies:
  ADHD, 342
  antisocial personality disorder, 184
  autistic disorder, 335
  cardiovasular health, 161
  familial alcoholism, 206

mood disorders, 259
panic disorders, 91
schizophrenia, 288–289
Type A behavior, 154

UCR (unconditioned response), 45
UCS (unconditioned stimulus), 45, 46
Unconditional positive regard, 52
Unconditioned response (UCR), 45
Unconditioned stimulus (UCS), 45, 46
Uncued panic attacks, 86
Underarousal, and antisocial personality disorder, 186–187
Underweight, *See* Eating disorders
Undifferentiated schizophrenia, 280–281, 284
Undifferentiated somatoform disorder, 126–127, 129–130
Undoing, as defense mechanism, 42
Unexpected panic attacks, 86
Unipolar disorders, 250, 264
  See also Depression and depressive disorders
"Uppers" (amphetamines), 200–201, 291
Urban children, asthma, 160
U.S. Advisory Board on Child Abuse and Neglect, 350

Vaginismus, 226, 231, 234
Validity, 22, 65–66
Valium, 200
Values, multicultural psychology, 19–20
Variables, experiments, 22
Vascular dementia, 313

Ventricular enlargement, schizophrenia, 292
Viagra, 229, 232
Vicarious conditioning (modeling), 45
Victorian era, 5
View-avoidance conflict, alcohol use and abuse, 208
Violence:
  anger-hostility-aggression (AHA) syndrome, 154–155
  child abuse, 326–327, 350–351
  conduct disorders, 344–345
  dangerousness, 381, 388
  pedophilia, 239, 242
  school violence, 346–347
Virtual reality therapy, 100
Visual hallucinations, 276
Voyeurism, 238, 239, 240, 242

WAIS, WAIS-III or WAIS-R (Wechsler Adult Intelligence Scale), 73, 323
Walden II (Skinner), 45
Warehousing schizophrenia patients, 298
Watson, John B., 45
Waxy flexibility, disorganized schizophrenia, 283–284
Weapon choice and suicide, 268
Wechsler Adult Intelligence Scale (WAIS, WAIS-III or WAIS-R), 73, 323
Wechsler Intelligence Scale for Children (WISC-III or WISC-R), 73, 323
Wechsler Preschool and Primary Scale of Intelligence (WPPSI-III), 73
Weight, and depression, 248
  See also Eating disorders
Weight and height tables, adult, 368, 369

Wernicke's encephalopathy, 308
Westin, Russell, Jr., 379, 380, 385
White Americans:
  alcohol use and abuse, 197, 207–208
  cultural bias in research, 20
  as label, 57
  mental retardation, 323
  models of psychopathology, 56, 58–59
  population composition, 19
  See also Race and ethnicity
WISC-III or WISC-R (Wechsler Intelligence Scale for Children), 73, 323
Witchcraft, 15
Withdrawal, substance, 194, 202
Withdrawn catatonia, disorganized schizophrenia, 283
Women, *See* Gender differences
World Health Organization, 286
Worldview, cultural considerations, 7–8
Worth, conditions of, 52
WPPSI-III (Wechsler Preschool and Primary Scale of Intelligence), 73

Xenophobia, 94
X-ray studies, 75

Youngberg v. Romeo, 389

Zoloft (sertraline), 262
Zoophilia, 244
Zoophobia, 94